The Making of Chinese
Foreign and Security Policy
in the Era of Reform, 1978–2000

The Making of Chinese Foreign and Security Policy in the Era of Reform, 1978–2000

David M. Lampton, Editor

STANFORD UNIVERSITY PRESS

STANFORD, CALIFORNIA

Stanford University Press
Stanford, California

© 2001 by the Board of Trustees of the
Leland Stanford Junior Univesity

Printed in the United States of America
on acid-free, archival-quality paper.

Library of Congress Catalog Control Number: 2001086970

ISBN 0-8047-4055-0 (cloth)
ISBN 0-8047-4056-9 (paper)

Original printing 2001

Last figure below indicates year of this printing:
10   09   08   07   06   05   04   03   02   01

Typeset by Princeton Editorial Associates
in 11/14 Adobe Garamond

In Memory of
A. Doak Barnett
Teacher, Colleague, Friend

Contents

Figures and Tables

Acknowledgments

As a teacher I found myself needing a volume that systematically addressed the question "How is Chinese foreign and national security policy made?" As a researcher I was interested in analyzing how the Chinese policy-making process had changed over time, whether changes were more evident in certain policy areas than in others, and what the consequences of such changes might be for Chinese external behavior. And personally I was determined to complete this, the third volume in a trilogy on the Chinese policy-making process, which includes a volume I edited entitled *Policy Implementation in Post-Mao China* (University of California Press, 1987) and another I edited with Kenneth Lieberthal entitled *Bureaucracy, Politics, and Decision-Making in Post-Mao China* (University of California Press, 1992).

It is only through the assistance of a number of persons and organizations that this volume reached completion. First I must acknowledge the Smith Richardson Foundation for both its financial and its conceptual support. In particular I thank Dr. Marin Strmecki and Dr. Samantha Ravich, who provided assistance throughout the period of this undertaking and who attended project conferences and meetings. The foundation not only supported the research that went into this undertaking but also was farsighted enough to see value in the project's unique design.

In 1996, when I began to conceive of this undertaking, I felt that the China studies field needed a collective endeavor in the area of foreign policy that would involve both younger and more senior scholars in a common enterprise. I believed that the endeavor should involve field investigation throughout Greater China. Consequently, with the foundation's support I assembled an advisory committee, we developed and refined an overall architecture for this volume, and we sent out a national request for proposals to numerous persons we hoped might be interested in submitting their ideas for chapters. Having received a great number of proposals, we selected approximately twelve authors who would undertake research funded by the project and who would then have their draft chapters evaluated and revised following two conferences (in 1998 and 1999). We also invited the participation in these conferences of past and current U.S. policy-makers who had dealt extensively with China in areas covered by this volume, to draw on their insights in order to create a volume of both theoretical and policy significance.

For their help in developing the design of the volume, selecting the chapter authors, and subsequently implementing the project, I wish to thank the advisory committee, which included the late A. Doak Barnett, to whom this volume is dedicated by the grateful field of Chinese studies and all of the book's contributors; Dr. Thomas Fingar of the United States Department of State; Dr. Harry Harding of George Washington University; Dr. Lyman Miller of the Naval Postgraduate School and the Hoover Institution; Dr. Michel Oksenberg of Stanford University; and Dr. Michael Swaine of RAND. Doak played a seminal role not only in the development of this volume, but, more important, in the evolution of the field of contemporary Chinese studies as a whole. In its quest to bring the worlds of scholarship and policy practice together this volume is a fitting memorial to an exceptional man who inspired all of the volume's contributors.

In addition to the contributors, I thank the National Committee on United States–China Relations in New York. I began this volume prior to leaving my post as president of that organization and coming to the Paul H. Nitze School of Advanced International Studies at Johns Hopkins University and The Nixon Center in late 1997. The committee's new president, John Holden; its chairman, Barber B. Conable, Jr.; and its board of directors were kind enough to consent to administer the project after my departure. The Committee's sponsorship of this undertaking was appropriate given its historical commitment to public education on China and United States–China relations. In particular I must express the authors' collective appreciation to Mr. Andrew Dorko of the National Committee staff, who provided the logistical and general support essential to the project's success, and to Ms. Ros Daly, National Committee vice president for administration and development, who so ably kept this undertaking on financial track.

Turning to the revision, editing, and production of this volume, I thank two anonymous outside reviewers commissioned by Stanford University Press for their trenchant, useful comments. Moreover, the chapter authors and I express our appreciation to Ms. Krista Forsgren Ahdieh for her help in editing and polishing the manuscript, as we all do to Princeton Editorial Associates and Mr. Peter Strupp. And finally, to Ms. Muriel Bell, editor at Stanford University Press, I offer my thanks for her support and guidance during the process of moving this volume toward the light of day.

In short, this book represents an enormous collective undertaking. Although the chapter authors and all of the persons and organizations involved in this undertaking may differ in their assessments of where China's policy-making process is heading and what those changes may mean for the future, all are united in their conviction that these will be among the central questions of the early twenty-first century.

David M. Lampton
Washington, D.C.

Abbreviations

ADB	Asian Development Bank
AFC	Asian Financial Crisis
AMS	Academy of Military Science
ANC	African National Congress
APEC	Asia Pacific Economic Cooperation forum
ARATS	Association for Relations Across the Taiwan Strait
ARF	ASEAN Regional Forum
ASEAN	Association of Southeast Asian Nations
BBC	British Broadcasting Corporation
CAIFC	China Association for International Friendly Contact
CASS	Chinese Academy of Social Sciences
CCGO	Central Committee General Office
CCP	Chinese Communist Party
CCTAO	Central Committee Taiwan Affairs Office
CD	Conference on Disarmament
CDM	Clean Development Mechanism
CICIR	Chinese Institute for Contemporary International Relations
CIISS	China Institute for International Strategic Studies
CMC	Central Military Commission

CNNC	Chinese National Nuclear Corporation
COSTIND	Commission of Science, Technology, and Industry for National Defense
CPD	Center for Peace and Development
CPU	central processing unit
CTBT	Comprehensive Test Ban Treaty
CWC	Chemical Weapons Convention
DPP	Democratic Progressive Party (Taiwan)
DPRK	Democratic People's Republic of Korea
DSS	Department of Strategic Studies
EI	economic interdependence
EOI	export-oriented industrialization
ESCAP	Economic and Social Commission for Asia and the Pacific
EU	European Union
FALSG	Foreign Affairs Leading Small Group
FAO	Foreign Affairs Office
FBIS	Foreign Broadcast Information Service
FCCC	Framework Convention on Climate Change
FDI	foreign direct investment
FETC	Foreign Economic and Trade Commission
FISS	Foundation for International Strategic Studies
FMPC	Fissile Materials Production Cutoff
GAD	General Armaments Department
GATT	General Agreement on Tariffs and Trade
GDBOI	Guangdong Board of Investment
GL	global logic
GLD	General Logistics Department
GPL	General Political Department
GSD	General Staff Department
IAEA	International Atomic Energy Agency
ICI	Imperial Chemical Industries
ICITO	Interim Commission for the International Trade Organization
ID	Investigation Department
IDA	International Development Agency
IGO	intergovernmental organization
ILD	International Liaison Department
IPR	intellectual property rights
ISI	import-substituting industrialization
ISS	Institute for Strategic Studies
KOTRA	Korean Trade Promotion Association
KWP	Korean Workers' Party

LD	Liaison Department
LSG	leading small group
MCI	Ministry of Chemical Industry
MEI	multilateral economic institution
MFA	Ministry of Foreign Affairs
MFN	most favored nation
MII	Ministry of Information Industries
MNC	multinational corporation
MND	Ministry of National Defense
MOFTEC	Ministry of Foreign Trade and Economic Cooperation
MSS	Ministry of State Security
MTCR	Missile Technology Control Regime
NATO	North Atlantic Treaty Organization
NCA	Nuclear Cooperation Agreement
NDC	newly democratizing country
NDU	National Defense University
NEPA	National Environmental Protection Agency
NGO	nongovernmental organization
NIC	newly industrialized country
NPC	National People's Congress
NPT	Nuclear Non-Proliferation Treaty
NTR	normal trade relations
NWFZ	nuclear weapon free zone
OCAO	Overseas Chinese Affairs Office
ODS	ozone-depleting substance
OPCW	Organization for the Prohibition of Chemical Weapons
PBSC	Politburo Standing Committee
PD	Propaganda Department
PFA	People's Friendship Association
PLA	People's Liberation Army
PNE	peaceful nuclear explosion
PNTR	permanent normal trade relations
PRC	People's Republic of China
PRO	Political Research Office
PTBT	Partial Test Ban Treaty
ROK	Republic of Korea
SCFAO	State Council Foreign Affairs Office
SAR	Special Administrative Region
SASS	Shanghai Academy of Social Sciences
SCTAO	State Council Taiwan Affairs Office
SDPC	State Development Planning Commission

SEF	Strait Exchange Foundation (Taiwan)
SEPA	State Environmental Protection Administration
SETC	State Economic and Trade Commission
SEZ	special economic zone
SIIS	Shanghai Institute for International Studies
SMA	State Meteorological Administration
SOE	state-owned enterprise
SPA	Supreme People's Assembly
SPC	State Planning Commission
SSTC	State Science and Technology Commission
START	Strategic Arms Reduction Talks
TALSG	Taiwan Affairs Leading Small Group
TARO	Taiwan Affairs Research Office
TIA	Transparency in Armaments (committee name)
TMD	Theater Missile Defense
TMN	transnational manufacturing network
TRADP	Tumen River Area Development Program
TRI	Taiwan Research Institute
TRIMS	trade-related investment measures
TTBT	Threshold Test Ban Treaty
UFWD	United Front Work Department
UN	United Nations
UNDP	United Nations Development Program
UNEP	United Nations Environment Program
UNROCA	United Nations Register of Conventional Arms
U.S.	United States
USFK	United States Forces in Korea
USTR	United States Trade Representative
VOA	Voice of America
WTO	World Trade Organization

The Making of Chinese
Foreign and Security Policy
in the Era of Reform, 1978–2000

China's Foreign and National Security Policy-Making Process: Is It Changing, and Does It Matter?

DAVID M. LAMPTON

When asked what he and other economic officials thought about the February 21, 2000, white paper on Taiwan that threatened a firestorm of reaction in Washington that might affect pending China-related legislation, a PRC [People's Republic of China] economic official responded as follows: "We [economic officials] said it would be bad for WTO [the World Trade Organization], but we were not the leading group creating this policy so ours was just a voice in a room. Nobody was going to listen to us. . . . Policies are created not by the whole government, but by parts in the government. We often don't know what the other side is doing."[1]

INTRODUCTION

The second half of the twentieth century witnessed a gradual and important change in the Chinese foreign and national security policy-making process as it successively moved through the eras of Mao Zedong, Deng Xiaoping, and Jiang Zemin. This shift is not only of theoretical importance; it also has significant consequences for China's international behavior in the early twenty-first century. The world involvement of the PRC is now much more extensive than in the earlier period, particularly in the domains of economics, culture, and multilateral organizations. Moreover, the role of expertise in government is much greater, the bureaucracy is more differentiated and complex, and therefore the way in which recurrent policy issues are handled is different. Concisely, the process for making recurrent, noncrisis decisions is more bureaucratic in character, with elite options constrained; decisions are often harder to produce. Frequently, as the quote opening this chapter suggests, the left hand does not know what the right is doing.

On the other hand, showing some continuity with the period of Mao, the most senior political elite, headed by General Secretary Jiang Zemin, continues to play the decisive role in establishing broad national strategy. It alone determines policy on issues such as China's big power alignments, whether or not to join the WTO, and whether or not to set a timetable for national reunification with Taiwan, potentially jeopardizing other important national goals.[2] With regard to these strategic questions, it is essential to know the arena in which decisions are made and who sits at the table.

The Chinese policy-making process, therefore, presents the analyst with two faces. With regard to major issues of strategy, the setting of broad agendas, and crisis management, the senior elite still has considerable latitude. As Nathan and Ross observe, "Of all the large countries, China has had the greatest freedom to maneuver, act on grand strategy, shift alignments, and conduct a strategic foreign policy in the rational pursuit of national interest."[3] Dramatic changes in policy are, therefore, possible, although the personalized authority of Jiang Zemin is dramatically less than that of Mao Zedong in the earlier era, and (as Bates Gill points out in his contribution to this volume), the elite is often hemmed in by the cumulative logic of previous, recurrent decisions.

At the same time, in its myriad dealings with the rest of the world on routine issues ranging from arms control to economic relations, Beijing increasingly speaks, often with multiple voices, in terms familiar to the rest of the world, and policy changes gradually. In this realm, decisions tend toward global and professional norms, against the ever-present backdrop of realpolitik and considerations of national interest.[4] Those who deal with Beijing, therefore, must be aware of the potential for abrupt changes arising from a system that is compartmentalized and personalized at the very top. At the same time, they may be reassured by the constraints that offer the prospect of a China that eventually may fit more comfortably into the international order.

Beyond change and continuity in China's foreign policy and national security decision-making processes and how these alterations have affected Beijing's declaratory policies and actual behavior, a number of questions animate the chapters that follow: Do nations learn from prior experience, and, if so, how? What is the relationship between bureaucratic structure and policy-making behavior? To what degree and how do professionalism, pluralization, decentralization, and globalization affect substantive Chinese policy and the policy-making process? What is the relationship between domestic politics and external action? How do foreign policy-making processes and behavior change as systems move from the hands of a charismatic, revolutionary leadership to a more technocratic elite? Are global economic, information, security, and technological interdependencies shaping the behavior of foreign policy leaderships, and, if so, how? How do transnational communities of experts ("epistemic communities") affect policy? What role does "national interest" play in the formation of foreign policy, and are state-centered (parochial) notions giving way to broader concepts of "cooperative security"? Why do some areas of a nation's foreign policy and behavior see pronounced change and others demonstrate great continuity? What factors account for the gaps between declaratory foreign policy pronouncements and actual behavior? And to what degree have China's foreign relations exceeded the capacity of its foreign policy apparatus to control such relations? In the latter respect, are we likely to see the emergence of formal institutions of government that are more dedicated to international cooperation just as the ability of such institutions to control society's behavior in the international context declines?

This volume explores these practical and theoretical issues by examining several domains. Part I addresses the changing structures and roles of institutions and localities. Part II assesses the changing patterns of elite and societal opinion, while Part III examines the influences of the international system. The volume concludes, in Part IV, by exploring how the preceding variables (institutions and localities, elite and societal opinion, and the international system) have played out in important cases: arms control, Taiwan policy-making, WTO entry, and Chinese policy-making with regard to the volatile Korean Peninsula. In short, this volume examines both the dimensions of change in PRC foreign and national security policy-making processes and the implications of those changes for system behavior in areas of substantive policy-making.

THE PROCESSES OF PROFESSIONALIZATION, CORPORATE PLURALIZATION, DECENTRALIZATION, AND GLOBALIZATION

Two broad changes in the Chinese policy-making process are documented in the chapters that follow: First, the number of actors, though still comparatively small, is increasing; in the words of Fewsmith and Rosen in their contribution to this volume, the elite is thickening. As part of this expansion, previously peripheral actors are becoming more numerous and more proximate to the decision-making arenas, particularly with respect to routinized, noncrisis categories of policy choice. Second, individuals, organizations, and localities not formally involved in the foreign and national security policy-making process nonetheless have more space to act internationally. Beyond changing the character of much foreign interaction with the PRC, the actions of somewhat autonomous Chinese individuals, groups, and localities increasingly generate issues and problems and exert pressures to which the central foreign policy elite must respond.

With respect to the latter dynamic, those not formally involved in the foreign policy-making and implementation processes often act internationally and thereby play a role (inadvertently perhaps) in setting the central elite's foreign policy agenda and establishing some of the broad parameters within which Beijing must make decisions. For example, somewhat autonomous exporters can transfer technology and hardware that raise security problems for the United States or others, thereby generating external pressure on Beijing to develop export controls and clamp down on those actors.[5] Similarly, local officials can turn a blind eye to the illegal trade in human beings smuggled abroad because the money remitted to their home locality by the emigrants (not to mention initial bribes) have become important sources of local revenue and personal income.[6] This trade, in turn, produces foreign pressure on Beijing to stop the illegal flow. Finally, as the chapters by Peter T. Y. Cheung and James T. H. Tang and by Samuel S. Kim amply demonstrate, in the case of policy-making related to the Republic of Korea, provinces can nudge central policy-makers either to move in directions in which they might not otherwise spontaneously move or to change policy earlier than was anticipated.

Four "-izations" (si hua)—professionalization, corporate pluralization, decentralization, and globalization—are driving the twin developments noted earlier in this section. It is with respect to these transformations that the following chapters are most illuminating. Using these chapters as my principal data, in this chapter I address these changes, assess their impact on policy formulation and implementation, and conclude with a discussion of what they mean for system behavior and our understanding of some basic theoretical issues.

Professionalization

Professionalization, as used here, refers to a number of related developments. These include the trend toward a higher level of specialized knowledge among Chinese elite and subelite foreign policy decision-makers; the proliferation of expert-based bureaucracies in the decision-making process; and the increased reliance by decision-makers on information provided by specialized bureaucracies (and their attention to the quality and diversity of such information). The baseline for understanding what happened in this dimension between 1978 and 2000 is presented in this volume in the chapters by Lu Ning, H. Lyman Miller and Liu Xiaohong, and Michael Swaine. Almost every contribution to this volume, however, speaks to professionalism and its profound effect on the Chinese foreign and national security policy-making process.

The character of China's elite has undergone a dramatic change in the post–Mao Zedong era. This evolution is apparent when one examines the distinct attributes of the leadership ranks at the Twelfth Congress of the Chinese Communist Party (CCP) in 1982, the first full-fledged congress with Deng Xiaoping at the helm, and at the Fifteenth Party Congress in 1997, the first at which Jiang Zemin was preeminent. Comparing the respective Politburos elected by each, the Jiang leadership was nearly a decade younger, on average, than that of the 1982 Politburo; more than half of the Fifteenth Congress Politburo did not join the CCP until after the PRC's founding in 1949; and, as Miller and Liu report, although none of the members of the 1982 Politburo had a university degree, 70 percent of the Fifteenth Congress Politburo did. Similarly, Lu Ning notes that although past senior leaderships included very few persons who spoke foreign languages, the Politburo selected by the Fifteenth Party Congress consisted entirely of members who could speak a foreign language, save one person. If one examines local leadership in China, the trend toward technocratic leadership is also apparent, suggesting that those in the promotion pipeline will reinforce an already evident technocratic trend.[7] As Cheung and Tang explain in their chapter on provinces, "The training and backgrounds of FAO [provincial foreign affairs office] officials has gradually improved. Young recruits tend to be graduates of foreign language universities or colleges, with a specialty in international studies. Some of the senior officials, such as those in Guangdong, have postgraduate degrees from Western countries or have received overseas training."

There is not an easily demonstrable linkage between aggregate attributes of the elite and subsequent policy-making behavior. Nonetheless, such statistics and generalizations take concrete form when one encounters central PRC leaders and officials from China's provinces. To meet General Secretary Jiang Zemin, for example, likely means that you will hear about the latest book he is reading. One of Jiang's closest confidants is former Shanghai Mayor Wang Daohan, who, beyond his many foreign policy–related responsibilities, periodically provides the general secretary with a list of books and articles containing new ideas. Indeed, a best-selling book entitled *Jiang Zemin's Counselors* includes Wang Daohan as the subject of the first chapter, "The Red Dynasty's Imperial Mentor Wang Daohan" (*Hong chao di shi Wang Daohan*).[8] As Swaine observes in his chapter, "Wang is widely viewed as Jiang's most trusted advisor on Taiwan affairs and a key channel for [expert] advice." From the elite on down, expert knowledge and information are part of the legitimating gestalt for leadership. The elite is in a constant search for information, and such information has resulted in policy change. Nonetheless, just because the elite seeks out information does not mean that it collects, processes, or uses that information to which outsiders might attach importance.

In September 1998, Jiang Zemin set up a foreign policy group of "wise men" composed of about twenty-five former Chinese ambassadors. With limited staff, this group discusses those foreign policy questions of most interest to Jiang (who is not only general secretary of the CCP and state president and chairman of the Central Military Commission, but also head of the Foreign Affairs Leading Small Group and the Taiwan Affairs Leading Small Group), conveying its conclusions back to the general secretary.[9] Jiang also relies on academic and policy advisors in Shanghai. Jiang's reliance on personal advisors, his creation of the group of wise men, and his close connections to the Shanghai intellectual community all represent efforts to obtain a broad range of information before issues are decided and to move beyond the perspectives provided by Beijing's permanent bureaucracies. In his chapter, Lu Ning summarizes the fundamental transition that has occurred in the elite in the 1990s; as Lu says, "The emergence of Jiang Zemin, Li Peng, and Zhu Rongji at the center of political power represents a transition of Chinese political leadership from a generation of revolutionary politicians to a generation of technocrat politicians."

Beyond the changing character of China's central (or "core") political and foreign policy elite that Lu Ning describes, changes in the Ministry of Foreign Affairs (MFA) are also important. The MFA, the agency with the day-to-day responsibility for policy recommendation and implementation in the area of foreign affairs, is singular among Chinese ministries. It has a deeply ingrained professional culture that dates back to the late 1930s and 1940s,[10] when Zhou Enlai began to build the CCP cadre (many members of which had had a Western education), first in Hubei, and later in Sichuan, during the war against the Japanese.[11] Even with this baseline, the movement of the reform-era MFA toward greater professionalization and internal differentiation during the eras of Deng Xiaoping and Jiang Zemin has been notable. This increased professionalism can be seen in the number of persons the MFA sends abroad for graduate-level training in international affairs and in the increasing introduction of foreign materials and lecturers into training programs such as those at the Foreign Affairs College. Increasing professionalization is also apparent in the MFA's extensive information-gathering and dissemination system, which is described in detail by Lu Ning in his contribution to this volume and evidenced in the fact that the ministry itself increasingly seeks outside expert advice.[12]

The MFA's professionalization and specialization is also reflected in the agency's bureaucratic structure. For example, as Gill points out in his chapter, the MFA has gradually created not only an arms control department (under the leadership of Sha Zukang), but has hired personnel who are increasingly conversant with the technical dimensions of arms control issues. This permits the MFA to be more effective not only in dealing with foreign negotiators, but also in acting as a counterweight to domestic constituencies in the military and arms industry that have an interest in looser export controls. As Gill writes: "The MFA became a more important and institutionalized participant in arms export decision-making, along with trade-related and military-related organizations. In the case of highly advanced exports and exports to 'sensitive regions,' the MFA takes part in a high-level interagency body . . . that was first established in 1989. If an export is expected to generate opposition abroad, the MFA is to write up a justification for the transfer for the leadership to consider. . . . Chinese export control regulations issued in the late 1990s likewise describe a prominent role for the MFA in vetting military-related exports." As the MFA has increased its capability to articulate its arms control interests, it appears that the military has likewise supplemented its in-house expertise to protect its equities. In short, there is something of a bureaucratic arms race going on in which the increasing specialization of one bureaucratic combatant requires others to increase their own expertise.

Professionalism and increasing bureaucratic specialization are apparent not only in the MFA, but also in the Ministry of Foreign Trade and Economic Cooperation (MOFTEC). With respect to proliferation and technology concerns, for instance, MOFTEC's Bureau of Science and Technology has become a pivotal control point for nuclear, dual-use, and chemical exports (though not weapons). Indeed, in December 1998 an expert delegation led by MOFTEC Director General Xu Fuxing visited Washington, D.C., to explain the PRC's export control regulations to Capitol Hill staffers. Among the notable characteristics of the delegation were its comparative youth and high professional caliber. As the expertise and professionalism of persons and institutions in the MFA, the People's Liberation Army (PLA), and other bodies grow, their advice is increasingly available to the upper reaches of the Chinese decision-making structure. Gill's chapter suggests that the perspectives of such bodies are playing an increasing role in shaping policy.

Nor are professionalism and specialization limited to policy-making in the areas of technical and economic issues; rather, they extend to regional and geographic concerns as well. With respect to policy regarding Taiwan, for instance, in his contribution to this volume Swaine points out that a number of new organizations have been created to manage policy (the CCP Central Committee Taiwan Affairs Office and the Taiwan Affairs Leading Small Group, founded in 1979 and 1980, respectively). Moreover, such policy-making and coordination organs have come to rely on both their own professional research bureaus and outside research agencies. Among the latter are the Chinese Academy of Social Sciences' Taiwan Affairs Research Office and the China Institute for Contemporary International Relations, as well as Xiamen University's Institute for Taiwan Studies and many other military and CCP research and intelligence organs. According to Swaine, the foregoing entities "have grown significantly in number and in importance to the policy-making process. They have become particularly significant since the early 1990s, when the third generation of party leaders came to the fore. The Jiang Zemin led leadership has come to rely on a wide range of 'external' policy inputs, including the expertise of research institutes, staff offices, and personal advisors, to make strategic assessments and effective policy decisions."

This growing reliance on internal and external research has been driven by the increasing complexity of contemporary technology transfer and arms control issues, as well as the need to know more about circumstances in specific localities such as Taiwan. Nonetheless, just because more—and more diverse—information is available to top decision-makers does not mean that basic strategic decision-making will be insulated from other powerful considerations, such as domestic political struggle, deeply embedded perceptions, or basic value or interest commitments. Beijing's seemingly counterproductive Taiwan policy of 1999–2000 may be a good case in point.

Another area of foreign policy that has required progressively greater personnel specialization and bureaucratic differentiation has been China's international economic relations and need to deal with international economic, development, trade, and financial organizations such as the General Agreement on Tariffs and Trade / World Trade Organization (GATT/WTO), the International Monetary Fund (IMF), and the World Bank, not to mention the global private financial community. The trend in this area began in the early 1970s with Beijing's efforts to develop the expertise it would need to be effective in the United Nations. To this end, for example, Premier Zhou Enlai sent Long Yongtu (who would later lead the negotiations on WTO entry) to the London School of Economics (in 1973–1974) for training in Western international economics. Premier Zhou realized that after its long years of isolation from the Western economy, China had virtually no senior government personnel who understood Western economics or international trade.[13]

The institutional landscape of MOFTEC has also changed internally in response to China's interaction with international economic organizations. As Margaret M. Pearson writes in her chapter: "The GATT organization itself gained a foothold in the bureaucracy when the GATT (now WTO) Division was set up in MOFTEC to handle the relationship with the multilateral institution and when the State Council created the GATT LSG [Leading Small Group]." Similarly, the Ministry of Finance had to create new internal organizations and capabilities to deal with the World Bank once Beijing joined the organization in 1980. According to Jacobson and Oksenberg, "Its [the Ministry of Finance's] External Finance Department grew to a fifty-member bureau consisting of four divisions. . . . Also at the Ministry of Finance, the Bureau of Education assumed responsibility for managing a major cadre training program sponsored by the World Bank's Economic Development Institute."[14] Discussing MOFTEC's GATT/WTO Division, Pearson says, "Although it is not true . . . that MOFTEC's GATT/WTO Division was 'in the pocket' of the global institution (though it sometimes is accused of such), the institutional norms of MOFTEC became increasingly aligned with the norms of the international regime, and its officials have become the strongest advocates within the government for China's adoption of international practices."

In the economic arena, as with arms control and Taiwan policy, the need for specialized research has become increasingly pronounced. As important, this research is valued for its analytical independence, not its political correctness. Thomas G. Moore and Dixia Yang note in their chapter, for example, that with respect to the Asian Financial Crisis (AFC) "studies are also more frequently commissioned without indicating the desired policy direction. One interviewee, for example, cited cases where the MFA had requested analysis without providing any information indicating prejudgment of the issue."

In the continual bureaucratic and personal struggle of Chinese politics, the need for greater expertise naturally disadvantages some preexistent organizations and favors other (often new) ones. As Lu Ning points out, for example, the drive to deal effectively with the outside world (and the collapse of communist regimes) has weakened the old propaganda and International Liaison Department functions of the CCP. For example, the party's Central External Propaganda Small Group was abolished in 1987 due to its "ineffectiveness." In its place, the State Council and the party have substituted the State Council Information Office and the Party International Communication Office, both of which are headed (and have been since 1998) by Zhao Qizheng, the cosmopolitan former vice mayor of Shanghai. In turn, Zhao is recruiting personnel who have spent time abroad, speak foreign languages, and better understand public relations.[15]

Professionalism, specialization, and bureaucratic differentiation are important to the development of Chinese foreign policy-making, as well as to the larger issue of how China is fitting into the structures of world affairs. In Chinese bureaucracy, one finds increasing interaction with specialists abroad and in so-called epistemic communities—transnational groups of like-minded persons with common knowledge, concerns, and interests. In this way, expert perspectives are becoming globalized. Elizabeth Economy most clearly addresses this important development in her chapter. She describes how the interaction of experts in China's National Environmental Protection Agency (since 1998 the State Environmental Protection Agency) and State Science and Technology Commission (SSTC) with counterparts abroad affected the course of China's debates over accession to the Montreal Protocol (the agreement to phase out ozone-depleting substances) and the Framework Convention on Climate Change. With respect to the Montreal Protocol, for instance, Economy writes: "The relatively high degree of international attention, scientific certainty, and interest of the Chinese scientific community persuaded the Chinese leadership to establish a working group under the auspices of the National Environmental Protection Agency (NEPA) to evaluate the costs and benefits of signing the Protocol. . . . According to one member of the working group, strong scientific evidence and interactions with the international scientific community were key components of the group's deliberations."

Epistemic communities introduce new perspectives into the system and create peer standards against which the Chinese may judge their own behavior. External expert communities also feed data and money into the system, providing resources that were previously unavailable (as in the case of the PRC's efforts to develop a research program on climate change). Economy points out that the NEPA drew on research from the international community to fight against the "outdated methodologies" and "conservative findings" of the State Meteorological Administration. As she says, "The international community thus expanded the range of environmental and economic scenarios developed by the Chinese and even contributed to a radical reorientation in the perspective of some officials." In this effort, the international scientific community, the NEPA, and the SSTC were implicitly allied against more conservative, domestically grounded agencies. In the economic area, Moore and Yang similarly point out that "the transfer of economic ideas and norms clearly has been an important channel of influence in areas such as customs law, trade and investment policy, and accounting practices." The formation of these "epistemic communities" or "cohorts" is evident in the arms control arena as well. Gill's chapter provides a glimpse into the formation of like-minded cohorts that cut across organizational lines and reveals an increased willingness to solicit and accept advice from outside—even foreign—institutional structures.

Although I examine the impact of this professionalizing trend on policy outputs (formulated policy) and outcomes (the actual effects of implemented policy) later in this chapter, a few words are necessary about what these trends signify. First, professionalism is only one of many contributors to the erosion in the role of the "preeminent leader," especially with respect to an enlarging zone of routinized decisions. Second, leaders at all levels of the Chinese system are beginning to look more like technical managers and less like the strategic visionaries of the PRC's first- and second-generation elite. Third, growing professionalization, mounting specialization, a more complex bureaucracy, and more information have together created a setting in which persuasion is an increasingly important tool of leadership; compulsion has correspondingly retreated as a leadership instrument, although it is never entirely absent.

As Swaine puts it when discussing the shift to post Deng Xiaoping foreign policy and national security leadership, "This transition reinforced the trend . . . toward a more extensive, bureaucratic, and consensus-oriented policy-making process. This process therefore supplanted the largely top-down, authoritarian, personalistic, and at times ideological pattern of decision-making of the Deng era."

On the other hand, China's trend toward professionalism does *not* mean that individual Chinese leaders, their policy preferences, and their personal connections are unimportant, nor does it mean that strategic decisions are highly participatory. Indeed, with respect to nonrecurrent, crisis, and strategic decisions, the personal and power dimensions remain absolutely crucial because these types of decisions are made in settings of fewer participants, greater time compression, less information, and they are decisions that demonstrably affect the fundamental interests of the regime. Furthermore, increasing professionalism, knowledge-based decision-making, and "epistemic community" participation does not mean that Chinese and Western interests (and therefore policies) will necessarily converge. Elizabeth Economy, for instance, shows how China resisted participation in global greenhouse gas restrictions, notwithstanding just such professionalism.

Corporate Pluralization

Corporate pluralization refers to the proliferation of organizations, groups, and sometimes individuals in the policy-making process. In the PRC, although there are tendencies that hold out the prospect that currently unsanctioned social organizations may one day be part of a broader pluralization process, today almost all of the central actors are "licensed" in corporatist fashion to participate, and therefore their numbers are still comparatively small and their participation contingent on elite decisions. Nonetheless, even this restricted, corporatist pluralization has a number of effects. On the one hand, pluralization can enhance system legitimacy and compliance with decisions inasmuch as organizations and individuals come to feel that their interests are being taken (even minimally) into account. Moreover, pluralization increases the chances that decision-makers will have heard a greater number of the considerations that will affect a policy's viability. As Moore and Yang point out: "The foreign policy system is more open to expert input than in the past. . . . The result, by all accounts, is that a greater diversity of views on international economic issues such as the AFC now reaches top decision-makers." Even more hopeful with respect to nonproliferation and arms control policy, Gill asserts that "the twin trends of pluralization and institution building at home" are impelling China toward policies that increasingly conform to widely accepted international norms and practices.

This corporatist pluralization, however, can be a mixed blessing. The need to solicit, digest, bargain, and balance a greater number of views slows down the policy formulation process, as I have argued with respect to domestic policy-making.[16] Further, corporatist pluralization proliferates the points at which implementation can be subverted. Finally, although the popular opinion component of pluralization is beneficial in many ways, one might also be apprehensive about the nationalistic passions that may emerge, as Fewsmith and Rosen suggest in their contribution to this volume. Concisely, as more and more actors have become germane to the making and implementation of Chinese foreign and national security policy, we see both the gains and pathologies of pluralization, albeit a pluralization in which the societal component is still minimal.

What is the evidence that pluralization exists and is growing? At the most abstract level, it can be seen in the occasional reference to the constraints that "public opinion" places upon China's leaders. It is also apparent in the proliferation of interagency coordination (that is, "small leading") groups. Such coordination groups reconcile subordinate agencies experiencing bureaucratic conflicts and seek to ensure that once the elite makes a decision its intent is followed throughout the policy implementation process. These coordinating groups are properly viewed as reflections of bureaucratic pluralism, as do Hamrin and Zhao.[17] The need for an increasing number of coordinators, then, arises from the creation of new agencies and the addition of divisions within existing bureaucracies, with the resulting need to collect and process information and to maintain the control of the central elite.

A broader, less corporatist, pluralization increasingly can be seen in the nascent development of civic organizations, only a few of which are beginning to touch upon foreign policy-making. For example, as Economy notes, "Nongovernmental environmental organizations have also emerged, some of which are now becoming involved in ensuring local implementation of international environmental commitments." Similarly, Pearson notes that local industries and government authorities concerned about the impact of WTO entry on their interests have begun to draw on the work of local research organizations, including the WTO Research Center of Shanghai, which draws analysts from Shanghai-area universities and claims to be a nongovernmental organization. Despite the fact that the emergence of civic organizations may ultimately transform Chinese politics and policy-making, however, they continue to develop only slowly and under the watchful eye of Beijing.

Before discussing the third major trend, decentralization, a few more words are appropriate on two of the ways in which pluralization has manifested itself—public opinion and the need for interagency coordination.

Public Opinion. None of the authors whose work appears in this volume would argue that public opinion is either measured or worshiped in China in the same way it is in contemporary American society, although increasingly sophisticated polling (both domestic and foreign) is occurring in the PRC. Rather, public opinion helps demarcate space within which the leadership has relatively wide latitude to operate, as Fewsmith and Rosen explain. Although this space is large, it is not unlimited. Therefore, some issues and some domestic circumstances allow the leadership less room to operate than others. Leaders understand which issues are so sensitive that to mishandle them could lead to social instability or could provide political competitors an avenue by which to undermine them; there is a vague concept of "boundaries of the permissible." In this vein, according to Fewsmith and Rosen, "One of the most important ways in which public opinion has been expressed is through nationalism." PRC leaders consequently understand that perceived weakness in the face of a Japan unrepentant about its pre–World War II invasion of China and insistent on its territorial claims against the PRC is enough to bring nationalistic students into the streets. Public opinion surveys in China validate the wisdom of this view, though admittedly it is difficult to tell when methodologically weak surveys are used to validate the elite's preferred policy or when such presumed popular attitudes are driving elite decision-making. As Fewsmith and Rosen report: "One survey of attitudes toward Japan, conducted at the end of 1996, surprised even the surveyors. For example, the word *Japan* 'most easily' made 83.9 percent of the [Chinese] youth surveyed think of the Nanjing Massacre and made 81.3 percent think of 'Japanese denial' and the 'war of resistance against Japanese aggression.' When asked which twentieth-century Japanese was most representative of Japan, first place (28.7 percent) went to Tojo Hideki of World War II fame. When asked to place a label on the Japanese, 56.1 percent chose 'cruel.'"

Therefore, after President Jiang Zemin's trip to Japan in November 1998, there was severe popular and elite criticism of Foreign Minister Tang Jiaxuan for not having secured concessions from Tokyo and for being insufficiently strong in the face of what the Chinese widely interpreted as Tokyo's intransigence. Indeed, for some time after the trip it was unclear whether the foreign minister would survive politically.

Another illustration is useful here. In speaking with a member of the Standing Committee of the Politburo in April 1993, a visiting American delegation suggested that Beijing needed to make some concessions on human rights or normal tariff treatment by the United States would be put at risk, given President Clinton's pledge to link the PRC's individual rights behavior to Washington's tariff treatment. The Politburo Standing Committee member responded: "But I don't think I can report what you told me to the Chinese people via television, because they would say that . . . [I am] making China's policy based on the American President, and they would overthrow me. So all I can say to the Chinese people is that the Sino-American relationship is very important. Even though the United States is much richer and stronger, nevertheless, our two countries are equal. We believe that Sino-American relations, including MFN [most-favored-nation tariff treatment], are all based on equality and mutual benefit. . . . So while thanking you, I can only tell the Chinese people what I have told you now."[18]

A similar state of affairs exists concerning the issue of Taiwan. A Chinese scholar explained why Chinese leaders, when in doubt, take a hard line toward Taiwan in this way: "Our American friends talk about the pressure the U.S. administration [faces] on the Taiwan issue, but no pressure can be larger than the pressure Chinese leaders face on the Taiwan issue. Given this pressure, they have very little latitude. Even if we suppose that there are two options [hard and soft] and they use tough measures . . . , and the leader fails to resolve [the problem], he is justified. But, if [he] uses too much honey, and he fails, you are regarded as guilty by all future generations."[19]

As Fewsmith and Rosen conclude: "A case can be made that public opinion as that term is usually understood has begun to play a role, albeit one that remains restricted and significant only under certain conditions." One reason for this trend is that the current generation of Chinese leaders lacks the revolutionary and charismatic authority that legitimized the rule of Mao Zedong and Deng Xiaoping. Consequently, the new elite must seek legitimacy elsewhere; taking account of popular aspirations (including a desire for economic growth) is one way to do so. Another reason for the growing role of public opinion is the increasing number of institutional actors that have perceived stakes in foreign policy decisions. As more groups are mobilized, the "space" in which the political leadership must operate has narrowed. Further, Chinese leaders can reference public opinion to resist foreign entreaties and make their own policy positions more credible to foreigners. In short, public opinion not only constrains Chinese foreign policy, but may occasionally strengthen it as well.

Pearson raises an interesting paradox, noting that there is no evidence that public opinion has been highly influential in shaping WTO policy. Nonetheless, she observes that then-MOFTEC Minister Wu Yi and her principal vice minister in charge of GATT/WTO negotiations "concluded that it was important to educate Chinese citizens about GATT and its benefits for China" and that "one former MOFTEC official reported that he flew all over China, making at least two presentations a week on the subject."

There are a couple of hypotheses to explain why MOFTEC officials would spend time trying to educate the public (or key organizational groups) about the advantages of WTO accession. One is that they may have been seeking public support for their position and seeking to deny that support to bureaucratic, social, and territorial opponents. Another possibility is that MOFTEC officials sought to protect themselves against subsequent public criticism once WTO accession occurred. Whatever the motive, it appears that people in MOFTEC thought public, territorial, and organizational opinion was worth influencing.

Pluralism is evidenced not only in public opinion, but also within the bureaucracy. Bureaucratic pluralism, in turn, creates a need for interagency processes both for developing policy and for ensuring subsequent implementation.

Building Interagency Processes. As a nation's international involvement increases, the number of agencies participating in the foreign policy-making process increases, as does the number of domestic constituencies with a perceived stake in decisions. These developments, in turn, require the central leadership (and ministries like MOFTEC) to expend a greater amount of energy reconciling divergent interests and seeking to coordinate, reconcile, harmonize, or bring into line (*xietiao*) various governmental and social organizations. This need is apparent in the creation of new coordinators or the empowerment of existing agencies with this responsibility. As more Chinese agencies act abroad, moreover, the central leaders will need the means to better supervise subordinate agencies. Finally, as decisions become more complex and technical, increasingly specialized expertise will be necessary to formulate and evaluate policy. Increasingly, this expertise may be available from economic and social organizations that are somewhat or wholly autonomous with regard to the government.

How organizational proliferation and heightened international activity can combine to exponentially increase the need for interagency coordination is nowhere more evident than in the area of arms control in the 1980s. As Lu Ning points out, in the early 1980s weapons sales were "regarded as a normal trade issue with little need for oversight." As the military saw its budget decline[20] and began to cut back on procurement from domestic weapons manufacturers, however, both the PLA and arms manufacturers developed an incentive to increase arms sales abroad. The PLA was selling weapons out of its inventory. Indeed, arms makers and the military (particularly the PLA's General Staff Department) became competitors in this trade in the 1980s and much of the 1990s.

As this occurred, the United States became increasingly concerned about the character of the regimes that were purchasing Chinese arms and technologies. With the United States applying increasing pressure on Beijing to curtail such sales, the State Council and the CMC Military Products Trade Leading Small Group (LSG) was created in September 1989. Its purpose was primarily to ensure that the activities of the arms industry and military organizations with weapons to sell were known to and coordinated by senior political leaders so that any impact on foreign relations could be taken into account before problems arose. Although the CMC Military Products Trade LSG was abolished in a 1998 State Council restructuring, as Lu Ning documents in his chapter, over time other export control coordinators have been created within the MFA and MOFTEC as well.

The need for interagency coordination may also increase as a growing number of Chinese actors with a perceived stake in foreign and national security policy seek to advance their interests. As Moore and Yang explain, "The expanding role of foreign trade corporations and provincial governments illustrates how a broader range of political/economic/bureaucratic interests has been introduced into the process." China's growing place in the international economy and the increasing impact of international developments on domestic interests has therefore mobilized new groups in the foreign policy-making process. Pearson notes, "The incorporation of a greater number of interests was accompanied by efforts to arrive at consensus among this diverse set of actors."

More specifically, China's mounting international economic participation has changed MOFTEC in two respects. First, the ministry has had to expend increasing effort reconciling the various policy positions of different domestic constituencies. Second, and more fundamentally, the role of

MOFTEC in the overall foreign policy-making process has expanded. Generally, as conflicts multiply among agencies, some entity (sometimes a ministry like MOFTEC and sometimes an LSG like that on financial and economic affairs) must be designated to help develop or implement a unified policy. These are the "parts in the government" referred to in the chapter by Moore and Yang. As Lu concludes in his chapter, "As the dynamics of China's domestic and foreign policy change, some CCP central LSGs assumed new roles in foreign policy, whereas others have been abolished, and additional LSGs have been set up to cope with changed circumstances and to handle new issues that cut across vertical government, party, and military systems."

Mounting international economic involvement has not only increased the need for ministerial-level coordination (and in the process made MOFTEC a central foreign policy player), but it has also increased the need for supraministerial coordination. This can be seen in the growing role of the Central Financial and Economic Affairs Leading Small Group. As Lu Ning says, "The Central Financial and Economic Affairs LSG has . . . become an increasingly important locus for the making of China's foreign economic decisions and for coordination of their implementation." Swaine also speaks to the issue of pluralization and interagency processes in his discussion of Taiwan policy. In that discussion we see how four policy arenas (formulation/oversight, administration/implementation, coordination/supervision, and research/analysis) interact in an intricate and "complex decision-making process marked by extensive horizontal and vertical consultation, deliberation, and coordination." The examples of the CMC Military Products Trade Leading Small Group, MOFTEC, the Central Finance and Economics LSG, and the making of Taiwan policy all reveal that pluralization requires coordination and that such coordination can be provided either by newly created organizations (as in the case of the Military Products Trade LSG) or by preexisting organizations (such as MOFTEC and the Central Finance and Economics LSG). In either event, the social and governmental pluralization that creates the need for coordination itself spawns new organizations (or new divisions of existing organizations) to provide such coordination. This, in turn, compounds bureaucratic complexity.

Taken as a whole, pluralization is having a contradictory impact on the policy-making process. To start, this trend enhances the chances that policy decisions will be reached based on more varied input. At the same time, because many of the new institutional actors are designed to bring China into conformity with international norms and regimes (for instance, international arms control and financial arrangements), as Gill says, "The pluralization and institution-building process in China . . . offers new opportunities for Beijing to bring its practice more in line with international norms."

Nonetheless, there are downsides as well. To start, these changes almost guarantee that it will take longer to reach decisions and that most of the time policy will be more difficult to change and to effectively implement. Second, if public opinion, for example, is gradually playing a greater role in the Chinese foreign policy-making process, and if it has the increasingly nativist or populist tinge that Fewsmith and Rosen describe, the "public opinion" aspect of pluralization may introduce substantial volatility into Chinese foreign policy. Nonetheless, as a whole, pluralization of the foreign and national security policy-making process is a positive development. As Swaine argues, "On a broader level, the increasingly pragmatic, bureaucratic, and consensus-oriented nature of policy-making in the post-elder [post–Deng Xiaoping] era has increased the overall influence of policy-coordinating mechanisms such as the TALSG [Taiwan Affairs Leading Small Group]."

Finally, one other potentially problematic aspect of pluralization should be highlighted and leads to the discussion of decentralization that immediately follows. That is, as greater numbers of societal and lower-level bureaucratic and territorial actors interact with the world, particularly in the context of still weak regulatory and oversight mechanisms, Chinese behavior may occasionally be predatory or unmindful of international rules. The PRC's inability to control smuggling and enforce its own tariff schedules, along with the odious trade in human beings and drugs, reminds us of two sets of examples.

Decentralization

Beyond professionalization and pluralization, a third major trend in policy-making has been the gradual decentralization of power (occasionally in policy formulation and more often in implementation) both within the central bureaucracies and from Beijing to the rest of the country. Decentralization has been most evident in the international economic arena and least so in the handling of high-level diplomacy and national security strategy. Decentralization and pluralization are, in fact, intimately related, inasmuch as the delegation of authority to lower-level actors (for example, provinces), and the toleration of increased initiative by them gives rise to the growing number of actors that influence Chinese foreign policy.

Post-Mao decentralization of foreign and national security policy-making has been manifest in various ways. There has been a gradual flow of authority from the core leader to the broader central collective, from the central leadership to the supraministerial and ministerial levels, from the MFA to other central bureaucracies, noticeably MOFTEC, and, particularly in the economic arena, from Beijing gradually to the provinces, municipalities, and corporations.

This pattern of decentralization reflects many converging developments. Most important has been the PRC's increased interactions abroad. In 1978, the PRC had relations with 113 countries, in 1999 with 161—a 42 percent increase.[21] In the 1970s, China belonged to twenty-one international governmental organizations and 71 international nongovernmental organizations; by 1997 the respective numbers were 52 and 1,163.[22] In 1978, foreign trade constituted 10 percent of GDP; by 1995, it had reached 40.4 percent (on an exchange rate basis, which may overstate the country's actual trade dependence).[23] In the face of such a rapid growth of contacts, leaders at each system level have had to delegate responsibility to lower levels of the system.

Decentralization also reflects the migration of economic power from the government to society, as reflected in the decline of the percentage of GNP represented by government revenues from about 35 percent in 1978 to about 11 percent by 1995 (a low from which it had risen to about 14 percent by 1999).[24] Similarly, the proportion of total government expenditures (including extra-budgetary funds) controlled by Beijing had fallen from 47.4 percent in 1978 to 27.1 percent in 1996, whereas provincial control increased from 52.6 percent in 1978 to 72.9 percent in 1996.[25] Finally, decentralization has also been encouraged by the growing complexity of foreign and international economic policy decisions.

The chapters of this volume that address the role of provinces and aspects of economic policy-making provide the greatest insight into decentralization. For example, Moore and Yang argue that the central government, and Premier Zhu Rongji in particular, maintained tight control over the broad parameters of China's response to the Asian Financial Crisis from 1997 to 1999, particularly the decision to keep the PRC's exchange rate stable. However, as provinces (most notably Guangdong) saw their export growth in jeopardy and their export targets unchanged, they made what amounted to new policy to prevent the erosion of their own economic positions. As Moore and Yang explain: "In Guangdong several actions were taken by the provincial government to cope with the effects of declining growth in exports and foreign investment.

Some merely involved the implementation of measures approved by the central government (for example, raising the rates for export tax rebates). Others, however, were defiantly creative, such as giving provincial assistance to encourage private enterprises to engage in direct export. . . . According to some interviewees, this policy was adopted without the authorization of MOFTEC."

This example illustrates that although policy formulation authority may not be expressly delegated to lower levels, it may nonetheless be exercised by them. This relates to the concept of policy "space," to which we will return shortly. Many more actors, at an increasing range of levels in China, have more space within which to affect policy, at least in implementation. As Cheung and Tang put it, "[Provinces] sought to achieve these goals . . . by exploiting new opportunities and maximizing their interests within the broad framework of existing policies of the central government. Hence, it would be misleading to view provincial initiatives in external affairs as moves that are necessarily in conflict with central policies." There is therefore both de jure and de facto decentralization of policy-making in China, which either serve the purposes of the central government or run counter to them. Sometimes, the central government may not even "know" what "it" wants.

Cheung and Tang discuss three examples of provincial involvement in foreign policy-making. In each case, the localities involved had been left behind in the coastal development strategy; each sought to influence the government to permit the establishment of economic, diplomatic, or project relationships with neighboring countries or international agencies serving local interests. As often as not, Beijing responded positively.

The first example was the 1984 convocation of a "southwest regional economic coordination conference" (Sichuan, Guangxi, Yunnan, Guizhou, Tibet, and Chengdu and Chongqing), which was intended to help these areas compensate for the greater advantage coastal provinces enjoyed in economic development in a variety of ways, including that of influencing the central government. As Cheung and Tang report, "They formed this coalition not only to coordinate their own external economic policy, foster interprovincial cooperation, and attract foreign investment, but also to influence the policy-making of the central government and to jointly lobby for more central investment." In response, the central government actively supported some of these efforts, recognizing that the desire of the southwestern inland provinces to establish stronger local economic ties with neighbors to the south would serve Beijing's strategic interests in Vietnam and elsewhere in Southeast Asia. In China as in America, the game of politics often is to show one's superiors how one's agenda serves their purposes.

Another instance of provincial involvement in foreign policy involved the northeastern province of Liaoning and the eastern province of Shandong, which are situated strategically adjacent to South Korea. Though Beijing and Seoul did not establish formal diplomatic relations until 1992, according to Cheung and Tang both "Liaoning and Shandong actively competed in opening up contacts between the two countries in 1988, when both provinces attempted to make arrangements for the first South Korean trade mission to China." Indeed, contacts between the two provinces and South Korea received central approval prior to the establishment of diplomatic relations. And one can see why these two localities were so anxious, with more than 85 percent of South Korean investments in the 1990s going to the Bohai Sea area (Shandong, Jilin, Liaoning, and Heilongjiang Provinces).

A final—and perhaps most revealing—example of provincial foreign policy initiative involves Jilin Province in China's northeast, which borders both Russia and North Korea. Jilin is an inland province whose only route to the Pacific is the partially Pyongyang-controlled Tumen River. Consequently, as Cheung and Tang explain, "Jilin has always been eager to get access to the sea. Since the mid-1980s Jilin's efforts to promote a regional cooperative [development] scheme around the Tumen River involving China, North and South Korea, the former Soviet Union, Japan, and Mongolia clearly reflected strong local desires to benefit from the country's coastal development strategy. In promoting local provincial interests, Jilin tried to influence the country's foreign relations to the province's benefit." Kim further shows how Jilin's desires resonated with central purposes: the Tumen Project was another means by which to stabilize the Yanbian Korean Autonomous Prefecture in Jilin Province, which was conceivably threatened by possible sociopolitical turmoil in North Korea.

Jilin's efforts to influence Beijing were multifaceted, protracted, and effective. They included undertaking research, drafting thoughtful recommendations for central decision-makers to consider, lobbying the Foreign Ministry to put sea access on the agenda with Moscow, and lobbying Huan Xiang (then director of the State Council's Center for International Studies), who in turn mobilized the head of the SSTC and Premier Li Peng. Through these efforts and others, as Cheung and Tang say, "eventually the province secured the central government's endorsement to negotiate for China's navigation rights on the Tumen River." Jilin also secured United Nations (UN) sponsorship for several conferences and UN Development Program involvement in some of the Tumen Project planning efforts.

Each of these examples of provincial involvement in the foreign policy-making process had its initial motivation in economic considerations. Nonetheless, these economic motivations had diplomatic and strategic consequences, inasmuch as the above provinces were proposing new relationships with countries with which Beijing has historically dealt carefully—Vietnam, Russia, North Korea, and South Korea. Therefore, provincial initiatives may have called the attention of the central government to new opportunities and encouraged policies that otherwise might never have been considered.

In her analysis of the WTO accession discussions, Pearson calls attention to another way in which provinces affect policy. Provinces may not only affirmatively seek permission for policy departures, but also seek to prevent the adoption of international economic policies they consider contrary to their interests. For instance, Pearson notes that some provinces opposed WTO accession because they perceived that they had nothing to gain, and much to lose, from global competition. Moreover, some provinces did not want to see the recentralization of power in MOFTEC that would come with China's commitments to abide by WTO rules. As one Chinese scholar explained it, many provincial trade corporations and local trade regulators believed that if Beijing adopted universal rules of trade administration, they would lose their capacity to extract "rents" for their required approvals. As he said, "Much of MOFTEC is opposed, and provincial and municipal [trade entities] are monopolies, so they are opposed" to universal rules and national treatment for foreign firms.[26]

The effects of decentralization have also been apparent in the arms sales and technology transfer area. As Gill reports, "For example, China's initial efforts at trade liberalization included the decentralization of trade authority from a handful of centrally controlled foreign trade companies to 'private' foreign trade corporations operating independent of the government's foreign trade plan." The entrepreneurship of these firms in the sale of arms to sensitive countries, however, created foreign policy problems that the central government has had, in turn, to address by exerting tighter control and oversight. Nonetheless, although this problem has been addressed, it has by no means been resolved. A 1999 Central Intelligence Agency Nonproliferation Center report covering the first half of 1998 makes clear that entities in Russia and China were still exporting chemical, biological, and nuclear weapons technology, as well as missile technology, although there is some indication that subsequently progress was made.[27]

All this brings us to the most important aspect of decentralization. Since provinces and other local actors have more space in which to operate, particularly in the international economic realm, these authorities and actors are increasingly taking actions that create problems for the central government to address. For instance, the smuggling of human beings from Fujian Province (in particular) has been a growing problem throughout the reform era.[28] Such trade in humans could not occur without the complicity of local officials, and this practice brings repeated protests from foreign governments. Similarly, many local governments and economic entities in the PRC feared Beijing would devalue the renminbi (RMB) in response to the AFC. They therefore kept hard currency outside the country or kept earnings in hard currency (often U.S. dollars) rather than RMB. The cumulative effect of these actions was to further weaken confidence in Beijing's pledge not to devalue the RMB; in turn, these moves led Beijing to impose foreign exchange control regulations that aggravated foreigners who now found it more difficult to exchange RMB for U.S. dollars. As Moore and Yang put it, "Subnational actors typically have greater input into policy *feedback* than into policy *formulation*."

Therefore, decentralization has had a number of effects on the Chinese foreign and national security policy-making processes. Most important, it has multiplied the points of initiative within the Chinese system and, according to Moore and Yang, "increased the prospects for widespread learning from China's participation in world markets." But these same beneficiaries of decentralization are often attached to the previous arrangements from which they have benefited; this can slow down the pace at which China conforms to global standards. Finally, decentralization can mean that the influence of lower-level participants comes primarily as policy is implemented, and thereafter through feedback. This feedback, in turn, shapes the agenda of central decision-makers.

Globalization

The fourth "-ization" that has figured prominently in the evolving character of the Chinese foreign and national security policy-making process since 1978 has been globalization, including economic globalization, information globalization, and the increasing degree to which national security must be multilaterally negotiated (not unilaterally secured). Because interdependence is a by-product of globalization and interdependence is presumed to foster cooperation, it is easy to assume that globalization will slowly erode Beijing's dedication to its narrow national interest and practice of realpolitik. Although there is plenty of evidence of increasing Chinese cooperation and conformity with international norms, there is little evidence that considerations of national interest and realpolitik figure any less prominently in Chinese thinking than they always have. As Thomas Moore remarked in 1998: "The Chinese are receptive to globalization as a means to become modern—it is not a goal, it is a means. Globalization is a limited, but positive, constraint on Chinese foreign policy. Policy and behavior has changed more than their [Beijing's] worldview."[29] Globalization has modified the PRC's behavior; because of it, China's leaders and citizens have developed a broader view of where their interests lie. This broader view does not always foster cooperation, however. Pearson, for example, points out that one of the principal effects of the protracted fight over the terms of the PRC's accession to WTO was to alert Chinese localities and industries to what they might lose if Beijing was too accommodating.

With respect to globalization's promotion of cooperation, there is no better example than that found in the analysis of Moore and Yang. In their case study of Beijing's response to the AFC, they suggest how a variety of considerations shaped China's policy and behavior. Of all these factors, however, China's integration into the world was primary. Take, for example, Beijing's persistence in maintaining the value of the RMB from 1997 to 1999. Beijing consistently characterized this decision as an example of its good citizenship, a move designed to avoid a spiral of competitive devaluations in the region and beyond. Good citizenship aside, Beijing's integration into the world economy made a devaluation of the RMB contrary to its own interests. Considerations of cooperative behavior and national interest thus coincided. As Moore and Yang explain, "Increased import costs [which would have occurred had there been a devaluation] were likely to inhibit the competitiveness of Chinese goods on the world market. Although devaluation would make finished Chinese goods cheaper on the world market, it would also raise the price of imported inputs [for instance, oil and components for assembly]. According to most estimates, about 50 percent of China's total exports depend on the processing of imported raw materials. . . . In this sense China's growing participation in TMNs [transnational manufacturing networks] reduced the efficacy of currency policy as an instrument for improving the competitiveness of 'Chinese' exports."

In short, China did not devalue the RMB because it was not in its interest to do so (though many Chinese exporters, including shipbuilders and steelmakers, vigorously called for it). Beijing defined its interests in the context of China's position in the global economic system and recognized that its behavior could create systemic instability contrary to its own overall interests. Therefore, China was acting based on its interests, but those interests were greatly influenced by China's role in the global manufacturing and trading system. Moore and Yang also explain how China's participation in international (largely private) capital markets and its incorporation into TMNs create "*private* conditionality driven by market forces that operates similarly to the *official* conditionality imposed on developing countries by foreign governments and MEIs [multilateral economic institutions]." If the PRC and its subordinate administrative units do not conform to norms acceptable to the broader international system and observed by its economic competitors, the capital available will flow to more congenial sites. As a result, because China has defined economic and technological modernization as its primary goal, conformance with international standards that put it in a favorable competitive position to obtain capital is often in China's interests even if interests are narrowly construed. According to Moore and Yang, the effect of this "global logic" is clear: "China finds itself today, contrary to its original plans, increasingly market oriented and deeply involved in the world economy." Market conditionality may therefore prove more important than the kind of political conditionality President Clinton tried (and failed) to impose by linking tariff treatment and human rights behavior from 1993 to 1994.

Another illustration of globalization is China's decision to join the signers of the Comprehensive Test Ban Treaty (CTBT). From 1994 to 1996, while negotiating over the terms of the CTBT, China joined France in not adhering to the self-imposed moratorium on nuclear testing observed by the United States, Britain, and Russia. Instead, Beijing conducted an accelerated testing program to modernize its nuclear forces before the treaty was to be signed in late 1996. China's leadership made a double calculation on the CTBT, believing that it could stand the international heat of continued testing for two years, but that its overall national security and international standing required it to ultimately sign the treaty. As Gill explains, "this decision [to sign the CTBT] was couched in the language of Chinese national interests, not an 'internationalist' or 'cooperative security' perspective. China's more cooperative position thus resulted from the limits imposed by the very processes of integration that the decision-makers sought to preserve and enhance." When China was faced with demands by both its Third World constituency and the other nuclear powers that it sign the CTBT, "this critical decision appeared to be driven largely by international pressures and a fractious internal debate that in the end favored accession—for the sake of China's international image and some possible relative gains in Chinese security." Therefore, Gill concludes that "China's policy-making is constrained by an intricate web of international dependencies, status relationships, and security realities it faces."

Finally, as Economy explains, it is certainly true that China's scientists, involved as they are in the international scientific community, have been progressively persuaded that ozone depletion is a problem affecting everyone, including China. But it was not simply an understanding of ecological interdependence or a sense of global obligation that resulted in Beijing's signing of the Montreal Protocol and subsequent participation in the regime. Rather, it was the combination of these considerations with more tangible interests—namely the desire to export appliances in conformance with international refrigerant codes and the promise of financial assistance as China adapted to the new regime—that proved decisive. In short, Chinese cooperative behavior is most likely when global interdependence creates a situation in which Beijing's own economic, security, and prestige interests are served by cooperation. Globalization often creates such circumstances, but not always.

IMPLICATIONS FOR POLICY BEHAVIOR

What are the implications of the four "-izations" for the policy and behavior of the PRC today? Of all the observations one can make, Fewsmith and Rosen make the one most central: "As compared to Chinese foreign policy in the Maoist era, the domestic context of Chinese foreign policy today has become both more important and more complex." This is reflected in the fact that the number of individuals and organizations at the Center that are involved in making major decisions, the circle of those involved in consultation and subsequent policy implementation, and the space in which "society" and local systems can operate have all expanded since 1978.

The effects of these changes on the policy-making process and behavior have already been significant and will become more so. As to process, the paramount leader has become less paramount and has been forced to consult more broadly. Lu Ning describes the evolution of a situation in which there is more equality among members of the decision-making bodies at the Center. Meanwhile, power over all but the broadest and most strategic decisions has moved from high-level central organs to government ministries. At the ministerial level, power has been diffused from the MFA to other (often economic) ministries. In turn, particularly in the economic realm, ministerial power has moved from Beijing to the provinces and industrial corporations. However, as Swaine reminds us, actors at any level but the highest have very little influence over grand strategy decisions.[30]

Turning to look at society more broadly, much of China's interaction with the world is no longer effectively controlled by the government at all. "Epistemic communities"—diffuse transnational groupings of like-minded individuals—are examples of one of the many nongovernmental channels for such interaction. Fewsmith and Rosen explain how "public opinion" can establish a delimited space within which the Chinese leadership must operate. Looming on the horizon, though still of scant importance except in the area of environmental monitoring (see the chapter by Economy), is the emergence of civic organizations that will advocate policies affecting China's behavior in the world.

In examining China's late-twentieth-century foreign and national security policy-making system, we are clearly faced with a system in transition. Its long-term direction, however, is clear, despite short-term perturbations: more constrained paramount leaders, more limited bureaucracies (constrained by the very complexity of their processes), and a society that has progressively more space within which to operate. Together, these put the formal policy-making process in a position of often reacting to issues and challenges imposed on it by society and the global system.

Because the Center has grown larger, the degree to which decisions are personalized has diminished. Because China's leadership has become more educated and cosmopolitan (technocratic), it tends to search ever more broadly for information upon which to fashion decisions. The instruments of this search are multiplying, as is the distance from the Center at which information is being sought. Finally, as the bureaucracy has become more specialized, much of its added capacity has come in areas that permit China to better "fit" into the international organizations and regimes in which it now participates. In this vein, Economy notes the international property rights (IPR) tribunals being created within China's judicial system. The policy-making process has therefore become less personalized, more specialized, and more compatible with global systems, notwithstanding the fact that issues of basic national strategy are highly personalized, as are crisis and major nonroutine decision-making.

Turning from process to behavior, we must address these questions: What changes have occurred? What is the direction of the changes? What have been (and will be) the effects of these changes? First, economic objectives have become the Chinese policy lodestone, although Taiwan could supersede it. Likewise, as Gill suggests, PRC leaders are coming to recognize that security cannot always be achieved unilaterally and will occasionally require multilateral cooperation. Again demonstrating the dual character of many phenomena, however, multilateral security cooperation is not simply an idealist conception, but rather a means by which to promote "realist" national interests. China is not unusual in this regard. The United States has also generally looked at multilateral cooperation as a way to promote its interests rather than as a determinative goal in and of itself. Similarly, China's increasing participation in the ASEAN (Association of Southeast Asian Nations) Regional Forum and its commitment to the United Nations Security Council are seen as ways to constrain the unilateralist tendencies of the United States, Great Britain, and NATO in the post–cold war world.

The developments in the policy-making process described earlier also have other implications. For one, foreign interlocutors will find it progressively harder to observe senior members of the Chinese elite single-handedly commit the PRC to a course of action without extensive prior domestic consultation and exhaustive efforts to ensure subsequent implementation. Several effects follow from this trend. First, policy innovation will likely be harder to achieve.[31] Second, stalemate on important issues—what Gill calls "some policy paralysis"—will be increasingly frequent. Third, foreigners may face mixed signals from an increasingly pluralized system. On the subject of WTO entry, for example, during the long negotiations in 1998 and 1999 one heard from some officials that Beijing was committed to entering the WTO quickly, yet at the very same time other equally credible officials conveyed just the opposite view. Similarly, in 1999 one could simultaneously hear from equally authoritative sources in China that Beijing wanted to "resolve" the Taiwan issue relatively quickly and that the PRC felt no particular urgency and could remain patient for a considerable period. When Americans point out these discordant voices to the Chinese, a frequent response is exasperation; the sentiment is that Americans wanted increasing openness and freedom of expression and should live with the consequences. Finally, it is becoming progressively more difficult for foreign interlocutors to know when they have spoken to an authoritative Chinese actor. As Pearson explains: "It is impossible to write about the structure of WTO decision-making without reference to the decision-makers that on an organizational chart would appear peripheral, but in fact exerted tremendous influence."

In sum, then, it is becoming progressively more difficult to know when one has heard the "last word." In fact, even when Beijing has reached an agreement (for example, to observe international intellectual property protection norms, WTO commitments, or the Missile Technology Control Regime), the pluralization of the implementation process has often meant that the relevant agreement has become the starting point for further negotiation and specification. Likewise, as Economy points out with respect to international environmental agreements, ensuring compliance with central commitments is a huge task.

Pearson provides an excellent example of how complex negotiations with a pluralizing China have become. China's WTO negotiating team from the late 1980s "ballooned in size" as relevant industrial and bureaucratic interests were incorporated. By March 1998, the team included "representatives of MOFTEC, the Ministry of Foreign Affairs, the SDPC [State Development and Planning Commission], the SETC [State Economic and Trade Commission], the Ministry of Justice, the Ministry of Agriculture, and the Ministry of Information Industry." In the face of this trend, the lead negotiator of the "team," MOFTEC's Long Yongtu, reportedly felt that "to invite them in was the same as inviting our enemies. They were just a drag on our legs." Ultimately, to energize the negotiations in 1999, Long had to get Prime Minister Zhu Rongji involved, thereby short-circuiting his own negotiating team.

Even with respect to the treatment of Taiwan, a high-priority issue with strong domestic and military overtones, the policy-making process has become more consultative and diffuse, as Swaine explains in discussing Jiang Zemin's role: "Despite his relative dominance over Taiwan policy, Jiang's overall position as 'first among equals' in the post-Deng leadership as a whole has meant that, in the formulation of basic policy, he must consult more extensively than did Deng Xiaoping with a wider circle of senior leaders, including individuals in the policy administration and implementation arena." In explaining that this consensus-building process can take a long time, Suisheng Zhao states, "Nonroutine decisions can be kicked around at lower levels for years without being resolved if no consensus can be reached or the top leaders do not want to take positions or do not know what position to take."[32]

Until now, I have described what the changes discussed herein have meant for Chinese foreign and national security policy-making behavior in the clinical language of political science. But there are more straightforward questions that dominate much of the policy and political discourse concerning China to which this volume also speaks: Will China increasingly conform to global norms? Is China becoming more or less expansionist, more or less cooperative? Are irreconcilable conflicts between China and other big powers, particularly the United States, growing? Is China gradually coming to recognize that security can often be achieved only cooperatively? The authors of these chapters would not all offer identical answers to these questions, but I believe that the weight of the evidence provided herein leads in the direction of cautious optimism. Nonetheless, the pattern of China's policy-making behavior remains highly reactive, grudging, based on national interest, and designed to test international limits. From a Western perspective, the overall direction is positive, but there is a substantial distance to go. The treatment of Taiwan remains a very dangerous issue regarding which the dangers of small group decision-making driven by nationalist sentiment could easily come together with tragic consequences.

WHAT DOES THIS RESEARCH ADD TO WHAT WE KNOW, AND WHAT ARE ITS IMPLICATIONS?

The contributors to this volume have built upon several broad literatures: the literature of the policy-making process; scholarship on China's bilateral and multilateral relations, substantive areas of policy, and the relationship between domestic and foreign policies; and writings on China's integration into the international order.

The landmark work on the foreign policy-making process was A. Doak Barnett's *The Making of Foreign Policy in China: Structure and Process* (1985).[33] Indeed, the present volume is dedicated to Barnett in recognition of his signal contribution to thinking in this area, as in so many others. Through exhaustive interviews with senior Chinese leaders in the mid-1980s, Barnett pieced together an institutional picture of the Chinese foreign policy-making process. In doing so, he threw light on how the various components of the process interrelated and how the personalities of specific leaders, particularly Zhao Ziyang, affected both the processes and outcomes.

Barnett's contribution was followed by two additions to our understanding of Chinese foreign policy-making institutions and processes, the first of which was Lu Ning's *The Dynamics of Foreign-Policy Decisionmaking in China*.[34] Another important contribution was Michael Swaine's *The Role of the Chinese Military in National Security Policymaking*.[35] Two other contributions to our understanding of the Chinese foreign policy-making process (though principally focused on domestic policy-making) have been *Decision-Making in Deng's*

China, edited by Carol Hamrin and Suisheng Zhao,[36] and Kenneth Lieberthal's *Governing China.*[37]

These works, along with a great deal of other research, have provided much greater detail about the foreign policy-making structure than Barnett was able to unearth and have revealed a system with a dual character—a system in which an increasingly professionalized, complex, and conflict-ridden bureaucracy has coexisted with a still very powerful, personalized senior-dominated elite. The present work by no means invalidates findings by scholars such as Christensen,[38] Nathan and Ross,[39] Alastair Iain Johnston,[40] Whiting,[41] and others who have been more impressed by the capacity of the central elite to control policy, manipulate popular passions, and resist the "imperatives" of international integration and specialization. However, this work does draw analytic attention to the tensions between the "new" forces and the old system.

A second body of literature from which this volume draws and to which it adds is research addressing the PRC's bilateral and multilateral relationships, the perceptions and history that have shaped those ties,[42] and Beijing's behavior in various functional areas (for example, arms control, trade, human rights, and international economic policy). Samuel Kim's *China and the World*[43] not only addresses China's bilateral relationships and specific policy concerns, but even tackles (in its first chapter) the policy-making process. The principal problem is that Chinese society and government, not to mention the PRC's role in the world, has changed considerably since that volume's initial publication.

Among the recent works of note in this more traditional foreign policy literature have been Robinson and Shambaugh's *Chinese Foreign Policy: Theory and Practice*[44] and Nathan and Ross's *The Great Wall and the Empty Fortress.*[45] Contributions by John W. Lewis and his team at Stanford University[46] and by Evan Feigenbaum,[47] in turn, have greatly increased our understanding of China's arms control and military modernization policies.

Another body of literature to which this volume addresses itself concerns China's integration into the global community as well as its impact upon the international system and the effect of this integration on China's own foreign policy behavior. Here one of the earliest and most comprehensive works was Jacobson and Oksenberg's *China's Participation in the IMF, the World Bank, and GATT: Toward a Global Economic Order.*[48] More recently, Alastair Iain Johnston has written a seminal piece that asks whether China's participation in international regimes and multilateral organizations is changing Beijing's goals and patterns of behavior or whether its more cooperative behavior is merely a tactical "adaptation" to be abandoned once China's realpolitik interests change.[49] In that piece Johnston ultimately concludes that Beijing's motivations and goals have not enduringly changed in the course of reform.

There are three theoretical areas to which this volume significantly contributes. The first concerns the relationship between domestic politics and foreign policy. Collectively, the chapters that follow not only reveal that domestic and foreign policy processes in China are similar (and appear to be gradually converging), but also indicate how these processes influence one another. This interpenetration has many origins, though two are key. The first is the fact that Beijing has declared that domestic economic growth is its overriding objective (if the Taiwan issue can continue to be set aside); foreign policy is intended primarily to create a hospitable international environment for such growth. To the degree that Beijing's foreign policy fails in this regard, it is a domestic issue.

The second factor contributing to the close linkage and interplay between foreign policy and domestic politics is the fact that Beijing's leaders are ultimately playing "two-level games."[50] How the Chinese leaders are perceived to be handling foreign affairs affects their standing in the domestic political struggle, and external perceptions of their domestic standing affect their potency with foreign interlocutors. Further, a country's leaders can use the specter of domestic opposition as a lever with foreign negotiators to extract concessions from them. Finally, some domestic actors use foreign pressure as an ally in their policy struggles at home, whereas others use it to discredit their domestic opponents on nationalistic grounds.

Thus does Swaine explain how Jiang Zemin's handling of Taiwan policy issues was carefully designed to position him well in his struggle to become China's preeminent leader after Deng Xiaoping's death. As Swaine puts it, "Any aspirant to supreme authority within the Chinese communist regime cannot afford to permit another senior leader to control Taiwan policy." On the flip side, one might note the example of New York Mayor Rudolph Giuliani's refusal to meet the man who was then mayor of Beijing, Li Qiyan, in part because he had been told that Mayor Li would soon be relieved of office. Giuliani did not want to expend his limited political capital on a relationship destined to be short-lived and controversial among his constituents.

These considerations, along with the increasing bureaucratization of the foreign policy-making process as a whole, mean that the foreign and domestic policy-making processes are intertwined and converging, though they will likely never be identical.

Samuel Kim's chapter is a seminal contribution to our understanding of Beijing's Korea policy in the reform era and to our understanding of the interpenetration of domestic and foreign policy. As Kim writes: "The making and implementing of China's Korea policy is best understood as an ongoing process of choosing among competing options rather than any finalized decision, even as Chinese central decision-makers, situated strategically between domestic and international politics, are constrained simultaneously by what the two Koreas will accept and what domestic constituencies will ratify. The making and execution of a foreign policy decision thus requires that China's decision-makers engage in a 'double-edged' calculation of constraints and opportunities in both domestic and international politics in order to achieve international accord and secure domestic ratification."

Several other chapters in this volume also analyze the tight embrace of domestic and international politics. Economy shows how the international scientific community has used its resources to shape the PRC's internal debate concerning Beijing's role in international environmental regimes and how Chinese advocates of international environmental cooperation use external pressure to strengthen their own positions in domestic battles. Similarly, Pearson clearly shows, as has my own contact with MOFTEC's Long Yongtu, that China's trade system reformers have promoted Beijing's accession to the GATT/WTO in order to secure international allies and the backing of a multilateral organization in their domestic battles over economic reform. Meanwhile, Chinese politicians, when negotiating the terms of China's adherence to the WTO and other global regimes, cited their domestic opposition in arguing for greater concessions by the international community.

Finally, Moore and Yang demonstrate how China's leaders sought to use their refusal to give in to domestic pressures to devalue the RMB to gain credit abroad (and perhaps secure more lenient terms for WTO entry) at the same time that they used the resulting prestige gained abroad to enhance their domestic positions. Yet all the while Beijing did not devalue the RMB *primarily* because of a realistic assessment of its own interests, including Beijing's fear of domestic bank runs, accelerated inflation, and loss of foreign investor confidence.

A second theoretical concern (although also a practical concern) addressed in this volume speaks clearly to the issue raised by Alastair Iain Johnston and Thomas Christensen: is Beijing "learning" (that is, genuinely internalizing and embracing) global norms and values, or is the PRC simply "adapting" to global norms to derive tactical benefits while maintaining the flexibility to reject them when they no longer serve PRC interests?[51] The answer that this volume provides is that such questions are misstated. The chapters that most clearly address this topic are those by Gill, Moore and Yang, and Pearson. The conclusion they suggest is that Beijing may initially be entering into encumbering international relationships based on tactical considerations, but that international involvement is a slippery slope. As a nation seeks to derive maximum benefit from the system, it becomes increasingly constrained. As it becomes increasingly constrained, the costs of withdrawal become progressively greater. What starts out as tactical adaptation may slowly change into "learning" (permanent change). "Adaptive learning" may be the most appropriate conceptualization.

The very nature of international involvement creates new interests where none previously existed. For example, with the reversion of Hong Kong to China in 1997, the fear of destabilizing the city's economy in 1997 and 1998 provided Beijing one reason (among many) not to devalue its currency. Were destabilization to occur, Beijing would naturally lose international prestige (and money, given the tens of billions of dollars the PRC has invested in Hong Kong). Moreover, such destabilization would also diminish the (already minimal) attractiveness of the "One Country, Two Systems" formula Beijing has used in the hope of drawing Taiwan back to the embrace of the motherland. Similarly, because the PRC had become so enmeshed in transnational manufacturing networks, it made less sense to devalue the RMB, even though powerful domestic interests vigorously argued that Beijing should do so. In short, the more international involvement a nation has, the more interests it accumulates and wishes to protect.

Further, in seeking to deal with the international community, the Chinese have developed new organizations. These new bureaucratic implants, in turn, have changed the nature of decision-making within the Chinese system itself. Therefore, the old argument about whether leadership composition, strategy, and perception or institutional structure is more important may not be as central a question as it may seem. Leadership decision-making shapes the structure of the bureaucracy, and the bureaucracy, in turn, shapes the context of perception and decision-making, especially in the process of making routinized and noncrisis decisions.

Domestic policy and institutional changes have been reinforced by international economic policy-making and globalization. All these forces combined have tended to promote institutional and economic policy convergence between China and her major trading partners.[52] This brings us to the question of whether China is likely to exhibit more cooperative behavior in the future or to persist in state-centric, realpolitik patterns of action. The answer that this volume provides is clear: Beijing will persist in pursuing its interests, as Kim makes clear in his discussion of the PRC's desire to keep North Korea as a buffer against U.S. power. Nonetheless, Beijing's global and regional interests are becoming progressively more complex, the struggles over their definition are becoming more protracted, and, as China becomes more interdependent, the costs of withdrawal are becoming progressively greater. In short, China's elite will show no less dedication to the PRC's interests in the future than in the past, but gradually, by fits and starts, even narrow calculations of national interest may produce progressively more cooperative behavior. A fitting conclusion to this introduction to the present volume is a quote from Moore and Yang as they describe China's foreign policy predicament: "What matters is the scope and degree of China's interdependence, not how it became interdependent (that is, through adaptation, learning, or adaptive learning). Whether Chinese leaders view interdependence mainly as a tool for economic modernization or as an independently valued goal, the reality of interdependence is the same. Indeed, the latter issue—whether interdependence is valued as an end in itself—matters only if the costs China is likely to incur in extracting itself from its current (increasingly) interdependent context are low or nonexistent. If the exit costs are high, the issue of adaptation versus learning arguably is less important. From this perspective, interdependence is a *predicament* countries must deal with, not a *world-view* or a foreign policy *strategy.*"

PART ONE

Institutions and Localities

TWO

The Central Leadership, Supraministry Coordinating Bodies, State Council Ministries, and Party Departments

LU NING

In order to understand fully the foreign policy establishment and its structure, it is necessary to first briefly examine the general power structure of the People's Republic of China (PRC). The governing regime of the PRC consists of three major vertical systems (*xitong*): the Communist Party, the government, and the military.[1] At the apex of these systems is the Political Bureau (Politburo) of the Chinese Communist Party, which is often further crystallized in the form of a leadership core (*lingdao hexin*), as during and after the Deng Xiaoping era, or of a single person, such as Mao Zedong, as during the Mao Zedong era. The three major systems operate on five levels: center (*zhongyang*); province (*sheng*) (for the party and the government) or army (*jun*) (for the military); prefecture (*di*) (civil) or division (*shi*) (military); county (*xian*) (civil) or regiment (*tuan*) (military); and township (*xiang*) (civil) or battalion (*ying*) (military).[2]

For the purpose of effectively controlling and running the political system, this structure is divided into six major functional sectors (*xitong* or *kou*) that cut across the three major systems. Each sector is supervised by a member of the Standing Committee of the Political Bureau of the Chinese Communist

Party (CCP). The six sectors are military affairs; legal affairs, which is responsible for legislative, judicial, and law enforcement affairs; administrative affairs, which is responsible for industrial and agricultural production, finance and commerce, foreign affairs, health, education, science, sports, and so on; propaganda, which is responsible for media and cultural affairs; United Front, which is responsible for noncommunist political parties, religion, and minorities, as well as Taiwan, Hong Kong, and Macao affairs; and mass organization affairs, which is responsible for unions, youth, women's organizations, and other associations. A member of the Politburo Standing Committee conducts direct sectoral supervision through an institutionalized body such as a committee or a nonstanding organ such as a leading small group (LSG) (*lingdao xiaozu*). Among the most important such organs are the CCP Central Military Commission (CMC) for military affairs, the CCP Central Political and Legal Affairs Committee (*zhongyang zhengfa wei*) for legal affairs, the Central Financial and Economic Affairs LSG (*zhongyang caijing lingdao xiaozu*), and the Central Foreign Affairs LSG (*zhongyang waishi lingdao xiaozu*).

This system of sectoral division for management, known as *guikou guanli*, is in most cases an internal mechanism that does not appear on any formal organizational charts of the party, the government, or the military.[3] Its purpose is to allow the CCP Politburo Standing Committee to exercise centralized control over the whole political system and its policy-making processes.

THE FOREIGN POLICY DECISION-MAKING STRUCTURE: THE PLAYERS AND THEIR ROLES

A horizontal view of the overall foreign policy decision-making structure reveals three basic types of actors: the central leadership,[4] major foreign affairs bureaucracies and institutions, and working-level officials in the foreign affairs establishment.[5] The following is an examination of this structure and of the roles played by the top political leadership and the foreign affairs establishment in the formulation of China's foreign policies.

The Central Leadership

There are four components of the central leadership: the paramount leader or leading nucleus, the nuclear circle, the members of the Politburo Standing Committee, and the other members of the Politburo, particularly those who live in Beijing and those who work in the Secretariat. Normally the leading nucleus and the members of the leading nuclear circle are all members of the Politburo Standing Committee. They collectively constitute the top leadership.

One of the major characteristics of the Chinese political system is the high concentration of political power in the CCP. Within the party, the power is further concentrated in the hands of one or a few leaders. Foreign affairs, military affairs, and party "organization work" (high-level appointments) have long been considered the most sensitive areas that demand an even higher concentration of decision-making power.

The Paramount Leader and Leadership Nuclear Circle. Foreign affairs has always been one of the areas in which ultimate decision-making power has been retained by the paramount leader or the leading nucleus.[6] This paramount leader may or may not be the chairman or general secretary of the party or the state president, but most often he controls the military as the chairman of the CMC. The paramount leader creates an informal leadership nuclear circle that surrounds him, consisting of one or two members he personally designates. In the Mao era this circle included Liu Shaoqi and Zhou Enlai from 1949 to 1966, Lin Biao from 1966 to 1971, Zhou Enlai from 1971 to 1974, Deng Xiaoping in 1975, and Hua Guofeng in 1976. In the Deng era there were Chen Yun, Hu Yaobang before 1986, Zhao Ziyang from 1986 to 1989, Jiang Zemin after 1989, and Yang Shangkun after 1990. Up until late 1992 the circle consisted of Deng, Chen, Yang, and Jiang.[7] After Yang retired in late 1992 and Chen died in April 1995, Deng, Jiang, and Li Peng made up the small circle. In reality, as Deng's health was deteriorating, Jiang and Li formed the new post-Deng leadership nuclear circle long before Deng's death in early 1997. After the election of Zhu Rongji as premier and Li Peng's move to head the National People's Congress (NPC) in March 1998, although Li has retained his number two position within the party, he has seen his policy role diminished, whereas Zhu's has been increased. Since 1999 most of the important foreign and defense policy decisions have been made by Jiang and Zhu in conjunction with their Politburo Standing Committee colleagues and their top aides in the party, government, and military systems. The paramount leader and the leadership nuclear circle wield the ultimate foreign policy decision-making power in China because they can, in reality if not in law, veto or ratify decisions made by the Politburo.

The Politburo and Its Standing Committee. The Politburo is the most important institution of political power in China. It stands at the apex of the formal, though unpublicized, foreign policy structure and under the informal, personalized arrangement of the paramount leader or leading nucleus. The Politburo consists of members resident in provinces and cities other than Beijing, and it is relatively large. These two factors make it too cumbersome for the body to decide foreign policy issues that often demand immediate attention. As a result, de facto foreign policy decision-making power rests with the Politburo's Standing Committee. However, the most important foreign policy decisions, such as whether to make war or peace or major shifts in foreign policy orientation, are generally still subject to deliberations by the full Politburo. This was true even during the Mao era, even if only for purposes of legitimization. In more recent years the Politburo has been used as a training ground for future senior political leaders.[8] Except for its Standing Committee members and those who oversee specific functional foreign affairs departments in the government and the party, most Politburo members are only marginally involved in the making of foreign policy.

Internally, the highest foreign policy decision-making institution is the Standing Committee of the Politburo. Normally the Standing Committee includes the chairman of the CCP, the chairman of the CMC, the premier of the State Council, the state president, the chairman of the Standing Committee of the NPC, and the chairman of the Chinese People's Political Consultative Conference. The party constitution adopted at the Twelfth Party Congress stipulates that the general secretary, the director of the Central Advisory Commission, the first secretary of the Central Disciplinary Commission, and the chairman of the CMC must be members of the Standing Committee. On the Standing Committee one member, usually someone with more experience in the field, takes charge of the foreign affairs sector (*waishi kou*) as head of the CCP Central Foreign Affairs LSG. From 1977 to 1987 this was Li Xiannian, from 1987 to early 1998 Li Peng. In March 1998, when Li Peng moved from the premiership to head the NPC Standing Committee, Jiang Zemin personally took charge of foreign affairs as the head of the Central Foreign Affairs LSG.[9] Therefore, for the first time in its history the Foreign Affairs LSG is headed by the paramount leader himself.

The Secretariat. In the official power structure, immediately under the Politburo is the CCP Secretariat. Its role, however, has been ill defined, and it has been changed from time to time. From the late 1940s until 1956 the Secretariat was the supreme decision-making body within the CCP, functioning as does the present-day Standing Committee of the Politburo.[10] As a consequence of the party restructuring at the Eighth Party Congress in 1956, the Secretariat as we know it today was created in subordination to the Politburo to carry out its day-to-day operations. It was later abolished during the Cultural Revolution, but reestablished at the Fifth Plenum of the Eleventh Party Congress in 1980 by Deng Xiaoping. Deng's main purpose at the time was to circumvent his political rival, Party Chairman Hua Guofeng, and the conservative-dominated Politburo.

In June 1958 the CCP Central Committee and the State Council issued a joint document entitled *Circular Concerning the Establishment of Financial and Economic, Political and Legal, Foreign Affairs, Science, and Cultural and Education Small Groups,* in which it stipulates the following: "The decision-making power concerning major policy orientations and principles and guidelines rests with the Politburo. The Secretariat is responsible for making detailed plans and overseeing (their implementation). . . . The actual implementation and decision-making authority regarding their details belong to government agencies and their party groups."[11] According to the 1982 CCP Constitution, the Secretariat is the executive body (*banshi jigou*) of the party center, which is designated to handle day-to-day work (*chuli dangzhongyang richang gongzuo*). Officially, therefore, the Secretariat is not a decision-making body. Rather, as the executive body of the Politburo, it plans and supervises the implementation of decisions made by the Politburo.

Of the three major systems, the Secretariat has always exercised direct leadership over the party bureaucracies, whereas its control of the government and, in particular, the military has not been consistent. When it was first re-created in 1956 under Deng Xiaoping, it managed all three systems, and the secretary general of the CMC, who was in charge of the day-to-day work of the military, was a permanent member of the Secretariat. When the group was revived in 1980 after the Cultural Revolution, it continued this broader encompassing of the military.

The Secretariat's power reached its zenith at the Twelfth Party Congress with a total of twelve members. But with the downfall of its general secretary, Hu Yaobang, in 1987, its influence declined. At the Thirteenth Party Congress, to further weaken the power of Hu's associates who remained in the Secretariat, the Secretariat's role was limited to running party affairs. Senior government and military officials were withdrawn from its ranks, and its size was reduced to six. This was done under the pretext of separating the party from government. After the events at Tiananmen Square on June 4, 1989, four members of the Secretariat were dismissed. Of the four members of the new Secretariat, three were concurrently serving as members of the Politburo Standing Committee. Therefore, the Secretariat came to exist only in name. For a time after CMC Secretary General Yang Baibing joined the body at the Fifth Plenum of the Thirteenth Party Congress in late 1989, it looked as though the Secretariat was going to regain some of its lost power. However, the subsequent Fourteenth Party Congress in 1992 confirmed that the role of the Secretariat was to remain restricted to managing party affairs. At the Fifteenth Party Congress in September 1997, Zhang Wannian, vice chairman of the CMC, joined the Secretariat. The reentry of a professional soldier indicated that the Secretariat might again be broadening its responsibilities.

Although in reality the Secretariat has at times been involved in making some major decisions, it has never played a major decision-making role in foreign affairs, which, prior to the Cultural Revolution, was overseen personally by Premier Zhou Enlai with Mao making the fundamental choices, and, during the Deng era, by Deng and members of his leadership nuclear circle. In the post-Deng era the locus shifted to the Politburo Standing Committee.

Although the relative weight of the Politburo and the Secretariat changes from time to time due to political shifts within the CCP leadership, the Politburo and the Secretariat generally serve as the providers of a rubber stamp to lend legitimacy to decisions made by the paramount leader, the leading nuclear circle, or the Politburo Standing Committee; a consultant to the paramount leader in making some key decisions; a forum for building consensus or constructing a coalition among the inner elite; an architect providing the blueprint for a new foreign policy orientation often outlined by the paramount leader; and a command center providing direction for achieving major foreign policy goals.

The central leadership makes key policy decisions that include decisions that determine the basic orientation of Chinese foreign policy; decisions over military operations that involve actual or potential conflicts with foreign powers; decisions regarding the formulation of regional policy and national policies toward key world powers such as the United States, Russia, and Japan; major decisions concerning the implementation of these national policies; and decisions concerning "sensitive" regions or countries and "sensitive" issues that can have a major impact on China's foreign relations.

THE LSGS AND OTHER COORDINATING
BODIES AND STAFF OFFICES

The body that takes overall charge of foreign affairs is the CCP Central Foreign Affairs LSG. This LSG is a nonstanding body consisting of a head, one or two deputy head(s), and ministerial officials from various foreign affairs bureaucracies. This body was first established in 1958 with Vice Premier and Foreign Minister Chen Yi as its head. During the Cultural Revolution this body, like many others, disappeared, and most of its members were in political hot water. When it was reestablished after the fall of the Gang of Four, Li Xiannian was appointed head and Zhao Ziyang deputy head of the LSG.

Following the Thirteenth Party Congress, Li Peng took over the premiership from Zhao Ziyang, who became the general secretary of the CCP. Li Xiannian was replaced by Yang Shangkun as state president. The Central Foreign Affairs LSG was subsequently reorganized after the reshuffle. Li Peng became the head of the LSG, and State Councilor and Foreign Minister Wu Xueqian became his deputy. Defense Minister Qin Jiwei also became a member of the organ.[12] Qin's membership was significant, since it represented the first time that the LSG had in its ranks a professional People's Liberation Army (PLA) soldier. Before the Cultural Revolution Chen Yi was officially a PLA marshal and a member of the CMC, and thus theoretically represented the PLA's interests. But through most of the 1980s the military had no official representation at this level. Qin's membership, therefore, represented an acknowledgment of the PLA's interest in foreign affairs and the need to bring it on board for improved policy coordination and implementation.

After Zhu Rongji was elected premier to replace Li Peng in March 1998, Jiang Zemin himself took charge of the Central Foreign Affairs LSG, whereas Premier Zhu Rongji and Vice Premier Qian Qichen served as deputy heads of the group. Qian would make day-to-day decisions, referring major decisions to Jiang and Zhu or the Politburo Standing Committee.[13] Members of the newly constituted LSG included Wu Yi, Foreign Minister Tang Jiaxuan, CMC Vice Chairman and Defense Minister Chi Haotian, and Minister of State Security Xu Yongyue.[14]

At the time of their creation in 1958, the functions of the LSGs were not very well defined. The circular issued to establish them emphasized that the LSGs were to be "directly subordinate to the CCP Politburo and Secretariat and report directly to the two bodies."[15] At the Second Plenum, held on December 16, 1987, a reform package was adopted for the CCP Central

Committee institutions. Under this reform package the roles of the organs of the Party Central Committee were redefined into three categories: decision-making consulting bodies (*juece zixun jigou*), executive bodies (*banshi jigou*), and service institutions (*shiye jigou*). All leading small groups fall in the first category. They are composed of leading members of the relevant government, party, and military ministerial ranking agencies, and in most cases have no permanent office or staff. They convene regular meetings to discuss issues, exchange ideas, and put forward proposals as policy alternatives for the Politburo and its Standing Committee to use to make decisions.[16]

The Central Foreign Affairs LSG provides a forum for the members of the central leadership in charge of foreign affairs—the politicians—to meet face to face with the leading officials of various party, government, and military foreign affairs institutions—the top bureaucrats. When necessary, department-level officials from relevant bureaucracies, academic specialists, and influential journalists are also invited to sit in on some of the LSG meetings. Although the LSG is not a decision-making body, its policy preferences and recommendations are likely to have an important impact on the final outcomes of the decision-making process. The ratification of these decisions by the central leadership is sometimes simply a formality. At other times decisions are made by the central leadership based on the recommendation of the LSG with minor modifications.[17] Decisions at this level often involve cross-ministerial jurisdiction or interest. Therefore, the Foreign Affairs LSG, in fact, plays a pivotal role in the decision-making process.

However, this body is not a standing *institution* and has no permanent staff. Instead it has traditionally relied on the Foreign Affairs Office of the State Council (SCFAO) for staff work and to exercise overall sectoral coordination. Therefore, the SCFAO, as the executive body of the Central Foreign Affairs LSG, served as the central processing unit (CPU) between the decision-makers and the implementing organs in the party, government, and military systems.[18] Similarly, all decisions that were beyond the mandate of a bureaucracy had to be submitted to decision-makers at the Center through this CPU, regardless of which of the three major systems originated them. From here, then, all foreign affairs activities of the PRC were coordinated. This concept is called *guikou,* and until September 1998 the SCFAO was the general entrance/exit point for the foreign affairs sector. Staffed mostly by former officials of the Ministry of Foreign Affairs (MFA), the SCFAO was always headed by a ministerial-ranking former official of the MFA. With a staff size of only twenty—mostly

MFA officials who would eventually return to the MFA—it was often regarded as a bastion of MFA influence.

When Liu Huaqiu became the director of the SCFAO, he tried to enhance the office by giving it a policy role fashioned after that of the National Security Council of the United States.[19] This plan apparently backfired. The office was stripped its title of the SCFAO in September 1998 and became instead the Party Central FAO. More significant, the council's policy-coordinating role and some of its staff moved to the MFA. Therefore, the FAO was reduced to a role of policy consultation.[20]

As the dynamics of China's domestic and foreign policy change, some CCP central LSGs assumed new roles in foreign policy, whereas others have been abolished, and additional LSGs have been set up to cope with changed circumstances and to handle new issues that cut across vertical government, party, and military systems. It is worth noting that not all LSGs are of equal rank; some are made up of ministerial-ranking officials, whereas others are made up of vice ministerial officials.

The Central Financial and Economic Affairs LSG has always been the most important organ in economic decision-making. Before 1979 the Chinese economy was largely closed. Therefore, except during the 1950s when economic cooperation between China and the former Soviet Union was key, this powerful LSG had little to do with foreign policy issues. At a time when foreign economic and trade relations were viewed as instruments serving the nation's foreign political and security policies, most foreign economic aid and trade issues were handled by the Foreign Affairs LSG. However, since the late 1970s, when China embarked on its program of reform and opening up to the outside world, the centrality of economic development has dictated that China's foreign political and security policies serve its economic interests, in a reversal of past practices.

Further, the Chinese economy has become increasingly integrated with the world economy. The Central Financial and Economic Affairs LSG has therefore become an increasingly important locus for the making of China's foreign economic decisions and for their coordination and implementation. For much of the 1980s the Central Financial and Economic Affairs LSG was headed by the then-Premier Zhao Ziyang. Since the early 1990s Jiang Zemin has been the official head, with Zhu Rongji his deputy. However, in reality Zhu has been in overall charge of the financial and economic sector.

Before 1988 there existed a CCP Central External Propaganda Small Group, with the CCP Propaganda Department as the lead institution.

However, at the Second Plenum of the Thirteenth Party Congress, held on December 16, 1987, it was disbanded due to confusion over its authority and its general ineffectiveness.[21] In its place, a State Council Information Office was created. After the Fourteenth Party Congress in 1992, the group was restored under the official name of the International Communication Office of the CCP Central Committee.[22] In the subsequent reorganization of the State Council in 1992, the State Council Information Office and the Party International Communication Office were officially declared a Party Central Committee organ, with one team of staffers and two nameplates.[23] After the group's restoration it was headed by Zeng Jianhui, an old Xinhua News Agency hand.[24] After the NPC meeting in March 1998, Zhao Qizheng, former administrator of Shanghai's Pudong New Area and vice mayor of Shanghai, was appointed head of the State Council Information Office, thus also becoming head of the Party International Communication Office.[25]

For a long time Taiwan-related work was personally handled by Liao Chengzhi, son of a founding member of the Kuomintang, who reported directly to Zhou Enlai and Mao Zedong. After Liao's death in 1983, Yang Shangkun, then executive vice chairman and secretary general of the general office of the CMC, was officially appointed first deputy head of the CCP Taiwan Work LSG, which was then headed by Deng Yingchao, wife of Zhou Enlai.[26] After her retirement, Yang Shangkun took over. In the 1992 reorganization, as in the case of the Central External Propaganda Small Group, the State Council and the Party Central Taiwan Work Office were officially made an organ of the party structure in another one-team, two-nameplates arrangement.[27] As of 1999 this LSG was headed by President Jiang Zemin, with Vice Premier Qian Qichen as his deputy. Following the NPC meeting in March 1998, the Taiwan Work LSG was enlarged from six to eight members, including CCP United Front Work Department Director Wang Zhaoguo, president of the Association for Relations across the Taiwan Strait Wang Daohan, PLA Deputy Chief of General Staff Xiong Guangkai, CCP General Office Director Zeng Qinghong, CCP Taiwan Work Office Director Chen Yunlin, and Minister of State Security Xu Yongyue.[28]

Purely defense-related issues are traditionally coordinated at the General Office of the CMC, with the CMC secretary general playing a pivotal role in running the day-to-day operations of the PLA. Before the Cultural Revolution Luo Ruiqing was the secretary general. After the Cultural Revolution Geng Biao was the first secretary general. Through much of the 1980s, Yang Shangkun was in charge. After June 4, 1989, Yang Baibing became CMC secretary general, but he was removed in 1992 and the post of CMC secretary general was subsequently abolished.[29] Thereafter, the day-to-day operations of the PLA have been handled by a vice chairman of the CMC.

On September 26, 1989, an additional LSG dealing with military sales abroad was created and called the State Council and CMC Military Product Trade Leading Small Group, with the CMC as the lead body.[30] In late 1997 the establishment of a State Military Product Trade Management Committee under the dual leadership of the State Council and the CMC was announced; its purpose was to supervise the export of military products. However, the comprehensive restructuring of the State Council bureaucracies initiated by Premier Zhu Rongji in March 1998 resulted in the abolition of this LSG. Its responsibilities were subsequently shifted to the Commission of Science, Technology, and Industry for National Defense (COSTIND),[31] which was itself placed solely under the civilian authorities of the State Council.

THE CENTRAL BUREAUCRACIES

Beneath the structures at the apex of political power, there are a number of institutions that operate somewhat independently in foreign affairs. Most of them are of ministerial/provincial/army rank. These bureaucratic institutions represent the foreign policy elements of the three major systems of Chinese political power: the party, the government, and the military. In the government system these include primarily the Ministry of Foreign Affairs, the Ministry of Foreign Trade and Economic Cooperation (MOFTEC), and Xinhua News Agency. In the party system there is the CCP Central (Committee) International Liaison Department (ILD). And in the military system there is chiefly the PLA General Staff Department. Until early 1998 COSTIND, which oversaw China's defense research and development and defense industry, straddled the government and military systems.[32] The government restructuring in early 1998 resulted in COSTIND's being placed solely under the State Council and assuming oversight of arms export control. Its functions that had been more closely related to the PLA were taken over by the newly upgraded PLA General Equipment Department.

According to their respective functions, the foreign affairs organizations can be placed into roughly three main categories: policy consultation, coordination, and supervision—the Central Foreign Affairs LSG and, until September

1998, the SCFAO; policy recommendation and implementation—the MFA, MOFTEC, the CCP Central ILD, and the Second Directorate (Intelligence) of the General Staff Department (GSD); (3) information and research—Xinhua News Agency, the Second and Third Directorates of GSD, and the Ministry of State Security.[33]

The Ministry of Foreign Affairs

The MFA plays a pivotal role in China's foreign policy decision-making. It is indisputably the most important foreign affairs institution in the formulation and implementation of China's foreign policy. Important roles are played by the MFA in the foreign policy formulation and decision-making process. First, it plays a decisive role in the "tactical" aspects of foreign policy decision-making. Second, it plays the role of a reliable provider of "processed" information to central decision-makers.

Policy Interpretation. When "strategic" foreign policy decisions are made by the central leadership, they often consist of no more than a vague concept, basic policy orientation, broad policy guideline, or long-term policy goal—just "the bones" of policy. It is consequently up to the MFA to make "tactical" policy choices and work out detailed plans for realization of leadership's policy goals, adding the "flesh and blood" to China's foreign policy. In September 1982, for instance, Hu Yaobang proclaimed at the Twelfth Party Congress that China was to pursue an "independent foreign policy" under which it would make decisions on international issues based on independent judgments of their individual merits. The interpretation and implementation of such a policy fell to the MFA.

Policy Control. Decision-making power with regard to the implementation of details of China's policies toward key countries has always been a prerogative of the central leadership. This has been particularly true during periods of policy adjustment and when implementation details could have affected the posture of China's overall relationship with the major powers. These key countries fall into two categories: those of strategic importance in world affairs and those of geographical importance to China—the states on the periphery. Countries in the first category include the United States, Russia, and Japan. Countries in the second category include Korea, Indochina (Vietnam, Laos, and Cambodia), India, Pakistan, and, more recently, Kazakhstan and Mongolia. Of course countries like Russia and Japan fall into both categories.

Once regional policies are worked out under the guidelines provided by the central leadership, country policies for minor states are decided by the MFA, which ensures that policies toward specific countries conform to China's overall strategy and regional policies. Most decisions in this category are made by the MFA. Exceptions to this general rule are policies toward a few minor countries that, if changed, might affect the carefully constructed balance of China's regional policies. In the 1980s these "sensitive" countries included Israel, South Korea, and South Africa. In these instances shifts in China's policy would, respectively, affect overall relations with the Arab world, alienate most of its friends in Africa, or offend North Korea, a key ally. Similar to policies toward sensitive countries, certain policies are also considered sensitive because of their wider implications in functional terms. For instance, when China began to export arms on a commercial basis in the early 1980s, it was regarded as a normal trade issue with little need for oversight. However, when exports of certain products and exports to certain regions of the world began to attract international reaction, these exports became a sensitive issue. (For more on this, see the chapter by Gill.)

Making policies with respect to sensitive countries and sensitive issues is the prerogative of the central leadership. However, it is almost impossible for the central leadership to micromanage the intricate details of each situation and make decisions accordingly. A system has been put in place to manage and control such sensitive policy decisions. Over time, for example, the central leadership made strategic decisions to readjust China's policies toward Israel, South Korea, South Africa, and the Vatican. (Since the main motivation behind these adjustments was largely economic, relations with the Vatican were not seriously pursued until the late 1990s.)[34] The Chinese leadership envisaged a long process of gradual and incremental changes leading to normalization rather than a sudden shift, which could cause major upheaval in China's traditional relations with allies. Rather than setting a timetable, it entrusted the MFA to control the overall processes and determine the pace and the timing of each subtle policy shift.

Ensuring the compliance of ministerial-ranking bureaucracies with MFA policy oversight is carried out through the issuance of a central joint document mandating that all matters concerning the designated sensitive countries have policy clearance from the MFA.[35] Similarly, during the Iran-Iraq War the two countries were designated as sensitive areas for Chinese arms exports. All direct arms exports were generally forbidden. Special cases and indirect imports had to have specific clearance from the MFA and be approved by the central leadership.[36] Beginning in the mid-1980s, exports of Chinese missiles, including Silkworm and ballistic missiles, were added to the "sensitive items" list. Such exports had caused an uproar in the West. In September 1989, when the aforementioned informal arrangements were no longer adequate to coordinate Chinese policies in this regard, a coordinating body was created to oversee China's arms exports—the Military Product Export Leading Group.[37]

Information Provision. In addition to the roles of policy interpretation and control of the implementation of foreign policy decisions, the MFA also plays an important role as an information provider for the central leadership. Among the Chinese bureaucracies, the central leadership has regarded the MFA as a more reliable provider of information than other sources. Much of the information provided by the MFA is processed as opposed to the raw material generated by Xinhua News Agency. As of 1999, the MFA maintained some 140 diplomatic missions abroad, whose cables reach the central leaders directly. The MFA's internal publications also provide a constant flow of up-to-date, concise, readable information. Therefore, the MFA input plays a significant role in shaping the central leadership's perceptions. As a result, the MFA's policy recommendations and opinions usually prevail over those of other bureaucratic institutions in the battle for the attention of the central leadership.

The Ministry of Foreign Trade and Economic Cooperation

MOFTEC is the primary bureaucratic institution responsible for designing China's foreign trade and economic aid strategies and planning and for studying and implementing the foreign trade and economic aid policies under the guidelines established by the central leadership.[38] Since decisions regarding China's foreign trade and economic relations with foreign countries often are considered less sensitive politically than foreign policy issues, MOFTEC often has a higher degree of control over these decisions than the MFA has over foreign policy issues, and these decisions often have a strong domestic linkage. MOFTEC's decision-making process is similar to that of the MFA, though many issues within its purview are run through the powerful Central Finance and Economics LSG. (For more on this, see the chapter by Pearson.)

The International Liaison Department

The ILD was established to manage the Chinese Communist Party's relations with other communist parties around the globe and was modeled after the Soviet system. Because communist parties were (until the late 1980s and early 1990s) ruling parties in the former Soviet Union and East European countries and still remain so in a few Asian countries and Cuba, the ILD has played a significant role in foreign policy decision-making regarding those states. The ILD's research and study regarding Russia and other East European countries has been considered high quality. It has also been instrumental in maintaining high-level contacts with the leadership of Asian communist countries such as North Korea and Vietnam. In the 1980s its information on the Khmer Rouge leadership was decisive in shaping China's Indochina policy. Since the late 1970s the ILD has begun to broaden its contacts to include noncommunist political parties in foreign countries. However, its impact on policies toward the noncommunist world is slight, and overall its influence has been declining. One indication of this loss of influence was the loss of its seat in the Foreign Affairs LSG in 1998.

Xinhua News Agency

With its widespread network abroad, Xinhua is the most important provider of unprocessed information to the central leadership and the broader foreign affairs establishment. Its daily publication *Cankao Ziliao* (Reference Material), each issue of which averages more than fifty pages, represents the most comprehensive world information coverage in China. Its sources are very diverse, including not only wire reports, but also articles and commentaries in major international and national newspapers, magazines, and other publications around the world. They are sent daily in their original languages by Xinhua's local offices and translated and compiled by the *Cankao Xinwen Bianji Bu* (Reference News Compilation Department) at its headquarters in Beijing. This publication is intended for the central leadership and foreign affairs professionals, as well as for senior officials at the provincial/army level. There are occasions on which certain information is considered so sensitive that it cannot even appear in *Cankao Ziliao*. It is then printed in a special edition called *Cankao Ziliao (Qingyang)* (Reference Material [Proof]). Almost always classified as top secret and highly restricted in its circulation, this special publication deals with such sensitive or embarrassing issues as Chinese arms sales, defections, and alleged Chinese espionage activities.

The same department also publishes a newspaper, once internally circulated, for mass consumption called *Cankao Xiaoxi* (Reference News). In the 1950s its circulation was restricted to high-ranking officials. In the 1960s it was extended to all officials and university students. In the 1970s Mao loosened the restriction further to include ordinary workers, and in the 1980s it became available to all Chinese citizens. Although its contents are more strictly edited than those of *Cankao Ziliao,* some criticism of nonsensitive aspects of Chinese society appears in the newspaper, but sharp criticism is usually edited out.

Xinhua is not limited to the role of a provider of raw information. It has its own research units, and its correspondents based in foreign countries also write in-depth analyses of important international developments and of the domestic situations of their resident countries and those countries' attitudes toward international and regional issues, particularly China. The internally circulated biweekly *Guoji Neican* (International Affairs for Internal Reference) provides a forum for these internal analyses by Xinhua's overseas correspondents.[39] In places where China does not have diplomatic representation, the reports and analyses by the resident Xinhua correspondents play a key role in shaping the perception of China's central leadership. Occasionally a correspondent is even mandated to carry out semiofficial functions, including contacting important local officials on behalf of Beijing and lobbying for China's interests.

The People's Liberation Army

Civilian control of the military is one of the most basic principles undergirding the Chinese armed forces.[40] The role of the PLA in China's foreign policy decision-making is largely confined to certain activities of its departments. It is a mistake to talk of a well-defined overall PLA interest in foreign policy or of well-established policy goals. Rather, various elements of the PLA are driven by their particular departmental interests: signal and imagery intelligence gathering for the GSD Third Directorate; human source intelligence and intelligence analysis for the GSD Second Directorate; arms purchases and, until 1998, sales abroad for the General Equipment Department; and Taiwan for the General Political Department Liaison Directorate.

With the exception of the Taiwan issue, serious involvement of elements of branches of the PLA in foreign policy issues started with the Chinese leadership decision in the 1980s to allow the PLA to sell surplus arms overseas.

However, following the subsequent decision by the leadership to demand that the PLA hand over all its businesses to civilian authorities by the end of 1998, this involvement by the PLA in foreign policy issues may prove only short-lived. Indeed, the PLA is likely to terminate all official involvement in overseas arms sales, with Norinco beginning to exercise oversight over the Poly Group[41] and with the transfer of control over overseas arms sales to COSTIND under the government bureaucracy restructuring program unveiled in March 1998.[42] The foreign affairs of different branches of the PLA are coordinated by the Foreign Affairs Bureau of the PLA General Staff Department.[43]

THE MINISTERIAL POWER STRUCTURE

In addition to limiting the decision-making power of the central bureaucracies and their party groups to implementing details, the 1958 CCP Central Committee and State Council joint circular further stipulated the following: "With regard to major policy orientation, principles, and guidelines, and to implementation planning and supervision, government organs and their Party groups have the power to make recommendations. But the decision-making power belongs to the Party Center."[44] This rule is still in effect today. Until recently the leadership structure within a government ministry or party department at the central level was almost a miniature of the central party structure and mechanism described earlier.

Officially, the system at the ministerial level was called *dangwei lingdaoxia de xingzheng shouzhang fuzezhi* (the system of administrative chief executive responsibility under the leadership of the party committee or party group).[45] Before the Thirteenth Congress of the CCP, the ministerial party group (*dangzu*), like the Politburo, was the highest decision-making body within each particular bureaucracy. It consisted of most of the vice ministers and assistant ministers. Within the party group there were also a very few persons—often only one or two—who were identified as key or nuclear members (*dangzu hexin chengyuan*), equivalent to the Standing Committee members of the Politburo.

However, at the Thirteenth Party Congress the party's constitution was revised to gradually abolish the party group from the leadership structure of government bureaucracies, which conflicted with the minister responsibility system introduced in the PRC Constitution.[46] This change was part of the political reform package introduced at the Thirteenth Party Congress in an attempt to separate the party from the government and thereby reduce party interference in government affairs. In the place of the party group the minister was designated as the chief executive under the "administrative chief executive responsibility system" (*xingzheng shouzhang fuzezhi*). A system of administrative conferences (*xingzheng huiyi*) has been instituted to replace the party group meetings as the chief venue for collective decision making.[47]

After the downfall of General Secretary Zhao Ziyang, who masterminded the political reform package introduced at the Thirteenth Party Congress, the decision to gradually abolish the party groups was not implemented. At the central government level, this failure does not make much of a difference. Unlike at the provincial level, where party secretaries and governors are not the same person, in central government bureaucracies the chief executive is concurrently the secretary of the party group, which is made up of ministerial officials. Therefore, the chief executive, the minister, assumes overall responsibility for running the bureaucracy, whether in the role of party secretary or minister.[48] Under him there is a division of labor among vice ministers and assistant ministers, with each taking charge of a number of regional and functional departments (*si*) or bureaux (*ju*) in an arrangement similar to the practice of sectoral control by the Politburo Standing Committee. Each department or bureau has one chief officer in charge of the overall work of the department and also the work of one or two divisions (*chu*). He is assisted by two deputy chiefs, each of whom takes charge of a number of divisions. In some bureaucracies, such as the MFA, there is a fourth departmental ranking officer who oversees the political work of the department (*zhengzhi gongzuo*); this individual is like a political commissar in the military, only with much less power. Further down the chain of command, a division chief is assisted by two deputy chiefs, with each in charge of a particular aspect of the division's responsibility. Finally, in a number of bureaucracies there is another layer in the power structure called a *ke*, or section.[49]

As a result of reforms of the 1980s, the responsibilities and decision-making powers of each bureaucratic post are explicitly defined in the form of internal regulations. For all foreign affairs policy matters, the decision-making power rests with the ministerial leaders and above. Departmental officials have the power to oversee the day-to-day operations that fall under their respective jurisdictions under established rules. Even in the case of those kinds of decisions with clearly established rules and precedents, the proposed course of action is often referred to the responsible ministerial leader for ratification. In the case of matters that have no rules or precedents to follow, it is usually up to the ministerial leadership (and above) to make the final call.

EMERGING TRENDS

The most fundamental change in the dynamics of foreign policy decision-making has been the shift of emphasis since 1978 on the part of the central leadership from the nation's physical security to its economic development. Although the Vietnamese invasion of Cambodia and the Soviet invasion of Afghanistan caused considerable concern over China's security, it soon became clear that the overseas misadventures of Hanoi and Moscow were such a painful drain on their own resources that any threats they posed to Beijing were manageable. By the early 1980s the leadership in Beijing reached a consensus that China was physically secure. Deng, however, invented "three main obstacles" to the normalization of relations between Moscow and Beijing, mainly to control the domestic pressure to trade with Moscow so as not to create a backlash in the West.

The impact of this shift toward economic development on foreign policy decision-making can be viewed along several lines. One is the gradual erosion of the preponderant role of the paramount leader in favor of the leading nuclear circle in the making of foreign policy decisions. (For more on this, see the introductory chapter by Lampton.) Deng Xiaoping retreated as the nucleus of the second generation of CCP leadership in three stages: in the late 1970s Deng retreated from active involvement in policy decision-making on issues ranging from the normalization of relations with the United States to the invasion of Vietnam; through much of the 1980s he allowed Zhao Ziyang and Hu Yaobang to make most of the important foreign policy decisions and intervened only occasionally; after 1989 and until his death in 1997, he intervened rarely and only when asked.

This shift came as a matter of objective necessity and subjective limitations, as well as personal style. As the nation's foreign relations grew increasingly complex in the two decades of reforms, retaining the same high level of concentration of decision-making power as during the Mao era became impossible. To manage such an extensive and complex relationship required technical expertise that Deng's generation of leaders did not possess. Furthermore, Deng did not possess the absolute authority that Mao once commanded. Deng alone could not dictate every major decision if there was serious disunity among the government elite. It was necessary for him to build consensus. Further, Deng's personal work style had never been that of a micromanager, like that of Zhou Enlai. Deng believed in the delegation of authority and placed his chief lieutenants on the front line of decision-making.

The emergence of Jiang Zemin, Li Peng, and Zhu Rongji at the center of political power represents a transition of Chinese political leadership from a generation of revolutionary politicians to a generation of technocratic politicians. This new group is characterized by its lack of any absolute authority based on charisma and prestige established through decades of wars and construction and by its relatively narrow power base. No single leader can command unquestioned authority simultaneously in the three major systems of China's political power—the party, the government, and the military. This has led to more of a collective decision-making process, with checks and balances reflected in the structure and composition of the Politburo Standing Committee, which has begun to represent more bureaucratic and regional interests.

Another trend that has emerged from the shift in focus to economic development is the centrality of economic factors in making foreign policy decisions. (For more on this, see the chapter by Pearson.) During the Mao era, because the focus was on national security, Beijing's political considerations dominated foreign policy decision-making. Foreign trade and economic aid were but instruments for the realization of China's international political and security objectives. By 1980 this order was reversed: China's diplomacy was required to serve the nation's paramount interest in economic development. When faced with choices, the decision-makers in the central leadership, particularly the premier, under great pressure to deliver economically, have been biased in favor of economic interests.

As a result of this economic bias, the third trend in the changing dynamics in foreign policy decision-making has emerged: the decentralization of decision-making power in favor of the foreign affairs establishment at the expense of the central leadership, in favor of other bureaucracies at the expense of the MFA, and in favor of trade corporations and local authorities at the expense of MOFTEC. (For more on this, see the chapter by Cheung and Tang.)

The subtle shift of authority from the central political leadership to the foreign affairs establishment has been driven by the same forces that have been responsible for the erosion of the power of the paramount leader in favor of the leading nuclear circle. The relative fluidity of the leading nuclear circle has also contributed to this process. Turnover at this level has been fairly frequent compared with the past. As a consequence of its relative inexperience, the political leadership has had to rely more heavily on professional bureaucrats to reach foreign policy decisions. The bureaucratic institutions, meanwhile, have become more assertive and have occasionally even resisted ill-conceived policy initiatives of members of the leading nuclear circle.

MOFTEC's growing influence is a contributing factor to the erosion of the MFA's power. MOFTEC, however, is itself losing some of its decision-making power over the conduct of Beijing's foreign economic and trade relations. This reflects the economic reform program that emphasizes decentralization of economic decision-making power from central to local authorities and from administrative bureaucracies to corporations and enterprises. Since the 1985 reform of the foreign trade structure, MOFTEC has eased its oversight of the business management of the sixteen Chinese foreign trade corporations, which until then had been under its direct control. In the meantime, various ministries of the central bureaucracy have set up their own corporations to conduct trade independent of MOFTEC. Similarly, MOFTEC has had to yield increased powers to trade departments in the provinces to allow them to conduct trade negotiations with foreign concerns independently. In this respect MOFTEC's power has been further undercut by the fact that, starting in 1999, all government, party, and army organs have been obliged to give up all businesses they controlled. China's entry into the World Trade Organization will simply accelerate all of these trends.

In the shifting of power in the central foreign affairs establishment, the emergence of the PLA's role in foreign affairs has garnered considerable attention in the West. Although the opening of the PLA to the outside world since the early 1980s has been unprecedented, the perception that the PLA has become an independent force in foreign policy decision-making is erroneous. The decision to sell arms abroad was a domestic economic decision, not an attempt by the PLA to extend its influence abroad or to encroach on foreign policy formulation. And with the restructuring of the government bureaucracy and the decommercialization of the PLA, even this limited role has officially come to an end.

The biggest loser among institutions involved with foreign policy has been the ILD. More than any other foreign affairs institution, the ILD has been susceptible to changes in the external environment. Its tentative revival in the late 1970s and 1980s, when Beijing began to mend its fences with the Soviet Union and the East European nations, where communist parties still dominated, soon fell victim to the demise of the communist regimes in Eastern Europe and the disintegration of the former Soviet Union in 1989–1991. With the Khmer Rouge fading into oblivion and North Korea and Cuba struggling to survive, it is doubtful that the ILD will ever regain its influence in the foreign policy-making process.

THREE

The Influence of the Gun: China's Central Military Commission and Its Relationship with the Military, Party, and State Decision-Making Systems

TAI MING CHEUNG

Mao Zedong's observation that political power flows from the barrel of a gun is as relevant in China today as when he wrote these words more than half a century ago.[1] The People's Liberation Army (PLA) is a core pillar of the Chinese power structure, although its influence in the running of the country's affairs is less significant and pervasive than in the past. It retains a powerful voice at the highest levels of the country's decision-making process, however, especially in the defense and national security arenas, as Lu Ning and Michael Swaine demonstrate in their contributions to this volume. But how the military brass formulates its views and exercises its influence is cloaked in a tight veil of secrecy. As China makes its presence increasingly felt on the international stage, increasing attention is given to the role the PLA plays in shaping the country's strategic posture. This has been highlighted by such events as provocative Chinese military exercises in the Taiwan Strait in 1995 and 1996.

Any examination of the Chinese military's involvement in policy-making must begin with the role of the Communist Party's Central Military Commission (CMC). The CMC is the country's highest-level military organ and is responsible for the making and coordination of defense policy. It also wields potent political influence, and it is an unwritten but general rule of Chinese politics that the country's paramount leader must also be in charge of the CMC. The CMC is the organizational embodiment of the relationship between political power and the gun.

This chapter examines the evolution, role, and internal workings of the CMC and its relationship with the military and civilian decision-making processes. Although there have been studies outlining the Chinese military's organizational structure and its general involvement in the formulation of foreign, defense, and national security policies,[2] remarkably little is known about how China's military chiefs actually make and carry out decisions. Even rudimentary information about how often the CMC meets is a closely guarded secret.

THE HISTORICAL EVOLUTION OF THE CMC

When Marxist revolutionaries founded the Chinese Communist Party (CCP) in 1921, one of their first acts was to establish an organ responsible for military affairs. This forerunner to the CMC was set up in 1924 in Guangdong with Zhou Enlai as its head. The CMC was officially established in 1926, although it took another four years before its functions and structure were properly defined. Ever since its establishment, the CMC has played a pivotal role in the CCP's rise to power and in shaping the development of the PLA. At the 1935 Zunyi Conference Mao Zedong won control of the Communist Party. He took over as CMC chairman shortly thereafter, a position he retained until near the end of his life. Throughout the civil war and anti-Japanese war years, the CMC was in operational charge of the Red Army. The army's headquarters command, which included the general staff and the political and supply departments, was subordinate to the CMC.

After the communists took power in 1949, the CMC relinquished its operational responsibilities to the PLA headquarters departments, which were also separated from the CMC's administrative structure. The CMC concentrated instead on the transition of the PLA from a wartime guerrilla outfit into a regular peacetime army. This included the demobilization of several million troops, the establishment of a military rank and salary system, the creation of a paramilitary internal security force, and the formulation of new military operational strategies.[3]

Nonetheless, the CMC remained a key center of political power during the early years of communist rule. Top CMC leaders were among the inner decision-making elite, including Mao and Marshal Peng Dehuai, who was in charge of the CMC from the early to the late 1950s. The CMC's political importance also meant that it became entangled in internal power struggles within the party and military leadership. In 1959, for example, Peng was charged with military fac-tionalism following his criticism of Mao Zedong's Great Leap Forward, was stripped of all his posts, and was forced out of the military in disgrace.

More political turmoil followed with the outbreak of the Cultural Revo-lution in the mid-1960s when the CMC was taken over by conservative hard-liners ("leftists" in the jargon of the time) led by Marshal Lin Biao, who had replaced Peng. Lin, Mao's hand-picked successor, allied with Jiang Qing, Mao's wife, and other leftist leaders and established a CMC Small Affairs Group that took control and left the rest of the CMC structure virtually paralyzed.

After an allegedly abortive coup by Lin in 1971, the CMC was placed in the hands of Marshal Ye Jianying and other top military elders close to Mao. The CMC Small Affairs Group was abolished, and the CMC resumed its pre–Cultural Revolution structure. The role and size of the CMC ballooned under Ye's tenure during the mid- to late 1970s.[4] More than sixty Long March revolutionaries and Maoist stalwarts were appointed to the CMC in 1977, for example. In addition, the CMC formed numerous committees and offi-ces to directly handle major military issues. These included a weapons science and technology committee, an education and training committee, and a leading group on wartime communications preparations.[5]

When Deng Xiaoping took over in late 1978, he moved to reduce the CMC's involvement in the running of the military establishment. During a meeting of the commission in July 1982, Deng complained about the CMC's bloated size and its confused lines of command: "The Military Commission and the various general departments should be streamlined. It is not yet completely clear how that should be done. But the present system, method of leadership and organization of work in the army are not very satisfactory; they are too complicated. We have the Military Commission, its Standing Committee, its regular working conferences and then the several general departments. The fact is, we should increase the responsibilities of the General Staff Headquarters, the General Political Department and the General Logistics Department, and have only a small co-coordinating organization above them. With too many leaders, not only do the comrades at lower levels find it hard to get things done, but we ourselves have trouble circulating papers for approval."[6]

At the Twelfth Party Congress in 1982, at which Hu Yaobang replaced Hua Guofeng as general secretary of the CCP, the CMC underwent a major streamlining with the abolition of its Standing Committee and a reduction in the number of its committees. Yang Shangkun, one of Deng's close confidants, took over as CMC secretary general and was given wide-ranging responsibility for the body's management. In the spring of 1983 a state CMC was established, along with the enactment of a state constitution, as part of the effort to separate state and party functions and to at least give the appearance of civilian control of the military. This new body, however, was an empty shell whose membership mirrored the leadership of the party CMC. Some observers believe, though, that the state organ has symbolic importance, because key orders and regulations are occasionally issued on official letterhead originating from this office.[7]

During the mid-1980s military planners were given the task of drawing up guidelines for the PLA's development to the end of the century. One of the main conclusions was that the state CMC should be given real authority or that a new state National Defense Council should be set up to work closely with a fully functioning Defense Ministry. Planners argued that this new defense organization was needed because the PLA's modernization had become too complex for the party CMC to handle alone.[8]

At the same time that these military reforms were being advocated, the political leadership was beginning to take steps to overhaul the political system. At the Thirteenth Party Congress in October 1987, top leaders agreed to separate the functions of the party and state apparatuses. This separation would have eventually given state bodies a greater role in defense issues. The National People's Congress (NPC), for example, considered the establishment of a special National Defense Committee.[9] These discussions came to an abrupt halt, however, with the June 1989 Tiananmen Square crackdown. The leadership moved quickly to reaffirm the party's exclusive control over the military and clamped down on any talk of separating the party and state apparatuses. The proposals to enhance the state CMC's role were indefinitely shelved.[10]

JIANG ZEMIN AS CMC CHAIRMAN

In November 1989 Deng handed over the CMC chairmanship to Jiang Zemin in an effort to shore up the weak power base of his newly chosen successor. Although Jiang had never served in the military, his appointment as the PLA's commander-in-chief was an honor that Deng had not bestowed on his previous heirs apparent. Following the appointment, Jiang devoted enormous energy to attending CMC and other PLA meetings to demonstrate to the top brass his interest in military affairs.[11] For example, he attended an average of two to three of the CMC's weekly work meetings each month during the early 1990s.[12] Although the routine work of the CMC proceeded normally, Deng's departure had a profound impact on the organ's political authority. Under Mao and Deng the CMC had owed its importance not only to its institutional clout, but also to the personal prestige of its chairmen. With Jiang at the helm a key source of the CMC's influence had been diminished, although if the party chief were able to solidify his hold on political power, this situation could be reversed.

Jiang had a difficult time securing control of the CMC in the early 1990s because Yang Shangkun and his half-brother Yang Baibing had built up a strong power base within the commission and other parts of the PLA high command. Only after Deng purged the Yangs at the Fourteenth Party Congress in late 1992 did Jiang begin to actively consolidate his support within the military high command. Jiang spent a considerable amount of time over the next few years cultivating personal ties with many leading generals in the PLA headquarters departments and the military regions. His top military supporters included Generals Zhang Wannian and Chi Haotian, who were appointed as CMC vice chairmen in late 1995 alongside two Deng loyalists, Generals Liu Huaqing and Zhang Zhen, who ran the CMC during this period. Chi and Zhang Wannian took full control of the CMC at the Fifteenth Party Congress in September 1997 when Liu and Zhang Zhen retired.

Jiang has been active in cultivating ties with PLA chiefs, but his interest in military affairs has been largely confined to political, welfare, and personnel issues. He has occasionally spoken out on matters related to military strategy and force modernization, but these pronouncements have tended to be scripted and lacking in substance. Jiang has also spent less time taking part in military activities since the mid-1990s. However, although he no longer attends working-level CMC meetings, Jiang continues to make high-profile appearances at important military events to show that he is paying attention to military affairs.[13]

With Jiang mostly preoccupied with party and state affairs, Chi and Zhang Wannian have enjoyed wide-ranging autonomy in running the CMC.[14] These officers are representative of the post-1949 generation of professional soldiers who have little interest in participating in politics. This distinguishes them from earlier generations of military leaders who were often intimately involved in the political process. This change has helped promote a growing sense of institutional identity in the upper echelons of the high command.[15]

Zhang is ranked ahead of Chi in the CMC lineup primarily because he is responsible for the modernization of the PLA's war-fighting capabilities. He is an experienced field commander and has been actively involved in revamping the PLA's training program and developing military contingencies against Taiwan. He has also overseen the formulation of strategic and operational doctrines and the streamlining of the PLA's force structure. Chi is in charge of political and external liaison work as well as defense science and technology. He has an extensive background as a political commissar and has also traveled widely overseas as defense minister, including to the United States in 1996. His main role is to oversee party work within the rank and file and to deal with the military's involvement in foreign relations. He is the military's representative in the party's leading small group on foreign affairs, which is discussed in greater detail in the chapter by Lu Ning in this volume. Chi is also a close political ally of Jiang and has played a leading role in building up the party chief's power base within the military.

Zhang and Chi appear set to retire at the Sixteenth Party Congress that is scheduled to take place in 2002. Leading candidates to replace them include General Fu Quanyou, currently PLA chief of the General Staff, and General Cao Gangchuan, head of the PLA General Equipment Department (GED). Two younger generals were appointed to the CMC as members in September 1999 in preparation for their elevation to the CMC's top posts within the next few years. They were Lieutenant Generals Guo Boxiong and Xu Caihou. Guo was formerly the commander of the Lanzhou Military Region, and Xu was the political commissar of the Jinan Military Region. Hu Jintao, a member of the Politburo Standing Committee (PBSC) and vice state president, was also appointed as a CMC vice chairman in September 1999. This was a clear indicator that he is being groomed to take over from Jiang as commander-in-chief in the coming years. Hu has had little previous experience in military affairs, though, and has spent most of his time involved in party organizational and youth affairs.

The access of the PLA's top representatives to the top levels of the party and state decision-making processes is unclear, though. Although Chi and Zhang are members of the full Politburo and Zhang is also a member of the Party Secretariat, they do not belong to the more powerful PBSC. The failure of either of them to replace Liu Huaqing on the PBSC at the Fifteenth Party Congress was considered a serious blow to the PLA's political clout.[16] The military also did not have a seat on the PBSC during the 1980s, but Yang Shangkun is believed to have regularly attended its meetings to ensure that the military's views were heard.[17]

Defense chiefs may have reservations about Jiang's commitment to backing their interests on the PBSC. As the CMC chairman has steadily consolidated his power base, however, his dependence on the military's support has lessened, as indicated by his willingness in 1998 to take on the PLA's business interests and clamp down on its smuggling activities. Although Jiang's backing of the military remains strong, since the mid-1990s he also has had serious disagreements with defense chiefs over how to deal with Taiwan. Jiang has been relatively keen to adopt a more flexible strategy to improve ties with Taipei, but the military has advocated a hard-line approach, because it believes that former Taiwanese President Lee Teng-hui and current President Chen Shui-bian are seeking independence. In his contribution to this volume Michael Swaine sees somewhat less tension between Jiang and the PLA than I believe to be the case.

To ensure the rest of the top leadership pays attention to their views, the military chiefs are actively seeking a wide range of channels to make their views heard. These channels include key policy-making forums such as meetings of the party leading groups on foreign affairs and Taiwan as well as small group deliberations at the annual sessions of the National People's Congress. There are reports that the military has sought to upgrade its representation in the party's Taiwan Affairs Leading Small Group from a deputy chief of general staff to a CMC vice chairman, but it does not appear to have achieved this objective thus far.

All four heads of the PLA headquarters departments are also CMC members, along with Deng Xiao-ping's former military secretary and deputy director of the General Political Department, Wang Ruilin.[18] They regularly participate in CMC functions, including key internal meetings, and have an influential say. The heads of other major military units, including the service arms, the National Defense University, the Academy of Military Sciences, and the seven military regions also occasionally participate in CMC discussions, although they are not members of the commission and have no voting rights.

General Cao Gangchuan, the head of the PLA's GED, is regarded as a rising star in the military hierarchy. He is now in overall charge of managing the PLA's weapons and equipment apparatus, including research, development, and procurement. This gives him considerable influence over budgets and input into the direction of the PLA's force modernization, which had previously been the responsibility of Zhang Wannian.

Another important figure in the CMC hierarchy is Jiang's personal military secretary and head of his General Office, Jia Tingan, who is also a deputy director of the CMC General Office. Jia has worked for Jiang since the late 1970s, but had only limited military experience before his appointment to the CMC general office in 1994.[19] Despite his lack of military credentials, Jia enjoys the rank of a major general and wields substantial influence within the CMC because of his direct access to Jiang.[20] With his commander-in-chief spending little time dealing with military or CMC matters, Jia has been avidly acting on Jiang's behalf and has begun to establish his presence in the military high command. Jia could eventually be in line for a senior military position, like his predecessor Wang Ruilin.

CMC STRUCTURE, WORKINGS, AND RESPONSIBILITIES

Although it is one of the most powerful institutions in China, the CMC is a small and trim bureaucratic organ that operates independent of the rest of the military high command. Some observers believe that the CMC operates in a similar fashion to party leading groups, as a forum for "facilitating coordination, communications, supervision and consultation" among leading military organs.[21] But the CMC wields far more power and responsibility; its status is more on a par with that of the PBSC and the State Council.

As the CMC is the supreme national organ in charge of military and defense affairs, its functions include the "formulation of military strategy, timely handling of contingencies and vital issues concerning defense building, comprehensive coordination of military, economic, political and diplomatic strategies, and formulation of guidelines and polices."[22] In the event of war the CMC "can take command of the whole army and quickly set up a wartime establishment while, at the same time, organizing the soldiers of the whole country to make a quick and effective response." The role of the CMC chairman is especially important, as "the particularity of military struggles requires . . . the practice of the system of personal responsibility for the chairman, so as to execute highly concentrated command of the armed forces."[23]

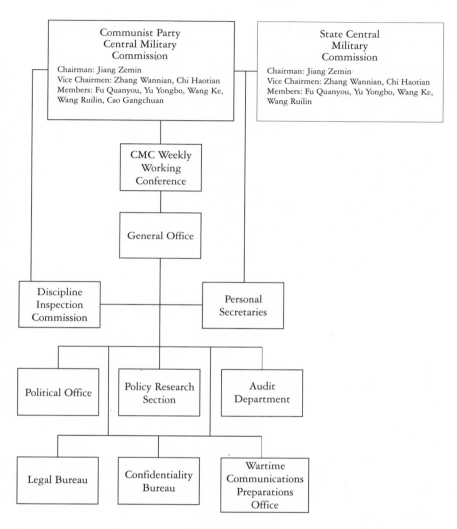

FIGURE 3.1
THE COMMUNIST PARTY CENTRAL MILITARY
COMMISSION, 1999

The structure of the CMC (see Figure 3.1) includes two parts: its permanent administrative structure and the various types of ad hoc committees and working groups that are convened under its auspices. The CMC's main bureaucratic structure is its General Office, which has a staff of between two hundred and three hundred and is headquartered in Sanzuomen, near the central leadership compound of Zhongnanhai in central Beijing. A new, more modern CMC headquarters building was opened up next to the Military Museum in western Beijing in October 1999.[24] It is called the August First Building and is an almost opulent structure. The General Office's main functions are to provide secretarial, administrative, and personnel support for the CMC leadership. The General Office is headed by a lieutenant general, and it has several components, including a discipline inspection commission, policy research section, audit department, military trade bureau, legal affairs bureau, and communications war readiness office.[25]

Although the General Office plays a marginal role in the CMC's policy-making, it wields considerable influence by controlling the flow of information and documents, as well as the organization and agendas of key CMC meetings.[26] Mao Zedong pointed to the unseen but influential role played by the CMC General Office when he commented in 1952: "In my understanding of the army's situation, no small part goes to comrade Xiao Xiang-rong [CMC General Office director], who delivered the materials."[27] The General Office collates reports from other PLA organs and circulates them to the CMC leaders in the form of reading material summaries, commentaries, and bulletins.[28] The General Office also liaises frequently with its counterparts in the party and state apparatuses. Some observers believe that the General Office's functions and clout are being expanded on account of the absence of a functioning CMC Secretariat; the future of that office was put in limbo with the sidelining of Secretary General Yang Baibing in 1992. In a related move, the number of General Office deputy directors has been gradually expanded, from three to four in the early 1990s to six in 1997.[29]

Ambitious staffers in the General Office have occasionally put forward policy initiatives of their own. When Major General Li Jijun headed the General Office's policy research section in the late 1980s, he wrote several policy papers advocating a new local war strategy as part of a general shift that was taking place in the PLA's strategic posture at that time. These proposals were well received by Li's superiors, including Yang Shangkun and Zhao Ziyang, who served as CMC first vice chairman between 1987 and 1989, notwithstanding strong bureaucratic opposition to his role from other parts of the PLA apparatus. Although Li's initiative was shelved after Zhao was ousted from power in the Tiananmen Square crackdown, it was eventually adopted in the early 1990s as part of the PLA's new operational strategy for fighting high-technology wars under local conditions.[30]

The chairman and vice chairmen have their own offices, each with a small staff of secretaries and personal advisors. Their chief personal secretaries are powerful figures within the CMC administrative system.[31] As already pointed out, Jia Tingan, Jiang's chief military secretary, is a deputy director of the CMC General Office and head of Jiang Zemin's general office.

CMC Meetings and Conferences

Meetings and conferences are the lifeblood of the CMC and are essential for policy coordination, formulation, and dissemination of directives. These gatherings come in several forms.

The Work Conference (Bangong Huiyi) / *Standing Conference* (Changwu Huiyi). The work conference is the CMC's executive forum. It is held every Thursday at the Sanzuomen complex and includes the commission's vice chairmen and members or their deputies if they are unable to attend. The chairman does not normally participate, but other PLA officials occasionally take part, depending on the topics being addressed, in an ex officio capacity. Conference attendees deal with routine administrative matters, such as adopting decrees and approving regulations, but are also active in policy-making.[32] Decisions on major military and defense issues are often made at these meetings and are later ratified at enlarged CMC gatherings. During several periods in the 1970s and 1980s a standing conference attended by the members of a standing committee replaced the work conference. In 1982, for example, a CMC standing committee was formed that consisted of the commission's secretary general and deputy secretaries general.[33] The standing conference is believed to have been replaced by a new work conference in the early 1990s. These constant name changes have not seriously affected the functioning of this key decision-making body.

The "Knocking Heads" Conference (Pengtou Huiyi). This is a brief working meeting that is intended as a forum for the exchange of information among senior CMC and PLA officers. Such meetings were especially popular during the 1960s and 1970s, but have been held less frequently since the 1980s.

The Discussion Conference (Zuotan Huiyi). Each session of this conference runs for several days or more and is held to allow CMC leaders and high-ranking military chiefs to candidly discuss major political, military, and foreign policy issues. They are often held shortly after party plenums. At one of these meetings in October 1984, for example, the CMC leadership decided to give preliminary approval to the demobilization of a million troops and to allow military units to take part in commercial activities.[34]

The Plenary Conference (Quanti Huiyi). An annual plenary session was occasionally convened during the Maoist years. Such sessions were usually held around the end of the year to review the past year's work and to set priorities for the following year. They were replaced by enlarged CMC conferences in the 1980s.[35]

The Enlarged Conference (Kuoda Huiyi). The enlarged conference comes in two forms, as annual year-end review sessions and as extraordinary meetings to unveil major initiatives. Since the early 1980s the annual enlarged meetings have been held at the end of each year and are attended by several hundred top commanders from around the country. Major policy announcements are occasionally made at these events, such as Jiang Zemin's appointment as CMC chairman in 1989. These meetings are analogous to the party's annual plenary session and the national economic work conference that is held around the same time. Extraordinary enlarged conferences take place once or twice every decade and are convened to announce major organizational reforms or shifts in the country's security posture. The most important of these meetings included the first enlarged conference in 1954, at which attendees ratified the PLA's peacetime organizational structure; a 1975 meeting that paved the way for a major streamlining of the armed forces; and an enlarged session in 1985 at which was announced the reduction of one million troops and the PLA's strategic shift to a post–cold war footing.

The Beidaihe Summer Conference. The CMC also gathers during the leadership's annual summer retreat in the coastal resort of Beidaihe, usually in July and August, to discuss work priorities to be announced at the December enlarged conference. The informal nature of these summer get-togethers may allow for more open debate among participants than do other CMC forums.

Because CMC meetings deal primarily with defense-related issues, the attendees are almost exclusively military personnel. Senior civilian leaders are sometimes allowed to participate in the enlarged conferences and give speeches. For example, Party General Secretary Hu Yaobang attended the 1985 enlarged session, and Li Peng occasionally took part in CMC events when he was premier.

Ad Hoc Working Groups and Committees

When the CMC decides to undertake major policy initiatives, it often organizes special ad hoc working groups and committees drawn from the PLA bureaucracy to develop policy recommendations. Some of the most important of these entities include the following.

The Drafting Group on the Five-Year Defense Plan. An ad hoc group of military specialists drawn from the General Staff Department (GSD), PLA think tanks, service arms, and other key central-level military units are convened once every five years to draft the defense component of the national five-year development plan. The PLA's portion focuses on defense modernization programs and budgeting issues. This group meets a year before the implementation of the new plan and spends six to nine months drawing up an outline and liaising with key government agencies such as the State Development and Planning Commission and the Ministry of Finance. The plan is first approved by the CMC and then reviewed and adopted by the government. Civilian agencies undertake a similar decision-making process.[36]

The Committees and Working Groups on Military Strategy, Training, and Force Restructuring. When major changes to military strategy, operational doctrines, or general threat assessments are required, the CMC may organize a special committee to formulate a general outline, which is then fleshed out by the GSD. During the early 1960s, for example, Marshal Ye Jianying was chairman of a committee for military training and military scientific research under the CMC. Under Ye's direction "a series of regulations for the PLA were formulated."[37] A special working group was also set up by the CMC in the late 1980s to coordinate the reorganization of the PLA's force structure, weapons research, and military training as part of the shift from fighting major wars to fighting local wars.[38]

The Working and Inspection Groups on Financial and Economic Discipline. Since the mid-1980s the CMC has regularly organized special working and inspection groups to oversee campaigns to clean up military units and enterprises involved in economic activities. In 1986, for example, a leading group on financial and economic discipline was established to crack down on corruption and other abuses by army enterprises and military units dealing with financial matters.[39]

THE CMC'S INVOLVEMENT IN DEFENSE AND NATIONAL SECURITY DECISION-MAKING

As China's role in international affairs grows, its defense and national security interests are also expanding. Acting as the nexus between the military and civilian decision-making apparatuses, the CMC has played a prominent role in areas that have a major impact on the country's defense and security postures, especially related to the safeguarding of the country's sovereignty and territorial integrity. These areas include arms exports, ties across the Taiwan Strait, strategic relations with major powers, and maritime sovereignty disputes.

Although the CMC and the rest of the military establishment is paying more attention to the external security environment, their involvement in the mainstream foreign policy arena appears to have diminished, as the chapters of this book by Lu Ning, Margaret Pearson, and Michael Swaine also suggest. This has allowed the civilian foreign policy establishment, especially the Ministry of Foreign Affairs (MFA), to become more assertive in advancing its own diplomatic interests and expanding its areas of responsibility. The MFA has, for example, assumed a leading role in international arms control negotiations[40] and, along with the Ministry of Foreign Trade and Economic Cooperation, a more prominent role in technology export controls.

But the onset of the Asian financial crisis in the summer of 1997 also led decision-makers in the CMC and other PLA organs to focus more attention on nonmilitary threats that could adversely affect the country's national security. Considerable interest was paid to the consequences of the Asian financial meltdown for China's overall security as well as its ramifications for the regional security regime.

Cross-Strait Relations

At the top of the military's list of priorities since the early 1990s has been the deterioration in relations across the Taiwan Strait. Policy-making toward Taiwan during the 1980s and early 1990s was primarily in the hands of paramount leader Deng Xiaoping and Yang Shangkun. As these two revolutionary veterans controlled the CMC, there was little need for PLA chiefs to be involved in the policy-making process. Under Deng, Beijing took a pragmatic and long-term approach to its dealings with Taiwan, focusing on economic and cultural exchanges in the hope that this would pave the way for eventual reunification.

This situation changed following the Fourteenth Party Congress. Yang, who also headed the Taiwan Affairs Leading Small Group (TALSG), discussed at length in the chapter by Swaine, was retired after losing a power struggle, and Deng's involvement in policy-making decreased sharply thereafter due to his failing health. The Taiwan portfolio was left open, and Jiang took charge of the TALSG. Military chiefs also moved to fill the vacuum, and they began to make their voices heard. The new leadership began to explore possible initiatives regarding Taiwan, and a far-reaching debate among policy-makers began on the future direction of cross-strait relations. Competing institutions represented in the TALSG put forward new proposals in response to the changing dynamics in China-Taiwan relations, especially in the following areas.

Deteriorating Sino-U.S. Relations. Ties between China and the United States began to worsen in the late 1980s as the cold war faded and Beijing became a less vital strategic partner to Washington. Relations plummeted further after the 1989 Tiananmen Square crackdown and have only slowly and partially recovered following a tortuous path, with highs represented by the 1997 and 1998 summits and lows exemplified by the May 1999 bombing of the Chinese embassy in Belgrade. More generally, as Sino-U.S. relations worsened, Washington began to improve its links with Taipei. A major turning point occurred in 1992, when U.S. President George Bush sold 150 F-16 fighter jets to Taiwan. Beijing regarded the sale as a breach of the joint 1982 Sino-U.S. diplomatic communiqué, in which Washington pledged to gradually reduce arms sales to Taipei and not increase their quality.

Sweeping Political and Social Change on Taiwan. Under Lee Teng-hui and his successor, Chen Shui-bian, Taiwan has forged an increasingly separate identity from the mainland, based on its new democratic system. New generations of locally born Taiwanese have taken over from Nationalist mainlanders who fled to the island after the communist victory in 1949. There is little enthusiasm among these younger, Taiwan-born leaders for reunification with China.

Taiwan's Rising International Status. In the mid-1990s Taiwan launched an aggressive campaign to expand its foreign relations. Using its abundant financial resources, Taipei offered generous economic assistance to international organizations and governments in Africa, South America, and other parts of the world (including small Pacific atolls and nongovernmental units) in exchange for diplomatic recognition. Lee used the guise of overseas vacations to break out of the isolation Beijing has sought to impose on Taipei. In addition, pro-Taiwan and anti-China sentiment has been growing in major Western countries, especially in influential political institutions such as the Japanese Diet and the U.S. Congress.

Moderates in the TALSG and in the State Council's Taiwan Affairs Office, which oversees the daily management of Taiwan policy, believed China needed to respond to these developments by offering concessions that would secure Taipei's agreement to a new framework on cross-strait relations. But skeptics, especially on the CMC, believed that Lee was seeking to create a separate Taiwanese state and argued for a tough response to deter him. The basis for the military's uncompromising views, according to my interviews in Beijing, was a comprehensive reexamination of cross-strait relations ordered by the CMC and conducted by policy planners and intelligence analysts in the first half of 1993.[41] The findings, which were adopted by the military leadership at a CMC meeting in May 1993,[42] were alarming:

— Lee Teng-hui was committed to seeking the creation of a separate Taiwanese state.
— The domination of Taiwan's ruling Nationalist Party (Kuomintang) by pro-reunification mainlanders was quickly ending; the influence of Taiwan-born politicians who opposed reunification was growing. Additionally, the staunchly independence-minded Democratic Progressive Party (DPP) was becoming a powerful political force.
— Taipei might make major breakthroughs in its aggressive campaign for international recognition in coming years.
— The situation across the Taiwan Strait was likely to become increasingly volatile with Taiwan's first-ever presidential election in March 1996 and Hong Kong's return to Chinese sovereignty in July 1997.

After lengthy deliberation, the party leadership decided to adopt a conciliatory approach. China would show greater flexibility on the issue of reunification if Lee were to accept that Taiwan was part of China and stop his diplomatic maneuverings. At the same time, the PBSC and the CMC ordered the PLA to quietly begin to upgrade preparations for military action against Taiwan should the "carrot" strategy fail. Combat training for select units was stepped up, and the PLA was allowed to resume major war games in areas of Fujian Province close to Taiwan-held islands.

Jiang unveiled his softer line in January 1995 in an eight-point proposal to Taiwan (*Jiang Ba Dian*), as is also discussed in the chapter by Swaine. "On the premise that there is only one China, we are prepared to talk with the Taiwanese authorities about any matter," he said.[43] Jiang added that "Chinese should not fight fellow Chinese," and he repeated an offer to officially end the state of hostilities that still existed between the two sides as a first step in a comprehensive agreement toward reunification. Lee responded several months later with a counter-proposal that Beijing regarded as a rejection of Jiang's offer. Lee said Beijing must renounce its threat to use force against the island before any negotiations could begin, a demand that China rejected.

Washington's decision in May 1995 to grant Lee Teng-hui a visa to make a private visit to Cornell University triggered an angry reaction from Beijing, especially from military and conservative hard-liners. Military chiefs pointed out that Lee's visit provided conclusive evidence that their assessments of trends in cross-strait relations were accurate. They argued that the conciliatory approach had failed and that the only way to deal with Lee was intimidation: specifically, through provocative military exercises and a savage propaganda assault in the period before crucial Taiwanese legislative elections at the end of 1995 and the presidential election the following year.

Military strategists had already begun advocating the incorporation of provocative displays of military force into the PLA's new strategy of local war under high-technology conditions several months earlier. At a military symposium on the initial stages of the new local war strategy held in November 1994, some policy planners and analysts argued that China should demonstrate its military might during a crisis to deter its opponent and avert war.[44] Military chiefs and hard-liners persuaded their more moderate civilian counterparts to act firmly against Lee, and the go-ahead was given for the PLA to conduct missile tests near Taiwan several weeks after Lee's U.S. visit. These missile tests were followed up by more missile firings and war games in August and by even larger military exercises on Pingtan Island in November, ahead of Taiwan's parliamentary elections. At the same time the Chinese media attacked Lee, condemning him as a traitor to the Chinese people. Beijing also suspended semiofficial contacts. Beijing further stepped up its saber rattling in the period before the Taiwanese presidential election in March 1996 with even larger-scale air, naval, and ground war games and missile firings within fifty kilometers of Taiwan's two main seaports, Keelung and Kaohsiung.

Arms Sales

China's arms sales, especially its export of missiles and nuclear technologies to Pakistan and Iran, have been a major source of friction in Sino-U.S. relations since the mid-1980s, as Bates Gill explains in detail in his contribution to this volume. Even the MFA reportedly complained about the lack of control on arms exports, which were being conducted by well-connected family members of the country's ruling elite,[45] a point developed in more detail in the chapters by Lu Ning and Bates Gill.

The CMC established an arms trade bureau in 1989 to tighten up supervision of the military's arms trading activities.[46] This bureau not only focused on overseeing arms exports, but since the early 1990s has also played an active role in the acquisition of advanced foreign arms and technology, especially from Russia. The bureau, for example, established an office in the Chinese embassy in Moscow to handle arms acquisitions and related technology transfers from Russia.[47]

The PLA's Views on Economic Security

The near-meltdown of many Asian economies in the late 1990s has led Chinese military planners to pay considerable attention to the importance of economic security as a critical component of the country's overall national security. This was apparent in the publication in the summer of 1998 of the country's first-ever Defense White Paper, which pointed out that economic security "was becoming more important" in shaping national security interests. The report said that the Asian financial crisis "has made the issue of economic security" more prominent, especially the volatility and destructive power of global financial markets.[48] The kinds of interdependence described by Thomas Moore and Dixia Yang in their chapter in this volume were of concern to the PLA high command.

As the Asian financial crisis deepened, the world's financial markets began to scrutinize the Chinese economy, especially the stability of the renminbi (the official Chinese currency). It was widely assumed that if the Chinese currency were devalued, it would have a domino effect on currency values in other Asian economies, most notably Hong Kong, and this could, in turn, have a devastating impact on the world economy. In the second half of 1998 the Chinese central leadership is believed to have ordered the GSD's Second (Intelligence) Department and the Ministry of State Security to investigate international currency and hedge fund speculators, especially those seeking to undermine the renminbi and the Hong Kong dollar.[49] Although China generally avoided the most severe economic effects of the Asian financial crisis, it nonetheless has serious problems in its domestic economic and financial system that could affect the country's stability. These include rising unemployment, a weak banking and financial system, and a chronically inefficient and bloated state industrial sector. There are mounting concerns that the country could face economic upheavals over the next few years if it is unable to tackle these deep-rooted defects.

The primary contribution of the Chinese military high command has been to avoid taking any actions that might lead to military tensions and scare away sorely needed foreign investments. PLA decision-makers, for example, debated in the summer of 1998 whether to organize military exercises in the period before the parliamentary elections in Taiwan in December to deter voters from supporting the DPP. They decided against authorizing these maneuvers because of the potential adverse impact on China's economy.[50]

DECISION-MAKING IN THE PLA HIGH COMMAND

At Deng Xiaoping's directive, the CMC's direct involvement in military operational decision-making has steadily decreased since the early 1980s. As a result, other military organizations have become more prominent in policy-making. The place of these organs in policy formulation falls into several concentric rings:

The Central Core. The CMC stands at the center of the military decision-making process.

The First Inner Ring. The PLA GSD is the chief executive arm of the CMC and provides critical support in information gathering, analysis, and policy formulation to its parent.

The Second Inner Ring. Other central-level military organs provide regular input into the policy-making process, but they normally participate in decision-making only regarding issues directly related to their areas of responsibility. These include the General Political Department (GPD); the General Logistics Department (GLD); the General Equipment Department (GED); the

Commission for Science, Technology, and Industry for National Defense (COSTIND), and the service arms.

The Third Outer Ring. The military regions are on the margins of the military decision-making apparatus, although they play an important role in policy implementation and in the adaptation of central-level operational doctrines to local conditions.

The General Staff Department

The PLA's general headquarters, especially the GSD, has become increasingly important not only in operational management and policy implementation, but also in shaping high-level decision-making. As the most powerful of the four general headquarters units, the GSD is a sprawling administrative organization divided into nine second-tier departments and several other bureaus and offices.[51] Its responsibilities include collection and analysis of strategic and tactical military intelligence, communications, operational management of frontline combat units, mobilization, and training. Officers from the ground forces dominate the GSD leadership, especially field commanders who earned their credentials in combat units. With the growing attention being given to joint and littoral operations, however, efforts have been made to bring in air force and naval officers, although this has met with only limited success.

GSD organs that have an important say in military policy-making, especially related to broader national security issues, include the following.

The Second and Third (Intelligence) Departments. These two departments are among the country's premier organs for the gathering and analysis of intelligence, not only on military matters, but also on strategic and foreign policy issues. The Second Department has several bureaus, including an international analysis wing, and units in military regions that report to it directly. The Third Department is primarily involved in gathering technical intelligence, as Lu Ning and Michael Swaine discuss in their chapters in this volume. A deputy chief of general staff, currently Lieutenant General Xiong Guangkai, oversees the activities of these departments. Xiong has played an influential role since the mid-1990s in shaping the external views of the military brass and Jiang Zemin, as well as being the point of contact for Sino-American military-to-military dialogue.

The Operations Department. The Operations Department is responsible for drawing up plans for fighting wars and is in operational charge of the deployment of the PLA's combat units. In drawing up contingency and war plans, the Operations Department has an important say in shaping the military's overall thinking on key issues. For example, the department has played an influential role in the crafting of the PLA's policy toward Taiwan since the early 1990s, especially in the saber rattling between the summer of 1995 and the spring of 1996.

The General Equipment Department

One of the GSD's most important subordinate organs was the Equipment Department, but a major organizational reform of the military-industrial complex led to the elevation of this department to the position of the PLA's fourth general department in April 1998. One of the GED's chief responsibilities is to oversee weapons procurement and the export of surplus arms. This has been an important, if controversial, component of China's foreign relations since the 1980s, especially with countries such as Russia, Pakistan, and Iran.

Two well-connected princelings, He Pengfei and He Ping (Deng Xiaoping's son-in-law), headed the Equipment Department during the 1980s and the first half of the 1990s. This added to its bureaucratic clout, particularly in securing permission to export missiles and other sensitive arms over the reported objections of the Foreign Ministry, as both Lu Ning and Bates Gill suggest in their chapters. He Ping's retirement from the military in 1996 and Deng Xiaoping's death the following year removed an important backdoor channel of influence to the senior civilian leadership.

To oversee and coordinate the activities of these often competing departments, the chief of the General Staff has several deputies directly responsible for planning and operations, intelligence, training, and other major issues. A small general office looks after their administrative needs. Although they meet regularly, no evidence exists of a formal executive or work committee. But the GSD Party Committee has a standing committee that holds an enlarged meeting toward the end of each year to set out work priorities for the following twelve months.

The General Political Department

Although the GSD is intimately involved in military and strategic policy planning, the GPD and the GLD play only a little role in these matters. One exception has been the GPD's Liaison Department, which has a special role in gathering and analyzing political and economic intelligence concerning Taiwan. The Liaison Department was originally established as the GPD's United War Front Department during the Anti-Japanese War in the late 1930s, and it played a key role in coordinating military operations against the Japanese with the Nationalist forces. The Liaison Department is also said to play an important role in the diplomatic war of recognition between Taipei and Beijing.[52]

One of the Liaison Department's principal means of gathering information has been through the commercial activities of its business conglomerate, the China Carrie Group, although the firm's ties with its military parent were severed at the end of 1998 following the PLA's divestiture of its business interests.[53] The Liaison Department's influence was also affected by the retirement of its longtime head, Major General Ye Xuanning, a son of the late marshal Ye Jianying, at the Fifteenth Party Congress. However, the Liaison Department continues to play an active role in policy-making toward Taiwan.

The Commission of Science, Technology, and Industry for National Defense

COSTIND has also played an important role in shaping the country's defense posture and external security relations through its management of the coordination of weapons research and development between the military and the defense-industrial complex. It has also been prominent in its purchase of advanced foreign technology with military applications through both overt and covert means.[54] It has played a leading role, for example, in forging a close arms-trading relationship between China and Russia, especially with regard to the acquisition of weapons and defense technology, in coordination with other agencies in the GSD and CMC.

But COSTIND was reorganized in early 1998 as part of a major effort by the military authorities to improve the lackluster performance of the defense industry, one indicator of which was the fact that the PLA had to rely increasingly on Russia for new generations of weapons. The military and civilian components of the original COSTIND were separated, and the military components were incorporated into the GED. The civilian element of COSTIND was retained and kept its name, although it is no longer regarded as part of the military establishment.[55]

The original COSTIND also had a small apparatus for the planning and analysis of policy, and this apparatus studied strategic and technical issues affecting the country's weapons capabilities. These elements are believed to have been transferred to the GED. Their work focuses on arms control, disarmament, and defense conversion. COSTIND researchers have also been in the forefront of efforts to assess the technological revolution in military affairs and its implications for China's military modernization.[56]

The Service Branches and Military Regions

The PLA's service arms and, to a lesser extent, its military regions also regularly participate in the decision-making process. The PLA Navy has played a prominent role in shifting the military's doctrinal focus from continental to littoral operations since the late 1980s. The naval chiefs were indebted to former navy commander Liu Huaqing, who strongly supported the navy's interests during his tenure at the top of the military high command. The navy has also been actively involved in the formulation of key national security policies, such as China's hard-line strategy toward the disputed Spratly Islands in the South China Sea during the late 1980s and early 1990s.

Despite its lack of bureaucratic clout and powerful patrons, the PLA Air Force has achieved remarkable success in winning budgetary battles for more funds to modernize its largely obsolete fighter fleet. Chinese arms purchases from Russia have been dominated by the acquisition of Su-27 fighter aircraft, high-altitude air defense missile systems, and more recent deals to acquire Su-30 combat jets. In part, the air force owes its good fortunes to the inability of domestic aerospace manufacturers to produce state-of-the-art warplanes and to the 1991 Gulf War, during which the United States and its allies demonstrated that airpower could decisively win modern conflicts. This was further demonstrated in 1999 when NATO was able to force Serbian forces out of Kosovo through the exclusive use of airpower. PLA Air Force commanders were able to use these events to convince the military chiefs of the central importance of airpower in modern warfare.

With the PLA's strategic focus on dealing with the potential outbreak of limited local wars, the seven military regions and their equivalent air force and naval commands have had a growing say in the formulation of plans, operations, and deployments in their areas of geographical responsibility. In the PLA's strategy toward Taiwan, the Nanjing and Guangzhou Military Regions—sometimes referred to as "War Zones"—have played a conspicuous role in coordinating exercises and other military activities in and near the Taiwan Strait with the aim of putting pressure on the Taiwanese authorities. Although these regional military commands have little clout with the central government, their implementation of directives and monitoring of developments in Taiwan gives them a small voice in policy-making.

The influence of the military regions may grow in the coming years, moreover, because one consequence of military modernization is to increase the decision-making autonomy and logistical responsibilities of the lower-level military commands, although under strict political supervision. In the past few years the military regions have been given more responsibility for the reform and modernization of the PLA's logistics networks and liaising with local governments in the construction of key infrastructure projects that may have defense applications, such as highways, airports, and telecommunications networks.[57]

INTERACTION BETWEEN THE MILITARY AND CIVILIAN DECISION-MAKING PROCESSES

The military decision-making system has traditionally been a highly insular and vertically integrated structure with few external linkages except with the party. But with China's economic liberalization and opening up to the outside world since the early 1980s, efforts have been made to increase the contacts between the military and civilian policy-making organs, principally the state apparatus, at different levels of the chain of command. At the same time, however, the military's interactions with the party have steadily diminished because of its focus on professionalism and its reluctance to become entangled in domestic affairs.[58]

Military-Party Ties

The highest level of interaction is between the CMC and the CCP, although these ties have diminished since the 1980s as the PLA has become less involved in party affairs and focused more on professional matters. The CMC has several channels of contact with leading party organs. Among the most important linkages are the personal ties between senior CMC members and party leaders. Because the CMC chairman is also the country's top political leader, he plays a pivotal role in liaising between the CMC and the PBSC. But because of his other responsibilities, the CMC chairman usually becomes involved only in major issues and delegates responsibility for handling routine matters to his deputy at the CMC, who is either the secretary general or the executive vice chairman.

Zhang Wannian took over as second in command at the CMC at the Fifteenth Party Congress in 1997. But because he is not on the PBSC and appears to have few personal ties with any of its members, his influence with the party leadership is instead through his official position on the full Politburo and, perhaps more important, on the party Secretariat. As the executive arm of the top party leadership, the Secretariat is responsible for refining the decisions made by the PBSC and supervising their implementation. The organ's influence also comes from its oversight of the activities of the central party bureaucracy, including the leading small groups.[59]

Zhang is the first military member of the Secretariat since Yang Baibing in 1992. Zhang and Defense Minister Chi Haotian's membership in the full twenty-two-member Politburo, though, is of more symbolic importance, because this organ generally lacks decisive political clout, as Swaine also notes in his contribution to this volume. In addition, Wang Ruilin was a deputy director of the Party Central Committee's General Office, a position largely derived from his role as Deng Xiaoping's secretary.

Below the Politburo level, the military has a presence in two key party leading small groups dealing with foreign affairs and national security matters.[60]

The Foreign Affairs Leading Small Group. Chi Haotian's membership in the Foreign Affairs Leading Small Group (FALSG) is ostensibly in his capacity as defense minister, although his CMC position accords him greater authority. Although the FALSG is primarily a forum for coordination and discussion among party, government, and military organs involved in foreign affairs, it can have an influential role in overall foreign policy decision-making.

The Taiwan Affairs Leading Small Group. The military's representative on the Taiwan Affairs Leading Small Group (TALSG) presently is Xiong Guangkai, the deputy chief of the general staff responsible for intelligence and external affairs, suggesting that he plays a primarily advisory role, especially as the other members are more senior civilian decision-makers, as described in the chapter by Swaine.

Military-State Ties

Relations between the military and state decision-making apparatuses are less focused on defense or security matters than on economic issues. The State

Central Military Commission and the Ministry of National Defense (MND) serve as the formal links between the government and the PLA. But although the state constitution makes the latter responsible for overseeing army building and military preparedness, in reality, they have no policy-making or administrative functions. The state CMC exists simply for symbolic purposes, and its members all serve concurrently on the more powerful party CMC, as described earlier in this chapter.

The MND's primary role is to liaise with foreign military establishments, and it has a small but growing administrative staff, including a foreign affairs bureau[61] and a conscription bureau. In a move that may suggest the MND could acquire more responsibility and influence in the future, the foreign affairs bureau (*Ju*) was upgraded (by a grade) to a general office (*Ting*) in 1997.[62] Additional duties might include liaising with local governments in the preparation of wartime contingency plans, because a growing number of provincial authorities have established defense mobilization committees since the mid-1990s.

As the government lacks representation within the military establishment, so the military also lacks a strong presence in the governmental hierarchy. Few senior government leaders have responsibilities that bring them into contact with the military. Before his retirement in 1998, Vice Premier Zou Jiahua was reported to be responsible for military-industrial matters, along with his oversight of sixteen other ministries.[63] Wu Bangguo has now taken over most of Zou's responsibilities and also regularly inspects military-industrial facilities around the country. The PLA claims a token representative among the government's top ranks since the appointment of Chi Haotian as a state councilor. This allows him to attend State Council meetings.

Most of the interaction between the government and the PLA, therefore, is between the PLA general headquarters departments and the government ministries and commissions. These ties are extensive, although narrowly focused:

— The GSD and GLD, for example, negotiate regularly with the Ministry of Finance over the size of the defense budget, although the political leadership makes the final decision on granting funding increases.

— COSTIND liaises with the State Development and Planning Commission and the State Science and Technology Commission regarding the activities of the defense industry as well as scientific research and development.

— The MFA and the military organs meet to discuss policies and co-ordinate action on foreign policy issues ranging from specific topics such as arms control and relations with major countries to broader analyses of the international strategic situation.

— MOFTEC liaises with the CMC, the GED, and other PLA organs in dealing with arms trade matters.

— The Ministry of Public Security coordinates with the paramilitary People's Armed Police and the GSD over internal security matters.

— The Ministry of Civil Affairs cooperates with the GPD and local military authorities regarding the resettlement of demobilized troops and the welfare of retired soldiers.

— The Ministry of Information Industry works closely with the GSD's communications department and the GED in the development of defense telecommunications and electronics systems.

The PLA's worry that economic reforms could erode its interests has led to increased dialogue with the government. Military leaders have been especially concerned that the government's moves to cut support to inefficient and loss-producing industrial enterprises could have an adverse impact on the country's sprawling defense-industrial complex. Defense factories are among the biggest loss producers in the state sector, and the military chiefs are concerned that reforms could lead to widespread closures and a shrinking of the defense production base. The military chiefs have lobbied the leaders of the central government to give defense-industrial enterprises special financial assistance.

But since Zhu Rongji took over as premier in 1998, he has taken an uncompromising line toward the military chiefs. This could have far-reaching implications for military-state relations in the coming years. Zhu, who has a reputation as a no-nonsense administrator, has been especially critical of the PLA's participation in business, which has led to rampant economic abuses. Zhu was particularly incensed about the involvement of major military firms in smuggling, and he played an instrumental role in ordering a nationwide antismuggling crackdown in June 1998. In a speech at an antismuggling conference, the premier explicitly highlighted the conduct of military-backed entities.[64]

Shortly after the antismuggling campaign was launched, the central leadership ordered the PLA's divestiture of its commercial activities because of its involvement in these illegal activities. Jiang Zemin personally ordered the PLA to halt its business operations, but Zhu has been largely responsible for implementing the decision through the State Economic and Trade Commission (SETC), which is one bastion of his power.[65] In a rare move, the party leadership ordered that civilian agencies manage the divestiture because it was felt that the military authorities could not be relied upon to carry out the orders.[66] The SETC was put in charge, with the GLD and other military bodies playing a supporting role. The military chiefs generally welcomed the PLA's separation from business, but they were concerned about the loss of earnings and assets and pressed for adequate compensation. The PLA apparently received a substantial reward in the form of double-digit increases in the defense budgets in both 1999 and 2000. This divestiture, which was officially completed at the end of 1998, appears to have been largely successful.[67] This is a remarkable feat, especially for Zhu, who has only limited ties with the military brass. He was able to gain access to the closely guarded military system and take charge of the crackdown. Moreover, Zhu appears to have retained cordial relations with the military chiefs.

Under the 1997 National Defense Law, the State Council has taken on expanded responsibilities for defense matters. This could pave the way for government ministries to play a more active role in supporting the military in coming years. These enhanced obligations include:

— The drawing up of programs and plans for national defense construction.
— The formulation of principles, policies, and administrative laws for national defense construction.
— The direction and administration of scientific research and production for national defense.
— The administration of expenditures and assets for national defense.
— The direction and administration of work related to national economic mobilization as well as mobilization of the people's armed forces, the people's air defense, national defense communications, and other related matters.
— The direction and administration of work in support of the army, the preferential treatment of families of servicemen and martyrs, and work concerning the placement of soldiers discharged from active duty.
— The direction of work concerning national defense education.
— The direction of work concerning the building of the People's Armed Police and the people's militia and the conscription and reserve

service, as well as the administration of work concerning frontier, coastal, and air defense in coordination with the CMC.[68]

The NPC is also becoming a more important forum for the military to use to lobby for its own interests and to exert influence on other issues. At the NPC's 1994 annual session, for example, the PLA delegates were prominent in voicing their concerns and submitting a series of bills on military spending, defense industry reforms, and a range of other topics.[69] This behavior was in marked contrast to the behavior of such delegates in the past, when the PLA delegates kept a low profile and voiced their opinions in private group gatherings.

As the NPC gains in independence and influence, the voice of the military representatives could also strengthen. Although the role of the congress has traditionally been to rubber stamp government decisions, it has shown increasing independence in policy-making and the drafting of legislation since the late 1980s. During Qiao Shi's tenure as chairman of the NPC Standing Committee between 1994 and 1998, delegates became increasingly vocal and critical of the government's track record, especially on issues such as crime and corruption. The NPC's annual sessions have also become an important arena for the exchange of views among central and provincial leaders. With the increasing outspokenness and strong representation of the military delegates—who account for 10 percent of total NPC membership—the PLA could play a growing role in congress debates. Finally, there has also been a revival of discussion about the establishment of a parliamentary defense committee.

CONCLUSION

This study of the structure and policy-making process of the CMC offers some useful insights into the military's changing role in national security decision-making during the reform era, especially under Jiang Zemin, which can be summarized as follows:

— The military decision-making process is increasingly institutionalized and bureaucratic, as Lampton's introduction to this volume suggests is the case, throughout the broader foreign and national security policy-making system. Although personal factors occasionally play an important role in shaping policies, they are generally no longer of great significance.

— Jiang Zemin has successfully solidified his control of the military, although he gives only limited attention to military affairs. This has allowed the PLA chiefs to exercise more autonomy in setting their own professional priorities and agendas, although they remain under tight party supervision.

— Decision-making among the military brass is consensus driven and is done by committee. Although there is ample room for debate, especially among competing bureaucratic entities at the lower levels, there tends to be a strong unity of views at the top of the high command.

— The PLA's influence in the national policy-making process remains strong, but its ability to be heard at the very top levels of the political leadership cannot be taken for granted except during major crises. The military chiefs have to rely on institutionalized channels of communication, such as the party Secretariat, to pass their views to the senior political leadership.

— Professional military interests largely shape the PLA's involvement in national security and foreign policy decision-making, which focuses on safeguarding sovereignty and territorial integrity. Its role in the mainstream foreign policy arena has diminished. In its domain, the PLA is powerful, but its influence in this sector does not translate into equal influence in other realms of policy.

— The PLA's organizational structure has been undergoing substantial reform throughout the 1990s to adapt to changing military missions and priorities. The traditional dominance of the ground forces is being gradually eroded, and other service branches, especially the PLA Air Force and Second Artillery, have begun receiving more funds for weapons procurements. This shift in the PLA's organizational makeup is likely to accelerate in the foreseeable future, because its chief challenges are increasingly offshore.

— The military carefully coordinates its decision-making with the civilian leadership and is not a freewheeling actor. Nonetheless, it is willing to put forward and stand by opposing views, such as on the issue of Taiwan, although it will act only with the permission of the civilian authorities.

— The military's ties with the state apparatus are likely to proliferate in the coming years, especially over economic-related issues such as bureaucratic fights for resource allocations and defense-industrial reforms. There will also likely be growing interaction over how to cope with China's vulnerabilities in the economic security arena, such as in the high-technology and financial sectors.

FOUR

The External Relations
of China's Provinces

PETER T. Y. CHEUNG AND JAMES T. H. TANG

China's provincial-level units have emerged as important political and economic actors since 1978.[1] Deng Xiaoping's economic reforms and open-door
policy (*kaifang zhengce*) have not simply decentralized economic power from
the central government to the provinces and other localities, but also increased
the latter's involvement in China's foreign affairs. Not only have such developments posed enormous challenges for the management of China's foreign
affairs system, but they have also generated a new dynamic in central-
provincial interaction, because the provinces have heightened their participation in the global economy and forged their own international links. This
increased assertiveness of China's provinces in the 1990s has significant
implications for the study of China's international behavior and foreign policy. Yet few scholars have systematically examined provincial involvement in
external affairs, apart from a few studies on provincial patterns of foreign trade
and on the prospect of China's disintegration.[2] In this chapter we analyze the
nature, organization, and changing pattern of provincial external relations in
the reform era, especially the 1990s, as well as the political implications of
these developments.[3] We conceptualize external affairs and relations in a broad

manner, encompassing the activities of subnational governments in establishing contacts with the outside world in the economic, social, cultural, and diplomatic arenas.

This chapter is divided into four sections. First we provide a historical perspective of the role of regional governments in China's foreign relations. Next we introduce the characteristics of the provinces and the overall policy framework set out by the central government, and we then proceed to examine the organization and operation of the provincial foreign affairs system. Finally we identify the pattern of provincial involvement in China's external relations. A discussion of the political implications of the growing role of the provinces in Chinese foreign affairs concludes the chapter.

HISTORICAL BACKGROUND

Because China is a unitary state, the conduct of Chinese foreign policy has traditionally been dictated by the central government. However, the vastness of China's territory and the absence of a clear concept of territorial boundary in the traditional tributary world order prior to the twentieth century left much room for local governments to pursue their own foreign economic and political interests. Attempts by both central and local authorities to control international trade, for example, have been a major source of central-local tensions throughout Chinese history. Reviewing historical developments from the middle of the fourth century up to the collapse of the traditional Chinese world order in the mid-nineteenth century reveals a rich history of central-local interactions in the conduct of China's foreign relations, with a pattern of centralization and local resistance.[4]

The collapse of imperial rule was marked by the intrusion of the West and the imposition on China of a treaty system through which the central government in Beijing surrendered its control over trade in the coastal provinces. During the Republican period central-local differences over foreign trade took a different form, because continuing foreign domination, civil wars, warlordism, and the war against Japan rendered central control of the localities in foreign trade matters ineffective. The communist movement was in part inspired by a strong nationalistic desire to respond to this trend and restore political order.

Therefore, when the Chinese communist leaders assumed power in 1949 they were determined to build a stable, unitary state free of foreign privileges and to restore China's former glory. The communist leaders were determined to seek proper recognition of China's international status. Foreign policy, therefore, was a matter of key importance that had to be concentrated in the hands of the top leaders. Even the Ministry of Foreign Affairs (MFA) had relatively little say in foreign policy matters, as Lu Ning indicates in his contribution to this volume.[5] However, if China's turbulent modern history impressed first-generation Chinese communist leaders with the importance of a unified China under strong central leadership, the country's premodern history demonstrated that maintaining absolute central control over localities in a country as large as China is impractical when foreign trade and other international activities are flourishing.

During the first three decades of the People's Republic of China (PRC), tight central control over foreign affairs at all levels was maintained. Even prior to the inauguration of the PRC, the Chinese Communist Party (CCP) had set up regional foreign affairs offices in cities that had significant foreign presences such as Tianjin and Shanghai.[6] Although the central government attempted to recruit cadres from local governments to serve in the Foreign Ministry during the mid-1960s, the central leadership has always dominated foreign policy-making, with perhaps the sole exception of the late 1960s, when the whole government machinery became paralyzed during the Cultural Revolution. Provincial authorities, especially in the border provinces, played a supporting role in receiving foreign visitors and supporting the efforts of the central government to manage relations with neighboring countries, but they did not have their own foreign affairs agendas.

Gradually, however, the provinces have become key agents in the initiation and implementation of China's foreign economic policy. For instance, leaders in Guangdong and Fujian provinces not only have actively lobbied the central authorities for special policies, but also have skillfully and flexibly implemented these policies since 1978.[7] If the coastal provinces have been far more privileged in exploiting the opportunities of the open-door policy by virtue of their location, social capital, and historical legacy, the inland and border provinces have been eager to catch up, especially in view of their late start. Yet these provinces have sought to achieve these goals not by encroaching upon the prerogatives of the central government in diplomacy or national defense, but rather by exploiting new opportunities and maximizing their interests within the broad framework of the existing policies of the central government. Hence it would be misleading to view provincial initiatives in external affairs as moves that are necessarily in conflict with the policies of the central government. As David Lampton points out in his introductory chapter, the policies of the central government have simply created broader "space" for a wider array of local actions.

PROVINCIAL CHINA: AN OVERVIEW

The province (*sheng*) has been a key political and administrative unit in China since the Yuan Dynasty in the thirteenth century. Since 1949 the number of provincial units has fluctuated over time;[8] however, the total number of provincial units remained twenty-nine from 1967 to 1987 (excluding Taiwan). The most important changes during the reform era were the hiving off of Hainan from Guangdong as a separate province and a special economic zone (SEZ) in 1988 and the upgrading of Chongqing from a centrally planned city (*jihua danlieshi*) to the fourth city directly administered by the central government in March 1997.

China's provinces are huge units in terms of population, size, and economic power, but they are marked by extreme disparities along a number of dimensions (Table 4.1). With over 1.6 million square kilometers, China's largest province, Xinjiang, is the size of a large country, whereas the smallest provincial unit, Shanghai, occupies only 6,431 square kilometers.[9] China's provinces, although smaller on average than the average province in Canada or Australia, are bigger than the average state in the United States. The population of an average province like Jiangxi or Zhejiang (about forty million) is the same as that of a medium-sized country.[10] The difference in provincial economic strength is even more striking. For instance, the gross domestic product (GDP) of Guangdong, the largest provincial economy in China, is ninety-five times that of Tibet, the smallest economy. On the basis of per capita GDP, Shanghai ranks first, with an annual figure of 25,750 yuan, which is about twelve times that of Guizhou, China's poorest province. These financial inequalities have only widened in the 1990s; the eastern region's share of China's GDP rose from 52.8 percent in 1978 to 58 percent in 1997, whereas the shares of the central and western regions fell from 30.7 percent to 28 percent and from 16.5 percent to 14 percent, respectively, during the same period.[11]

The provinces can be divided into three types, according to their geographical locations: border, inland, and coastal. There are a total of eight coastal provinces, four coastal/border provinces, twelve inland provinces, and seven inland/border provinces.[12] In the prereform era the inland provinces benefited from the allocation of resources by the central government, whereas the

TABLE 4.1
BASIC STATISTICS OF CHINA'S PROVINCIAL-LEVEL UNITS, 1997

Province	Size (square km)	Population (10,000)	GDP (100 million yuan)	GDP per capita (yuan)	Agricultural output (100 million yuan)	Industrial output (100 million yuan)	Foreign investment (U.S.$ million)
Beijing	16,807	1,240	1,810	16,735	171	1,993	1,627
Tianjin	11,305	953	1,240	13,796	149	2,838	2,524
Hebei	180,000	6,525	3,954	6,079	1,437	5,980	1,107
Shanxi	156,000	3,141	1,480	4,736	341	2,351	281
Inner Mongolia	1,280,000	2,326	1,095	4,691	489	1,075	131
Liaoning	145,700	4,138	3,490	8,525	921	6,499	2,458
Jilin	180,000	2,628	1,447	5,504	585	1,597	409
Heilongjiang	469,000	3,751	2,708	7,243	845	2,703	760
Shanghai	6,431	1,457	3,360	25,750	204	5,654	4,602
Jiangsu	100,000	7,148	6,680	9,344	1,816	12,542	5,595
Zhejiang	100,000	4,435	4,638	10,515	1,005	10,380	1,548
Anhui	130,000	6,127	2,670	4,390	1,227	4,317	453
Fujian	120,000	3,282	3,000	9,258	926	3,858	4,202
Jiangxi	166,600	4,150	1,715	4,155	786	1,573	448
Shandong	150,000	8,785	6,650	7,590	2,232	9,984	2,778
Henan	167,000	9,243	4,079	4,430	1,710	5,648	759
Hubei	180,000	5,873	3,450	5,899	1,244	5,977	853
Hunan	200,000	6,465	2,993	4,643	1,322	3,817	1,010
Guangdong	178,000	7,051	7,316	10,428	1,656	12,331	12,639
Guangxi	230,000	4,633	2,015	4,356	980	2,040	931
Hainan	34,000	743	410	5,698	234	231	725
Chongqing	82,000	3,042	1,350	4,452	445	1,285	453
Sichuan	485,000	8,430	3,320	4,029	1,395	3,469	310
Guizhou	170,000	3,606	793	2,215	418	715	64
Yunnan	390,000	4,094	1,644	4,042	612	1,440	170
Tibet	1,200,000	248	77	3,194	41	12	n.a.
Shaanxi	200,000	3,570	1,326	3,707	464	1,312	638
Gansu	450,000	2,494	781	3,137	325	957	52
Qinghai	720,000	496	202	4,066	59	162	10
Ningxia	66,000	530	211	4,025	73	221	44
Xinjiang	1,600,000	1,718	1,050	5,904	476	771	45

Sources: *Zhongguo Tongji Nianjian 1998* (China Statistical Yearbook 1998) (Beijing: Zhongguo Tongji Chubanshe [China Statistics Press], 1998), pp. 63, 65, 107, 390, 434, and 642; *Sichuan Nianjian 1998* (Sichuan Yearbook 1998) (Chengdu: Sichuan Nianjianshe [Sichuan Yearbook Press], 1998), p. 8; Zhou Shunwu, ed., *China Provincial Geography* (Beijing: Foreign Languages Press, 1992).

Notes: (a) Size = square kilometers; (b) population = 10,000; (c) GDP = gross domestic product (current prices); (d) GDP per capita = gross domestic product per capita; (e) agricultural output = gross output value of farming, forestry, animal husbandry, and fishery; (f) industrial output = gross industrial output value; (g) foreign investment = total foreign capital and investment actually acquired in U.S.$ million.

coastal provinces were denied investment by the central government and heavily taxed, in part to foster equality and in part for strategic distribution of industry. In the reform era, however, state-owned enterprises, ideological egalitarianism, and conservatism have hindered economic reform in the inland and border provinces. Shaanxi and Sichuan are typical examples of lagging inland provinces.[13] By contrast, the coastal provinces have prospered more under Deng Xiaoping's reforms because of better location, more diversified economic structures, overseas Chinese connections, and a wave of foreign direct investment. Therefore, the poor access of most inland and some border provinces to the outside world has constrained their ability to conduct provincial external relations. In the case of Heilongjiang, the economic decline of its natural trade partner (Russia) has been a major liability.

The border provinces constitute a special category. The management of borders is as much a concern of the central government as of the border provinces. Historically China had engaged in conflicts with its neighbors, ranging from border disputes to full-scale wars. Whenever the relations between China and its neighbors were smooth, border trade prospered. Most border provinces also have sizable minorities, further raising the central government's concern over their stability. For instance, a quarter of China's total land border (5,500 kilometers) is in Xinjiang, the province farthest away from China's political and economic capitals. Political separatism, especially in Tibet and Xinjiang, as fomented by dissident groups in exile, has reinforced the central government's predisposition to exert tight control over political and military affairs in these regions.

The levels of economic development of China's neighbors have a major impact on the way border provinces conduct their external affairs. Provinces with economically advanced neighbors can often utilize such linkages for their own economic development. Guangdong and Fujian, for example, have taken advantage of their social and cultural affinity with Hong Kong and Taiwan, whereas Heilongjiang and Jilin have fostered closer economic ties with neighbors like Russia and Japan. On the other hand, Yunnan and Guangxi's poor neighbors can offer only limited trade opportunities for those two provinces, except in the anomalous case of the drug trade among Myanmar, Laos, and Yunnan.

POLICIES OF THE CENTRAL GOVERNMENT
TOWARD THE PROVINCES SINCE 1978

Provincial involvement in external affairs in the reform era is influenced by at least three factors: their physical attributes (especially their geographic locations), the policies of the central government, and provincial development strategies. If differences in provincial conditions largely determine a province's resources and policy agenda, the policies of the central government still constitute the most significant factor shaping the framework for provincial external relations. Foreign policy and national defense are the prerogatives of the central government. Although the provinces share revenue with the Center and play key roles in supporting China's foreign policy, the formulation of foreign policy, defense policy, and foreign economic policy still rests with the central authorities.

The central government's preferential policies toward specific provinces are among the most critical factors influencing a province's external relations. Although Guangdong and Fujian were formally granted special policies in 1979, other coastal provinces received only limited preferences in 1984, when some of their cities were designated as among China's fourteen coastal open cities. In 1985 the three deltas in the coastal region, namely the Pearl River Delta, the Yangtze Delta, and the Minnan Delta, were opened to the outside world. In 1988 General Secretary Zhao Ziyang articulated his coastal development strategy and bestowed more preferential treatment upon the coastal regions generally. By contrast, preferential policies were granted to the inland and border provinces only in the 1990s.

The inland and border provinces began to lobby for the universalization of preferential policies as early as the mid-1980s.[14] After the promulgation of the coastal development strategy in 1988, the bandwagon moving toward greater opening to the outside world gained momentum. The 1989 Tiananmen incident did not reverse this trend. Lobbying by interior provinces thus continued, especially over the formulation of the Eighth Five-Year Plan (1991–95) in late 1990. Although the interior provinces could not establish SEZs as had Guangdong or Fujian, they demanded free trade zones, economic development zones, and other kinds of special zones to attract foreign investment. After the fall of Zhao Ziyang in 1989, China shifted from the pro–coastal development strategy of the 1980s to one that stressed the industrial sectors in the 1990s. Since the emphasis of this new strategy was on agriculture, energy, and other basic industries, it reflected a change in favor of the interior regions, dropping the pro–coastal development biases in the Sixth and Seventh Five-Year Plans. These moves in opening up China were not simply economic reform measures, but were also part of an effort to achieve diplomatic breakthroughs in the early 1990s.

Aside from the changing intellectual and political climate and the growing gap between the inland and the coastal regions, two other considerations compelled the central government to open up the interior. First, the collapse of communism in the former Soviet Bloc and the attendant rise of ethnic nationalism in those areas heightened concern over the precarious stability of China's border provinces, especially Tibet, Xinjiang, and Inner Mongolia. A senior Xinjiang official even openly argued that closing the gap between the coastal region and the inland and border regions was critical to maintaining national unity.[15] Second, it was feared that the economic stagnation of the inland and border regions would create difficulties for the central government and the coastal provinces, which would be most immediately apparent in the flow of surplus labor to the east coast.

China's open-door policy was fully expanded from the coastal provinces to the inland and border provinces after Deng Xiaoping's southern tour in early 1992. Although Deng's tour provided further stimulus to the coastal region, such as additional policy support for Shanghai and the creation of bonded zones in five coastal provinces in 1992–93, the inland and border regions clearly benefited most from the new wave of opening. In 1992 five cities along the Yangtze River and eighteen provincial capitals of interior areas received the same preferential treatment as the coastal open cities.[16] Border provinces such as Guangxi, Yunnan, Heilongjiang, Jilin, and Xinjiang were allowed to have open cities, which received preferential treatment in foreign trade and investment akin to that enjoyed by the coastal areas. In 1992–93 various cities in the inland and border provinces, such as Chongqing, Wuhan, Weihai, Changchun, and Harbin, were empowered to establish economic and technological development zones. Further modifying the earlier pro–coastal development strategy, the Ninth Five-Year Plan (for 1996–2000), approved in March 1996, proposed various measures to address interregional inequalities.[17] In fact, the Fourteenth and Fifteenth National Congresses of the CCP, held in 1992 and 1997, focused prominently on inland development as a key agenda item.

THE MANAGEMENT OF PROVINCIAL EXTERNAL RELATIONS

The organization and operation of the provincial foreign affairs system have expanded and become more professional since 1978. The framework for local foreign affairs activity in the reform era was authoritatively spelled out by Li Xiannian, former president and head of the Foreign Affairs Leading Small Group of the CCP, in 1981. He stipulated that local external affairs constituted an integral part of Chinese foreign policy and had to supplement the efforts of the central authorities.[18] China's provinces conduct their external relations through an elaborate set of organizations and mechanisms. The provincial Foreign Affairs Office (*waishi bangongshi*, FAO) is the key organ responsible for conducting provincial foreign affairs. FAOs are part of the provincial government establishment and are entirely funded and staffed by the local authorities; hence, they are under the dual leadership of the MFA and the provincial governments.

According to a key State Council document issued in 1981, the FAOs at the provincial, ministerial, and commission levels served as "the functional departments [*zhineng bumen*] for the government's external affairs and the secretariat [*banshi bumen*] of the local party committee and its leading group on external affairs work."[19] They were established to implement the principles and policies of the central government in foreign affairs under the dual leadership of the MFA and its respective party committee and government, to manage and coordinate external affairs and other external activities (*shewai huodong*) at the local level, and to handle political affairs with an external dimension (*zhengzhisheng shewai shixiang*). The major duties of the FAOs are as follows:[20]

— Implement the foreign policies of the central government and, together with relevant units, suggest concrete measures, and supervise their implementation.

— Analyze and follow external affairs, as well as the general conditions of sister cities, counties, or neighboring foreign areas, and make suggestions on these issues.

— Organize the reception of state guests, guests of the party, friendly personnel, and other important guests; receive and manage diplomatic personnel and foreign correspondents who come to the province in their official capacities; and manage consulates and foreign news agencies.

— Manage the external business of provincial leaders.

— Manage overseas visits, including the approval and checking of overseas tours authorized by the provincial government (including tours to Hong Kong and Macao); handle applications of foreign visitors to the province; approve and issue visas and passports for people who go abroad on official business; and supervise the work of cities that have the power to issue passports and visas.

— Manage nongovernmental exchanges and relations with sister cities.

— Supervise and coordinate border affairs, as well as official and unofficial civilian exchanges.
— Assist and coordinate with the party committee and party disciplinary committee in supervising foreign affairs discipline and confidentiality, and handle those who violate the rules in these areas.
— Carry out other business as prescribed by the provincial government, the MFA, and other central units.

Three features of the scope of the FAO system merit attention. First, the local FAOs must serve local and national interests at the same time. The MFA exercises professional leadership (*yewu lingdao*) over the provincial FAOs, but the FAOs are mainly responsible for the execution of foreign affairs, as well as internal administration such as financing and personnel matters. Although the provincial FAOs have considerable room to maneuver, they have to be mindful of Beijing's concerns.[21] Second, although the CCP has an International Liaison Department under the Central Committee (see the chapter by Lu Ning) that liaises with communist and other socialist parties abroad, the local FAOs have to serve both the party and the government at the same time.[22] Third, although the FAOs are given a broad mandate over external affairs, they are more geared toward political affairs, because other local government organs take care of economic and trade matters. Nonetheless, the conduct of provincial external affairs has been expanding to include an increasing number of economic issues since the mid-1980s, as provinces have been competing for foreign trade and direct investment. The provincial FAOs also have to arrange external activities on behalf of provincial party and state leaders. Provincial leaders often do not have foreign affairs expertise, but they would like to use external ties to boost their own careers and business opportunities for their provinces. An FAO provides expertise not only in arranging such economic functions, but also in performing more mundane tasks such as public relations and translation.

As noted, however, the FAOs do not and cannot monopolize all dimensions of external relations, because other provincial governmental and nongovernmental organs also play significant roles in their respective arenas. The FAO in a province is one of the forty to fifty or so provincial bureau-level (*ting*) organs. Other important provincial organs that play an active role in foreign affairs include the Foreign Economic and Trade Commissions (*duiwai jingji maoyi weiyuanhui*, FETCs) and the Overseas Chinese Affairs

Offices (*qiaowu bangongshi*, OCAOs). The FETCs are responsible for the management of foreign trade, the acquisition of foreign investment, and the supervision of foreign enterprises. Some provinces, such as Hebei and Liaoning, also have additional offices on external opening (*duiwai kaifang bangongshi*). Meanwhile, in some border provinces, such as Heilongjiang and Yunnan, border economic and trade management bureaus are common.[23] Communist Party organs such as the United Front Work Department and the Propaganda Department are also involved in provincial external relations.

Policy-making regarding foreign affairs is managed by a small leading group on provincial foreign affairs (*waishi gongzuo lingdao xiaozu*), which is under the provincial Communist Party Committee and is headed by a ranking official.[24] In Sichuan, for instance, the provincial party secretary led this group, with three other senior provincial party and government officials (the governor, a vice governor, and the director of the FAO) serving as deputy heads.[25] In Henan foreign affairs was conceptualized as part of an overall strategy to open up the province and was therefore put under the purview of a small leading group on external opening (*duiwai kaifang*) of the provincial government.[26] Whether the provincial party secretary or the governor takes the lead in handling foreign affairs varies. The day-to-day conduct of foreign affairs, meanwhile, is usually under the supervision of a vice provincial governor.

Several aspects of the provincial foreign affairs system deserve attention. First, the sizes of the provincial organs involved in foreign affairs vary significantly. The staff of Shanghai's FAO, excluding the nonprofit units under its control, consists of 238 persons and is the largest among provincial-level units. The border provinces also tend to have fairly large staffs because of their work on border issues. Guangxi's FAO, for instance, has more than 150 staff members. The coastal provinces have sizable offices as well. For instance, the staffs of the FAOs of Zhejiang and Guangdong are 64 and 104, respectively.[27] The inland provinces and some border provinces that are not very active in external affairs have far smaller establishments, and their ability to conduct foreign affairs is consequently more limited. Hubei, Guizhou, and Xinjiang, for example, manage both foreign affairs and overseas Chinese affairs in one office.[28] On the other hand, Guangdong's FETC (230 staff members) is twice as big as its FAO, which reflects the significance the province attaches to this portfolio.

Second, the staffing of FAOs' administration also varies substantially. For instance, two recent directors of the FAO of Shanghai were former diplomats. But senior officials of other provincial FAOs are recruited locally and are seldom from the MFA. For instance, Guangdong's FAO is currently headed by a key provincial official, the director of the General Office of the provincial government. Overall, however, the training and backgrounds of FAO officials have gradually improved. Young recruits tend to be graduates of foreign language universities or colleges, with a specialty in international studies. Some of the senior FAO officials, such as those in Guangdong, have postgraduate degrees from Western countries or have received overseas training. The head of Guangxi's FAO is a former English language professor who later developed a career in local foreign affairs. Among the fifty-eight officers (*zhuanzhi waishi ganbu*) in Zhejiang's FAO in 1992, 74 percent had a college education, and 45 percent spoke at least one foreign language.[29] Aside from training in language and other fields, annual training classes on the conduct of foreign affairs have been organized, sometimes with participation by veteran Chinese diplomats.[30] Similarly, provincial FAO cadres regularly attend training courses on foreign affairs at the Foreign Affairs College in Beijing. Many of them have also been sent abroad to serve in China's embassies. Yunnan's FAO, for instance, sends its officials to serve in the Chinese embassy in Laos.[31]

Third, in addition to the FAOs, other provincial government or party organs whose functions have an external dimension also play a role in foreign affairs. Most obviously, the OCAOs and Taiwan Affairs Offices deal with overseas Chinese as well as Taiwan residents. Provincial party organs such as the Propaganda Department or the United Front Work Department also are engaged in receiving foreign guests. Reflecting the importance of overseas Chinese links in Guangdong, Fujian, and other coastal provinces, separate OCAOs and FAOs are commonly established, whereas some inland or border provinces, such as Guizhou and Xinjiang, combine these offices. In fact, the OCAO in Guangdong (108 staff members) is larger than its FAO (104).[32]

Fourth, gaining access to Beijing and other important localities is a central element of provincial external strategies. In 1995, for instance, Guizhou hosted forty-two foreign ambassadors and representatives from international organizations.[33] Provinces also regularly invite Chinese ambassadors to observe their recent socioeconomic developments so that they can facilitate contacts with foreign businesspeople and potential investors. Similarly, provincial officials seek out foreign diplomats when they visit Beijing and invite them to tour their provinces. Hebei also lobbies government agencies in Beijing to permit their leaders to make more overseas trips.[34] Further, the provinces utilize their own network of offices (*zhuwai banshichu*) in other parts of the country to conduct external affairs. For instance, Henan's Beijing office is established as a bureau-level organ with six division-level units, one of which focuses on foreign economic issues and foreign affairs.[35] In addition to a Beijing office, provinces often set up offices in Shanghai, Guangzhou, Guangdong's SEZs, and other coastal cities such as Dalian and Tianjin. Heilongjiang and Shandong, for example, have established, respectively, nine and ten such offices.[36] Guizhou, an inland province, set up a total of thirteen such offices.[37] Although their primary duty is to liaise with other localities and foster domestic economic intercourse, these provincial offices are also responsible for networking with foreign enterprises and other foreign agencies in China and conducting public relations activities.[38]

Fifth, "nongovernmental" or quasi-governmental organs such as People's Friendship Associations (PFAs) and institutes of international studies are also part of the functional system (*xitong*) managed by the FAO. Some of these, such as the PFAs, fall under the direct leadership of the FAO, whereas other units, such as universities, may have their own foreign affairs offices. Especially in the prereform era, the PFAs were actively involved in people-to-people diplomacy, notably with countries with which the PRC had no diplomatic relations, as in the case of Japan. In the reform era the provincial PFAs have continued to participate extensively in important external activities.

Finally, it should be noted that provincial expenditures in foreign affairs have increased significantly in the reform era, especially for active provinces. For instance, Jiangsu's foreign affairs expenditure rose from 3.7 million yuan in 1978 to over 8 million yuan in 1990 and 59 million yuan in 1996.[39] The amount of foreign affairs expenditure, unsurprisingly, closely correlates with the level of external activities. The coastal and coastal/border provinces spend much more than their inland counterparts, whether in absolute or per capita terms. In 1996 the twelve coastal provinces spent more than 70 percent of China's total expenditure on local foreign affairs, each spending an average of over 40 million yuan. Liaoning, Guangdong, Jiangsu, Shanghai, and Shandong were the top five spenders, with foreign affairs expenditures in the range of 45 to over 100 million yuan. Among the inland and border provinces Jilin's expenditure was also high (37 million yuan) because of its keen interest in foreign affairs. Seven of the inland and inland/border provinces, meanwhile, spent between 10 and 24 million yuan, whereas the remaining ten spent just a few million. Nonetheless, although there is great variation among provinces, the share of this item still amounts to a negligible fraction of provincial budgets.

THE CONDUCT OF PROVINCIAL FOREIGN AFFAIRS

The pattern of provincial involvement in China's external relations is identified and examined in this section. Local governments in China support national foreign policy in a variety of ways. As the international relations of China expand, provincial authorities must manage the expanding foreign diplomatic presences within their jurisdictions. Border and coastal provinces are often involved in border talks and cross-border management. Provinces also provide expertise and research support to the central government, with the most notable example being the Shanghai Institute of International Studies. Further, provinces sometimes conduct informal diplomacy on behalf of the central government with countries with which Beijing has no diplomatic links or when formal diplomatic relations are strained.

Provincial foreign affairs work is no longer conducted merely for the interests of the central government, however. Rather, provinces now also conduct external relations in order to enhance their own international images and pursue their own economic interests. For instance, in 1996 Guangxi's primary goal in foreign affairs was defined as "positively serving the overall national foreign policy and Guangxi's strategy for economic and social development."[40] Therefore, the locations and economic conditions of the provinces strongly shape the direction of their pursuit of international links. For instance, Liaoning's priorities in 1995 were defined as: the promotion of exchange and cooperation with Japan and South Korea, the expansion of links with North America, and the strengthening of relations with North Korea to establish a stable environment in the province's neighborhood.[41]

In pursuing their individual interests, provinces engage in a variety of foreign affairs activities of varying significance. Several of the most important elements of provincial foreign affairs are discussed in the subsections that follow.

The Management of Foreign Diplomatic Presence

By mid-1997 there were almost sixty foreign consulates general or consulates or other diplomatic offices in the PRC. The cities of Shanghai and Guangzhou, major commercial centers with strong international economic links and overseas connections, are favorite locations for foreign consulates. The Japanese set up their consulate general in Shanghai in 1975, and the Americans opened theirs in Guangzhou in 1979. In July 1997 thirty-one countries had diplomatic representatives in Shanghai.[42] The diplomatic community in

Guangzhou is smaller, but still significant. By mid-1997 there were twelve consulates general or consulates in the city.[43] Most of the consulates general or consulates cover several neighboring provinces. Therefore, the jurisdictions of consulates in Guangzhou often include Fujian, Guangxi, and Hainan, and the jurisdictions of those in Shanghai usually include Jiangsu, Zhejiang, and Anhui.[44]

Although the provinces are responsible for managing foreign diplomats stationed in their jurisdictions and for maintaining and recruiting foreign affairs personnel, the MFA not only provides guidance and advice, but also sets the direction for national foreign policy. National meetings on local foreign affairs are regularly convened to communicate directives of the central government concerning the management of external relations at the local level. The MFA also briefs local authorities on the international situation and advises them on China's foreign policies. For example, during Assistant Foreign Minister Wang Guozhang's ten-day visit to Xinjiang in October 1995 he instructed the FAO on how to improve its work. Likewise, during Vice Foreign Minister Wang Yingfan's meeting with the FAO officials of Gansu in June 1996, he explained the central government's position on the international situation, the principles and implementation of China's foreign policies, and the need to revise Gansu's foreign affairs work plan.[45]

Informal Diplomacy

Provinces will often engage in informal diplomacy at times when formal diplomacy is difficult or inappropriate. One example is then–Shanghai Mayor Zhu Rongji's trip to the United States in 1990 and to Western Europe in 1991, when China was still trying to repair Tiananmen-related damage to China's foreign relations. The latter trip (covering Italy, the Netherlands, Belgium, France, Germany, Spain, and the European Union Commission) was seen widely as a major diplomatic breakthrough for the PRC in the aftermath of the Tiananmen incident.[46] Many provinces, in fact, conducted high-profile overseas visits in 1991. During this period, for example, the PRC's contacts with Canada, one of the strongest critics of the 1989 crackdown, were dominated by provincial-level visits. Although no senior Chinese leaders or high-ranking central government officials were invited to visit Canada, eight senior provincial leaders, including the vice governor of Jilin and the vice mayors of Beijing, Shanghai, and Tianjin, among others, visited the country.[47]

The development of closer relations between the PRC and post-apartheid South Africa is another good example of informal diplomacy conducted by China's provinces.[48] Although the PRC had supported Nelson Mandela's African National Congress (ANC) during the apartheid era, the Mandela administration maintained diplomatic relations with Taiwan when the ANC came to power and dismantled apartheid. Prior to the establishment of formal diplomatic relations between the PRC and South Africa in 1997, organizations such as friendship associations and provincial delegations were important elements of the PRC–South African bilateral relationship. In 1995, for example, the PRC maintained an active program of exchanges and mutual visits with South Africa, with the support of the provinces. At the beginning of 1995 the premier of Free State was invited to visit Hainan. In March a Beijing municipal government team visited Gauteng. When the premier of Gauteng went to Beijing in May, Politburo member Wei Jianxing was present at the premier's meeting with the mayor of Beijing. In December 1995 the vice president of the Chinese People's Friendship Association led a provincial-level trade delegation to South Africa consisting of provincial representatives from Jiangsu, Tianjin, Ningxia, Qinghai, and Sichuan. Although the intention of South Africa to establish diplomatic relations with the PRC became clear in 1996 and direct, high-level political contacts between the two countries intensified, provincial-level exchanges maintained the momentum of the interactions they had enjoyed prior to formal normalization. This practice can cut both ways. Therefore, following a row over the sale of sixty Mirage 2000-5 jets to Taiwan in the early 1990s, the French consulate in Guangzhou was closed and French companies were reportedly barred from bidding on the construction of the Guangzhou subway system.[49]

Border Management

During times of conflict with neighboring countries, border provinces have to bear the costs of direct military confrontations, as did Tibet during the border war with India in 1962, Xinjiang and Heilongjiang during Sino-Soviet conflicts throughout the 1960s, and Guangxi during the Sino-Vietenamese "defensive counterattack" in 1979. At other times they must mobilize their own resources to support China's neighboring allies, as did Jilin and Liaoning during the Korean War and Guangxi and Yunnan in the 1950s and 1960s in support of the Vietnamese communist forces.

In addition, the provinces are often involved in negotiations between the PRC and neighboring countries over border issues. In recent years, as China's relations with its neighbors have improved, the border provinces have been increasingly active in border control and management. The Chinese team on the joint Sino-Pakistan border commission, for example, was organized and led by the Xinjiang authorities, with the technical support of central government agencies. Yunnan supported the 1992–95 border discussions with Myanmar and has been involved with the Mekong Delta cooperation project. Together with local cities and counties, Guangxi directly conducted talks with Vietnam on liberalizing cross-border traffic between the two countries in 1996. With the support of the central government, Guangxi entered agreements with the Vietnamese authorities to open three border checkpoints.[50] Finally, the territorial demarcation between Hong Kong and Guangdong was actually directly negotiated by the Guangdong authorities and the Hong Kong government.[51]

Research Work

The provinces also support national foreign policy by providing the research services of various institutes and provincial organizations. One example is the Southeast Asian research network in China. Although international research institutes linked to the central government have become more interested in Southeast Asia in recent years and have expanded their capacities and expertise in the area, major academic research institutes on Southeast Asian studies are still based in southern China because of geographic proximity and traditional links.

The Research School of Southeast Asian Studies (formerly the Institute of Southeast Asian Studies) based at Xiamen University in southern Fujian, for example, is one of the leading centers of Southeast Asian studies in the country. The school, the institutes of Southeast Asian studies at Zhongshan University and Jinan University in Guangzhou, the Guangxi Academy of Social Sciences in Nanning, and the Yunnan Academy of Social Sciences in Kunming, are collectively known as China's five major institutes of Southeast Asian studies. In early 1996 Hainan set up a South China Sea Research Center (located at the provincial foreign affairs office in Haikou), which is the national base for South China Sea research in China. The Center also organized a national academic conference on problems in the South China Sea in November 1996. Additionally, in support of the Foreign Ministry Hainan also conducted research projects on the Gulf of Tonkin and the South China Sea.[52]

Establishing External Links

Unlike sovereign states, local governments do not have formal diplomatic representation overseas. Rather, they rely on unofficial or quasi-official channels to establish links with foreign countries. Some common strategies include sister city and province arrangements, reception of foreign guests, establishment of campuses and representative or business offices abroad, and dispatching of delegations. The conduct of provincial foreign affairs in such social and economic arenas shows great variation. By taking advantage of their particular location, social and cultural connections, and the preferential policies of the central government, the coastal provinces have established extensive overseas social and economic links since 1978. The inland and border provinces have been trying to catch up in these areas, especially since 1992.

Establishing Sister City and Province Arrangements. The coastal provinces have established the largest number of overseas sister city arrangements (*youhao chengshi*).[53] By establishing such relations, provinces and their localities find it more convenient to organize official visits, carry out social and economic exchanges, and conduct other business in a regular manner. The increasing number and variety of such relations testify to the growing international profile of China's provinces. For instance, Jiangsu has established a total of eighty-one sister city relationships with twenty-one countries, the largest number among the provinces, whereas Shandong has established seventy-five such pairs. The fact that seven of the most dynamic provinces have each established between thirty and eighty-one sister relationships, meanwhile, demonstrates a strong correlation between such sister ties and the level of foreign relations activity.

Although the central government has the power to authorize the establishment of sister relations, the actual local-to-local "diplomacy" often depends on the initiative of provincial units themselves rather than the central authorities.[54] Therefore, overseas Chinese connections and personal initiatives by leaders seem to be critical. For Guangdong, for example, the assistance of overseas Chinese has been important in its establishment of sister city relations with many foreign cities or states that have large Chinese settlements, such as Manila and Vancouver.[55] The MFA may occasionally serve as middleman, as reflected in its role in helping Qingdao establish sister relations with Long Beach, California, in 1984.[56]

The development of friendly overseas ties may also take a more personal form. For instance, FAOs in coastal cities regularly honor foreign nationals or overseas Chinese as a sign of appreciation of their contributions. By 1996 Tianjin had conferred honorary citizenship on nineteen foreign nationals and had invited another thirty-seven prominent foreign businessmen to serve as economic advisors to the city.[57] This parallels the appointment of citizens of Hong Kong, Macao, and Taiwan to local Chinese People's Political Consultative Conferences and other public bodies, a practice common in provinces such as Guangdong and Fujian. Although conferring such honors furthers the central government's united front strategy toward elites in Hong Kong and Taiwan, this practice also promotes the interests of the provinces by cultivating closer ties with investors and contributors to their localities.

To similar effect, conducting overseas Chinese relations remains a critical task for provinces with large numbers of overseas Chinese, such as Guangdong, Fujian, and Hainan. Thus, Hainan spent its own funds to receive over three thousand overseas Chinese in 1995 alone.[58] In fact, attracting overseas Chinese investment has become an integral part of the development strategies of these areas. The OCAOs and related units in Hebei and Shandong, for instance, secured, respectively, over U.S.$150 and U.S.$200 million worth of investment contracts in 1996 alone.[59]

Receiving Foreign Guests. The reception of state guests and other delegations in the provinces is as important for the central government as it is for the provinces. For the central authorities, regular tours to localities showcase the economic accomplishments and business opportunities brought about by reform. These functions not only open up business opportunities and are sources of valuable advice for the provinces concerned, but also highlight the provinces' pivotal role in China's open-door policy. Hence, Guangdong, Fujian, and their SEZs were regularly selected as sites for foreign delegations to visit after visits to Beijing in the 1980s. In the 1990s, however, Guangdong lost out to Shanghai, and its officials even complained to Western diplomats that they ought to help arrange more visits to the province.[60] The volume of such visits and their costs to the provinces are substantial. On average, municipal leaders in Shanghai met a senior visitor every other day in 1995.[61] That same year Jiangsu invited over 130,000 foreign guests and over 400 groups of official guests at the vice ministerial level or above.[62]

The provinces also take advantage of China's open-door policy by sending official delegations abroad, mostly in search of business opportunities. The number of official delegations going abroad skyrocketed in the 1990s, with thousands (if not tens of thousands) of such visits every year. Following efforts by the central government to restrict such visits in the mid-1990s because of waste and abuse, overseas visits by provincial leaders were limited to one visit per year of less than two weeks' duration.[63] Nonetheless, visits by provincial party and state officials have now become a regular and important part of provincial foreign affairs. In the early days of reform Hubei's party secretary, Chen Pixian, characterized his visit to Ohio in 1979 as an eye-opening experience. Later he turned this relationship into a catalyst for promoting Hubei's economic development.[64]

International exposure is equally important for the coastal provinces. During a visit to Massachusetts, a sister state of Guangdong, in the summer of 1997, the Guangdong governor was so impressed by the advanced information technology he saw during his trip to Boston that he determined to develop similar industries back home.[65] Although most inland and coastal provinces' visits are directed at Hong Kong, Japan, North America, and the European Union countries, which are often their key export markets and sources of foreign investment, the border provinces tend to cultivate closer ties with their immediate neighbors.

As noted, the pursuit of provincial external relations often serves the interests of both the central government and the provinces. For instance, in support of the central government's efforts to develop closer relations with China's neighbors in the 1990s, the border provinces have actively pursued their own local interests. In 1995 Yunnan officials made a record 4,339 visits—about 46 percent of its official visits abroad—to neighboring Laos, Vietnam, Myanmar, Thailand, Malaysia, and Singapore.[66] Cross-border cooperation has also become a necessity in dealing with smuggling, drug trafficking, illegal immigration, and other crimes. In these areas the border provinces have carried out active local-to-local "diplomacy" by liaising directly with local governments on the other side of the border. In 1995 Guangxi alone carried out over 400 visits and sent more than 200 official letters or documents to Vietnam.[67] Liaoning sent its leaders to North Korea and received at least eight delegations from the other side, and additionally it provided a modest amount of food assistance following a severe flood in 1995 in order to improve ties.[68]

Conducting Tourism and Other Activities. Tourism has become a major means for the provinces to open up, promote their image, attract foreign investment, and generate income. Tourist festivals and events oriented to business promotion are already quite common in coastal provinces such as Guangdong, Fujian, and Hainan.[69] The inland and border provinces have sought to follow suit.

Hubei promoted the province as a tourist destination when international attention to the Three Gorges increased.[70] Similarly, Xian's majestic reception of U.S. President Bill Clinton in 1998 helped showcase its cultural heritage and tourist attractions to the world. The border provinces have also begun to capitalize on the potential of cross-border tourism. Therefore, local governments in border regions of Yunnan and Guangxi have begun to organize cross-border tours to Southeast Asia and Indochina as China's relations with these countries have improved. To these ends these provinces have even relaxed their control over immigration, sometimes without the approval of the central government at the initial stage.[71]

The level of provincial external contacts generally is reflected in the number of international tourists, including those from Hong Kong, Macao, and Taiwan.[72] This pattern, furthermore, roughly parallels the geographic locations and the volume of external economic relations of the provinces. For instance, remote inland and border provinces such as Ningxia and Qinghai attract only a few visitors each year (3,700 to 13,300), whereas the most visited inland provinces, Sichuan and Shaanxi, attract, respectively, about 380,000 and 440,000 visitors because of their cultural relics or scenic beauty. Most coastal provinces, on the other hand, boast 400,000 to 2 million international visitors annually, with Guangdong in the lead with approximately 7.4 million. The only coastal exceptions to this rule are Hainan, which is quite small in size and more remote, and Tianjin, which is dwarfed by the nearby capital.

A variety of formal cultural and social exchanges are also organized to promote provincial external affairs. Beijing and Shanghai, of course, are most active in utilizing their cultural assets to develop external ties, but many coastal provinces have done so. In 1995 Jiangsu had over 1,600 students, 600 economic specialists, and 980 teachers and experts in its colleges and universities from overseas.[73] The inland provinces have taken steps to catch up in this area. Shanxi is a case in point.[74] Despite its remote location, the province established a provincial international relations association to "market Shanxi internationally and to bring the world to Shanxi." The province established an educational endowment to fund its students to study overseas in 1984, supporting the postgraduate studies of about 100 graduate students every year.[75] Similarly, Yunnan sponsored a conference on the development of the Mekong River region at the World Economic Forum held in April 1995 and took the initiative to host the International Horticultural Exposition in 1999.[76] Such activities coincide not only with the national government's open-door policy and desire to develop the border regions, but also with its foreign policy objectives to sustain cooperation with neighboring Asian countries.

Promoting Foreign Trade and Acquiring Foreign Investment

With the decline of central planning during the reform era, foreign investment has become a significant source of capital, employment, and technology for China's provinces.[77] Foreign trade, meanwhile, enables the provinces to play to their comparative advantages, loosening central government restrictions and developing greater access to overseas markets. Indeed, expanding foreign economic relations has become the most important theme of provincial external affairs. The provinces not only have identified economic development as a key component of their foreign affairs, as suggested earlier, but also are making use of provincial foreign affairs activities, such as the reception of foreign guests and informal diplomacy, for economic purposes.

Diversifying Foreign Trade. Given the advantage of their geographic location and economic strength, as well as their already extensive external ties, the coastal provinces have most fully utilized the opportunities created by Deng Xiaoping's 1992 southern tour. During the period from 1990 to 1997 most coastal provinces more than tripled their exports. Some, like Fujian, Guangdong, Jiangsu, and Zhejiang, increased their exports five to seven times. Although uneven, export performance among the inland and border provinces is weaker, with most having just doubled their exports between 1990 and 1997.

Provincial trade patterns shed light on a key dimension of provincial external relations by revealing the trading priorities and dependencies of the provinces. In a pioneer study of provincial trade patterns using 1990 data, Brantly Womack and Guangzhi Zhao offered several interesting observations.[78] First, they found that although neither the border nor the inland provinces are heavily dependent on trade, foreign trade is more consequential for the border provinces. Second, the border provinces differ from the coastal provinces in that the former are usually more interested in securing their own special arrangements with their neighbors, whereas the latter have a greater stake in open channels for international trade. In short, opening to the international economy is more critical for the coastal region.

Comparing our work with the data provided by Womack and Zhao, several interesting developments can be discerned since 1996. The overall dependency of the coastal region on foreign trade has not changed dramatically, because exports already constituted about 15 percent to 20 percent of the GDP of most coastal provinces in 1996. By comparison, the share of exports in the GDP was in the range of 5 percent to 10 percent for most inland and border provinces.[79]

Other observations merit attention as well. First, although it served more as an entrepot, in 1990 Hong Kong was the top export destination for all but seven of the provinces. Japan was the top market for only four provinces.[80] Even in 1996 Hong Kong still stood out because it was the largest export partner of fourteen provinces and the second or third largest of another thirteen provinces. Because of geographical proximity, southern provinces such as Guangdong and Guangxi, as well as central-south provinces such as Jiangxi and Hunan, particularly rely upon Hong Kong as an export partner, with the special administrative region (SAR) receiving 40 percent to 50 percent of their exports. The unique case of trade dependency is Guangdong, because over 86 percent of its exports went to Hong Kong. Again, however, although about 40 percent of China's total exports were destined for Hong Kong, the bulk of these commodities were either directly reexported or further processed for export, especially to Taiwan, North America, and Western Europe.[81]

Second, by 1996 Japan already was ranked the largest export market for twelve provinces, the second largest for twelve, and the third or fourth largest for another five. Japan has undoubtedly established a strong commercial presence throughout the PRC's provinces, but especially in northern border areas such as Inner Mongolia and all coastal provinces in central or northern China. Japan's share of provincial exports ranged from 25 percent to 40 percent in most coastal provinces, with lower proportions in the inland and border areas. Hong Kong's once-dominant share in provincial exports has also declined somewhat since 1990 as the provinces have developed their own infrastructure and export linkages abroad.

Third, although the United States remains the third-ranking destination for exports from China's provinces, South Korea has replaced the former Soviet Union as their fourth-largest export partner. Finally, the border provinces have continued to increase their exports to neighboring countries. For instance, Heilongjiang sent 39 percent of its exports to Russia, Yunnan sent 30 percent of its exports to Myanmar, and Xinjiang sent over 30 percent of its exports to Kazakhstan and 30 percent to Kyrgyzstan. In short, with the improvement of transport links and the development of provincial foreign affairs, the provinces have diversified their export markets. The trend toward regionalization of trade seems to be proceeding even further because East Asian countries such as Japan and South Korea have gained significance as Chinese export markets.

Competing for Foreign Investment. With the gradual opening up of China, provincial competition for foreign investment intensified in the 1990s. The number of foreign-funded enterprises jumped rapidly after Deng's 1992 southern tour. Between 1992 and 1997 the total number of registered foreign-funded firms in the coastal region more than doubled, whereas those in the inland and coastal regions jumped more than three times. However, in 1997 the coastal provinces still boasted close to 200,000 foreign-funded enterprises, whereas the inland and border provinces accommodated, respectively, only about 30,000 and 13,000. More important, the coastal region absorbed the bulk of foreign investment. At the same time, however, the domination of Guangdong and Fujian in the acquisition of foreign investment has diminished. Nonetheless, five coastal provinces, namely Guangdong (20 percent), Jiangsu (9 percent), Fujian (6.5 percent), Shanghai (7 percent), and Shandong (4 percent), contributed almost half of the national total in 1997.[82] If the other coastal provinces— Beijing, Tianjin, Hebei, Liaoning, Zhejiang, Guangxi, and Hainan—are combined, the coast accounts for over 63 percent of the total foreign direct investment acquired by China as a whole. Despite the overall expansion of provincial external relations, this situation is unlikely to change soon. Aside from their much better investment environment in terms of transportation, communication, and human resources, the coastal provinces have benefited from more than a decade of preferential policies and accumulated a great deal more experience in attracting foreign capital.

Owing to the intensifying competition for foreign capital, the coastal provinces have set up a variety of mechanisms and a network of organs to promote trade and investment. In an effort to show that Shanghai is friendly to foreign business, since 1988 the municipal leadership has held an annual meeting of the Mayor's International Business Leaders' Advisory Council, which is comprised of leading foreign businessmen.[83] In Guangdong there is the high-powered Guangdong Board of Investment (GDBOI), chaired by the governor, with three specialized departments devoted to Asian, European, Oceanian, and American countries. In 1995 the GDBOI organized investment seminars and business fairs in Southeast Asia and the United States. In 1996 such activities were extended to Japan, Canada, Europe, and South Korea. Other coastal provinces such as Jiangsu have tried to capitalize on special projects with the support of the central government. For example, the Suzhou Industrial Park, inaugurated in Februrary 1994, was used not only as a major site for attracting foreign capital, but also as an area in which to highlight a special relationship with Singapore. Hainan has attempted to assume the role as the link between Southeast Asia and the rest of China. In 1994 the China–Southeast Asia Commercial Committee was inaugurated in the province's capital, Haikou. In 1997 the committee organized a series of seminar programs for enterprises and government departments to discuss economic opportunities in Southeast Asia and economic development in the region. At the end of 1997 the committee raised 10 million yuan from enterprises and government agencies all over the country to set up a company in Beijing to invest in and trade with Southeast Asia.[84]

The provinces also extend their reach overseas by setting up companies and offices abroad. Although most provinces have set up companies in Hong Kong and Macao, they also try to establish their own overseas offices, often under a provincial company. Again, coastal provinces have been most aggressive in this regard. For instance, as of 1994 Shandong had already set up sixty-four offices in seventeen overseas countries, which were managed by the provincial government, various enterprises, and subprovincial units.[85] The province also had a total of eighty-seven overseas trading firms and had invested in a total of 115 factories abroad.[86] Even an inland province such as Sichuan maintained seventeen small offices in Germany, Pakistan, Nepal, the Middle East, Southeast Asia, and various African countries.[87]

Owing to the problems facing the state-owned enterprises, inland provinces such as Shanxi also emphasized greater efforts to attract foreign investment in order to speed up enterprise reform and technical innovation.[88] Nonetheless, the central government has been keen to keep the external financing of the provinces under central purview and to stamp out financial irregularities that can shift loan liabilities to the Center, as reflected in the tough stance of Beijing in handling the collapse of the Guangdong International Trust and Investment Corporation and the subsequent disclosure of the financial problems of other provincial companies in Hong Kong in late 1998 and early 1999.

Expanding Interprovincial Cooperation. The expansion of external economic relations by the inland and border provinces also takes the form of interprovincial cooperation, reflecting their fear of being left behind. Various regional groupings were organized to compensate for the growing economic prowess of the coastal provinces and their ability to influence the central government. One prominent example was the convening of the Southwest Regional Economic

Coordination Conference comprised of five provinces (Sichuan, Guangxi, Yunnan, Guizhou, and Tibet) and two cities (Chengdu and Chongqing) in 1984.[89] Two offices to promote this region were set up in Kunming and Nanning in 1992. The high-profile Kunming trade fair, which began in 1993 with extensive participation by businesspeople from Southeast Asia and South Asia, has now become an annual event. Since these southwestern provinces were less affluent and did not have great influence in Beijing, they formed this coalition not only to coordinate their own external economic policy, foster interprovincial cooperation, and attract foreign investment, but also to influence the policy-making of the central government and to jointly lobby for more central investment.[90] The central government, recognizing the importance of this region to national defense and the stability of the border area, supported this regional group by sending officials at the vice premier level to its meetings. As was aptly stated in a State Council report, the opening of the southwest region not only would foster the unity of minorities in the area, but would facilitate closer economic ties with neighboring countries in Southeast Asia and South Asia.[91]

Similarly, Liaoning, Jilin, and Heilongjiang have promoted the concept of a "Northeast Economic Circle" since the early 1990s.[92] Despite their obvious competition, these provinces agreed to cooperate. In 1992 the provincial party secretaries of the three northeast provinces agreed to strengthen their economic cooperation by promoting uniform policies. For instance, they decided to share information, cooperate on technological development, reduce interprovincial protectionism and duplication, and adopt similar preferential policies for each constituent member.[93] In response, a major report by the State Planning Commission in 1996 supported the opening of the northeast region to neighboring countries (as through border trade) and the Tumen River Project (see the chapter by Kim in this volume). Again, these examples suggest that the objectives of the central government's foreign policy and provincial interests are not always in conflict. Rather, provincial cooperation and the expansion of external economic ties serve the national objective of cultivating better ties with neighboring areas.

Examining the Role of Central-Local Dynamics in Provincial External Relations. Central-local dynamics is a driving force in provincial external relations. China's provinces have utilized the opening of new diplomatic opportunities to promote their local economic interests, whereas the central government has used such contacts to foster bilateral and multinational cooperation. The cases of Shandong and Jilin are revealing and illustrate the complex interplay of provincial, central, and foreign interests.

The normalization of diplomatic relations between the PRC and South Korea in 1992 can be attributed to both diplomatic and economic considerations, as Kim discusses in his contribution to this volume. The concept of the Yellow Sea Economic Circle, encompassing South Korea and Japan as well as Liaoning, Shandong, and neighboring provinces in Northern China, seemed appealing to both the PRC and South Korea. Shandong was seen as a convenient venue to attract South Korean investment to the needy northeast. Aside from its geographic proximity, the province could play well to the overseas Chinese community because over 90 percent of the Chinese in South Korea were from Shandong.[94] The State Council decided to designate Shandong as the key province for developing nongovernmental and business links with South Korea in December 1987. Liaoning and Shandong actively competed in opening up contacts between the two countries in 1988, when both provinces attempted to make arrangements for the first South Korean trade mission to China.[95] In fact, various special arrangements were approved by the central government to facilitate economic contacts between South Korea and Shandong even before both countries had established normal diplomatic ties. These measures included the provision of ferry services between Weihai (Shandong) and Inchon (South Korea) and the issuance of entry visas to South Korean businesspeople on their arrival in China. After Sino–South Korean relations were normalized in 1992, Shandong fully utilized this diplomatic opening to accelerate its own development. Although South Korea's role in Shandong's foreign trade and investment was insignificant in the 1980s, this changed dramatically in the 1990s. In fact, South Korea replaced Hong Kong as Shandong's second most important export market and overtook Taiwan as the second most significant source of foreign direct investment in 1995.[96]

The involvement of Jilin, a land-locked province, in the Tumen River Project is another interesting case showing provincial participation in multinational cooperation. Sharing common borders with Russia and North Korea and located only fifteen kilometers from the Sea of Japan, Jilin has always been eager to gain access to the sea. Since the mid-1980s Jilin's efforts to promote a regional cooperative scheme around the Tumen River involving China, North and South Korea, the former Soviet Union, Japan, and Mongolia clearly reflected strong local desires to benefit from the country's coastal development strategy.[97] In promoting local provincial interests, Jilin tried to influence the country's foreign relations to the province's benefit.[98] The fact that Jilin has a large concentration of ethnic Koreans facilitated this strategy.

The idea of regaining Jilin's access to the Sea of Japan through the Tumen River was raised in 1984, when scholars and specialists in the province formed a study group on the possibility of developing trade between Jilin and the Soviet Union. In November 1986 researchers from the Institute of Northeast Asian Geography at the Northeastern Normal University in Changchun conducted field research in the area and recommended several options for gaining access to the Sea of Japan through the Tumen River. Although the proposal was made at a time when difficulties in Sino-Soviet relations were still significant, scholars and specialists urged the MFA to put the question of sea access for Jilin on the agenda of the Sino-Soviet negotiations. Following the conference the China Center for International Studies, a coordinating and research institute under the Foreign Affairs Office of the State Council, convened a meeting in Changchun to inaugurate the Northeastern China Research Center on Soviet and Eastern European Studies during which the question of sea access for Jilin was again discussed. The director of the China Center for International Studies, Huan Xiang, referred the recommendation to party leaders and the State Council. Jilin's proposal also secured the support of Song Jian, head of the State Science and Technology Commission, who wrote to the elder statesman, Yang Shangkun, and Premier Li Peng in April 1989. Song's recommendation was endorsed by Li, who asked the MFA to explore the possibility of putting this issue on the agenda of the Sino-Soviet talks.

Jilin later set up a special task force to investigate the feasibility of the Tumen River Project and organized a special boat trip down the river in 1990. Through its provincial office in Beijing, Jilin made arrangements for the task force to report its findings to relevant ministries including the MFA, the Ministry for Foreign Economic Relations and Trade, and others. Eventually the province secured the central government's endorsement to negotiate for China's navigation rights on the Tumen River. Jilin ensured subsequent involvement in the regional cooperation scheme by following up with surveys and international conferences under United Nations sponsorship. Jilin thus influenced the Sino-Soviet talks and promoted itself in this regional cooperation scheme.

Although the Tumen project did not, in the end, succeed because of mutual suspicion among the key countries involved and a lack of investment, the Jilin example demonstrated that this type of provincial lobbying strategy can be a highly complex endeavor. First, Jilin pressed its interests at an opportune moment. In the late 1980s Sino-Soviet relations were beginning to improve and the two countries were about to enter negotiations on cross-border issues. The political situation in northeast Asia was also relatively stable, and most countries were interested in regional economic development. Second, Jilin's initiative was in line with the country's overall development strategy and interest in gaining maritime access. Third, the province secured allies in the central government by winning the support of heavyweight figures such as Huan Xiang and Song Jian, who subsequently persuaded other senior leaders to pay attention to Jilin's request. Fourth, the provincial authorities worked diligently through the complex policy-making machinery. Also, the province did not rely on any one central government agency; instead it took the initiative to discuss the proposal directly with several agencies with an interest in the issue. Finally, the province used its own resources to support research and fact-finding missions, sought international resources for its scheme, and maintained a high profile domestically as well as internationally.

CONCLUSION

Several conclusions can be drawn from the material discussed in this chapter. First, China's provinces are becoming increasingly active in foreign relations. Since the central government's leadership opened a window to the world in 1978, the provinces have strengthened their foreign affairs systems and extended their reach to neighboring as well as faraway communities. They have done so using many strategies, including establishing friendly overseas ties, promoting foreign trade and investment, and developing bilateral and multinational cooperation projects to support their own local development. If the coastal provinces have been most effective in such endeavors, their counterparts in the inland and border areas have nonetheless been trying to catch up.

Second, the provinces have not generally pursued their own foreign policies independent of Beijing. In fact, the growing assertiveness of China's provinces should not be confused with independent foreign policies conducted at the local level. Although foreign governments should take China's provinces more seriously, as many have argued, China is still a unitary state ruled by a hierarchical and dominant political party.[99] At the subnational level only the Hong Kong SAR comes close to conducting its "foreign policy" under the "one country, two systems" arrangement. Moreover, even Hong Kong's autonomy in international economic affairs is granted to the SAR by the central government and does not extend to defense and diplomatic issues. The Hong Kong model is unlikely to be extended to give other localities similar privileges in foreign affairs.

Third, the provinces still are important partners for the central government in its foreign relations efforts. The opening up of China's provinces, together with greater provincial discretion in the acquisition of foreign capital, helps to boost their influence over that of business lobbies in many foreign capitals. The special treatment of Guangdong and Fujian is thus directly tied to China's objectives vis-à-vis Hong Kong and Taiwan. Likewise, the opening of the coastal provinces attracts considerable investment from Japan, South Korea, and Southeast Asia, and the development of economic cooperation in the border regions of southwest, northwest, and northeast China have enhanced cooperation between the PRC and neighboring countries. The establishment of a stable regional security environment, in turn, is essential not only to China's economic development, but also to its management of relations with other great powers.

Finally, the international interactions of China's provinces have added new dimensions to its foreign relations in the reform era. A dichotomous view of central-local relations, however, may not always be a useful framework of analysis, because the national and local roles of the provinces in Chinese foreign policy are not necessarily always in conflict. The opening of China since 1978 is a national strategy that has benefited the provinces immensely. In the 1990s the provinces became more important players in the complex web of Chinese foreign policy-making as the nature of Chinese foreign policy underwent significant changes, including greater emphasis on economic matters, keener competition among government agencies, and increasing multilateral international interactions. Although the central government still dominates foreign policy-making, the expansion of provincial foreign affairs, driven by competing economic interests and diverse strategic considerations, is already making an impact on the international behavior of China.

PART TWO

Elite and Societal Opinion

FIVE

The Foreign Policy Outlook of China's "Third Generation" Elite

H. LYMAN MILLER AND LIU XIAOHONG

The leadership that now presides over China's foreign and domestic policies is unlike any that has governed the People's Republic of China (PRC) since its founding in 1949. Often called China's "third-generation" leadership, the cluster of top leaders around Party General Secretary Jiang Zemin is the product of two concurrent transitions. On one hand, it reflects the cumulative outcome of a deliberate process of succession to a post-Deng leadership managed by Deng Xiaoping himself to put into place younger leaders recruited according to criteria befitting China's postrevolutionary agenda. On the other hand, it reflects a signal turnover of elite generations, bringing to the top a group of postliberation leaders whose life experiences and career paths differ profoundly from those of their predecessors.

How much the new third-generation leaders will address the problems of governing China, assess China's place in the post–cold war world, and manage Beijing's foreign relations in ways distinctly different from their predecessors may be known with certainty only with the passage of time. But a very broad-gauged examination of who these leaders are, together with a very large-scale assessment of the political context they inherit and a preliminary look at their foreign policy record so far, allows one to make provisional judgments about their outlook on the international system, their approaches to state-craft, and their foreign policy inclinations. Looking to the future, we need not only to explore more fully the views, policy-making style, and effectiveness of third-generation leaders such as Jiang Zemin, Li Peng, and Qian Qichen, but also to begin to assess their likely successors among the "fourth-generation" leadership.

A POSTLIBERATION LEADERSHIP

The present Chinese leadership is distinctly new. Of the twenty-four leaders appointed as full or alternate members of the Chinese Communist Party's (CCP's) Politburo at the Fifteenth National Congress in September 1997 (Table 5.1), only six had served in that body before 1992. Of those six, two (Li Peng and Tian Jiyun) were first appointed to the Politburo at the extraordinary party conference in 1985, the other four at the Thirteenth Congress in 1987. Of the remaining eighteen, nine were first appointed to the Politburo at the 1992 Fourteenth Party Congress, and one (Shanghai party chief Huang Ju) was appointed at the 1994 Fourth Plenum. The remaining eight achieved Polit-buro standing only in 1997.[1]

The twenty-four members of the Fifteenth Congress's Politburo, therefore, share a combined total of sixty-eight years of service in that body or an aver-age of less than three years per member. From this perspective the leaders who now constitute China's domestic and foreign policy decision-making leader-ship are of very recent and relatively short tenure. It is worth noting in this context that the foreign policy leadership of the other great powers of the post–cold war era—Clinton in the United States, Blair in Great Britain, and Putin in Russia—are comparably inexperienced in foreign affairs. The pres-ent leaders also differ from those who dominated China's politics and foreign relations during the Deng era, and more broadly since 1949, in a number of other significant ways. In terms of regional origin and experience, education, career path, foreign travel, and military service the present leadership differs starkly from the preceding two generations of PRC leaders.

How different the present leadership is may be seen from comparing them with the top leadership appointed at the CCP's Twelfth National Con-gress in 1982. The leadership appointed in 1982 reflected the consolidation of power of Deng Xiaoping and a coalition of veteran party leaders who there-

TABLE 5.1
CHINA'S NATIONAL PARTY LEADERSHIP, MARCH 2000

CCP Politburo Members	Age (2000)	Other principal posts	Province of origin and university degree, if any
Standing Committee leaders (rank order)			
Jiang Zemin	74	CCP general secretary; chairman, CCP and PRC Central Military Commission; PRC president	Jiangsu; electrical engineering
Li Peng	72	NPC chairman	Sichuan; hydro-electrical engineering
Zhu Rongji	72	Premier	Hunan; electrical engineering
Li Ruihuan	66	Chairman, CPPCC	Tianjin; construction engineering
Hu Jintao	58	PRC vice president; president, Central Party School	Anhui; hydraulic engineering
Wei Jianxing	69	Secretary, Central Discipline Inspection Commission; Secretariat; president, All-China Federation of Trade Unions	Zhejiang; mechanical engineering
Li Lanqing	68	Vice premier	Jiangsu; enterprise management
Regular members (stroke order)			
Ding Guan'gen	71	Secretariat; director, CCP Propaganda Department	Jiangsu; railroad engineering
Tian Jiyun	71	NPC Standing Committee vice chairman	Shandong
Li Changchun	56	Secretary, Guangdong CCP Committee	Liaoning; electrical engineering
Li Tieying	60	President, Chinese Academy of Social Sciences	Yanan/Hunan; physics
Wu Bangguo	59	Vice premier	Anhui; electrical engineering
Wu Guanzheng	62	Secretary, Shandong CCP Committee	Jiangxi; electrical engineering
Chi Haotian	67	Minister of National Defense; state councillor; CMC vice chairman	Shandong; Third Field Army
Zhang Wannian	72	CMC vice chairman; Secretariat	Shandong; southern Fourth Field Army
Luo Gan	65	Secretariat; state councillor	Shandong; metallurgical engineering
Jiang Chunyun	70	NPC Standing Committee vice chairman	Shandong]
Jia Qinglin	60	Secretary, Beijing CCP Committee; mayor, Beijing	Hebei; electrical engineering
Qian Qichen	72	Vice premier	Shanghai

(continued)

TABLE 5.1 (*continued*)

CCP Politburo Members	Age (2000)	Other principal posts	Province of origin and university degree, if any
Huang Ju	63	Secretary, Shanghai CCP Committee	Zhejiang; electrical engineering
Wen Jiabao	58	Secretariat; vice premier	Tianjin; geology
Xie Fei	68	NPC Standing Committee vice chairman (deceased October 27, 1999)	Guangdong
Alternate members			
Zeng Qinghong	61	Director, CCP Organization Department	Jiangxi; engineering
Wu Yi	62	State councillor	Hubei; petroleum engineering

Sources: *Renmin Ribao,* Sept. 20, 1997, p. 1; Xinhua News Agency, Sept. 19, 1997; and *Who's Who in China: Current Leaders* (Beijing: Foreign Languages Press, 1994).

after dominated China's politics in the 1980s and, as retired elders, in the early 1990s. The 1982 leadership, in fact, shared many basic characteristics with China's leaders during the period from 1949 to 1976, despite the profoundly different orientation of the policies it espoused in the reform era from those of the Mao years. Many of them—Chen Yun, Peng Zhen, Li Xiannian, Yang Shangkun, Nie Rongzhen, Xu Xiangqian, Ye Jianying, and Deng himself—had been members of China's top elite in the 1950s. Their policy views in the 1980s derived in part from outlooks they had developed and shared on China's domestic and foreign policy during the earlier decades, and those views, of course, had made most of them targets of Mao's ferocious attacks in the 1960s and 1970s. Their appointment to the party's top leadership in 1982 therefore marked a restoration of their power, not the arrival of a new elite. In this sense it is misleading to speak of two leadership generations preceding the present third-generation leadership with Jiang Zemin as "the core," because both of the first two generations drew from the same pool of veteran revolutionaries. In comparing the present Politburo leadership to the 1982 leadership around Deng Xiaoping, then, we are in fact safely drawing comparisons that hold generally across both the first- and second-generation elites that governed the PRC over its first forty years.

It is also misleading to describe the present leadership as composed solely of third-generation leaders. The twenty-four full and candidate members of the Politburo appointed in 1997 really constitute two roughly equal groups of third- and fourth-generation leaders. The third-generation group includes twelve men who were sixty-seven or older by 2000 and who therefore may be expected to retire from the Politburo by the party's Sixteenth Congress in 2002 if prevailing practices continue. The remaining twelve leaders younger than sixty-seven include nine who are sixty-two or younger and who therefore may continue in formal leadership roles after 2002, and in some cases well beyond. Judgments about potential differences in the foreign policy outlooks of these third- and fourth-generation leaders are deferred to the last section of this chapter.

The differences between the present leadership around Jiang and the 1982 leadership around Deng Xiaoping are stark and dramatic. First, the present Jiang leadership is on average a decade younger than the leadership installed in 1982 around Deng. The average age of the twenty-four members of the Jiang leadership on appointment in 1997 was sixty-three years. By contrast, the average age of the twenty-five leaders appointed to the Politburo with Deng Xiaoping in 1982 was in that year seventy-two.

Second, following directly from the relative youth of the Jiang leadership, most of its members began their careers after the founding of the PRC. Of the twenty-four leaders in the present Politburo, fourteen joined the Communist Party after 1949. These include two who joined between 1950 and 1955, three between 1956 and 1959, and nine between 1960 and 1965. Of the ten who joined before the establishment of the PRC, six joined during the 1946–49 civil war; of the remaining four, three (Li Peng, Tian Jiyun, and Zhang Wannian) entered the Communist Party in 1945, and Qian Qichen joined in 1942. By contrast, most members of the 1982 Politburo were drawn from among the party's founding generation. Among its twenty-five members, twenty-three joined the party before the mid-1930s Long March, including sixteen who joined during the 1921–28 First United Front period.

Third, the present leadership is far better educated than that of 1982. Among the twenty-five leaders appointed to the Politburo in 1982, none had university degrees. Two (Nie Rongzhen, from the Red Army Academy in Moscow, and Xu Xiangqian, from the Whampoa Military Academy in Canton) had studied at military academies, and two more (Ulanfu and Yang Shangkun) had studied at Sun Yat-sen University in Moscow. Two others, Hu Qiaomu and Liao Chengzhi, had at least two years of university-level study but never completed degree programs. By contrast, seventeen of the twenty-four members of the present Politburo leadership have university degrees. The educational background of the present leadership, moreover, is overwhelmingly technical. Of the seventeen holding university degrees, sixteen studied in scientific and technical fields; fourteen of the sixteen, in fact, are engineers. (The odd man out among the seventeen is Li Lanqing, who holds a degree in enterprise management.) Among the six with any university training in the 1982 leadership, only two majored in technical areas (Nie Rongzhen in chemical engineering and Hu Qiaomu in physics).

Fourth, the present Jiang leadership is strongly associated with the progressively reformist provinces on the Chinese coast. Among the twenty-four members of the present Politburo, thirteen trace their regional origins to the five coastal provinces of Shandong, Jiangsu, Zhejiang, Fujian, and Guangdong and two province-level coastal cities, Tianjin and Shanghai. Of the remaining eleven who do not come from these coastal provinces, four (Zhu Rongji, Zeng Qinghong, Jia Qinglin, and Wu Bangguo) worked substantial portions of their careers in these provinces and cities during the 1980s and 1990s, the heyday of Deng's coast-oriented reforms. By regional origin or work experience, seventeen of the twenty-four, therefore, are associated with the coastal backbone of reform. By contrast, only six of the twenty-five members of the 1982 Deng leadership hailed from the coastal provinces and cities. The reform years under Deng were dominated by men associated with Deng's home province of Sichuan and the provinces in the party's old Central-South Bureau, together with a smattering of a "Shanxi gang."

Last, the Jiang leadership appointed in 1997 is virtually devoid of military experience. Only the two professional military leaders, Zhang Wannian and Chi Haotian, who both fought in the civil war and in the Korean War, have firsthand military experience. (Zhang and Chi are discussed in the chapter by Tai Ming Cheung in this volume.) The remaining twenty-two have none at all. By contrast, among the twenty-five members of the 1982 Deng leadership, twenty had military experience by way of past military leadership positions or direct combat, and seven had followed military career paths after 1949.

Therefore, the consolidation of the Jiang leadership at the Fifteenth Party Congress in 1997 marked the arrival at the top of China's political hierarchies of a generation of leaders whose life experiences and careers set them apart from the preceding party leaderships around Deng Xiaoping and, before that, Mao Zedong. Most of the present leaders came of political age during the "ten glorious years" of the PRC's first decade after rising steadily through the various institutional hierarchies amid the social transformations created by the communist revolution. Many endured the Cultural Revolution decade rather than prospered from it, and so they are mindful of the policy disasters of the last two decades of Mao Zedong's rule. All saw their careers take off with the Dengist restoration of the late 1970s and 1980s. By education most are technically trained, and, as part of the managerial elite created in the 1950s and early 1960s, they are by profession technocratic in administrative experience, not heroic social revolutionaries. In a China where in modern times security has remained the foremost priority and where political power has rested in part on military foundations, the Jiang leadership is an unprecedentedly civilian leadership.

A POSTREVOLUTIONARY LEADERSHIP

Leaders sharing these general characteristics, of course, have been the kind that Deng Xiaoping consciously sought to promote from the beginning of the reform era under his leadership, and their arrival at the top levels of the political system reflects the culmination of his efforts to match personnel to the policies he promoted. The recruitment and promotion criteria that Deng applied, together with the broader changes in institutions, political process, and policy context that he spearheaded throughout this period, provided the ladder by which all of the members of the Jiang leadership advanced into the top ranks of the party and state hierarchies. The broader changes in the political process he brought about, emphasizing party discipline, institutional routine, and professionalization, provided the context in which their careers flourished.

The watershed event in all these respects, and in PRC political history in general, was the Eleventh Central Committee's Third Plenum in December 1978, at which the committee decided to shift the focus of party work from the "revolutionary" agenda of promoting social transformation by waging continued class warfare to the "postrevolutionary" agenda of putting foremost priority on promoting economic growth and managing overall modernization.[2] This transformation of the party's mission had immediate consequences in terms of the kind of cadres to be admitted to the party and the kind of leaders to be promoted at all levels. No longer did the party need cadres recruited and promoted according to criteria suited to Mao Zedong's Cultural Revolution–era policies of "continuing the revolution under the dictatorship of the proletariat," emphasizing political "redness" over substantive expertise and a capacity for mass mobilization in political campaigns using the "struggle" tactics favored by Mao. The party's postrevolutionary transformation from an agent of class warfare to a manager of modernization required, instead, cadre recruitment and leadership promotion criteria emphasizing formal education, technical training, administrative experience, and managerial skill. Accordingly, successive reorganizations of the State Council and Central Committee departments, beginning in 1982 and 1983, together with comparable efforts to engineer the turnover of leaders at the provincial level and below, produced an increasingly technocratic corps of leaders at middle levels of the political order.

The personnel changes pressed by Deng also emphasized "rejuvenation" (*nianqinghua*) of the leadership ranks. In a talk to provincial party secretaries following the June 1981 Sixth Plenum, Deng stressed that failure to address the problem of rejuvenating the party's leadership ranks would immediately lead to "chaos" within three to five years as veteran leaders died off or became incapacitated because of age. He specifically cited the example of Liu Lanbo, who proposed that a "younger comrade" with a strong technical background and administrative experience succeed him as minister of electronics. The younger comrade to whom Deng referred may in fact have been Jiang Zemin, who became vice minister in 1982 before assuming the post as minister in the large-scale State Council turnover at the Sixth National People's Congress (NPC) in 1983.[3] In step with this emphasis on rejuvenation of the leadership ranks, throughout the Deng era and continuing into the post-Deng period Xinhua News Agency accounts of successive leadership changes have publicized the steady lowering of the average ages of adjusted leadership bodies at central and provincial levels.

In conjunction with the profound postrevolutionary reorientation of the party's agenda and its attendant consequences for policy and leadership personnel that Deng brought about, two other transformations for which Deng pressed had a significant influence on the kind of leadership that has emerged in the post-Deng era. First, Deng promoted the professionalization of the People's Liberation Army (PLA) and its withdrawal from politics, a development that Michael Swaine's contribution to this volume also addresses. Deng's efforts in this regard preceded the reform era, going back to his efforts after his rehabilitation in 1973 to help Mao to reduce military influence from its Cultural Revolution high point—which is reflected in PLA membership on the Ninth Central Committee at over 40 percent—and to break the entrenchment of military leaders in the provinces in the New Year's Day 1974 rotation of military region commanders. In 1975 and repeatedly in the early post-Mao years Deng stressed the need to reduce the size of the PLA in favor of better-trained and, later, better-equipped troops. These emphases were extended by the redefinition of China's security needs at the landmark 1985 Military Commission meeting, leading to the call in the early 1990s for a military force capable of fighting "limited wars under high-tech conditions." Parallel with the comparable emphases on cadre recruitment and promotion, PLA recruitment and promotion began to emphasize institutionalized military education—focused on the consolidated military academies—and technical skills.[4] In 1988 ranks were finally restored.

These reforms aimed at professionalizing the PLA and altering its role in the larger political process were not without resistance and were met with setbacks. Deng's 1981–82 effort to transfer authority over the Military Commission from the party to the state, which he saw as appropriate to a "mature" socialist institutional structure, instead produced parallel party and state commissions, with the same cast of leaders serving on both simultaneously. (Tai Ming Cheung's chapter explains this aspect in greater detail.) The resort to using the PLA to suppress the Tiananmen demonstrations in 1989—in the name of preserving domestic peace and order, as a duty alongside the PLA's external mission of meeting foreign security threats to the country—seemed for a time to bring the military back into politics after two decades of trying to get it out. Subsequent themes in military political education stressing the army's "absolute loyalty" to the party somewhat diluted the professionalizing import of the earlier military reforms.

But the Deng military reforms have continued, despite the setbacks, and promise an increasingly professional and technically competent military force that is in step with the broader trends in the foreign policy and national security system that David Lampton identifies in his introductory chapter to this volume.[5] As in the party itself, these professionalizing reforms in the PLA have proceeded in step with a generational change in the PLA's leadership ranks. Through institutionalized retirement systems and systematic promotions the long-standing veteran military leadership whose direct combat experience had been in fighting the Kuomintang and Japan rapidly gave way in the 1980s and 1990s to younger officers in the middle and upper ranks whose benchmark combat experience was the Korean War. With the retirement of Liu Huaqing and Zhang Zhen in 1997 and the promotions of Chi Haotian and Zhang Wannian two years earlier, this turnover of military generations reached the very top of the military hierarchy. General Xiong Guangkai (discussed in the chapters by Tai Ming Cheung and Michael Swaine) typifies the more cosmopolitan and professional leaders emerging at the top of the PLA.

One far-reaching implication of this evolution has been a significant change in the channels and mechanisms of military influence in the political arena. Formerly, with veteran revolutionaries who had long military experience, such as Mao and Deng, at the top of the party and with veteran military leaders such as Ye Jianying as very high-ranking party leaders, much of the party and military elite was indistinguishable. PLA influence permeated politics easily through informal ties with leaders such as "Uncle Ye." Party influence reached with comparable ease into the PLA informally through the network of relationships—the influence of Second Field Army members in the 1980s being the case in point—that Mao and Deng had built up over the decades. Now, thanks to the concurrent civilian cadre and military reforms under Deng Xiaoping, the PRC now has for the first time separate political and military elites. On one hand, the cadre recruitment and promotion reforms have produced a top party and state leadership that by 1997 was almost completely civilian. On the other hand, the retirement and deaths of the veteran revolutionary generations, together with the military reforms of the Deng period, have produced a younger and increasingly professionalized military leadership that must increasingly rely on institutional routines and formal channels to interact with the party leadership.

The other transformation that has profoundly affected PRC political processes has been a creeping institutionalization of politics in general, of which the just-cited change in party-military relations is one example. In contrast to Mao's preference for "revolutionary" spontaneity and skepticism regarding institutions, Deng Xiaoping, consistent with his "postrevolutionary" focus on governing and modernization, emphasized organizational discipline, administrative routines, and deliberative policy-making. In contrast to the irregularity of party processes under Mao, party congresses and Central Committee plenums in the Deng era met according to statute. Convening NPC sessions again became an annual routine. Restoration of the annual budgeting processes stimulated the regularization of state accounting and economic forecasting, and there was a resumption of the late 1950s project of setting down codes of law to mediate social conflicts arising in the course of accelerated modernization. Under the aegis of "soft science" approaches to policy planning and decision-making, think tanks proliferated throughout the political hierarchy under Zhao Ziyang, producing position papers and feasibility studies for a broadened, much more consultative, decision-making process.[6]

As a consequence of this evolution pressed by Deng, China's politics have become much more routinized, predictable, stable, consensual, and, in the words of one observer, "normal."[7] This is not to say that leadership conflict has disappeared; it is just that it has become increasingly institutionalized and embedded in rules that are adhered to far more rigorously than during the last two decades of the Mao Zedong era. Deviations from explicitly prescribed processes still occur, but they are increasingly occasional and stand out as aberrations from expected norms.

A case in point has to do with the fate of Qiao Shi at the Fifteenth Party Congress. Qiao lost a game of musical chairs sparked by the leadership's intent to live up to the prescription of the 1983 PRC constitution (rather than rewrite the constitutional provision or ignore it altogether, as was done before the Deng era) that no one serve longer than two five-year terms as premier. Appointed premier in 1988 at the Seventh NPC, Li Peng was therefore expected to step down at the forthcoming Ninth NPC in March 1998. The problem going into the 1997 Fifteenth Party Congress had been to decide the fate of Li Peng, a leader whose political weight had diminished perceptibly but had not altogether been eclipsed as the 1990s proceeded and who retained some political utility to a rising Jiang Zemin. Among the Politburo Standing Committee members holding top posts outside the party, none was required by term-limit provisions, as Li was, to step down: Qiao as NPC chairman, Li Ruihuan as Chinese People's Political Consultative Conference chairman, and Jiang himself as PRC president had each served a single five-year term. Within the Politburo, however, Qiao was vulnerable to the informal expectation that leaders over seventy years of age, aside from the "core leader," retire. Aside from seventy-year-old Jiang Zemin, only Qiao, at seventy-one, among this group faced this constraint (Li Peng was sixty-nine and Li Ruihuan sixty-three), so the obvious course, unless compelling political considerations dictated otherwise, was for Qiao to step down as NPC chairman in favor of Li. Judging by the proliferation of rumors and leaks purveyed in the Hong Kong press, a number of political factors made resolution of the question contentious. But the fact is that none of these factors was sufficient to warrant deviation either from the term-limit stipulations of the PRC constitution or from the solidifying informal rule on age limits for Politburo membership. In the end all six leaders dropped from the Politburo at the Fifteenth Congress, including Qiao, were older than seventy. In short, rule-following won, establishing in this instance an important precedent for institutionalized leadership turnover.

More broadly, the resolution of the fate of Qiao Shi comports with the style of leadership politics practiced in the transition to a post-Deng era. The Jiang leadership has faced a daunting agenda of recomposing popular confidence in the party leadership in the wake of Tiananmen, maintaining order over a fragmenting party and a society undergoing rapid social change and economic transition, pressing ahead with economic reforms that portend serious social unrest, and managing an uncertain post–cold war foreign policy context— all as Deng Xiaoping's health and political activity declined. Although in the 1990s there have been clear-cut indications of policy debate—over the shape of the Ninth Five-Year Plan, for example—and political conflict—as repeated blasts from an increasingly marginalized but still vocal conservative intraparty opposition suggest—policy-making in the Jiang leadership has not been characterized by the symptoms of open political conflict that pervaded the Mao transition in the early 1970s or even the more stable politics of the 1980s under Deng and his reform coalition. This overall capacity of the Jiang leadership to contain political differences and policy debates within a facade of stability and consensus threatens to give collective leadership a good name.[8]

Most broadly, under Deng Xiaoping's leadership and postrevolutionary agenda the process of managed succession and institutionalization has delivered an orderly, almost business-as-usual leadership succession that stands in stark, universal contrast to the process at comparable moments of leadership succession in the experience of ruling communist parties everywhere. Orderly and arranged leadership succession has been everywhere absent among the communist states. In no major ruling communist party has the top party leader retired voluntarily from his predominating formal posts, turning power gradually over to successors in the normal course of political routine. Paramount leaders have either died in office or been pushed out in internal power struggles.

In the former Soviet Union, for example, no Soviet leader retired voluntarily. Lenin died in place in 1924 as the architect of the Bolshevik Revolution, leading to a prolonged struggle for power among Stalin, Trotsky, and Bukharin. Stalin's death in 1953 also led to a power struggle, which Nikita Khrushchev finally won in 1957 after the purge of the "antiparty group." Khrushchev was himself overthrown in 1964 after a turbulent tenure and a visibly building power struggle. Leonid Brezhnev gradually emerged as the foremost leader of the succeeding triumvirate, and he held power until his death in 1982 despite the creeping senility of his leadership during what became characterized later as the "era of stagnation." His successors, the reform-inclined Yuri Andropov and the Brezhnev loyalist Konstantin Chernenko, were of his own generation, and each held onto the top post in the Communist Party of the Soviet Union (CPSU) for less than two years before expiring. The younger Mikhail Gorbachev emerged from a tight contest for power in 1985, only to see his own tenure end with the fragmentation of the CPSU and the collapse of the Soviet Union itself. In Vietnam Ho Chi Minh died in place as leader of the Vietnamese Communist Party (VCP) in 1969, at a critical point in the Vietnamese revolution. His successor, Le Duan, also died while still serving as VCP general secretary in July 1986, at a turning point in Hanoi's relations with Beijing and Moscow and amid mounting domestic problems. Le Duan's death led to the immediate "unanimous" election of VCP veteran Truong Chinh as his successor on the eve of the VCP's Sixth Congress, which was scheduled for later that year. But Truong Chinh's tenure was as a brief caretaker. Amid abundant indications of internal party conflict the Sixth Congress unseated him and appointed a new party chief, Nguyen Van Linh. The congress also deposed several other members of the VCP old guard in favor of younger reform-inclined leaders and authorized a marked shift in policy orientation, inaugurating the *doi moi* reforms. Linh ceded his post to Do Muoi in 1991 only as his health failed. The dynastic succession of Kim Chong-il to Kim Il-song in Pyongyang requires no comment here.

China's experience, before the present instance, had been no different. Mao Zedong's attempts to name his own successor and to institutionalize orderly processes of leadership retirement fell afoul of his own machinations. First his implicit designation as his successor of Liu Shaoqi in 1956 and then his explicit designation of Lin Biao in 1969 ended in the disgrace of both. Hua Guofeng's claim as Mao's successor rested on his appointment as party first vice chairman in April 1976, accompanying the second purge of Deng Xiaoping, and on a flimsy interpretation of a note supposedly scrawled by Mao that year confiding to Hua, "With you in charge, I'm at ease." Hua's effective tenure lasted only two years. More broadly, in 1956 Mao and the senior CCP leadership also began to demarcate first and second lines of leadership that were intended to bring about the gradual withdrawal of party veterans into back-bench advisory roles and the succession of a younger generation of leaders to responsibility for the day-to-day management of party and state affairs. But these efforts at orderly succession also foundered amid the accelerating leadership conflicts growing out of the Great Leap Forward and its aftermath, leading to the Cultural Revolution. Despite the dramatic setbacks reflected in the fall of Hu Yaobang in 1987 and then Zhao Ziyang in 1989, the order-liness of the Deng succession contrasts starkly with Mao's. It also poses the test that Jiang faces: will he be willing and able to follow the norm for rou-tinized succession, presumably at the Sixteenth Party Congress in 2002 and the Tenth NPC in 2003?

In summary, the post-Deng leadership of Jiang Zemin is the product of several trends promoted by Deng Xiaoping through the reform years. Their membership emerged from a deliberate process of selection according to cri-teria driven by Deng's postrevolutionary purposes. They advanced to the top levels of the political system thanks to Deng's efforts to establish orderly processes of leadership turnover and succession. Their work style solidified in the con-text of the increasingly institutionalized processes of postrevolutionary pol-itics that Deng worked to instill. The relative smoothness of the post-Deng transition is due in part to the passing from the scene in the early 1990s of most of the veteran leadership elders who, with Deng, dominated politics in the 1980s and who, had they survived Deng, might well have mobilized a potent challenge to Jiang. Deng, however, once again demonstrated his adroit politi-cal skill in passing from the scene only after most of his peers among the elders—Hu Qiaomu, Li Xiannian, Deng Yingchao, Chen Yun, and Peng Zhen—had already died. Luck was therefore not an irrelevant element of the post-Deng succession. But the smoothness of the transition also manifests how success-ful Deng was in transforming the severely polarized and fragmented politi-cal system he had inherited himself only twenty years before. Both in terms of their own ascent and of the political context they inherit, the legacy Deng bequeathed the Jiang leadership is enormous.

FOREIGN POLICY ORIENTATION

On the basis of the preceding considerations, what kind of approaches to state-craft and policy outlook should we expect from the post–Deng Xiaoping leader-ship? A number of predilections (but still rather less than deterministic predictions) suggest themselves:

— The Jiang leadership is likely to be very pragmatic. Engineers see political issues as problems to be solved based on hard data and hard interest, not as conflicts driven by ideological principles.[9] In many ways, if the larger economic and political context permits, the Jiang leadership is likely to push fundamental reform of the economy dramatically farther than was politically feasible in the Deng period. At a minimum, in the hands of this leadership the era of egalitarian social revolution in China is over. Just one bit of evidence of how far the leadership is willing to go was seen in its decision to join the World Trade Organization (WTO), which is chronicled in Margaret Pearson's chapter in this volume.

— The strong association of the post-Deng leadership with China's coastal region suggests that they will remain deeply committed to the "coastal strategy" of economic reform and development launched in the Deng era. It is true that Jiang has repeatedly announced programs to reduce interprovincial inequities and to develop China's West. Nonetheless, the Jiang leadership has continued to emphasize the role of the coastal provinces in leading the way in overall national development.

— Because of their coastal regional association and reformist outlook, and drawing on their much broader experience in dealing with the international order during the later Deng years, the Jiang leadership is likely to be thoroughly internationalist in its approach to the international community. They will remain convinced of the necessity of integrating China into the international economy as the best way to address China's developmental needs. Additionally, because they matured as leaders during the period when the PRC began to establish and consolidate its position as a fully sovereign and recognized member of the international community, the Jiang leadership may be expected to sustain and expand that standing. As Bates Gill's chapter shows, Beijing's readiness to expand Chinese participation in arms control and other security forums manifests this impulse.

— In international politics the Jiang leadership is likely to understand international power in realist terms and therefore be acutely sensitive to China's relative strengths and weaknesses with respect to the regional and global context in which they operate. As engineers who already have had considerable international experience, they are disposed to understand politics in terms of national interest, not idealistic visions of some alternative world future, as would romantic revolutionaries.

— As technically trained reformers the Jiang leadership will undoubtedly attach great priority to the technological transformation of the PLA into a fighting force that attains advanced contemporary standards. Increasing military budgets and the incorporation of new technologies into a leaner force are fully consistent with these views, as

Michael Swaine's and Tai Ming Cheung's chapters suggest. The new leadership will be attentive to patterns of military modernization around China in East Asia, especially in Japan, and, more broadly, to the implications of the revolution in Western military affairs.[10] Given their other political priorities, however, they will be sensitive to the broader economic foundations and budgetary costs such technological advances entail. Doctrinally this leadership generation will continue to support the evolution of PLA strategy away from the "people's war" tactics employed by Mao in favor of the more modern Western concepts of fighting wars that the PLA has adopted since the mid-1980s, leaning more toward Moltke and less toward Sunzi and outdated Soviet doctrines. And, most specifically, combining their appreciation of the requirements of modern warfare and their bias toward the economic centers on the China coast, they will probably continue to back the development of a "green" or "blue water" navy that can defend China's vulnerable coastline much farther out at sea, make credible its threat of the use of force against Taiwan to support its pursuit of reunification through political means, and make its Southeast Asian neighbors respect its claims in the South China Sea pending a larger settlement of the issue.

— With respect to decision-making processes as they relate to foreign policy and security issues, the Jiang leadership is fundamentally a civilian leadership accustomed to operating in the institutional context that Deng established in the post-Mao period. They are inclined to rely on staff work by aides, professional bureaucrats, and experts to provide background information and intelligence and on various formal and informal mechanisms, such as standing bodies and task forces, to debate policy options.[11] Reflecting the broadened spectrum of domestic interests and competing institutional agendas involved in major foreign policy and security questions in China since the late 1970s, they will likely continue and even deepen consultative consensus-building approaches in policy formulation while preserving as much as possible Beijing's long-standing capacity for coordinated and disciplined implementation. Because most in the Jiang leadership lack real military experience of their own, they are likely to take all the more seriously the advice of China's military leadership. Because the PRC's military leadership has become increasingly professionalized, however, its advice and policy prescriptions are likely to be carefully defined and limited to areas of clear-cut military purview.[12] Nonetheless, in combination, the civilian party and military leaderships are likely to be cautious, not adventurous about the use of military force in foreign affairs, but decisive, not tentative, once the decision to use it has been made.

Taken together, these propensities suggest that the foreign and security policies of the Jiang leadership will continue along the general lines set down by the leaders whose reforms brought them to the top, which is to say that they will be Dengist without Deng. Freed from some of the political limitations that Deng faced, moreover, they may be prepared to move considerably farther along paths established in the Deng period, as their readiness to press state-owned enterprise reform for the sake of WTO entry already suggests.

THE PRELIMINARY JIANG RECORD: CONTINUITY WITH DENG

As speculative as the preceding judgments based on shared leadership characteristics may seem, the Jiang leadership's conduct of foreign policy has generally borne them out. The arranged succession managed by Deng proceeded over the years since 1989, with the installation of Jiang as general secretary and Deng's own complete retirement from his formal posts in the spring of 1990. The Fifteenth Congress in 1997 consolidated the process of transition to the present leadership that had begun at the Fourteenth CCP Congress in 1992. The years of Jiang's leadership before 1997, while Deng was still alive, and the years since 1997 under Jiang's consolidated leadership thereby provide a preliminary record that complements the preceding analysis based on shared leadership characteristics.[13]

First, the foundations of PRC foreign policy in the immediate post-Deng period and in the five years since the Fourteenth Congress have remained those that had framed the PRC's foreign policy since the beginning of the Deng period. Those premises, as endorsed at the watershed Third Plenum in December 1978, are, first, that China's accelerated economic modernization is essential to the survival of the PRC in the contemporary world and so is the "center" of all leadership work. The second premise is that China's economic modernization requires both its integration into the broader international political and economic order and a stable international context over a prolonged period of time. On the basis of these premises Deng normalized relations with the three powers that have traditionally constituted the main threats to PRC security—Japan, the United States, and the Soviet Union. Under his leadership China joined the international economic order, becoming a rapidly rising trading power and major site for foreign investment. Under Deng's leadership Beijing made significant progress in advancing its reunification agenda, securing an agreement for the reversion of Hong Kong from British rule, and preparing the way for an explosion of cross-strait relations with Taiwan by the late 1980s. On all three main items on Beijing's long-standing foreign policy agenda—security, development, and reunification—Deng Xiaoping's foreign policy made major advances and brought China to its most secure and prosperous period since the eighteenth century.

As Jiang took up his top leadership posts during Deng's last years, however, several events and trends arising in the late 1980s and maturing in the early 1990s raised questions about the viability of sustaining this foreign policy direction. First, Soviet-American détente, symbolized by the 1987 agreement on intermediate nuclear forces, and then the collapse of the Soviet Union altogether had the effect of marginalizing China's strategic significance in world affairs. Instead of a bipolar system evolving slowly toward multipolarity, as Chinese analysts described the structure of world power in the 1980s, Beijing now faced a potentially hegemonic system dominated by the remaining superpower, the United States. Since 1949 Beijing had strategically tilted away from the strongest pole in the international order.[14] In the post–cold war era it faced the dilemma of how to balance itself against American hegemonic power while at the same time sustaining productive bilateral ties with that preponderant power for the sake of China's development.

Second, despite its reduced global stature, China paradoxically looked bigger in the East Asian region with Soviet influence in eclipse (and Beijing's own economy experiencing growth), sparking anxieties over an emergent "China threat" in Southeast Asia and elsewhere. Third, the end of the cold war complicated Beijing's bilateral ties with important capitals because a diverse array of bilateral economic, human rights, and other political issues that previously had been subordinated to the overriding priority of strategic collaboration against Moscow came to the fore. Fourth, in the United States and elsewhere the success of the East European and Soviet revolutions demonstrated that former United Nations Ambassador Jeanne Kirkpatrick had been wrong, that communist states can be brought down as easily as right-wing authoritarian states, an empirical truth that made the international image of the Beijing regime, already blackened by its suppression of the 1989 Tiananmen protests, even darker. Perceived in the 1980s as the most dramatically progressive of reforming communist states, China now seemed to be a political fossil governed by a brutal, aging leadership at a time when democratization was sweeping the world. Finally, Taiwan's domestic evolution—its rapid democratization since 1987 and the Taiwanization of its politics—was changing Taipei's approach to the international order in ways that raised fundamental doubts about prospects for national reunification.

Beijing appears to have debated the implications of these events and trends, all of which emerged in 1989–91, for continuing the foreign policy line of the 1980s at least four times—in 1989–90 (in the wake of Tiananmen), in 1991 (following the collapse of the Soviet Union), in 1995–96 (in the context of the Taiwan Straits crisis and uncertainties over U.S. policy toward China), and in 1999 (in the wake of the American and NATO air war over Yugoslavia and the bombing of the Chinese embassy in Belgrade). In each case the debate concluded with a renewed commitment to Deng's policy of placing primacy on China's domestic economic development, though this position was modified by an accelerated effort to modernize China's defense capacities.

In short, the Jiang leadership has continued to reaffirm and act on the internationalist premises of the "independent foreign policy line" established in the early Deng period and articulated by General Secretary Hu Yaobang at the Twelfth Party Congress in 1982. In most areas around China's periphery Beijing has seen stability as best serving its security and economic interests. With respect to Russia, Central Asia, and South Asia it has tried to defuse tensions through diplomatic activism and by setting aside or resolving territorial disputes and expanding economic ties as a foundation for political relationships. On the Korean peninsula Beijing's foremost interest appears to remain stability and only gradual change. Beijing's creeping expansionism in the Spratly Islands is the notable exception to these foreign policy tactics as they apply in Southeast Asia. In this situation Beijing's ultimate goal may be to respond to efforts (since the 1980s) by other claimants, particularly Hanoi, to substantiate their own claims by taking possession of some islets. But in any case Beijing's approach to the Spratlys did not begin in the Jiang period.

The most serious post–cold war challenges to continuing the Deng foreign policy approach arose in relations with Tokyo and Washington, but there, too, the essentially Dengist framework has continued to prevail. Beijing's uneasiness regarding Japan, which in the late 1980s and early 1990s stemmed from its suspicions of Tokyo's increasing foreign policy activism, was exacerbated thereafter by the demise of Liberal Democratic Party domination of Japan's national politics, allowing what Beijing perceived to be more extremist voices to gain a greater audience in Tokyo's fragmented political arena. Reflecting these concerns, Beijing employed tactics of public confrontation against the first Hashimoto government, strongly objecting to the April 1996 modifications to the U.S.-Japan alliance, protesting Hashimoto's visit to the Yasukuni Shrine the following August, and protesting the building of a lighthouse on one of the Senkaku (Diaoyutai) outcrops by right-wing Japanese. Beijing meanwhile sought to preserve ongoing Sino-Japanese economic and financial ties and took no steps to intervene in the Senkaku affair while seeking to restrain popular protest in China itself. Once Hashimoto, following the elections in the fall of 1996, began to make active preparations for a summit with Beijing and to reestablish stable foundations for bilateral relations, Beijing's public stance warmed. Despite abiding Chinese suspicions regarding the implications for Taiwan of the modified U.S.-Japan alliance and the corresponding adjustments to the bilateral defense guidelines, the Hashimoto-Jiang summit in Beijing produced an agreement to convene bilateral summits annually. Momentum stalled during Jiang's 1998 Tokyo visit, but appeared to resume when Prime Minister Obuchi visited Beijing in 1999.

The evolution of Sino-U.S. relations followed a comparable course over the same period, beginning with the efforts of the Clinton administration after the March 1996 Taiwan Straits confrontation to restore stability to bilateral relations through an approach of active engagement and "strategic dialogue," culminating in Jiang Zemin's official visit to Washington in October 1997 and President Clinton's visit to China the following year. All of these Sino-U.S. and Sino-Japanese summits have underscored the fundamentally internationalist premises of the post-Deng leadership's foreign policy and its continuing interest in regional stability for the sake of China's development. In turn, Beijing now trumpets the benefits to regional stability of a summit diplomacy with all of the region's major powers.

Meanwhile, a strain of realism complements this abiding internationalism, as is reflected in Beijing's effort to establish "strategic partnerships" among some capitals based on a shared hope for emergent "multipolarity" in the international order and opposition to "hegemonism." These commitments were reflected first in the Sino-Russian joint statement produced at the end of Jiang Zemin's Moscow visit in April 1997 and a Sino-French declaration during President Jacques Chirac's May 1997 Beijing visit, and they have since been repeatedly reaffirmed in subsequent summits with Russian and some European leaders. At first glance these efforts seem reminiscent of the balance-of-power tactics used by Beijing in the 1950s to build an "international united front against U.S. imperialism" and in the 1970s against Soviet "hegemonism."[15] However, the present effort to build "strategic partnerships" differs in fundamental ways. In contrast to the earlier efforts to build "united fronts" against a "main enemy," the present focus on "strategic partnerships" stops short of designating the United States as such a threat. Instead, Beijing agreed to describe its shared policy with Washington as "building toward a constructive strategic partnership" during the 1997 summit.

On balance, the omnidirectional attempt to establish partnerships seems intended to serve two interrelated purposes with respect to the United States. First, indicating the enduring realism of the Jiang leadership's outlook, these partnerships serve as a hedge against preponderant U.S. power in an international system in which China is now a well-established and increasingly important participant. Second, they reflect an attempt to redress through diversification Beijing's essentially weak and vulnerable position with respect to a Washington whose cooperation and collaboration it needs and desires.[16]

BEYOND DENG XIAOPING

In summary, the Jiang leadership's approach to foreign policy and security issues in the years up until Deng's death and the Fifteenth Congress in 1997 built firmly on the premises and relied on the tactics of the foreign policy approach of the Deng era that it is now applied to an evolving post–cold war context. Given the attributes that the members of the Jiang leadership share generally, given the political context they inherit, and barring dramatic changes in the international context they must address, the probability is high that they will continue these approaches as the general framework of Chinese foreign and security policies.

In a number of significant ways, however, Jiang Zemin has moved beyond Deng Xiaoping, introducing new themes and emphases to Beijing's foreign policy since Deng's death in February 1997. All of these themes are extensions or shadings of the framework set down by Deng, not clear departures from it. On every appropriate authoritative occasion, Jiang and other leaders have repeatedly and firmly declared continuity with the premises and goals of the Deng approach.[17] The new themes and emphases appear to constitute Jiang's attempt to elaborate his own vision for a post-Deng foreign policy in a changing post–cold war, "cross-century" world order and thereby give China's foreign relations his own stamp.[18] Jiang's initiatives in this regard are evident in several broad areas:

— Beijing now routinely stresses the responsibilities of the "great powers" (*daguo*) in shaping a stable international order for the next century. Beijing continues to voice its long-standing call, first expounded by Deng Xiaoping in 1988, for a "new international political and economic order," but since 1997 it has also begun to call on the most powerful capitals to establish strategic partnerships that embody a new type of relationship based on interest, consensus seeking, cooperation, and shared long-term commitments to stability in the international system. In contrast to the great power and superpower relationships of the cold war era, however, the emerging new type of relationship is not an alliance that presumes confrontation against third parties. Beijing itself pioneered such new partnerships with Moscow and Paris in 1997, and then with Washington later the same year. Since then others have emerged amid the pattern of accelerating bilateral summits among the powers. Beijing's list of great powers now includes the United States, the European Union, Russia, Japan, and, of course, China, and it adds Brazil, India, and the nations comprising the Association of Southeast Asian Nations (ASEAN) as emerging candidate great powers. But Beijing views the relationships among the United States, Russia, and China as the most critical.[19]

— The emerging strategic partnerships among great powers, Beijing predicts, will help consolidate an international order for the twenty-first century based on a "new security concept" shared by all states in the international system to replace the "outmoded" cold war mentality of power politics. This new security concept is based on the recognition that security in the post–cold war world will rest not simply on unalloyed calculations of military power, but also on broader political, economic, and technological foundations. The new security architecture, Beijing argues, should incorporate state-to-state relations based on the "five principles of peaceful coexistence" first articulated among China, India, and Burma in 1954—territorial integrity and sovereignty, mutual nonaggression, noninterference in internal affairs, equality and mutual benefit, and peaceful coexistence—as well as recognition and promotion of mutual interdependence in economic ties and a commitment to resolving problems and disputes through multilateral consultations and dialogue.[20]

— Since the summer of 1998, beginning with Jiang Zemin's keynote speech to the eighth conference of diplomatic envoys, Beijing has stressed the importance of "economic globalization" as a central and enduring feature of the emerging twenty-first-century world order. In step with this, and prompted in part by the financial crises in Asia,

Russia, and Brazil, Beijing has called for multilateral steps by the economic powers in particular, premised on free market principles, to provide for "economic security" within an increasingly interdependent world of national and regional economies interlocked by computerized capital flows, rapidly shifting exchange rates, and diversified trade balances.[21] The Jiang leadership's appreciation of globalization trends also reinforces its decision to press for entry into the WTO.

— Since 1997 Jiang has taken considerably farther the defense modernization effort begun under Deng Xiaoping. Jiang and PLA leaders now routinely refer to an emerging revolution in military affairs. Jiang is personally credited with leading the way toward the establishment of a "new defense mechanism" that enhances collaboration between the PLA and China's scientific and technical community and brings about "greater compatibility between military and civilian products and greater convertibility between peacetime and wartime production," points developed in the chapter of this book by Tai Ming Cheung. In line with these priorities, Jiang called for a further reduction in PLA force levels by half a million at the Fifteenth Party Congress in September 1997, announced the creation of a new "General Armament Department," began the reconfiguration of defense industries in April 1998, launched a drive to divest the PLA of commercial sideline enterprises the following summer, and thereafter pursued an antismuggling campaign directed at activities in which some PLA units were deeply involved.[22]

These new themes and emphases also coincide with Jiang's effort since 1997 to take stronger hold of the foreign policy apparatus. With the retirement of Li Peng as premier in March 1998, Jiang took over the position of chairman of the party's Foreign Affairs Leading Small Group (FALSG), a position that would otherwise have gone by tradition to the new premier, Zhu Rongji.[23] Also at the March 1998 NPC session, Jiang's candidate Tang Jiaxuan succeeded Qian Qichen as foreign minister, not Li Peng's presumed candidate, State Council Foreign Affairs Office Director Liu Huaqiu. The FALSG now includes a roster of members sharing close working relationships with and personal ties to Jiang: Vice Premier Qian Qichen, Premier Zhu Rongji, Foreign Minister Tang Jiaxuan, former Ministry of Foreign Economic Relations and Trade Minister Wu Yi, Defense Minister Chi Haotian, and Minister of State Security Xu Yongyao. In addition, as discussed in the Swaine chapter, Jiang continues to head the party's Taiwan Affairs Leading Small Group, directing Taiwan policy together with Qian Qichen and Wang Daohan. Finally, a reconfiguration of the foreign policy coordinating apparatus has taken place, as reflected by the creation of the Central Committee Foreign Affairs Office, which is attached to the Foreign Affairs Leading Small Group and has taken over the administrative and coordination functions of the State Council Foreign Affairs Office.[24]

Also emerging under Jiang's aegis is an apparent provision for freer public debate of foreign policy issues within a controlled framework, a step of startling freshness given the penchant of both the Mao and Deng periods for nearly complete secrecy in foreign policy deliberations. The most prominent manifestation of this new openness is the emergence of a growing public literature on foreign policy problems that airs explicitly competing policies and frameworks. The book that has caught the greatest attention outside China, though not written by foreign affairs specialists, is the highly sensational, nationalistic, anti-U.S. polemic *China Can Say No: Political and Emotional Choices in the Post–Cold War Era,* which calls on China to stand up to American pressures.[25]

More directly significant in policy terms, however, are several other recent books by specialists in the foreign affairs apparatus. The panoramic survey *China's Rise: An Assessment of the International Environment,* written by China Institute for Contemporary International Relations (CICIR) Foreign Policy Research Center Director Yan Xuetong and others, offers a broad geopolitical and historical analysis of the implications of China's rise from a thoroughly realist perspective. Yan, who studied political science and international relations theory as a graduate student at Berkeley, also offered a comparable assessment in his *Analysis of China's National Interest.*[26]

Another CICIR specialist, North America Research Office Deputy Director Xi Laiwang, published a comparably realist assessment, *The Grand Plan of China's 21st Century Strategy,* that countered the popular *China Can Say No* by advising that, although China has historically said no to both of the world's superpowers in the past and of course can say no to the United States in the future as an expression of China's independence and growing international standing, Beijing cannot simply say only no; it must also manage China's interests realistically in an international order in which the United States remains a world power.[27]

The most policy-relevant book, however, may be Shen Jiru's *China Should Not Be "Mr. No": Issues in Contemporary China's International Strategy,* published in 1998 as part of the "China's Problems" series. "In a world in which the economic interdependence of various countries is increasing and their cultural exchanges are proliferating, erecting barriers and sealing off the country to defend oneself is absolutely impractical," Shen declared. China cannot pursue "a narrow nationalistic strategy of noncooperation with others that is based on a string of 'nos.'" Sounding themes consonant with those associated with Jiang, Shen argues that the great powers and large country blocs like the European Union share responsibility in shaping the emerging multipolar world. China should not make the mistake of the former Soviet Union in contesting the United States for world hegemony, a choice that distorted both Moscow's foreign and domestic policies and that led to Soviet ruin. Instead, Beijing should seek a constructive partnership with Washington based on the interests in stability they share and that "helps America bid farewell to its past and create a new era without hegemonism and hegemonic powers." The most dangerous "adverse current" against prevailing world trends in favor of cooperative multipolarity is not the United States, but Japan's latent militarism. "The Japanese government over and over says it seeks to strengthen Sino-Japanese friendship, however its actions are contrary," Shen states, adding that "the historical lesson of World War II is that appeasement abetted the aggressive ambitions of Nazi Germany and Japanese militarism," enjoining "vigilance" in the present circumstance.

As all books in the "China's Problems" series do, Shen's book carries a preface by then–Academy of Social Sciences Vice President Liu Ji, whom Jiang moved up into the central propaganda apparatus in 1995 from his position in the Shanghai CCP Committee propaganda office. A part of Shen's book was published as the first chapter of the sweeping survey of the issues post-Deng China confronts, *A Crucial Moment,* whose title is taken from a landmark speech by Jiang Zemin. Both in his preface to his own book and in his chapter in *A Crucial Moment,* Shen states that Liu Ji's invitation to write a book on China's international strategy counts as "a big step forward in freedom of speech and political democratization in China," because discussion of this topic had previously been limited to internal (*neibu*) channels. But the particular themes Shen stresses are largely congruent with those pressed by Jiang since 1997.[28]

Taken together, these several steps underscore and bear out the foreign policy predilections of the Jiang leadership derived from the analysis of their shared attributes. These include an abiding internationalist and system-sustaining commitment to activism in the international system, an enduring realist sense of international politics tempered by an increasingly clear-cut appreciation of

interdependence and the role of multilateralism, and a technocratic understanding of the changing criteria of national security. The toleration of public expositions of alternative foreign policy strategies is consonant with a
policy-making style of building consensus through institutional channels. In
all of these respects they build on but move beyond the outlook of Deng Xiaoping and his generation of leadership.

From a longer-term perspective they also underscore trends in the evolution of PRC foreign policy. First, the eclipse of Marxist-Leninist ideology as
a factor relevant to PRC foreign policy seems almost complete and has given
way to considerations of national interest. This evolution has been apparent
in the authoritative explications of foreign policy at successive party congresses.
At the Ninth Congress in 1969 Lin Biao declared that Chinese foreign policy
is based on Marxism-Leninism–Mao Zedong Thought and on proletarian internationalism; at the Twelfth Congress in 1982 Hu Yaobang declared that
PRC foreign policy is "based on the scientific theories of Marxism-Leninism
and Mao Zedong Thought" and "proceeds from the fundamental interests of
the Chinese people and the rest of the world"; at the Fifteenth Congress Jiang
Zemin stated that PRC foreign policy is formulated on the basis of "the fundamental interests of the people of China and other countries" and made no
reference at all to Marxist-Leninist principle. This evolution, as the preceding party congress citations attest, has been gradual. The great watershed in
Beijing's international outlook, of course, came in 1971, when China joined
the United Nations and so became a fully sovereign legitimate member of the
international political order for the first time since the Opium War. As a consequence of this evolution Beijing could pursue its international agenda of
security, national reunification, and development using the full panoply of
diplomatic, economic, and state-to-state instruments and, gradually, with access
to the international economic system. In step with that watershed change, Beijing rapidly dropped its previous revolutionary class-based foreign policy
vocabulary in favor of a nation-state-based lexicon that increasingly focused
on issues of "interest" rather than revolutionary principle.[29]

Second, in place of this ideological component and paralleling a profound reembracement of China's past after sixty years of May 4 cultural
iconoclasm, there has emerged a "wealth and power" nationalism (described
in the chapter by Joseph Fewsmith and Stanley Rosen) that in foreign relations discourse expresses an increasingly modernist appreciation of China's cultural traditions as a basis for Beijing's interactions with the world. Although
neither Qian Qichen nor Jiang Zemin has cited Marx, Engels, Lenin, Stalin,

or Mao in presentations of PRC foreign policy to the United Nations in the 1990s, they have several times referred to adages of Confucius and other sources of Chinese tradition.[30] Similarly, in his speech at Harvard University during his October 1997 tour of the United States, Jiang explicated at length the relevance of Chinese tradition to contemporary China's foreign policy principles. In his speech to the December 1997 informal ASEAN summit in Kuala Lumpur he suggested that East Asian peoples generally share cultural traditions that value the virtues of "self-respect and self-strengthening, arduous effort, industriousness, frugality, modesty and eagerness to learn" as well as "harmony in human relations and peaceful coexistence in international relations."[31]

Third, the consolidation of the central coordinating position of the Ministry of Foreign Affairs (MFA) and its long-term, steady ascent to preeminence at the expense of other bureaucracies related to foreign policy and national security has been challenged by the growing stature of other institutions as the diversity and complexity of China's foreign relations have grown. In the 1950s and 1960s the MFA's role was blunted by the fact that Beijing enjoyed formal diplomatic relations with only about forty capitals, a small minority of the capitals in the international system, most of them either bloc allies or Third World states in Asia and Africa. Bloc relations were handled through party channels, giving prominence to the Party Central Committee's International Liaison Department (ILD). In step with the wave of diplomatic recognitions after 1970, the role of the ministry grew, and the ILD took on a steadily declining, complementary role. During the same period the international contacts of the PLA and the Ministry of Foreign Trade and Economic Cooperation in its various incarnations also grew, but mostly in step with the elaboration of official ties managed through the MFA. As the foreign interactions among the PRC's economic, military, provincial, and other institutions have since multiplied, however, the MFA's central coordinating role appears to have been overrun, as several chapters in this volume suggest.

Looking ahead, perhaps at the party's Sixteenth Congress slated for 2002, another generational turnover may begin, in which the present "third-generation" leadership gives way to a "fourth generation." If present indications hold, the transition is likely to be managed in favor of extending the trends that have built on the framework set down by Deng Xiaoping and that have been extended and shaped by Jiang Zemin. The designation of Hu Jintao as PRC vice president at the Ninth NPC in March 1998 both confirmed his unofficial designation as Jiang's successor and provided Hu with increased visibility in the international arena. His public appearances in receiving international visitors and representing Beijing abroad have expanded since his appointment, although he has yet to travel to the United States. Although it is far too early to predict his smooth succession as China's paramount leader, it seems likely that fourth-generation leaders, whoever they may be, will use Jiang's foreign policy preferences as points of departure, modified by their own proclivities, the successes of their domestic policies, and the international environment with which they must deal.

SIX

The Domestic Context of Chinese Foreign Policy: Does "Public Opinion" Matter?

JOSEPH FEWSMITH AND STANLEY ROSEN

Discussions of Chinese foreign policy decisions rarely take into account in more than a cursory fashion the domestic context in which those decisions are made, yet that context is important for understanding China's foreign policy. Thomas Christensen's recent book argues that domestic factors were central to Mao's decision to inaugurate the second Taiwan Strait crisis in 1958.[1] Previous studies of Sino-Soviet and Sino-U.S. relations have likewise seen the domestic context, albeit in the more limited sense of elite conflict, as important in realigning China's foreign relations.[2] Moreover, it is important to recognize that the international environment China faces, and particularly the leadership's evaluation of that environment, has an important impact on its domestic politics, which in turn influences its foreign policy.[3]

As compared to that of the Maoist era, the domestic context of Chinese foreign policy in recent years has become both more important and more complex, as the chapters in this volume by David Lampton, Margaret Pearson, and Peter Cheung and James Tang amply demonstrate. These chapters show that as China's relations with the world have become more extensive and more domestic interests have been affected by that interaction, the number of voices trying to influence policy has grown. As Lu Ning's chapter shows, as the number of bureaucratic interests involved in formulating foreign policy has also grown, so the points of access—for both domestic and foreign interests—have multiplied. A case can be made that public opinion, as that term is usually understood, has begun to play a role, albeit one that remains restricted and significant only under certain conditions, a point Margaret Pearson makes in her analysis of China's efforts to join the General Agreement on Tariffs and Trade / World Trade Organization (GATT/WTO).

The task of this chapter is to better define the context in which foreign policy decisions are made. It traces some of the changes in that arena in the reform period and suggests the ways in which the broad domestic context either coincides with or differs from the preferred views of the foreign policy "establishment."

In thinking about the ways in which the domestic context or "public opinion" affects the content and conduct of Chinese foreign policy, it is useful to distinguish three levels of opinion—elite, subelite, and popular—only the last of which resembles public opinion as that term is generally used in the West. At the elite level there are two dimensions that are relevant. First, there are inevitably differences of opinion among elite political actors. In the reform era differences in political opinion are usually seen as spanning from "conservatives," who seek to uphold the ideological, economic, and social orientations associated with traditional socialism, to "liberals," who believe that the system has to open up more either economically or politically or both. In between are "moderates," who try to bridge these differences, hoping to open up enough to invigorate the system but not so much as to threaten its fundamentals. Although there are differences of opinion within each of these three broad levels of opinion, and the "center of gravity" of the system shifts to the "left" or "right" over time (with the general tendency over the past two decades being to the right), the continued existence of political cleavages among the elite has been one of the constants of elite politics. Such differences mean that the preferences of the supreme leader (Deng Xiaoping for most of the reform era and Jiang Zemin in recent years) are subject to challenge and negotiation. Indeed, as will be argued below, elite conflict is one of the ways in which "public opinion" gets injected into the policy-making process.

Second, over time there has been a "thickening" of the elite, as Lampton's introduction to this volume explains. In the Maoist era, at least with regard to foreign policy, the elite stratum was a very thin one, consisting of Mao, Zhou Enlai, and a remarkably small number of other officials.[4] Although Deng Xiaoping continued to dominate the making of foreign policy until his death, a rather large and diverse "foreign policy establishment" has grown up over the past two decades. The content and conduct of Chinese foreign policy today are far more complex and detailed than previously, and as China has become involved in an increasing number of international organizations requiring greater expertise, it has developed a new generation of foreign policy specialists who are far more knowledgeable of the outside world and of specific issue areas than were their counterparts in the past.[5] This development is well detailed in this volume by Bates Gill with regard to arms control and by Elizabeth Economy with regard to environmental policy.

Whereas in the past foreign policy decision-making tended to revolve around the great issues of strategic alliances and of war and peace, today foreign policy also includes a vast array of issues, often quite technical in nature, ranging from global warming to international trade regimes to weapons proliferation. There is an important difference between a China that is trying to develop nuclear weapons in order to have a credible retaliatory capability and one that is engaged in serious international negotiations regarding the size, capabilities, and deployment of nuclear forces. The latter requires a familiarity with and participation in the development of international norms and concepts that are simply not necessary for the former. Similarly, as trade and international finance have taken on greater importance in China's foreign policy, trade expertise has become increasingly important, and the changing composition of China's foreign policy elite reflects this trend, a point H. Lyman Miller and Liu Xiaohong make in their chapter. An issue such as whether or not to join the WTO is not simply an issue of deciding whether or not to have better relations with the United States and other Western countries (although that is involved), but also of determining, on an issue-by-issue basis, the terms for such relations. The need for specific expertise in addition to strategic judgments is apparent.

Below the top policy-making level one can distinguish a stratum of subelites who might best be defined as "public intellectuals," people who take part in public discourse and try to influence informed public opinion and government policy on a range of issues. Such intellectuals exist across a broad range of fields, including economics, politics, and culture. The growing importance of this stratum is suggested by a request of the Foreign Affairs Leading Small Group in 1998 for a list of important academics in order to broaden the range of thinking available to the leadership. It is also suggested by President Jiang Zemin's assembly of a group of about twenty-five former ambassadors to advise him on foreign policy.[6] Whether or not the policy advice of these individuals is accepted by the government, they participate in a public discourse that is part of the domestic context in which foreign policy decisions are made. Moreover, although foreign policy is often thought of as an arena insulated from other areas, we would argue that there is a constant interchange between foreign policy specialists and specialists in other areas of intellectual inquiry. Sometimes the inputs of these different areas are mutually reinforcing, whereas at other times there is tension between them. In either case, the importance of this "public arena" has increased during the reform era, though its influence remains limited.

The boundaries of this subelite are difficult to define. On the one hand there are a number of influential intellectuals who are close to the government (indeed, part of it, since many think tanks are government organs), whose views are sometimes sought by officials, and who direct their views upward, to the policy elite. In some cases, such as economics, it might be difficult to draw a clear boundary between the policy elite and the subelite. On the other hand there are other intellectuals who deliberately write for a broader audience. Such individuals appeal to the public and often position themselves as articulators of public opinion. In this case it becomes difficult to draw a clear line between the subelite and the broader public. In between, of course, are those intellectuals who write primarily for each other. But such activity is not without policy ramifications. Such subelites are part of a broad policy community, and influencing the discourse of that community can be important.

Although we normally think of the subelite as composed of individuals, important interests, such as enterprises, can also be thought of as existing at this level—outside of the policy-making elite, but above the general public. Particularly in a period of rapid economic change and globalization, enterprises try to defend their interests by influencing policy, as Pearson describes in her chapter. As we argue later, economic interests come into play when international economic issues are at hand, as when foreign capital is acquiring significant interests in China and when issues related to the WTO come up. Again, the boundaries of this group can be vague. Some enterprises can be seen as almost part of the government, whereas the views of other enterprises may diverge substantially from those of the government because they ally themselves with their workers' interests.

Finally, we can look at public opinion more or less as that term is understood in the West, namely, as what the public thinks about various policy issues, including foreign affairs. It should be noted at the outset that China is not a democracy and that public opinion does not have much direct impact on policy, particularly in the area of foreign policy. Nevertheless, public attitudes are worth inquiring about for several reasons. First, it could be argued that public opinion has become more important in recent years. Certainly the Chinese government expends a great deal of effort commissioning opinion polls to allow it to understand better what the public thinks.[7] Mostly, of course, the government cares about public opinion because it is concerned with political stability, suggesting that the role of public opinion is mostly a negative one. Nevertheless, the effort the government puts into understanding public opinion suggests that the role of public opinion is somewhat broader. For instance, Premier Zhu Rongji and other leaders are regular watchers of television shows such as *Focus Interview*, which report on abuses by local officials and sometimes touch on foreign affairs. Many leaders read controversial best-sellers to understand the public mood.[8]

Moreover, as will be argued further below, public opinion is relevant to the extent that elites or subelites can mobilize broader support, often reported through internal channels or public opinion polls, to support their policy positions. For instance, in recent years conservatives have tried to position themselves as the protectors of the working class and have used workers' fear of layoffs to argue for a slower pace of economic reform. A recent instance in which public opinion may have affected specific policies was China's response to the Asian financial crisis. In 1998, as the impact of the crisis began to affect China more deeply, the government adopted new policies to expand domestic demand. These and related policies were based in part on fears that worker layoffs would lead to demonstrations and social disorder.[9] By the same token, there is ample evidence that China's domestic concerns have influenced Beijing's position on WTO entry, making it less willing to join the organization without protection against the forces of economic globalization. As these examples suggest, Chinese public opinion tends not to be effective as an independent force, but it can have an impact when joined with the concerns or interests of those higher in the system.

Having said this, it is nevertheless useful to consider what is known about Chinese public opinion, particularly on issues related to foreign policy. Since survey research was introduced into China in the late 1970s, it has moved far from its prior status in Maoist China as part of bourgeois social science.[10] Improvements in survey methodology have been accompanied by a corresponding expansion in the range of topics investigated. Most areas of domestic political, social, and economic life—with some notable exceptions—can now be investigated.[11] Questions relating to China's foreign relations, however, have always been politically sensitive. It was only in the late 1980s that it became possible for Chinese researchers to conduct surveys that asked about foreign countries, and even then they could do so only so long as the questions were relatively innocuous. One survey from that time, for example, solicited respondents' opinions on South Korea, which had been chosen to host the 1988 Olympics.[12] A recently published compendium of surveys conducted in China over the past few years contained one whole section entitled "How Chinese People See the World." The editors compared the situation a decade ago, when the expression *foreign country* (*waiguo*) was as mysterious to ordinary Chinese as the moon (*yueliang*), with the current situation, in which there is a substantial flow of goods and people in and out of China daily.[13]

But whether contact with the West has been less (as in the 1980s) or more (as now), the authorities have had reason to regard surveys that touch on foreign relations with caution. In the 1980s, as Chinese students were being introduced to intellectual concepts from the West for the first time, widespread suspicion, documented in surveys, began to develop concerning some of the core collectivist values of the regime.[14] Such suspicion extended to the Chinese media and the government's conduct of foreign policy. Traveling to university campuses in eastern China in the mid-1980s, Rosen was frequently accosted by groups of students asking for reliable information on the outside world. Was it true that China was selling arms to Iran and Iraq? Was it true that China secretly supported apartheid in South Africa? This suspicion of their own government was often accompanied by an almost reflexive trust in Western reporting from the Voice of America (VOA) and the British Broadcasting Corporation. In that era of student unrest—with major demonstrations in 1985, 1986, and of course 1989—the number of people listening to such foreign media broadcasts increased dramatically. One Chinese public opinion specialist has cited unpublished surveys to demonstrate this phenomenon. One found that 13 percent of China's university students regularly listened to the VOA before the 1986 student demonstrations, but the number jumped to 30 percent during the demonstrations. Although about 70 percent believed the VOA reporting, 75 percent distrusted the official Chinese media.[15] This attitude toward the West and the foreign media, as we shall see below, changed dramatically in the 1990s.

So what do Chinese citizens know of the outside world? Survey research suggests that most Chinese, like citizens in other countries, simply lack

TABLE 6.1
CHINESE CITIZENS' RECOGNITION OF
INTERNATIONAL ORGANIZATIONS, 1995

International organization	No response	Heard of it, but don't know what it does	Heard of it, know what it does	Haven't heard of it
Security Council	0.2	37	50	12.9
World Trade Organization	0.2	37	42.8	20.1
European Community	0.4	42.6	43.8	13.2
Asia Pacific Economic Cooperation Council	0.6	41.3	30.1	28
Nonaligned movement	0.6	39.3	31	29.1
United Nations	0.4	21.1	74.3	4.2
Association of Southeast Asian Nations	0.6	43.4	25	31
North Atlantic Treaty Organization	0.5	38.4	35.4	25.6
International Olympic Committee	0.2	17.7	76.4	5.7
World Bank	0.3	31.6	49	19.1

Source: *Guancha Zhongguo*, p. 45.
N = 1,050, values in percent.

knowledge of or interest in foreign affairs. One extensive survey conducted from March to May 1995 in five major Chinese cities examined knowledge of and views about the outside world.[16] One question asked respondents to identify various international organizations. The results can be seen in Table 6.1. In only two cases—the International Olympic Committee and the United Nations—did more than 50 percent of respondents claim to know the function of the organization.

Another study, conducted among 1,000 students at twenty universities in Beijing, asked respondents to name the ten most newsworthy individuals and the ten news reports to which they paid most attention in 1997. The results suggest that international popular culture has made serious inroads into China. Among the individuals chosen, the first three were Chinese (Deng Xiaoping, Jiang Zemin, and Hong Kong's Tung Chee-hwa), but fourth place— chosen on 78.27 percent of the ballots—went to Princess Diana. The next six choices were also foreigners—Diana managed to triumph over Bill Clinton, Kofi Annan, Hun Sen, Tony Blair, Boris Yeltsin, and Benjamin Netanyahu.

In terms of news events, again the first three choices were "China-related" (the reversion of Hong Kong, Deng Xiaoping's death, and the Fifteenth Party Congress), but Princess Diana's death was fourth. Indeed, her death was chosen by 77.32 percent of respondents, far ahead of the fifth choice, Jiang Zemin's trip to the United States (47.48 percent). The Asian financial crisis (29.71 percent) and the qualifying matches for the Soccer World Cup (27.48 percent) drew roughly the same amount of interest from the university students.[17]

NATIONALISM AND ITS DIMENSIONS

One of the most important ways in which public opinion has been expressed is through nationalism. Although Chinese nationalism has attracted a great deal of attention in recent years, it is hardly new. In fact, nationalism has been one of the basic *leitmotifs* of twentieth-century China, undergirding the Revolution of 1911, the May 4 Movement of 1919, the reorganization of the Guomindang in 1924, and the communist revolution.[18] It has received renewed attention in recent years, however, because as Marxism-Leninism has faded as a legitimizing rubric, nationalism has emerged as the major pillar supporting the government. In addition, heated expressions of nationalistic feeling—such as that which erupted following the bombing of the Chinese embassy in Belgrade—have caught the outside world by surprise, thus drawing attention to contemporary manifestations of this modern political phenomenon.[19]

The expression of nationalistic feelings in the 1990s should be seen neither as something new nor as simply a retreading of old ideas, but rather as a transformation of previously existing emotions. Indeed, it could be argued that nationalism was one of the primary forces behind the inauguration of reform in the late 1970s. Deng and his colleagues regarded the twenty years in which Mao's revolutionary romanticism had gotten the better of him, leading first to the Great Leap Forward and then to the Cultural Revolution, as a "waste" that had diverted China from its century-old goal of attaining "wealth and power." In the 1980s, as China turned from Maoist nativism, there was a natural turn toward the outside, as Deng rallied support around the goal of the "four modernizations" through "reform and opening up." The leadership, and even more so the intellectuals, looked to the West for models, whether in economics, culture, or increasingly politics. This outward orientation, however, did not mean that China was not nationalistic.

A closer look at nationalism in the 1980s suggests the need to disaggregate emotional responses to the outside world. The dominant trend, exemplified by Deng Xiaoping, fit very well within China's century-old tradition of "self-strengthening," the notion that China could absorb what is useful from the outside world while rejecting what it deemed harmful. In Deng's colorful metaphor, it is a matter of opening the windows but putting up screens to keep the flies out.[20] At the subelite level, however, as China's intellectuals were exposed to Western ideas and became increasingly critical of China's own tradition, they went beyond the self-strengthening tradition to carry out a real "cultural revolution." The mood was well captured by Gan Yang's paean to cosmopolitanism and cultural renovation: "China must enter the world, so naturally its culture must also enter the world; China must modernize, so naturally we must realize the 'modernization of Chinese culture'—this is the common faith of every person of foresight in the 1980s, this is the logical necessity of the great historical take-off of contemporary China."[21]

This "cultural fever" culminated in the 1988 television series *River Elegy*. In this series the dry, arid, exhausted soil—and culture—of the northwest (the cradle of Chinese civilization) was contrasted with the fertility, dynamism, and openness of the blue sea. If China hopes to revitalize its ancient civilization, the program suggested, it must look to the outside world, and particularly to the West. The outward orientation of the series, however, did not mean it was not nationalistic. On the contrary, it betrayed its nationalism with such questions as "Why did China fail to maintain the *great lead it used to have?* Why did China fail to maintain its *cultural and political domination* over the world?"[22] As Jing Wang comments: "The modern elite are, after all, dreaming the same dream as their forebears of the dynastic past: wealth, power, and hegemony."[23] *River Elegy*, like other efforts to renovate China's culture, was clearly rooted in a nationalistic response to China's problems, but a nationalism that was cosmopolitan in its orientation, one that aspired to remake China in the image of the outside world.[24]

If the dominant impulses of the 1980s were Deng's self-strengthening and the cultural elites' cosmopolitanism, the type of nationalist expression in the 1990s has been significantly different—leading to the greater notice that nationalism has attracted. First and foremost, the trauma of Tiananmen, followed in close order by the collapse of socialism in Eastern Europe and the disintegration of the Soviet Union, brought a resurgence of the sort of "leftist" thinking associated with such ideologically orthodox Marxists as Hu Qiaomu (Mao's former secretary, who died in 1992) and Deng Liqun (former head of the Propaganda Department). Drawing on nativist impulses, such leftists (now referred to as the "Old Left" to distinguish them from a younger group of intellectuals, known as the "New Left," who share nativist tendencies but not Marxism-Leninism) view the situation of the world not only as highly conflictual but as having direct ramifications for the domestic order of China, and vice versa: if socialism (as understood by such people) cannot be maintained domestically (that is, if political power is not in the hands of the "working class"), it can hardly prevail internationally. Therefore, state security (and ideological purity) is rooted in the preservation of the socialist system, including public ownership of industry and Marxist ideology.

It is often argued that the influence of this "Old Left" is much diminished, yet as the publication of *Crossed Swords* makes clear, it continued to be a potent political force at least up until the Fifteenth Party Congress of 1997, and perhaps enjoyed a resurgence following the bombing of the Chinese embassy in Belgrade in May 1999.[25] There are at least five reasons for this. First, the old guard draws much of its strength from people who have spent their careers in the propaganda system. In a political system that still bases its legitimacy, at least formally, on Marxism-Leninism, few can wield the symbolic language of that system as well as the Old Left. Second, because many of these people are first-generation revolutionaries—"old cadres" who have devoted their lives to "building socialism"—they have credentials and status that are hard to dismiss. Third, much of China's bureaucracy has an interest in maintaining a more orthodox understanding of Marxism-Leninism. This is true not only of the propaganda *xitong* (system), but also of much of the economic *xitong*. Bureaucracies can use the vocabulary of Marxism-Leninism to justify their continued importance: upholding the "leading position" of state-owned industry continues to be invoked, even as that sector of the economy fails. Fourth, reform and opening up have brought about competition threatening various interests; the latter find at least some of the rhetoric of the left appealing, or at least useful. Finally, the left's critique of income inequality, corruption, declining moral values, privatization (often seen as connected with corruption), and the influx of foreign capital has stirred a sympathetic response in the broader public, which resents corruption, fears for its jobs, and yearns for (and romanticizes) the "good old days" before reform, when people were said to have had ideals and to have cared for one another.

If Tiananmen and the subsequent tension in Sino-U.S. relations resuscitated the Old Left, other changes have altered the intellectual atmosphere in China as well. One is the broad disillusionment with the West in recent years.

In part, as Suisheng Zhao comments, the "demythification" that took hold in the post-Tiananmen period was, ironically, the product of wider and more frequent exchanges with the United States. As intellectuals have come to know the United States better, they have acquired the knowledge and the boldness to become more critical.[26] As discussed below, they also learned post-modernist and other cutting-edge critiques of capitalism.

The resulting view of the West has been reflected in public opinion surveys conducted by the *China Youth Daily*, which has been conducting investigations of youth attitudes since the mid-1990s.[27] Taking advantage of the fiftieth anniversary of the end of the war against Japan, *China Youth Daily* conducted a large-scale public opinion poll in May 1995, which found that 87.1 percent of respondents believed that the United States was the country "least friendly" to China, whereas 57.2 percent responded that the United States was the country toward which they felt most negative. Reflecting cynicism about American motives, 85.4 percent responded that they believed that the United States engaged in the Gulf War "out of its own interests."[28]

A concluding essay argued that the nationalism reflected in the survey showed that China "still has hope." Setting the results of the survey against recent discussions of globalization, the author (or authors) declared—in the best realist tradition—that the world was still divided into nation-states and that the dividing line separating nation-states was far stronger than any other, including—with reference to Samuel Huntington—culture. There was, however, the article concluded, one division that did not fall neatly into the realist paradigm, namely that between the haves and the have-nots. The West, the article explained, is guided by self-interest and fears not only that the rest of the world is too poor, which could trigger a wave of immigration, but also that the rest of the world is too prosperous, which could "threaten their [the West's] superiority." Those in the "have-not" camp, the article asserted, "love our camp, love our China."[29]

Although there were obvious methodological problems in the way this widely cited survey was conducted, the basic trends reported appear to have reflected reality.[30] Indeed, another survey taken in the summer and fall of 1999—another politically sensitive time, coming only months after the U.S. bombing of the Chinese embassy—revealed that the United States still had the highest negative rating of any country. This survey, taken among 1,589 junior and senior high students in Beijing, Shanghai, Guangzhou, Foshan, Suzhou, and Baoding, combined favorable and unfavorable rankings of different countries to derive an overall rank order. The United States came in fourth in terms of favorable ratings (trailing France, Singapore, and Japan), but easily ranked first in terms of unfavorable ratings. Combining the scores, the United States came out as the country with the highest unfavorable rating, followed by Japan and Vietnam.[31]

It should be noted that the United States was not the only target of popular Chinese opprobrium. One survey of attitudes toward Japan, conducted at the end of 1996, surprised even the surveyors. For example, the word *Japan* "most easily" made 83.9 percent of the youth surveyed think of the Nanjing Massacre and made 81.3 percent think of "Japanese denial" and the "war of resistance against Japanese aggression." When asked which Japanese person in the twentieth century is most representative of Japan, first place (28.7 percent) went to Tojo Hideki, of World War II fame. When asked to place a label on the Japanese, 56.1 percent chose "cruel."[32] In the 1999 survey, as just noted, Japan scored second highest in unfavorable ratings, and in follow-up seminars some of the negative statements about Japan referred to its previous invasion of China, hegemonist ambitions (*baquan yexin*), and discrimination against Chinese people.[33]

This "national memory," as the surveyors put it, raises potentially serious issues for the Chinese leadership. Indeed, the gap between the government's Japan policy and the views of Chinese youth is particularly wide and has been manifest on several occasions, including the September 1985 student demonstrations in Beijing and, more recently, the protests over the occupation of the disputed Diaoyu (Senkaku) Islands. There have been widespread reports of government efforts to curb student attempts to organize public protests against Japan. In one well-publicized case the government moved to control computer communications after one message on a "bulletin board" called for protests at the Japanese embassy in Beijing.[34] In addition, the State Education Commission reportedly issued an internal document stating that Jiang Zemin had ordered university officials in Beijing and Shanghai to prevent students from staging protests over the Diaoyu Islands issue. Jiang was quoted as being appreciative of the patriotism of the students, but arguing that maintaining stability and unity was among the most important tasks of the government and suggesting that the dispute would be better handled through diplomatic channels.[35]

Public dissatisfaction two years later had, if anything, gotten worse. According to a Hong Kong source, a poll conducted by the Chinese Academy of Social Sciences and the Communist Youth League, and reported by the State Council Policy Research Office not long before Jiang Zemin's November 1998 visit to Japan, revealed that 82 percent of mainland citizens are opposed to the government's policy toward Japan, noting that the government has departed from principle on such issues as the Diaoyu Islands' sovereignty, Japan's compensation for its aggression against China, and the Japanese-U.S. Security Treaty.[36] Such widespread public feelings may have led Jiang to push for more concessions on his trip to Japan than Tokyo was willing to give and may have contributed to the sense that the summit meeting was less than successful.[37]

It was in this same political atmosphere that *China Can Say No* was published. Written by five young authors, *China Can Say No* reflected a broadening of mass culture (discussed below) as well as the bubbling up of nationalist feeling. The book was striking not only because of its highly emotional tone, but also because the authors all claimed to have been strongly influenced by the United States, only to have become disillusioned with it in the 1990s. They cited American efforts to block China's bid to host the 2000 Olympics, the *Yinhe* incident, protracted and seemingly onerous negotiations over China's GATT/WTO bid, the Taiwan issue (especially Lee Teng-hui's visit to the United States), American support for Tibet, and alleged Central Intelligence Agency activity in China to account for their changed attitudes.[38] They had come to realize, they claimed, that the United States was not the bastion of idealism that it claimed to be; "human rights" was merely a facade behind which Washington pursued its national interests. In fact, far from championing ideals in the world, the United States was an arrogant, narcissistic, hegemonic power that acted as a world policeman; now it was doing everything in its power to keep China from emerging as a powerful and wealthy country.[39] Although many intellectuals argued that the book was shallow, poorly written, and overly emotional, many read it and perhaps even enjoyed venting the frustrations they shared with the authors, albeit not necessarily to the same degree. The book quickly became a best-seller, selling perhaps as many as two million copies, and one survey showed it to be the most influential book in the period after 1993.[40] The authors quickly followed with a sequel,[41] and imitators sprouted up "like bamboo shoots after the rain."[42]

There was, however, another side to *China Can Say No* that was apparent to Chinese readers, but has gone largely unremarked in the United States, and that is that the populism of the book had a distinctly antigovernment edge to it as well. The authors charged that the Chinese government had been naive and soft in its dealings with the United States, that it should be more forthright in just saying no, and that the government was neither confident nor competent; it was too wrapped up in the past and not bold enough in engineering China's modernization.[43] Government officials may have welcomed such an expression of nationalism, but they also realized that the populism of books like *China Can Say No* could be turned against them, as it had been so many times in the twentieth century. In the wake of the embassy bombing in 1999 there was another spate of nationalistic publications, led by *China's Road under the Shadow of Globalization,* in which the same combination of nationalistic outrage and criticism of the Chinese government appears.[44]

Indeed, part of the post-Tiananmen turning away from the cosmopolitan orientation of the 1980s was a turn toward populism. For instance, Chinese neoconservatives have argued forcefully that the "liberal" intellectual currents prevalent prior to Tiananmen were in fact a form of self-abasement or "reverse racism" (*nixiang zhongzu zhuyi*) and indeed were fostered by the Chinese government because of policy needs. As Wang Xiaodong, using the pen name Shi Zhong, put it in an article that appeared in a leading Hong Kong journal because it was then too politically sensitive to be published at home, "China in the 1980s needed to open its doors quickly and take in all kinds of things from the West, including investment, technology, ideas and even forms of entertainment." Encouraging liberal intellectuals to criticize China, according to Wang, was therefore part of an elite strategy designed to prepare public opinion to support this opening to the West. Wang found the post-Tiananmen development of Chinese nationalism a "healthy" response to the distorted self-abasement of the previous decade. Openly critical of Westerners who are "very sensitive to and outspoken about what they claim is the Chinese government's use of nationalism to 'fill an ideological vacuum' in the 1990s," Wang argued that the Chinese government's control over public opinion "has already greatly weakened."[45]

If neoconservatives have rejected the cosmopolitan orientation of the 1980s as a sort of "reverse racism," others have turned inward, reviving an interest in Chinese history and culture. In the 1980s, as noted above, the dominant mood was to renovate Chinese culture. A decade later a major trend in intellectual circles has been to look to Chinese history and culture, hoping to recover values that are of use today. This trend has found a number of notable expressions, including the establishment of a Center for the Study of Traditional Culture at Beijing University, the publication of influential journals such as *Modernity and Tradition* and *National Studies Research,* and the growing influence of such overseas Chinese intellectuals as Yu Yingshi, Lin Yusheng, and Tu Wei-ming (all of whom are articulators of China's Confucian heritage).[46] Some intellectuals, speaking in ways that were in direct contrast with ways they had spoken in cultural discussions of the 1980s, began to talk about how Chinese civilization was necessary to save the world.[47]

Perhaps ironically, this turn toward tradition was accompanied by a growing acceptance of postmodernist discourse. As works by such influential scholars as Edward Said, Michel Foucault, and Fredric Jameson were introduced into China, there was a growing interest in and acceptance of postmodernism and deconstructionism. These concepts were used to develop a new "Chinese discourse" that rejected Western categories. As one commentator observed: "Although Western academic thought continued to be introduced in large amounts [in the 1990s], a considerable portion of what was introduced was non-mainstream Western critiques of mainstream thought; opposition to Western colonial hegemonism and cultural colonialism became a central focus attracting peoples' attention. Academic and cultural nativism was enthusiastically promoted by people and became a rather influential trend of thought."[48] The same trend was apparent in the turn away from neoclassical economics as some scholars tried to incorporate what they saw as the positive message of the communist revolution and Maoism with postindustrial critiques of the West.[49]

Such scholars, who are often referred to in China as the "New Left," are part of a broad-gauged effort to redefine China's national identity. Efforts to define China's national identity in terms distinct from Western categories of thought seem inevitable, but the turn away from the cosmopolitanism of the 1980s can lend itself to extreme nationalism, even xenophobia, even as the very absorption of postmodernist discourse reflects an international awareness.[50]

Still another response to Tiananmen has been to engage in introspection. Many intellectuals have concluded that their previous enthusiasms were precisely that: enthusiasms ungrounded in a sober assessment of reality. In the wake of Tiananmen intellectuals have come to see the task of reform as more complicated and longer term than they expected in the 1980s. Whereas reform was largely conceived in the 1980s as a moving away from the old Maoist system (in ideological, cultural, economic, and political terms), by the 1990s there was a greater sense of the problems that have emerged with the deepening of reform. If breaking up the old system seemed adequate in the 1980s, today the difficult task of building new structures preoccupies the thoughts of intellectuals. In this regard the models of the West are less beguiling. For instance, although democratic practices, institutions, and ideals continue to have appeal, there has been a movement away from democracy in the abstract and toward focused efforts to make at least limited democratic practices, such as village elections, work in the context of China's social and political reality.[51] The China of the 1990s is more interested in problems than in -isms.[52]

Along with these various intellectual responses to the West in post-Tiananmen China has come an important change in the status of intellectuals. The television series *River Elegy* can be seen as epitomizing an intellectual project of a cultural elite, one that conceives of itself as carrying on an intellectual and cultural mission of enlightenment, including science and democracy, that stems from the May 4 Movement. In contrast, the trend of the 1990s has been toward a commercialization and popularization that is inherently marginalizing of the elite. An important turning point in this regard was the television series *Yearnings,* which began broadcasting in November 1990. China's first domestically produced soap opera, *Yearnings* was put together hastily by a group of writers, including the respected authors Zheng Wanlong and Wang Shuo, in a self-conscious effort to create a commercial success, something that does not come naturally to Chinese intellectuals. Starting with stock characters—the kindly, filial daughter, the "sappy intellectual," the "shrew," and so forth—the scriptwriters added flesh and blood and created a television drama that drew huge audiences.[53] In her brilliant portrait of the contemporary intellectual scene, Jianying Zha quotes Li Xiaoming, the chief scriptwriter, as saying: "If you're a television writer, and you know that the majority of your Chinese audience had to save up for years to buy a TV set, then you'd better come to terms with them."[54] Commercialism had come to the Chinese intellectual scene, and it was a painful transition for many. Commercialism destroyed the "feeling that a writer is the beloved and needed spokesman of the people and the conscience of society."[55]

Finally, the opening of China has, particularly in the 1990s, brought in a massive influx of foreign investment associated with globalization, and the growth of international awareness and pop culture also threatens specific interests and provokes economic nationalism in response. For instance, starting in June 1996 China's leading economic newspaper, *Economic Daily,* ran a series of fifteen articles examining foreign pressures on China's national enterprises, a process that Thomas Moore and Dixia Yang in their chapter refer to as the "conditionality" of the international marketplace. As the commentator article that accompanied the opening article in the series reported, the role of foreign investment in China's economy was growing rapidly. Imported capital, it said, accounted for about 20 percent of all investment in fixed assets in China; foreign-invested enterprises (*sanzi qiye*) accounted for 39 percent of China's exports; and foreign trade equaled some 40 percent of domestic production, suggesting a high degree of dependence. Opening up to the outside world was good, the commentator said, "but looking across the various countries of the world, [one can see] that opening up definitely cannot be without certain principles and certain limits." It is important, the commentator concluded, to "pay attention to protecting national industries."[56]

The nationalistic tone of the articles was evident in a description of the refusal of Yanjing Beer to form a joint venture. The enterprise's decision was presented as not just an economic one, but a patriotic one. As Li Fucheng, general manager of the Yanjing Beer Enterprise Group, put it: "Would I let others eat me up? . . . Creating our own labels and developing national industries is our historical mission."[57] Other articles in the series discussed the difficulties facing Chinese brand names, how the United States, Japan, and France had protected their markets while their economies were growing, and how a well-known Shanghai cutlery business had refused foreign offers to form a joint venture.[58] A letter to the editor, featured on the front page, declared that the series in *Economic Daily* was doing "a great thing to protect [China's] national industries. There should have been this type of discussion long ago!"[59]

Indeed, the issue of "cultural colonialism" (*wenhua zhimin zhuyi*) has become a major theme in the Chinese press in items ranging from the type of economic nationalism just described to missives defending the honor of Chinese citizens against the encroachment of foreign privileges. For example, a recent discussion in the widely circulated Shanghai newspaper *New People's Evening News* was entitled "Chinese Are Not Inferior to Foreigners" and began with a letter to the editor as follows: "Shopping in the Baijia supermarket, customers with prominent noses and green eyes saunter in grandly with their bags and satchels, whereas yellow-skinned, black-haired customers with bags are refused entry." The author, an overseas Chinese living in the United States, described his humiliation when, traveling, he was told that, based on regulations from above, only foreigners were allowed to carry their bags into the store to shop. The letter evoked a visceral response in readers throughout China and led to a "demand that national self-respect be upheld." After a week of attacks from readers, Chinese lawyers, and managers of other supermarkets, the manager of the Baijia supermarket (a Chinese-foreign joint venture) apologized for what was considered a "misunderstanding" and a "mistake" by lower-level security personnel.[60]

These trends all stand in some tension with the foreign policy "establish-ment" that is institutionally charged with overseeing the conduct of China's foreign relations and that, as we suggested above, stands within China's self-strengthening tradition. Recognizing the inevitable diversity within this establishment, one can nevertheless hazard three broad generalizations that seem to characterize it. The first is that suspicions of and negative impressions about the United States are deeply imbedded. In a recent survey of Chinese perceptions of the United States, Wang Jisi, director of the Institute of American Studies at the Chinese Academy of Social Sciences (CASS), has presented a bleak picture of informed Chinese citizens holding uniformly negative views of the United States. As he put it, "No one of political weight in China would actually portray the United States as playing a generally con-structive role in maintaining world peace." He added that "the depth and inten-sity of China's elite and popular disenchantment with the United States is difficult to fathom" and emphasized that such perceptions "do make an impact on policymaking."[61]

The second generalization that one might make is that, despite such neg-ative views, the foreign policy establishment views the United States as the single most important issue with which it has to deal. Therefore, Wang and others note the importance of the United States in the contemporary world and that developing a better relationship with it is essential to the achieve-ment of China's economic and security goals. Similarly, Zhang Yunling, head of the Institute of Asia-Pacific Studies at CASS, has argued in his recent book on Sino-U.S.-Japanese relations that there are many sources of insta-bility in the region, including the belief that the real American policy is to contain China over the long run. Nevertheless, as he put it, although China does not like American policy, it has to cope with it. "If China and the U.S. become adversaries," Zhang wrote, "it will not only have serious conse-quences for those two countries but also for the entire world."[62]

Third, there has been an evolution in the way international relations are conceived among foreign policy specialists. Older analysts and national secu-rity specialists are influenced by Marxist-Leninist assumptions and tend to view both domestic and international politics as part of an overall class struggle. This does not by any means preclude their viewing the world in "realistic" terms (Leninists can be good practitioners of realpolitik), but younger ana-lysts who emphasize "national interest" more clearly approximate the assump-tions of realist thinkers in the West in that they view the international system in state-centric terms.[63] As Yong Deng has pointed out, Chinese realists "view the world as almost exclusively an arena of interactions between sovereign states engaged in merciless competitions."[64] The difference between the older generation and the rising generation of realpolitik thinkers might be best illustrated by contrasting the reaction to the August 1991 attempted coup d'état in the Soviet Union of older conservatives, who hoped at the outset that the coup would restore "real" socialism in that country, with that of younger people (neoconservatives), who pointed out that China's national interests would be better served by having a weak state to the north, even if it was nonsocialist, than having a strong, socialist one.[65] National interests were more important than ideology. At the same time that realpolitik is being strongly espoused by a number of younger analysts, however, there is also a rising school of liberal thinking that, like its counterpart in the West, stresses the interdependence of the world. For such thinkers competition among nations need not be seen in the zero-sum terms of realism; interdependence can be positive.[66]

In general, those in the foreign policy establishment have a stake in preserving and expanding Sino-U.S. relations, despite whatever reservations they may have about American intentions. This generalization appears to apply most strongly to the economic bureaucracies, particularly the Ministry of Foreign Trade and Economic Cooperation (MOFTEC), but also to the Ministry of Foreign Affairs, which is charged with dealing with the United States. It is perhaps this stake in guiding Sino-U.S. relations that makes the foreign policy establishment subject to harsh criticism by other bureaucratic interests and popular opinion, much as the U.S. State Department is often accused by Capitol Hill of having been coopted by foreigners.

At the risk of oversimplifying the trends we have been discussing, it is useful to consider Chinese nationalism as lying across two important dimensions. First, as we suggested earlier, there are different orientations toward the outside world: nativist, self-strengthening, and cosmopolitan. Second, there are different levels of response within Chinese society: elite, subelite, and popular (or, better, populist). In Table 6.2 we have set up a three-by-three grid to locate representative trends of thought.

Some comments on this matrix are necessary. If one starts with the "elite" row, the placement of the foreign policy elite in the "self-strengthening" column seems appropriate, although, as the brief discussion earlier suggests, there are within this community both those who lean toward the "nativist" side and those who lean toward the "cosmopolitan" side. The placement of the Old Left—those orthodox Marxists associated with the Hu Qiaomu and Deng Liqun

TABLE 6.2
NATIVIST DIMENSIONS OF
CHINESE NATIONALISM, 2000

	Nativist	Self-Strengthening	Cosmopolitan
Elite	Old Left	Foreign policy establishment	Arms control advocates; MOFTEC
Subelite	He Xin; economic nationalism	New Left	*River Elegy*
Populist	*China Can Say No*	*Gang-Tai* pop culture	Globalized pop culture

wing of the party—as both elite and nativist also seems straightforward. Finding "cosmopolitans" at the elite level is more problematic. MOFTEC officials, who see China's economic future as linked to its integration into the international economy (see the chapters of this book by Pearson and by Moore and Yang), should be placed here, although both pressures from domestic industries and their natural efforts to secure the best deal possible for Chinese industry suggest that they draw from China's "self-strengthening" tradition as well.[67] Alastair Iain Johnston, Paul Evans, and Michael Swaine have recently studied China's arms control community and found a group of people who have come to see China's participation in an international arms control regime as being in China's interest, a point illustrated as well in the chapter by Gill.[68] Such people might well be seen as standing in the cosmopolitan tradition, at least in part.

Looking at the "subelite" level, authors such as He Xin, the literary critic turned political apologist who vociferously defended the government and launched broadsides against the United States in the years following Tiananmen, qualify as nativist.[69] On the opposite extreme, the cultural fever of the 1980s, including the television series *River Elegy,* exemplified a cosmopolitan orientation. We can place the New Left in between. Such scholars reject both nativism and cosmopolitanism, though in their turn away from cosmopolitanism there is a distinct note of nativism in their writings. Despite the populist bent of some of their writings, the sophistication of their methodologies makes it difficult for them to represent the vox populi, though they do influence those who write for a broader audience, as well as those who write for policy elites.

Finally, looking at populist expressions of nationalism, one can distinguish between the almost xenophobic expressions found in a book such as *China Can Say No* and *China's Road* and the very cosmopolitan adoption of Western pop culture among some circles. Ironically, these different orientations, which exist on the opposite ends of the heuristic spectrum, are often held by the same types of people and perhaps by the same individuals. This reflects the desire of many people, particularly the young, who want both the benefits of globalization and the rise of China as a major power. At least potentially— or perhaps one should say under "normal" circumstances—this popular cosmopolitanism might be expected to ameliorate expressions of virulent nationalism. Finally, "self-strengthening" attitudes seem not to lend themselves easily to populist expression, though perhaps the adoption of Hong Kong–Taiwan (*Gang-Tai*) pop culture could be seen as fitting here.

There is a certain artificiality in any such typology; the complexities and nuances of various nationalist expressions are lost, and the boundaries separating the various dimensions are never as clear in reality as they appear on paper. Nevertheless, it makes clear that nationalism is not a unified, monodimensional phenomenon. Both the sociology of nationalism (who does the expressing) and the attitude toward the outside world (imitative, hostile, or in between) need to be taken into account. Such a typology also makes it easier to visualize the changes in social mood that have occurred in China over the past decade or so and thus to identify the different pressures that the foreign policy establishment has faced over time. This typology better identifies the domestic context in which Chinese foreign policy decisions are made. In general, as China has moved from the 1980s to the 1990s, the cosmopolitan orientation of intellectuals has been replaced by the theoretical explorations of postmodernists, deconstructivists, traditionalists, neoconservatives, and populists (or some combination of these often overlapping categories). At the same time, nativist expressions at the elite, subelite, and populist levels have increased. The "center of gravity" on our grid has generally shifted downward and to the left.

If this has been the general trend over the past decade, there have been counter-trends as well. In particular, as Sino-U.S. relations warmed up in 1997 and 1998 (with the exchange of visits by Presidents Clinton and Jiang Zemin), a number of works were published that reflected a continuing liberal, cosmopolitan strand in Chinese thinking. This trend started with books such as *China Should Not Be "Mr. No,"* which defended domestic reform and improved relations with Washington by contrasting China's successful implementation of reform and opening up with the failure of the former Soviet Union to do either until it was too late.[70] This was soon joined by other calls for reform, including the controversial best-seller *Crossed Swords,* which traced the conflicts between "conservatives" and reformers over the past two decades; *Beijing University's Tradition and Modern China,* which compiles important articles on political liberalism from the twentieth century; *Fire and Ice,* which reflects on the state of politics and culture in contemporary China; *Political China,* which brings together a number of recent liberal essays on politics and political reform; and *Turbulence: A Memoir of China's Economic Reforms (1989–1997)* by *Crossed Swords* co-author Ling Zhijun.[71]

PUBLIC OPINION AND FOREIGN POLICY

In his now classic study James N. Rosenau noted in 1961 that "we have little reliable knowledge about the role of public opinion in shaping foreign policy."[72] Now, some forty years later, the publication of impressive correlational studies have demonstrated that when public policies change, the shifts are predominantly in the direction favored by the public. Nevertheless, Ole Holsti's recent review of the case study literature revealed varied findings and mixed results, raising far more questions than answers. Surveying this literature, Holsti suggested the continuing need for more substantial evidence of a causal nature, arguing that by far the least well-developed area of public opinion research—and the most important one as well—has been the opinion-policy link.[73] Generally speaking, however, in democratic countries public opinion is thought of as providing broad limits, sometimes thought of as "dikes," that establish "the boundaries of the permissible."

If it is difficult to specify the role of public opinion in democratic countries, it is far more difficult to do so in a nondemocratic country such as China. The concept of public opinion "dikes" may have some applicability; after all, the Chinese government pays a bit of attention in trying to manage public opinion, as when a number of books and articles portraying the United States in a more positive light were published in the period before the exchange of summits between Presidents Jiang and Clinton. Often the management of public opinion is negative, as when the Chinese government shut down Internet servers to prevent students from taking to the street during the Diaoyu Islands controversy.

A good example of such government manipulation of public opinion, and the inherent risks involved in trying to do so, was seen relative to the presidential election in Taiwan in March 2000. Prior to the election leading officials, most notably Premier Zhu Rongji in remarks made during a televised press conference marking the close of the National People's Congress (NPC), warned the Taiwanese voting public not to make the mistake of voting for a candidate who advocated Taiwan's independence. After the victory by Chen Shui-bian of the Democratic Progressive Party, the candidate most objectionable to Beijing, some five thousand students were reported marching through the streets of Chongqing demanding a tough response. The government was apparently able to prevent similar protests from developing in Beijing.[74]

Nevertheless, the authorities found themselves compelled to dampen the fervor generated by their own rhetorical excesses. They faced a complex situation in which their efforts had stirred up domestic passions over Taiwan, but had not produced a favorable electoral outcome. They were further constrained because of important legislation relating to Taiwan's defense and Sino-American trade relations pending before the U.S. Congress. Under these conditions the government reportedly issued an "internal circular" that was considerably tougher than the official moderate response to Chen's victory. The circular pledged Beijing's "determination and ability" to recover Taiwan within a certain (albeit still unstated) time frame. Significantly, the circular urged the public, including students and soldiers, not to take any rash actions such as engaging in demonstrations. Reflecting the leadership's acknowledgement of the potential danger of unchecked public outrage, the circular reportedly went on to say: "We understand the angry reaction of the public to the rise of the Democratic Progressive Party. However, the nation must concentrate on economic construction and remain in unison with the center. The masses should trust the central leadership's determination and ability to accomplish unification."[75]

In extreme cases the government has sought to more directly channel public opinion, as when the government provided buses for student demonstrators in the wake of the Chinese embassy bombing in Belgrade, understanding full well that students were going to take to the streets in any event and that if they did not throw stones at the American embassy they would throw them at Zhongnanhai (the leadership compound).

Such generalizations are a useful starting point, but we would like to suggest three dimensions that seem important in allowing public opinion to enter the arena of elite politics and thus affect Chinese foreign policy either

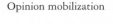

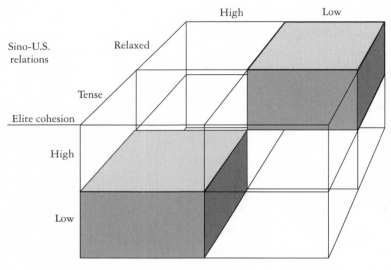

FIGURE 6.1
INTERACTION BETWEEN DOMESTIC POLITICS AND
THE INTERNATIONAL ENVIRONMENT

positively (by pushing it in one direction or another) or negatively (by constraining it). These dimensions are elite cohesion, Sino-U.S. relations,[76] and popular mobilization. The basic hypothesis is that a high degree of elite cohesion sharply limits the impact of public opinion, whereas a high degree of tension in Sino-U.S. relations or of popular mobilization are, ceteris paribus, more likely to render public opinion more salient. This can be understood through the three-dimensional schematic in Figure 6.1.

This figure depicts eight boxes or combinations. Two extremes are of greatest interest to our inquiry: the combination of a low level of elite cohesion, tense Sino-U.S. relations, and a high level of opinion mobilization on the one hand and of a high level of elite cohesion, relaxed Sino-U.S. relations, and a low level of opinion mobilization on the other. The first situation suggests the possibility of events spinning out of control, leading to a potentially dangerous situation for the political elite, the second to a much more controlled situation in which the elite would be free to manage foreign policy without much regard to public opinion.

It should be noted that this figure does not imply directionality. Presumably the causal arrow could run from elite conflict to opinion mobilization to tense Sino-U.S. relations, but it could also run from mobilized opinion to elite conflict to tense Sino-U.S. relations or from tense Sino-U.S. relations to opinion mobilization to elite conflict. This suggests that one might expect to see a different dynamic relating domestic politics to Sino-U.S. relations over time and across issues.

Keeping in mind both this diagram and our previous discussion of the dimensions of nationalism, can we establish any correlation between these observations and the course of Chinese politics and foreign policy in the real world? We believe that we can.

PUBLIC OPINION AND CHINESE POLITICS, 1995–99

Chinese politics from 1995 through 1999 make for an interesting study of the ways in which domestic politics and international relations affect one another. Those five years can be broken down into three distinct phases, each one of which displayed a different interaction between the variables just discussed. In the 1995–96 period, elite conflict coincided with an increase in Sino-U.S. tensions to generate a wave of popular nationalism. Although the expression of popular nationalism did not result in China's decision to respond with military exercises (described in the chapter by Swaine), it may have facilitated the making of that decision by making it difficult to resist appeals to "do something." Following the crisis in the Taiwan Straits, from the spring of 1996 through 1998 the forces worked in the opposite direction; that is, a reduction of elite conflict and an improvement in Sino-U.S. relations tended to calm public attitudes and make public opinion less important. This cooling was primarily an elite-driven process hinging on governmental efforts to improve Sino-U.S. relations. But there was also an effort to turn around public opinion at least at the subelite level and, to some extent, the popular level. Finally, in the third phase, 1999, the WTO issue and especially the tragic bombing of the Chinese embassy in Belgrade provoked new tensions in Sino-U.S. relations, unleashed a new wave of nationalistic emotion, and set off a new round of elite conflict. In this period public opinion had a clear impact on both the conduct of elite politics and on Chinese foreign policy.

The Impact of Domestic Politics, 1995–96

In 1995, as Deng's health was obviously in decline and leadership fell to the "third generation" headed by Jiang Zemin (discussed in the chapter by Miller and Liu), a new round of political debate and struggle broke out. The primary cause was the crisis facing the state-owned enterprises (SOEs) and the rapid expansion of private enterprise. Just how far and how fast should China go to embrace those trends? It is certainly true that by the mid-1990s there were few, if any, true believers in Marxism-Leninism, but abandoning ideology is different than simply not believing in it. Legitimacy—and interests—were at stake. "Upholding socialism" protects the interests of some, just as abandoning it promotes the interests of others.

These conflicts became "public" when leftists (the Old Left) circulated a "ten thousand–character manifesto."[77] This sharply worded document, entitled "Several Factors Influencing China's National Security," warned that the proportion of state-owned enterprises in China's aggregate industrial output value had fallen sharply (from 76 percent in 1980 to 48.3 percent in June 1994), that the number of private enterprises had grown rapidly, and, most important, that a "new bourgeoisie" had appeared.[78] Only about three months after this first manifesto was circulated, the U.S. government granted a visa to Taiwan President Lee Teng-hui so that he could visit his alma mater, Cornell University. This trip fueled new and sharp tensions in Sino-U.S. relations and resulted in the crisis in the Taiwan Straits.

What is noteworthy is that it was during this period of elite discord and heightened tensions with the United States that nationalistic views became particularly widespread in Chinese society. It was at this time, in the summer of 1995, that the *China Youth Daily* surveys cited earlier were conducted (and were allowed to be conducted), and it was in this atmosphere that *China Can Say No* and its imitators were published. Interviews confirm that there was widespread criticism within party and government circles of the Ministry of Foreign Affairs (denigrated as the *maiguobu*, "ministry for selling out the country") for its supposedly "weak" handling of Sino-U.S. relations. The convergence between popular expressions of nationalist feelings and similar criticisms within elite and subelite circles placed a certain amount of pressure on the leadership. Those with more moderate views on Sino-U.S. relations found it difficult to express their opinions.[79]

A second leftist manifesto, circulated in late summer or early fall of 1995 as tensions built up in the Taiwan Straits, extended the critique of reform to international issues. This document maintained that China faced a hostile international environment made up of "monopoly capitalists" who viewed China as an enemy and a domestic environment that was changing rapidly, bringing about trends that were threatening China's national security and social stability.[80] Like the first document, this one argued that the private economy was growing very quickly, that a "new capitalist class" had appeared, and that class polarization was taking place. Such trends, the author surmised (hoped?), might cause class struggle to again become China's primary contradiction. The threat of "peaceful evolution" was the critical issue.[81] Reliance on the international economy had weakened China's "national" (domestic) industries.[82] Given the ideological confusion in the party, the article maintained, it was possible that a Gorbachev-type leader might appear within the next ten to twenty years,[83] though presumably the author was hinting at troubles within a much shorter time frame.

Moving Toward the Middle, 1996–97

These manifestos put real pressure on Jiang.[84] Not to respond would be to acquiesce. Ultimately, Jiang responded in three steps. First, he tried to reduce his vulnerability by tacking to the left, stressing ideological correctness by calling on cadres to "talk politics" (that is, to emphasize ideology and uphold discipline). Second, he moved to stake out a defensible middle ground in China's political spectrum. Finally, in 1997, Jiang criticized the left in an important speech at the Central Party School that would set the tone for the Fifteenth Party Congress, to be held in September of that year.

Jiang stressed "talking politics" from the Fourth Plenary Session of the Fourteenth Central Committee in October 1994 and in early 1995. In late 1995, however, Jiang delivered a series of internal speeches in which he called for drawing a line between Marxism and anti-Marxism in seven areas, including the dichotomies of socialist democracy and Western parliamentary democracy; a diverse economy with a predominant public sector and privatization; studying what is advanced in the West and fawning on the West; and so forth. These distinctions were trumpeted in an important series of commentator articles carried in *Liberation Army Daily* between April 1 and May 6, 1996, although the tone of these articles was apparently more conservative than Jiang desired.[85]

In June 1996 Xing Bensi, vice president of the Central Party School, published a long article in *People's Daily*. In trying to define what constituted "real" Marxism (and thus refute the Old Left that positioned itself as the defenders of the faith), Xing argued that a great deal had changed since the birth of Marx 150 years ago. Although "some" of the "fundamental principles" (*jiben yuanli*) of Marxism are still applicable, he said, "indeed a considerable portion of the principles" of Marxism has changed. Xing juxtaposed "Deng Xiaoping theory" against leftist thought and, referring explicitly to the first "ten thousand–character manifesto," criticized those who declared that reform had brought about a "new bourgeoisie." Xing's article was clearly written in anticipation of the Fifteenth Party Congress, which determined that the party should "hold high" Deng Xiaoping theory.[86]

At the same time that Xing criticized the left he defined a "right" that was just as anti-Marxist as the left. Xing cited several manifestations of rightism, including "privatization" and revisionist interpretations of Chinese history that implied that China had taken the wrong road in pursuing the revolutionary path and that it was now necessary to say "farewell to revolution" (*gaobie geming*). This reference was to a well-known book of the same title by prominent philosopher Li Zehou and leading literary critic Liu Zaifu, both of whom were then living in exile in the United States.[87] By defining and criticizing a "right" Jiang and his defenders were able to carve out a middle course—just as Deng had secured his authority in the post–Cultural Revolution context by abandoning the "struggle *between two lines*" in favor of a "struggle *on two fronts*" (that is, both left and right).[88] As Chinese politics had polarized in the late 1980s, it had been increasingly difficult to prevent it from reverting back to a struggle between two lines, as indeed the harsh criticism of Zhao Ziyang in the wake of Tiananmen suggested it had. Now, after six years as general secretary and after being able to slowly build his personal authority, Jiang began to try to define a new center.

An effort to define Jiang's program in more positive and systematic terms—and to influence public opinion—became visible with the October 1996 publication of *Heart-to-Heart Talks with the General Secretary*. The most notable feature of this book was its unrestrained defense of reform; the title of the second chapter put it as bluntly as Deng Xiaoping ever did: "Reform, Reform, Reform: There Is No Other Road for China." Implicitly joining the ongoing debate about the cause of socialism's collapse in the former Soviet Union, the authors clearly placed the blame on Brezhnev rather than on Gorbachev, as the Old Left did. Brezhnev-type leaders easily appear in difficult circumstances, the authors argued, but the result of Brezhnev was eighteen years not of "stability," but of stagnation. They declared that the lesson to be drawn from the experience of Brezhnev is that without reform there will indeed be instability.[89]

The decision to bring together a number of young intellectuals to write *Heart-to-Heart Talks with the General Secretary* was a self-conscious effort to rebut the leftist criticisms that had been made in the first and second "ten thousand–character manifestos" as well as the rising tide of nationalism. It was clearly recognized that such trends would, if not refuted, severely constrain Jiang Zemin's range of policy choices and his effective power.[90] The rapid improvement in Sino-U.S. relations since March 1996—fostered through exchanges between Liu Huaqiu, head of the State Council Foreign Affairs Office, and Anthony Lake, then national security advisor for President Clinton—clearly facilitated this effort to respond to critics. U.S. Secretary of State Warren Christopher was due in Beijing in November 1996, only weeks after the publication of *Heart-to-Heart Talks with the General Secretary,* to finalize plans for Jiang Zemin and Clinton to exchange summits.[91]

Criticizing the Left, 1997–98

Jiang moved further to the "right" after Deng's death, with the Fifteenth Party Congress looming (it was held in September 1997). In his funeral eulogy for Deng, Jiang set a clearly reform-minded tone. Although great praise of Deng was to be expected on such an occasion, Jiang appeared to go out of his way to emphasize Deng's bold leadership and his pragmatic economic policies. For instance, Jiang quoted Deng as saying at the time he was restored to his posts in 1977 that there are two attitudes toward work: "One is to act as a bureaucrat; the other is to work." This appeared to be a risky quotation for the cautious Jiang to cite, but in retrospect one can see it as a declaration of Jiang's own intention to be more than a caretaker general secretary. Jiang went on to endorse the still controversial Thirteenth Party Congress of 1987, which had elaborated the notion of the initial stage of socialism, and to highlight Deng's 1992 tour of Shenzhen.[92]

A draft of the Fifteenth Party Congress report was circulated among the top leaders in March. The reaction from the left was reportedly scathing.[93] Jiang had reached a real turning point: either he had to step back from the direction he had been cautiously charting over the previous months or he had to push forward, directly challenging the left. Jiang chose the latter course. In his May 29 speech to the Central Party School Jiang finally began to move toward an open split with the left, something that he had avoided since coming to Beijing in 1989.

Judging from the published excerpts of his speech (*People's Daily* published approximately four thousand characters of a reported twenty thousand),[94] Jiang focused on the issue of enterprise reform, particularly the formation of joint stock companies, which became one of the centerpieces of his report to the Fifteenth Party Congress. But major changes in economic policy such as this one had to be justified in ideological terms, and therefore Jiang's report raised two important issues that similarly became major themes in the fall: the role of "Deng Xiaoping theory" and the "primary stage of socialism." Jiang's decision not only to "raise high" the banner of Deng's theory, but also to emphasize that Deng's approach was built on a continuation and development of "Mao Zedong Thought," was intended to refute leftist critics (who liked to cite Mao) by suggesting that Deng's "theory" was higher than Mao's "thought." Jiang also left room for himself (trying to avoid the "two whatever" problem) by saying that Deng Xiaoping theory was itself subject to further development. Thus Jiang stressed that "Marxism will definitely continue to develop with changes in real life as it is impossible for it to remain unchangeable." Accordingly, Jiang took a jab at the left, saying, "There is no way out if we study Marxism in isolation and separate it and set it against vivid development in real life."[95]

Although Jiang's movement to the right in this period was driven first and foremost by domestic concerns, particularly the problems with the SOEs, there is little question that his effort to promote domestic reform was facilitated by the more relaxed international environment that was being created in this period. The government obviously worked to cool nationalist passions, as the publication of *Heart-to-Heart Talks with the General Secretary* showed, and to justify its foreign policy, as the publication of Shen Jiru's *China Should Not Be "Mr. No"* demonstrated. The improvement in public opinion supported the pursuit of better relations with the United States—culminating in Jiang's trip to the United States in September 1997 and President Clinton's visit to China in June 1998—just as better relations with the United States worked to calm public opinion in China. In 1999 these trends were suddenly and unexpectedly reversed.

The Impact of the Embassy Bombing, 1999

Only six months after President Clinton's trip to China, new tensions emerged to plague the relationship—a new wave of arrests of democratic activists in China, allegations of illegal Chinese contributions to Clinton's 1996 campaign for the presidency, and accusations of nuclear espionage. Such issues raised again for the Chinese public the image of the United States as overbearing in its conduct toward China and hostile to China's emergence as a world power. Therefore, the atmosphere was well primed for the events of spring 1999, events that would mark that year as truly an *annus horribilis* in the history of Sino-U.S. relations.

A downward spiral of events started on March 24 as a frustrated Clinton administration began bombing Serbia in an effort to stop ethnic killings in Kosovo. Traditionally opposed to international interventions in trouble spots around the world, a legacy of its painful experience in the Korean War, China has become more open to multilateralism in recent years. It sent peacekeepers in support of the United Nations (UN) mission in Kampuchea, and it abstained from voting on the UN resolutions that called for a military response to Iraq's invasion of Kuwait.[96] When the North Atlantic Treaty Organization (NATO) acted unilaterally in Yugoslavia, however, China quickly condemned the action. Conservatives argued that Premier Zhu Rongji's trip to the United States should be postponed in response. Therefore, there was already controversy within the Chinese leadership before Zhu's plane touched down in Washington on April 6.

Zhu had come largely to put the finishing touches on China's accession to the WTO, as Pearson describes in her chapter. The failure to secure an agreement, however, left Zhu exposed to withering criticism when the office of the United States Trade Representative (USTR) posted an outline of the trade commitments China had made. The degree of division within China's leadership and among its ministries became apparent when Wu Jichuan, head of the Ministry of Information Industries, tendered his resignation (which was not accepted).[97] For a minister to publicly criticize a premier was simply unheard of in China, and certainly would have been impossible without high-level political backing, which came from NPC head and former premier Li Peng and parts of the military. Almost immediately the Internet was filled with denunciations of Zhu. What is interesting in light of our discussion of public opinion is that upon the USTR posting the Chinese government lost control over the flow of information. People from students to factory heads to provincial leaders and perhaps even State Council ministers gained direct access to information that had previously been tightly controlled. Public opinion was quickly inflamed, and it soon began to play a role.

There had been no time for passions to cool when on May 8 (Beijing time) five bombs from an American bomber slammed into the Chinese embassy in

Belgrade, killing three and wounding more than twenty others. Public outrage was so great that the Chinese authorities had no choice but to yield to
the demand to take to the streets, despite the very real danger that demonstrations could get out of hand (especially since many of the early demonstrators
were young working-class males). Buses were dispatched to bring students from
the Haidian district of northwest Beijing (where the universities are concentrated) to the American embassy. Nationalism in China is very much a
double-edged sword; if students and others had not been permitted to vent
their feelings against the United States, they no doubt would have found release
through criticism of the Chinese government.

There is no question that the failure to conclude a WTO agreement,
compounded by the bombing of the Chinese embassy, set off major rifts within
the Chinese government—Zhu Rongji's authority was visibly reduced over
the summer—and that new questions about China's foreign policy were
opened up. Within the subelite, foreign policy specialists previously well
disposed toward the United States expressed new skepticism; for instance, Shen
Jiru, the author of *China Will Not Be "Mr. No"* worried openly about omi-
nous trends in international relations.[98] Within the broader populace, a new
and deeper wave of nationalism dominated public opinion.

Just as in the 1995–96 wave of nationalism, new books began to appear.
The most important of these so far has been *China's Road under the Shadow
of Globalization*. The main author was Wang Xiaodong, whose views on
nationalism were mentioned earlier. In *China's Road* he took every opportunity to denigrate and mock the political and intellectual elite of China, especially "liberals." He depicted them as lapdogs, saying that they "support the
United States, support everything about the United States," whereas the
reality is that the interests of China and the United States clash.[99] The
United States, fearing China's growing strength, simply will not let China join
the world; indeed, it has made clear its intention of using NATO to control the
world in the twenty-first century.[100] Against this unsentimental view of
power politics, Wang saw China's elite as selling out the interests of China for
their own selfish purposes. The foreign policy elite, he said, have long cherished excessively high hopes for Sino-U.S. relations,[101] but the fact of the matter
is, he said, that the United States simply does not care about Sino-U.S. relations, that the United States pursues its own selfish interests, and that it is simply
laughable to believe (as some Chinese liberals supposedly do) that Americans
have a higher sense of morality.[102] One of the interesting things about this
book is that previously Wang Xiaodong had kept his distance from the

authors of *China Can Say No;* here one of the authors of that book, Song Qiang, is included as co-author. So the line between a more restrained expression of nationalism and populism and an unrestricted appeal to mass populism was breaking down.

Whereas Wang Xiaodong rarely invoked the language of postmodernism or even Marxism (he was too focused on national power to care much about Marxist theory), his primary co-author, Fang Ning, a professor at Capital Normal University, wallowed in the vocabulary of dependency theory. According to Fang, colonialism was replaced following the Second World War by neocolonialism—the use of foreign capital to bind and exploit the third world. But neocolonialism was losing its grip as some nations escaped dependency and others carried out revolutions. Thus the world was moving toward postcolonialism (*houzhiminzhuyi*), which will use more military force to shore up the position of the Western "core" nations.[103] U.S. actions in Iraq and Yugoslavia reflected this logic.

Although Wang Xiaodong did not use the language of postmodernism, he shared many of the perspectives of those who employ that approach, just as they share, to a greater or lesser extent, Wang's nationalism. Just as concerns with nationalism and postmodernism flow horizontally through the intellectual community (that is, the subelite level), one finds some of the same language being adopted by those in policy-making circles (the elite level). For instance, Wang Huning, now deputy director of the Policy Research Office of the Central Committee, offered a critique of Samuel Huntington's "Clash of Civilizations?" article that drew both on Joseph Nye's concept of "soft power" and on the broader discussions of culture found in the literature on Orientalism. Cultural influence, Wang said, was directly related to political and economic strength, so developed countries were often comfortable talking in terms of an "erosion of sovereignty" and the declining importance of sovereignty, whereas developing countries found that such "cultural expansionism" often ended up threatening political stability and national sovereignty. Furthermore, cultural influence was directly related to the construction of international norms and regimes, which were not always in the best interest of the developing nations. As Wang put it, "If one nation-state is able to make its power appear reasonable in the eyes of another people, then its desires will encounter less resistance. If the culture and ideology of one nation-state is attractive, other people will voluntary follow it. If one nation is able to establish international norms (*guifan*) that are consistent with its domestic society, there is no need for it to change itself. If one nation-state is able to support an international regime, and other nation-states are all willing to go through this regime to coordinate their activities, then it [the first nation-state] has no need to pay the high price of hard power." Cultural imperialism, in short, is a cheap way of achieving the goals states used to employ hard power to attain.[104]

One finds the same argument articulated by Fang Li, a bureau chief in the same office, in an internal article written shortly after the bombing of the Chinese embassy. According to Fang, during the cold war America's "cultural diplomacy" became a very important tool for "dividing" (*fenhua*) and "Westernizing" (*xihua*) socialist countries. In trade negotiations the United States tries anything it can to get other nations, "especially developing nations," to open their cultural markets. The result, Fang concluded, is that "whether from a macro-perspective or a micro-perspective, the United States' cultural expansion is bound tightly with its economic expansion, so that in the course of economic exchange it (cultural expansion) can achieve the effect of 'politics in command' (*zhengzhi guashuai*)."[105]

One also finds links between popular nationalism and elite politics. When *China Can Say No* appeared in 1995 it had an afterword by Yu Quanyu, the very conservative deputy head of China's Human Rights Commission at that time (and later head of the CASS Institute of Journalism). Yu, a long-time reporter with Xinhua, has close ties to the Old Left. When *China's Road* appeared in 1999 it had a preface by Yu Quanyu. One should not assume that this demonstrates that elites are seeking to manipulate public opinion (though that is, no doubt, part of the story); self-designated articulators of public opinion clearly seek out elite support.

CONCLUSION

This brief overview of Chinese politics since autumn of 1995 draws out the interaction of the variables discussed earlier. Elite politics—particularly elite discord—was an important feature. In the earlier part of the period the prospect of the forthcoming Fifteenth Party Congress, the very real tensions with the United States, and the difficulties in China's domestic economy set the stage for a period of heightened conflict. It is interesting to note, contrary to the prevailing wisdom, how much the terms of the debate at that time were set by the left and its more orthodox understanding of Marxism-Leninism.[106] The various "ten thousand–character manifestos" cannot be dismissed as inconsequential, because we have the clear evidence of top ideologues (such as Xing Bensi) and eventually Jiang Zemin himself responding explicitly to the charges raised.

The heightened elite conflict and international tensions both in 1995–96 and again in 1999 provided an opening for the broader discussion of foreign policy under the rubric of nationalism (of the nativist variety). How much of this expression of public opinion was spontaneous and how much was generated from the top is open to debate; both elements seem to have been present. Certainly there were elements in the government that believed that a certain degree of mobilized public opinion would be useful in dealing with the United States, although there seems to have been a division between those who wanted to use public opinion to negotiate a different, more equal relationship with the United States and those who wanted to use such public opinion to damage relations with the United States and therefore distance China from the various influences—cultural, economic, and political—that America represents. There were also others, especially those in the foreign policy establishment, who worried deeply about the opening of such public discussions, viewing them as a double-edged sword that would make the management of foreign policy more difficult. The effectiveness with which Jiang and his allies moved in 1996–97 to respond to the challenge from the left, and the reduction in tensions with the United States as relations improved and an exchange of summit meetings was put on the table, in turn, made it easier for the government to contain nativist-type nationalism. Indeed, with the exchange of presidential visits a veritable torrent of books touting the new "strategic cooperation" between China and the United States appeared. The evolution of Chinese domestic politics and the improvement in Sino-U.S. relations removed some of the most controversial issues from the public agenda and allowed the management of foreign policy to be confined again to the foreign policy establishment.

By the mid-1990s it was much more evident that Jiang Zemin was playing a two-level game in which domestic politics constrained his actions, but the conduct of foreign policy also had important ramifications for domestic politics.[107] For instance, as tensions with the United States increased first in 1993–94 and then again in 1995–96, those who sought a more cooperative approach found it difficult to speak up lest their patriotism be questioned.[108] Conversely, the improvement in Sino-U.S. relations beginning in 1996, and particularly Jiang Zemin's visit to the United States in 1997, fed back into Chinese domestic politics, facilitating a cautious liberalization of the political atmosphere.[109]

The failure to reach a WTO agreement in April 1999 and the subsequent bombing of the Chinese embassy reversed this progress. Not only did students take to the streets to express their nationalistic feelings, but also the assumption of American hostility toward China became much more deeply implanted in Chinese consciousness at the popular and subelite levels than ever before. The subsequent agreement on WTO accession, reached in November 1999, and the agreements for compensation for material and personal damages to Chinese and American diplomatic compounds should not be allowed to obscure the deep and long-lasting damage that was done to the relationship. The continuing tensions over the Taiwan Straits have only exacerbated this situation. Public opinion seems destined to play a more important—and more difficult—role in Chinese foreign policy in the future.

This sense that Chinese public opinion will play a greater role in the future accords with public opinion surveys that show a palpable sense of public expectation that contrasts with that of earlier periods. A public sense of China's "rightful" place in the international arena has emerged alongside the country's economic development and has been cultivated by the Chinese government as part of its patriotic education campaign since 1993.[110] Indeed, it was this consciousness of China's status in the international community that underlay much of the emergent nationalism of the 1990s and that makes nationalism such a double-edged sword—critical both of countries that are seen as denying China its "proper" status as well as of the Chinese government, which is seen as weak in the face of foreign pressures.[111]

The *China Youth Daily* surveys cited earlier included one question that was particularly revealing in this regard. The question asked the youth to assess China's current place in the world and to predict where China would be in thirty years. The results are reported in Table 6.3. As the table shows, respondents saw great improvements in China's political, economic, and military status over the next thirty years. A regime that is unable to meet such high expectations may find, to use an old Chinese expression, that in playing the nationalism card it has "mounted a tiger and can't easily dismount (*qihu nanxia*)."

The pull of such high expectations, if not excessively disappointed, might well be ameliorated by pulls in the opposite direction as the population increasingly enjoys the benefits of globalization. These different pulls suggest a government that faces the contradictory expectations of a citizenry that wants to participate in the economic, social, and cultural activities of the international community but also to see China assert its interests against that same order.

TABLE 6.3.

PERCEPTIONS OF CHINA'S STATUS, 1995

	Low	Low-middle	Middle	Upper-middle	High
What do you think is China's current level internationally?					
Political status	0.5	3.4	16.9	50	29.2
Economic status	4.5	41.4	41.5	11.8	0.8
Military status	0.95	6.3	25.6	47.3	19.8
What do you think China's level will be internationally thirty years from now?					
Political status	0.3	0.4	3.2	21.6	74.5
Economic status	0.4	1.9	17.6	43.9	36.3
Military status	0.4	0.7	7.1	32.6	59.1

Source: *Zhongguo Qingnian Bao,* July 14, 1995, p. 8.
N = 10,018, all 30 province-level units represented, values in percent.

Although the former expectation can help pull China into the world, the latter can form a reservoir of hostility that could be tapped in future conflicts, especially given the increasing diversity of interests and subelite opinion in China. Renewed tensions in the Taiwan Straits, U.S. foreign policy decisions that are perceived as "anti-China," and friction with Japan could all trigger nationalist reaction from China's subelites or the broader public. Such a response could make it very difficult for China's political elite to compromise, as indeed happened over the course of 1999.

PART THREE

International System Influences

SEVEN

Empowered and Restrained: Chinese Foreign Policy in the Age of Economic Interdependence

THOMAS G. MOORE AND DIXIA YANG

This chapter derives its inspiration from a deceivingly simple question: What is the impact of China's deepening participation in the world economy on its foreign policy-making process and behavior? A popular hypothesis among many observers of contemporary China, including foreign leaders, businesspeople, and scholars, is that growing economic interdependence (EI) is gradually creating a diplomatic context in which significant constraints are placed on Chinese behavior. From this perspective, EI will lead not only to a basic shift in how China understands the nature of international politics, but also to more cooperative behavior in its foreign policy. In this sense, the webs of interdependence spun by China's growing participation in the world economy will serve as the best guard against Beijing's becoming a source of instability in East Asia. Other observers are far more skeptical, however, as to whether EI can play such a role in managing China's emergence as a great power. According to this view, China will be able to resist much of the mutual influence posited by interdependence theory, thereby retaining foreign policy options that include both cooperative and uncooperative behavior.

This chapter is designed to provide a rather broad-brush approach to the subject of EI as an international system influence on Chinese foreign policy. Although the chapter is not a case study per se, we use China's response to the Asian Financial Crisis (AFC) to illustrate the dynamics of EI.[1] Although China was relatively insulated from the direst effects of the AFC, the crisis undoubtedly represented the most serious external economic shock experienced during the first two decades of the reform era. And given China's limited participation in the world economy under Mao Zedong, it could be argued that the AFC was the most serious international economic challenge China had faced in half a century. State Councilor Wu Yi, in a speech on the effects of the AFC, described it as a "shockwave" that "caused a definite deterioration in the international climate for Chinese economic development."[2] Moreover, as the crisis unfolded across the region, China found itself in one of the most pivotal international roles it had played since the Korean War.

This chapter represents an initial effort to address some basic questions about the impact of EI on Chinese foreign policy. For example, are the constraints imposed by deepening EI best understood as permanent and largely irreversible or simply as a diplomatic context from which China can extract itself over time? Indeed, many observers have expressed concern that China's calculation of the costs and benefits of EI will change in the future. This raises the issue of China's commitment to EI processes. Specifically, has China's conception of its national interest changed (for example, through learning or value change), or is it simply adapting to new circumstances whereas its fundamental long-term objectives remain unchanged? In terms of dynamics within the international system, the payoff question is whether the constraints of EI are sufficiently powerful to alter China's behavior from the historical pattern exhibited by other emerging great powers.

In this chapter we argue that China has become increasingly, if still somewhat cautiously, receptive to EI as a means of pursuing national economic revitalization. It has not, however, fully embraced EI as a world-view or substantially changed its strategic focus on national power in response to EI. In this sense interdependence is largely a tool for becoming modern, not an end in itself. At the margin, however, there have been some significant changes in Chinese perceptions, changes that raise the possibility of a more fundamental transformation of Beijing's world-view in the future. That said, EI's influence thus far has been greater on China's official foreign policy and actual external behavior than on its weltanschauung. Indeed, the fact that important changes in policy and behavior have occurred despite the persistence of China's basic world-view constitutes perhaps the strongest evidence of EI's impact. This also suggests that China's deepening participation in world affairs could lead, through a process of foreign policy "learning," to a substantial change in world-view if norms do, in fact, follow behavior.[3] In sum, although EI is best character-ized at present as a positive but limited source of cooperative behavior in the Chinese case, it is simply too early to conclude that EI cannot or will not have a more profound impact on Chinese foreign policy in the long run. In this sense we reach conclusions similar to those Bates Gill reaches in his chapter on nonproliferation and arms control policy-making.

For data the chapter relies heavily upon interviews conducted in Hong Kong, Guangzhou, Shanghai, and Beijing in August 1998. All told, we met with nearly three dozen academics, journalists, businesspeople, policy analysts, government bureaucrats, and (in the case of Hong Kong) political leaders. To protect the anonymity of these individuals, they are not identified by name or institu-tional affiliation. Whenever possible, however, we provide a general descrip-tion of our interviewees in the text. In addition to interviews, the chapter also relies upon a careful review of China's foreign relations literature, including speeches by Chinese leaders, policy analysis published in the Chinese media, and scholarly articles written for academic and policy discussion in China.[4]

CHANNELS OF INFLUENCE

Even restricting our focus to China's participation in the world economy, there are many channels through which the outside world influences China: person-to-person contacts, the transfer of economic ideas and norms, multi-lateral economic institutions, the policies of foreign governments, multinational corporations, transnational manufacturing networks, and finally China's par-ticipation in global markets more generally. Although a single chapter on a subject such as EI cannot provide exhaustive discussion of all these influences, we can provide a typology of channels through which EI operates, offering a brief analysis of how each affects China's foreign policy.

Person-to-Person Contacts. One of the greatest changes in the post-Mao era has been the enormous increase in person-to-person contacts between Chinese and foreign citizens. China has sent more than two hundred thousand students abroad during the past two decades, whereas a more modest (but ever-growing) num-ber of foreign students are taking advantage of opportunities to live and study in China. Although many Chinese students have not returned to China, the sheer scope of academic exchanges—of scholars as well as students—suggests a major channel of outside influence. Equally important, contact between Chinese officials and their interlocutors in foreign governments and international institutions has also increased substantially over the past two decades.

Given this chapter's focus on EI, commercial relations are another major source of person-to-person contacts that deserves special mention. With the steady growth of joint ventures, especially in the 1990s, an unprecedented number of foreigners are now living in China. Even greater numbers visit China regularly for business. Although the numbers are still modest by comparison, business trips abroad by Chinese citizens have also grown more frequent. All told, perhaps nothing epitomizes China's deepening participation in the world economy better than the proliferation of business contacts across national borders and the Taiwan Strait.

Virtually every individual we interviewed confirmed that person-to-person contacts among academics, businesspeople, and government officials have been among the most important channels of influence through which EI has operated on China during the reform era, especially as regards learning about the world economy. From local leaders and factory managers to foreign policy bureaucrats and national leaders, individual learning on the basis of person-to-person contacts has been a critical input into the policy-making process. According to this view, individual learning is transformed over time into both institutional learning and political learning within the foreign policy system.

Multilateral Economic Institutions. First analyzed extensively by Harold Jacobson and Michel Oksenberg and later researched by a host of other authors, multilateral economic institutions (MEIs) have been an important channel of external influence throughout the post-Mao period.[5] Indeed, Margaret Pearson's chapter in this volume provides a case study of China's accession to the World Trade Organization (WTO) in which she examines, among other things, the role of international influences on Chinese economic policy-making. Overall, the strategy of MEIs has been to condition China's full integration into the world political economy on Beijing's willingness to conform its policies and institutional structures to the norms of the international system over time. Specifically, the MEIs are trying to transmit the principles and rules of economic liberalism to China. The rich literature on this subject documents that MEIs have served as a significant source of domestic and foreign policy change in China.

The Transfer of Economic Ideas and Norms. Another channel of influence, related to the first two but sufficiently distinct to warrant separate consideration, is the flow of economic ideas and norms. Examples include the idea of comparative advantage discussed in Pearson's chapter, as well as the belief, which proved central to China's decision to join the WTO, that deregulation is necessary to spur development in high-technology industries. While ideas often flow as a direct result of China's increasing participation in MEIs and growing numbers of person-to-person contacts more generally, it should be noted that their transfer has also been facilitated by advances in telecommunications and transportation. From fax machines and the Internet to satellite television and expanded air travel, technology has increased the salience of ideas and norms as a channel through which EI operates on China.

One application that emphasizes expert discourse as a mechanism through which ideas and norms are transferred is the concept of epistemic communities.[6] According to this approach, communities of experts form—either transnationally or at least at the domestic level—in specific issue areas such as environmental protection, arms control, and trade policy. As the chapters by Elizabeth Economy, Bates Gill, and Margaret Pearson show, there is evidence that expert discourse in these areas has led to communities of this kind in China, at least in an incipient form. As far as EI is concerned, the transfer of economic ideas and norms clearly has been an important channel of influence in areas such as customs law, trade and investment policy, and accounting practices.

Intergovernmental Pressure. The policies of foreign governments are another important channel through which EI operates on China. Examples include bilateral U.S. trade actions on market access issues, intellectual property rights, prison labor exports, and textile fraud. Indeed, it is precisely this kind of interdependence that China arguably fears most. From the formerly annual debate over American renewal of China's most-favored-nation status (now called normal trade relations) to Washington's influence over Beijing's accession to the WTO, vulnerability to policy influence by great powers such as the United States and the European Union has long been a major concern of Chinese leaders. As China's participation in the world economy has grown, so too have issues of bilateral interdependence (and even dependence) in Chinese foreign relations.

Multinational Corporations. Foreign investment has had a profound impact on post-Mao China, especially since so much foreign capital has been received in the form of direct investment rather than portfolio investment. For example, Hong Kong and Taiwan industrialists have played an immeasurable role in the economic transformation of Guangdong and Fujian Provinces, respectively. More recently, a similar dynamic has begun to emerge between South Korea and Shandong Province, albeit one temporarily interrupted by the AFC. Although Western and Japanese multinational corporations (MNCs) lagged significantly behind overseas Chinese as a source of foreign investment in the early stages of the post-Mao era, their presence in China grew steadily through the 1990s. All told, more than two hundred *Fortune* 500 companies are active in China today, operating some forty-five thousand factories, branches, and offices (not including those in Hong Kong).[7] Their deepening involvement in the Chinese economy, although still limited in certain respects, represents an increasingly important channel of outside influence.

Although inward foreign investment justifiably captures most of the attention, the impact of outward foreign investment should not be overlooked either. By one recent count there are 4,800 Chinese companies operating in more than 180 foreign countries.[8] Although much smaller than the operations of foreign MNCs in China, the activities of these companies represent yet another means through which the outside world affects China. As more and more Chinese companies locate abroad, their managers gain firsthand experience conducting business in foreign markets, experience that is often transmitted back home.

Transnational Manufacturing Networks. Few changes in the world economy have been more profound for East Asia than the emergence of regional and global manufacturing systems in which the production, distribution, and marketing of many goods—including such staples of the East Asian "miracle" as consumer electronics, garments, athletic footwear, and housewares—now span several countries or territories. Although developing countries have long specialized in labor-intensive production, most accounts suggest that the transnational manufacturing networks (TMNs) that have emerged in recent years constitute a new form of economic interaction across national borders. Indeed, the world economy is now characterized by an ever-widening variety of production arrangements, so much so that some Western observers argue that "globalized networks of production and exchange" should join traditional conceptualizations focusing on national economies and territorially defined political states as the appropriate units of analysis for studying the world political economy.[9] Along the same lines, an approach that focuses on TMNs also transcends the study of MNCs per se.

From this perspective the most important story of economic integration in East Asia during the 1990s would not be the genesis of the Asia-Pacific Economic Cooperation (APEC) forum so much as the accelerated incorporation of China, Indonesia, Malaysia, Thailand, and other latecomers into TMNs originating in Japan and the Four Dragons (Hong Kong, Taiwan, South Korea, and Singapore). To be sure, TMNs represent an informal rather than formal mode of economic integration, but their implications for China's development strategy and foreign policy are profound all the same. And although the highest concentration of Chinese participation in TMNs may still be at the regional (that is, East Asian) level, especially given the extensive relocation of industrial production from Hong Kong and Taiwan, one should not underestimate China's deepening incorporation into global manufacturing systems that originate in North America and Western Europe as well.

Global Markets. A final and often underestimated channel of outside influence is the policy discipline exerted by global markets (namely, capital and goods markets). Consider, for instance, the role of foreign investors in shaping China's domestic and foreign economic policies. From commercial laws and investment regulations to product standards and managerial practices, the activities of foreign investors have been an unusually important channel through which the pressures of an interdependent world economy have influenced China. As mentioned earlier, it would be difficult to overestimate the role of Hong Kong and Taiwan industrialists in the economic transformation of South China, not just in terms of creating wealth, but also in terms of economic reform and industrial restructuring in the broadest sense.[10] On numerous occasions foreign investors have been consulted in the drafting of reform measures concerning investment policy, just as MEIs have been consulted on reform proposals for the foreign trade and foreign exchange systems. Recent research has also shown that international norms in areas such as business ethics, management-employee relations, and human rights are having a substantial impact on Chinese enterprises with foreign involvement.[11]

Less directly, but perhaps even more significantly, the increasing mobility of capital has been an enormous force in impelling liberalization among developing countries. Although the degree of financial integration in the world economy is sometimes overstated, capital is now freer than in the past to use the territorial divisions of the international system to extract concessions and otherwise regulate the conditions of global production. The result has been a pattern of competitive liberalization in which China and its neighbors in

Southeast Asia, not to mention other latecomers around the world, have on the whole responded in an accommodating fashion to the demands of global capital.[12] In this sense economic change is driven by market discipline, whether that discipline is imposed by an overseas Chinese investor looking for a new production site in East Asia or by a credit agency such as Moody's assigning risk to China's sovereign debt. In short, growing capital mobility means that there are certain (increasingly restrictive) requirements that national and local economies alike must meet in order to secure foreign investment.

As an impetus for change, the globalization of goods markets operates in a way similar to capital mobility: competitive forces in an increasingly transnational production structure provide powerful incentives for national and local economies to adopt "best practices" that reduce economic inefficiencies. Although the result certainly falls short of a total convergence of policies and institutions, increasing conformity to internationally accepted economic norms and practices can be seen across a wide range of countries. (See the chapter by Elizabeth Economy for a discussion of developments in the environmental realm.) In order to make themselves more attractive as locations for new production links in the TMNs that increasingly define contemporary global capitalism, reforming state socialist countries such as China have had to undertake substantial economic change.[13]

In sum, there is a *private* conditionality driven by market forces that operates similarly to the *official* conditionality imposed on developing countries by foreign governments and MEIs. Especially in an era characterized by a high level of capital mobility and a deepening transnationalization of production, private conditionality exerts pressure on countries such as China along a wide variety of economic fronts, from macroeconomic stability and trade policy to industrial restructuring and laws governing foreign investment.[14] Just as China's participation in MEIs is conditioned upon conformity to certain standards, so too is China's participation in capital and goods markets conditioned in a similar way upon domestic reforms and changes in foreign economic policy.

ECONOMIC INTERDEPENDENCE, DEVELOPMENT
STRATEGY, AND CHINESE FOREIGN POLICY:
THE GLOBAL LOGIC OF CHINA'S OPEN POLICY

Clearly, the outside world has been a powerful force in organizing economic life and shaping foreign policy in China. Some channels of influence, such as the policies of foreign governments and MEIs, are well recognized. Others, such as China's incorporation into TMNs—and its participation in capital and goods markets generally—have received somewhat less attention. The private conditionality associated with these latter channels, in particular, suggests that there is a "global logic" (GL) to the evolution of China's open policy (*kaifang zhengce*), just as others have identified an "economic logic" or "political logic" to reform and opening.[15]

The Idea of a Global Logic

The main point of the GL is simple: much of China's foreign economic policy and foreign economic relations, not to mention its domestic economic change, can be understood as a function of its position in the regional and global political economy.[16] Although it is certainly difficult to identify specific imperatives that all latecomers must heed, China's behavior fits the basic pattern exhibited by other developing countries that have been integrated into the world economy in recent years. Indeed, one of the main virtues of the GL is its ability to explain how China finds itself today, contrary to its original plans, increasingly market oriented and deeply involved in the world economy. After all, the original idea behind economic reform had been rather simple: make limited use of markets as a supplement to the plan, and undertake a partial opening to benefit from the modern technology, management skills, and production practices available in the world economy. The goal was neither to marketize substantial economic activity nor to insert China into the international division of labor. As far as development strategy was concerned, the aim was to continue pursuing an import-substituting industrialization (ISI) strategy, financed by selected exports, in which the industrial core of China's economy would remain insulated from foreign contact. Simply put, the essence of state socialism was to be retained.

However, just as China's economy is said to have "grown out of the plan," so too has China's development strategy "traded out of ISI," without any antecedent change in official policy.[17] To be sure, the state has adopted reform measures that have validated this shift along the way, but it was not a policy change originally intended by China's leadership. Here it is necessary to draw a distinction between the state as a (perhaps grudging) agent of change and the state as a strategic catalyst for change. From this perspective, the state did not so much *plan* a change in development strategy as much as it *presided over* the transition to a new export-oriented industrialization (EOI) strategy (or, perhaps more accurately, a quasi-EOI strategy). In this sense the state deserves credit mainly for legitimating successful changes that localities, firms, and individuals were making, at least in part, in response to powerful forces in the world economy.

Although there has not been a single response to the geoeconomic pressures associated with globalization, even among similarly situated developing countries in East Asia, the world political economy does provide strong incentives and disincentives for certain types of economic policies, institutional changes, and foreign policy strategies. In this sense, deepening EI in world affairs increases both the potential returns from effective state action and the likely costs of incompetence. Specifically, Jeffry Frieden and Ronald Rogowski argue that globalization has increased incentives for greater economic openness by raising substantially the opportunity costs of economic closure.[18] As Peter Evans recently observed: "The increasing weight and changing character of transnational economic relations over the course of the last three decades have created a new, more constraining context for state action."[19] According to the GL, this context requires that China expand its open policy as the centerpiece of its development strategy. For instance, if participation in TMNs is the primary means by which countries can take part in the new globalized industrial order, the efficacy of ISI and other development strategies based on traditional concepts of "national development" becomes questionable.

By examining the GL behind competitive liberalization in East Asia we can see just how critical the regional (and global) context of development is for understanding not only broad trends across countries, but also specific outcomes within individual countries. Given the general disadvantages of being a latecomer, China and other developing countries in East Asia have a strong incentive to adapt to whatever economic opportunities present themselves at a given time. Development strategy has always been time sensitive, but the connection between historical context and policy choices may be especially powerful today given the scope and pace of technological change, the financial requirements for participating in global industrial activity, and the evolving nature of transnational economic relations.[20]

As a systemic influence, EI has given profound shape to China's development strategy and, by extension, its foreign policy. Once economic development was identified as the overriding national priority—a decision that itself arguably originated in part from an assessment of China's external environment—the parameters of successful and unsuccessful development strategies were largely set. For China the only effective option was to pursue modernization through reform and opening. As regards foreign policy, the necessary corollary was co-operative foreign relations that would allow China to achieve the economic revitalization necessary to ensure its long-term national security (or, alterna-tively, regime survival). To be sure, there are many important questions about the pace, sequence, and specific content of various economic and for-eign policies that cannot be answered by the GL alone. That said, the effects of external factors—and EI especially—on China's development strategy and foreign policy should not be underestimated.

Conditions Favorable to the Global Logic

Under what conditions is the GL most (and least) powerful? Although a thor-ough examination of the issues surrounding this question lies beyond the scope of this chapter, we can offer a brief assessment related to this volume's focus on the policy-making process. As regards the impact of centralization versus decentralization, the power of the GL has varied both across time and across different channels of outside influence. Early in the reform era, for instance, relatively high levels of centralization favored the operation of the GL, insofar as China's leaders were predisposed to experiment with reform and opening. With decision-making authority relatively concentrated at the top, the com-mitment of Deng Xiaoping and other reform leaders to economic modern-ization allowed the GL to operate fairly strongly. Indeed, reform and opening might well have failed to achieve its initial momentum in a more decentral-ized environment. If nothing else, centralization thus suggests the possibility of rapid, deep change under the right conditions.

Later, as decentralization progressed, points of access to the Chinese politi-cal economy multiplied. On the one hand, decentralization increased the prospects for widespread learning from China's participation in world markets. This, in turn, led both to more reform initiated from below and to greater local implementation of reforms initiated from above. For certain channels of influence, however, decentralization does not appear to be so propitious. Consider China's bid for WTO accession. Until 1999, when the top leader-ship intervened decisively on this issue, the pluralization of the foreign policy-making process had impeded negotiating progress as resistance to the costs associated with WTO membership grew, especially among certain local and sectoral interests (see the chapter by Margaret Pearson). As a result of changes in China's domestic structure, therefore, the role of MEIs in transmitting liberal economic ideas could actually weaken, at least in terms of directly affecting policy outcomes. By contrast, other channels of influence, such as TMNs and global markets, could become more important as sources of reform due to the effects of economic decentralization. Put differently, private conditionality may be more efficacious than official conditionality in the future.

ECONOMIC INTERDEPENDENCE AND THE CHINESE FOREIGN POLICY-MAKING PROCESS

The preceding discussion of the GL reinforces the premise that any consideration of EI as an influence on Chinese foreign policy must begin with an examination of its impact on the policy-making process. Indeed, as David Lampton's introduction to this volume describes, the conventional wisdom is that Chinese foreign policy is now made in a more pluralized environment, at least partly as a result of reform and opening.

A "Pluralization" of the Chinese Foreign Policy-Making Process?

EI is assumed to have increased both the desire and the ability of diverse groups to influence domestic and foreign policy. To cite just two examples, the expanding role of foreign trade corporations and provincial governments illustrates how a broader range of political/economic/bureaucratic interests has been introduced into the process (see the chapter by Peter Cheung and James Tang). By accelerating reform and opening in China's economy, EI has helped reshape the dynamic of both central-local relations and relations among various subnational entities (provinces, industries, and so on). In this sense, decision-making power is generally understood to have been decentralized not only from China's top leaders, but also from the Ministry of Foreign Affairs (MFA), the Ministry of Foreign Trade and Economic Cooperation (MOFTEC), and other traditional power centers in the foreign policy system.

Although changes to the formal structure of the foreign policy system have been relatively minor, traditional institutions are now thought to operate in a broader policy-making environment in which linkages between policy formulation, policy implementation, and policy feedback have become more extensive. The received wisdom is that EI has broadened the de facto foreign policy system to include new actors, new interests, and new identities. This, in turn, has complicated policy implementation considerably. Furthermore, as the number of stakeholders in China's foreign economic policy has expanded, the feedback stage of the policy-making process has also become more important. All told, China's deepening participation in the world economy is seen as having profoundly transformed the conduct of its foreign relations. Specifically, a wide variety of forces other than the formal institutions of the foreign policy system—sectoral (such as factory managers), provincial (such as local economic policies), international (such as MEIs), transnational (such as MNCs), and global (such as capital markets)—now shape China's foreign *relations* and, by extension, its foreign *policy.* From this perspective, the changing nature of China's foreign relations has affected both the substance of its policy (that is, EI can be seen as a source of policy constraints) and the way its foreign policy is made (that is, EI can be seen as a source of change in the policy-making process).

In the section that follows we use the AFC as a case study to examine whether the description provided earlier—which we believe represents the conventional wisdom about the impact of EI—is consistent with actual changes in the foreign policy-making process.

The Asian Financial Crisis and the Chinese Foreign Policy System: Underestimating the Threat

When asked about the policy-making process, interviewees frequently began by commenting on how badly the AFC was underestimated within the Chinese foreign policy system. By all accounts, the Chinese leadership was not seriously concerned about the AFC until the Hong Kong dollar came under speculative attack in October 1997. Shortly thereafter, on November 18, 1997, Jiang Zemin, Li Peng, Zhu Rongji, and other high-ranking central and provincial leaders attended a financial summit organized by the State Council to discuss China's financial system and ways to avoid the currency crises and general economic turmoil plaguing its neighbors. Until then China had watched closely but without alarm as financial distress spread through the region. Currency policy and reform of the banking system were reportedly among the leading topics discussed at this meeting, although devaluation of the renminbi was apparently considered unnecessary given China's existing capital controls and strong economic fundamentals. According to interviewees, Beijing's pledge to maintain currency stability looked like an easy way to bolster its regional image at the time. (In fact, a Chinese expert on international finance acknowledged that the decision to adopt a "no devaluation" policy reflected Beijing's confidence that the AFC would have only a negligible impact on the

Chinese economy.) Another outcome of this meeting was the establishment of a high-level task force under Zhu to monitor China's financial sector. It was also around this time that the state-run media began to publish articles drawing parallels between the challenges faced by China and the problems experienced by China's neighbors in the Association of Southeast Asian Nations (ASEAN).

That said, some interviewees claimed that the AFC did not become a serious priority in leadership circles until January or February 1998, after policy-makers finally recognized the threat to Chinese economic growth in the final weeks of 1997. As one Beijing-based reform intellectual put it, the AFC was underestimated "from top to bottom" within the foreign policy apparatus. Another interviewee, a high-ranking foreign policy bureaucrat, described how analysts and decision-makers alike were always a step behind as the turmoil evolved, first from a currency crisis into an economic crisis, then into a sociopolitical crisis, and finally into a full-blown international crisis. Although everyone seemed aware that the whole world had underestimated the AFC, including the U.S. Treasury, most interviewees believed that the Chinese foreign policy system had been especially egregious in its failure to understand the nature and implications of the crisis.

Not only was China's foreign policy community slow to anticipate the severity of the AFC for the region, it also grossly underestimated the impact the AFC would have on China. China's economic fundamentals were thought to be so good—high rates of economic growth, high savings and investment rates, relatively low levels of external debt (especially short-term debt), strong exports and favorable current account balances, and bountiful foreign exchange reserves—that the AFC was not anticipated to have much impact on China. As late as February 1998 a Chinese Academy of Social Sciences (CASS) study estimated that China's export growth would be 17.5 percent for 1998, down only slightly from 21 percent in 1997.[21] (As it turned out, its export growth in 1998 was less than 1 percent.) Along the same lines, interviews and press accounts have indicated that analysts of the Japanese economy underestimated the possibility that the yen would continue to decline through most of 1998. According to one report, Zhu raised the issue in internal discussions early in 1998, well ahead of experts in the foreign policy system.[22]

Interviewees and press accounts indicated that concern about the declining yen, and worsening economic turmoil in the region generally, led directly to the focusing of attention on the crisis as the spring months passed and the prospect of global financial disorder grew. In mid-June 1998 the Chinese Communist Party (CCP) Central Committee set up a Central Financial Work Committee (*Zhongyang Jinrong Gongzuo Weiyuanhui*) under the auspices of Zhu Rongji, with Vice Premier Wen Jiabao as secretary, to combat the possibility of "financial floods" from abroad. This institutional development reportedly came after a special session on financial security held by the CCP Central Committee on May 12, 1998. The timing also suggests that the declining yen and fears about the weak prospects for successful multilateral coordination among the leading financial powers (namely Japan and the United States) finally provided the impetus for the AFC to be regarded as the most pressing foreign policy issue facing the Beijing leadership at the time. From that point forward the AFC received sustained attention at all levels of the foreign policy system.

The Influence of China's Top Leaders on China's Response to the Asian Financial Crisis

By all accounts, Premier Zhu Rongji presided over a highly centralized decision-making process in charting Beijing's response to the AFC. Although he certainly did not act unilaterally within the political system, Zhu did, in the opinion of many interviewees, personally dominate Chinese policy from the very beginning of the crisis. For instance, Zhu exercised considerable influence as head of the Finance and Economy Leading Small Group (*Zhongyang Caijing Lingdao Xiaozu*). One Hong Kong interviewee with access to top leaders in Beijing was adamant that Zhu initiated all policy vis-à-vis the AFC. In his words, "Zhu must consult Jiang Zemin, of course, but he is definitely running the show. [Central Bank Governor] Dai Xianglong and [Finance Minister] Xiang Huaicheng are just following his orders." Indeed, many observers thought the unyielding nature of China's no devaluation policy reflected Zhu's personal resolve to deliver on at least one of his two promises: currency stability and 8 percent economic growth during 1998. Both goals were desired, of course, but in case the country fell short of Zhu's growth target he could at least point out that China had avoided devaluation.

Beyond Beijing, another key to Zhu's centralized management of AFC policy was an adept personnel strategy, begun long before the crisis, in which he placed many of his protégés in critical positions in Guangdong, Shanghai, and other important localities. According to interviewees, these connections were important to Zhu's ability to manage an increasingly pluralized system. As we discuss later, local (and sectoral) interests articulated their views strongly within the system, so Zhu's personal control over the process should not be overstated, but AFC policy did, in the end, conform to his preferences.

Although foreign policy was not Zhu's main area of responsibility, he is widely seen as having contributed during the AFC to a growing shift away from the Dengist dictum on international affairs that China should "never take the lead, keep a low profile, and watch changes with a cool head." As one Shanghai scholar noted with reference to the AFC: "The Zhu/Jiang leadership is taking China toward a more interdependent view of international relations." Although this remains to be seen, Zhu certainly seems to support the idea of responding more assertively to international events such as the AFC. As we discuss in detail later, China sought to capitalize on the opportunity provided by regional economic turmoil to flex its foreign policy muscle. Foreign Minister Tang Jiaxuan and other high-ranking officials were careful to deny that China's response to the AFC represented an effort to take a "leading role in the region," but it is clear from Zhu's performance at international events such as the Asia-Europe Meeting in April 1998 that his vision of Beijing's leadership in world economic affairs is quite proactive.[23]

In comparison to the role of Zhu Rongji, Jiang Zemin's role in formulating specific responses to the AFC appears to have been much more modest. (The same can be said for the roles of Li Peng, Qian Qichen, and other top leaders involved in foreign policy.) As general secretary of the CCP, chair of the Central Military Commission, president, and head of the Foreign Affairs Leading Small Group, Jiang obviously dominates the foreign policy system in a formal sense. Aside from his reported participation in top-level deliberations, however, Jiang seems to have played a largely consultative role through much of the crisis. (As noted earlier, Zhu apparently was allowed to use the Finance and Economy Leading Small Group as the focal point for policy-making in response to the AFC.) Not surprisingly, Jiang's participation seems to have been greatest when China's relations with major powers such as the United States and Japan were at issue. For instance, in June 1998, just prior to President Clinton's visit to China and in the midst of global concerns about the declining yen, Jiang used an interview with *Newsweek* to chide the U.S. government for commending one country (China) for maintaining currency stability while tacitly giving its approval to another country (Japan), which allowed the value of its currency to fall.[24]

Bureaucratic Politics and the AFC Policy-Making Process

Interviewees confirmed that the general trend in China's foreign policy system is toward greater institutionalization, both in terms of the roles played by long-standing bureaucratic actors (for example, ministries) and in terms of new actors brought into the policy-making process (for example, foreign trade companies, industry groups, and provincial economic interests). Compared with earlier generations of top leaders, the current group must heed more diverse interests within the system. That said, every indication is that the AFC policy-making process was not especially defined by bureaucratic politics. (As such, this case is consistent with the cross-national expectation that crises are typically addressed in higher-level, more personalized decision-making arenas.) Interviewees generally agreed, for instance, that none of the primary ministerial-level actors (such as MOFTEC, the Ministry of Finance, the People's Bank of China, the MFA, and the State Administration of Foreign Exchange) was particularly effective in independently influencing policy. Although their input surely mattered, the consensus is that top leaders, especially Zhu Rongji, were the driving force in shaping Chinese policy. Several interviewees emphasized, for instance, that the MFA played a very minor role throughout the AFC. Similarly, as indicated above, the Ministry of Finance and the People's Bank of China were perceived as following Zhu's lead very closely. For its part, MOFTEC was active administratively in the wake of the AFC, commissioning reports and organizing myriad seminars on the impact of the crisis on China's export and foreign investment prospects. In terms of political influence, however, MOFTEC is not regarded as having significantly affected policy.

Expert Input into the AFC Policy-Making Process

In the case of the AFC, input from scholars and policy analysts was somewhat less than usual due to early failures in anticipating the severity and duration of the economic turmoil. As we discussed earlier, the top leadership was gravely disappointed with the quality of information and analysis made available by the foreign policy system. That said, interviewees from CASS and SASS (the Shanghai Academy of Social Sciences) claimed that analysis produced by their institutes on currency policy, multilateral economic coordination, and other matters related to the AFC had, in fact, reached the desks of high-level decision-makers in Beijing and the mayor's office in Shanghai, respectively.

Whatever their earlier displeasure, Chinese leaders apparently had little choice but to rely at least in part on economic experts and foreign policy specialists given the technical nature of many financial issues surrounding the AFC. Specifically, Zhu's brain trust is known to include several leading academic economists.

Overall, there seems to be wide agreement that the foreign policy system is more open to expert input than in the past. Some interviewees, especially those who themselves enjoy regular input, argued that the decision-making system has changed greatly in recent years, with many new opportunities for expert analysis to influence policy. Others saw more modest change, arguing that the policy-making process is still very centralized at the top. For scholars and policy analysts alike, a major avenue of influence is participation in the many seminars, meetings, and conferences organized by ministerial and provincial bodies. (Not surprisingly, research institutes directly affiliated with the central government serve as the main source of expert advice.) As one Beijing-based expert on international finance described it, "if government departments see your ideas as being in their interest, then they may be transmitted to higher levels."

The result, by all accounts, is that a greater diversity of views on international economic issues such as the AFC now reaches top decision-makers. Although academic institutes such as CASS do not play a direct role in the decision-making process, analysis provided by its experts appears to enjoy a broader audience, and perhaps a more elite audience, than in the past. Studies are also more frequently commissioned without indicating the desired policy direction. One interviewee, for example, cited cases where the MFA had requested analysis without providing any information indicating prejudgment of the issue. Although this means that scholars must exercise caution in presenting their ideas, it also contributes to the genuine enthusiasm, albeit one tempered by realism, that scholars and policy analysts feel about the increased input they now have into the foreign policy-making process. As one such expert stated, "The channels are still limited, but the system is more pluralized and the channels are more diversified."

Local and Sectoral Input into the AFC Policy-Making Process

As we discussed earlier, the foreign policy-making process was highly centralized in formulating China's response to the AFC. Nonetheless, there also was substantial give and take between Beijing and a variety of local and sectoral interests. As one interviewee put it, "China's policy toward the Asian Financial Crisis has been characterized by remarkably open debate." He proceeded to recount events at a well-attended meeting in Guangdong at which officials from Beijing presented the case for the no devaluation policy. The subsequent exchange with the audience was quite rancorous, as one Guangdong representative after another spoke in favor of devaluation. As it turns out, many of the most outspoken members of the audience were official and quasi-official representatives of Guangdong's export-oriented industries (or, more precisely, those export-oriented industries that were not reliant primarily upon import-intensive export processing). The no-devaluation policy threatened the foreign sales of these industries.

These industrial interests were not alone as proponents of devaluation, however. Provincial leaders from some coastal areas also favored devaluation as a means to sustain the high level of export growth that has played such a central role in their prosperity during the reform era. In fact, calls from below to change China's currency policy increased markedly once it became apparent that declining export growth would make it difficult for localities to achieve the targets for economic growth assigned to them as part of Beijing's goal to achieve 8 percent growth nationally. Managers of many state-owned enterprises (SOEs) were also supportive of devaluation since the resulting change in China's terms of trade would give heavy industry at home a better chance to compete with imports.

By most accounts, Zhu Rongji was unusually receptive to input from below during the AFC, although, as one interviewee conjectured, this encouragement of discussion was "perhaps mainly to make them [local leaders and industry officials] feel good." On the whole, interviewees found it difficult to generalize about the degree of local and sectoral input into foreign policy decisions. There was broad agreement that the policy-making process has been more "open" or "pluralized" in the reform era, and some interviewees even maintained that policy rarely proceeds without substantial support from below. Others, however, argued that although there is much greater discussion, Chinese foreign policy in the case of the AFC reflects just how little substantive input local and sectoral interests enjoy in the formulation of national policy. Even when the material interests of specific provinces or industrial sectors are directly at issue, some observers explained, key policy decisions are made at the very top. In the AFC, Zhu and his team were able to ignore a vocal pro-devaluation lobby.[25] For all the debate that surrounded currency policy during the AFC, the decentralization of economic power did not translate into an influential foreign policy profile for local and sectoral interests.

That said, the combination of local and sectoral interests aligned against Beijing's currency policy was not politically insignificant. Some interviewees suggested that pressure from these sources played an important role in shaping certain aspects of China's response to the AFC (for instance, those related to export tax rebates, increased export financing, and improvements in foreign investment policy). According to this view, these measures were taken to compensate for the lack of devaluation. It is unclear, however, to what extent these steps were taken preemptively by Beijing in the national interest (out of concern for declining export growth and foreign investment flows) or taken as the result of bargaining and compromise in a more pluralized foreign policy-making process. Here, unfortunately, interviews and press accounts offer inconclusive evidence. At the margin, however, it appears that Beijing was not significantly constrained by the pro-devaluation lobby in its policy-making. First, proponents of devaluation seemed quite dissatisfied with the alternative measures taken by Beijing to stimulate exports and foreign investment. Although this could simply have been a bargaining tactic to extract still more concessions, there is every indication that devaluation was greatly preferred to the alternative measures offered by Beijing. Second, there is evidence that certain policies, such as increased export financing, were not the generous compensation one might think. One interviewee in Shanghai argued that this measure was critical only for industries such as shipbuilding that produce big, expensive machinery. For most industries, he explained, "if you have a market for your goods, credit is not a serious problem. A devaluation would, without question, make a much bigger impact." When asked whether pro-devaluation forces in Guangdong were satisfied with China's policy, another interviewee simply responded that "they have to accept what they can get."

In the end it would be reasonable to conclude that Beijing took few measures in responding to the AFC that it would not have taken even in the absence of pro-devaluation voices in China. That said, interviewees consistently suggested that the foreign policy-making process is more pluralized than in the past, especially with regard to routine, noncrisis matters. In this sense, the new dynamic that has emerged in central-provincial relations during the reform era does extend, albeit in a limited way, to foreign policy. As China's response to the AFC demonstrates, however, the policy-making process can still be operated in a highly centralized fashion when necessary, even if the vital interests of decentralized actors are at issue. Consistent with the chapter by Peter

Cheung and James Tang, it seems that localities and sectors are still limited in how they can pursue their interests through the foreign policy system. As we discussed earlier, a key aspect of Beijing's ability to retain a high degree of central control is personnel management. Although the structure of the foreign policy system still favors the central government, Zhu Rongji's success in putting his team in place at the provincial level suggests an indispensable strategy for further manipulating the policy-making process in cases such as the AFC when there is great diversity of local, sectoral, and national interests.

Local Adjustment to Chinese Foreign Policy during the Asian Financial Crisis

Although provinces and other subnational actors in China cannot have their own foreign policies, they can make changes in local economic policy and readjust certain aspects of their foreign economic relations in response to international phenomena like the AFC. Interviews in Guangdong, a province known for its independent and even rebellious policies, were particularly revealing in this regard. In meetings with us, academics, businesspeople, policy advisors, and government officials confirmed both the limits of provincial influence in the decision-making process at the national level and the extent to which a narrow focus on the formal foreign policy system fails to capture important aspects of China's response to the AFC. In Guangdong several actions were taken by the provincial government to cope with the effects of declining growth in exports and foreign investment. Some merely involved the implementation of measures approved by the central government (for example, raising the rates for export tax rebates). Others, however, were defiantly creative, such as giving provincial assistance to encourage private enterprises to engage in direct export. Caught between the Scylla of declining exports and the Charybdis of economic growth targets well above the national average, Guangdong chose to promote direct export among private enterprises as a means of increasing both the volume of exports and the efficiency of foreign trade. According to some interviewees, this policy was adopted without the authorization of MOFTEC.[26]

At a more general level, Guangdong used the economic pressures created by Beijing's currency policy as an impetus for internal readjustment. At a series of meetings convened by the provincial government, including a special conference in November 1997 (a month after Hong Kong's currency travails), Guangdong officials decided to adjust their development strategy. One initiative was to diversify the province's trade and foreign investment relations away from their traditional focus on East Asia. Provincial officials and businesspeople worked together to expand export markets in North America, Western Europe, Latin America, and even Africa. Efforts were also intensified to court foreign investors from all over the world, especially large Western multinationals that had been underrepresented in the past. In the wake of the AFC, business as usual could not suffice. Although Guangdong arguably had little influence over the formulation of official foreign policy, it could adjust its foreign economic relations in an effort to better serve its interests.

Press reports, as well as additional information gleaned from interviews in Hong Kong, Guangdong, Shanghai, and Beijing, suggest that this pattern of local response was played out across China. With varying degrees of success and independence from central authorities, provinces and other subnational actors adjusted their economic policies, development strategies, reform agendas, and foreign economic relations in response to the AFC. In Fujian, for instance, where more than 70 percent of the province's overseas capital has traditionally come from Taiwan, Hong Kong, and Macao, local authorities introduced preferential policies on tax refunds and land use to counter the negative effects of the AFC on foreign investment.[27] All over China, local governments, which in the past had been cautious about granting foreign trade rights to foreign-funded enterprises, now actively encouraged these enterprises to apply for such rights. (In essence, these rights allow foreign-funded enterprises to become foreign trade companies that can sell goods other than their own.) Furthermore, approval requirements were relaxed for other types of enterprises as well, all in an effort to reinvigorate China's exports.[28]

From all indications it appears that provinces and other subnational actors face formidable constraints in pursuing their interests through the formal foreign policy system. As the example of the AFC demonstrates, their ability to influence the formulation of national policy is still quite limited. This case is somewhat unusual, since Zhu committed himself to a currency policy that could be reversed only at tremendous domestic and international cost, but it seems from interviews that subnational actors typically have greater input into policy *feedback* than into policy *formulation*. In addition to direct feedback, such as appeals through the system itself, another method of providing feedback is through making local adjustments in other domains to cope with the consequences of national policies (for instance, foreign trade companies' holding onto their hard currency earnings during the AFC as a hedge against devaluation rather than selling it to banks). By changing local economic policy and recalibrating foreign economic relations at the provincial or firm level, subnational actors can both minimize the impact of national foreign policy and perhaps even shape the formulation of future foreign policy.

"Pluralization" Redux: Economic Interdependence and the Chinese Foreign Policy-Making Process

This examination of China's response to the AFC suggests that we should not overstate the degree of change in the foreign policy-making process. Although the policy process has, by virtually all accounts, become more pluralized during the reform era, the impact of decentralization on the actual output of the foreign policy system was relatively minor in the case of the AFC. The fact that a formidable pro-devaluation lobby of local and sectoral interests was resisted with relative ease suggests that the power of China's top leaders should not be underestimated, even in the post-Deng era. Indeed, everything we know about China's response to the AFC confirms the ability of the central leadership to control key foreign policy decisions.[29] This finding is especially important since the challenges posed by the AFC epitomize the nexus of foreign and domestic economic policy, where one might expect to find the greatest change in the policy-making process. Yet in this case the impact of EI was arguably greater on policy content than on the process. (Indeed, it could be argued that certain elements of the policy-making process were effectively *recentralized* during the AFC.)

This discussion, however, leaves several questions at least partially unanswered. For example, it remains difficult to measure either the degree of decentralization in the foreign policy-making process or the significance of EI as a source of this change. Another issue that will require further study is the likely impact of a more pluralized policy-making process on the prospect for new foreign policy initiatives. Does the inclusion of a broader range of interests bode well for, say, greater reform and opening (and cooperative foreign relations generally)? Or will the increasingly contested nature of the decision-making process result in more frequent instances of policy stalemate, except perhaps in critical cases such as that of WTO accession when the top leadership intervenes decisively? One effect of deepening EI is that almost no foreign policy issue falls easily into a discrete functional category. Although this was partially true even prior to the reform era, China's deepening participation in the world economy—and the growing exposure to EI that results—means that almost every actor in the system has an interest in any given foreign policy issue. Jurisdictions (functional, institutional, and regional) that used to be relatively discrete now overlap in complex ways.

Finally, consider the question of whether deepening EI increases or decreases the influence of the outside world on Chinese foreign policy. On the one hand, domestic politics in China may become more "internationalized" as external forces (such as MNCs, goods and capital markets, international norms and institutions) further penetrate China's political economy and render its borders increasingly porous. Even if one rejects the most deterministic globalization scenarios and related prognostications about the obsolescence of the nation-state, it is easy to see how deepening EI might increase the importance of external sources to Chinese behavior. On the other hand, EI could actually increase the relative weight of domestic structures as determinants of Chinese foreign policy. If EI continues to reinforce domestic economic reform and administrative decentralization, the foreign policy-making process might over time be characterized by ever increasing pluralization. From this perspective, which again is not strongly supported by the AFC case, as the rational actor model of foreign policy-making declines in utility, bureaucratic and political process models—which focus, respectively, on the institutional landscape of decision-making processes and questions of modern political economy—become more relevant. In this sense, "domestic structure" could gain explanatory weight vis-à-vis "international system influences" in the study of Chinese foreign policy, as Pearson's chapter argues was the case with regard to China's WTO policy until 1999, when the top leadership intervened decisively in favor of an intensified bid for membership.

ECONOMIC INTERDEPENDENCE AS A SOURCE OF CHINESE FOREIGN POLICY: THE CASE OF THE ASIAN FINANCIAL CRISIS

As documented in this section, Chinese foreign policy related to the AFC was motivated by a large number of considerations—economic, political, international, and domestic. Our review of the evidence here is designed to address the following question: How important was EI as a source of Chinese behavior in this case?

Economic Sources of China's Foreign Policy in Response to the Asian Financial Crisis

The main economic advantage of devaluation was clear from the onset of the AFC: Chinese exports would become more competitive in world markets, thereby allowing export expansion to continue as a stimulus for economic growth. (Most estimates suggest that export growth accounted for a quarter to a third of economic growth in China in the years immediately preceding the AFC.) Robust economic growth was, in turn, seen as critical to keeping unemployment under control, especially given the leadership's commitment to a reform agenda highlighted by SOE restructuring and government downsizing. Moreover, an economic slowdown of any magnitude carried the threat of financial crisis given the tenuous nature of China's banking system.

Despite its potential to stimulate the economy, however, a change in currency policy was not pursued. As detailed in the sections that follow, there were several economic disadvantages to devaluation. Before surveying these sources of China's currency policy, however, we should note that China's financial condition, unlike that of many other nations, did not require devaluation. Specifically, Beijing did not face a balance-of-payments crisis during 1997 and 1998. In fact, China earned a record trade surplus in 1998 ($43.6 billion), and foreign exchange reserves remained at high levels ($145 billion) despite slowing inflows of foreign capital, widespread currency fraud, capital flight, and smuggled imports. Debt management was good (for example, foreign exchange reserves exceeded total foreign debt, which stood at only 15 percent of the gross domestic product), and the macroeconomic situation was generally favorable. Finally, speculation against the renminbi was difficult, if not impossible, given its lack of convertibility for capital account transactions. Therefore, although devaluation was a viable policy option, it was not financially necessary.

Competitiveness Issues. The advantages of devaluation notwithstanding, several factors also militated against such a move. First, there were serious questions about whether devaluation would improve the competitiveness of Chinese exports. Most notably, it was feared that even a modest devaluation of the renminbi would lead to a destabilizing round of competitive devaluations among China's neighbors, thereby wiping out the benefits devaluation was supposed to create in the first place. Worse still, a series of competitive devaluations was almost certain to plunge the region into a substantially deeper recession, or even depression. In this sense Beijing was faced with the possibility that devaluation of the renminbi would do great damage to the regional economy and thereby its own economic fortunes. Even fears of a Chinese devaluation periodically sent jitters across Asia's stock and currency markets during the AFC. In this sense, the stakes were far higher than whether devaluation would provide a competitive boost to China's exports.

Even if a Chinese devaluation would not set off a round of destructive devaluations, the positive impact it might have on Chinese sales was still questionable. Chinese exports were declining mainly in East and Southeast Asia, regions where depressed demand could not be offset by cheaper prices. In other words, the issue was a loss of purchasing power rather than a lack of competitiveness on the part of Chinese goods. If these countries simply were not buying, nothing could make Chinese exports more competitive. By contrast, exports to North America and Western Europe continued to grow even without devaluing the renminbi.

As far as Japan was concerned, the minimal overlap between Chinese and Japanese exports also weakened the case for devaluation. Although a declining yen adversely affected China's exports to Japan, Beijing understood how the effects of the declining yen varied significantly from product to product. For many goods exported by China, there was little or no domestic Japanese production. Interviewees confirmed that Chinese exports to Japan were one motivation behind China's private and public diplomacy at critical junctures in the AFC, but they were not Beijing's primary concern in urging Tokyo (and Washington) to stop the yen's slide. Indeed, the greatest danger was not the decline in Chinese exports per se—whether to Japan or to third-country markets—but the implications of a declining yen for Japan's role as the economic engine of the whole region. The fall of the yen was worrisome, to be sure, but devaluation of the renminbi was not going to address the underlying problem.

Another disadvantage of devaluation was the negative impact it would have on import costs. First, more expensive imports would slow, at least marginally, rising Chinese living standards at a time when difficult economic reforms loomed on the horizon, reforms destined to increase financial hardship in many Chinese households. Second, devaluation was likely to be inflationary, especially given the higher cost of critical imports such as oil. Third, and perhaps most important, increased import costs were likely to inhibit the competitiveness of Chinese goods on the world market. Although devaluation would make finished Chinese goods cheaper on the world market, it would also raise the price of imported inputs. According to most estimates, about 50 percent of China's total exports depend on the processing of imported raw materials. Consequently, devaluation would raise production costs, perhaps even disadvantaging China's exports in certain cases. In this sense China's growing participation in TMNs reduced the efficacy of currency policy as an instrument for improving the competitiveness of "Chinese" exports.

As this analysis suggests, one advantage of renminbi stability when currencies elsewhere in the region were declining was the prospect of less expensive imports, which would lower production costs in China and thereby increase the competitiveness of Chinese goods. For example, less expensive purchases of machinery imports from Japan, South Korea, and other advanced economies augur well for lower production costs, and therefore enhanced competitiveness, well into the future. More generally, many observers argued that devaluation was an inefficient way to strengthen the economy. From this perspective China's long-term competitiveness stood to gain considerably from currency stability, because Chinese firms would feel intense pressure to become more efficient.

This logic extended not only to imported goods, but also to imported capital. Consider the case of the yen. Since Japan is the largest source of China's overseas borrowing, the combination of renminbi stability and a declining yen would lower the costs of principal and interest repayment substantially. This easing of the debt burden was quite welcome, especially given China's experience at the other end of the exchange rate game in the late 1980s, when the yen appreciated substantially after the 1985 Plaza Accord. At that time China learned the hard way how currency realignments can increase debt burdens and thereby increase the costs of financing development.

Defending the Hong Kong Dollar's Peg. Another major disadvantage of devaluing the renminbi was the belief among China's leaders that it would put unbearable pressure on the link between the Hong Kong dollar and the U.S. dollar. The end of the peg system would, in turn, seriously jeopardize Hong Kong's status as an international financial center, a position critical not only to Hong Kong's well-being, but also to China's economic development. Some observers argued that there was no inherent link between the renminbi and the Hong Kong dollar, but the international consensus was still that devaluation by Beijing was likely to cause speculators to attack the Hong Kong currency. In the case of an attack, Hong Kong officials would have to choose between raising interest rates, and thereby risking a larger recession, and delinking from the U.S. dollar. Rather than erode confidence in Hong Kong, it was argued, China should pursue alternative measures to cope with the AFC. Whereas Hong Kong was vulnerable to speculative attack, China neither had to devalue (the renminbi is inconvertible on the capital account) nor needed to devalue (Beijing's foreign exchange reserves were three times larger than China's short-term foreign debt and six times larger than the debt actually due in 1998). Therefore, China should avoid such a policy at all cost, many observers argued, in order to spare Hong Kong.

Domestic Confidence. A final disadvantage was the destabilizing effect devaluation could have had on China's domestic market at that time, particularly in terms of public confidence. In the wake of repeated promises early in the crisis that Beijing would not devalue the renminbi, any change in currency policy would likely have shaken domestic confidence badly, possibly leading to the hoarding of imported goods and a slowdown in bank deposit growth, which in turn could have sparked a financial crisis of uncertain magnitude. As documented in Nicholas Lardy's research, China's banking system was so weak in the late 1990s that Beijing undoubtedly wished rather desperately to avoid undermining monetary confidence.[30] For this reason alone, some observers argued that devaluation simply was "not a choice" as the crisis unfolded. Although this is probably an overstatement, Zhu Rongji is reported to have said in August 1998 that "the negative impact on confidence at home" was a leading reason behind the decision not to devalue the renminbi.[31]

Political Sources of China's Foreign Policy in Response to the Asian Financial Crisis

One of the most striking, though by no means surprising, aspects of Beijing's response to the AFC was the salience of political factors, domestic and international alike, in the formulation of Chinese foreign policy. As important as economic considerations were, political considerations were equally powerful. Especially in the early stages of the AFC, and particularly as regards the international dimensions of China's response, Beijing's actions were highly political in origin.

Taiwan's "Villainous Role." Much of Beijing's focus in terms of regional foreign policy during the AFC centered on Taiwan. Not surprisingly, Taiwan relations figured prominently, albeit indirectly, in the way Beijing handled AFC issues involving Hong Kong. Although most foreign observers do not believe

Taiwan has any interest in reunification, several interviewees, including two individuals with access to top leaders in both Hong Kong and Beijing, noted that China deliberately crafted its Hong Kong policy during the crisis in a way that strongly reaffirmed its support for the "one country, two systems" formula.

More directly, a wide range of interviewees emphasized that the no devaluation policy was motivated, especially in the early months of the crisis, largely as a political response to Taiwan's campaign to exert pressure on the renminbi and the Hong Kong dollar. After nearly eight years of stability vis-à-vis the U.S. dollar, Taiwan officials announced a major devaluation of the New Taiwan dollar on October 17, 1997. (According to an interviewee with access to high-level Chinese policy advisors and decision-makers, Beijing believed the timing of the devaluation was intended to disrupt Jiang's impending visit to the United States.) Although Taiwanese authorities denied any attempt to destabilize the renminbi and the Hong Kong dollar, Chinese officials later denounced the action as a conspiracy to sabotage regional currency markets.[32] Hong Kong interviewees and U.S. government officials confirmed that Beijing was largely justified in viewing Taiwan's currency policy as a competitive devaluation intended to pressure the renminbi and the Hong Kong dollar. Moreover, these sources also confirmed that "Taiwan voices" were the first to predict publicly that China would need to devalue the renminbi. As one influential Hong Kong economist recalled, it was this "badmouthing" of the renminbi and the Hong Kong dollar by Taiwan that speculators seized upon in stirring up the financial storm that hit Hong Kong in the second half of October 1997. So significant were these developments that Chinese observers generally point to Taiwan's devaluation as the beginning of the "second wave" of the AFC.[33]

In the face of this perceived political plot by Taiwan, the no devaluation policy quickly became a matter of pride to the Beijing leadership. Several interviewees indicated that the resolute nature of official Chinese statements on the renminbi is best explained as a response to the implicit challenge issued from Taipei. Given Taiwan's antagonistic behavior, China did not want to lose face. Politically, the best option—both domestically and internationally—was to stand strong at all cost, refusing to devalue. For the same reasons, China strongly opposed Taiwan's broader efforts to play the "finance card" during the AFC. For instance, it rejected an April 1998 proposal that Taipei and Beijing co-host a regional meeting to discuss the economic turmoil in East Asia. It also rejected suggestions that Taiwan provide financial aid to neighboring countries in its capacity as an APEC member. From the Chinese perspective, these initiatives represented a transparent effort to upgrade Taiwan's international status and use economic relations to develop substantive contact with ASEAN countries. All told, the goal was to deny any victory to Taiwan.

Protecting Hong Kong: "One Country, Two Interdependent Currencies." Beijing certainly cannot be accused of neglecting Hong Kong's interests in formulating its foreign policy in response to the AFC. As described earlier, the possibly negative effect of a renminbi devaluation on Hong Kong was among the chief reasons Beijing offered for its currency policy. Specifically, Premier Zhu, Finance Minister Xiang, Central Bank Governor Dai, and other high-ranking officials explained time and again that Hong Kong would not be able to keep its pegged exchange rate system if China devalued the renminbi. Although the substantive issues were ostensibly economic, China's motivation in trying to protect Hong Kong was equally political in nature. Interviewees in China confirmed the great importance Beijing placed on defending Hong Kong, both to demonstrate its effective guardianship over the new Special Administrative Region and to preserve Hong Kong's critical role in China's economic development. To this end Chinese officials not only ruled out devaluation of the renminbi, but also repeatedly pledged, among other things, to spend a considerable portion of Beijing's foreign exchange reserves to defend the Hong Kong dollar. In short, it would be difficult to overestimate the resolve with which China's leaders approached the defense of Hong Kong during the AFC. They believed devaluation of the renminbi would wreck Hong Kong's economy, thereby sullying Beijing's international reputation and ruining the credibility of the "one country, two systems" formula as a model for reconciliation with Taiwan.

Driven by Image: The Asian Financial Crisis and China as a "Responsible" International Partner. As the last point suggests, another important source of China's behavior in the wake of the AFC was Beijing's desire to improve its status internationally. As widely noted, Chinese foreign policy has been characterized in recent years by a new emphasis on cultivating its image as a responsible power. For instance, in the early stages of the AFC, when Chinese observers at all levels underestimated the severity of economic turmoil in the region and its likely impact on China, Beijing's foreign policy was motivated in no small measure by a desire to improve relations with its ASEAN neighbors. According to several well-placed interviewees, China's currency policy was regarded at the highest levels as an important instrument for pursuing China's long-term strategic interests in the region. One key objective was to address fears of a "China threat" that had emerged during the 1990s, reaching an apex in 1996 with China's military exercises off the Taiwan coast. Simply put, interviewees suggested that China's currency policy was designed in part to make China look good. Regional politics in the wake of nuclear testing by India and Pakistan in May 1998 only increased the opportunity for China to improve its international status during this period. Indeed, Beijing uncharacteristically took the initiative in organizing a meeting of the nuclear powers in Geneva shortly after the detonations on the subcontinent.

Beijing also sought to use its response to the AFC as a means to improve its relationship with Washington. As a U.S. government official explained in an interview about China's currency policy: "China wants the U.S. to be grateful, to regard China as an important partner, one that can be counted upon and deserves rewards." Indeed, it was obvious that Beijing hoped to receive, and may even have expected, favors from Washington in return for "paying a price" during the AFC. By most accounts, one motivation for China's foreign policy during the AFC was a calculation that its "responsible" behavior (for example, maintaining its no devaluation policy; aiding Thailand, South Korea, and Indonesia; and supporting Hong Kong) would establish the credentials Beijing needed to receive more favorable terms for WTO accession and lower entry costs for full participation in the world economy generally. As one Shanghai-based scholar put it, "The main political goal [of China's currency policy] may be to demonstrate its WTO worthiness."

Here devaluation also carried the disadvantage of introducing greater strain in Sino-American relations, because a declining renminbi was certain to increase the already politically divisive U.S.-China trade imbalance, which was expected to worsen even without devaluation. This, in turn, could have jeopardized Sino-American cooperation in a number of areas, including WTO accession, by creating the perception that China sought to advantage itself at the expense of others, thereby reinforcing the mercantilist image Beijing had worked so assiduously to dispel.

There can be little doubt that China's response to the AFC was motivated significantly by its desire for international prestige. In sum, three landmark opportunities for image making stand out: China's contribution to the International Monetary Fund (IMF) bailout of Thailand, its efforts to stand firm in the face of Taiwan's "predatory" devaluation, and Beijing's effort to contrast its "responsible" behavior with Tokyo's failure to provide regional and global leadership in managing the AFC (its offer to organize an Asian Monetary Fund notwithstanding). Beijing's $1 billion contribution to the IMF's Thai bailout was unprecedented in Chinese foreign policy, marking the first time it had participated in a multilateral effort of that kind. All told, China contributed more than $4 billion to assist Thailand, Indonesia, and South Korea. (As we discussed earlier, Chinese leaders were also determined to preempt a ruinous cycle of competitive devaluations across the region by withstanding devaluation pressures created by Taipei's October 1997 salvo.)

Beijing believed that, in combination with its currency policy and Keynesian efforts to pump prime the domestic economy, its financial contributions to recovery efforts in neighboring countries would improve its image as a responsible power. Furthermore, China's leaders clearly hoped their actions would invite favorable comparisons with Japan's resistance to domestic economic expansion. Given China's relatively small economic size, it would be an exaggeration to say that Beijing hoped to inherit the mantle of regional economic leadership from Tokyo, but it clearly saw an opportunity to fill leadership space left vacant by Japanese (and, for that matter, American) neglect. Indeed, many interviewees stressed that China was committed, once the opportunity arose, to play a more active role regionally than Japan (and South Korea) in managing the AFC. According to a well-connected scholar in Beijing policy circles, to understand Chinese foreign policy during the AFC one must first realize that "China is driven by image and wants badly to be seen as a good participant" regionally.

Chinese Foreign Policy in Response to the Asian Financial Crisis: Weighing the Role of Economic Interdependence

The evidence presented earlier suggests that EI did, in fact, play a role in shaping Chinese foreign policy in the wake of the AFC. Indeed, EI arguably informed both China's economic considerations (such as concerns about the impact of a renminbi devaluation on the Hong Kong dollar's peg) and its political considerations (such as the dynamics of interdependence in the context of Sino-American relations). That said, the evidence also suggests that several important sources of Chinese foreign policy during the AFC were completely unrelated to EI. This indeterminacy is not surprising, but it does raise enormous challenges for anyone trying to assess the impact of EI on Chinese foreign policy. For example, did China's "responsible" behavior during the AFC reflect the deepening impact of EI on Chinese foreign policy or simply

Beijing's strategy for improving its international image, increasing its regional influence, and competing with Taiwan? Indeed, from the latter perspective Beijing's cooperative behavior during the AFC may be part of a larger strategic shift in Chinese foreign policy that is consistent with, but not driven by, the constraints of EI.

Unfortunately, these issues are not easily sorted out. One approach would be to identify benchmarks for assessing the impact of EI on Chinese foreign policy. One benchmark used in the past to gauge China's commitment to international regimes has been the dedication of financial resources. One could therefore argue that Beijing's aid to Thailand, Indonesia, and South Korea represented a watershed in Chinese policy, a clear benchmark in the development of its interdependent foreign relations. From this perspective China's stake in the regional economy had become so great that Beijing had a self-interest not only in resisting devaluation of the renminbi, but also in contributing financially to the recovery of its neighbors. These contributions were unprecedented, to be sure, but the source of Chinese policy was nonetheless unclear. As we discussed earlier, interviewees suggested that Chinese policy might have been driven as much by concerns of image and reputation—not to mention Taiwan policy—as by the constraints of EI.

Another possible benchmark would be the adoption of policies that impose clear self-constraints, such as burden-sharing in international economic adjustment (for instance, acceptance of slower growth) and restraints on sovereignty (for instance, pledges not to exercise policy autonomy) that could easily have been avoided. In the case of the AFC, it could be argued that China's currency policy represents a critical instance where Beijing accepted self-imposed costs and otherwise limited its ability to chart an independent policy. As Beijing declared so often during the crisis, China "paid a great price" for its "responsible" international behavior. Even if Beijing was merely trying to make a virtue out of necessity, there was still some truth to its claim that China absorbed significant costs as the result of its foreign policy during the AFC. In the absence of devaluation, for example, Beijing had to subsidize Chinese exports through programs such as increased tax rebates and wider access to export credits, both of which negatively affected government coffers. In this sense the AFC was costly. At a broader level, there was also the opportunity cost of lost exports and delayed reforms associated with Beijing's no devaluation policy, neither of which should be underestimated. Finally, China had to pump prime its economy, mainly through increased commitments to public works projects and other forms of government investment, in order to compensate for economic growth arguably lost as a result of Beijing's decision not to devalue the renminbi. In short, China's currency policy during the AFC was certainly not cost free, even if China did not "pay a price" in exactly the way Beijing claimed.

On the other hand, the alternatives would likely have been even more costly. As we discussed earlier, a Chinese devaluation would have had devastating consequences regionally. These, in turn, would have damaged Chinese interests. To be sure, other countries might have been hurt more seriously, but China too would have suffered. In this sense devaluation of the renminbi might have been self-defeating. If China did in fact pursue the most cost-effective policy, how do we assess its response to the AFC against the interdependence benchmark of self-imposed costs? Does the fact that China adopted the least costly policy invalidate the AFC as a critical case in the evolution of China's interdependent foreign relations? Or is the benchmark satisfied by the fact that China accepted substantial costs—financial and otherwise—that it could easily have avoided? After all, China's response to the AFC imposed significant constraints on its domestic economic policy as well as its currency policy.

In the end, the fact that China's own economic interests led it to resist devaluation surely signifies a milestone of some kind in the evolution of its interdependent foreign relations. As we documented earlier, many of the considerations underlying Beijing's decision (such as its reliance on imported inputs and regional capital markets) hinged directly on China's increasing participation in the world economy. Put another way, even the fact that China acted with restraint to preserve its own interests during the AFC showed how much has changed, inasmuch as Chinese interests are now significantly intertwined with those of its neighbors, at least compared to the past.

CHINESE FOREIGN POLICY IN THE AGE
OF ECONOMIC INTERDEPENDENCE

As we described earlier, the essence of the global logic (GL) is a process in which latecomers respond in patterned, although by no means completely uniform, ways to pressures for change in their foreign trade systems, investment policies, and broader development strategies. From this perspective, reform and opening is best understood as a "discovery process" in which China has attempted, through trial-and-error experimentation, to improve its performance in the world economy. According to this conceptualization, the open policy has been an exercise in problem-solving, one best understood not as a coherent reform program, but as a series of ad hoc policies taken over the past two decades to address specific problems as they have arisen.

Adaptation, Learning, and Interdependence: A Conceptual Assessment

Earlier we argued that deepening EI in the international system induced, or at least reinforced, China's long-term development strategy of reform and opening. Even if EI has contributed in this way, however, it is not clear that the shift in priorities epitomized by the open policy reflects foreign policy learning, a process in which the ends as well as the means of foreign policy change. Indeed, EI is seen by China's leaders primarily as a tool for pursuing national economic revitalization, not as a goal in itself. (By contrast, one could argue that interdependence, as embodied by the European Union, is an explicit goal of certain countries in Western Europe. Additional arguments could be made, perhaps more controversially, that EI represents an independently valued goal in U.S. foreign policy.) Simply put, China has neither fully embraced EI as a world-view nor changed its strategic focus on national power. In this sense, the moderate, relatively cooperative behavior that has generally accompanied China's deepening participation in the world economy seems to reflect "adaptation" rather than "learning."[34]

That said, there have been some changes both in China's understanding of international politics and in its actual behavior that raise the possibility of a more fundamental transformation in the future. For instance, the persistence of a realpolitik approach within China's foreign policy community should not be mistaken for either a monolithic or a static view of world affairs. The range of views within the basic realist framework has grown progressively richer in China, especially in the 1990s. This widening of realist views—as well as some limited support for neoliberal institutionalism—has included many subtle (and some not-so-subtle) departures from the traditional emphasis on political-military relations in favor of greater attention to economic competition as a fundamental dynamic of international relations. Indeed, this would seem to be the lesson of Beijing's decision to make the concessions necessary to join the WTO, a policy shift clearly designed (at least in part) to use forces associated with economic globalization as a lever to accelerate domestic economic change, with national strengthening as the fundamental objective.

Along with other characteristics of China's external environment, such as the lack of imminent security threats and the low probability of war among the major powers, deepening EI in the international system has provided China with a strong incentive to make civilian economic development its top priority. As we suggested earlier, it may well be that this shift was designed not to achieve goals such as individual welfare, as economic liberalism would suggest, but to enhance China's economic strength so it can pursue great power aspirations in the long run, as political realism or economic mercantilism would suggest. That said, it is difficult to ignore the significance of China's changing priorities, regardless of its actual objectives. In this connection the adoption of a more comprehensive concept of national security is especially significant. As long as China's leaders view security at least partially in terms of sustained economic growth, Beijing will be inclined to maintain positive relations with as many countries as possible in order to take full advantage of the benefits that accrue from wider participation in the world economy. In this sense China's expanding economic and diplomatic ties, especially in East Asia, cannot be fully understood without reference to an international system characterized by deepening EI. From Beijing's efforts to diffuse conflicts in Cambodia and the Koreas to its efforts to cultivate better relations with Indonesia, Singapore, and South Korea (see the chapter by Samuel Kim), EI has arguably facilitated the taking of new directions in China's bilateral relations.

Consider also China's limited but growing support for multilateral initiatives, especially those that promote greater economic cooperation. Chinese participation in multilateral forums such as APEC has become increasingly institutionalized, and there is some evidence that Beijing is beginning to adopt the "habits of consultation and dialogue" expected by interdependence theory. Although we must be careful not to overstate this trend, there has arguably been a modest shift in China's approach to international politics from a realist-centered bilateralism (or even unilateralism) to a greater emphasis on cooperative problem-solving. In some cases, at least, China seems to view its interlocutors as partners as well as rivals. To the extent that these trends have increased in recent years, EI has undoubtedly contributed.

What all of this suggests is that the dichotomy between "adaptation" and "learning" may be overdrawn. As argued in different ways in the chapters by Gill, Economy, and Pearson, we should perhaps instead think in terms of "adaptive learning."[35] In this conceptualization, adaptation and learning are not mutually exclusive: adaptation can, over time, provide a new context—both domestically and internationally—in which learning can emerge. As China's experience with the open policy shows, adaptation has created interdependence. Although interdependence does not *necessarily* lead to learning, in the sense of value change, it is a slippery slope indeed. At the very least, room for tactical maneuver narrows as adaptation proceeds.

For example, although there were many considerations behind China's response to the AFC, the interdependent nature of currency relations in the region did constrain the "independence" of Chinese foreign policy. In fact, several interviewees noted that the AFC represented a watershed in Beijing's understanding of interdependence issues in China's foreign relations. As we discussed earlier, China's top leaders understood well the risk that a devaluation of the renminbi would set off a round of competitive devaluations among its neighbors. Although it is impossible to know whether this factor would have carried the day in the absence of other factors militating against a devaluation, a review of official speeches, public comments, and articles from leading newspapers and journals, as well as numerous interviews on the subject, suggests that there is a heightened awareness among Chinese leaders that the external impact of foreign policy decisions needs to be considered in responding to events like the AFC. At a minimum, China's experience during the AFC seems to have demonstrated to political leaders and policy elites alike that China's position is different now, with its influence on the outside world somewhat greater than in the past. This development, of course, both enables and constrains China's strategic options in foreign policy-making.

On the other hand, the effect of the outside world on China is also greater due to EI. In the case of the AFC, interviewees emphasized that China's ability to achieve economic growth targets and pursue specific reform plans depended to an unprecedented degree on international developments such as the value of the yen. Even those who argued that the no devaluation policy was adopted mostly for domestic reasons readily admitted that China's currency policy—and its economic policy generally in the wake of the AFC—was, in the words of one interviewee, "conditional upon the behavior of the United States and Japan." As the result of growing integration among the economies of East Asia, especially the integration achieved through increased capital flows in the 1990s, government policies and corporate strategies adopted in one country (such as Japan) now have a greater impact in shaping policies and strategies adopted elsewhere (such as in China). This, of course, is the essence of interdependence. Although care should be taken not to overstate the degree of such interdependence, especially for a large continental power like China, EI is now widely seen by Chinese observers as an important context for understanding Beijing's economic policy, reform plans, and foreign relations. Simply put, the predicament of interdependence is now exerting a greater, albeit still fairly modest, influence on China. Rhetoric about globalization had been growing for years in China, but in many ways it took the AFC to make the phenomenon tangible.[36]

The preceding discussion suggests that the most critical issue (for policy if not for theory) is the nature of China's interdependence with the outside world, not questions about adaptation versus learning. Put another way, what matters is the scope and degree of China's interdependence, not how it became interdependent (that is, through adaptation, learning, or adaptive learning). Whether Chinese leaders view interdependence mainly as a tool for economic modernization or as an independently valued goal, the reality of interdependence is the same. Indeed, the latter issue—whether interdependence is valued as an end in itself—matters only if the costs China is likely to incur in extracting itself from its current (increasingly) interdependent context are low or nonexistent. If the exit costs are high, the issue of adaptation versus learning arguably is less important. From this perspective, interdependence is a *predicament* countries must deal with, not a *world-view* or a foreign policy *strategy*. What matters most is China's behavior in coping with interdependence, not whether this behavior reflects adaptation or learning as such.

Economic Interdependence in Contemporary World Politics: Empowering and Restraining China

As much as EI empowers China, most notably by enabling its economic development, it also restrains its behavior in certain ways. Since the legitimacy of the Chinese regime is now heavily dependent upon economic performance, and given the additional fact that the open policy could be reversed only at great political as well as economic cost, EI can be expected to have a substantial, albeit not easily predicted, long-term impact on China's foreign policy-making process and behavior. The process of reform and opening has, over the course of two decades, already led to reduced economic sovereignty vis-à-vis the outside world and a weakening of central control over certain aspects of economic decision-making. From the perspective of interdependence theory, these kinds of conditions, in China and elsewhere, augur well for a furtherance of EI processes. At the very least, deepening EI suggests that China faces a strong incentive to cooperate with a broad group of nations, especially at the regional level. Indeed, the record over the past two decades shows that China is remarkably willing to be engaged, at least when compared to the past.

Although the constraints associated with EI are growing, they remain somewhat limited. This means that fundamental strategic choices remain before China's leadership and, on balance, Beijing must still be characterized as resisting, or at least trying to resist, the logic of EI wherever possible, even in light of its decision to accept the costs of WTO membership.[37] Although all countries try to resist the constraints of EI, or at least try to minimize the costs of EI (while readily accepting the benefits), this observation still applies to China with more than the usual force. From its mixed record of abiding by agreements on arms proliferation and intellectual property rights to its unwillingness to commit the South China Sea dispute to processes of international law, China continues to vigorously guard its economic autonomy and political sovereignty.

From this perspective, Chinese foreign policy reflects a country accommodating itself to the realities of international power rather than one that embraces the constraints of EI with palpable enthusiasm. In this sense China's moderate, relatively cooperative behavior in world affairs denotes not so much a new world-view informed by EI, but a world-view that recognizes the viability of the interstate system for meeting China's goals. (This in itself represents a significant change from the Mao era.) Despite a modest broadening of views within China's foreign policy community, the conventional framework of Chinese realpolitik still applies on the whole. At least in the short term, EI is not alone likely to transform either Chinese world-views or Chinese foreign policy. (Indeed, its impact is still arguably greatest on China's foreign relations.) If this is the case, EI cannot be relied upon as the only (or perhaps even the primary) means for managing China's rise as a great power in the international system. At a minimum, more time will be required for EI to sink its roots even deeper into China.

EIGHT

The Impact of International Regimes on Chinese Foreign Policy-Making: Broadening Perspectives and Policies . . . But Only to a Point

ELIZABETH ECONOMY

During the past two decades the domestic political and economic landscape of China has altered dramatically. Equally striking, however, has been the sea change that has occurred in Chinese foreign policy. Specifically, China has shifted from an insular, autarkic state into one that has assumed a prominent role in global affairs, seeking to participate in the full range of debates regarding relations among sovereign nations. The number of international governmental organizations of which China was a member therefore increased from twenty-one in 1977 to fifty-two in 1997.[1] Moreover, in virtually every policy arena China has joined or is seeking to gain entrance to the key accords and treaties that regulate states' behavior, as the chapters by Bates Gill and Margaret Pearson in this volume also amply demonstrate.

For both the scholarly and policy-making communities this rapid increase in Chinese participation in the institutions of global governance has raised a range of questions concerning the precise nature of Chinese involvement. What values and policy priorities does China bring to the table? What is the impact of China's evolving political and economic system on Chinese behavior and the policy-making process? What role does the international community play in shaping Chinese preferences? How effective is China's implementation of the global accords that it has ratified? What does all of this mean for the United States and other countries?

A rich literature has developed that addresses a number of these questions, and no purpose would be served in devoting too much time to repeating its findings. This chapter briefly reviews some of the key points concerning China's overall approach to international regimes and then focuses primarily on a relatively understudied question, namely: What role does the international community play in shaping Chinese preferences and policy choices in international regimes? Moreover, this chapter considers not only the preferences and choices of Chinese actors, but also the underlying policy process that leads to those choices. As David Lampton has indicated, "The key task is not simply . . . to identify discrete influences on Chinese foreign policy, but also to weave these various influences into a more coherent and integrated analysis of the Chinese national security and foreign policy-making process(es)."[2]

This chapter, therefore, illuminates the ways in which international regimes may influence the evolution of foreign policy-making in China through the establishment of new institutions, the emergence of new foreign policy actors (or the enhancement of others), and the development of new ideas, values, or orientations among Chinese decision-makers. It also offers some thoughts as to the long-term implications of such evolution in the policy-making process for China's interest in and capacity to adhere to its international agreements, a topic of concern not only in the environmental realm, but in the arms control and economic realms as well.

Although this chapter draws on the findings of prior studies of this subject,[3] it focuses on two case studies: China's accession to and implementation of the Montreal Protocol on Substances that Deplete the Ozone Layer (1991) and its initial decision to sign the Framework Convention on Climate Change (1992) and subsequent rejection of international pressure to assume any firm commitments or permit activities, such as joint implementation, that would imply even informal participation in the regime.[4] Through these two cases the chapter elucidates the salient aspects of the role of the international community in Chinese foreign policy-making and its outcomes, as well as suggests some of the factors that limit such influence.

CHINA'S OVERALL APPROACH TO
INTERNATIONAL REGIMES

As I noted earlier, numerous scholars have attempted to shed light on the values and priorities that China brings to the negotiating table and the nature of Chinese participation once it has joined an international regime. Despite significant differences in methodology among the scholars, this scholarship has resulted in a high degree of consensus. At one level, most analysts have concluded that despite an overall reorientation toward more active participation in global regimes, China remains ambivalent, if not suspicious, of global governance. Thomas Christensen argues in a recent *Foreign Affairs* article: "Chinese elites are suspicious of many multilateral organizations, including those devoted to economic, environmental, nonproliferation, and regional security issues. In most cases, China joins such organizations to avoid losing face and influence. . . . Chinese analysts often view international organizations and their universal norms as fronts for other powers."[5] Harry Harding and David Shambaugh similarly suggest that although China may now be far more integrated into the international community than previously, its "ambivalence toward cooperation has not been completely resolved." They further argue that "Chinese leaders will continue to view international regimes with suspicion, especially those whose rules they did not help write."[6] In this volume Bates Gill and Thomas Moore and Dixia Yang likewise argue that deep ambivalence characterizes China's participation in such international regimes.

Another facet of China's approach to international regimes can be summarized by what Samuel Kim has termed the "maxi-mini principle"—maximization of rights and minimization of responsibilities. Although Kim acknowledges that during the reform period Chinese elites have articulated a foreign policy orientation of "international cooperation and global interdependence," he also finds that the involvement of the People's Republic of China (PRC) in international regimes is directed at "state-enhancing, not state-diminishing functionalism." In essence, the PRC is interested only in "free rides" and in gaining access to technical expertise, foreign aid, and information in order to further its goal of economic development.[7]

More specifically, encompassed within this maxi-mini principle is a set of enduring foreign policy values that the PRC brings to the negotiating table across a range of issues. In their historical analysis of China's outlook on international relations Harding and Shambaugh suggest several such values, including protection against infringements on "territorial integrity and commercial viability, limiting foreign cultural and intellectual influences on their society," and maintenance of a "monopoly of organized political power such that all politically active organizations would be sanctioned by and loyal to the central government."[8] These same points are largely echoed by Alastair Johnston in his study of Chinese thinking on nuclear weapons: "The preferred ends have predominantly remained the preservation of territorial integrity and foreign policy autonomy, the defense of political power by the communist leadership in Beijing, and the growth of China's influence commensurate with its self-ascribed status as a major power."[9]

Other studies, most notably that resulting in a recent Council on Foreign Relations report on Chinese behavior in international regimes, further illuminate the extent to which these values have become embedded in Chinese thinking and strategy concerning international regimes.[10] For example, the report concludes that with regard to the maintenance of sovereignty, Chinese leaders remain vigilant against the incursion of unwanted foreign influence in areas as disparate as telecommunications, human rights, and the environment. Therefore, although embracing the technological advantages of participating in the telecommunications regime, Chinese leaders have engaged in a continuous battle against the "spiritual pollution" that such technology brings.[11] In the realm of human rights, China has generally "defied the efforts of international organizations and individual governments . . . to judge China's performance and impose international standards on its political system."[12] In the environmental area, China's consistent refusal to allow formal monitoring of its implementation of environmental accords, on sovereignty grounds, has earned it a reputation for advocating agreements that "have no teeth."[13] Similarly, M. Taylor Fravel argues that although China has generally adopted a more positive outlook toward peacekeeping since 1981, "as peacekeeping norms have evolved from traditional to non-traditional (e.g., don't have consent of all parties), China has maintained a traditional view by stressing the importance of sovereignty and emphasizing consent and impartiality."[14] This view was clearly governing when China agreed on the deployment of United Nations (UN) peacekeeping forces (and eventually allowed its own personnel to be sent) to East Timor in 1999 only after the Jakarta government, however reluctantly, "invited" the UN to do so.

Along with a defense of Chinese sovereignty, maintaining national security as traditionally understood is a top priority for Chinese decision-makers in negotiations with other states. Michael Swaine and Alastair Johnston have detailed the extent to which Chinese leaders continue to apply a state-centered, balance-of-power approach to their negotiation of arms control regimes. They conclude that China's growing involvement in arms control negotiations has "primarily taught it to use the arms control arena more effectively for its state-centric purposes rather than promoting a reconsideration of how best to attain security."[15] From their perspective China has been slow to adopt cooperative concepts of security and to accept the need to place real restrictions on Chinese military capabilities.[16] Johnston additionally notes, in a separate study, that for China "the world is, in the main, a threatening place where security and material interests are best preserved through self help or unilateral security."[17]

A third underlying value identified by a number of researchers is the protection of economic stability and growth. Since the initiation of reform in the late 1970s and early 1980s, the legitimacy of the Communist Party has rested primarily on the pillars of nationalism and economic growth. To the extent that international economic organizations are seen as supporting these twin goals, integration has proceeded relatively smoothly. Margaret Pearson, for example, building on the work of Susan Shirk, Harold Jacobson, and Michel Oksenberg, has described a two-stage process of Chinese integration into the primary international economic organizations. The first stage, partial integration, encompassed the period from 1978 to 1994 and was a relatively straightforward process in which "the short-term goals of the PRC reformers meshed to a significant degree with the workings of the trade and investment regime."[18] The second stage, full integration, requires opening the Chinese economy to the degree present in most free industrial economies. Chinese negotiations to join the General Agreement on Tariffs and Trade (GATT) and now the World Trade Organization (WTO) were emblematic of this second stage. As Margaret Pearson discusses in her contribution to this volume, this stage requires a far more painful set of economic and political adjustments, and at least some Chinese leaders are not convinced that the economic benefits of accession will outweigh the economic and political costs.[19] Nicholas Lardy's work on Chinese banking reform points to a related tendency of Chinese leaders to resist the steps necessary to make their banks competitive internationally[20] for fear of slowing economic growth and causing dramatic increases in unemployment. Not surprisingly, it took China's reformers such as Zhu Rongji considerable time to develop an agreement domestically and with the WTO members. Indeed, the more Chinese constituencies found out about the consequences of WTO membership, the more political resistance there was to an integrationist agenda.

Notwithstanding the tendency of Chinese leaders to "minimize their responsibilities while maximizing their rights," China's concern with its international image, especially among developing countries, has occasionally engendered a more proactive stance in its participation in international regimes. For example, as the Council on Foreign Relations report notes, "China's decision to accede to the Comprehensive Test Ban Treaty resulted in large measure from pressure from the developing world, a point made in more detail by Gill. . . . In addition, China has relinquished some of its claim on International Development Agency (IDA) loans so as to leave more money for loans to disaster-stricken Africa, thereby both making itself look good in the developing countries and demonstrating a commitment to internationalist values."[21] Nonetheless, image is likely a secondary concern to China's core values, and in 1999 China "graduated" from its IDA eligibility by virtue of its past successful economic growth. In the case of the Framework Convention on Climate Change, for example, despite substantial pressure from some developing countries to limit its production of the "greenhouse gases" that contribute to climate change, China's concerns about the infringement of Chinese sovereignty through monitoring requirements and the possibility that the treaty would limit economic development outweighed China's interest in fostering a more positive international image.[22]

The literature I cited earlier highlights the continuity in Chinese values and approaches to international regimes across both issue and time. On one level these analyses suggest a relatively static picture of Chinese participation in regimes, giving the scholar or policy-maker a fairly high degree of predictive ability concerning future Chinese behavior. Yet none of the scholars I cited earlier would subscribe to such a static picture. In fact, Chinese participation in regimes—from accession through implementation—is a highly dynamic process, with implications regarding both the mechanisms by which China makes its foreign policy and the evolution of that policy. By the very nature of the ongoing interaction between Chinese domestic institutions and those of the international arena, China's involvement in international regimes represents a nexus of domestic and foreign policy.

This chapter looks at half of this equation: the impact of the international community on Chinese foreign policy-making processes and policy outcomes. What changes have been wrought through the efforts of the international community? What are the sources of such changes? And what is the potential for such changes to yield a longer-term and broader shift in China's foreign policy orientation? In other words, how, why, and when do international linkages matter in shaping policy-making and influencing policy outcomes on Chinese participation in international regimes?

THE IMPACT OF INTERNATIONAL REGIMES ON THE POLICY-MAKING PROCESS

International regimes and the process of establishing international regimes may influence the manner in which a participant formulates policy. Such influence is important for several reasons: the transmission of new ideas and knowledge from the international community can contribute to the learning process and to changes in behavioral norms by domestic actors, the requirements of the regime may result in the proliferation of new domestic actors or the establishment of new bureaucratic linkages that will influence policy outcomes, and regimes often provide training opportunities, financial transfers, and technological advances that enable policy change.

International actors will often attempt to influence expert discourse within states. In the fields of trade, arms control, and the environment, for example, there are a growing number of international linkages among nongovernmental organizations (NGOs), experts, and policy-makers. In the environmental arena, Peter Haas argues that transnational expert groups, or what he terms "epistemic communities," have emerged around specific policy concerns, such as Mediterranean Sea pollution.[23] These expert communities link scientists, bureaucrats, journalists, and representatives of NGOs who share common concerns and expertise in an area and share certain values and norms. Often these linkages arise from the regime itself. The roles of these communities in affecting policy, in turn, depend to a significant extent on their access to key decision-makers. However, they are most likely to be effective in issue areas where technical expertise is necessary in the decision-making process, such as trade, arms control, and the environment.[24]

For developing countries such as China, international experts have proven instrumental in contributing to the establishment or enhancement of a domestic expert community with shared values. By identifying Chinese experts or potential experts and drawing them into the international discourse, the international regime may therefore contribute to the development of a domestic community of experts.[25] In the trade arena, Jacobson and Oksenberg found strong evidence that the World Bank and the International Monetary Fund (IMF) contributed not only to deepening the expertise of Chinese trade and foreign policy analysts and to establishing an epistemic community but also to reconfiguring the balance of power among various individuals and groups of Chinese economic experts; Pearson's findings in this volume also make this point.[26] In some cases Chinese leaders themselves may decide that the technical demands of a regime necessitate the development of domestic expertise and then decide to send individuals abroad for training and research opportunities. Garrett and Glaser, for example, have identified such a community of foreign-trained arms control experts in China.[27]

The international community may also provide resources to domestic actors either to ease the process of accession to a regime or to help ensure implementation of the regime's goals. Kim notes that the World Bank, for example, is viewed as providing "free technical assistance not available from other commercial banks . . . [serving as] a kind of global repository of scientific knowledge on economic development."[28] Jacobson and Oksenberg's study further elaborates the importance of the World Bank in this regard. One Chinese official they interviewed noted: "With the Bank's assistance, we have come to understand that just importing equipment is not enough. Management is also important. So, the Bank insists that with every project, there must be a training component. This focus on how to manage a project is crucial. Previously there had been much waste of material in capital construction projects, but foreign management techniques help us to reduce waste. So, competitive bidding, foreign consultants, training of personnel have changed our minds about undertaking projects and taught us how to reduce costs and improve quality."[29]

A third way in which international regimes or institutions influence domestic processes and outcomes is by helping to establish institutions and laws that address new activities relevant to the international regime. The demands of entering into a new regime often include meeting a wide range of requirements. Data collection, monitoring of implementation, and reporting results typically necessitate the establishment of new bureaucratic linkages and even permanent institutions. These institutions also provide a means by which domestic actors become inculcated with the values of the regime.[30] In turn, these actors may become advocates for deeper and broader reforms in Chinese foreign policy and attitudes.

Oksenberg and I cite a range of examples in which new institutional arrangements have been established to meet the demands of a regime. With regard to national patent, copyright, and trademark protection, for example, intellectual property rights tribunals are being created within the court system.[31] In the environmental realm, for each treaty China has signed, the leadership has established a complex institutional arrangement to ensure that all relevant agencies are involved in the decision-making and implementation processes.[32] Typically the Chinese leadership will establish a leading group including representatives of the bureaucracies with the greatest expertise on the issues involved in the regime and those whose interests will be affected by the regime, a bureaucratic procedure that Lu Ning, Margaret Pearson, and Michael Swaine also describe in their chapters in this volume. Under the auspices of this leading group, numerous additional agencies and regional actors may become involved in the policy-making process, either by being tapped to provide data and input or by participating in preparatory meetings for the international negotiations. A range of offshoot activities may also be initiated under the auspices of these individual agencies. Nongovernmental environmental organizations have also emerged, some of which are now becoming involved in ensuring local implementation of international environmental commitments.[33] Swaine and Johnston have also delineated how, in response to technical arms control issues, the Ministry of Foreign Affairs increasingly sought input from technical specialists at the Commission of Science, Technology, and Industry for National Defense, the China Academy of Engineering Physics, and other math and physics institutes. This marked the beginning of an interagency process that brought new actors into the policy-making process and contributed to the broader pluralization of the policy-making process that Lampton describes in his introduction to this volume.[34]

INTERNATIONAL REGIMES AND CHANGES IN POLICY OUTCOMES

If China's accession to and participation in international regimes does in fact engender new institutions, bureaucratic processes, and heightened state capacities, the question remains: Does participation in regimes actually affect the values and preference ordering of leaders? Do norms of behavior evolve in ways that are consistent with the regime? Kim has articulated an overarching theory on the mechanism by which international institutions affect Chinese behavior. He says: "Most IGOs [intergovernmental organizations] can have influence through their own global agendas on the shaping or reshaping of Chinese national agendas. Most IGOs both give and take information, thereby gradually affecting Chinese foreign policy makers' perception of self-interest and their calculations of the costs and benefits of norm-abiding and norm-defying behavior."[35] He further notes that compliance with international agreements "inevitably calls for readjustment or restructuring of certain values, principles, norms and institutions of Chinese foreign policy."[36] Finally, he argues that "Post-Mao Chinese global learning does not have clearly demonstrated starting and ending points in time. Instead, it can be better explained as a form of learning process itself, an ongoing cognitive and experiential re-evaluative process in which both domestic and external variables interact and mediate between actors' perceptions of national needs, interests and beliefs."[37]

This interplay is revealed most clearly in the economic realm. Jacobson and Oksenberg stress a process of "mutual learning." They note several policies that the Chinese adopted based on information and advice from the World Bank and the IMF. These included increasing interest rates, improving China's data management, and expanding the policy of price reform related to coal.[38] At an even more basic level, they note that the PRC's acceptance of Ricardo's theory of comparative advantage allowed Chinese economists to communicate more effectively with Western economists.[39] Indeed, trade has moved from the periphery of China's development strategy to the center. Pearson also illuminates the extent to which Chinese officials adapted their domestic legislation to increase foreign involvement in China's economic development. In 1988 they removed restrictions on profit repatriation by joint ventures.[40] Similarly, in their drive to gain admission to GATT, the Chinese lowered the tariffs on twenty-two imported goods in 1991; the following year they opened many service industries to foreign investment.[41] Additionally, in adapting to international norms for the protection of intellectual property norms, Wang Yangmin notes that the Chinese implemented a number of reforms based on Western practice, such as "extension of copyright protection . . . and the removal of the prohibition against the patenting of pharmaceuticals and chemicals."[42]

Even in the most sensitive foreign policy area, arms control, there is some evidence that the Chinese have learned from contacts with the West and that this has affected behavioral norms (albeit in a limited sense), a point Gill makes in his contribution to this volume. Swaine and Johnston argue that contact between Western and Chinese arms control experts has "helped buttress arguments in favor of signing the NPT [Nuclear Non-Proliferation Treaty] and CTBT [Comprehensive Test Ban Treaty] and joining the FMPC [Fissile Material Production Cutoff] talks. They [Western experts] have also exposed some members of the community to ideas about minimum deterrence, ideas that run contrary to much of the thinking in the uniformed PLA [People's Liberation Army] about limited deterrence."[43] Through their discussions with Chinese arms control experts Garrett and Glaser discovered an important shift in Chinese perceptions of the NPT following China's accession. They noted a "major change in thinking among scientists, analysts and officials in China during the early 1990s after China had signed on to the NPT," representing a "growing appreciation in China of the value of arms control in enhancing Chinese security."[44]

International theorists, however, have warned against assuming that policy shifts are accurate signals of long-term changes in behavioral norms. It is important, therefore, to distinguish learning in which beliefs and values change along with policies from simple tactical learning, in which policy changes but beliefs remain the same[45] (or, as Johnston terms it, "adaptation versus learning").[46] In his analysis of Chinese policy shifts in the arms control arena, Johnston concludes that there has been no paradigm shift in Chinese thinking concerning arms control that would signal learning. He states: "The learning explanation does not appear to account for many of the key features of Chinese arms control behavior . . . [whereas] the adaptation model does appear to account for 'more' variance in Chinese arms control behavior. The basic defect–free ride decision rule that characterized Chinese behavior in the early 1980s persists into the 1990s."[47]

The implications of Chinese adaptation rather than learning may have long-term consequences for actual foreign policy. For example, Hung-yi Jan refers to the PRC's decision to sign the intellectual property rights agreement in February 1995 as an example of "forced learning of international reciprocity." He states that in order to avoid punitive tariffs imposed by the United States, the PRC undertook a number of "immediate steps to curtail infringements on intellectual property of American manufacturers covered by copyrights, patents, and trademarks, and improve enforcement methods to prevent future abuses."[48] Although Jan views this as a successful exercise and an example of how intense international pressure can bring about change in PRC behavior, the question arises as to whether such "forced learning" actually produces sustained change in PRC behavior. At least two Chinese foreign policy analysts suggest not, noting: "If a country thinks that the treaty is unfair and that it adversely affects its security, it will find a way around it."[49] This is supported by George Schaller's experience in assisting the PRC's efforts to control trade in endangered species. Schaller discovered that even with education, training, and economic incentives, knowledge may not be absorbed in such a way as to produce a long-term, sustainable transformation of behavior. In this case apparently significant changes in the behavior on the part of Chinese actors were the result of short-term, immediate economic incentives. When those incentives were no longer present, attitudes and practices reverted to previous norms.[50]

THE CASE STUDIES

Chinese participation in two environmental treaties—the Montreal Protocol on Substances That Deplete the Ozone Layer[51] and the Framework Convention on Climate Change[52]—offers the opportunity to understand whether and how China's interaction with international regimes may contribute to evolution in the policy-making process and to substantive policy change. Beyond simply adding one more voice to the choir, however, these case studies can help to sort out which variables within the interaction of the international regimes and China are relatively significant in determining the Chinese negotiating stance and behavior.

The Montreal Protocol

China, like all developing countries, was not involved during the early stages of international negotiations on ozone depletion in the 1970s. In fact, it was not until immediately prior to the Vienna Convention (1985)[53] that the Chinese scientific community was prompted to explore the issue of ozone depletion already being studied by the international community.[54] Pressed by the discovery of a growing ozone hole only six months after the Vienna Convention, the Chinese expert community, led by Beijing University atmospheric chemist Tang Xiaoyan, undertook a number of studies that eventually caught the attention of China's top science official, Vice Premier Song Jian, head of the State Science and Technology Commission (SSTC). Likely at Song's behest, in 1987 the Chinese leadership sent an observer to attend the next round of negotiations, which culminated in the formulation of the Montreal Protocol. Once the protocol had been signed by the advanced industrialized states, the international community, specifically the United Kingdom, began to encourage the Chinese to consider joining it as well.

The relatively high degree of international attention, scientific certainty, and interest of the Chinese scientific community persuaded the Chinese leadership to establish a working group under the auspices of the National Environmental Protection Agency (NEPA) to evaluate the costs and benefits of signing the protocol.[55] This group concluded that there were three reasons China should sign the Montreal Protocol. The most important reason was its potential sanctioning mechanism. China was interested in becoming a major exporter of light industrial products (such as refrigerators) that used ozone-depleting substances (ODSs). The protocol, however, forbade signatories from purchasing such products and sanctioned those countries that traded in them. Other concerns included a belief that as a member of the international community China should contribute to the resolution of this international environmental problem and that it would serve China's image to sign. According to one member of the working group, strong scientific evidence and interactions with the international scientific community were key components of the group's deliberations.

Once China joined the international deliberations,[56] however, there was little evidence of the cooperative or proactive attitude expressed by the working group. The bottom line for the Chinese participants was the financial implication of joining the Montreal Protocol. Along with India, China refused to sign the accord without significant financial support and transfers of technology from the international community. Both countries argued that given the historical responsibility of the industrialized nations for ozone depletion, as well as the need for developing nations to place a higher priority on meeting their populations' basic needs, the industrialized nations should bear the brunt of financing India's and China's abatement measures aimed at chlorofluorocarbons.

In response to the Indian and Chinese demands, the international community agreed to establish a multilateral fund to offer assistance in the form of both financial compensation and technology transfers. The agreement of the international community was undoubtedly due to the ability of China and India, as large countries with potentially significant ODS production and consumption capacities, to negate the impact of the Montreal Protocol if they did not participate. China ratified it in 1991.

In the wake of the international negotiations China moved rapidly to fulfill its international obligations by developing a vast bureaucracy to manage its ozone protection effort, including a fourteen-agency leading group and a full-time office under NEPA's auspices with seven full-time and thirty-four part-time employees. To date China has received positive marks from the international community for its "proactive" approach and the concrete measures it has taken to phase out ozone-depleting substances (including closing factories that produce and consume ODSs). Thus far the multilateral fund has contributed almost $200 million to this effort. This funding, coupled with the strong commitment of State Environmental Protection Administration (SEPA) officials to phase out ODSs, has produced significant results.

Nonetheless, there have been indications that the strongest supporters of the Montreal Protocol are encountering obstacles in their efforts. Bureaucratic politics is one source of difficulty. In 1996 a Ministry of Foreign Affairs (MFA) official with some oversight responsibility for environmental issues indicated that the Ministry of Public Security, which is responsible for the production and consumption of the ODS halon for use in fire extinguishers, was refusing to comply with a state mandate to utilize substitutes. Its local public security bureaus derived substantial income from a monopoly on the production and sale of fire extinguishers using halon.[57] Since that time, however, China has applied for and received an additional $66 million grant from the multilateral fund to pay for the replacement of halon. Reportedly this grant has energized the Ministry of Public Security toward greater compliance.[58]

The nature of the Chinese economic and political order poses a second challenge to Chinese proponents of the Montreal Protocol. The industries that consume ODSs are small and dispersed, making enforcement difficult. Some Chinese officials fear that neither China's market mechanisms nor its regulatory abilities are adequate to enforce implementation over the long term. Local officials have little incentive to enforce regulations that will limit their revenues. In the foam sector (foams are used in the automobile and construction industries), for example, despite $31 million in grants from the multilateral fund to develop and implement foam substitutes, by 1997 only seven projects had been completed. The vast majority of a thousand small foam-manufacturing enterprises have had no access to this money, to alternative technologies, or even to information about ozone depletion and the multilateral fund.[59] Without such information and financial assistance, implementation and enforcement have been poor. Finally, China's interactions with the communities of international experts and IGOs have been strained. Chinese scientific experts claim that the World Bank, United Nations Development Program (UNDP), and Asian Development Bank consultancy processes do not support indigenous Chinese technological development, but force the Chinese to accept Western consultants who utilize technologies from Dupont or Imperial Chemical Industries. Moreover, the Chinese ministries responsible for various aspects of implementation (such as the Ministry of Light Industry and the Ministry of Electronics) are consequently required to devote manpower and financial resources to such things as translating relevant materials, negotiating, and hosting foreign experts.

The Framework Convention on Climate Change

At the outset of the scientific negotiations on climate change (1988–90),[60] China had conducted little climate change research with the exception of a long tradition of paleoclimatology, which is generally considered only marginally useful as a predictor for future global climate change. In order to meet the demands of the international negotiations, therefore, China suddenly had to develop a highly sophisticated research effort. The State Environmental Protection Commission brought together four agencies—the SSTC, NEPA, the State Meteorological Administration (SMA), and the MFA—to develop a research program. By 1989 China's program encompassed forty projects and involved about twenty ministries and five hundred experts.

The international community was instrumental in funding this scientific research. The World Bank, the Asian Development Bank, the United Nations Environment Program, the UNDP, Japan, and the United States took steps to provide monitoring equipment for greenhouse gas emissions, share computer modeling techniques, offer technological assistance in developing response measures, and train Chinese environmental officials. For example, the State Planning Commission's (SPC's) Energy Research Institute became a focal point for international work on energy and climate change (despite having no history of such research) when the U.S. Department of Energy's Pacific Battelle Memorial Labs identified a few talented economists from the institute and trained them in the United States. China eventually used a variation of one of Battelle's models for estimating emissions of carbon dioxide in preparation for the political negotiations.

The international expert community also had an important impact on the ideas expressed by the domestic expert community. As the research program progressed, serious differences in approach and understanding emerged among the Chinese scientists concerning the implications of climate change for China. Many researchers, especially those within the SMA, relied on outdated methodologies such as paleoclimatology, which yielded more conservative findings concerning the impact of climate change. In contrast, NEPA and the SSTC, which had no tradition of climate research, relied heavily on the international community for their education and training, resulting in a far more proactive set of recommendations. The international community thus expanded the range of environmental and economic scenarios developed by the Chinese and even contributed to a radical reorientation in the perspective of some officials. One SSTC official, for example, stated that his basic knowledge of climate change came almost entirely from contacts with scientists and officials from abroad. This interaction transformed his thinking and encouraged him to assert a proactive position as to how China should respond to the threat of global warming.

However, there is some evidence that there was limited transmission of new ideas from Chinese experts to officials within the energy sector, which was central to the Chinese research effort and received substantial attention from the international expert community. According to one prominent energy specialist, Chinese energy officials typically could not understand the computer models generated to explain projections of energy usage and pricing, ignored complex reports detailing energy efficiency options, and relied on their traditional methodologies for assessing the makeup of China's energy structure, thereby avoiding serious consideration of alternative energy sources.

From the range of ideas and research produced by the scientific community, the NEPA and SMA each submitted a report to a core Chinese decision-making committee for climate change. The emphasis and concerns of the reports, however, varied significantly.[61] The NEPA report substantially credited the research and thinking of the international community on climate change in China. The report concluded that global warming would affect every aspect of Chinese society—agriculture, forestry, animal husbandry, marine life, and industry. Overall, NEPA experts believed that agricultural productivity would suffer a 5 percent loss and that there would be an increase in forest fires, soil erosion, and pestilence, all affecting public health. In contrast, the SMA report, although acknowledging a relationship between carbon dioxide and an overall warming of the global climate, stated that given regional discrepancies, it was essentially impossible to predict the overall impact of global warming for China. The results of China's research effort on global climate change were inconclusive, so the message the scientific community sent to the political elite was a mixed one.

Immediately on the heels of the domestic and international scientific deliberations, Chinese leaders began to focus on the political negotiations. As early as the spring of 1990 the seven organizations with primary responsibility for arriving at China's negotiating position—primarily the SSTC, the SPC, the MFA, and NEPA and secondarily the Ministry of Energy, the Ministry of Forestry, and the Ministry of Agriculture—had arrived at a set of five principles to guide the Chinese negotiating effort. These principles reflected familiar themes of Chinese participation in other international regimes: sovereignty (no country may interfere with the decisions of another as to its use of natural resources), the primacy of economic development (as opposed to environmental protection), the historic responsibility of the advanced industrialized states for the problem at hand, the necessity that the advanced industrialized states bear the financial and technological burden of responding to the problem, and the concern that the technology to remedy the problem be transferred at below-marginal cost.

Despite general agreement among the various ministries, there were significant differences of opinion concerning the degree to which China ought to contribute to the international effort to respond to climate change. For some officials in NEPA and the SSTC the potential access to technology, management techniques, and environmental management practices, combined with a sense that China had a responsibility to participate because it was a major contributor to the problem,[62] created a more proactive attitude. At the same time, others in the SPC and the MFA believed that economic development and sovereignty concerns necessitated a limited Chinese response. In reconciling these views the SSTC, which was originally charged with drafting the final report for the negotiations, was replaced by the politically more powerful SPC. However, not only did the SPC lack the expertise to develop a sophisticated analysis; in fact it did not even have a bureaucratic mandate to examine the issue of climate change until after the scientific negotiations. Its first departments devoted to climate change (and the environment generally) were established in 1991.

The result of this domestic bargaining process was that China quickly earned a reputation as one of the most recalcitrant participants in the international political negotiations, advocating the weakest reporting obligations and no concrete measures or timetables for reducing greenhouse gas emissions. China also vociferously opposed proposals by the advanced industrialized states for joint implementation, allowing the advanced industrialized states to "get credit" for their share of decreased emissions by undertaking projects in other countries. The Chinese claimed this would permit the advanced industrialized states to avoid the painful economic adjustments they were asking of the developing world.

Therefore, despite the wide-ranging impact of the international community on the development of domestic Chinese institutions, the establishment of an epistemic community, and a flow of funds to China for scientific research, China's stance on climate change was among the least proactive of any participant involved in the political negotiations. In part this was likely because, unlike the circumstances surrounding the Montreal Protocol, the centrality of science was limited during the actual formulation of China's negotiating position on climate change. As one science official commented, "The policy making on climate change depends on social issues, not science." In addition, the potential economic costs of taking action on climate change were far greater than those involved in reducing ozone depletion. A meaningful Chinese response to global climate change would have required a complete reorientation of the Chinese energy industry and substantial investment in new energy-efficiency technologies; indeed, similar concerns have been partially responsible for the U.S. Senate's balking at the Kyoto agreement. A third factor that perhaps contributed to China's maintenance of a highly noncooperative approach to the negotiations was the lack of any real image costs to the PRC. After some initial criticism by the developing countries (which China managed to coopt early in the negotiation process), only the NGO community appeared ready to criticize the PRC for its inaction.[63]

The conclusion of the political negotiations left China without having undertaken any substantive commitment to reduce its impact on global climate change. Moreover, eight years and three additional rounds later, China has still managed to avoid adopting any formal or voluntary targets or timetables that would commit it to reducing emissions. Initial signs that China might have been putting into place the bureaucratic means by which new policies on climate change could emerge have proven disappointing. In the wake of the meeting for signing of the Framework Convention on Climate Change and the UN Conference on Environment and Development (held simultaneously in Rio de Janeiro in 1992), China developed a master environmental plan for the entire country (based on an international model), China's Agenda 21. This plan was designed to meet China's international environmental obligations (including several projects on climate change), as well as to address the full range of domestic environmental challenges confronting China. Under the auspices of the SSTC and the SPC,[64] a vast bureaucracy, including bureaus down to the city level, was established. The agenda relies heavily on external sources of knowledge, funding, and technology. The possibility of receiving funding and training from the international community has apparently provoked fierce bureaucratic rivalries in which the quality of the scientific endeavor proposed is secondary to the likelihood of gaining access to funds or training opportunities. Thus far, moreover, agenda projects have been primarily focused on local environmental quality issues, such as responding to air pollution in Benxi, rather than addressing global environmental concerns.[65]

During 1998 significant changes in China's leadership on climate change policy also suggested that there might be a shift in China's posture. Thus far, however, no such evolution has occurred. At the top, Li Peng's 1998 replacement as premier, Zhu Rongji, might have had some impact. Zhu reportedly indicated to foreign and domestic scientific and policy elites alike that China should find a constructive role to play on the issue of climate change. As of yet, however, Zhu has not introduced any significant innovations in China's climate change policy.[66] In addition, of the four leading agencies in the Climate Change working group—the State Development and Planning Commission (SDPC), the State Economic and Trade Commission (SETC), the MFA, and the Ministry of Science and Technology—as of 1998 three had new leaders, suggesting the potential for revisiting China's stance. Meanwhile, the growing role of the SETC in the wake of the 1998 changes in the State Council has reportedly given a greater presence to those in the working group who are interested in a more proactive climate change policy in order to gain access to new technologies from abroad. According to one Chinese scientist, there is increasing dissatisfaction among some of the industrial and scientific agencies with the MFA's hard stance at the climate change negotiations. The sentiment is that China is missing significant opportunities to advance its technological know-how because of a reluctance to agree to any sort of cooperation.[67]

A new Climate Change Coordinating Committee also has been established under the auspices of the SPDC, with four officials assigned to coordinate the projects and activities of the fourteen agencies involved in climate change research and policy development. Unfortunately these officials have little expertise in climate change.[68] There has also been a burst of activity on climate change within the scientific community. In 1996 the Chinese Academy of Sciences hosted a major conference on climate change and its effects on China. The resulting 560-page report, *Studies on Climate Change and Its Effects,* includes a number of articles that point to the potential devastation climate change will wreak on the PRC. However, its policy recommendations still tend to support adaptation rather than mitigation,[69] with a continued call for more scientific research to reduce the uncertainties inherent in climate change.[70]

Moreover, the gap between the scientific community and even the most proactive members of the policy-making community remains significant. At a Chinese conference on technology transfer that brought together Chinese, Japanese, and American scientists to discuss climate change and environmental technology, the scientists reached consensus on the need to reform barriers to internal and external technology transfer. However, the participating policy-makers—including Qu Geping, head of the National People's Congress's Committee on Natural Resources and Environmental Protection; Zhang Kunmin, deputy head of the SEPA; and Zhou Fengqi, director of the SDPC's Energy Research Institute—acknowledged only the external barriers and criticized the participating scientists for not stressing the need for developed countries to pay the cost of technology transfers and to devote a greater part of their GDP to environmental protection in developing countries.

Therefore, without any significant pressure from these domestic actors, China's negotiating stance at the most recent round of negotiations, the Conference of the Parties IV in November 1998, reflected the same set of interests the delegation had articulated in the early 1990s: the need for the developed countries to take action first, continued technology transfer from the developed countries under favorable terms, and no commitment on targets or timetables for emission reductions. An additional concern, however, arose with the defection of Argentina from the alliance of developing countries that China had established in 1991. When Argentina agreed to set voluntary commitments, China protested vehemently, stating that such commitments would "create a new category of Parties under the FCCC [Framework Convention on Climate Change] and could destroy the unity of the G-77/China."[71] China also repeatedly called to task those developed countries that were not going to meet their reporting or emissions reduction targets by the year 2000.[72]

There are, however, signs of some movement in China's position toward a version of the Brazilian proposal for a Clean Development Mechanism (CDM) as an alternative to joint implementation. A CDM would permit the same type of emissions reduction activities as joint implementation, but would not involve crediting the sponsoring advanced industrialized country. Therefore, China would receive the benefit of externally funded projects to advance energy efficiency or reforestation without assuming any obligations or permitting other countries to take credit.

In this regard, continued initiatives by the West to educate and cultivate Chinese policy-makers may have yielded some results. Since 1996 the United States has engaged in a regular dialogue with China under the auspices of Vice

President Al Gore's Office on Climate Change.[73] In 1997 Gore and Premier Li Peng established the U.S.-China Forum on Environment and Development. The forum, which has met twice since that time (most recently in December 1999 in Hawaii), has dealt extensively with both the scientific and political aspects of climate change. Currently, within the science working group of the forum there are plans to pursue highly focused climate change impact studies for various regions within China in the hopes that this may further heighten Chinese interest in undertaking mitigation efforts. There is also a separate high-level dialogue on climate change sponsored by the U.S. Department of State designed to engage senior Chinese negotiators and policy-makers.[74] Still, reports from the forum sessions suggest that future progress will remain difficult: the Chinese believe that the U.S. focus on climate change is misplaced given the myriad environmental issues China confronts, and they are frustrated by the lack of U.S. financial assistance to implement the many proposals of Chinese action emanating from U.S. negotiators and forum participants.[75]

The nongovernmental communities' interaction with Chinese policy-makers and scientists also continues to be a crucial element in the development of Chinese thinking on climate change. Prior to the June 1998 summit between President Clinton and President Jiang, a paper authored by Chinese and U.S. environmental scientists reportedly contributed to the decision of the Chinese government to add environmental issues (including climate change) to its agenda proposal.[76] In addition, the U.S.-based World Resources Institute hosted one of the new Climate Change Coordinating Committee officials, Sun Cuihua, for two months to help develop her expertise on climate change issues.[77] The value of such an inexpensive, long-term investment has become increasingly clear in recent years. For example, one of the SDPC's economists educated on climate change by Battelle in the early 1990s was a member of the Chinese delegation to the climate change negotiations in 1998.

In addition to efforts of the international community to educate and train their Chinese counterparts, changes in the international arena may place additional pressure on China to be more flexible in its negotiating posture. Argentina's defection from the ranks of the developing countries' united front has weakened the Chinese position and will likely contribute to increasing pressure from domestic actors who are concerned that Argentina will benefit disproportionately from access to technology and assistance from the advanced industrialized countries for its proactive stance.[78]

CONCLUSION

China's participation in both the ozone and climate change regimes supports the findings of previous studies of China's interaction with international regimes. The regimes must not hinder China's economic development, infringe on its sovereignty (either through monitoring by external actors or determination of how China utilizes its resources), or permit the advanced industrialized countries to further the already unequal technological or economic advantages they enjoy. Perhaps the only contrary finding is that China will sign onto accords it did not have a role in designing so long as the rules are consistent with its interests as stated earlier. A primary finding is that China's interaction with international regimes shapes the context in which decisions are made rather than the specific decisions (that is, it introduces new actors and ideas). However, where international actors involved in the regimes provide funding and technology, these regimes, in fact, can induce fundamental changes in policy. In terms of developing the policy-making framework, international regimes spur the emergence of new bureaucratic arrangements to manage China's involvement in the regimes and encourage the introduction of new actors from the scientific and expert communities into prominent policy-making positions. In both the ozone and climate change cases, these new bureaucratic arrangements have been maintained in order to continue to address the needs of the regimes.

The impact of the epistemic community on Chinese thinking on both ozone depletion and climate change—at least within some institutions of the Chinese bureaucracy—has been substantial. Twenty years ago China had only a very small scientific community specializing in these issues, and these researchers had to actively pursue access to cutting-edge technologies, monitoring techniques, and equipment. The international scientific community was instrumental in developing the expertise of these researchers and, in the case of climate change, identifying talented scientists who could quickly come up to speed on the complex issues and serve as China's experts in the negotiations. Moreover, through formal and informal channels these Chinese scientists have gained direct access to the Chinese leadership and have had a significant impact in encouraging Chinese consideration of climate change in bilateral discussions with the United States.

At the same time it is clear that the international scientific and policy-making communities played little role in determining the outcomes of the decision-making processes. In the case of global climate change, despite scientific evidence that climate change would have a substantial negative effect on the Chinese economy, especially in agriculture, the science of climate change remained incidental to political decision-making. China's negotiation strategies reflected the core values outlined in the first section of this chapter. Although initially the relatively high degree of scientific uncertainty on climate change (in contrast, for example, to the science of ozone depletion) may have contributed to Chinese reluctance to take action, Chinese scientists and policymakers alike appear to remain focused overwhelmingly on questions of equity and the protection of their right to continue to develop economically. In the case of ozone depletion, although the epistemic community played a role in domestic deliberations, it was not until its economic demands were met that China assumed a more proactive orientation toward accession. Ultimately, then, the key to Chinese accession and compliance was the international community's willingness to finance its implementation efforts.

In both cases Chinese institutions and actors proved remarkably resistant, and the international community was not always effective at reaching the level at which it might alter domestic politics. In the case of global climate change, the international community lacked the tools—both financial and educational— to recruit support from the key economic and industrial actors. Therefore, Chinese cooperation was unlikely. As Oksenberg and Economy have noted, "Participation in an international regime ultimately is in the hands of Chinese bureaucracies. . . . To understand China's policies, one must understand the bureaucratic politics and interests at work."[79]

Both the ozone reduction and climate change regimes involved a number of ministries and government agencies. Throughout the accession and implementation processes these bureaucracies held competing perspectives and interests with regard to the regimes. In the case of global climate change, a bureaucracy that felt threatened by the potential demands of the regime— the SPC—was able to capture the issue. The perspective of its successor organization, the SDPC, has been similarly conservative; however, the emergence of a second powerful player (the SETC) with a different set of priorities suggests that there may be new opportunities for a reorientation of the Chinese negotiating posture. In the case of ozone depletion, the lead agency, NEPA, was eager to support the goals of the regime for environmental reasons and to improve its own domestic and international standing. Even after the top leadership endorsed the regime, however, a recalcitrant bureaucracy—the Ministry of Public Security—hindered implementation until it secured what it deemed adequate compensation.

In the cases of both regimes the international community exerted a set of relatively discrete influences that shaped China's foreign policy-making process and, to a lesser extent, the policy outcome. This interaction between the regimes and domestic actors and institutions continues, however, and may yet produce more substantial changes in both process and outcome. Moreover, the relatively high degree of institutionalization of an entirely new and broad-based environmental bureaucracy with direct and extensive ties to the international community suggests the potential for the type of "paradigm shift" needed for learning to occur among a large segment of the Chinese policy-making community. Still, without adequate financial and technological compensation, China will likely continue to resist a dramatic change in its positions.

PART FOUR

Case Studies

Two Steps Forward, One Step Back: The Dynamics of Chinese Nonproliferation and Arms Control Policy-Making in an Era of Reform

BATES GILL

Over the past fifteen years, and particularly since the early 1990s, Chinese non-proliferation and arms control policy has shifted remarkably, drawing closer to widely accepted international norms and practices. Moreover, owing to the reform era policy of openness abroad and the twin trends of pluralization and institution building at home, this transformation appears to be gaining strength within the Chinese foreign policy decision-making structure. However, because these developments receive little attention in Western academic literature or mainstream media, our understanding of Chinese decision-making in this area is not well developed.[1] Chinese sources on nonprolifer-ation and arms control do not ameliorate this problem. Although increasing in number, Chinese sources on these topics tend to be descriptive rather than analytical and rarely address the Chinese policy-making process.[2]

The aim of this chapter is to partially fill this gap by identifying the prin-cipal Chinese policy-shapers in nonproliferation and arms control, their roles within the decision-making hierarchy, the principal international and domestic influences that guide them, and how these players and influences have changed and will continue to change over time. This chapter takes a case study approach to connect these issues to real policy. The case studies address three key aspects of nonproliferation and arms control for China: strategic arms control, military technology proliferation, and military transparency issues that have been hotly debated within the Chinese policy-making system and involve policy choices at the multilateral, bilateral, and unilateral levels. The three case studies reveal a number of important findings about Chinese non-proliferation and arms control decision-making:

— Beijing's reform and opening up have critically affected China's non-proliferation and arms control policy. The decision-making system in this area has opened up to and is being buffeted by far more plural-ization and omnidirectional influences both abroad and at home.

— Chinese nonproliferation and arms control policies of the early to mid-1990s, which most closely match widely accepted international norms, indicate the strong influence of external (usually multilateral) consensus as a factor.

— A reform-oriented, increasingly open policy-making structure allows for a greater degree of pluralized discussion, but also results in more bureaucratic in-fighting, difficulties in implementing and monitoring decisions, and some policy paralysis.

A "realpolitik" and "adaptive" approach dominates Chinese decision-making in this arena. However, China's policy-making is constrained by an intricate web of international dependencies, status relationships, and security realities. Taken collectively, these factors illustrate the fact that Chinese nonprolifer-ation and arms control policy-making is in a critical period of transition char-acterized by debates, pluralization, and institution building. This situation explains the often disjointed nature of Chinese decisions, which is characterized here in the notion of two steps forward, one step back.

STRATEGIC ARMS CONTROL: THE CASE OF THE COMPREHENSIVE TEST BAN TREATY

As early as 1963 China called for a halt to nuclear testing.[3] Once it had nuclear weapons of its own, however, China increasingly viewed test bans such as the Partial Test Ban Treaty (PTBT) of 1963 and the U.S.-Soviet-U.K. Thresh-old Test Ban Treaty (TTBT) as ploys intended to monopolize nuclear weapons and solidify the larger nuclear powers' advantages. In 1982 China put forward its "three halts and one reduction" proposal—a proposal that the United States and the Soviet Union halt the testing, improvement, and manufacture of weapons and reduce the number of existing nuclear warheads by 50 percent—as a condition for other states with nuclear weapons to halt testing and to enter into disarmament talks.[4] In 1986 China announced that it would no longer conduct tests in the atmosphere—a de facto acceptance of the PTBT. Also in 1986 and again in 1990, China indicated it would participate in an ad hoc group of the Conference on Disarmament (CD), if one were created, in working on a Comprehensive Test Ban Treaty (CTBT). In July 1990 it stated: "China sympathizes with, and understands, the ardent desire of the vast number of third world countries and other non-nuclear-weapon states for the early realization of a complete prohibition of nuclear tests. . . . China will take an active part in the work of the Ad hoc Committee and together with all other delegations work for the early materialization of a nuclear test ban and effective nuclear disarmament."[5]

In spite of these positive declarations regarding a possible CTBT, China abstained from a United Nations resolution calling for such a treaty in 1990. China had its eye on disturbing developments among other states with nuclear weapons: the series of tests by the United States in the mid-1980s to develop "third-generation" warheads, the proposed development of strategic defenses in the United States, and the nuclear modernization programs elsewhere. Faced with these conditions, China was not prepared to enter into negotiations that would prevent it from modernizing its nuclear deterrent.[6] Indeed, on May 21, 1992, China conducted its largest underground nuclear test ever. U.S. sources initially estimated the yield to be 700 kilotons to 1.8 megatons, noting that the test was well over the limits provided for in the TTBT (to which China was not a signatory) and claiming that it was meant for a new warhead that would arm China's next-generation intercontinental ballistic missile.[7] Subsequently China has conducted only eight tests, each in compliance with the TTBT (with yields below 150 kilotons).

On October 5, 1993, following its thirty-ninth nuclear test, China announced its support for a CTBT: "China fully understands the sincere desire of the non-nuclear states for an early conclusion of a comprehensive test ban treaty through negotiations and believes that such a treaty has its positive significance." Furthermore, in the statement China pledged to work to conclude the treaty "no later than 1996."[8] In December 1993 China joined the other nuclear powers in a General Assembly consensus resolution calling for a CTBT, and negotiations began in January 1994. Initially China indicated that it would support a CTBT in the context of a move toward complete nuclear disarmament and only in exchange for a no-first-use pledge from the other nuclear powers. Later, however, China dropped this latter requirement for its CTBT participation, but still called on all nuclear powers to adopt a no-first-use pledge and instead focused on two other concerns through the CTBT negotiations: the possibility of future "peaceful" testing and the means for verification of the ban.[9]

China consistently argued for an exemption allowing peaceful nuclear explosions (PNEs) under the final treaty, insisting that China and other developing nations should not be forced to foreclose the possibility of using nuclear explosions for peaceful purposes with economic benefits. According to Chinese Foreign Ministry spokesman Shen Guofang: "We believe nuclear explosions are one of the ways mankind makes peaceful use of nuclear energy. . . . In fact, experts on nuclear matters still have differing views on this matter. Therefore we believe that the door to nuclear explosions should not be closed, at least for now."[10] On June 6, 1996, Chinese Ambassador to the Conference on Disarmament Sha Zukang said that in order to "facilitate the conclusion of the treaty" China would allow for a "temporary ban" on PNEs in the CTBT. However, he added that China intended to revisit the PNE issue at a review conference scheduled for ten years after the CTBT enters into force.

China also objected to the use of "national technical means" (NTM) of verification of the CTBT. NTM refers to countries' use of their own verification methods—such as the use of satellites, technical measures, or other forms of surveillance, such as espionage—to verify other parties' compliance. China preferred that verification be conducted through an international monitoring system that would be open to all parties to the treaty. Beijing was especially concerned that allowing on-site inspections on the basis of intelligence information would amount to "espionage." China also argued that on-site inspections should be conducted only when thirty of fifty-one members (rather than a simple majority) of the Executive Council of the CTBT agreed.[11] This provision, which makes on-site inspections more difficult to launch, was eventually incorporated into the treaty (Article IV, paragraph 46) after China dropped its support for PNEs.

China signed the CTBT on September 24, 1996 (it was the second country to do so, after the United States), but has not yet ratified it. In the declaration accompanying its signature China expressed its opposition to "the abuse of verification rights by any country, including the use of espionage or human intelligence to infringe on the sovereignty of China." Subsequently, at the October 1997 U.S.-China summit, the two countries noted in a joint statement: "The United States and China agree to work to bring the Comprehensive Test Ban Treaty into force at the earliest possible date."[12] However, even by the end of 2000 neither side has ratified the treaty: the U.S. Senate rejected CTBT ratification in late 1999; the Chinese leadership claims it will ratify the treaty, but may await U.S. ratification.

However, the nuclear tests by India and Pakistan in May 1998 put possible future Chinese and American ratification of the CTBT in jeopardy, along with the entry into force of the treaty. Interestingly, though some Indian leaders stated that the tests were intended as a deterrent against China, Beijing has continued to comply with the de facto test moratorium among the Big Five nuclear powers. China's concerns prompted it to side with the United States in opposing the tests. Indeed, in a rare show of proactive initiative Beijing led the drafting committee that issued the June 1998 Perm-5 consensus document condemning the tests.[13]

CTBT Decision-Making

China's decision to go along with the CTBT is particularly intriguing because, along with its accession to the Chemical Weapons Convention, it marks the first time China has agreed multilaterally to place effective limits on its weapons capabilities. This is especially important given the weight China has attached to its nuclear arsenal as a symbol of its status as a great power and the ultimate guarantor of Chinese sovereignty. Although China has signed a number of nuclear nonarmament agreements, including the Outer Space Treaty, the Seabed Arms Control Treaty, the Antarctic Treaty, and the relevant protocols of a number of regional nuclear weapon free zone agreements, these treaties and agreements do not present a realistic limitation upon China's nuclear arsenal or deployment practices. In cases where real limits might be imposed—such as if Beijing were to join the Strategic Arms Reduction Talks with the United States and Russia—China has steadfastly declined participation.

Placed in the uncomfortable position of opposing an achievement that had nearly universal support, China was compelled to "go along" with the international community despite deep reservations within its military-scientific community and live up to decades of its disarmament rhetoric. This critical decision appeared to be driven largely by international pressures and a fractious internal debate that in the end favored accession for the sake of China's international image and some possible relative gains in Chinese security.

International Pressures. The negotiations over the CTBT from January 1994 to August 1996 took place in the framework of growing international opprobrium of nuclear proliferation and testing. Normative pressure not to test had built up both in the developing world and in several states with nuclear weapons. An informal testing moratorium among four of the latter—the Soviet Union / Russia, the United States, France, and the United Kingdom—had already been in place for several years.[14] The United States was particularly vocal in urging the Chinese to join the testing moratorium. At the end of 1995 China made the difficult choice to oppose the General Assembly resolution urging the halt of nuclear testing.[15] Meanwhile, following France's last test in January 1996, China was left as the sole country still testing.

China was also pressured by several of its Asian neighbors. Following the Chinese test of May 1995, Japan suspended the grant portion of its Chinese foreign aid program. Later, in August 1995, the Japanese Diet passed a resolution protesting China's testing and froze government grants for the remainder of 1995. Concern over testing gathered momentum in the Asia-Pacific region with the resumption of French explosions in September 1995.[16] After China's July 1996 test, Japan considered extending its aid ban to include soft loans (the majority of Japan's official funding for China), but in the end took no action. Instead, once China announced its testing moratorium and signed the CTBT, the two sides began negotiations on a fourth loan package of about $5.3 billion in late 1996. On March 28, 1997, Japan's foreign minister stated that Japan would restore grant aid to China.

To China's west, countries near China's Lop Nor test site—Kazakhstan, Kyrgyzstan, and Uzbekistan—sternly criticized Chinese testing in 1994–96. Numerous protests were staged at Chinese embassies in the respective capitals, and officials from each lodged formal protests and raised concerns over possible environmental damage. The protests were enough to lead Chinese President Jiang Zemin to state that "China fully understands the concerns of Central Asian states over the possible negative impact of atomic testing on the environment," although he added that there was no evidence of such negative effects.[17]

In its moratorium announcement in July 1996 the Chinese government acknowledged the pressures from the international community. The statement noted that the decision to halt nuclear testing was in part "a response to the appeal of the vast number of non-nuclear-weapon states" and also a positive step toward disarmament.[18] Therefore, evidence suggests that China's CTBT decision was influenced by its concern with international opinion. However, the decision rested primarily on a difficult calculation of constrained Chinese national interests rather than a powerful commitment to the international non-proliferation and disarmament norms embodied in the treaty.

Internal Debates. Based on interviews and observation of the public record, it is evident that the decision to sign the CTBT occasioned substantial debate within the Chinese arms control decision-making apparatus. The debate split roughly along "political" and "military" lines, although this distinction cannot be drawn too starkly. Here the reform era effects of openness, pluralization, and institution building were clearly at work, as the introduction to this volume argues more generally.

On one side were those associated with the People's Liberation Army (PLA) and the defense-industrial community, particularly the nuclear weapons research and development complex. They did not necessarily oppose the signing of the treaty per se, but they argued that China was "not technically ready" to sign.[19] China required more tests to improve its nuclear weapons capability, especially given the more extensive and sophisticated program of testing that the other nuclear powers had already conducted. Particularly in the face of the superiority of the U.S. nuclear weapons program and the possibility that the United States would deploy effective missile defenses in the future, thus widening further the technological gap between the United States and China, deep concerns arose among Chinese strategists and nuclear scientists tasked with ensuring that the country could credibly maintain a basic counter-value retaliatory capability.

In a departure from its normally terse boilerplate, the language used by the government in announcing its moratorium on nuclear testing suggests its desire to assuage the concerns of its military and nuclear weapons scientists:

> Over the past three decades and more since its first nuclear test on 16 October 1964, China has established a capable and effective nuclear self-defense force. In a pioneering spirit of self-reliance, sustaining hardships and personal sacrifices, a large number of Chinese workers, scientific and technical personnel, officers and soldiers of the People's Liberation Army, as well as all the staff working on the front of national defense have made strenuous efforts under extremely difficult conditions in the research, manufacture and development of China's nuclear weapons. Their indelible historical feats have greatly boosted

the morale of the Chinese people and enhanced China's capability to safeguard peace. The Chinese Government and people wish to extend cordial greetings and pay high respect to them.[20]

The importance of the military and strategic scientists' views is suggested by several developments. First, China continued testing throughout negotiation of the CTBT in the face of enormous international pressure. In fact, the pace of Chinese testing in 1994–96 increased. China's six tests during the period of twenty-five months from June 1994 to July 1996 more than doubled China's average testing pace. This period was also the only time in Chinese history that nuclear weapons were tested twice in three successive years.[21] Additionally, this period marked the only time in Chinese testing history that blasts occurred in July or August—outside the typical Chinese testing "season"—also indicating a sense of urgency within the military and scientific communities. Finally, the initial bargaining positions put forth by China, especially on PNEs and on verification procedures, offered the military the possibility of further testing and succeeded in stalling the negotiation process to allow China's testing program to continue. Shortly after China announced that it would end its testing program following one more test, it backed away from these objections to the treaty and made a number of key concessions.

On the other hand, persons and institutions associated with the Ministry of Foreign Affairs (MFA) appeared to take the lead in arguing for signing the CTBT in spite of the problems it posed for Chinese nuclear deterrence. But not only MFA officials held this view. For example, a Chinese military officer presciently recognized in early 1994 that a CTBT was "an inevitable development."[22] Indeed, from the outset of CTBT negotiations in early 1994, Chinese leaders consistently asserted their desire to conclude a treaty by the end of 1996, suggesting that a political decision to sign the treaty had been made by 1993 or earlier.

Sha Zukang, China's lead negotiator on the CTBT and the chief arms controller in the MFA, went directly to military leaders to discuss the CTBT and make the case for Chinese adherence. The ministry, tasked with promoting Chinese interests abroad, argued that China's international stature and image as a responsible great power were at stake and required a constructive position on the CTBT. Specifically, the ministry argued that supporting the CTBT would promote the goals of the nonproliferation regime by demonstrating good-faith efforts under Article VI of the Nonproliferation Treaty (which stated that the nuclear powers would work toward general and complete disarmament), would create more favorable conditions for Chinese economic development, and would contribute to further disarmament on the part of the major nuclear powers.[23]

In the end the Chinese leadership was convinced by the MFA arguments and decided against the military's recommendation for continued testing. It is important to note, however, that this decision was couched in the language of Chinese national interests, not an "internationalist" or "cooperative security" perspective. China's more cooperative position thus resulted from the limits imposed by the very processes of integration that the decision-makers sought to preserve and enhance.[24]

PROLIFERATION OF MILITARY TECHNOLOGY: THE CASE OF IRAN

As in the case of strategic arms control, China's record on the proliferation of military technology is mixed in spite of relatively encouraging developments. Debates have heightened in China over the relative merits of nonproliferation, often pitting powerful constituencies against one another. Decisions to abide by nonproliferation agreements and regimes most often derive from recognition of clearly discernible national security interests rather than from acceptance of international norms. This is especially true when nonproliferation is assessed as a "Western" or "American" concern targeted largely at the developing world. However, there is evidence that the international normative concept of nonproliferation is slowly gaining ground in China. As this debate continues, China's nonproliferation record will continue on a path of "two steps forward, one step back."

Over the past fifteen years Chinese policies regarding arms and export of military technology have changed significantly. First, the volume of Chinese arms and military technology exports has drastically declined, particularly since the late 1980s.[25] At present China's only major recipients of military technology are Iran, Pakistan, and Myanmar; China captured less than a 4 percent share of total conventional arms exports worldwide for the five-year period from 1992 to 1996, falling to about 3 percent from 1993 to 1997 and to just below 2 percent from 1995 to 1999 (for 1999, China's conventional arms exports accounted for less than 0.5 percent of all arms exports worldwide).[26]

Second, China has taken steps to join a number of international regimes, has committed itself to certain bilateral pledges with the United States, and has undertaken certain unilateral measures, all of which aim to stem the spread of militarily-relevant technology. These steps include (1) joining the Nuclear Non-Proliferation Treaty (NPT; to which it acceded in 1992 and for which it supported indefinite extension in 1995), the Chemical Weapons Convention (CWC; which it signed in 1993 and ratified in 1997), and the Zangger Committee (which it joined 1997); (2) providing bilateral pledges to the United States regarding the Missile Technology Control Regime (MTCR; to which it adhered in 1992, then accepted the "inherent capability" concept in 1994 and agreed to cutting off nuclear-capable ballistic missiles and technology to South Asia in June 1998); (3) halting assistance to unsafeguarded nuclear facilities in 1996; and (4) cutting off nuclear and antiship cruise missile–related trade with Iran in 1997. In addition, China has taken unilateral steps, especially since 1995, to strengthen its export control regulations for nuclear, chemical, missile, and military products.[27]

On the other hand, Chinese export of sensitive military and dual-use technologies continues, and the country's compliance with certain international, bilateral, and unilateral commitments often comes into question. Of special concern is not the quantity of Chinese exports, but their nature and the degree to which they consequently contribute to the development of weapons of mass destruction and advanced conventional weapons in recipient countries. In addition, it is not clear that China's stated adherence to regimes necessarily equates to full acceptance of the norms, concepts, rules, and details that govern them. For example, although China officially associates itself with the MTCR and the Zangger Committee, it also argues that "existing discriminatory and exclusive export control mechanisms and arrangements should be overhauled and rectified."[28]

This tension between encouraging developments and continuing concerns is especially well illustrated in China's military-technical relations with Iran. Chinese military-technical exports to Iran began in 1981, shortly after the beginning of the Iran-Iraq War. This trade has included thousands of tanks, armored personnel vehicles, and artillery pieces; several hundred surface-to-air, air-to-air, cruise, and ballistic missiles; thousands of antitank missiles; more than a hundred fighter aircraft; and dozens of small warships. In addition, China has assisted Iran in the development of its ballistic and cruise missile production capability and has provided Iran with military-related scientific expertise, production technologies, blueprints, and possibly assistance in the development of clandestine chemical and nuclear weapons programs.

In recent years, however, China's conventional arms trade with Iran has been curtailed dramatically. Over the two years prior to the U.S.-China summit of October 1997, under significant pressure from the United States, China took a number of steps to curtail particularly sensitive transfers to Iran. Although it appears that Chinese arms exports to Iran diminished, concerns persist that China continues to provide Iran with critical subsystems, technologies, and expertise, contributing to further development of its cruise and ballistic missile capability and to its alleged nuclear, chemical, and biological weapon–related programs. As in other areas, external and internal influences combine to result in contradictory Chinese policies and practices.

International Influences

China's strategic rationale for providing military assistance to Iran has changed considerably since the end of the Iran-Iraq War (1988) and especially since the end of the cold war (1990–91). Contrary to widely held views, it is clear that Beijing's desire to build stronger ties to Iran (including through the provision of weapons) had as much or more to do with strategic considerations as profit. Whether under the shah or the ayatollah, Iran held a vital place in China's strategic frame of reference in the late 1970s and through most of the 1980s. Iran's position on the Persian Gulf, in the middle of the world's most oil-rich region, and on the Soviet southern flank had long made it strategically important for China.

However, with the monumental changes in the international environment during the early 1990s the strategic rationale for strong Sino-Iranian ties also changed, and therefore the military trade component of that relationship also subsequently shifted. With the threat from the Soviet Union / Russia greatly diminished, Iran's utility as an obstacle to Soviet expansionism waned. In addition, Iran's revolutionary positions no longer appealed to Chinese leaders who saw in them the seeds of discontent among China's own Muslim population. Also, as China became increasingly dependent on a stable Persian Gulf for its own modernization and energy imports, it may have wished to curb trade activities that might embolden Iran to make destabilizing moves or others to take preemptive steps. Perhaps most critically, as China has tried to break out of its post-Tiananmen isolation and move forward in establishing a more friendly international environment that is conducive to its economic modernization program, it has become far more important for Beijing to maintain a good relationship with the West. This has resulted in China's accession to strong pressure from the United States to curtail military-technical relations with Iran.

Bilateral Influences: U.S. Pressures

Although U.S. pressure is a significant factor in stemming China's military-technical relations with Iran, it is also a significant cause of irritation and outright recalcitrance among the Chinese nonproliferation and arms control decision-making authorities and uppermost political leadership. For example, since the early 1990s and particularly in the run-up to the U.S.-China summit of October 1997, the two sides were able to hammer out a number of nonproliferation agreements, mostly related to Iran. In spite of these agreements, however, China has provided Iran with a range of nuclear- and missile-related assistance, including alleged technical assistance for uranium mining, enrichment, and conversion and for the development of nuclear research reactors, as well as other technical training and support. China "went along" with the United States, but in subsequent interpretations of their nonproliferation agreements fell short of U.S. expectations.

Antiship Cruise Missiles. U.S. pressure on China related to military-technical exports began in the late 1980s with the Reagan administration's October 22, 1987, decision to freeze further liberalization of technology sales to China in response to Chinese exports of the HY-2 "Silkworm" missile to Iran.[29] Under this pressure and with intelligence information linking China directly to Iranian Silkworm imports, Beijing pledged to prevent the diversion of Silkworms from other countries, such as North Korea, to Iran. By March 1988, in exchange for lifting the high-tech embargo, China gave private assurances to the United States that it would stop exporting the Silkworm to Iran.

In January 1996, when Iran tested an advanced Chinese C-802 antiship cruise missile, the United States pressured Beijing to halt these shipments as well. The Clinton administration even considered imposing sanctions against China under the 1992 Iran-Iraq Arms Nonproliferation Act.[30] In response to U.S. criticism, Chinese Foreign Ministry spokesman Cui Tiankai defended the transfers, stating that China's "engagement with other countries, including Iran, in small amounts of conventional weapons is totally appropriate and legal."[31]

The Clinton administration decided against sanctions and instead tried to persuade China that sales of advanced conventional weapons to Iran were contrary to China's own self-interest. With reports in June 1997—only a few months before the U.S.-China summit in October 1997—that Iran for the first time was able to fire Chinese antiship cruise missiles from fighter aircraft, even greater pressure was brought to bear on the Chinese.[32] U.S. and Chinese negotiators apparently reached an agreement on the sales during a meeting in New York City between Secretary of State Madeleine Albright and Chinese Vice Premier and Foreign Minister Qian Qichen on September 23, 1997, when Qian pledged that China would halt future sales. In an October 18 statement the White House confirmed, "Secretary Albright has raised in all her meetings with the Chinese foreign minister our deep concerns about the sale of conventional weapons and cruise missiles to Iran." However, the spokesman had "no comment" about the Chinese response to these concerns.[33] At the summit itself a White House official noted: "The U.S. and China discussed the danger posed by the provision of advanced conventional weapons to Iran which threaten maritime activities and regional stability. China has agreed to take steps to address U.S. concerns. The United States will continue to monitor this issue."[34] Chinese president Jiang Zemin and Defense Minister Chi Haotian provided further assurances to U.S. Secretary of Defense William Cohen during his visit to China in January 1998.

Ballistic Missiles. In the case of ballistic missiles it appears that U.S. pressure paid off in preventing the transfer of certain M-series ballistic missiles to Iran. Evidence suggests that China and Iran may have discussed the transfer of complete M-9 (600-kilometer-range) and M-11 (300-kilometer-range) missiles and that those transfers were imminent in late 1991 and again in late 1992. However, China backtracked as a result of U.S. pressure, especially in the period from 1989 to 1991. In 1991 alone the United States sent six high-level officials to China to discuss M-series missile exports.[35]

After it was sanctioned by the United States in June 1991 for M-11 transfers to Pakistan and planned M-9 transfers to Syria, China agreed with the United States in November 1991 to abide by the MTCR, which prohibited the export of any missile capable of carrying a 500-kilogram warhead at least 300 kilometers. This pledge was provided to the United States in writing in February 1992. In return, the United States lifted the June 1991 sanctions, which had prohibited U.S. satellite launches on Chinese carrier rockets and restricted trade in certain technologies. In spite of pledges and U.S. pressures, however, China has continued to assist in the indigenous development of Iran's ballistic missile program through technology transfers, scientific advice, and assistance in the construction of a missile production facility.

Nuclear-Related Transfers. The United States also placed great pressure on the Chinese not to provide Iran with nuclear-related assistance and technologies. China and Iran have argued since 1992 that Chinese nuclear assistance is fully consistent with the provisions of Article 4 of the NPT, which allows for peaceful nuclear cooperation, and that Iranian nuclear facilities are under International Atomic Energy Agency (IAEA) safeguards. To date, based on its full-scope safeguards agreement with Iran, the IAEA has found that Iran is in full compliance with its NPT obligations not to develop nuclear weapons. Nevertheless, the United States has strongly urged China (and other countries) to halt ongoing nuclear cooperation with Iran, arguing that any form of nuclear assistance would contribute to Iran's clandestine nuclear weapons program.

A U.S. strategy of pressures and inducements appears to have had some success in limiting and perhaps ending Chinese nuclear-related transfers to Iran. Specifically, in order to certify to Congress that the 1985 U.S.-China Peaceful Nuclear Cooperation Agreement (NCA) should go forward, the Clinton administration pointed to a number of concessions and agreements from China. First, in May 1996, following revelation of the export from China of ring magnets to unsafeguarded nuclear facilities in Pakistan, the United States secured pledges from China that it would not assist such facilities in any country, a pledge China has complied with according to the Clinton administration. Second, China was asked to issue and implement a detailed set of nuclear export control regulations, a process initiated by the promulgation of new nuclear export controls by China in September 1997. Third, China agreed to join the Zangger Committee, a multilateral body concerned with nuclear export controls, on October 16, 1997. Finally, for the certification process to go forward, China was also required to provide written assurances that it would not engage in new nuclear cooperation with Iran.

U.S. pressure had already stalled several China-Iran nuclear-related transactions. For example, although a 20-megawatt research reactor project was reportedly already under way, China cancelled the deal in October 1992, citing "technical reasons." Some observers believe that U.S. opposition directly influenced China's decision, suggesting that China cancelled the sale in order to maintain its most-favored-nation trading status with the United States.[36] Similarly, in 1992 the United States pressured China to cancel its proposed sale of two Qinshan 30-megawatt civil nuclear power reactors to Iran. Sino-

Iranian discussions and preparations continued, with the United States step-ping up its pressure, including using the possible implementation of the NCA as leverage. On September 27, 1995, Chinese Foreign Minister Qian Qichen told U.S. Secretary of State Warren Christopher that China had unilaterally decided to cancel the Qinshan reactor sales.[37] Some believe that the Chinese and Iranian explanation of the reason for the cancellation—that the two sides differed over technical and financial issues—was basically accurate. Nonethe-less, U.S. pressure may have played a significant role. According to one U.S. official involved in negotiations with China, after Washington asked China to terminate the sale, a face-saving mechanism allowing China to back out of its agreement with Iran was discussed. "After that," the official reports, "China started making noises about how Iran didn't have enough money to pay for the reactors and that there were problems with the seismic safety of the site."[38] In any event, U.S. pressure, including use of the NCA as an incen-tive, may have convinced China to let the deal collapse due to existing tech-nical and financial problems.

During the U.S.-China summit in October 1998, "authoritative, written communications" were confidentially provided to the United States stating that China would provide no new nuclear assistance to Iran. U.S. National Security Advisor Sandy Berger stated: "We have received assurances from the Chinese that they will not engage in any new nuclear cooperation with Iran and that the existing cooperation—there are two projects in particular—will end. That is the assurance we have received."[39] Under the summit agreement China would complete two existing projects not of proliferation concern to the United States: the construction of a zero power research reactor that uses natural uranium and heavy water and of a zirconium cladding production factory. Following completion of these projects, which was expected soon there-after, China was not to provide new follow-up assistance to Iran. Specifically, the United States and China agreed that China would not provide the power reactors and uranium hexafluoride conversion plant that had been under discussion.[40]

Internal Policy-Making Dynamics. It appears that the Chinese government, although forthcoming on a number of nonproliferation issues, faced internal disagreement over how to deal with U.S. pressure. This pressure apparently prodded Chinese decision-makers into action, but in several instances China subsequently sought to reinterpret and circumvent the spirit and letter of its commitments with the United States. For example, following its 1988 pledge to stop exporting Silkworm missiles to Iran, China continued to provide the technology and assistance to help Iran develop its own version of the missile.[41] Therefore, China's internal policy-making is often at odds with its declared policy.

With regard to nuclear-related assistance, the official Chinese line on the Qinshan reactor deal is that it has "suspended," not halted, the sale. Similarly, just three days after the White House announcement regarding Chinese assurances not to provide new nuclear assistance to Iran, the Chinese MFA spokesman stated: "The question of assurance does not exist. China and Iran do not have any nuclear cooperation," thereby calling into question the precise nature of the Chinese commitment.[42] Furthermore, in a discussion with an authoritative MFA official in late 1997 it emerged that China had not agreed to halt nuclear exports to Iran, but retained the option to restart such trade in the future.[43] Therefore, although the most obvious examples of Chinese transfers of sensitive weapons and technology to Iran have halted or slowed, the issue is still debated within China.

Although it is difficult to precisely identify the root of the divergent domestic views, the information available suggests at least three possible sources within the internal decision-making dynamic: bureaucratic in-fighting, devolution of authority, and problems associated with reform-oriented organizational restructuring and institution building. As to bureaucratic in-fighting, it is important to note that interagency tension and bargaining is not new to China, although the more open and complex policy environment of the reform era has made consensus more difficult to reach. In the case of military technology exports, the differences often involve the MFA on one side and military-technical interests on the other. The PLA (when selling inventory surplus, as in the 1980s) and the defense industries stand to gain the most from exports, especially given budgetary cutbacks. The MFA, on the other hand, gains little direct benefit from arms sales, yet is tasked with addressing the negative effects such sales have on China's diplomatic relations, as with the United States. (See the chapter by Lu Ning in this volume for further discussion of this dynamic.)

As Chinese arms exports became more controversial in the mid- to late 1980s, and therefore raised more complex foreign policy questions, the MFA became a more important and institutionalized participant in arms export decision-making, along with trade-related and military-related organizations. In the case of highly advanced exports and exports to "sensitive regions," the MFA takes part in a high-level interagency body—possibly the so-called Military

Exports Leading Small Group (*Junpin Chukou Lingdao Xiaozu*) that was established in 1989.[44] If an export is expected to generate opposition abroad, the MFA is to write up a justification for the transfer for the leadership to consider.[45] A 1995 Chinese white paper on disarmament notes that the MFA, as a member of the State Administrative Committee of Military Products Trade, plays a "leading role" in the development and implementation of regulations governing arms transfers.[46] Chinese export control regulations issued in the late 1990s likewise describe a prominent role for the MFA in vetting military-related exports.[47]

China's export of DF-3 medium-range ballistic missiles to Saudi Arabia in 1988 offers a good example of the bureaucratic differences between the MFA and the military over military technology sales abroad. The PLA was eager to go forward with the deal as it involved the export of aging missiles already in the Chinese inventory, the sale of which would financially benefit the military. Lewis and colleagues note that the MFA was opposed to this sale due to diplomatic concerns. Lu Ning states that the MFA supported the sale, but raised concerns about how it might affect China's relations with Washington and Moscow.[48] In either case, the MFA was involved in this decision and was able to raise its concerns over the deal, which eventually went forward.

The second internal decision-making factor concerns the devolution of authority in the reform era. Systemic changes associated with the restructuring of China's economy since the early 1980s have complicated implementation of China's nonproliferation policies. For example, China's initial efforts at trade liberalization included the decentralization of trade authority from a handful of centrally controlled foreign trade companies to "private" foreign trade corporations operating independent of the government's foreign trade plan. With such changes Beijing lacks sufficient resources to implement and enforce its export controls.[49] Although China's leaders had taken the major political step of creating export controls consistent with international standards—indeed, one Chinese expert noted that the country's nuclear export control regulations were explicitly crafted to meet international norms—it faced the difficult challenge of seeing that these rules were disseminated, adhered to, and properly enforced throughout China. The ring magnet transfers to Pakistan in 1996 provide a good example of this accountability problem. In response to U.S. protests over the sale, Chinese officials privately explained that they had been unaware of the transfer. Washington accepted this point, but in subsequent years China has publicly adopted more stringent export controls related to nuclear, chemical, and conventional weapons.

The third important component of the internal decision-making dynamic related to military transfers concerns problems associated with governmental restructuring and institution building. In particular, decisions to restructure the Chinese defense industry that were made at the March 1998 National People's Congress and Jiang Zemin's July 1998 declaration ordering the PLA to abandon its business activities have important implications for Chinese military-related exports. As part of the restructuring, several organizations and ministries, such as the Chinese National Nuclear Corporation and the Ministry of Chemical Industry, were abolished; and, as of the end of 2000, the responsibilities of their successor organizations were not yet fully known. Discussions with Chinese experts revealed the uncertainties created by this reorganization, especially with regard to the lines of authority within and among defense industries and related military organizations.

The debates and changes that characterize present Chinese nonproliferation decision-making raise questions about the effectiveness of Chinese policy commitments and help explain the phenomenon of "one step forward, two steps back." At worst, this phenomenon will mean that as the Chinese grapple with how to handle military-related exports, their decision-making will continue to hinge on basic Chinese interests and not move toward a broad acceptance of international nonproliferation norms or understandings of "cooperative security." A less skeptical interpretation would note Chinese acceptance and implementation of controls on military exports, in many cases as a result of U.S. pressure, but recognize that Beijing simply lacks the resources to fully implement its commitments. In either case, the pluralization and institution-building process in China's nonproliferation and arms control sectors offers new opportunities for Beijing to bring its practice more in line with international norms. We see similar trends under way in environmental policy (see the chapter by Elizabeth Economy in this volume) and in China's entry into global economic regimes (see the chapter by Margaret Pearson).

MILITARY TRANSPARENCY: THE CASE
OF THE CHINESE WHITE PAPERS

Another component of arms control that China has considered more actively in recent years involves military-related transparency. According to views held predominantly in the West, transparency contributes to arms control and security by alleviating the suspicions and clarifying the intentions and capabilities among potential adversaries.

The baseline Chinese view of military transparency runs contrary to that of the West, emphasizing the potentially destabilizing effect that transparency can generate in certain circumstances. When he was Chinese ambassador to the Conference on Disarmament, Sha Zukang argued that it is "impossible to have absolute military transparency" and that China "opposes the pursuit of military transparency that disregards a nation's real condition."[50] In other words, transparency is not universally beneficial or applicable, particularly as it may expose the vulnerabilities of weak nations.

In spite of such reluctance, the Chinese government has taken steps to open the door to various aspects of its military-industrial system, a process that has accelerated since the early 1990s and may continue as several nonproliferation and arms control verification regimes are put into place in the years ahead. These developments suggest that in the face of widespread international practice and norms China will be more forthcoming, although still within conservative limits.

For example, in November 1991, China agreed to report to the International Atomic Energy Agency (IAEA) any export or import of one effective kilogram or more of nuclear materials from or to a state without nuclear weapons. And in July 1993 China voluntarily agreed to further report all exports of nuclear equipment and related non-nuclear materials. China has also made some of its civilian nuclear facilities subject to IAEA safeguard inspections, which, as a state with nuclear weapons, it is not obliged to do under existing international agreements. On the other hand, Beijing has resisted calls to reveal even basic information on its strategic weapons and fissile material stockpile.

In another example, the Chemical Weapons Convention (CWC) includes an intrusive monitoring and verification regime, including "challenge inspections" of suspected chemical weapon sites. China has submitted its initial and subsequent declarations to the Organization for the Prohibition of Chemical Weapons (OPCW), which reportedly included a declaration regarding two former chemical weapons sites, in addition to reporting the abandoned Japanese chemical weapons on Chinese soil. By 1999 China had hosted nine inspections by the OPCW, two of them reportedly related to former Chinese chemical weapons production sites.

In the area of conventional arms, China was a consistent contributor to the United Nations Register of Conventional Arms (UNROCA) in the form of both annually submitting its arms imports and exports and participating in negotiation of the original Register and subsequent reviews of the process.[51] On the other hand, China has not always fully supported the development and expansion of the UNROCA and has questioned its usefulness. For example, the December 1991 General Assembly resolution establishing the UNROCA passed by a vote of 150 to 0; Cuba and Iraq abstained, whereas China and Syria did not vote. Moreover, China has opposed measures by which states would be requested to provide more information in their annual submissions or to include procurement via national production; in submissions for the years 1992–95 China provided no background or additional information.[52] In some cases Chinese submissions to the UNROCA have omitted transfers that other countries have listed as imports from or exports to China or that appear in other open-source registers such as the *SIPRI Yearbook.*[53]

In June 1997 China opposed the establishment of the Ad Hoc Committee on Transparency in Armaments (TIA). Noting that the UNROCA was already in place and functioning, the Chinese ambassador to the Conference on Disarmament (CD) said, "If the CD continues to seek or explore some abstract or sweeping TIA measures, my delegation does not see any practical meaning in this. My delegation is not against transparency as a matter of principle. We only feel that all transparency measures are in fact treaty-specific."[54] As to another mechanism of military transparency—the United Nations register of military budgets, which was established in 1980—China had yet to file a return as of the end of 1997.[55]

In August 1997, in filing its submission to the UNROCA, China attached a *note verbale* saying it "note[d] with regret that the United States has included its arms transfers to Taiwan, a province of the People's Republic of China, in the footnote of its annual reports provided to the Register for the calendar year 1995 and 1996."[56] When the United States filed its 1997 report a year later and again included its arms transfers to Taiwan, China responded by not filing with the register for the first time since the mechanism's creation. Interviews with senior Chinese arms control officials make it clear that this decision was made at the highest levels of the Chinese government based on the advice of the Arms Control and Disarmament Department of the MFA.[57]

Therefore, as with the other case studies in this chapter, China's record on military transparency is mixed. Its approach to the issues has been to provide some limited information, usually when pressed or confronted with a significant international consensus. However, even in the case of broad consensus, such as that of the UNROCA (on average, about eighty to ninety UN members have participated in the UNROCA each year), China is willing to with-draw its participation to signal annoyance on a matter of national sensitiv-ity. As to military transparency measures undertaken on a bilateral or unilateral basis, China appears less likely to be forthcoming. Its participation in mili-tary transparency measures seems to be driven more by the need to preserve China's international image than by the need to make a significant contribution to confidence building or to help bolster the norms of transparency as an arms control tool.

The Chinese White Papers

Two examples of Chinese military-related transparency—its white paper on arms control and its white paper on national defense—plainly illustrate China's penchant to respond to international prodding, but to do so within conservatively circumscribed limits. In November 1995 China issued a thirty-four-page document entitled *China: Arms Control and Disarmament.*[58] This white paper focuses on nonproliferation, arms control, and disarmament mat-ters and was designed to promote Chinese views and contributions in these areas. However, some sections include limited information on numbers of troops, force structure, military equipment and facilities, military spending, and defense conversion, in line with traditionally defined defense white papers. Most of the information in the document was already known through various open sources; as a form of military transparency, therefore, the doc-ument had limited utility. On the other hand, it had an important symbolic meaning. Its publication indicated an initial willingness (albeit limited) on the part of the Chinese government to accept transparency as a necessary arms control and confidence-building measure.

It would appear that China's concern with its image, particularly among its neighbors in the Asia-Pacific area, played an important role in the publi-cation of the arms control white paper. In 1994–95, in the intersession preparations for the Association of Southeast Asian Nations (ASEAN) Regional Forum (ARF) meeting, it became apparent that the group would urge its members to issue defense policy papers, or "white papers," as a confidence-building measure. Many members of the ARF—including Aus-tralia, Canada, Japan, New Zealand, Singapore, South Korea, and the United States—had issued defense white papers for many years. Thailand had issued its first defense white paper in 1994, and Malaysia had issued a glossy hard-cover report on its armed forces that year. Indonesia had followed suit in 1995, and the Philippines and Vietnam were said to be contemplating the publication of defense white papers.[59]

The ARF chairman's statement concluding the forum meeting in August 1995 enunciated the group's consensus to promote greater transparency in the region in various ways, including through the issuance of defense white papers. At the meeting, participating ministers agreed to encourage dialogue on political and security cooperation, to take note of the increased participation in the UNROCA and to encourage those not participating to do so, to increase the number of high-level contacts and exchanges between military academies and staff colleges, and to urge every ARF member to submit, on a voluntary basis, an annual statement of its defense policy.[60] Three months later the Chinese white paper on arms control was issued.

The United States also strongly encouraged Chinese transparency in its military affairs and urged China to release a defense-related white paper. The U.S. position on this issue is most closely associated with former Secretary of Defense William Perry, who, beginning with his November 1994 visit to China, launched an effort to engage the Chinese military. Notably, China's issuance of its arms control white paper in mid-November 1995 coincided with the arrival in China of U.S. Assistant Secretary of Defense Joseph Nye, who was also a strong advocate of transparency as an arms control and confidence-building measure. Taken together, the external pressures on China—especially those exerted in the ARF—were important factors in moving China toward the publication of its white paper on arms control and disarmament.

A publicly available white paper on national defense was more difficult for China to produce. In January 1996, during the third set of bilateral security talks between China and Japan, the Chinese side noted the country's intention to issue its first white paper on the PLA. This followed a previous statement of its intention to "issue a report on Army buildup at a proper time."[61] Discussions with Chinese military officials in 1996 also suggested that a second white paper, focused on military issues and more in line with defense white papers as they have been traditionally understood, was in the works. Although reportedly making the rounds among Beijing specialists in draft form in 1996, this document did not appear until more than two years later.[62] Beginning in 1995, the preparation of the document was initially coordinated within the PLA Second Department (intelligence) and its associated think tank, the China Institute for International Strategic Studies (CIISS). Including input gathered from the Academy of Military Sciences and other research circles, the document was later approved by the Ministry of Foreign Affairs and then sent to the Central Military Commission (CMC) and the State Council for final approval. (See the chapter of this volume by Tai Ming Cheung for further analysis of the CMC.)

In contrast to the arms control white paper, the July 1998 white paper on national defense had a wider scope, including a discussion of the international security situation, national defense policy, national defense construction, international security cooperation, and arms control and disarmament. It describes China's new concept of regional security, explains the intent behind some elements of Chinese military modernization, broadly outlines China's defense organization, provides some information on China's defense budget and arms trade, and spells out official positions on arms control and nonproliferation. Containing information culled from official statements and documents, however, the document contains little new information. According to well-positioned Chinese sources, Beijing will continue to issue white papers, probably ones similar in scope to the July 1998 publication on national defense, on a regular, but not annual, basis.[63]

The release of the national defense white paper came in response to international pressures on the one hand and shifts in domestic bureaucratic politics on the other. As noted earlier, pressures had built up for at least three years for China to issue a white paper on national defense. The timing of the release of the document to coincide with the ASEAN Ministerial Meeting and the Fifth ARF meeting in Manila in late July 1998 strongly suggests China's concern that the white paper impress its ASEAN neighbors and meet the ARF call for greater transparency. PLA officials further note that the issuance of a white paper on national defense gained some momentum in the wake of the unexpectedly strong international response to the first Chinese white paper on arms control.[64]

Release of the white paper also followed a leadership shuffle at the CIISS, which brought Lieutenant General Xiong Guangkai to the organization's directorship, and the broader effort of reorganization and professionalization in PLA-related bodies in early 1998. Such trends are very much in line with David Lampton's discussion in this volume on professionalization and with the chapter by H. Lyman Miller and Liu Xiaohong, which addresses the more advanced education of leaders at all levels. Several PLA interlocutors suggested that Xiong's more open leadership style and his interest in initiating defense-related ties to the West were important factors in the long-awaited release of the Chinese defense white paper.

Looking ahead, China's approach to military-related transparency will have important implications for the success of certain arms control and nonproliferation regimes. The CTBT calls for a relatively intrusive verification regime once it enters into force; as noted earlier, the Chinese forcefully negotiated the CTBT to constrain the ability of the treaty's governing body to launch on-site inspections. In addition, both the protocol to the Biological Weapons Convention and the proposed treaty to end the production of fissile materials for weapon-production purposes will presumably require robust verification procedures to be successful. China's position on these and other arms control and nonproliferation initiatives will continue to show cautious acceptance, spurred by the degree of international consensus but restrained by internal considerations of secrecy and the costs of verification.

ANALYZING CHANGE AND IMPLICATIONS FOR POLICY

China's nonproliferation and arms control policies have taken a dramatic turn, especially since the early 1990s, to come more in line with international norms and practices. Although the changes are obvious, it is difficult to elegantly frame the fundamental sources, motivations, and processes involved. In one of the best analyses of the subject to date, Iain Johnston asked whether the changes in Chinese arms control policy can be attributed to "learning" or "adaptation."[65] The analysis presented here is not contrary to that approach, but finds that the reality of Chinese nonproliferation and arms control decision-making is more complex than the "learning versus adaptation" model implies. Rather than representing an "either/or" dichotomy, it appears these processes occur interactively ("learning *and* adaptation" or "learning to adapt" and "adapting to learn").

In short, although a "realpolitik" or "adaptive" approach to nonproliferation and arms control appears to dominate Chinese decision-making, the independence and unilateralism of that approach should not be overstated. The realpolitik approach is increasingly constrained and shaped by the intricate web of international dependencies, commitments, status relationships, and security realities that China faces, many of which are themselves a product of previously calculated "realist" choices. As this process goes forward, the imperative to "learn" becomes more pressing for Chinese national interests. This process of both adaptation and learning has set China on a path toward nonproliferation and arms control policies more consistent with broader international norms and practices. However, given the trends of increased pluralization and internal debate over the appropriate course of Chinese policies in this area, the process will not be smooth; it will involve bumps, stops, and backtracking. Again, the image of "two steps forward, one step back" is apt.

As the case studies in this chapter suggest, the principal developments to watch for will be those related to the role of external influences, the influence of the United States, and the interplay of domestic institutions.

External Influences

The impact of external influences on Chinese nonproliferation and arms control decision-making might best be encapsulated in the notion that China has increasingly become a greater stakeholder in the international economic and security system. Therefore, the more Chinese leaders make calculations intended to promote Chinese aims in that system, the more they become enmeshed within it. First, there is a growing recognition among Chinese leaders that the country's interest in achieving stable relations with leading members of the international system can be assisted through constructive engagement in global nonproliferation and arms control regimes. This recognition is most clearly evidenced by the plethora of Chinese declaratory statements, "strategic partnerships" of various types, implementation of confidence-building measures, and adherence to multilateral and bilateral agreements limiting horizontal and vertical weapons proliferation.

Second, there is the increased understanding that past policies that ignored or undermined international arms control and nonproliferation initiatives must be radically reordered to reduce the rapid diffusion of weapons and military technology worldwide, often on China's doorstep (in India, North Korea, and Pakistan). Third, as arms control and nonproliferation initiatives have advanced the Chinese leadership has recognized the need to be involved in order to maximize limitations of the military capabilities of others while limiting potential constraints on Chinese capabilities. It is no accident that China has become a more pronounced advocate at the Conference on Disarmament of banning weapons in space and has weighed more forcefully into the global debate about missile defenses at the same time that the United States seeks to enhance its security through the development of missile defense systems.

Taking all of these factors into account, it is clear that politics and economics—rather than strictly technological and military considerations—will play an increasingly important role in the fields of nonproliferation and arms control as China becomes increasingly enmeshed in a lengthening list of international and domestic commitments. China finds itself on a "slippery slope" regarding nonproliferation and arms control, leading to increased constraints on China's ability to act unilaterally in the face of strong international consensus. Even though the fees for entry to the "club" of international non-proliferation and arms control regimes have in some cases been costly and inter-nally contentious—such as those related to decisions to join the CTBT and the CWC—the costs of China's absence are becoming even greater for a China concerned with international stature, improved international relations, and greater access to the international financial and trading system.

But juxtaposed against this trend will be the continuing influence of a more cautious approach to international nonproliferation and arms control regimes. In a review of trends in international arms control it can be seen that some of China's leading arms control experts argue that in the current post–cold war condition of U.S. strategic dominance, "the West controls the subject, process, and even the results" of arms control discussions that are typically aimed at preventing proliferation in "Third-World countries" and promoting "re-gional security cooperation," arrangements that are in the West's interests. These analysts warn that "in reality, some measures in Western arms control nego-tiations are first and foremost targeted at China."[66] According to one observer at the United Nations, the Chinese even suspect that UN-initiated disarma-ment efforts are actually intended to target proliferation in the developing world, including China.[67]

And yet Chinese strategists recognize that many aspects of the present-day international arms control and nonproliferation situation benefit China: U.S.-Russia arms control and nonproliferation efforts reduce the relative threat to China; the control of nuclear, chemical, and biological weapons pro-liferation among its neighbors reduces the threat to China; and China's international position has been elevated with many arms control and dis-armament questions requiring China's participation and cooperation.[68] These "benefits" also correlate to Chinese national security interests, but in recog-nizing them China takes another step toward the realization that the promotion of multilateral aims entails payoffs for China as well. China's initiative in lead-ing the P-5 effort to condemn the Indian and Pakistani nuclear tests is a case in point.

Multilateral arms control efforts such as the CTBT and the CWC are likely to see the greatest degree of constructive Chinese policies. The case of the CTBT demonstrates that narrowly defined, traditional understandings of military or security interests may have less influence in major multilateral negotiations.

More than in the case of military technology proliferation, China is likely to see universal disarmament efforts as global in nature, hence offering greater value for its participation. Further progress in this regard can be expected, then, when a strong international norm can be identified and clearly conveyed as such to the Chinese leadership, when Chinese participation is a matter of international prestige, and when the developing world supports such efforts. Some Chinese confidence in this process was eroded with the U.S. Senate's rejection of the CTBT in late 1999, but the overall approach by China to such questions seems set.

U.S. Influence

The United States has a critical role in influencing Chinese nonproliferation and arms control decision-making. However, this influence cuts both ways, promoting cooperation on nonproliferation goals on the one hand, but potentially exacerbating suspicions in China and thereby undermining U.S. nonproliferation efforts on the other. This is especially a problem with regard to specific types of technology transfers to specific countries, such as Iran, with which the United States has particular nonproliferation and security concerns.

The United States has been most effective in influencing Chinese decision-making in several specific ways. First and foremost, as the CTBT decision and the white papers suggest, Chinese agreement with U.S. views on nonproliferation and arms control is most likely when U.S. positions are consistent with a strong international consensus. That consensus should be truly international, with a significant degree of support from the developing world and among China's neighbors, and not simply a diplomatic offensive pressed by the United States alone.

Second, U.S. nonproliferation initiatives with the Chinese stand the best chance of success when they are linked to credible and concrete inducements or disincentives. Halting or preventing the transfer to Iran of such items as Silkworm antiship missiles (1988), complete M-series ballistic missiles (1991–92), C-801 and C-802 antiship cruise missiles (1997), and future nuclear-related assistance (1997) came in the face of credible disincentives and inducements. These included the possibility of targeted sanctions against Chinese economic entities, of Chinese access to advanced U.S. civil nuclear technology, of Chinese membership in international decision-making regimes (such as the Zangger Committee), of valued U.S.-China summits, and of U.S. statements on Taiwan, such as the "three nos."[69] Similarly, China often links its adherence to and possible membership in the MTCR to U.S. inducements such as limits on theater missile defense development and reduced political and military-technical relations with Taiwan.

Third, Washington appears to experience greater success when it can make a convincing case to Chinese interlocutors that certain nonproliferation and arms control activities will produce a direct benefit for Chinese national interests (for instance, improved U.S.-China relations, a stable security and economic environment, and enhanced Chinese global prestige). The United States has also appealed, with some success, to broader internationalist concerns as a means to promote Chinese cooperation on issues of military technology transfers, especially in light of the South Asian nuclear tests of May 1998. However, nonproliferation is still widely viewed in China as a Western or American issue.

The cases herein clearly show that Chinese cooperation is not always forthcoming and that numerous questions remain about China's nonproliferation record. However, approaches to China that stress its national interests while also promoting the broader benefits of a cooperative approach to nonproliferation have had encouraging results.

Internal Dynamics: Pluralization and Institution Building

In China today, bureaucratic entities, scientific institutions, and strategic research organizations are broadening their engagement in nonproliferation and arms control policy research and implementation. The growth of such "epistemic communities" is similar to trends noted in the Lampton and Economy chapters in this volume. These internal developments are marked by greater openness to change and outside opinion, reduced rhetoric, the establishment and strengthening of agencies and institutions concerned with nonproliferation and arms control, a diffusion of expertise, and more sophisticated and pragmatic assessments and policies. Prominent manifestations of this more open atmosphere appeared in the case studies above, and they include a more obvious degree of intra- and interagency bargaining on issues of nonproliferation and arms control, the nascent formation of like-minded cohorts cutting across organizational lines, and an increased willingness to solicit and accept advice from extrainstitutional actors, including foreigners.

The very need for China to be more active in the increasingly dynamic and complex international nonproliferation and arms control regime of the post–cold war era has in turn created a basic demand for more institutions, individual experts, and sources of expertise. Although it is certainly necessary to promote Chinese interests, this diffusion of expertise also contributes to the pluralization of the decision-making process inside China and to the exposure of a growing cadre of Chinese specialists to the international community.

The multiplication of Chinese organizations and institutions concerned with nonproliferation and arms control is well known. A brief look at the case of export controls offers a prime example of the diffusion of decision-making authority. According to a Chinese arms control official, a centralized system of "executive decrees" previously sufficed to effectively implement export controls. In the face of reform, however, the Chinese government has had to implement a new system that is more authoritative, consistent with international practice (including licensing procedures and export control lists), and dispersed among various government ministries housing necessary expertise and enforcement capacities. Under these new conditions responsibility for the export of sensitive materials and military products falls to myriad organizations, including the Chinese Atomic Energy Authority, the General Equipment Department, the Ministry of Foreign Trade and Economic Cooperation (MOFTEC), the MFA, and the State Customs Administration.[70]

Among these and other players, however, several play a prominent role in policy development. Most prominent among China's arms control and nonproliferation bodies is the Department of Arms Control and Disarmament within the MFA. Based on a review of publicly available Chinese export control regulations, on discussions with the department's personnel, and on the department's structure, this organization is likely to have more clout in the area of internationally negotiated treaties and regimes than in that of the implementation of domestic nonproliferation export controls or the promotion of military-related transparency measures.

The PLA and bodies associated with it are among the other key players in the nonproliferation and arms control decision-making process. As elsewhere in the Chinese foreign policy decision-making system, however, the role of PLA-associated organizations in arms control and nonproliferation is in a process of transition. Two organizations in particular—the Commission on Science, Technology, and Industry for National Defense (COSTIND) and the General Armaments Department (GAD) (*Zong Zhuangbei Bu*)—have experienced considerable reorganization. The organizational reform of these two bodies obscures the precise scope of their influence in decision-making on arms control and nonproliferation policies. However, it appears that with the reorganization COSTIND lost its place in arms control and nonproliferation decision-making; it was formally abolished and subsequently reconstituted during the March 1998 National People's Congress. COSTIND was placed under civilian leadership, tasked with implementing defense production orders, and given continuing oversight of the civilian production side of the defense-industrial base.

Nearly all military-related functions of the old COSTIND were handed over to the GAD, which was established in April 1998. The GAD pulls together uniformed personnel from the old COSTIND, the former equipment/armaments directorate of the General Staff and General Logistics Departments, and the Special Arms Directorate of the PLA ground forces. The GAD is the fourth PLA general department, joining the General Staff Department, the General Political Department, and the General Logistics Department. The Arms Control Department within the Foreign Affairs Office of the old COSTIND has also been transferred to the GAD Foreign Affairs Office; its staff includes several uniformed arms control experts with considerable international experience.

More specifically, the GAD will likely wield greater influence through three channels. First, through the Arms Control Department noted earlier the GAD will conduct research and staff delegations on a range of nonproliferation and arms control topics, including proliferation and disarmament. This will presumably include the provision of recommendations to the PLA General Staff and the CMC, to uniformed personnel staffing embassies abroad, and to participants in bilateral and multilateral negotiations. Second, the GAD will have an advisory role in reviewing export licenses for nuclear materials, missile-related technologies, and conventional weapons technologies and systems.

Finally, prominent persons associated with the GAD will have the opportunity to influence high-level policy debates within the CMC and the State Council. These persons include the head of the GAD, Lieutenant General Cao Gangchuan (formerly head of COSTIND), who was appointed in an ex officio capacity to the CMC in October 1998. Other key personalities are Zhu Guangya, Major General Qian Shaojun, and Lieutenant General Shen Rongjun. Zhu, a prominent nuclear physicist and leading light in China's nuclear weapons program, heads the GAD's Science and Technology Committee, an advisory body that previously served COSTIND, and is also vice chairman of the Chinese People's Political Consultative Conference. Qian, another physicist and a member of the GAD Science and Technology Committee, is the military's leading voice on arms control issues. Formerly one of the deputy directors of the old COSTIND and then transferred as a deputy director to GAD, Shen has long been associated with China's missile and astronautics programs. Although the military thus remains influential on issues of arms control and nonproliferation, the increased prominence of other players can be expected to counterbalance the PLA's interests. These include the MFA, MOFTEC, regulatory bodies within the civilian COSTIND, and others, depending on the issue, who will come to the interagency bargaining table.

The case studies presented earlier and this brief description of the pluralizing community of Chinese nonproliferation and arms control specialists suggest a need to be cautious about simplistically framing the current debate on these issues in China as the "military establishment versus the political establishment," just as Michael Swaine warns us with respect to Taiwan policy in his contribution to this volume. If it is true that concerns of prestige and relative rather than absolute gains in security can prevail over narrow military and technical considerations in certain cases, new paths toward constructive dialogue with China on nonproliferation and arms control appear possible, particularly through the engagement of military-related bodies. Ultimately, such engagement between the international community and the community of specialists in China will further diversify the range of opinion and expertise available to Chinese decision-makers.

CONCLUSION

The remarkable shifts on the international stage during the past fifteen years, not the least of which have occurred in China, have had a profound effect on Chinese nonproliferation and arms control decision-making. These effects might be summed up in the understanding that China has—by fits and starts, but nonetheless steadily—become an increasingly invested stakeholder in international security and economic systems. This process, which was accelerated by China's post-Tiananmen "break-out" strategy, has resulted in a far greater tendency to pursue China's national interests through the exercise of nonproliferation and arms control policies. At the same time, these efforts within the international community have entwined China in a web of relationships, expectations, commitments, and perceptions of prestige that have indirectly benefited Chinese interests. These lay the groundwork for more constructive policies in these areas in the years ahead.

However, this kind of change will take time and will not be without backtracking and continued internal debates in China concerning the means and ends of nonproliferation and arms control at the international, bilateral, and unilateral levels. The Indian and Pakistani nuclear tests and U.S. missile defense plans are just two of the many recent challenges China must debate in this arena. But it appears that through a contentious process of "two steps forward, one step back," Chinese foreign policy in this area will continue at its own pace to become more consistent with China's aspiration to be a leading member of the international community.

TEN

Chinese Decision-Making Regarding Taiwan, 1979–2000

MICHAEL D. SWAINE

This chapter analyzes the changing structure and content of the Chinese policy-making process regarding Taiwan from 1978 to early 2000.[1] It examines how Chinese Communist Party (CCP), government, and military leaders and their subordinate institutions and advisors interacted to produce a sequence of four basic policy decisions made by the People's Republic of China (PRC) toward Taiwan during this period. These four decisions were first, the decision to shift from the confrontational, military-oriented "liberation" policy of 1949–78 to a policy of patient negotiation aimed at peaceful reunification with Taiwan under the "one country, two systems" formula; second, the decision to make an effort to achieve a breakthrough in reunification discussions with Taiwan through the enunciation of a more flexible, conciliatory set of proposals, which was contained in Jiang Zemin's Eight Points of January 1995; third, the decision in late 1995 or early 1996 to shift to a hard-line stance toward Taiwan that combined greater political and economic pressure with overt military intimidation; and fourth, the decision, which emerged in 1997, to implement a less openly coercive, more balanced policy regarding Taiwan that attempts to utilize both carrots and sticks in a more effective manner.

This chapter's analysis of the factors that produced and shaped these decisions is divided into two parts. Part I is a discussion of the major individuals and organizations involved in formulating and implementing the aforementioned features of PRC policy regarding Taiwan. Part II consists of an assessment of how the decision-making process actually operated to produce the four basic policy decisions. The chapter concludes with a section based on the preceding analysis, which summarizes the major features of the Chinese decision-making process regarding Taiwan.

PART I: THE PRC'S TAIWAN POLICY APPARATUS

The Chinese policy apparatus related to Taiwan can be divided into four separate but interrelated policy arenas, each defined by a distinct set of policy functions: policy formulation and oversight, policy administration and implementation, policy coordination and supervision, and research, analysis, and intelligence. The key individuals and institutions responsible for these four policy arenas are depicted in Figures 10.1 and 10.2.

Policy Formulation and Oversight

This policy arena includes those senior leaders who determine the fundamental strategic principles and goals guiding China's policy regarding Taiwan and who exercise ultimate oversight authority over that policy. Since at least 1979 this arena has included three sets of actors: the most senior (or "paramount") leader and his closest personal advisors and associates, the paramount leader's senior associates on the Politburo Standing Committee (PBSC) and in the party Secretariat and State Council, and the most senior leaders of the Chinese military responsible for defense policy relating to Taiwan.

Among this group of senior leaders, the paramount leader has exercised ultimate decision-making authority over Taiwan policy, with support from his close political associates and advisors. Between 1978 and 1993 Deng Xiaoping was paramount leader and made all major decisions regarding Taiwan, albeit in consultation with other senior party and military leaders.[2] Senior party leaders who wielded notable influence over Taiwan policy included Hu Yaobang (before 1986), Zhao Ziyang (before 1989), Jiang Zemin (after 1989), and Yang Shangkun (before 1992), as well as various senior active and formally retired party and military elders, including Chen Yun (before 1995),

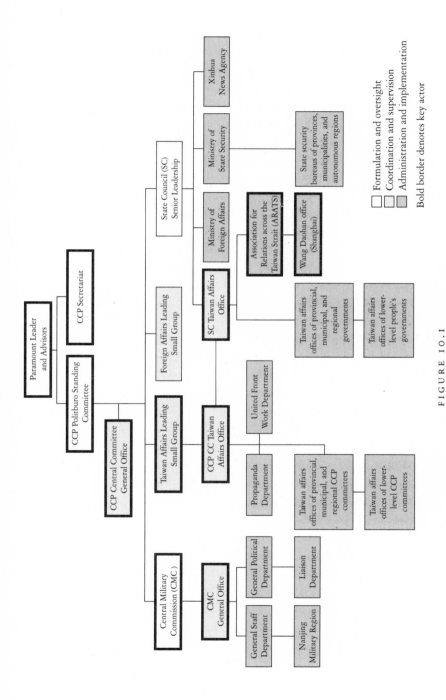

FIGURE 10.1

TAIWAN AFFAIRS POLICY APPARATUS MINUS RESEARCH, ANALYSIS,
AND INTELLIGENCE ORGANS, 1998

Source: Primarily from author interviews, conducted in China in 1998.

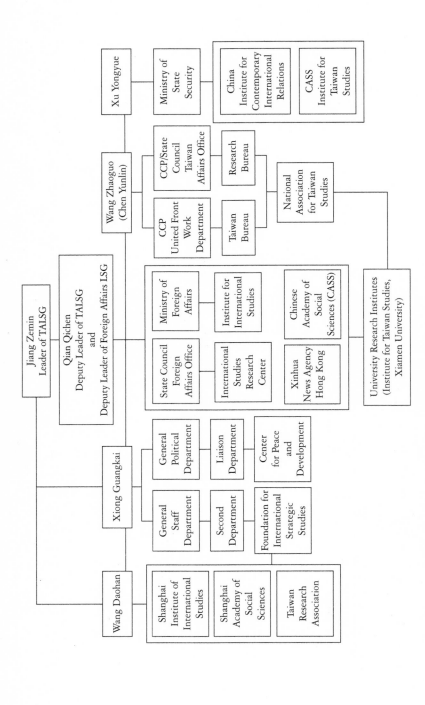

FIGURE 10.2

RESEARCH, ANALYSIS, AND INTELLIGENCE ORGANS ASSOCIATED
WITH THE TAIWAN AFFAIRS LEADING SMALL GROUP, 1998

Source: Adapted from source listed in note 5.

Li Xiannian (before 1992), Ye Jianying (before 1985), and Liu Huaqing and Zhang Zhen (both after 1992).[3]

Since mid- to late 1994 Jiang Zemin has held ultimate responsibility for policy toward Taiwan as party general secretary, chairman of the CCP Central Military Commission (CMC), and head of the CCP's Taiwan Affairs Leading Small Group (TALSG).[4] Although Jiang took control of the TALSG in June 1993, he did not fully assert his power over Taiwan policy (and other key policy arenas) until Deng's health began to seriously decline and other party elders had passed from the scene. This transition to the post-Deng, post-elder era did not occur completely until the Fourth Plenum of the Fourteenth Central Committee in the fall of 1994, when the third generation of party cadres had finally achieved firm control.[5] Since that time Jiang has served as the key locus of decision-making authority and policy coordination between the PBSC, the TALSG, and the CMC.

Jiang, like Mao Zedong and Deng Xiaoping, must retain control over the Taiwan policy arena for symbolic and substantive reasons. Given the close linkage between Mainland-Taiwan reunification and Chinese nationalism,[6] proper handling of the Taiwan issue is critical to the maintenance of regime legitimacy and political stability. Moreover, since Mao and Deng determined the basic contours of policy toward Taiwan, any aspirant to supreme authority within the Chinese communist regime cannot afford to permit another senior leader to control Taiwan policy.[7] And finally, Jiang frequently tells foreign visitors that Deng placed him in charge of relations with the United States, a relationship inextricably linked to both China's economic modernization and the Taiwan issue.

Yet despite his relative dominance over Taiwan policy, Jiang's overall position as "first among equals" in the post-Deng leadership has meant that in the formulation of basic policy he must consult more extensively than did Deng Xiaoping with a wider circle of senior leaders, including officials in the policy administration and implementation arena.[8] This point is also made in the introduction to this volume and several other chapters, most notably those by Margaret Pearson, Lu Ning, and H. Lyman Miller and Liu Xiaohong. Jiang's closest senior party associates and advisors on Taiwan policy include Li Peng (as second-ranking PBSC member and former State Council premier and leader of working-level State Council organs with responsibility for Taiwan policy and foreign policy in general); Qian Qichen (as Politburo member, State Council vice premier in charge of foreign affairs, former minister of foreign affairs, and deputy head of the TALSG and the Foreign Affairs Leading Small Group

(FALSG); Wang Daohan (as a close confidant, advisor, and political mentor to Jiang Zemin, director of the Association for Relations Across the Taiwan Strait [ARATS], TALSG member, and former mayor of Shanghai); and Zeng Qinghong (as a close personal advisor to Jiang Zemin, director of the Party Central Committee General Office, and head of the CCP Organization Department).[9]

Senior military officers responsible for Taiwan policy during the Jiang Zemin period include, from 1992 to 1997, Generals Liu Huaqing and Zhang Zhen (former first-rank CMC vice chairmen and military officers in charge of strategy and military modernization) and, since late 1997, Generals Zhang Wannian and Chi Haotian (successors to Liu Huaqing and Zhang Zhen in the CMC)[10] and, to a lesser extent, Fu Quanyou, chief of the People's Liberation Army (PLA) General Staff Department. With the exception of Fu, these officers have provided input on defense aspects of Taiwan policy as members of the CMC Executive Committee, an informal body comprised of the chairman and vice chairmen of the CMC.[11] They receive information and advice on these matters from General Xiong Guangkai, the military's representative on the TALSG,[12] the deputy chief of the General Staff in charge of military intelligence, and an increasingly close confidant of Jiang Zemin on military affairs.

Among these senior leaders, Jiang's most important associates on Taiwan policy, given their senior political and military rankings and direct responsibility for Taiwan-related functional areas, currently include Li Peng, Qian Qichen, and Generals Zhang Wannian and Chi Haotian. The latter two primarily influence defense-related decisions regarding Taiwan, not overall basic strategy (neither officer is a member of the PBSC). Of course other members of the PBSC and the CMC may exert significant influence over certain decisions, especially when there is disagreement among Jiang, Li, Qian, Zhang, and Chi or when the leadership is confronted with a crisis.[13] Although Wang Daohan lacks formal decision-making authority, he exercises significant influence over Taiwan policy as a result of his close association with Jiang Zemin. Wang is widely viewed as Jiang's most trusted advisor on Taiwan and a key channel for advice from a variety of Shanghai-based research institutes. As both the head of ARATS and a TALSG member, Wang is also able to handle sensitive contacts with Taiwan and important third-party countries (such as the United States and Japan) on behalf of Jiang, and he reportedly looks after Jiang's personal political interests in the Taiwan policy-making process.[14]

However, Wang's influence over final decisions on fundamental issues is probably less than that of PBSC members. Qian Qichen, in particular, almost certainly exerts greater influence than Wang over many aspects of Tai-wan policy given his Politburo ranking, his critical position as the senior govern-ment official in charge of foreign affairs, his role as sole deputy head of the TALSG and FALSG, and perhaps his alleged association with Li Peng.[15] Next to Jiang himself, Qian reportedly remains the most critical government offi-cial linking the foreign affairs and Taiwan policy arenas.

Policy Administration and Implementation

This policy arena includes the major ministry and commission-level party, gov-ernment, and military organizations and subordinate bodies responsible for administering and implementing Taiwan policy. Major actors include the lead-ers of these organs and those subordinate, bureau-level heads responsible for the day-to-day aspects of Taiwan policy. As depicted in Figure 10.1, the most important central bureaucratic organs involved in administering Taiwan policy are the Ministry of State Security, the Ministry of Foreign Affairs, the PLA General Staff Department, the Liaison Department of the PLA General Political Department, and the CCP Central Committee United Front Work Department.

The Ministry of State Security (MSS) is responsible for the collection and assessment of civilian intelligence relevant to national security issues and for conducting counter-espionage against foreign countries. When the CCP Investigation Department (*Diaocha Bu*) was abolished in 1983–84, the MSS took over many of its duties. Hence, the MSS conducts a wide variety of Taiwan-related activities, including the analysis of domestic Taiwanese political, social, and economic developments and of international trends relevant to cross-strait relations, as well as counter-measures against Taiwan's espionage.

As the premier state body responsible for foreign diplomatic and political relations, the Ministry of Foreign Affairs (MFA) is directly responsible both for relations with countries that may influence the international status of Tai-wan and for the increasingly intense diplomatic competition between Taipei and Beijing.[16] The Taiwan Affairs Office of the MFA is the working-level unit responsible for these activities.

As the chief executive arm of the PLA leadership, the General Staff Depart-ment (GSD) is responsible for developing military policies to ensure that Tai-wan remains free from foreign domination and incapable of permanently separating itself from the Mainland. The General Political Department (GPD) of the PLA has maintained a strong interest in Taiwan issues since the

1940s, when Red Army political operatives and intelligence agents were active on the island. Since that time GPD agencies have conducted a wide range of intelligence activities concerning Taiwan. The GPD Liaison Department (LD) is the primary office responsible for such intelligence. However, in recent years various offices in the GSD have eclipsed the GPD in the Taiwan policy arena, especially in the areas of policy research and analysis.

The United Front Work Department (UFWD) is the primary organ responsible for developing party-to-party and people-to-people contacts between the Mainland and Taiwan. Although its activities during the Mao Zedong era were largely limited to propaganda, the expansion of cross-strait contacts in the late 1980s and the 1990s has led to major growth in UFWD-related activities. Other significant but secondary central bureaucratic organs include the CCP Central Committee International Liaison Department (ILD), the Central Committee Propaganda Department (PD), and the Ministry of Foreign Trade and Economic Cooperation (MOFTEC). Of these three units, MOFTEC is undoubtedly the most important entity given the enormous expansion of cross-strait economic activity, not to mention its growing role in foreign policy-making, as explained in the Lampton, Lu, and Pearson chapters.[17]

During the Deng Xiaoping era the leaders of most of the aforementioned central organs were members of the TALSG, although they exercised authority only over their respective bureaucracies and not policy generally.[18] Under Jiang Zemin the MFA, MSS, GSD, and UFWD have come to perform the most important bureaucratic roles in the Taiwan policy-making process, and they alone are represented today on the TALSG. As a result, their influence over basic policy decisions is greater under Jiang than it was under Deng.

Although formally at a lower level in the bureaucratic hierarchy than the previously mentioned organs and "non-governmental" in status, ARATS, led by Wang Daohan, should also be noted as a significant bureaucratic player in Taiwan policy. Since its formation in the early 1990s, ARATS has been responsible for conducting all major political contacts and discussions with the Taiwan authorities. For example, the "semi-official" on-again, off-again discussions between Wang Daohan and C. F. Koo, head of Taiwan's Strait Exchange Foundation (SEF), the counterpart to ARATS, were carried out under the auspices of ARATS. These talks occurred in 1993 and 1998. The association is staffed by government officials on a temporary basis.[19]

Policy Coordination and Supervision

This policy arena is closely related to the previous arena, as most of its component organizations also administer and implement Taiwan policy. However, the primary function of these bodies is to coordinate and supervise interactions among the responsible leaders, senior bureaucratic and administrative organs, and research, analysis, and intelligence institutions of the party, government, and military. Many organs within this policy arena are also charged with developing policy proposals and documents at the request of administrators and senior leaders.

As depicted in Figure 10.1, the most important such organizations during both the Deng Xiaoping and Jiang Zemin periods have included the CCP Central Committee's Taiwan Affairs Leading Small Group; the CCP Central Committee's Taiwan Affairs Office; the CCP Central Committee General Office; the Central Military Commission General Office; and the State Council Taiwan Affairs Office. Because of the obvious relevancy of Taiwan affairs to China's relations with other countries, the Central Committee's FALSG also plays an important, albeit secondary, role in Taiwan policy-making.

The TALSG was established in January 1980 following the creation of the CCP Central Committee's Taiwan Affairs Office. It functions as a key policy coordination and supervision mechanism between the PBSC and the system (*xitong*) of functionally associated party, state, and military organs responsible for Taiwan affairs. Although formally under the party, the TALSG straddles the jurisdiction of both government and party structures, a pattern of institutional design Lu Ning discusses in his chapter. It is considered a "squad (*banzi*)-level" leading small group because it is led by one or more members of the top leadership "squad."

However, the TALSG is not a full-fledged bureaucratic organization. Like other leading small groups, it does not have any subordinate administrative offices or permanent staff.[20] Its total membership consists of leading party, state, and military officials responsible for administering key elements of Taiwan policy. Therefore, the TALSG functions almost exclusively as a policy deliberation, coordination, and at times decision-making body.[21] It conveys policy decisions downward to various organs of the Taiwan affairs *xitong* and transmits essential information, perspectives, and proposals upward to the senior party leadership. Although its individual members are responsible for carrying out aspects of Taiwan policy relevant to their subordinate offices, the TALSG as a body does not usually take direct responsibility for the implementation of specific policy decisions. However, it does coordinate the overall implementation of key elements of Taiwan policy by its major component systems.[22]

In general, the important place of the TALSG in the policy-making process has increased significantly over time. It was originally established primarily in response to the renewed stress placed on reunification by Deng Xiaoping.[23] However, the TALSG's policy-making role during the Deng era was largely limited to conducting research on Taiwan policy guidelines, submitting policy recommendations to the party leadership, overseeing implementation of major policy decisions, and providing administrative support to Deng and other senior leaders.

During much of the 1980s the leadership of the TALSG reflected its subordinate administrative role. It was originally directed by relatively senior yet less influential officials such as Deng Yingchao (deputy chair of the National People's Congress and wife of Zhou Enlai), who directed the TALSG from 1980 to 1987, and Liao Chengzhi (director of the State Council Overseas Chinese Affairs Office and of the State Council Foreign Affairs Office), who served as deputy head from 1980 to 1983. Neither individual wielded high-level political power or decision-making authority within the ultimate seat of power—the party apparatus.[24]

Beginning in the late 1980s, the membership and policy-making role of the TALSG increased somewhat as cross-strait contacts expanded and Beijing's hopes for significant improvement in relations with Taiwan increased.[25] The increasing scope and importance of Taiwan affairs was reflected in the promotion of Yang Shangkun from deputy head to head of the TALSG after Deng Yingchao became incapacitated in 1987. As president of the PRC, a Politburo member, a long-time senior party apparatchik with strong ties to the PLA,[26] and Deng Xiaoping's close associate, Yang was a much more powerful figure than either Deng Yingchao or Liao Chengzhi had been. During Yang's tenure (1987–93) the TALSG-led process of bureaucratic consultation became more thorough and systematic, the overall authority of the TALSG increased, and additional offices responsible for Taiwan policy (such as the State Council Taiwan Affairs Office) emerged. As a result, the operational aspects of Taiwan policy were placed more fully under the TALSG's control. During his tenure as head of the TALSG, Yang was also an important liaison with the military regarding Taiwan policy. Yet despite his significant powers, Yang Shangkun did not exercise any independent authority over major Taiwan policy decisions. In other words, the TALSG under Yang Shangkun continued to serve primarily as a policy coordination and consultation body for Deng Xiaoping and, to a lesser extent, other senior party leaders.[27]

Since 1993, however, the TALSG has become the locus of most decision-making on Taiwan, largely as a result of Jiang Zemin's emergence as the "core" of the post–Deng Xiaoping party leadership. Under Jiang's leadership[28] the membership of the TALSG has been reduced from twelve to six or seven members.[29] Members now include leaders of the most important party, state, and military organs responsible for the political dimensions of Taiwan policy: the supreme leader of the party apparatus (including the supreme party organ in control of the Chinese military), currently Jiang Zemin; the senior state official responsible for foreign affairs and relations with Hong Kong, Taiwan, and Macao, currently Qian Qichen; the head of the state security apparatus, currently Xu Yongyue; the director of the leading party and government working-level offices responsible for Taiwan affairs, currently Chen Yunlin; the head of the leading party office responsible for united front work, currently Wang Zhaoguo; a senior military officer in charge of foreign military relations and strategy and military intelligence, currently Xiong Guangkai; and the leading nongovernmental official responsible for cross-strait dialogue, currently Wang Daohan.[30]

The streamlining of the TALSG membership under Jiang Zemin has significantly increased its importance in the policy-making process and strengthened Jiang's personal influence over Taiwan policy. As Chu Yun-han points out, with Jiang Zemin's personal involvement the TALSG became, with a few exceptions noted later, "the real inner circle where all important matters dealing with Taiwan were discussed and policy proposals formulated."[31] In addition, the decision-making function of the TALSG became more focused and delineated, involving "only key members representing systems which carry out 'essential' political, military and intelligence functions in the Taiwan policy domain."[32] On a broader level, the increasingly pragmatic, bureaucratic, and consensus-oriented nature of policy-making in the post-elder era has increased the overall influence of policy-coordinating mechanisms such as the TALSG in the policy-making process, a point one sees reiterated repeatedly throughout the chapters in this volume and highlighted in the introduction.

The Central Committee Taiwan Affairs Office (CCTAO) was established in 1979 after the normalization of relations between the United States and China, reportedly at the suggestion of party elder and former PLA marshal Ye Jianying.[33] Like the TALSG, the CCTAO was created largely in response to the emphasis placed on Taiwan by Deng Xiaoping. It serves as the core party office charged with overseeing implementation of Taiwan policy. In particular, this ministry-level unit plays a critical policy role as the key administrative and secretarial agency supporting the TALSG. Indeed, since the TALSG does not hold regular meetings and has no permanent executive, the CCTAO performs many critical policy functions on behalf of the TALSG, serving as a general office (GO) for that body.[34] In this capacity the CCTAO prepares the agenda for all TALSG and Taiwan Central Work Conference meetings,[35] coordinates document flows and bureaucratic interactions among the members and subordinate bureaucracies of the TALSG, and provides analysis and policy suggestions to senior TALSG members, especially Jiang Zemin. It also supervises policy implementation by Taiwan affairs officers of provincial, municipal, and autonomous regional party committees and supports the activities of non-TALSG party organs charged with Taiwan policy responsibilities.[36]

In addition to performing a role of overall importance in the Taiwan policy-making process throughout most of the 1980s, the CCTAO most likely also served as a major conduit of PLA views and influence on Taiwan policy. This was largely because the head of the CCTAO at that time was Yang Side, a PLA officer with significant experience in Taiwan intelligence work via the PLA GPD Liaison Department. Due to Yang's presence, as well as the influence exerted by Yang Shangkun when he headed the TALSG, the CCTAO staff reportedly included many PLA officers and might have conveyed, in its policy papers, many of the more "hard line" military views of Taiwan.[37]

However, the level of PLA influence on the CCTAO decreased significantly after Yang Side retired in 1991 and Jiang Zemin became head of the TALSG in 1993. At that time Wang Zhaoguo was selected to serve as head of the CCTAO and secretary general of the TALSG.[38] From 1993 onward the personnel of the CCTAO included a variety of cadres from the military, diplomatic, security, united front work, and government departments. Moreover, its authority was expanded to include review of nearly all major Taiwan-related policy documents and information from party, government, and military organs.[39] In addition, in 1990 the personnel and work responsibilities of the CCTAO were merged with those of the State Council TAO, largely to resolve conflicts between the two offices that had emerged after the establishment of the latter in 1988.

The Central Committee General Office (CCGO) is a ministry-level policy coordination and oversight office under the CCP Secretariat. It serves both the party Secretariat and the Politburo, as well as the most important leading small groups, including the TALSG and the FALSG. Specifically, the CCGO performs critical liaison and communication functions among top-tier senior political leaders, between the top leadership and subordinate *xitong* and constituent agencies, and between the senior executive leaders of these agencies and their working-level functionaries and analysts.[40] Equally important, the office exerts significant influence over daily decisions and processes and at times even takes positions on specific issues, including policy toward Taiwan. The Policy Research Office of the CCGO is particularly important and is responsible for reviewing and distributing policy reports to the senior leadership and for drafting policy speeches. Although undoubtedly less central to the Taiwan policy-making process than the CCTAO, the CCGO, through its bureaucratic and personal interactions, can thus shape policy toward Taiwan in subtle yet decisive ways.[41]

As with the CCTAO, the policy role of the CCGO and its influence on Taiwan policy in particular has almost certainly increased greatly during the Jiang Zemin period. This is largely due to the fact that one of Jiang's closest advisors, Zeng Qinghong, has headed the CCGO since the early 1990s. Aside from Wang Daohan, Zeng has been identified as the most significant of the key advisors to Jiang Zemin on Taiwan policy. He often meets with Taiwanese political and economic figures visiting the Mainland and is responsible for supervising and coordinating much of the Taiwan-related analysis that is submitted directly to Jiang's office.[42] Zeng's overall political clout undoubtedly increased, moreover, after he was named an alternate Politburo member at the Fifteenth Party Congress in the fall of 1997 and head of the CCP Organization Department in the spring of 1999.

The Central Military Commission General Office (CMCGO) performs in the military realm a similar policy coordination and oversight function to that of the CCGO. It facilitates personal interactions among the senior members of the PLA leadership (especially members of the CMC), manages the external activities of the Ministry of National Defense (MND), coordinates bureaucratic interactions among the core PLA agencies and their subordinate systems, and supervises the daily operations of the CMC departments. It is also the key coordination, evaluation, and distribution point for strategic research and assessments developed within the PLA bureaucracy, including those relevant to Taiwan policy. In general, the CMC does not carry out policy research and analysis, but rather depends on agencies within the GSD and GPD for military-related assessments and proposals concerning Taiwan. These and other views on Taiwan issues are normally submitted to the CMC via the CMCGO.[43] Therefore, as in the case of the CCGO's relationship to the party leadership, the CMCGO likely exerts significant, albeit indirect, influence on the CMC leadership and in many areas of military policy, including Taiwan policy.[44]

The State Council Taiwan Affairs Office (SCTAO) also plays a critical role in coordinating Taiwan policy issues for senior leaders and in overseeing aspects of policy implementation by subordinate government agencies. The SCTAO was established in 1988 with State Planning Commission Deputy Director Ding Guan'gen as its first head. Ding was succeeded by Wang Zhaoguo in 1990, and Wang was in turn succeeded by Chen Yunlin in 1997. Tang Shubei has served as a very able deputy to both Wang and Chen. The ministry-level SCTAO was created to oversee the growing government (as opposed to party and military) aspects of Taiwan policy, including the development of cross-strait exchanges. The size and significance of the SCTAO has increased over time, however. Originally the office included only four or five departments, staffed mainly by Taiwan affairs cadres from the CCTAO, the United Front Work Department, the MFA, various economic and trade agencies, and even offices of the PLA. In recent years the number of internal bureaus has expanded to total at least eight, including bureaus responsible for news and propaganda, cross-strait exchanges, research, and economic relations.[45] As a result of this expansion the SCTAO's functions have grown to include a significant role in analyzing Taiwan affairs and in providing key policy recommendations to both the TALSG and the PBSC, often with the support of analysts within the MFA's Taiwan Affairs Office. It also provides such services directly to the leaders of the State Council, especially the premier. The SCTAO has a very active Research Bureau that produces and commissions a wide variety of Taiwan-related analysis and policy proposals (discussed later).[46]

Since 1990 the importance of the SCTAO has increased as a result of the merging of much of its staff and work duties with the CCTAO. To all intents and purposes the two TAOs now operate as a single unit, although party-relevant policy activities are usually conducted in the name of the CCTAO, whereas state-relevant activities (including the activities of ARATS) are conducted in the name of the SCTAO.

Policy Research, Analysis, and Intelligence

This policy arena includes central, provincial, and municipal party, state, and military units engaged in the production of research and analysis,[47] as well as units engaged in intelligence gathering. These units also provide policy recommendations and proposals, which are evaluated and revised by policy coordination and supervision organs. They provide information and analysis that is of direct relevance to the PRC's grand strategy toward Taiwan, including assessments of the global situation, relations between Taiwan and major world powers, cross-strait relations, and Taiwan's domestic environment.

Since the establishment of the CCTAO and the TALSG (in 1979 and 1980, respectively), Taiwan-related research, analysis, and intelligence organizations have grown significantly in number and in importance to the policy-making process. They have become particularly significant since the early 1990s, when the third generation of party leaders came to the fore. The Jiang Zemin–led leadership has come to rely on a wide range of "external" policy inputs, including the expertise of research institutes, staff offices, and personal advisors, to make strategic assessments and policy decisions.

At present the most significant agencies in this arena are under the auspices of the Party Central Committee, the State Council, the Ministry of State Security, the Shanghai Municipal Government, the Ministry of Foreign Affairs, the PLA General Staff Department, and the PLA General Political Department. As such, these entities are mostly associated with the five major organs represented on the current TALSG.[48] As depicted in Figure 10.2, these include the research bureaus of the CCTAO and the SCTAO, the Taiwan Affairs Research Office of the Chinese Academy of Social Sciences, the Chinese Institute for Contemporary International Relations, several Shanghai-based Taiwan research institutes, the Taiwan Affairs Office and Political Research Office of the Ministry of Foreign Affairs, the Second Department of the PLA GSD, and the Center for Peace and Development Studies of the PLA GPD's Liaison Department. An additional research organ of significance is the Institute for Taiwan Studies located at Xiamen University in Fujian Province.

The GSD Second Department, which is in charge of military intelligence, is superior to all other civilian or military organs as a source of national security and defense intelligence and military-related strategic analysis for the senior leadership. Hence, part of its responsibilities include the gathering and processing of intelligence on Taiwan's military capabilities and the capabilities of other countries (such as the United States and Japan) that might intervene militarily in a confrontation or conflict between Beijing and Taipei. Indeed, the Second Department constitutes the core of Taiwan-related research and analysis within the GSD.[49] Most GSD Second Department researchers use a "front" affiliation when interacting with foreigners, notably the China Institute of International Strategic Studies (CIISS).[50] Although the Second Department has been directed by Major General Luo Yudong since September 1999, ultimate authority over its activities is exercised by Lieutenant General Xiong Guangkai.

The GPD's Center for Peace and Development (CPD), under the Liaison Department's China Association for International Friendly Contact (CAIFC), carries out a wide range of intelligence activities concerning Taiwan's political situation. The GPD Liaison Department enjoys a very strong reputation for strategic analysis and intelligence on Taiwan, Hong Kong, and Macao, dating from the period before 1949, when Red Army political operatives and intelligence agents were active in all three areas. In fact, the GPD traditionally has played a more significant role in analysis of Taiwan issues than the GSD.[51] However, in recent years the research and intelligence arms of the GSD have reportedly eclipsed the GPD, largely due to the rising influence of Xiong Guangkai. As with the GSD Second Department staff, most researchers attached to the CPD use a "front" affiliation when interacting with foreigners.

In addition to the above units directly attached to the GSD and the GPD, scholars at the Academy of Military Science (AMS) and the National Defense University (NDU) also conduct research on Taiwan-related matters. Although formally under the MND, both units are directed by the CMC and the GSD. Their activities are limited to strategic and operational analysis (not intelligence gathering), including analysis of Taiwan defense matters. NDU's Institute for Strategic Studies (ISS) has two functions: to produce analysis for the CMC and the GSD and to conduct research on strategic issues in support of the university's officer instruction programs. In carrying out these duties the ISS reportedly enjoys considerable flexibility. In contrast, the activities of the AMS's much larger Department of Strategic Studies (*Zhanlue Yanjiubu,* or DSS)[52] do not include an instructional component and are more closely directed by the CMC and the GSD. Hence, the resulting analyses usually reflect the more operationally oriented concerns of those leading military organs.[53] Research on defense-related issues is also conducted by the Foundation for International Strategic Studies (FISS), a nominally "independent" think tank that is in reality associated with the GSD Second Department and Xiong Guangkai.

Although formally presented as the major research unit of the Chinese Academy of Social Sciences (CASS) on Taiwan affairs, the Taiwan Affairs Research Office (TARO) is actually funded and directed entirely by the MSS and receives its information through MSS channels. The TARO was established in September 1984 and evolved out of the Taiwan Research Institute of the CCP Investigation Department (ID). When the ID was abolished its personnel and duties were transferred to the newly established MSS and the GSD Second Department. As a result, the Taiwan Research Institute was attached to the MSS.[54]

As a result of its connection to a State Council ministry, the TARO plays a significant role in Taiwan-related policy discussions. In July 1985 the TARO began to publish the monthly Taiwan Research Reference News (*Taiwan Yanjiu Sankao*), an internal publication that has become very influential in the Taiwan policy community. At present the TARO has over ninety members. It is widely regarded as the premier civilian research institute on issues relating to Taiwan's domestic situation.[55] The TARO's assessments of the scope and pace of change on Taiwan are generally regarded as more orthodox and conservative than those of research institutes in Shanghai and other regions outside Beijing, such as Fujian. The importance of the TARO within the Taiwan affairs policy arena is also suggested by the fact that it has the same ministerial-level bureaucratic ranking as the SCTAO.

The China Institute for Contemporary International Relations (CICIR) is similarly attached to the MSS, and with over five hundred people working in ten regional research offices it is the largest research institute on international relations in Asia. The institute collects information from a variety of open and internal sources; prepares analyses of global, regional, and country-specific trends; and submits its findings to the MSS, which in turn provides analysis and policy views to the State Council and party leadership. The CICIR also has a direct channel to the offices of the FALSG and those of several PBSC members, including Jiang Zemin. These senior leaders often incorporate parts of CICIR analyses directly into their formal policy speeches.[56] Although the CICIR does not have a dedicated Taiwan research office, it produces analysis relevant to Taiwan affairs. Within the MSS system the CICIR generally provides the analysis of international issues relating to Taiwan, whereas the TARO analyzes Taiwan's domestic situation.[57]

As indicated above, the now merged CCTAO and SCTAO have become key producers of research, analysis, and policy recommendations on Taiwan for the TALSG, the State Council, the party Secretariat, and the PBSC.[58] Moreover, both offices gather, evaluate, and synthesize intelligence and analysis on Taiwan policy provided by other agencies within this policy arena. Given its strong research capabilities, the SCTAO Research Bureau is responsible for collecting information, conducting policy research, and supplying policy proposals concerning the most critical Taiwanese policy issues. Much of its information is obtained through analysis of the Taiwanese media, various intelligence channels, and first-hand contacts. The bureau often prepares Taiwan policy reports for senior leaders and articles on Taiwan for PRC and Hong Kong publications.

The GPD's Center for Peace and Development (CPD) was historically the major military unit engaged in research and analysis on the general political situation on Taiwan, whereas CASS's TARO is almost certainly the leading civilian unit. Yet the CPD has reportedly been eclipsed in its policy influence, as well as in the quality of its analysis, by the research organs of the GSD Second Department, as already indicated.[59]

The most important Shanghai-based research institutes include the Shanghai Government's Institute of International Studies (*Shanghai Guojiwenti Yanjiusuo,* or SIIS), the Taiwan Research Institute of the Shanghai Academy of Social Sciences, the Shanghai Municipal Taiwan Research Association (*Shanghai Taiwan Yanjiuhui*), and the Shanghai Institute of International Strategic Studies (*Shanghai Guoji Zhanlue Wenti Yanjiuhui*). The SIIS, which has several research offices and over one hundred personnel, is considered by many observers the most important of these units, in part because of its close association with Wang Daohan. Although the SIIS does not have a Taiwan research office, all of its components work on Taiwan-related diplomatic issues.

This Shanghai network of Taiwan research units was developed in the 1990s under Wang Daohan's patronage, largely in response to Jiang Zemin's desire to develop a source of analysis and policy viewpoints independent of the mainstream Beijing establishment. In general, the Shanghai network seems to generate less conservative assessments of domestic change on Taiwan than, for example, the TARO. Shanghai observers often stress the rapidity of the political reform process on the island, and hence the widening gap that is emerging between Taiwan and the Mainland.

The Taiwan Affairs Office (TAO) of the Ministry of Foreign Affairs is jointly responsible to the MFA and the SCTAO, which hold the same bureaucratic rank. It reportedly employs only a small number of researchers and produces few reports, but its products are usually of very high quality and are often sent to senior MFA and party offices. The TAO's reports are usually developed through the analysis of political intelligence reports provided by overseas offices of the New China News Agency or by PRC embassies. The MFA's Political

Research Office (PRO) plays an important, albeit secondary, role in the Taiwan policy arena. Based at Qinghua University, this unit is closely affiliated with Vice Premier Qian Qichen and therefore exerts sporadic influence over Taiwan policy.

Established in July 1980, Fujian's Xiamen University Institute for Taiwan Studies (ITS) was the first Taiwan research unit to appear in China. Although originally focused almost entirely on the study of Taiwanese history and culture, the Xiamen University ITS has gradually increased its focus to include Taiwanese politics, economics, and society. As a result of its location in Fujian Province, a major contact point with Taiwan, this institute has increasingly focused on the study of cross-strait and general Taiwan-related economic and trade issues in recent years. In fact, the ITS's long history, close proximity to and developing contacts with Taiwan, and involvement with Mainland-Taiwan economic issues have caused some observers to conclude that the ITS is a source of pro-Taiwan views within the larger policy community. In particular, observers often contrast the more orthodox views of the TARO with the allegedly more progressive, pro-Taiwan views of the ITS. This impression is reinforced by the fact that some leading figures within the latter are now institutionally associated with Wang Daohan's Shanghai policy network.[60]

The foregoing description suggests that the overall process by which Taiwan policy is formulated and implemented has become highly regularized, bureaucratic, and consensus oriented over time, reflecting the growing complexity of Taiwan policy, the changing nature of leadership authority in China, and the complexity of change on Taiwan. The rapid expansion of cross-strait economic and cultural ties, the initiation of quasi-governmental bilateral negotiations, and the challenges to Beijing posed by Taiwan's growing economic capabilities and diplomatic activities have all increased the number and breadth of responsibilities of the Chinese party, state, and military actors involved in Taiwan affairs. The creation of various Taiwan policy organs has also occurred in response to Deng Xiaoping's identification of the Taiwan issue as one of the three great issues to be resolved during the 1980s. By the end of that decade all the individual and institutional policy actors of the four functional policy arenas just described were in place and interacting in a complex decision-making process marked by extensive horizontal and vertical consultation, deliberation, and coordination.

Yet the most important transition in the PRC policy-making process regarding Taiwan during the two decades examined in this chapter occurred in the early 1990s with the departure from the political scene of Deng Xiaoping and his elder associates and the ascension to power of the so-called third generation of leaders led by Jiang Zemin. The authority of the Mao Zedong / Deng Xiaoping generation of revolutionary leaders derived primarily from their revolutionary credentials, individual prestige, and personal relations. The leadership group that replaced them consisted largely of more pragmatic, bureaucratically trained technocrats whose authority depended primarily on policy successes, substantive policy expertise, organizational controls, and the ability to persuade rather than dictate. This transition reinforced the trend discussed earlier in this chapter toward a more extensive, bureaucratic, and consensus-oriented policy-making process. This process therefore supplanted the largely top-down, authoritarian, personalistic, and at times ideological pattern of decision-making of the Deng era.

As a result of these developments, the content of individual policy decisions (including decisions relating to grand strategy) has been shaped by a wide range of individuals and organs since the early 1990s. At times subordinate actors initiate policy proposals, albeit under the general principles established by the senior leadership. In other cases these secondary actors respond to initiatives of the leadership. Regardless of the origin of the proposed initiative, however, the individual central, provincial, and municipal party, government, and military organs responsible for Taiwan affairs utilize the intelligence and analysis provided by the aforementioned research, analysis, and intelligence units to engage in detailed internal deliberations and consultations on the specific issue presented. These bureaucratic deliberations sometimes produce significant differences of opinion and require coordination meetings to achieve consensus. If consensus is not reached at such meetings, differing proposals are then simultaneously submitted to higher-level units for resolution.

Eventually, ministry- and commission-level units within each party, state, and military system submit Taiwan-related policy reports and recommendations to those high-level organs responsible for coordinating policy views within each system (the CCTAO, the SCTAO, and the CMCGO). These higher offices, in turn, provide formal reports or recommendations on various aspects of Taiwan policy (such as diplomacy and politics, defense, government, and societal contacts) to senior party, military, and government leadership bodies, specifically the TALSG, the CMC Executive Committee, and the top leadership of the State Council.[61] The policy views and recommendations submitted by these three bodies are then collected, summarized or synthesized, and conveyed to the offices of the senior party leadership by the CCGO.[62] At the uppermost level of the policy-making process differing party, government, and military views are resolved or muted through a process of informal deliberation among the senior leadership, as is also explained in the chapters by David Lampton, Lu Ning, and Tai Ming Cheung.

This entire policy-planning and consensus-building process can last for weeks or even months. Once a particular policy is determined, directives are then issued in the name of the Central Committee, the State Council, or the CMC, and implementation is coordinated and supervised by the TALSG and the leaders of its constituent units. As I indicated earlier, under Jiang Zemin the TALSG has come to play an increasingly critical role in this policy-making process as the core mechanism for coordinating and arbitrating the views of the most critical bureaucratic actors in the Taiwan policy apparatus. However, this does not mean that the TALSG has become the final decision-making body determining grand strategy toward Taiwan. Formal decision-making power concerning the most fundamental policy issues and initiatives still resides with the PBSC. Under most conditions, however, Jiang Zemin exercises effective control over agenda setting, proposal formulation, and implementation oversight through the TALSG. This means that he is often able to influence the policy-making process in ways that greatly limit the ability of other PBSC members to counter his views or undermine his policies. This is particularly the case when Jiang is able to convince the major state and military representatives in the TALSG to support his position. These individuals represent top power holders with a vital interest in the Taiwan issue.

The features of the Taiwan policymaking process discussed previously relate primarily to decision-making during noncrisis periods. In the event of a political or military crisis (such as the confrontation with the United States in 1995–96), senior political bodies such as the PBSC become more directly involved in daily decisions and thus supplant the activities of the TALSG. Moreover, if the crisis involves a significant military dimension, senior military leaders and the CMC will also become involved, as was the case during the 1995–96 confrontation. However, the net assessment presented herein is that Jiang Zemin is far more influential in the Taiwan policy arena than is often thought and that military control of the arena is less than is often assumed.

PART II: THE EVOLUTION OF CHINA'S GRAND
STRATEGY TOWARD TAIWAN

China's policy regarding Taiwan since the advent of the reform era in late 1978 can be divided into four major phases. Each is characterized by a different set of basic policy decisions regarding Taiwan and the U.S.-China-Taiwan relationship (as indicated in the introduction to this volume), and each is founded upon a different mix of political and bureaucratic calculations. The four phases are 1978–92, the shift to peaceful reunification; 1993–April 1995, the formulation of Jiang Zemin's Eight Points; May 1995–March 1996, a response to crisis; and March 1996 to the present, a modified peace overture. Beginning in spring and summer of 1999, Beijing again began to inject more coercive elements into its overall approach to Taiwan, largely as a result of actions taken by Lee Teng-hui (discussed later). However, it is too early to say whether this constitutes the beginning of a fifth policy phase.

1978–92: The Shift from Confrontation to Peaceful Reunifiication

The most significant change in PRC policy regarding Taiwan took place in the late 1970s, when Beijing formally shifted from a confrontational stance based on the notion of the "liberation" of Taiwan to a policy emphasizing peaceful reunification through negotiation. In support of this policy shift the PRC government ceased shelling the off-shore islands, dropped all propaganda references to the liberation of Taiwan, appealed for discussions to end the military confrontation, and suggested the establishment of a variety of direct cross-strait links.

Ralph Clough has identified nine basic elements of this policy line regarding Taiwan, including several that emerged as the policy evolved during the 1980s and early 1990s:[63]

— There is only one China; Taiwan is a part of China and cannot become an independent state.
— The reunification of Taiwan with China is necessary and inevitable, and the sooner it is accomplished the better.
— Reunification should occur under a formula of "one country, two systems," in which Taiwan will be permitted to retain its existing political, economic, and military systems in exchange for Taipei's recognition of the PRC government in Beijing as China's sole

national government and of that government's sole responsibility for Taiwan's defense and diplomatic relations.

— Reunification talks should begin as soon as possible.

— Reunification talks can be conducted on an equal basis by representatives of the Nationalist and Communist Parties, but not by representatives of Beijing and Taipei as two equal governments, because the Taiwan authorities administer only a provincial government.

— The two sides should promote people-to-people interactions to prepare for a smooth reunification.

— The so-called three links (direct mail, trade and shipping, and air services) are required to facilitate people-to-people interactions.

— Although the PRC favors peaceful reunification, it nonetheless reserves the right to use military force against Taiwan if necessary to prevent the island from permanently separating from the Mainland.

— Only the PRC has the right to represent China internationally, so Taiwan can have only economic and cultural relations with foreign countries, not diplomatic relations.[64]

Most of these principles were enunciated by Chinese leaders in key speeches and documents between 1978 and 1982, including Deng Xiaoping's public formulation of the "one country, two systems" concept in September 1982.

Elements of this policy line first emerged in the 1950s, when the PRC offered the prospect of "peaceful liberation" through negotiation. There followed the establishment of secret links between Beijing and Taipei in the early 1960s and repeated public offers to open talks on reunification in both the 1960s and the 1970s. Indeed, the concept of "one country, two systems" and other elements of this policy line (such as the stress on developing people-to-people contacts and direct links) evolved from these early efforts to seek a peaceful resolution of the long-standing struggle between the PRC and Taiwan.[65]

However, the decision to shift the basic thrust of China's Taiwan policy from confrontation to peaceful reunification through negotiations did not emerge fully until the late 1970s and early 1980s and was the logical consequence of other major policy initiatives, including the normalization of Sino-U.S. relations and the adoption of economic reform and open-door policies. The former development led to Washington's acknowledgment of Beijing's "one China" stance toward Taiwan and the abrogation of the U.S.–Republic of China (ROC) mutual defense treaty.[66] The latter policy required the development of a peaceful and stable external environment conducive to economic growth, including amicable ties with the major powers and with Asian neighbors, including Taiwan.

These developments made it possible for Beijing to adopt a nonconfrontational policy regarding Taiwan and increased the likelihood that such a policy would be accepted by Taipei. The Chinese leadership apparently reasoned that Taiwan's loss of U.S. political and military support and the development of closer ties between Beijing and the rest of Asia, combined with an offer to permit the continuation of Taiwan's existing political and economic order under the "one country, two systems" formula, would eventually force Taipei to drop its confrontational stance (marked by a nearly complete refusal to interact with Beijing) and enter into reunification negotiations. The Chinese leadership further believed that China's open-door policy and the ensuing rapid economic development would increase Taiwanese dependence on the Mainland and thus create even greater reasons for Taiwan to move toward reunification.[67] Therefore, from 1978 to 1992 various noncoercive cross-strait elements of Beijing's peaceful reunification policy line were uniformly emphasized.

Deng Xiaoping, having identified the resolution of the Taiwan issue as one of three major tasks to be accomplished during the 1980s,[68] was in complete control of Taiwan policy during this period and thus was the driving force behind this shift in strategy. Therefore, the reasons for the shift in strategy were closely associated with Deng's larger reform and open-door policies and with the normalization of relations with the United States. Deng also exercised ultimate control over defense-related issues concerning Taiwan as a result of his contacts with the military.[69]

However, Deng certainly did not decide on this major policy shift on his own, nor did he formulate all its supporting elements. He consulted extensively with several of his senior colleagues and associates, including Marshal Ye Jianying and Li Xiannian, on the logic, significance, and substance of a more conciliatory policy regarding Taiwan.[70] These senior leaders eventually accepted the new policy and formed a strong consensus with Deng on the need to end the policy of confrontation and draw Taipei into negotiations. This consensus persisted among the key leaders of the successor generation, including Hu Yaobang, Zhao Ziyang, Jiang Zemin, and Li Peng and has lasted to the present day, even though it has been subject to considerable strain in recent years. Indeed, the three subsequent policy shifts examined later constitute either modifications—but not abandonment—of Deng's basic strategy or responses to perceived challenges to the strategy.

Policy actors below the senior leadership level played an increasingly important role in the decision-making process as the policy of peaceful reunification evolved and developed in the 1980s. During the initial formulation of the policy line in 1978–82 the most important bureaucratic player was the newly established CCTAO. This critical policy body was created by Deng and his colleagues in 1979 to coordinate subordinate units in their efforts to operationalize the basic elements of the new policy line. Hence, recommendations to the senior leadership on the content of the "one country, two systems" formula were developed through a process of bureaucratic consultations led by the CCTAO. However, the bureaucratic policy-making process below the top leadership remained rudimentary in the early 1980s. Although the TALSG, established in 1980, was functioning as a research and support organ for Deng and the senior leadership, most substantive policy interactions occurred exclusively between Deng, his senior associates, and the CCTAO.[71] This general "nuclear core" consultation process is thoroughly described in Lu Ning's chapter in this volume.

The process of bureaucratic consultation and support for the senior leadership became more thorough and systematic during the late 1980s and early 1990s as the authority of the TALSG over the policy-making process increased and additional offices responsible for Taiwan policy (such as the SCTAO) were created. By the late 1980s, although ultimate authority over Taiwan policy remained in the hands of Deng Xiaoping, operational aspects of this policy were largely under the control of the TALSG under the leadership of Deng's close associate, Yang Shangkun. Yang also served as an important contact with the military leadership regarding detailed aspects of Taiwan policy during his tenure as head of the TALSG.[72]

1993–April 1995: Formulation of Jiang Zemin's Eight Points

Deng's grand strategy of peaceful reunification under the "one country, two systems" formula underwent a significant adjustment in the early 1990s, which was marked by the promulgation of a major policy initiative regarding Taiwan in January 1995—the so-called Jiang Zemin Eight-Point Initiative (known as *Jiang Ba Dian*, the Jiang Eight Points). This initiative became the basic guideline for cross-strait relations in the post-Deng era.[73] Although based on the core principles laid out by Deng, the Jiang Eight Points focused primarily on the modalities of cross-strait discussions leading to reunification. Specifically, the initiative listed various special proposals, such as regarding the convening of a cross-strait dialogue between equal representatives and an agreement to end hostilities, and emphasized the need for a phased process of rapprochement and negotiations leading to reunification. Unlike Deng's policy shift of 1978–82, which reflected a desire to resolve the Taiwan issue during the 1980s, the Jiang Eight Points did not anticipate such "speedy" reunification; rather, it sought only agreement on a transitional framework that would stabilize the status quo, facilitate economic exchanges, and generally preempt any permanent separation of Taiwan from the Mainland.[74]

Basically, the Jiang Eight Points constituted a highly conciliatory document. It suggested that as long as Taiwan would negotiate under the principle that there is only one China and Taiwan is a part of China, Beijing would consider all of Taiwan's concerns, presumably including its preconditions for lifting the ban on direct links with the Mainland (that is, renouncing the use of force, accepting Taiwan as an equal political entity, and permitting Taiwan to have a reasonable degree of international "space"). The Jiang Eight Points were formulated in response to various new domestic and external developments confronting the Chinese leadership in the early 1990s. These included changes in Taiwan's self-identity and international posture because of political developments on the island, apparent adverse (to the PRC) shifts in the U.S. stance toward the island (such as Washington's September 1994 limited "upgrade" in relations with Taipei), and various structural and personal opportunities for policy change resulting from the Chinese leadership succession process. Together these developments led to significant adjustments in China's grand strategy toward Taiwan.

Beginning in the late 1980s, the gradual democratization of Taiwan's political process, symbolized by the emergence of Taiwan-born President Lee Teng-hui and the growing influence of pro-independence political forces centered on the Democratic Progressive Party (DPP), had led to a shift in Taiwan's approach to the international community and its stance toward cross-strait relations. Under Lee's leadership, and using the increased leverage provided by its booming economy, Taiwan embarked on a diplomacy drive to achieve greater international recognition of Taiwan as a political entity separate from the Mainland. This included efforts to strengthen Taiwan's bilateral relations and to obtain a form of dual recognition for Taipei in international bodies.[75] Within Taiwan, Lee Teng-hui was apparently moving to redefine the core identity of the Chinese Nationalist Party (Kuomintang, or KMT) by replacing Mainland-born conservatives who believed strongly in reunification with individuals who supported his attempt to create a separate Taiwanese political identity. Lee was also pressing for constitutional amendments that would effectively end the Taiwan government's long-standing claim to sovereignty over all of China. At the same time a growing number of Taiwan residents were voicing support for outright independence while apparently rejecting their Chinese identity.

Beijing's concern with these developments was exacerbated by U.S. actions at the time, such as the October 1992 decision to sell 150 F-16 fighter-bomber aircraft to Taiwan. This action suggested to Chinese leaders that the United States had significantly weakened, if not reversed, its previous cautionary stance on arms sales to Taiwan, although in reality the principal motive for this decision was domestic, in particular the need during the presidential campaign of 1992 for President Bush to obtain votes in Texas, where the aircraft would be manufactured. Many Chinese leaders saw the U.S. sale as a violation of the 1982 Sino-U.S. communiqué in which Washington had pledged to gradually reduce arms sales to Taipei. Moreover, for many the U.S. action suggested that Washington was modifying its past "one China" stance to encourage pro-independence sentiment on Taiwan.

Events in 1993 and 1994 provided the final confirmation that the "Taiwan problem" had reached a critical stage. In early 1993 Taipei launched an effort to obtain a seat in the United Nations General Assembly as a political entity separate from the PRC.[76] At the same time recently initiated talks between Beijing and Taipei had stagnated. Also during 1993 Lee Teng-hui's major conservative opponent among Mainland KMT conservatives, General Hao Bocun, was ousted from office. This gave Lee the freedom to push forward with his domestic and international policies without significant KMT opposition.[77] Some Chinese leaders even feared that Lee would move to form a tacit alliance with the moderate wing of the DPP to permanently marginalize reunification supporters and ensure the creation of a separate Taiwanese state.[78] However, for many Chinese leaders (including Jiang Zemin) the confirmation of Lee's separatist intentions came in 1994. During that year the tragic Thousand Island boat incident (in which several Taiwanese tourists traveling in China were robbed and murdered, and the incident was allegedly covered up by Chinese officials) resulted in harsh rhetoric from Lee Teng-hui. Taipei subsequently rejected efforts by Beijing to continue the cross-strait dialogue begun in 1993. A final incident was Lee Teng-hui's interview with the Japanese journalist Ryutaro Shiba in April 1994. In this interview Lee confirmed, in the minds of the Chinese leadership, his support for an independent Taiwan with a pro-Western and pro-Japan diplomatic policy.[79]

From the Chinese perspective, it was obvious by the early 1990s that Deng's policy line had not brought about a narrowing of the political gap between Beijing and Taipei. To the contrary, the aforementioned events of 1993–94 indicated that the Taiwan government under Lee Teng-hui had rejected the modus vivendi that had ensured stable cross-strait relations for over forty years, which was centered on a joint PRC-ROC affirmation of Taiwan's status as a province of China. In its place Lee was apparently seeking to legitimate, both domestically and internationally, a "one China, one Taiwan" arrangement that would likely result in the permanent separation of the two. Deng's general strategy, of course, could not have foreseen such challenges arising from Taiwanese democratization and the rapid growth of the Taiwanese economy. By the early 1990s most Chinese observers recognized that further policy measures were required to stabilize the relationship.

Policy strategists, reportedly with the support of both Deng and Jiang, began to discuss how to respond to the new challenges posed by Taiwan.[80] According to Chinese interviewees, three basic approaches to Taiwan emerged in 1992–93. One approach argued that China should attempt to accelerate the reunification process by seeking to strictly limit Taiwan's international options and placing greater pressure (including military coercion) on Taiwan to enter into meaningful reunification talks. Major proponents of this viewpoint reportedly included many strategists within the Chinese military and various tough-minded civilians within both the MSS and the MFA research institutes. The second approach suggested the need to gradually move through at least two stages to resolve the Taiwan problem, combining any increase in pressure on Taiwan with positive political incentives. The first stage would involve the signing of a peace agreement between Taipei and Beijing, whereas the second would include discussions on reunification. Both steps would be stimulated by the clear enunciation by Beijing of a flexible approach to cross-strait contacts. Key proponents of this view included many civilian researchers, as well as strategists and officials in the TALSG, in the recently merged CCTAO and SCTAO, and in the Fujian provincial government. After 1993 this view was also expressed by many Taiwan specialists who were part of Wang Daohan's Shanghai network.

Finally, the third approach, less coherent and of only minimal influence within the policy apparatus, arose from the fatalistic attitude that neither gradual progress centered on greater concessions nor an acceleration of the reunification process was possible. It argued that the gradualist strategy would require major increases in Chinese economic and political leverage, which would take a long time. The accelerated strategy relied on the possession of coercive instruments that China did not presently possess and would not acquire for many years. Hence, for these individuals China's only option was to adopt a reactive stance, seeking only to prevent Taiwanese independence. This viewpoint was reportedly held by a minority of strategists and policy officials in both civilian and military research institutes.

Despite the emergence of this policy debate, the political environment in China did not initially facilitate the formulation of a systematic policy response to the Taiwan situation. From 1989 to 1992 China's leadership was distracted by urgent domestic priorities: the need to restore political and social stability to China following the Tiananmen incident of June 1989 and Deng's struggle to defeat the internal opponents to the next stage of his economic reform policy. In addition, Deng's health was declining during this period, limiting his ability to focus on less urgent issues. Moreover, Deng's newly anointed successor, Jiang Zemin, did not yet have the authority to formulate new approaches in key policy arenas.

Hence, the initial reaction of the Chinese government to the developments just described was disjointed and reactive at best. For example, in mid-1993 Beijing issued a white paper titled "The Taiwan Problem and China's Unification" that presented an optimistic assessment of the cross-strait relationship overall, meanwhile rejecting Taiwan's efforts to participate in the international community. Although promulgated in mid-1993, as Jiang Zemin was taking control of the Taiwan policy apparatus, the white paper had actually been formulated earlier, under Yang Shangkun's aegis as head of the TALSG, and likely represented a less flexible line than the one favored by Jiang Zemin.[81] It was only after the two critical domestic challenges were largely resolved and Deng had considerably reduced his direct control over the policy-making apparatus (between mid-1993 and mid-1994) that Jiang Zemin turned to the Taiwan problem. Indeed, by late 1993 Jiang had both the opportunity and the incentive to develop a new policy regarding Taiwan.

Jiang undoubtedly believed that a peaceful breakthrough on Taiwan would confirm the continuity of his policies with Deng Xiaoping's, boost his stature among the public, strengthen his position among his colleagues and rivals for power, and defuse military concerns over an increasingly independence-minded Taiwan.[82] Moreover, Jiang Zemin's ability to use Taiwan policy to achieve his political aims was increased by the fact that he had taken over the chairmanship of the TALSG from Yang Shangkun in mid-1993 and had restructured that body to facilitate its use as a key policy mechanism, as I indicated earlier. Therefore, by late 1993 Jiang and his close associates were seeking to turn the earlier deliberations among Taiwan specialists into a formal process designed to produce a new Taiwan policy. Wang Daohan reportedly first proposed the notion of drafting a new policy initiative on Taiwan in the second half of 1993. The formal decision to formulate the Jiang Eight Points was adopted soon thereafter, at the first meeting of the restructured and streamlined TALSG.[83]

The actual procedure involved in formulating the Eight Points reflected the extensive process of bureaucratic consultation and consensus building that had emerged in the late 1980s and early 1990s. All members of the new TALSG, including the military, were reportedly involved in the formulation process, with each member providing conceptual input and recommendations generated by his bureaucratic system. The actual writing group consisted of Taiwan experts from all the major civilian and military research institutes,[84] whereas the leading role was reportedly played by the CCTAO/SCTAO (and their head, Wang Zhaoguo) and Wang Daohan. A draft was circulated to all TALSG members and then to Politburo members for comment. A final draft was produced by October 1994.[85] This draft was then reviewed by the CCGO Policy Research Office and given final approval by the PBSC soon thereafter.[86] The formal proposal was then publicly announced by Jiang Zemin during the Chinese Spring Festival—when Chinese families come together—to emphasize Beijing's desire to reunite the larger Chinese national family.[87]

The Jiang Eight Points incorporated many of the gradualists' views. Jiang had apparently supported this approach when it was first presented in 1992 and 1993 because it presumably offered the best prospect for attaining his aforementioned personal and political objectives. Some observers speculate that the Chinese military leadership argued during the more formal policy deliberations of 1993 and 1994 for a hard-line stance toward Taipei that incorporated many of the views of the first of the three approaches noted earlier. At least one analyst argues that the Taiwan problem had been placed much higher on the PLA's list of national security concerns following a formal military reassessment of the situation in Taiwan in early 1994.[88]

However, there is no readily available corroboration of such a PLA reassessment concerning Taiwan or of any concerted military opposition to the Jiang Eight Points. As I indicated earlier, both military and party circles were concerned about political developments on Taiwan and the efforts undertaken by Lee Teng-hui to raise Taiwan's international profile. Moreover, both groups were fully involved in the formulation of the Jiang Eight Points. Therefore, it is unlikely that the military leadership directly opposed the conciliatory approach presented in the Jiang Eight Points. It is more probable that individual officers, such as Generals Liu Huaqing and Zhang Zhen, strongly urged that the initiative be coupled with specific improvements in PLA deployments and capabilities vis-à-vis Taiwan as an important "stick" to go along with the "carrots" contained in the Jiang Eight Points.[89] In fact, beginning in 1993 and 1994, the PLA gradually increased its presence in the Nanjing Military Region across from Taiwan, thus reversing a long-standing trend toward the demilitarization of the Taiwan Strait area. Such developments almost certainly occurred with the concurrence of Jiang Zemin and the party leadership.

Lee Teng-hui's response to the Jiang Eight Points was presented in April 1995 in the form of a counter-proposal for talks. In his response Lee demanded that Beijing renounce its threat to use force against Taiwan before any talks could begin. This was an unacceptable demand from the Chinese perspective and was viewed by most Chinese leaders as an outright rejection and a slap in the face. As a result, it generated concern within the Chinese leadership circles regarding the efficacy of the new strategy and hence increased pressure on its strongest supporters to ensure that no further slippage occurred. For example, the Ministry of Foreign Affairs exerted strenuous efforts to ensure that Washington would not provide further assistance to Lee's pragmatic diplomacy by permitting him to visit the United States in 1995. These developments set the stage for the next phase of China's approach to Taiwan.

May 1995–March 1996: A Tough Response to a Sudden Crisis

The conciliatory policy embodied in the Jiang Eight Points was soon eclipsed by the events of spring 1995. Cross-strait relations had shown some signs of improvement in early 1995, marked by Taipei's acceptance of a second round of semiofficial talks between Wang Daohan and C. F. Koo in Beijing and its decision to continue to hold such talks on an annual basis. However, the U.S. decision in May 1995 to permit Lee Teng-hui to visit his alma mater, Cornell University, precipitated a crisis.[90] This decision was seen by many Chinese leaders as a clear indication of Washington's support for Lee's strategy of "creeping independence" and tantamount to a reversal of U.S. policy on "one China."[91]

This Chinese assessment was strengthened by the actual circumstances of Lee Teng-hui's visit, namely: the apparent fact that the visit was treated by the Taiwanese authorities as an official visit, with little U.S. protest, and described as a "breakthrough" in Taiwan's efforts at pragmatic diplomacy; Lee Teng-hui's use of the term "Republic of China on Taiwan" many times in his Cornell speech; Taiwan's subsequent effort to advance its diplomatic strategy by offering $1 billion for a UN seat and by sending Premier Lien Chan on a series of visits to European capitals; and U.S. State Department officials' occasional reference to Lee Teng-hui as "President Lee."

These developments ultimately precipitated Beijing's adoption of a tough-minded, multipronged strategy that was designed to halt Lee's forward momentum, communicate Beijing's grave concern over Washington's (apparently changing) stance toward Taiwan, convey its commitment to preventing Taiwanese independence by any means necessary, and ultimately create a more durable foundation for Beijing's Taiwan policy. This strategy centered on four key elements:

— Efforts were made by Beijing to weaken support on Taiwan for what was then unanimously viewed as a pro-independence strategy by launching unremitting criticisms of Lee as a traitor to Chinese nationalism and a supporter of foreign (read Japanese and U.S.) interests. On the positive side, Beijing informally floated flexible reunification formulas that appeared to go beyond those presented in the Jiang Eight Points and continued to emphasize the importance of economic links across the strait.

— Beijing backed up its propaganda campaign against Taiwanese pro-independence sentiment by canceling the second round of the semiofficial cross-strait talks and expanding the scope of the intended military exercises near Taiwan. These exercises included war games simulating amphibious landings on Taiwan and unprecedented ballistic missile "tests" in waters near Taiwan, all timed, in part, to influence public opinion prior to Taiwanese legislative elections in December 1995 and the presidential election in March 1996. They were also intended to convince the United States and Asia that China was serious about preventing Taiwanese independence, even to the extent of deploying military forces.

— Beijing decided to pressure the United States not to support Lee's pro-independence strategy by taking limited diplomatic actions against Washington (such as recalling the Chinese ambassador to Washington, suspending military exchanges and high-level visits, and lodging a formal protest), meanwhile criticizing the United States in the public media for attempting to contain China. The Chinese also sought a pledge from Washington not to allow further visits of Lee Teng-hui or other senior Taiwanese officials.

— Beijing launched a diplomatic offensive across Asia, Russia, and Europe to reduce U.S. diplomatic leverage regarding Taiwan among third countries and to generally minimize collateral damage to China's basic policy line of cooperation, peace, and economic development. This offensive was designed to improve ties and assure anxious observers that the Taiwan issue was sui generis and did not portend a more aggressive Chinese foreign policy line. This reassurance effort was also directed at Taiwan businessmen, who were told that their investments and interests in the PRC would not be affected.

Some observers have suggested that this strategy was a consequence of the rise of a hard-line faction of military leaders (and Jiang opponents) within the party who were committed to a more coercive stance toward Taiwan. According to this interpretation, Taiwan's actions in April and May 1995 permitted these hard-line forces to wrest control of Taiwan policy from Jiang, who was thus forced to accept the decisions just listed, which amounted to a reversal of the Jiang Eight Points.[92] Deng's deteriorating health was also part of this scenario of internal struggle.

My research does *not* support this interpretation. As suggested by the previous overview of the policy-making process, the military does not dictate Chinese policy in any area, including those surrounding sensitive territorial issues such as Taiwan. Both military and civilian leaders know that direct military intervention in key policy areas would prove highly destabilizing to the regime as a whole and would possibly result in a violent power struggle or social unrest. Moreover, from a decision-making perspective, informants insist that military leaders seldom directly present formal policy recommendations on any issue, including Taiwan. Although PLA research and intelligence organs often submit reports to the CMC, such documents do not constitute the position or assessment of the military. The military leadership, by contrast, will issue a report on a sensitive issue only if Jiang Zemin requests it.[93]

The four policy elements previously listed represented a crisis response to what was perceived by all relevant policy actors as a serious challenge to a core Chinese national security interest. The events of May and June 1995 convinced most Chinese leaders that Lee Teng-hui was seeking de facto, if not de jure, independence for Taiwan. In addition, many leaders by that time suspected that Washington was attempting to use Taiwan policy as a means to keep China down politically and economically. Most officials, including Jiang Zemin and

Li Peng, consequently agreed that China must intensify the military, diplomatic, and political pressure to weaken Lee's position, deter his continued pursuit of pragmatic diplomacy, and halt further U.S. support for him.[94] Although this certainly required a much tougher approach to the Taiwan problem, few officials viewed the ensuing policy moves as a reversal of the Jiang Eight Points. Beijing reportedly remained committed to the peaceful resolution of the Taiwan problem that had been laid out in that initiative and recognized that cordial relations with Washington remained a critical element of China's strategy, to be preserved if at all possible.

This is not meant to imply that the decisions listed previously were made without debate or that Jiang Zemin's leadership was not put to the test by the events of April 1995–March 1996. Serious differences existed among civilian and military leaders over the timing and nature of the measures to be employed and the relative emphasis to be placed on coercive and noncoercive approaches. This was especially true because a larger number of senior party and military leaders became involved in formulating and implementing Taiwan policy than under more routine circumstances. Specifically, key decisions were made during the crisis by the PBSC (in particular, Jiang Zemin, Li Peng, and Liu Huaqing) and not via the TALSG.[95] As a result, some elements of the four-point strategy were doubtless a product of compromises between moderates on Taiwan policy generally within the MFA and the CCTAO-SCTAO and hard-liners (generally within the military). Nonetheless, the decisions arrived at during this crisis period were by and large the consequence of a collaborative policy-making process led by Jiang Zemin and not the outcome of a factional struggle.[96]

Although we do not possess most of the details of how these decisions were made, several significant features of the policy-making process are evident. The U.S. decision to grant a visa to Lee Teng-hui evidently caught the Chinese leadership by surprise given U.S. assurances and Qian Qichen's repeated assertion that President Clinton would successfully resist congressional pressure to grant a visa, and this decision seemed to confirm that Washington was indeed playing the "Taiwan card" against Beijing. An internal debate therefore ensued among senior party leaders, with input from TALSG members and subordinate specialists, concerning how best to respond to the visa issuance.

According to several informants, Jiang Zemin and other leaders such as Li Peng and Liu Huaqing were convinced, from the early stages of the crisis, that Beijing had to take a tough stand to prevent other countries from following the U.S. lead.[97] Foreign Minister Qian Qichen supported this tough response by May 1995,[98] although he and other Chinese leaders differed over the type and degree of toughness required. As might be expected, civilian MFA officials tended to stress the need for tough political and diplomatic responses. Many individuals were concerned that an overly harsh military reaction would precipitate a major clash with Washington, which might seriously weaken Sino-U.S. political and economic relations and thereby undermine Chinese growth and stability.[99] In contrast, other leaders, including military figures such as Liu Huaqing and Zhang Zhen, suggested the need for a significant military dimension to any response, possibly including missile "tests."[100] Supporters of this view reportedly argued that any possible U.S. response to such actions would not seriously threaten the Sino-U.S. economic relationship given Washington's apparent desire to protect major U.S. business interests in China, but that in any event it was worth risking possible economic damage to China in order to prevent the loss of Chinese territory.

The Chinese leadership initially decided to take a firm but restrained stance on the U.S. issuance of a visa to Lee. Beijing ceased all contacts with Washington at the time, including ongoing military-to-military visits, and lodged a strong protest. However, Jiang Zemin also decided, reportedly with the concurrence of other party leaders, that Beijing would permit preparations for the second round of cross-strait talks, scheduled for August, to go forward. Hence, Tang Shubei was permitted to travel to Taipei in late April as part of those preparations. Jiang and other leaders hoped that this action would show Beijing's commitment to the talks and, more important, deter Lee Teng-hui from actually traveling to the United States or at least from making provocative statements once there. The party leadership reasoned that Lee might show such restraint in order to avoid precipitating a breakdown in the cross-strait dialogue.[101] If so, they clearly miscalculated.

Lee Teng-hui not only traveled to Cornell, but made what were viewed by the Chinese leadership as highly provocative statements. These actions convinced Jiang and others that the military's recommendations should be implemented. Hence, in early July Jiang Zemin directed the PLA leadership to develop, and be prepared to implement in short order, plans for a military display directed at Taiwan. In mid-July the PLA leadership proposed a series of military exercises and short-range ballistic missile firings before the Taiwanese legislative elections in December 1995 and the presidential election in March 1996.[102] The PLA was prepared to conduct the first missile "tests" in a matter of days—that is, before the end of July—and they were to be followed by naval exercises in August and November and by more missile firings and exercises in February and March 1996. The military and civilian leaders calculated that these actions would chasten Taiwanese politicians and convince the populace of the dangers of Lee's pro-independence approach, resulting in votes against pro-independence legislators and Lee. The displays were also intended to demonstrate to all parties that China was (and is) deadly serious about preventing Taiwanese independence.[103]

The specific elements of this policy response were reportedly finalized at the annual expanded CCP work conference in Beidaihe in late July and early August of 1995. Some observers have reported that at this meeting Jiang Zemin's previous strategy for dealing with Taiwan was strongly criticized and that he was forced to make a statement amounting to "self-criticism" to hard-liners.[104] It is more likely, however, that Jiang simply presented a frank assessment of the difficulties of relying on a purely diplomatic strategy to deter Taiwanese independence and woo Taipei into reunification talks and willingly acknowledged the importance of military pressure.

At the same time, the Beidaihe meeting also apparently resulted in a decision to focus Chinese pressure on Taiwan and Lee Teng-hui and to reduce tensions with Washington. Although Chinese leaders at this meeting reconfirmed their view that the United States likely sought to contain China, they also recognized that Beijing needed to maintain workable relations with Washington. Both Jiang Zemin and Li Peng espoused the argument that China could not afford to confront the West and that Deng Xiaoping's long-standing emphasis on economic reform and development must remain dominant in China's overall strategy.[105] This theme was repeated by Jiang Zemin in a series of leadership meetings held in August and September, at which he "strongly defended a moderate stance toward the United States and was successful in achieving a consensus behind such a stance, despite deeply felt skepticism and criticism from other leaders urging a harder line toward the United States."[106]

From July 1995 to March 1996 the Chinese leadership implemented the strategy just described. The CMC played a major role in this effort, overseeing execution of the agreed-upon exercises and ballistic missile "tests," the latter of which were conducted in late July 1995 and early March 1996. However, the military cannot be said to have directed the overall Taiwan strategy. Once the basic strategy had been approved, moreover, there were no indications of debate or fundamental changes in policy. Although several developments must have raised doubts among some civilian Chinese officials as to the wisdom of an essentially militaristic approach, other events seemed to validate this approach. Specifically, four key milestones occurred during this period:

— In late October and early November 1995 Beijing largely succeeded in reducing the likelihood of further adverse actions by Washington in the near term. China had obtained firm commitments from the Clinton administration to uphold the "one China" policy and to limit further trips to the United States by high-level Taiwan officials. This commitment was reflected in public and private statements made by senior U.S. officials and by Washington's continued stance on limited arms sales to Taiwan.[107] This must have given both moderate and hard-line officials cause for optimism in placing further diplomatic and military pressure on Taiwan.[108]

— In Taiwan's legislative election of December 2, 1995, the KMT lost 5 of its 89 seats in the 164-seat legislature, whereas the DPP gained just 3 new seats, for a total of 54. The pro-reunification New Party trebled its number of seats in the legislature for a total of 21 seats. This development arguably vindicated the efficacy of China's tough-minded strategy, especially the missile tests of July and the naval exercises of August and November.[109]

— During February and March 1996 there was a significant escalation of tensions, marked by the third and fourth sets of Chinese military exercises; very strong statements by senior U.S. officials (including Secretary of Defense William Perry) describing the Chinese military activities as "reckless and provocative" and referring to the strength of the U.S. Navy and to the "grave consequences" of any attack on Taiwan; the deployment of two U.S. carrier battle groups to the vicinity of Taiwan; and private expressions of concern by regional governments regarding China's belligerent behavior. At the same time, senior U.S. security policy officials met in Washington with the director of the Chinese State Council Foreign Affairs Office, Liu Huaqiu, to warn that serious consequences would ensue if China did not exercise restraint.

These U.S. and regional actions quite possibly moderated the final stage of China's military exercises and missile firings. Although bad weather played some role in curtailing the March exercises, some observers believe that the Chinese cut these exercises short and reduced the number of missile firings to avoid further confrontation with Washington. There are also some indications that the Chinese leadership disagreed over how to respond to the U.S. actions. For example, the U.S. response apparently angered, not chastened, the military. Some military officers reportedly expressed a belief that Clinton's decision to deploy the carriers amounted to a "betrayal" of China by breaking a U.S. commitment to avoid the direct use of force in the defense of Taiwan and by ignoring China's assurances that its exercises were not intended as a prelude to an invasion of Taiwan.[110] Moderate Chinese officials within the MFA and the TAOs apparently took a different stance, however, arguing that the aggressive U.S. reaction belied the assumption, held by many hard-liners prior to February or March, that the United States would not utilize its forces to defend Taiwan because of domestic political constraints. These individuals wanted Beijing to explain more clearly that it did not intend to attack Taiwan and to cancel the remaining military exercises.[111] Therefore, China's behavior during this period probably reflected a compromise between these differing views, albeit with a continued emphasis on the military approach. Beijing carried out its missile tests and exercises, but fired only four missiles and apparently curtailed the last two days of exercises (March 24 and 25).

— On March 23, 1996, Taiwan held its first direct presidential election. The DPP earned only 21 percent of the vote, down from one-third in earlier elections. The KMT and Lee Teng-hui earned 54 percent of the vote, whereas two pro-reunification candidates earned 15 percent and 10 percent. The election, as well as opinion polls, suggested an apparent surge of political support for Lee Teng-hui as an embattled leader and symbol of Taiwanese nationalism. Even DPP supporters had increased their support of Lee. The pro-reunification New Party was the apparent loser. However, the results did not suggest that Lee had received a clear mandate for further movement toward independence.

By late March the outcome of the presidential election, combined with the results of the earlier legislative election and the energetic U.S. response to China's military displays, presented the Chinese leadership with a mixed set of consequences. The good news was that coercive diplomacy had produced some very positive benefits. First, the electoral blow to the DPP, combined with cautionary remarks by senior officials of the Lee Teng-hui government and Asian leaders' remarks critical of Lee, were viewed as indications of a slowing pro-independence movement and a restraint on Taiwan's pragmatic diplomacy. Second, the Taiwanese economy showed extreme vulnerability to prolonged Chinese political-military pressure, as proved by capital flight and declining stock market movement during the crisis period. Third, China's actions showed Taiwan, the United States, and Asia that China was serious about the use of force against Taiwan. In addition, China's strategy did not produce a strong negative reaction from Asian states. Instead, the events of May 1995–March 1996 suggested to many Chinese leaders that Asian states would likely remain passive in response to future tensions over Taiwan. Finally, the Chinese military and other more relatively hard-line elements argued that the military exercises strengthened China's military capabilities and thereby improved the credibility of its threat to use force against Taiwan.

On the other hand, the hard-line approach clearly did not achieve one of its key purposes—a reduction in public support for Lee Teng-hui. Beijing's actions actually drove Taiwan voters to back Lee in unexpectedly high numbers. Moreover, this approach also prompted an unexpectedly vigorous U.S. response and suggested that Washington might increase its military support for Taiwan. In addition, Taiwan emerged from the events of May 1995–March 1996 retaining the initiative in the China-Taiwan-U.S. relationship because no renewed modus vivendi for cross-strait relations resulted from Chinese pressure. Further, the Chinese leadership was doubtless aware that the Taiwanese public and other Asian leaders in countries such as Japan and Southeast Asia were alarmed, and in some cases angered, by Beijing's actions. And finally, although it had been long in the works, the April 1996 agreement between Tokyo and Washington to strengthen their alliance was given added significance. Therefore, sustained pressure by Beijing on Taiwan might generate more anti-China attitudes in Asia, accelerate arms acquisitions, and even increase future diplomatic support for Taiwan. Relative moderates in the Chinese leadership used these concerns to argue for a renewed emphasis on diplomatic approaches to Taiwan.[112]

March 1996 to the Present: A Modified Peace Overture

After the tensions of November 1995–March 1996 the Chinese leadership gradually revived the diplomacy-centered Taiwan policy embodied in the Jiang Eight Points, albeit with two key differences. First, certain military-related policy elements that emerged in 1994 and 1995 have remained in place in order to maintain pressure on Taiwan and to gradually strengthen Beijing's ability to resolve the Taiwan problem, by force if necessary. Second, the Chinese leadership lowered its short- and medium-term expectations of the objectives to be attained via the Jiang Eight Points. Beijing's immediate intention in pressing for talks was to gain the upper hand, showing the Tai-wanese public and the international community that China is flexible and remains committed to a peaceful solution to the Taiwan problem. However, the Chinese leadership, and Jiang Zemin in particular, still ultimately desires to achieve substantive progress in cross-strait relations on the basis of some version of the Jiang Eight Points.

In sum, the Jiang Eight Points is now part of a larger strategy designed to constrain Taiwan's freedom of action internationally; weaken Lee Teng-hui's influence within Taiwan both at present and after he leaves office in spring 2000; increase the political and military incentives for a post–Lee Teng-hui government to begin a genuine process of political negotiation;[113] achieve China's objectives by force if the previously mentioned efforts fail and Taiwan moves unambiguously toward independence; and deter Washington from inter-vening militarily in the event of a future Taiwan-Mainland confrontation.

Beijing is attempting to attain these objectives through a variety of means. From March 1996 to the middle of 1997 the Chinese leadership focused pri-marily on efforts to stabilize the regional situation and contain Taiwan. Inter-nationally Beijing sought to reassure the Pacific Rim that China remained committed to the peaceful resolution of the Taiwan problem and would not threaten the peace, stability, and growth of Asia. Chinese civilian and mili-tary leaders traveled to cities in Asia and Europe in support of these efforts. They also attempted to portray Lee Teng-hui as the instigator of the recent tensions and as a threat to regional stability.

With regard to Taiwan, Beijing utilized a variety of diplomatic, political, and economic carrots and sticks. First, it sought to maintain pressure on Lee by demanding that he unambiguously state his commitment to the "one China" policy and agree to discuss political relations between the two sides as a pre-condition for the resumption of cross-strait talks. China also sought to strengthen moderate elements within the Taiwan business community by increasing Tai-wan's economic links with and dependence on the Mainland. Finally, Beijing made it clear that the conciliatory initiatives contained in the Jiang Eight Points remained Beijing's basic approach to cross-strait relations.[114]

These efforts have apparently achieved some success. During his inaugu-ration speech in May 1996 Lee Teng-hui offered what some Taiwan observers regard as major concessions to Beijing. For the first time Taiwan did not demand, as a precondition of political talks between the two sides, that China relin-quish its threat to employ force against Taiwan. In addition, Lee showed no preference for meeting in a neutral area outside Taiwan and China as he had demanded in the past. At the same time Chinese leaders maintained pressure on Lee to make an unambiguous assertion of the "one China" policy.[115]

However, the key to Beijing's efforts to stabilize the situation and "box in" Taiwan rested with the United States. Given Lee Teng-hui's presumed commitment to achieving Taiwan's permanent separation from the Mainland and the increasingly unpredictable nature of domestic politics on the island, the Chinese leadership recognized that the only effective way to restrain Taiwan (and to convince Taiwan that it had little alternative other than to begin negotiations with Beijing) was to ensure that the United States would no longer encourage or support Taiwan separatism. And the best way to attain such U.S. cooperation was to improve China's overall relationship with Washington. Hence, Beijing responded to Washington's efforts, undertaken after the November 1995–March 1996 crisis, to reduce tensions and improve bilateral relations through sustained, high-level "strategic" dialogue. During this period the long-standing Chinese interest in a summit between President Clinton and President Jiang Zemin was again raised. Beijing thus intensified its efforts to attain a clear reaffirmation of the U.S. commitment to the three Sino-U.S. communiqués and thus to the "one China" policy.

The most important component of this effort consisted of an attempt to obtain a formal pledge from Washington that it was unambiguously opposed to Taiwan's political independence, would not support a "one Taiwan–one China" solution, and would not back Taiwan's efforts to enter international bodies that required statehood for entrance.[116] In addition, the Chinese sought assurances from Washington that it would reduce its level of military assistance to Taiwan. Beijing's ultimate objective was not only to "box in" Taipei, but also to persuade Washington to encourage Taipei to begin talks under the "one China" principle.[117]

Given the unpredictability of U.S. policy, however, Beijing did not rely entirely upon American cooperation. The Chinese leadership also intensified its efforts to enhance its military capabilities vis-à-vis both Taiwan and the United States. These efforts were designed to raise the credibility of a use of force against Taiwan and thus deter the United States from providing direct military assistance to Taiwan in the event of a future military confrontation across the strait, or at the very least to delay the deployment of such assistance.[118]

Intense efforts to resume cross-strait talks on the basis of the Jiang Eight Points commenced in the fall of 1997. Beijing began to show some flexibility on the preconditions of a Beijing-Taipei dialogue. In September Qian Qichen unambiguously stated that the talks should resume, albeit under the precondition of the "one China" principle. However, by the end of the year Qian had dropped the usual reference to the PRC as the sole legitimate government of all of China.[119] This was the first time that a senior Chinese official had explicitly omitted any reference to the PRC in the standard definition of one China. Wang Daohan provided less formal indications that Beijing was prepared to entertain rather flexible variants of the cross-strait relationship as long as Taiwan accepted the notion that there was only one China. In February 1998 for the first time the ARATS sent a formal, faxed reply to an SEF proposal, agreeing to resume the cross-strait dialogue without any explicit, formal preconditions.[120] Overall, this peace initiative was intended to pressure Taipei to begin political talks with Beijing by presenting Taiwan as the more rigid, unreasonable party in the continued stalemate.

Beijing and Taipei finally agreed to resume the cross-strait dialogue in the latter half of 1998, with Wang Daohan and C. F. Koo meeting on the Mainland in October. This was followed by plans for Wang to travel to Taipei in the fall of 1999. However, in early 1999 cross-strait relations again deteriorated significantly. In July Lee Teng-hui publicly characterized Mainland-Taiwan relations as a "special state-to-state relationship."[121] This was taken by Beijing as a deliberate attempt to strengthen both domestic and international acceptance of Taiwan as a sovereign nation entirely separate from and equal to Beijing and to prevent Lee's successor from pursuing a more accommodating policy toward the Mainland.[122] Beijing responded by canceling Wang's trip to Taiwan while Chinese officials at various levels gave the impression that China was considering some form of military action against Taiwan. This prompted heated rhetoric between Beijing and Washington, thus further worsening what had again become, by mid-1999, a tense relationship.[123] But Beijing's more calculated response to Lee Teng-hui's July statement took the form of a second white paper on Taiwan, issued in February 2000.[124] This document provided the most complete explanation to date of Beijing's position on Taiwan's status, Lee Teng-hui's supposed "splittist" behavior, and future cross-strait talks. It was a clear statement of Beijing's overall carrot-and-stick approach to Taiwan, albeit with an increased emphasis on the stick. While providing an extensive set of intended incentives to resume the stalled cross-strait dialogue, the white paper nonetheless also stated, for the first time in an authoritative policy document, what Chinese officials had been saying less formally for years—that Beijing would consider using force if Taipei avoided entering into meaningful talks with the Mainland indefinitely.

Some observers of China's Taiwan strategy after the November 1995–March 1996 crisis believe that the apparent shift from the high-pressure diplomatic offensive of April 1996–fall 1997 to the far more flexible approach of late 1997 and 1998 and the subsequent formal introduction in the 2000 white paper of a new threat to use force against Taiwan reflected an internal power struggle between hard-liners and moderates. According to this argument, the military and conservatives in the party retained a dominant role in the Taiwan policy-making process for many months following the crisis, eclipsing Jiang Zemin and his moderate supporters within the TAO and the Wang Daohan–led Shanghai expert community. It was only in the fall of 1997, after Jiang consolidated his control of the party apparatus and laid the groundwork for the retirement of the two most powerful figures in the PLA (Liu Huaqing and Zhang Zhen), that he was able to regain control of Taiwan policy and resurrect his peace overture. However, following Lee Teng-hui's provocative July 9 statement and the general downturn in Sino-American relations that had occurred in late 1998 and 1999, hard-liners were again able to gain the upper hand.

As in the case of the 1995–96 crisis, such an interpretation significantly distorts the nature of China's Taiwan policy-making process. Although the locus of decision-making temporarily shifted to the PBSC and, in the implementation of the military exercises and missile tests, to the CMC, Jiang Zemin never "lost control" of Taiwan policy during the 1995–96 crisis. As I indicated earlier, Jiang was a key supporter of the tough policy responses implemented during the crisis. At the same time, Jiang could not simply dictate any particular policy course to the senior leadership either during the crisis or afterward. He had to balance the interests and preferences of the major leaders and organizations involved in Taiwan security issues, in particular those of the PLA on the one hand and the MFA and other civilian officials on the other.

Indeed, the serious confrontation with Washington that resulted from Beijing's military displays exacerbated the natural contrast in policy preferences between these two groups. Following the crisis the MFA and other civilian entities reportedly stressed the feasibility of containing Taiwan and moving toward attainment of the Jiang Eight Points through political and diplomatic means, particularly the improvement of relations with the United States. Although in agreement on the ultimate objectives, the military and some hard-liners within the party stressed the need to continue developing China's military capabilities. However, these were not mutually exclusive views, and the resulting strategy clearly reflected elements of both sets of preferences.[125] In fact, the military leadership supported efforts to reinforce Beijing's continued emphasis on a peaceful solution, as indicated by the unprecedented involvement of senior military officers in official trips to Asia and Europe.[126]

The apparent revitalization of the Jiang Eight Points in the latter half of 1997 (albeit alongside more coercive elements) occurred not because moderates had regained control of the policy-making process, but because significant progress had been made and other events had taken place that permitted a renewed focus on the peace initiative. Three developments were of particular importance. First, Sino-U.S. relations had improved by mid-1997. This development significantly advanced Chinese objectives concerning Taiwan, and in fact Washington ultimately agreed to a public affirmation of the "three noes" described earlier during the second summit of 1998. Second, the reversion of Hong Kong to Chinese rule was successfully completed in July. This achievement had enormous implications for Taiwan; it suggested that Beijing could implement a "one country, two systems" formula without jeopardizing the peace, stability, and continued economic growth of the formerly separate entity. Moreover, once completed, the reversion permitted both Jiang Zemin and Qian Qichen to focus greater attention on the Taiwan issue. Third, Jiang Zemin finally consolidated his control of the party leadership at the Fifteenth Party Congress in the fall of 1997 and his control of the FALSG soon thereafter. Jiang was able to orchestrate the retirement both of his major rival within the PBSC, Qiao Shi, and of the two PLA elders remaining in formal positions of power, Liu Huaqing and Zhang Zhen. He was also able to place several of his supporters in the Politburo and on the PBSC. This added strength undoubtedly gave Jiang greater confidence in pressing forward with a revitalized peace initiative.

As early as the winter of 1996–97 Jiang had directed the Taiwan policy community to begin analyzing how to renew an emphasis on the Jiang Eight Points. This process of analysis and deliberation, under the aegis of the TALSG, continued for nearly a year. By the fall of 1997 Jiang and his senior colleagues on the PBSC had decided to stress three core elements in their effort to revive the Jiang Eight Points: resumption of the stalled cross-strait dialogue through the adoption of a somewhat more flexible stance, the development of closer contacts with more moderate elements within the DPP, and greater efforts to understand the dynamic political and social environment within Taiwan. These elements and the overall decision to pursue greater engagement with Taiwan were sanctioned at an Enlarged Work Conference on Taiwan Affairs held in

May 1998. This event, originally scheduled for 1995, had been delayed because of the 1995–96 crisis. At the same time Jiang and the senior leadership continued their ongoing efforts to improve China's military capabilities vis-à-vis Taiwan. Hence, elements of both basic approaches remained components of the leadership's core Taiwan strategy. Moreover, the issuance of the white paper in February 2000 constituted a continuation of this basic strategy, combining both highly flexible elements with a heightened emphasis on coercive elements, largely as an agreed-upon effort to repudiate Lee's stance and to both pressure and entice a post-Lee leader to resume the cross-strait dialogue.[127]

CONCLUSION

From the preceding analysis of the structure, process, and policy history of China's grand strategy toward Taiwan between 1978 and 2000, we can deduce several conclusions concerning the overall decision-making process. First, like policy-making in other policy areas discussed in this volume, the Taiwan policy-making process has become increasingly bureaucratic, pragmatic, and consensus oriented. This reflects the overall institutionalization of the policy-making process and the emergence of the successor generation of bureaucratic technocrats (see the chapter by Miller and Liu).

Second, the extreme sensitivity of the Taiwan issue meant that decisions on grand strategy toward Taiwan were tightly controlled by the paramount leader (Deng Xiaoping) throughout the 1980s. Although other senior leaders, advisors, and even some lower-level specialists provided their views to Deng and both senior leaders and policy administrators were able to shape specific policy features over time, Deng's control of grand strategy remained absolute. Hence, the growing number of policy structures that were established in the early and mid-1980s to manage the Taiwan policy-making process performed mainly policy coordination and implementation functions. These features are reflected in the process involved in the adoption and refinement of the "one country, two systems" policy during the 1980s and in the role played at that time by the TALSG and by the CCTAO and SCTAO.

Third, the greatest transformation in both the structure and outcome of the Taiwan policy-making process occurred when Deng left the scene and Jiang Zemin consolidated his power and authority somewhat before Deng's death, in 1993 and 1994. The critical importance of Taiwan to supreme leadership authority, the changed nature of that authority (that is, less charismatic, less personal, and more success based), and the overall trend toward the institutionalization of authority led Jiang to center decision-making on Taiwan in a restructured, more powerful TALSG. Under Jiang the TALSG became a smaller, more efficient policy-making mechanism, including representatives of only the most critical bureaucratic systems involved in Taiwan policy and, in at least two cases (Qian Qichen and Xiong Guangkai), figures with close ties to core party and military power holders. Although a deliberative PBSC became the ultimate decision-making authority over Taiwan strategy in the post-Deng era, Jiang Zemin has been able to utilize his chairmanship of the restructured TALSG, as well as his formal and informal interactions with key party and military leaders on the PBSC and CMC, to ensure his control of Taiwan policy. This is most clearly shown in the formulation of the Eight Points and the renewed peace overture of 1996–97.

Fourth, Jiang's ability to decisively influence, if not control, grand strategy toward Taiwan has been enhanced by the fact that the Chinese leadership as a whole is in agreement on the basic assumptions underlying Taiwan policy. Although political and bureaucratic interests serve as a basis for debate in a consensus-oriented policy-making process, such differences have largely arisen over timing and emphasis, not fundamental direction. Efforts to explain the evolution of China's grand strategy toward Taiwan in terms of struggles between sharply opposed personal or bureaucratic factions (for example, Jiang Zemin versus Qiao Shi or the PLA versus Jiang and the Foreign Ministry) greatly exaggerate the level of contention, overlook the basic consensus among Chinese elites on grand strategy toward Taiwan, and neglect the preponderant influence exerted by Jiang Zemin after 1994.

This is not to say that the 1995–96 crisis could not have provoked sharper conflicts among the leadership and ultimately weakened Jiang's power if it had been grossly mishandled or deemed a failure. In addition, Jiang's ability to control policy decisions during a crisis was probably impacted by the changed policy-making process in effect at that time. As I noted earlier, supreme political bodies such as the PBSC become more directly involved in making and supervising daily decisions during a crisis, supplanting the TALSG. Moreover, because the crisis involved a significant military dimension, senior military leaders and the CMC became more directly involved in making daily decisions, especially those involving the use of military instruments. Overall, Jiang Zemin had to play a deft game to maintain a general consensus. But he was largely successful in maintaining that consensus and in keeping control of the policy-making process, in part because he also favored a tough-minded approach.

We can also draw several generalizations regarding the narrower aspects of the Chinese process of policy-making regarding Taiwan. First, Jiang Zemin's views on Taiwan policy are not determined by or dependent on the views of Wang Daohan and the Shanghai-based Taiwan policy community. Wang plays an important role in the Taiwan policy-making process as a personal advisor to Jiang Zemin, as a patron of the Shanghai policy community, and as the head of ARATS. He especially helps ensure Jiang's control of the TALSG. But his views, and those of the Shanghai community and the Xiamen University Institute for Taiwan Studies, merely represent alternative sources of policy assessments to those of the mainstream Beijing policy community, which is centered on the CCTAO/SCTAO and the CASS Taiwan Research Institute. Since Wang Daohan's formal role in the decision-making process is concerned primarily with implementation issues via ARATS, he must tread very cautiously when expressing his views on Taiwan policy.

Second, Qian Qichen and the MFA are not as "moderate" in their approach to Taiwan policy issues as some outside observers might believe. In fact, Qian is generally regarded as a hard-liner on Taiwan issues, although primarily within a diplomatic framework. In other words, he believes that a tough policy can be implemented without relying on military instruments. His views thus overlap in many ways with those of senior military leaders, but he differs from them over how much emphasis to place on military versus diplomatic measures. This is not to deny that Qian antagonized some military leaders over the issue of the Lee Teng-hui visa issuance, but he is not viewed as an inveterate soft-liner on Taiwan policy.

Finally, the military does not dictate policy regarding Taiwan. During the Deng era military views on major issues were channeled almost exclusively through him. Lower-level PLA members were involved solely in the implementation of policy. However, the military has generally been very attentive to Taiwan policy because of its obvious institutional responsibilities. This attentiveness only increased in the 1990s, as a result of the growing capabilities and pro-independence orientation of the Taiwan leadership. Overall, the PLA's most active role in the policy-making process is limited to providing intelligence on and assessments of the domestic situation on Taiwan, the U.S.-Taiwan and U.S.-Japan-Taiwan security relationships, and the military balance across the strait; pressing for support from the civilian leadership for the acquisition of weapons and equipment to more effectively deal with Taiwan-related security contingencies; and applying various types of military pressure on Taiwan. Most of the concrete, operational dimensions of these functions have been handled in the policy-making process through the military representative in the TALSG.

However, the military has also become increasingly concerned with China's general strategic approach to Taiwan. Military leaders (including retired PLA elders) have apparently expressed criticism of what they have viewed as overly conciliatory approaches adopted by the MFA. Yet the standing PLA leadership does not formally develop and present "positions" on overall grand strategy toward Taiwan. Moreover, as head of the CMC, Jiang Zemin serves as the primary channel for the expression of the military's views to the senior party and state leadership. The decision to develop what eventually became the Eight Points and the decision to conduct military exercises and missile tests in 1995–96 both illustrate how the military interacted with, but did not dictate to, the civilian leadership.

ELEVEN

The Case of China's Accession to GATT/WTO

MARGARET M. PEARSON

In November 1999 the People's Republic of China (PRC) signed an agreement with the United States that guaranteed bilateral market access and committed China on many of the most difficult issues of China's accession to the World Trade Organization (WTO). By signing this agreement China cleared the biggest hurdle to joining the WTO, even though it still had to sign an important bilateral agreement with the European Union (EU) and agree on a final protocol for accession with the WTO itself before admission would be final.[1] The Sino-U.S. bilateral agreement took thirteen years to negotiate, starting with China's efforts in 1986 to accede to the General Agreement on Tariffs and Trade (GATT) and then, beginning in 1995, efforts to join GATT's successor, the WTO. By examining the record of events leading up to this bilateral agreement, this chapter seeks to shed light on the question of what factors have proven most important in the making of Chinese foreign trade policy.

The analysis identifies changes in the process of foreign policy-making over the course of the reforms, as well as significant areas of consistency with past practice. Three variables have been primary in explaining China's decision-making on GATT/WTO membership. First, a central role has been retained for the variable that in the past has been foremost in Chinese foreign policy-making: elite preference. China's top leaders inserted themselves into the GATT/WTO admission process at decisive times and in ways that trumped the rest of the process. Second, despite the continued and obviously important role for elite preference, there was a pluralization of domestic actors, that is, an increased and influential role for actors who were once peripheral to the foreign policy-making process, especially industrial interests. The incorporation of a greater number of interests was accompanied by efforts to arrive at consensus among this diverse set of actors. The weight that must be given to both the role of top-most leaders and the pluralization of the decision-making process makes it clear that, as in the United States and elsewhere, an understanding of domestic politics is crucial to understanding China's foreign economic policy-making as a whole.[2]

The third critical variable is external influences. China's economy has of course become more open to the global economy over the past two decades, but just as important for the GATT/WTO case has been the influx of norms of globalization and the market. Although pressure from foreign governments, especially bilateral pressure from the U.S. government, has pushed the GATT/WTO negotiations along, progress toward accession could not have been made without the adoption by Chinese reform officials of global market norms. These latter two variables—pluralization and international factors—are notable both because they represent an opening up of the policy-making process and because the strength of their influence is a relatively recent phenomenon.

A fourth variable is worth noting not because it played a decisive role in the Sino-U.S. bilateral agreement, but because it too reflects greater openness in the Chinese foreign policy-making system: public opinion. Public opinion on WTO accession played a greater role in the domestic debate over WTO accession than in the past on other issues, but in limited ways that are consistent with the circumstances highlighted in the chapter in this volume by Joseph Fewsmith and Stanley Rosen.

A case study of China's GATT/WTO accession process contributes to the overall objectives of this volume in several ways. As trade, direct investment, and monetary matters have moved toward the center of China's policy agenda, it has become crucial to understand the making of China's foreign economic policy. Moreover, because Chinese policy-making has been most transparent in the realm of economic policy, it has been possible to gain greater insight into this arena than in more secretive domains. Although the GATT/WTO policy has been confined to the reform era, it nonetheless has spanned that entire period; this case study, therefore, can provide us with evidence of how policy-making has changed during this period.

Yet it also is important to keep in mind the limits of this case study. The dynamics present in economic policy-making may not be replicated in other arenas, such as policy-making on military and security matters, Taiwan, and the environment. This arises in part from one of the aforementioned advantages: the relative transparency of economic policy-making. Likewise, because WTO accession affects myriad economic interests in China both positively and negatively, we can expect more groups (particularly local governments, state-owned enterprises, and industrial ministries) to seek active involvement in that area than in other foreign policy areas.

Before turning to an analysis of the formal organizational structure of China's GATT/WTO decision-making, it should be noted that the unfolding of the negotiations has been affected by many factors other than those highlighted in this chapter. Indeed, the GATT/WTO accession process has been dynamic and complex, affected by broad political and economic cycles at both the international and domestic levels and by a complex dance of bilateral and multilateral negotiations. For example, the years of negotiations leading up to the signing of the bilateral agreement with the United States in November 1999 were repeatedly buffeted by the overall cyclical nature of Sino-U.S. relations.[3] Negotiations received momentum in the run-up to presidential summits, whereas they tended to stall after conflicts such as the annual debate in the U.S. Congress over renewal of China's most-favored-nation status (MFN, now called normal trade relations, or NTR) and around uncertainties in U.S. presidential campaigns. China's external negotiations have lost and gained momentum in tandem with the ebb and flow of domestic economic reforms, succession politics, and economic nationalism. The international-level negotiations took place not only between China and the United States, but also between China and the WTO organization in Geneva and bilaterally with Japan and the European Union (EU). China's accession negotiations with the United States also took place in the context of competition with Taiwan for admission to the WTO.

These complex factors are noted in this chapter when relevant, particularly in the following thumbnail sketch. Exhaustive attention to them, however, is sacrificed in favor of more focused consideration of the decision-making structure and of the variables of elite politics, pluralization of the policy process, international influences, and public opinion.

A THUMBNAIL SKETCH: NEGOTIATING THE BILATERAL
SINO-U.S. AGREEMENT OVER GATT/WTO

China's first contact with officials representing GATT coincided with the beginning of its "open" policy. The decision of China's reform government in the
late 1970s to "open to the outside world" and introduce market reforms to
the domestic economy led to efforts to engage China with key international
economic organizations, including GATT.[4] Therefore, in 1980 China resumed
its place on the United Nations Interim Commission for the International
Trade Organization, a body whose function was to appoint the GATT Secretariat. In the next two years the PRC became an observer both at the Multifiber Arrangement meetings and at some GATT meetings. China joined the
Multifiber Arrangement in 1983.[5] It took on permanent observer status at GATT
in 1984, which Chinese officials felt would facilitate the country's admission
as a full member. In 1985 and early 1986 high-level GATT officials visited China
to explain what would be required of the PRC in the application process.

These early contacts provided China with experience in the organization,
as well as information about the technicalities of the international trade
regime. They also set the stage for China's application to "recover" (*huifu*) full
membership, which was made in July of 1986.[6] The GATT Working Group
on China began to meet in 1988 and made considerable progress. Prior to
the events at Tiananmen in 1989, it appeared that the GATT contracting parties would not force China to adopt market principles to become a member.[7]
Rather, the parties appear to have assumed that reform within China would
continue to progress enough to allow the country to take on the obligations
of GATT and in addition would enhance foreign business opportunities in
China. Nevertheless, GATT members were prepared to push China to make
substantial changes in its economy to gain accession. From the start of negotiations the GATT contracting countries, particularly the United States, the
European countries, and Japan, attempted to establish more stringent, "com-
mercially viable" terms for China's accession than they had secured from other
communist countries. The reference point was the experience with accession
of Eastern European countries in the 1970s, when a political interest in
luring these countries away from Soviet dominance trumped commercial interests and led to their admission on what subsequently was believed to be overly
generous terms.[8] The ensuing negotiations were protracted. They focused on
tariff reduction, something the Chinese were prepared to consider, and to some
degree on nontariff measures, which would prove more difficult.

If in the mid-1980s there was cautious optimism in Chinese government circles about China's smooth accession to GATT, it was gone by the end of the decade. A series of events significantly changed the attitude toward China held by the GATT contracting parties, especially the United States. Indeed, strained Sino-U.S. relations became a significant obstacle for Chinese negotiators. The events at Tiananmen in 1989 paralyzed China's GATT negotiations and entangled these negotiations in the annual battle in the U.S. Congress over China's MFN status and China policy more generally. Even when serious consideration of China's application formally resumed in 1991, the worsening bilateral trade deficit between the United States and China and the growing fears in some segments of the U.S. government of a "rising China," exacerbated existing strains. Such bilateral tensions strengthened the U.S. government's resolve to force China to make clear and specific commitments as to how it would adhere to WTO rules and to adopt these rules on a faster timetable than China desired or than was previously accorded "developing" countries.

Chinese advocates of GATT accession began to regain hope about China's admission in 1992–93. Internationally, China's post-Tiananmen effort to break out of its diplomatic isolation appeared to be bearing fruit, especially after the Gulf War. Agreements in 1992 between Washington and Beijing on market access and intellectual property rights (IPR) were a sign of momentum. The Chinese were encouraged by Washington's assurances, made at the time of the 1992 market access accord and at the 1993 Seattle meeting of the Asia Pacific Economic Cooperation forum (APEC), that it would "staunchly support" China's admission to GATT. Domestically, Deng Xiaoping's "southern tour," during which he declared the reform experience "excellent," as well as Party Secretary Jiang Zemin's greater consolidation of power following the 1992 Party Congress, gave more confidence to those favoring GATT accession.

In this domestic context China's reform leaders decided in 1994 to make a final push to join GATT before the organization was superseded by the WTO in 1995. If they were successful, this would allow China to become a founding member of the WTO. The fact that China would have to make far greater commitments on reforming its economy in order to be admitted later to the WTO provided even further incentive to move quickly. This strategy was sanctioned by Jiang Zemin, who was increasingly vocal in his support for China's entry to GATT.

What characterized Beijing's effort in 1994, however, was not wide-ranging concessions on substantive issues. Such concessions would have proven difficult in the context of a promised austerity program to combat inflation. Moreover, Li Peng used his position throughout this period as China's premier and chair of the State Council to block concessions that would have been acceptable to the United States.[9] Therefore, the push came in the form of a stepped-up pace of negotiations. China also engaged in a game of alliance politics designed to get Japan and the EU to pressure Washington to make concessions; the gist of the strategy was to emphasize that China, with its size, growing economic power, and ongoing reform program, should not be kept out of the organization.

The effort failed, because Washington declared Beijing's offer inadequate, particularly on the grounds of trading rights, market access, and other national treatment issues.[10] This failure created a backlash among policy-makers in Beijing, even among Chinese officials who previously had been enthusiastic about China's admission, as well as among informed citizens. It was felt that the United States had unfairly "raised the bar" for China's membership and had reneged on promises to facilitate China's admission.[11] Some of this anger was undoubtedly a tactic to protect Chinese advocates of entry to GATT from the perception that they had failed, yet much of the anger was genuine. It was compounded by a number of other things, including the perception that Washington had foiled China's efforts to host the 2000 Olympics and the broader view that the United States was playing the role of a global "hegemon" that desired to keep China weak. Serious questions began to be raised in many quarters, such as economic think tanks and government offices, about the necessity and desirability of WTO membership.

China's failure to be admitted to GATT in 1994 was not merely a problem of politics and pride. The terms for entry to the WTO would be, in fact, significantly more rigorous than those for GATT. The inauguration of the WTO forced China into negotiations over not only the run-of-the-mill tariff and nontariff measures covered by GATT, but also IPR, investment mechanisms, dispute resolution, and market access. Moreover, WTO rules applied to a whole new range of industries, particularly telecommunications, services, and distribution.

In 1995 the United States Trade Representative (USTR) provided China with what it called a "road map" of detailed liberalizations China would need to agree to in order to get Washington's approval for WTO admission. Although the U.S. "map" was carefully studied in Beijing, Chinese negotiators failed to respond to it. The Chinese negotiators had lost momentum, but argued, in addition, that election-year politics prevented Washington from engaging in productive negotiations. Strains over U.S.-Taiwan relations in 1996 after Taiwan President Lee Teng-hui's controversial visit to Cornell University further clouded the situation. Serious negotiations on WTO entry were essentially stalled for a year.

It is important to note, however, that even during this period China made policy changes and agreements designed in part to facilitate its WTO entry. In early 1995 China and the United States reached an agreement to open Chinese markets to American movies, music, and software. Late in the year, at the Osaka APEC meeting, China announced that it would cut tariffs by 30 percent and eliminate quotas on 170 products.[12] Zhu Rongji's announcement that the PRC's currency would be made convertible for trade transactions in 2000 (a date later postponed) was also touted as a step toward WTO compliance. Mid-1996 saw another deal between Washington and Beijing on IPR enforcement. Nevertheless, China's trade partners viewed these moves as minimal and continued to focus on market access, subsidies, national treatment, and other issues.

It was not until late 1996 that the U.S. trade negotiators began to feel that their Chinese counterparts were finally getting serious. It was said that Jiang Zemin was ready to see a deal closed, and—with U.S. election-year politics over and a presidential summit scheduled for October of 1997—a new momentum was felt. The U.S. trade negotiators returned from WTO-PRC talks in Geneva in March 1997 believing an agreement was possible and claiming that a sizable number of issues had been resolved; China had agreed to adhere to all terms of an IPR deal upon accession (rather than on a lengthened timetable) and to adhere to the deal on trade-related investment measures beginning two years after accession. The accession protocol, which lays out the major principles of agreement, was said to be 80 percent complete. Most significantly, the U.S. negotiators felt that there had been a breakthrough on the important issue of trading rights for foreign firms.[13]

But despite continuing negotiations, a deal was not concluded; Beijing still failed to make the key concessions required by Washington. Shortly after chief negotiator Long Yongtu returned to Beijing, China reneged on the trading rights offer. It appeared that Long had exceeded his authority in making the offer, and he was forced by his superiors to declare the discussion a misunderstanding. Tensions arose from a sense of betrayal, this time by China. By April 1997 WTO officials in Geneva were stating that China had "made very few compromises on key issues."[14] At the same time, in Washington the question of clandestine funds from Beijing being used to support election bids by U.S. officials was coming to light, and anti-China sentiments were being voiced ever more loudly in Congress. Chinese officials became pessimistic as to whether in this environment the political will could be found in Washington to ensure China's accession.

Chinese negotiators tried to break the deadlock on the eve of Jiang Zemin's summit visit to Washington in October 1997. China announced another round of tariff reductions to an average of 17 percent on 4,800 items and then committed to an average tariff of 10 percent by 2005.[15] It continued to reiterate its commitment not to devalue the yuan during the ongoing Asian financial crisis, a commitment designed to showcase China as a "responsible" economic power. Chinese negotiators further tried to press Washington behind the scenes to commit to China's accession. These efforts were unsuccessful, for even as China made further offers on tariffs, the United States became more focused than ever on areas that were extremely sensitive for China, particularly market access in the areas of agriculture, distribution, telecommunications, and services. Yet the domestic economic environment prevented Beijing from going further. Following the September 1997 Party Congress and Zhu Rongji's elevation to premier in March 1998, the top item on the economic agenda was state-owned enterprise restructuring and protection against a recession induced by the Asian economic crisis. Zhu viewed the foreign competition that would come with WTO membership as likely to worsen these existing economic problems, and therefore treated the WTO negotiations with caution.

Still another round of negotiations ensued in advance of President Bill Clinton's trip to China in June 1998. In this round, as well as in those carried out through the remainder of 1998, the U.S. side continued to claim that China's offers were insufficient.[16] Despite what on the surface seemed to be an impossible climate for signing a deal, changes were occurring that pushed a deal forward, though not immediately. Politically, Sino-U.S. relations were once again gaining a more stable footing after Clinton's successful visit to China in June 1998. Moreover, the Chinese government recognized that a 1999 deal might avoid clouding the congressional vote on permanent normal trade relations (PNTR) with election politics in 2000. In terms of economic logic, it made sense for Beijing to close a deal by the end of 1999, because the conditions for WTO entry would likely be set higher when the WTO members began another round of trade liberalization at its next meeting in Seattle. Beijing also hoped that the boost in its economic image expected from WTO membership would stem the slowdown in incoming foreign direct investment and Chinese exports that was occurring as a result of the Asian financial crisis. These factors strengthened the commitments of Zhu Rongji and Jiang Zemin to China's WTO accession.[17]

Zhu Rongji arrived in Washington in April 1999 with a package that, in all likelihood, reflected directives given to him by Jiang and the Politburo. The concessionary offer Zhu brought—containing favorable terms on nearly all issues to which the United States gave priority—pleased the U.S. negotiators and the business community and at the same time caught them by surprise.[18] At least in part because there was insufficient time for Washington to digest and then gain political support for the deal, Clinton walked away from it, a mistake that he almost immediately recognized. Immediate efforts by Washington to rectify the mistake were hampered by Chinese pride and the bureaucratic, industrial, and public opposition within China to the terms Zhu had offered—terms seen publicly for the first time only after Zhu had presented them in Washington. Having failed, Zhu Rongji reportedly was vilified in official meetings and in public discussion. He bore some of the political heat for Jiang Zemin, who for a time distanced himself from the agreement. Other officials long associated with the WTO agreement, including Wu Yi, stepped back from the offer Zhu had made, and Zhu himself hinted that parts of the offer were likely to be withdrawn.

U.S. efforts to gain a deal were made even more difficult by yet another downturn in Sino-U.S. relations that followed close on the heels of Zhu's failed trip. Strains caused by China's opposition to the U.S.-led NATO air attacks on Serbia were soon compounded by Chinese outrage over the U.S. bombing of the Chinese embassy in Belgrade in May 1999. The WTO negotiations became caught up in the enormous political outcry over this assault. Any appearance of being "in cahoots" with foreigners made pro-WTO officials subject to attack.

The odds against a deal once again seemed too great to overcome. Negotiations in Washington in September 1999, carried out on the Chinese side without longtime chief negotiator Long Yongtu, produced nothing. By October, however, Jiang reacted favorably to a telephone call from Clinton urging a resumption of negotiations. Clinton sent USTR Charlene Barshefsky and Gene Sperling (a top economic advisor who had urged rejection of the April offer) to Beijing in November. Six days of intensive negotiations produced a deal much like the one the United States had walked away from in April.[19]

THE ORGANIZATIONAL STRUCTURE
FOR WTO DECISION-MAKING

The organizational framework that governed decision-making on China's GATT/WTO negotiations was in many ways an extension of standard bureaucratic processes for domestic decision-making in China. Therefore, the model of "fragmented authoritarianism" applies broadly to this case study.[20] Just as fragmented authoritarianism posits, a complex matrix of relevant bureaucracies and interests produced decisions through extensive bargaining and coordination; efforts to gain consensus dominated. Once basic strategic decisions were made by the Standing Committee of the Politburo (as depicted in the chapter by Lu Ning in this volume), the bulk of formal decision-making responsibility rested within the State Council structure. It is perhaps easiest to view this structure as having a core, where most formal decision-making authority lay, and a set of orbiting organizations that were involved and sometimes had a decisive impact. At any point in time the specific locus of decision-making varied, depending on the importance of the issue presented and the constellation of organizations involved.

The standard policy-making processes described hereafter were employed for most of the period during which the bilateral agreement between Beijing and Washington was being negotiated. I shall show, however, that this process led to stalemate. Ultimately, Jiang Zemin and Zhu Rongji stepped in to break this stalemate and ensure that an agreement with the United States was struck. In other words, many of the expectations as to the process and structure that are laid out in this section were in the end thrown aside in favor of elite preference and authority.

The Core Backbone

The core organizational structure for WTO decision-making is comprised of three levels. At the bottom of the hierarchy is the Ministry of Foreign Trade and Economic Relations (MOFTEC). MOFTEC, and particularly its WTO division under chief negotiator Long Yongtu, was responsible for most of the day-to-day work on China's GATT/WTO bid. The WTO division has been responsible for conducting bilateral negotiations (for instance, with the United States, the European Union, and Japan) and negotiations with the WTO itself. It receives basic guidance from higher levels, determines the specific implications of this guidance, collects reports and analysis from research institutes, proceeds to negotiations, and reports back up the hierarchy on the results of negotiations.[21]

At the same time the WTO division was required to coordinate China's negotiating positions with other interested domestic bureaus and industries. Parties interested in a particular aspect of negotiations were actively involved in formulating China's negotiating position on that topic, and MOFTEC therefore had to be responsive to these external interests. In the United States the office of the USTR was in constant touch with various industry and government interests in the course of its bilateral negotiations with China. MOFTEC's duty to be responsive to domestic interests was even greater, and fulfilling this responsibility for "coordination" (*xietiao*) consumed an even greater amount of its time. Interagency disputes that could not be resolved at the division level were referred to the MOFTEC minister (Wu Yi until March 1998, and thereafter Shi Guangsheng), who then engaged in the bargaining and coordination necessary to reach consensus. The WTO division was also responsible for conducting a public relations campaign on behalf of China's entry into WTO, as I discuss later. Officials working in the MOFTEC departments responsible for trade relations with the West, and particularly officials in the WTO division, were the strongest advocates of China's accession within the Chinese bureaucracy during the 1980s and 1990s. This is unsurprising, because the careers of officials in such departments hinged on smooth trade relations in the long term.[22]

Despite MOFTEC's expansive role in the negotiations, its authority was limited. Its need to attend to the interests of peripheral organizations is discussed later. Two additional limits can be highlighted here. First, MOFTEC did not have a formal responsibility to negotiate or coordinate certain issues in the WTO negotiations. For example, under GATT the People's Bank of China had primary responsibility for negotiations on finance (banking and securities), and this division of labor continued with the WTO negotiations. For sectors that were new to the WTO agenda, some specialized bureaucracies also took the lead. This was true of the Ministry of Information Industries (formerly the Ministry of Post and Telecommunications) on telecommunications, the Ministry of Finance on accounting and insurance services, and the Ministry of Internal Trade on distribution. Therefore, MOFTEC's direct authority for the negotiations became more diffuse as the range of issues increased with the change to the WTO.

Second, as would be expected, MOFTEC did not have final authority to make the major decisions on issues related to WTO negotiations; this authority rested with the two levels superior to MOFTEC in the WTO decision-making hierarchy. Directly superior to MOFTEC were the various relevant leading small groups (LSGs)—joint party-state ad hoc coordinating bodies comprised of representatives of major governmental and sectoral interests on a particular issue. Most important in this regard was the now-defunct GATT/WTO LSG. From 1993 until its abolition in March 1998 (as a result of Premier Zhu Rongji's State Council reorganization), this LSG was chaired by Vice Premier Li Lanqing and included top figures in the bureaucracies interested in the negotiations. Members from the foreign economic policy bureaucracy included MOFTEC Minister Wu Yi (as vice chair), a MOFTEC vice minister, Sun Zhenyu (the major USTR interlocutor for some period), and heads of Customs and the Machinery and Electronics Export/Import Commission. It also included officials from agencies with a domestic economic focus, such as the Ministry of Finance, the State Development Planning Commission (SDPC, formerly the State Planning Commission), the State Economic and Trade Commission (SETC), the People's Bank of China, the State Price Commission, and the Foreign Exchange Control Commission. The LSG sanctioned most of the formal negotiating positions, such as the 1994 decision on the last-ditch negotiating stance regarding GATT entry. It also served as a forum for resolving disputes that could not be settled through MOFTEC processes. The GATT/WTO LSG also coordinated with and received input from two other LSGs that were more powerful, the Foreign Affairs and the Finance and Economics LSGs (see the chapter by Lu Ning).

To the extent that the WTO LSG acted primarily as a clearinghouse for issues and was, in fact, only an ad hoc body, power rested less in it than in its individual members. Vice Premier Li Lanqing and Wu Yi, the top specialists in the area of trade, clearly had a major influence on policy, Wu as MOFTEC minister for much of the relevant period (she was named a state councilor in March 1998) and Li as the state councilor responsible for foreign trade. Although they were themselves favorably inclined toward WTO accession, their role more often than not was to arbitrate the interests of other vice premiers. Much of their responsibility was to gain the agreement of others in the State Council and on the Politburo Standing Committee. As this implies, other vice premiers and ministers had de facto veto power in their jurisdictions, requiring that consensus among them be sought.

Because Li and Wu were trade specialists, and Wu especially was seen as strongly pro-accession (and pro-foreign), their voices were said to carry less weight with more conservative and industrial officials. Moreover, the abolition of the GATT/WTO LSG has been interpreted as an attempt to under-mine Li Lanqing's power in this area in favor of Zhu Rongji, who, when he assumed the post of premier in early 1998, appeared to weigh domestic pro-tectionist interests more heavily in the calculus of WTO accession.

At the apex of the core WTO decision-making structure were the premier and the paramount leader, in the context of the Politburo and its Standing Committee. Deng Xiaoping, the "paramount leader" until his death in 1997, sanctioned the decision in the mid-1980s to seek GATT membership, and Jiang Zemin, as party secretary general, kept that commitment. In interviews in 1997 and 1998, trade officials contended that the premier (Li Peng until 1998, Zhu Rongji thereafter) had authority to make major decisions related to the negotiations and, ultimately, to approve a package. Jiang was expected to defer to the opinion of Zhu on the decision as to what constituted an accept-able bilateral accession package.[23] The premier, of course, would receive input from interested parties, including reports from MOFTEC, the WTO LSG, and the Foreign Affairs and Finance and Economics LSGs. Zhu would also serve as the final arbiter of conflicting interests at the vice premier level. In this regard, he had tremendous authority, but also responsibility to be sure important interests were not abridged, or, if they were, that an accession pack-age as a whole served China's national interest—in other words, to ensure that China's interests were not sold out to foreigners.

The implications of Zhu Rongji's great authority in this matter for Li Lan-qing and the MOFTEC negotiators were substantial. The negotiators believed that Zhu Rongji would not assent to a WTO package unless they consulted with and gained the consensus of most (if not all) domestic interests. There-fore, MOFTEC and Li Lanqing would not send an accession deal up the hier-archy without accompanying documents demonstrating the agreement of key domestic interests (for example, the assent of the grain bureau to the parts of the deal related to agriculture). This only heightened the need for MOFTEC to do a thorough job in its domestic negotiations. If a package were to be sent upward without such signatures or with dissents, Zhu would be expected to seek some explanation. He might take on the burden of trying to hammer out a compromise with the relevant constituencies, but he more likely would refer the problem back down the hierarchy, and the seemingly endless coordinating meetings would begin again.

This highly bureaucratic decision-making process—a product of the need to generate agreement from many potentially hostile units—played a large part in creating the stalemate that engulfed the negotiations with the United

States during the late 1990s. It is this process that was essentially scrapped in the months of 1999 leading up to a bilateral agreement.

The Influential Periphery

It is impossible to write about the structure of WTO decision-making without reference to the decision-makers that on an organizational chart would appear peripheral, but in fact exerted tremendous influence, as David Lampton notes in his introductory chapter. As in other cases examined in this volume (for example, Michael Swaine's case on Taiwan and Bates Gill's case on arms control), the list of parties involved was long, although perhaps even longer in the WTO case. Most of these parties had equal rank with MOFTEC, though some were formally subordinate and some superordinate. The major peripheral players involved in decision-making on the WTO included the economic commissions of the central government, nearly all industrial sectors, and provincial and local governments—a huge number of entities.

The national economic commissions and cross-functional (rather than sectoral) bureaus charged with ensuring China's overall economic interests were actively involved both in negotiations and in coordinating meetings. The SDPC was a key voice, particularly on trading rights issues and agriculture. Historically the SDPC was "the single most important force upholding China's planned economy and defending the 'conservative' position. . . . It had a strong institutional interest in resisting, deflecting, and enervating the market-oriented reform policies put forth by reform-minded leaders."[24] After the March 1998 restructuring of the State Council, the profile of the SETC rose greatly vis-à-vis the SDPC, and it became more active in WTO negotiations. The Customs Tariff Commission had a key voice in tariff negotiations, whereas the Ministry of Finance had an interest in policies affecting state revenues. The Ministry of Foreign Affairs (MFA) also played a broad-based role in the negotiations.

Industrial bureaus and ministries as well as corporations tended to become involved when negotiations directly impinged on their business interests. As a result, individual bureaucracies often had strong power in narrow issue areas. For example, the China Animal and Plant Quarantine Bureau was a major voice in the negotiations over phyto-sanitary standards, whereas the National Machinery and Electronics Import and Export Office was central to China's position on quotas and licenses. On certain issues, of course, many organizations were involved. For example, those involved in the negotiations on retail issues included the Ministry of Internal Trade (which operates and registers many retail outlets), the SDPC (because retail is a critical sector of the economy), MOFTEC, and the SETC. More broadly, several bureaucracies were simultaneously on the front line of reviewing offers from Washington. For example, in June 1998 when USTR Barshefsky presented a list of conditions Washington required be met to the new MOFTEC minister, Shi Guangsheng, the document was reviewed by officials from MOFTEC, the MFA, and the SETC. They reported to their superiors, and ultimately to Vice Premier Li Lanqing, that the U.S. demands did not provide a basis for negotiation, and the conditions were rejected.

Local industries and governments over time became increasingly active in the negotiations as they grew aware of the potential impact of WTO accession (and trade integration more generally) on their economies. Indeed, some of the most detailed analyses of the potential impact of WTO membership were done by local organizations, including local academies of social sciences, provincial offices located in Hong Kong, the Shanghai Institute of Foreign Trade, and the WTO Research Center of Shanghai.

A bureaucratic interest model in which narrow economic interests of industries and ministries dictate their positions on the WTO appears to apply to the WTO negotiations. It is true that the views of the various peripheral actors toward the WTO sometimes evolved over time as circumstances changed; for example, the Ministry of Machinery and Electronics softened its initially negative view of integration into the global economy as China's electronics industry became more export oriented.[25] Still, this does not override the basic fact that narrow economic interests had the strongest influence on bureaucratic positions. Moreover, protectionism appeared equally strong in developed Chinese markets (such as textiles and grain), developing markets (such as automobiles), and new markets (such as insurance, telecommunications, retail, and banking).

Lobbying with Chinese Characteristics

How did the various economic players outside the core structure voice their interests and affect outcomes? There were both formal and informal channels. The formal process, as noted previously, consisted of consultation of affected interests by MOFTEC and MOFTEC's attempt to gain their assent or acquiescence to the portions of a deal relevant to their industry. As a rule, representatives of these interests took part in negotiations directly. Indeed, Chinese negotiating teams sent to Geneva and Washington ballooned in size during the late 1980s and the 1990s and came to include industry representatives in addition to the expected negotiators from MOFTEC and other interested commissions (such as the SETC). For example, delegates from the General Customs Administration, the State Statistical Bureau, and the State Commission for Restructuring the Economic System attended working group meetings in 1988 and 1989.[26] A March 1998 delegation to Geneva further included representatives of MOFTEC, the Ministry of Foreign Affairs, the SDPC, the SETC, the Ministry of Justice, the Ministry of Agriculture, and the Ministry of Information Industry.[27] Industry voices were also heard through the membership of ministers in the key LSGs. Vice premiers in charge of industry— notably Wu Bangguo and Wen Jiabao in the late 1990s—also were said to be conduits for industry views at the highest levels of the State Council.

Informal articulation of interests occurred in unsurprising ways: personal networks, particularly informal ties between ministers and vice premiers, were key mechanisms for expressing views. Similarly, local officials depended on their personal connections to central officials. This process was a Chinese version of lobbying. Indeed, trade politics in China seems to have been nearly as porous and subject to competing interests during this period as U.S. and European trade policy–making. The key difference was that most Chinese interests resided somewhere within the governmental or quasi-governmental structure. Indeed, because each minister's goal was to see his or her ministry flourish, the built-in involvement of industries in the relevant government bargaining structure virtually guaranteed that industry protectionism would have a voice. Unlike in the United States and Europe, however, there was no evidence that private interests, including private businesses, labor groups, or consumers acting independent of the government, weighed in on the WTO issue in China.[28]

THE KEY VARIABLES INFLUENCING CHINA'S
GATT/WTO DECISION-MAKING

Out of the highly complex story of the negotiations for a bilateral agreement with the United States over China's GATT/WTO accession, three variables stand out as particularly important and influential: international influences, pluralization of domestic actors, and elite politics. Public opinion, although far from decisive, is worth commenting on insofar as it, like international influence and pluralization, is a relative newcomer to the Chinese process of foreign policy decision-making and signifies an opening up of the foreign policy-making system.

International Influences

Foreign policy-making is, by definition, influenced by international pressures; Chinese foreign policy is no exception. Yet with the opening that occurred during the reform period, foreign policy-making in China became subject to even more types of external pressure, and at more levels of the decision-making structure. Nowhere was this more apparent than in the area of foreign economic policy, an area in which the leadership sought to adapt China to an existing international market and to existing multilateral organizations, including the World Bank, the International Monetary Fund (IMF), and GATT/WTO. Indeed, the rules for accession to these organizations were set by the institutions themselves and their members, and the accession process was largely a matter of China's willingness to abide by standards set by existing members.

During the 1980s China's GATT policy was therefore influenced by outside actors to a relatively new degree, and Chinese policy-makers' energies were directed to responding to the GATT requirements. For example, in early 1987 China was required to submit a memo to the GATT Working Party describing the Chinese foreign trade regime. Subsequently, GATT contracting parties submitted written questions—over 1,200 by mid-1989—to be answered by the Chinese.[29] The information China provided was incomplete and strategically selective; nevertheless, the first steps toward integration were being made.

Beyond a mere response to the explicit requirements imposed by GATT, a deeper dynamic of external influence was also at work. As Elizabeth Economy's chapter in this volume suggests, there are several mechanisms through which international norms and rules can influence the beliefs and behaviors of domestic decision-makers, and ultimately their policies. The mechanism of international influence that appears most important in this case is international learning. The concept of learning suggests that genuine (if often incremental) transformation of elite perceptions can occur as a result of exposure to international economic norms or rules.[30] (This theme is also developed in the chapter by Bates Gill.) To show that learning has occurred, we need to show first that new ideas about economic integration have been transmitted to a country either through the business community or through agents of international organizations. Hence, when learning about the international market system occurs, outside ideas bring about a shift in the dominant thinking among elites about the value of integration into the world economy. When it is most effective, this "new thinking" leads to policy change in a direction consistent with the new ideas, although policy change may be blocked by bureaucratic or other types of opposition.[31] The influence of international ideas can also be generational, as when ideas are adopted by a younger generation that comes to power. In fact, in the late 1970s and early 1980s there was just such a genuine adoption of ideas on the part of reformers in the Chinese leadership responsible for foreign economic policy. This change in outlook, which was significant enough to warrant the label "paradigm shift," went far beyond China's WTO accession. It involved the basic acceptance of comparative advantage as a "global law" rather than a tool of capitalism and the concomitant acceptance of trade and markets as legitimate and beneficial for China's development.[32] These conceptual changes enabled Chinese reformist officials and economists to be much more receptive to marketization and thereby legitimized China's participation in the GATT/WTO system. It is important to emphasize that the impetus for this paradigm shift was internal, not the result of international learning. And yet the initial decisions laid the groundwork for subsequent penetration of external ideas in a process that, as I shall show, can reasonably be interpreted (if not without certain difficulties, as I discuss later) as a form of learning. Moreover, ideological and political acceptance of these economic theories was bolstered as China began to reap clear benefits from participation in global markets.

Exogenous influences that led to learning in the area of international trade policy came in a number of forms as early as the first half of the 1980s. The Chinese government attempted to create a pool of experts—an epistemic community of the sort described in the chapter by Economy—that could better understand GATT and interpret it domestically. Many of the younger and highly educated officials MOFTEC attracted into its ranks had experience abroad in school, in multilateral institutions, or in foreign businesses. Other means used over the years included, for example, sending officials to take commercial policy courses organized by GATT and sanctioning the formation of study groups at the University of International Business and Economics in Beijing (sponsored by MOFTEC) and the Shanghai University of Finance and Economics. Dialogues between Chinese leaders and officials of multilateral economic institutions, as well as publications by these organizations, presented information on China and offered policy recommendations relevant to

GATT membership that sometimes were adopted.[33] Representatives of foreign businesses, foreign governments, and multilateral economic institutions were consulted about draft laws in the areas of foreign investment, trade, IPR, and currency convertibility. Many of their suggestions, as well as international market rules generally, made their way into the rules promulgated. Thus, for example, in 1985 China revised its customs regulations, whereas the second half of the decade saw the beginning of a long-term process of lowering its tariff rates, both at least in part in anticipation of its GATT membership bid. The adoption of GATT-oriented trade policies further suggests that the ideas embodied in global economic institutions began to carry weight in Chinese policy debates—an important test of the effectiveness of learning.

The sources of learning multiplied as domestic Chinese institutions were forced to adapt to exogenous pressures and foreign institutions. The GATT organization itself gained a foothold in the bureaucracy when the GATT (now WTO) division was set up in MOFTEC to handle the relationship with the multilateral institution and when the State Council created the GATT LSG. The creation of such new bureaucracies legitimated articulation of the views and interests of a foreign international organization directly to key government actors, much as the chapters by Bates Gill and Lu Ning show was the case in arms control policy. (Institutional expansion of existing ministries was also part of the response to the need to deal with the IMF and the World Bank.) Although it is not true that MOFTEC's GATT/WTO division was "in the pocket" of the global institution (although it sometimes is accused of such), the institutional norms of MOFTEC became increasingly aligned with the norms of the international regime, and its officials became the strongest advocates within the government of China's adoption of international practices.

The channels of international influence that appeared in the 1980s continued to influence China's policy on GATT/WTO accession in the 1990s, and in fact deepened. As the domestic environment for foreign policy-making became more decentralized, moreover, points of access for international influences multiplied. The clearest evidence of deepening influence was that ideas from outside affected ever-greater numbers of policy outcomes and pushed China ever further toward an open market economy. Beijing adopted a plethora of market norms. Multiple tariff reductions were made, as noted previously. The foreign trade plan was largely phased out. Direct subsidies for exports were eliminated, although some were restored in 1998 in order to boost exports without devaluation. Nontariff barriers, particularly import quotas, were gradually eliminated on a large number of products after the early 1990s. Bilateral agreements negotiated with Washington on market access and IPR starting in 1992, though agreed to by China begrudgingly and flawed in their implementation, nevertheless dovetailed with WTO requirements. Pressure from the U.S. negotiators was also important in bringing China closer to agreement in early 1997 on issues of nondiscrimination and transparency, both of which are important for accession to the WTO.[34] Thus, China's adoption of the norms and rules of the international economic regime was extensive and protracted. Most of these changes would not even have been considered seriously by Chinese officials in the 1980s.

Foreign influences appeared in forms that were quite direct, including bilateral negotiations and consultations with individual outside experts and organizations. Alliance politics involving multiple foreign countries also played a role. China felt concerted and unified pressure from the United States and Europe, especially since 1995, on the accession standards. There was remarkably little complaining outside of China about the fact of Washington's lead role or the content of its negotiations. Indeed, after at least mid-1997 the USTR coordinated informally with Canada, Australia, and the EU to share the offers being made to them by China and to be sure their responses to China were consistent. This coordination came in response to China's efforts to divide WTO members, particularly by attempting to convince others that it was close to a deal with the United States in the hope that these other countries would rush to conclude their own deals with Beijing, and thereby isolate Washington.[35]

The external influences that were equally important, if not more important, in allowing China to make the changes necessary for WTO accession were the gradual but continuous adoption of the norms of marketization and globalization and the acceptance of the rules of the global economic system. The November 1999 bilateral agreement shows how deeply China was affected by the notion of building a world-class industry through international market competition.

The adoption of these norms has not been without continuous controversy, of course. It may seem an ironic twist that the same learning process that contributed to a more positive view of economic integration simultaneously contributed to the expansion of opposition interests within China. For as China gained increasing experience with the international economy, "learning" was not only about whether or not to open to the global economy, but also about individual sectors' economic interests in protectionism. This learning process itself created a negative feedback loop by helping mobilize domestic political actors to oppose WTO accession. This dynamic is analyzed in greater detail in the following section.

The Domestic Political Context: Toward Pluralization of Influences on Policy-Making

The initial impetus for China's 1986 application to join GATT was internal; that is, it was not forced on China from the outside. Unsurprisingly, given the significant turnabout from past practice that the application represented, the decision to pursue membership was apparently made by the leadership at the highest levels. Indeed, Chinese writings on the initial decision emphasize the personal involvement of then-premier Zhao Ziyang, particularly his meetings with GATT Secretary Arthur Dunkel.[36] The decision appears to have been made "in a relatively centralized fashion so that it could not be blocked by opposition from industry."[37]

The decision to seek GATT membership appears to have been made for political and geostrategic reasons, as well as for economic ones. A key tenet of Deng Xiaoping's economic reforms was to expand exports to help pay for the modernization program. It was also seen as helping China gain market information already available to GATT members.[38] To this end Chinese negotiators were directed to make tariff reductions the centerpiece of their entry protocol and to argue that such reductions would reduce foreign pressure to increase market access—a more onerous request. China also argued that it should be accorded "developing country" status, under which state intervention was more tolerated and which allowed longer transition times for compliance with GATT rules.[39]

The GATT application was defined as a matter of foreign policy rather than economic policy, and advice was primarily sought from sectors of the foreign policy bureaucracy, including MOFTEC, the MFA, the Bank of China, the tourism administration, and the office in charge of special economic zones. The strategy was to draw on offices that would be sympathetic to the move and outflank industrial ministries that might pose opposition. Even with the relative centralization of the decision-making process and MOFTEC's dominance, however, a number of non–foreign policy bureaucracies were included in the earliest negotiations. As I discussed previously, the State Council established the interagency GATT LSG, which included most of the major institutional players in overall foreign trade policy-making as well as in key areas of the domestic economy.

A number of these economic bureaucracies, of course, could be expected to oppose GATT membership. It is possible that the inclusion of potentially recalcitrant bureaucrats was intended to dampen their opposition. At the same time there was considerable internal coordination among these bureaucracies. Ultimately, the pro-GATT forces were strong enough to ensure that the negotiations continued. Although industrial bureaucracies had interests that conflicted with GATT membership, these interests appear not to have been fully appreciated, vocalized, or acted upon in the 1980s. GATT membership was depicted almost universally as beneficial for China. It was not then, as it would be later, risky for the officials in charge of GATT negotiations to be seen as favoring rapid integration into the body.

From the start of the negotiation process, Chinese officials recognized that GATT would be more intrusive in its admission requirements than the World Bank or the IMF had been, and that GATT member countries were subject to substantial pressure to liberalize their trade regimes and submit to significant international scrutiny. The State Council gave Chinese negotiators very little leeway in negotiations, however, keeping the process quite centralized compared to what it would later become and allowing virtually no concessions.[40] Apparently the assumption was that China would be given relatively lenient treatment. As will be seen, in light of the changing political image of China following Tiananmen and China's mounting trade surplus and foreign exchange holdings, this assumption was naive.

As this discussion implies, despite the formal decision in favor of seeking GATT membership and more generally to integrate China into the world economy, considerable controversy surrounded the decision and the negotiation process. This controversy had ideological roots that tracked the classic debate over liberalism versus mercantilism, although for both sides the goal of strengthening China was key.[41] What did "liberal" and "mercantilist" interests look like in the context of the Chinese GATT/WTO accession debate? Liberal reform officials, particularly officials in MOFTEC responsible for the negotiations, believed that China should actively engage in international trade and that at least some competitive pressure was good for the Chinese economy. They agreed with the view Thomas Moore and Dixia Yang, in their chapter in this volume, attribute to many Chinese foreign economic policy analysts that, on balance, economic integration and market competition is good for China. The related idea that China, given its size and importance, *should* be a member of the world's trading body also held considerable sway. Moreover, Chinese leaders believed that GATT membership would free China from the annual certification of its MFN trade status by the U.S. Congress, a process China found degrading and unsettling. Finally, PRC leaders wished to be admitted to GATT ahead of Taiwan, which formally applied for membership in 1991.[42] A generally "integrationist" line on WTO accession was presented in many Chinese publications. Indeed, most publications on the WTO were from economic think tanks and research institutes (many of which had ties to MOFTEC) devoted to foreign trade issues. The ministry's own publication, *Guoji Maoyi* (International Trade) also featured this position in its articles.[43]

The mercantilist strain of economic nationalism was distinct from the autarkic beliefs of Maoism, but was most concerned to see the control of China's economy remain in Chinese hands. Mercantilists were concerned that domestic industry not be trampled on the way it was perceived to have been after the Opium Wars of the nineteenth century.[44] Indeed, prevention of undue foreign competition in the Chinese domestic market was perhaps the foremost value of advocates of this view. The role of multinational corporations operating on Chinese soil was also questioned due to the belief that multinationals, inevitably self-interested, would harm China's interests. A key role in this vision was reserved for state-owned enterprises (SOEs), state planners, and industrial policy, a position that of course dovetailed with the bureaucratic interests of the state-owned economy and state planning organizations.

The ideological outlook of both liberals and mercantilists evolved as the negotiations dragged on in the 1990s. In the aftermath of Tiananmen, liberals—who felt the burden of international isolation—came to believe that China needed a strong role in world markets to counter U.S. attempts to isolate China. GATT membership would provide a hedge against protectionist tendencies in developed countries. Chinese officials most directly involved in foreign trade also came to have a more realistic appreciation of the costs and benefits of WTO membership. Although a desire for international prestige remained important in the 1990s, the political benefits came to be seen as fewer in number. Chinese trade officials, in particular, internalized the fact that WTO membership would not guarantee that the U.S. Congress would grant them unconditional permanent NTR status, eliminating what was once perceived as a major benefit.

Liberals also came to see WTO membership as a way to achieve their domestic reform agenda. Particularly in the second half of the decade, they recognized that China's membership would allow them to use WTO rules as leverage to press for further trade reforms against recalcitrant local governments and foreign trade corporations.[45] Further, some industries came to recognize that they stood to be *helped* by WTO accession, and they supported accession. This was especially true of the export-oriented textiles and apparel industries, which favored the phased elimination of the tariffs imposed by the MFA, and also portions of the transport industry.[46]

It is important to note that the Chinese liberal position on GATT/WTO entry remained less than pure market liberalism even in the 1990s. The goal of membership was to create a strong Chinese economy and thereby to strengthen the Chinese state. Liberal support could waver, moreover; particularly when caution was espoused by top reform leaders, liberal officials, especially in MOFTEC, followed suit. For example, when in 1998 Zhu Rongji expressed concern about the need to make WTO entry consistent with slower state-led restructuring of domestic SOEs, MOFTEC officials echoed the view. Advocates of WTO accession also worried about the impact of membership on key industries. As one former Chinese negotiator argued in 1998 with regard to the auto industry: "*All* people in China believe China should have its own car industry. The car industry argues with the government that it has spent lots of money, and a domestic car industry can create jobs and stimulate other sectors. So the industry needs protectionism until it is stronger. Even half of our negotiators believed that if China opens quickly, the auto industry will be killed."[47] As this comment suggests, even though those in favor of GATT/WTO membership viewed it as beneficial for China in the long run, worry remained about the costs and how to ameliorate them.

The mercantilist argument also evolved in the 1990s, as criticism of WTO membership came more often to center on the specific economic costs of membership than on nationalism. Chinese planners and industry officials became increasingly cognizant of the potential competition to state enterprises that would result from the dismantling of barriers to the domestic market. Nationalist sentiments did not fade away, however. The range of opposition voices was particularly expansive at times of more general outrage at the United States, such as after China's failure to enter the WTO as a founding member in 1995, and also after Zhu Rongji's failure to conclude a deal in April 1999. At these times, opposition voices included many officials who previously had not opposed GATT/WTO membership, as well as many in the general public. Some argued that China already possessed most of the advantages that WTO membership would bring (particularly unconditional MFN from most countries, if not the United States) without the obligations of formal membership or the pressure for change that membership would entail.

In addition to these ideological evolutions on the part of both liberals and mercantilists, the domestic environment for GATT/WTO policy-making changed substantially in the 1990s. The growing understanding of the economic costs to China of WTO membership went hand in hand with an increased pluralization of interests. Indeed, pluralization of the policy-making process, which began in the preceding decade, moved front and center in the 1990s, as Lampton's introduction to this volume notes. The most significant dimension of pluralization was the consolidation and growing activism of a more sophisticated bureaucratic opposition to accession among industries that stood to lose from foreign competition. Even though from the beginning the Chinese decision-making process on GATT included bureaucratic actors with interests potentially opposed to membership (primarily at the GATT LSG and the State Council levels), those in opposition gained a more sophisticated understanding of the negative ramifications of WTO membership as well as a greater role in the decision-making process.

Protectionist interests ranged across a broad spectrum of Chinese industry, from old, established industries such as machinery and agriculture to growing industries such as automobiles, telecommunications, and chemicals and infant industries such as financial services, insurance, retailing, and information.[48] Some of the strongest opposition was from ministries that were to benefit from the promulgation of industrial policies.[49] Protection of these "pillar" industries, largely through special funding and preferential tax policies, was considered vital to the development of not only a strong economy, but also a strong military. Resistance to WTO entry and the bilateral agreement was therefore especially strong among SOEs and their representative ministries. Yet opposition also existed among provincial-level governments, which for much of the period believed that they bore little of the cost of failing to join the WTO. Such anti-WTO attitudes at the provincial and local levels were communicated in myriad studies on the implications of WTO membership that were commissioned by local governments and ministries.[50]

There were substantial opportunities for industrial interests at the central and local levels to make their voices heard in domestic economic policy-making. As discussed previously, lobbying occurred through channels formally set up to receive and coordinate various opinions (including the coordinating meetings of MOFTEC and the LSGs), through contacts between relevant ministers and vice premiers or other top leaders, and through direct participation of ministries in the negotiations.

The efforts of the telecommunications industry to shape its treatment in the negotiations illustrate several of these types of lobbying. One near-monopoly, China Telecom, dominates the Chinese market. A smaller company, China United Telecom (China Unicom), was set up by the government as a domestic competitor, although it has struggled to compete effectively. After Zhu's reorganization of the State Council in March 1998 the telecommunications industry in China came under the authority of the Ministry of Information Industries (MII).[51] MII had long benefited from China Telecom's strong position and wished to avoid competition from either domestic or foreign entities. The ministry's influence within the government was based on its representation of a growing and potentially vital industry, but also on that industry's creation of substantial revenues and employment. Because of the importance of this industry, MII minister Wu Jichuan had access to the highest levels of government and routinely made "his" firm's interests known there. Wu was said not only to speak directly to both Zhu Rongji and Li Lanqing, but also to be included in interagency meetings to coordinate negotiations with the United States on telecommunications, including the WTO LSG meetings. In one such meeting Wu is reported to have yelled at chief negotiator Long Yongtu, claiming that in negotiations with Washington Long was "selling out China's interests to foreigners" and that the WTO threatened China's national interests. At the level of day-to-day coordination and negotiations on telecommunications, moreover, MOFTEC was quite weak—so weak, in fact, that representatives of the telecommunications industry invited to coordination meetings and even negotiations sponsored by MOFTEC often did not show up. Because in the formal decision-making process on the WTO negotiations it was expected that the ministry would need to approve any deal on telecommunications, progress could not be made without its participation. Even after Zhu made his failed offer on a bilateral agreement to Clinton in April 1999, Wu attempted to stonewall future progress by tendering his resignation and making his opposition clear at the highest levels.

Because the desire to accede to the WTO was official policy, lobbying efforts with regard to the bilateral agreement could not be based on the notion that WTO membership would harm a particular sector. Rather, industry arguments needed to be framed in terms of national interest. The telecommunications industry, simply wishing to avoid competition (both domestic and foreign), therefore argued that WTO accession would harm China's national security, in part because it would give foreign Internet providers access to China. Industry officials claimed foreign Internet providers would use access to China's Internet markets to steal economic information, disseminate propaganda via e-mail, and use the Internet to support dissidents or undermine the party. Such arguments tapped into deep worries about loss of Chinese sovereignty to foreign powers. Widespread fear of social unrest made such arguments especially potent.

It is clear, therefore, that the ability to shape China's negotiating stance extended beyond the core organizational hierarchy described earlier, to a point where the fate of negotiations could be affected and often determined by interested industries. The inclusion of the affected industry in negotiations on a particular issue was originally seen as a natural extension of the need to consult with and gain the support of that industry. Over time, however, Long Yongtu reportedly came to feel it was a big mistake to invite such broad participation. Long acknowledged in 1994 that the last-ditch GATT offer was "the best we could get from the various [Chinese] ministries," thereby giving credence to the growing challenges of the domestic game.[52] He was said to feel increasingly that, as one trade officer put it, "to invite them in was the same as inviting our enemies. They were just a drag on our legs."[53] As of late 1998, Long was said to be seeking permission to remove industry representatives from the negotiating team. He also was said to have sought permission to report directly to Zhu Rongji so as to bypass the bureaucratic morass he came to feel bogged him down.

Elite Politics: Jiang and Zhu as Dei ex Machinae

Politicians at the apex of power were never very far from this highly bureaucratic process, and they set the tone for much of what occurred in the bureaucracy. Deng Xiaoping's basic policy decision to seek GATT/WTO membership initiated the process, which was continued by Jiang Zemin. Zhu Rongji's caution about harming the domestic economy when he took over as premier in 1998 set the tone of the MOFTEC negotiators during that period, as I noted previously.

By 1999 Jiang and Zhu, for different reasons, decided it was necessary to insert themselves decisively into the negotiation process. Jiang had long voiced general support for WTO accession, but had held back from pressing hard for it, perhaps because of insecurity about his role in leading economic policy. As the 1990s were ending, however, he became more willing to take political risks for a deal. Already basking in the success of Clinton's June 1998 trip, Jiang was encouraged further by personal and confidential letters from Clinton in November 1998 and in February 1999 stating the hope that the

WTO issue could be resolved quickly. He also seems to have been influenced by a desire to build a legacy as the leader who brought China into the new world economy rather than suffocating it under the old economic system. Zhu Rongji, driven more by economic imperatives, shifted away from his previously cautious attitude about the costs to the domestic economy of WTO accession and toward a full-scale acceptance of the leverage argument—the notion that the only way to break the hold of the "old" economy and its champions was to force change on it via the stringent requirements imposed by WTO rules.

In late February 1999 Jiang reportedly convened an expanded Politbuto meeting at which, despite the presence of opponents to WTO membership and likely due to Jiang's strong expression of support for it, approval was gained for the broad concessions Zhu would take with him to Washington two months later. Opposition within China was not won over, as had been attempted for the previous thirteen years, but rather run over.

Public Opinion

Chinese public opinion, distinct from industrial and bureaucratic interests, has traditionally been considered unimportant in the foreign policy-making arena. This assumption held true in the decision-making process on GATT during the 1980s. During the 1990s, however, public opinion toward GATT/WTO was expressed to a greater extent. The government attempted, and had some minor success at, generating positive public opinion through its press and mass media monopoly. Yet negative views of the WTO, stirred up by government sources that opposed membership, proved much stronger.

By 1992 and 1993 Long Yongtu and Wu Yi are said to have concluded that it was important to educate Chinese citizens about GATT and its benefits for China. Cadres in MOFTEC's WTO division were dispatched to universities, radio stations, and Chinese television to give presentations on why China should join GATT. One former MOFTEC official reported that he flew all over China, making at least two presentations a week on the subject. As part of this campaign, moreover, many popular books on the WTO were published and favorable articles were placed in the press. The number of publications skyrocketed after the mid-1990s.[54] Many of these publications were supportive of China's GATT/WTO membership, attempting to explain why membership would be beneficial despite the costs. Emphasis was often placed on the idea that WTO membership would translate into lower prices for consumers.[55] The campaign to bring attention to GATT was so successful, one official claimed, that "even taxi drivers knew about it."

Such a campaign had strong logic behind it. The conventional wisdom on trade politics in industrial countries suggests that anti-GATT sentiment could be expected to be more vocal than opinion in favor of membership because the benefits of open trade would be broadly dispersed, whereas the costs would be concentrated. To educate consumers as to the potential benefits of membership and to emphasize the national pride aspects of China's membership was therefore essential to creating a more vocal pro-GATT constituency. Yet this strategy was not terribly effective. As is true in most countries, no strong independent consumer groups exist in China, so there was no societal organization to take up the call. Even those urban groups who tended to believe that China's GATT bid was a good thing—groups such as businesspeople involved in trade or foreign-funded enterprises—failed to mobilize in favor of GATT membership.[56]

MOFTEC's strategy to create public support for the treaty may even have backfired. Although public opinion toward the WTO at first seemed to respond as intended (if only weakly) to MOFTEC's public relations blitz in 1992–94, positive opinion gradually eroded. At least some in MOFTEC feel this negative trend was piqued by all the attention focused on GATT; the publicity about GATT led the interested public to discover more about why GATT might hurt China. It also appears to have spurred industrial interests opposed to a deal to discuss more publicly—albeit in a constrained manner, given that an outright campaign against WTO membership remained taboo—the costs of membership to individual industries. Negative opinion reached a high point in 1995 and 1996, after China's bid to join GATT before it was converted to the WTO was rejected. Some outright anti-WTO sentiment was even expressed at that time, although MOFTEC claimed that such sentiment was the view of "left-wing" extremists and not broadly held. Yet even discussions with more "liberal" academics and researchers in the fall of 1996 revealed hostility toward the United States and its perceived efforts to keep China out of the WTO.

WTO division officials acknowledged another unintended consequence of the public relations strategy it launched. Each time China and the United States failed to reach agreement in the negotiations (especially China's 1994 push to join GATT), MOFTEC portrayed the failure as a reflection of the unreasonable demands of Washington. As a result, negotiators boxed themselves into a corner from which, unless the United States were to make major public concessions, any agreement that was reached would appear to be a product of Chinese concessions and would greatly harm the domestic reputations of those responsible for the deal.

By 1995 Long and his superiors reportedly had decided that the public relations strategy was a bad idea. From that point on, any public discussions of the WTO by MOFTEC with Chinese audiences had to be authorized, and the overall number was greatly curtailed. But by this time the public was much more attuned to debates about the WTO, and negative sentiment was much closer to the surface of public discourse. Views of the WTO also became linked in the public mind to other "evidence" that the United States was striving to keep China weak, such as Beijing's failed effort to win the bid to host the 2000 Olympics. The organization thus became a symbol of broader grievances about China's international status.

Although the degree of hostility ebbed throughout much of the late 1990s,[57] it came to the fore again, and with a vengeance, when Zhu Rongji returned from Washington without a signed agreement in 1999. Compounding the fact that Zhu had been humiliated, the USTR posted the deal it said Zhu had offered at its Web site, allowing industrial interests in China to see precisely how they had been "sold out." Although the official press gave little space to Zhu's trip, the debate on the Internet was merciless in declaring Zhu a "traitor" (*maiguozei*), often implying the same of Jiang Zemin.[58] Hostility to the deal was compounded by the embassy bombing the following month, as once again WTO membership became symbolic of a larger concern about China's sovereignty. Prominent intellectuals and intellectual journals also weighed in against the agreement, often claiming that the "globalization" inherent in WTO membership was a guise for "Americanization."[59]

Consistent with the argument made in the chapter by Fewsmith and Rosen, the confluence of elite conflict over the WTO issue, tension with the United States, and education of the urban populace as to the relevance of WTO entry for the Chinese economy facilitated the outpouring of negative opinion in early 1999. This negative public opinion, in turn, helped dictate a hiatus in public support from Jiang Zemin and other top reform leaders. Zhu took on a much lower profile in the WTO issue, whereas Jiang took the WTO portfolio for himself. As I noted previously, chief negotiator Long Yongtu's role in negotiations with Washington was greatly diminished in favor of that of the more conservative MOFTEC minister, Shi Guangsheng. Most significant, Jiang was not in the political position to respond to U.S. efforts to restart the negotiations. It was only several months later, with public emotion signifi-cantly cooled and broader steps taken to repair the rift in Sino-U.S. relations, that Jiang took the steps noted earlier to produce an agreement. With the deal signed, there was little public voicing of opposition.

What is interesting about the role of nationalistic public opinion in 1999 is that, whether mobilized by anti-WTO forces or genuinely independent, it helped force the reformers at the top of the system to make a strategic retreat from the deal they wanted. Jiang Zemin ultimately did not allow negative pub-lic opinion to get in his way, and the deal that he agreed to in November 1999 (after the upsurge in negative opinion) was essentially the same as that offered in April. Yet public opinion affected the timing of dealing with Washington and tarnished the glow that Jiang seems to have hoped would surround China's admission to a global organization.

CONCLUSION: CHANGE AND CONTINUITY IN THE MAKING OF CHINA'S FOREIGN ECONOMIC POLICY

The assumption that the study of Chinese foreign policy-making is coterminous with the study of elite preference has deep roots in the field of Chinese for-eign policy. Although elite preference clearly remains relevant, the Chinese policy environment is not as simple as it once was. The foregoing discussion shows that newly influential international forces, the pluralization of foreign policy-making, and (though to a significantly lesser extent) public opinion must be added to elite preference as important influences on China's policy regarding GATT/WTO accession.

As in the other cases examined in this volume, external forces have had an important influence on China's GATT/WTO policy; foreign policy-making is more porous to outside influences. Policy-makers have become increasingly willing to expose China to outside influences as a prerequisite for its fuller parti-cipation in the international system. Perhaps the most significant role of out-side influences has been that ideas and norms of the market and the GATT/WTO system have both been adopted by Chinese policy-makers and reflected in policy reforms. This role of external ideas is similar to the dynamic iden-tified in Gill's chapter on arms control and in Economy's discussion of "epis-temic communities." In other words, "learning" occurred. Learning occurred directly through channels of influence, such as the need for China to adopt GATT/WTO standards in order to join the organization, and indirectly as more and more Chinese officials became convinced that deeper economic integration was both beneficial and necessary.

As important as international influences were, though, they did not etch on a blank slate. They were fed through the perceptions of Chinese policymakers. In any country that is relatively centralized and excludes societal interests, it has been said that "international rules will only affect national policy when and if authoritative officials are predisposed to the prescriptions and proscriptions embodied in international institutions."[60] International influence may also be fed through domestic structures, depending on the degree of political centralization and the pattern of state-society relations (that is, whether policy-making is participatory or exclusionary of societal interests).[61] In the early and mid-1980s, Beijing was intrigued with and in some respects naive about engagement in GATT. In turn, the relatively centralized and exclusionary nature of foreign policy-making meant that, once the idea of membership captured the fancy of a few influential policy-makers (especially in MOFTEC), the path to membership appeared relatively straightforward. Once the narrow group of reformers at the apex of the system bought into the idea, movement toward membership was relatively easy. Over time, however, as the points of contact between Chinese policy-makers and the GATT/WTO system (and global markets generally) expanded, and as the international context evolved, the Chinese perception became more sophisticated. As international influences deepened, they created stronger domestic alliances in support of the organization, but also a backlash—the growth of forces opposed to or skeptical of GATT/WTO membership.

It would appear, therefore, that the process of learning was not as straightforward as the international relations literature would suggest. The learning process in China was more complex in at least two respects. First, learning was neither linear nor steady. Rather, throughout the 1980s and 1990s it occurred through many small, incremental steps—such as those taken on currency convertibility, tariff reductions, codification of laws, and transparency. Yet, especially beginning in the mid-1990s, a variety of forces stifled the ability of Chinese negotiators to close a deal. The Chinese government also learned to play a more sophisticated game of alliance politics to try to undermine the U.S. position. However, these trends occurred simultaneously with incremental steps toward adopting global norms, leading to a complex pattern of forward and backward movement that echoes the dynamic found by Bates Gill in his chapter in this volume.

Second, the direction of learning was both positive and negative as seen from the normative position taken by China's foreign interlocutors. Once the paradigm shift toward integration occurred in 1978, incremental changes began in a direction outsiders generally approved of, even if at too slow a pace. At the same time, the reluctant attitude toward rapid integration that was partially responsible for stalls in the negotiations was based on learning about the costs of integration. Such learning interacted with long-standing concerns over sovereignty and of course was supported by (though distinct from) protectionism voiced by industrial interests. Although it did not, for a significant period, move Chinese policy in the direction favored by WTO members, it was learning nonetheless.[62]

Although international influences came to affect Chinese economic policy more in the 1980s and 1990s than at any other time since the revolution, policy changes occurred in large part, and perhaps predominantly, as a result of domestic forces. This important role of domestic forces was particularly apparent in the original impetus for the policy of openness and for GATT accession, when Chinese policy communities favoring integration formed independent of international pressures and unilaterally decided to pursue membership in various multilateral organizations. This trend has remained in place even as international influence has grown. One of the two strongest domestic influences noted in this case study was the pluralization of policy inputs and the related role of internal lobbying. Actors beyond the core structures placed a brake on WTO accession. Organizations peripheral to the formal decision-making structure became far more influential over time; even if it did not ultimately prevent an agreement with the United States, this periphery certainly shaped the process.

The Chinese bureaucratic decision-making system of "fragmented authoritarianism" contends that the incorporation of multiple voices in decision-making is deeply entrenched in the Chinese political system. But expansion of the range of voices to the degree that occurred in the area of GATT/WTO negotiations was a relatively new development. The range of voices was expanded as a result of three factors. First, the transition from the tariff-oriented GATT to the more broadly targeted WTO drew many more issue areas and sectors into the negotiations. Second, MOFTEC made it a conscious policy to involve other actors very directly in negotiations (a policy that proved burdensome). Third, there was increasing sophistication of these parties about the impact of integration into the trade regime on them—namely, increased competition. Thus domestic politics became much more porous and diffuse.

The policy stalemate that set the stage for paramount leaders to step in shows how perceptions of top policy-makers remain decisive, or at least highly important; one or several top leaders can bring about major policy change or movement toward it. Yet elite preference appears more constrained in the Jiang era compared to the days of Mao Zedong and Deng Xiaoping. If nothing else, the bureaucratic genie has been let out of the bottle in ways not seen previously in Chinese foreign policy-making, particularly in involvement in the national debate and in the negotiations themselves. Although stuffed back in the bottle by Jiang Zemin, this genie appears destined to reappear in the implementation phase of WTO compliance and in future trade politics.

TWELVE

The Making of China's Korea Policy in the Era of Reform

SAMUEL S. KIM

On August 24, 1992, after more than four decades of cold war adversity but a decade of expanding informal relations, the People's Republic of China (PRC) and the Republic of Korea (ROK) signed a joint communiqué in which each country agreed to recognize the other and establish full diplomatic relations "in conformity with the interests and desires of the two peoples." In a single stroke a newly legitimated East Asian state officially known as *Da Han Min Guo,* or simply *Hanguo* (ROK), entered into—and *Nan Chaoxian* (South Korea) left—Beijing's diplomatically correct lexicon.[1] This shift from a one-Korea to a two-Koreas policy is one of the most momentous changes in China's post–cold war foreign policy.[2]

The making and implementation of China's two-Koreas policy is a critical case study for examining China's role in the shaping of a new international order in Northeast Asia and foreign policy-making in Beijing. History, geography, and North Korea's recent emergence as the loose cannon of Northeast Asia have combined to make the peninsula one of the central geostrategic and geoeconomic concerns of post-Mao Chinese foreign policy. Northeast Asia is the only region in the world with both the economic and the technological capability to support high-tech arms racing and the deep-seated (albeit currently attenuated) historical and national identity enmities. It is this combination of a high level of capability, abiding animus, proximity, and the absence of any multilateral security regime that explains the international community's response to North Korea's nuclear missile brinkmanship. Indeed, in Chinese strategic thinking the Korean peninsula is singled out as the "core problem" (*hexin wenti*) of Northeast Asia.[3]

Against the backdrop of its unsettled security environment and contemporary pressures of globalization and localization, China's response to the Korean problem is a key indicator of its emerging role in the transition to a post–cold war order. China's two-Koreas policy decision provides a point of departure for understanding the process China goes through in formulating its foreign policy in general and for addressing a set of specific questions of both theoretical and practical significance. What kind of bargaining and what time period were involved in arriving at the normalization decision? Based on what logic or cost-benefit calculus? How did domestic and external regional and global systemic factors interact and influence broader Chinese foreign policy?

Although we know more than ever before about the structure of Chinese foreign policy decision-making,[4] two major gaps remain. We know little of the making of relatively recent foreign policy decisions, including that leading to China's two-Koreas policy and of the interaction of domestic and international politics with diplomatic, security, and economic factors in the making of foreign policy decisions. Given the problems posed by secrecy and the lack of relevant archival data and interview access to key decision-makers, there is little sense in endlessly parsing independent variables—both structural and ideational—of decision-making unless such analysis is linked to manifest behavior. Since it is not possible to observe Beijing's decision-making process directly, we can only draw causal inferences and certain basic rules about its decision-making from its patterns of manifest action. However, we may hypothesize what decision-making axioms and rules would have been necessary in order for given observable outcomes to have occurred.

This chapter starts with the premise that both domestic and international factors are the significant determinants of foreign policy. Any single level or causal explanation seems insufficient because Chinese decision-makers have clearly not arrived at their two-Koreas decision for any single reason. Beijing often pursues multiple mutually competitive goals on multiple fronts. These goals include maintaining peace and stability on the Korean peninsula, promoting economic exchange and cooperation, helping North Korea's regime survive, preventing dominance of Korea by any external power, halting the flow of North Korean refugees and South Korean Christian missionaries into Jilin Province, stopping the rise of ethnonationalism among ethnic Chinese Koreans, and preventing the formation of any anti-China coalition in East Asia.

As in Putnam-like "two-level games," I will use an integrative domestic-external linkage approach to find answers to the above-mentioned questions. Domestic and external factors are considered in a relative and probabilistic rather than an absolute and deterministic manner to delineate the range of foreign policy choices available. In this regard, the making and implementing of China's Korea policy is best understood as an ongoing process of choosing among competing options rather than any finalized decision, even as Chinese central decision-makers, situated strategically between domestic and international politics, are constrained simultaneously by what the two Koreas will accept and what domestic constituencies will ratify. The making and execution of a foreign policy decision thus requires that China's decision-makers engage in a "double-edged" calculation of constraints and opportunities in both domestic and international politics in order to achieve international accord and secure domestic ratification.[5] To apply the two-level approach to the present case study, then, is to redefine the making of China's two-Koreas policy as an ongoing negotiating process in which Chinese decision-makers are striving to reconcile domestic and external imperatives.

The two-level model is not a perfect "fit" for fully capturing the complex dynamics of domestic and international politics at work in China's two-Koreas policy. Because of the Korean peninsula's centrality to Northeast Asia and China's deepening involvement in the global system, various international actors with different sets of interests have sought to "participate" in the shaping of China's foreign policy goals. Once the simplicity of bipolar superpower conflict disappeared there emerged various triangular patterns of varying dimensions and sizes—for instance, a China-U.S.-Korea triangle in which the geostrategically pivotal Korean peninsula became a geostrategic and geoeconomic battleground of Sino-American rivalry involving three sets of asymmetrical mutual interests and perceptions.[6] As a result, since 1992 China's Korea policy has constituted at least a triangular game of varying patterns and dimensions. The main problem with the two-level game approach in the China case is that the behind-the-scenes bargaining for domestic ratification is inherently harder to parse than the more manifest international bargaining.

Using a modified two-level approach as its framework, this chapter seeks to do three things. The first section examines the domestic and external forces behind Beijing's two-Koreas decision from 1978 to1992. The second section analyzes the practical challenges encountered in the implementation—and continual remaking—of Beijing's two-Koreas policy at the bilateral, regional, and global levels. In the third and final section the patterns of negotiating behavior are examined and some major challenges of Chinese foreign policy decision-making in the era of globalization are suggested.

THE MAKING OF THE TWO-KOREAS POLICY

Unlike China's October 1950 decision to intervene in the Korean War, the 1992 decision lacked all the hallmarks of a foreign policy crisis—surprise, high stakes, short response time, and limited number of options and participants in decision-making.[7] By fits and starts, China's Korea policy in the Deng Xiaoping era (1978–92) evolved through several phases—from the familiar one-Korea (pro-Pyongyang) policy to a one-Korea de jure / two-Koreas de facto policy and finally to a two-Koreas de facto and de jure policy. The 1992 decision was the culmination of a process of balancing and adjusting post-Mao foreign policy to fit changing domestic, regional, and global circumstances.

Although China's Korea policy is multilayered and complex, one useful approach is to prioritize the major factors at work and assess the relative importance of certain variables at a given time. For analytical convenience I characterize domestic and external factors as independent variables to explain China's normalization decision (the dependent variable). The independent variables are further characterized as either long-term causes or short/medium-term causes. The long-term or underlying causes of China's two-Koreas decision were largely internal—the rise of Deng as paramount leader at the Third Plenum in late 1978 and his new policy of reform and opening to the outside world. In contrast, the short/medium-term proximate causes that explain the normalization decision were external changes in China's security environment.

External Factors

What were the external factors that called for Beijing's response? Moscow, Seoul, Pyongyang, Taipei, Washington, and Tokyo were all involved in different stages and to varying degrees in the reshaping of China's external environment that called for a major readjustment of China's one-Korea policy. China's changing definition of and response to the external situations, as far as the Korean peninsula was concerned, were framed by three main concerns. First, the Korean peninsula was viewed as a significant element of China's security environment. Second, South Korea was viewed as a fitting if unspoken model for China's state-led development strategy, as well as a source of support for China's modernization drive.[8] Increasingly South Korea was seen as a potential partner in countering American economic pressure and Japanese economic hegemony in East Asia. Third, China wanted a Korea—divided or united—that posed no challenge to the legitimacy of the PRC as a socialist state and multinational empire.[9]

Gorbachev's Pacific Overtures. Mikhail Gorbachev's foreign policy was the single greatest factor in the reshaping of China's strategic context for the two-Koreas decision in at least three separate but related ways—by ending cold war bipolarity, by effecting Sino-Soviet renormalization, and by establishing Soviet-ROK normalization. By addressing nearly all Chinese and American security concerns through a series of unprecedented unilateral actions Gorbachev removed beyond recall the strategic raison d'être of the Sino-Soviet-U.S. triangle. "All of this had happened by 1990," as Robert Legvold writes, "two years before the collapse of the Soviet Union, and largely as the result of the revolution that Gorbachev brought about in his country's foreign policy. . . . In the end, the demise of the triangle, which had been a profound manifestation of the old order, became one of the profoundest manifestations of its passing."[10]

When the Sino-Soviet conflict ended, so did the logic of the strategic triangle in global politics and Sino-Soviet competition in North Korea. The rapid progress and improvement in Moscow-Seoul relations, coupled with an equally rapid decompression of Moscow-Pyongyang relations, took the sting out of the long-standing Sino-Soviet rivalry over North Korea. Accordingly, on September 1, 1990, Chinese Foreign Minister Qian Qichen and Soviet Foreign Minister Eduard Shevardnadze agreed, following extensive discussion in Harbin, that "without a solution to the Korean Peninsula question, it is impossible to achieve genuine security and stability in Northeast Asia" and that "the dialogue between North and South parts of Korea is important in the easing of the tensions."[11] Previously, ever since the deepening of the Sino-Soviet conflict from the early 1960s to the mid-1980s, Kim Il Sung had pursued an indeterminate line strategy. With the end of cold war bipolarity, however, Pyongyang's leverage in Moscow and Beijing dissipated, at least in the short run.

The 1988 Seoul Olympics was a watershed event in accelerating functional cooperation between Seoul and Moscow, as well as between Seoul and Beijing. The Soviet interest in Korea shifted from a passive desire to avoid confrontation with the United States to a more active solicitation of South Korean support for Soviet Far Eastern development. Indeed, a combination of Gorbachev's Pacific overtures, the deepening economic crisis at home, and Seoul's promise of $3 billion in aid seemed ready-made to provide a cost-effective means to move swiftly toward full diplomatic relations in September 1990. Moscow made it clear that it would no longer veto Seoul's bid to become a member of the United Nations (UN), leaving Beijing the only obstacle standing in the way of Seoul's entry into the UN.

The Soviet decision had major consequences for the North-South Korean dialogue and Pyongyang's international conduct. Like the Sino-American rapprochement of 1971–72, the normalization of Seoul-Moscow relations over Pyongyang's vehement public denunciation of it as "socialist betrayal" proved to be a major catalyst for the resumption of high-level North-South dialogue and led to several historic accords in late 1991 and early 1992. For China the Soviet tilt toward Seoul provided an escape from the entrapment of its one-Korea policy or at least a convenient cover for its own shift from a one-Korea policy to a two-Koreas policy. "In recent years," as two PRC scholars aptly put it, "it has been China's practice to let Moscow take the lead in approaching Seoul while it avoided lagging too far behind."[12] What Moscow did in a sweeping fashion, Beijing undertook at a more measured pace.

Roh's Nordpolitik. If Gorbachev's new foreign policy had the greatest restructuring impact on China's external security environment, Seoul's nordpolitik (northern policy) played a major role in the double-edged calculations of Beijing's one-Korea policy. In the reform era the two Koreas presented challenges for Chinese foreign policy, because Pyongyang and Seoul both saw Beijing as critical to their quest for international legitimization. Both President Park Chung Hee and then President Chun Doo Hwan pursued nordpolitik with the North and with China, but without success. It was not until President Roh Tae Woo's administration—the Sixth Republic (1988–92)—that nordpolitik was officially inaugurated, was vigorously pursued, and began to pay diplomatic dividends. Inspired by the West German ostpolitik, the policy called for the improvement of inter-Korean relations as well as South Korea's relations with other socialist powers in conformity with the principles of equality, respect, and mutual prosperity. That nordpolitik was proclaimed in a presidential declaration of July 7, 1988 (just two months before the 1988 Seoul Olympic Games and as South Korea was seeking to manifest its new identity as a newly industrialized country and newly democratizing country), suggests the underlying logic of nordpolitik. Indeed, the policy was designed to diversify and globalize South Korea's foreign relations—rectifying its image as an indebted Third World client regime.

Nordpolitik may be seen as Seoul's pragmatic strategy of comprehensive engagement with Beijing—indeed, as South Korea's answer to China's Five Principles of Peaceful Coexistence.[13] Even before the July 7, 1988, declaration, cooperative initiatives by Seoul at bilateral, regional, and global levels had produced the nontrivial effects of progressively modifying Beijing's perceptions of and attitudes toward South Korea. Despite the absence of official ties, the levels of indirect Sino-ROK trade grew dramatically in the 1980s, rising to $434 million by 1984—approaching the level of China's trade with North Korea ($498 million)—and, after the 1988 Olympic Games in Seoul, increasing to $3.1 billion by 1989 (about 80 percent of Seoul's total trade volume with all socialist countries at the time). By 1991 the total Sino-ROK trade volume had reached $5.8 billion, almost ten times that of Sino-DPRK (Democratic People's Republic of Korea) trade that year. Faced with this pattern, in October 1990 Beijing agreed to the establishment of trade relations between the Korean Trade Promotion Association (KOTRA) and the Chinese Chamber of Commerce, marking a shift from the one-Korea policy to a de facto two-Koreas policy.

Sports diplomacy followed along the same developmental lines and then expanded along with trade relations. Despite Pyongyang's objections, Beijing sent the largest delegation (some 350 athletes) to the 1986 Asian Games in South Korea. Two years later, thanks to Chinese and Soviet participation, the 1988 Seoul Olympic Games were among the most successful since the end of World War II, quite a "coming-of-age" party for South Korea's new national identity. One spillover of sports diplomacy has thus been a diffuse reciprocity and mutual adjustment of public adversarial attitudes.[14]

To reciprocate Beijing's participation in the 1988 Olympics and buttress its comprehensive engagement strategy, the South Korean government refused to follow the lead of the United States, Japan, Europe, and some international organizations in imposing sanctions on China for the Tiananmen carnage. To the contrary, the Roh government went to extraordinary lengths to promote Chinese tourism, a sector that had been badly hurt by Tiananmen, and to support the 1990 Asian Games in Beijing by providing $15 million in advertising revenues and other donations.

A succession of incidents in the 1980s—especially the May 1983 hijacking of a Chinese civilian airliner to South Korea—compelled Beijing to gradually suspend its untenable policy of separating politics from economics. In the hijacking crisis the Chinese government dispatched a thirty-three-member delegation headed by Shen Tu, general director of the Civil Aviation Administration of China, to resolve the crisis. For the first time, according to Seoul's account of the event, South Korea was referred to as "the Republic of Korea" in the official request for an entry permit as well as in the negotiated memorandum for the release and return of the airliner and its 102 passengers. The successful handling of this potentially explosive incident came as an unexpected windfall for Seoul's engagement strategy and proved significant enough to rattle both Pyongyang and Taipei.[15] The successful management of the 1983 hijacking crisis, the 1986 Asian Games in Seoul, and 1988 Seoul Olympic Games were the chief catalysts for the ensuing surge in cooperative aviation between the two countries.

Seoul's engagement strategy was also extended to multilateral forums and organizations, particularly the Asia Pacific Economic Cooperation (APEC) forum, the Association of Southeast Asian Nations, Post-Ministerial Conference, and many of the specialized agencies of the United Nations. In August 1991 South Korea played such a major role in the negotiations for the admission of all three "Chinese" applicants to the twelve-member APEC that when Chinese Foreign Minister Qian Qichen came to Seoul for the first time, to attend the November 1991 APEC conference, he thanked Seoul for its delicate diplomatic surgery, which had dovetailed with Beijing's party line (Beijing had been admitted to APEC as "the People's Republic of China," Taipei as "Chinese-Taipei," and Hong Kong as "Hong Kong").

Overcoming Pyongyang's Angst. Disconnecting Pyongyang's quest for absolute international legitimization (its one-Korea angst) from Beijing's own quest for absolute international legitimization (under the one country, two systems formula) was the major problem to be overcome before Beijing could begin normalization talks with Seoul. In 1990 and 1991 Beijing seized several opportunities to assure Pyongyang that their "traditional friendship" and "revolutionary loyalty" would endure many generations while simultaneously responding to Seoul's repeated diplomatic prodding with the refrain "Conditions are not ripe." Against this backdrop Seoul's all-out campaign for UN membership began.

Greatly buoyed by a series of triumphs in its nordpolitik, in November 1989 Seoul submitted documents to UN member states explaining its post-1973 position that both Koreas should be allowed to enter the world organization as member states. Thus the issue of Korean membership that had remained dormant for many years was reopened only to provoke Pyongyang's opposition. However, the rapid Moscow-Seoul rapprochement in the wake of the Seoul Olympics, leading to full diplomatic relations in September 1990, altered the dynamics of Seoul's foreign relations. The Soviet Union made it clear that it would no longer veto Seoul's application for membership. In late 1990 Seoul was further encouraged by the support expressed by many speakers at the UN General Assembly session. Of the 162 heads of state and other delegation leaders who spoke, a record 71 (up from 49 in 1989) backed Seoul's proposal of separate membership for both Koreas. In the end, however, Seoul decided to delay its formal membership application, partly because of the Security Council's preoccupation with the Persian Gulf crisis and partly to give it more time to prevent a Chinese veto.

By March 1991, having failed to obtain Beijing's explicit support, Seoul decided to proceed regardless. On March 8 Foreign Minister Lee Sang Ock announced that his government would soon apply for UN membership. Assuming China would not risk its international reputation and economic interests by casting the veto, Seoul decided to take a chance. This diplomatic gamble paid off, and with Pyongyang's dramatic reversal of its long-standing position on May 27, 1991, and initiation of its own application, the issue became moot.

The China factor was certainly among the major determinants—perhaps the most crucial one—in the reversal of Pyongyang's long-standing opposition to the separate-but-equal UN membership formula. As late as November 1989 the Chinese Foreign Ministry continued to reaffirm its support of the Pyongyang line. In 1990 Beijing was following an indeterminate line, arguing that the international community should encourage both Koreas to settle the issue through consultation. Seoul's March 1991 announcement of open diplomacy, however, set off a flurry of behind-the-scenes Sino–North Korean consultations. Premier Li Peng's visit to Pyongyang on May 3–6, 1991, confirmed that Beijing had extracted Pyongyang's grudging acceptance that Beijing would not permit Pyongyang to dictate its UN voting behavior, especially when separate Korean membership enjoyed the support of an overwhelming majority of UN member states. With Beijing's reversal on South Korean membership, Pyongyang was left with little choice but to submit its own membership application.[16]

Apparently Premier Li Peng was a key player in a two-level game of persuading President Kim Il Sung both that the costs of Seoul's solo entry would be too high and that Pyongyang's membership would bring benefits including wider diplomatic recognition and an enhanced eligibility to obtain multilateral aid. The major benefit of dual membership from Beijing's perspective, however, was to provide a plausible legal and diplomatic basis for differentiating a divided Korea from the Chinese case: there is only one China in the state-centric world of international organizations, whereas there were now two Koreas de facto and de jure. In a frantic race for diplomatic recognition both Koreas soon abandoned in practice, if not in principle, the Hallstein Doctrine (which had stemmed from West Germany's demand in the 1950s and 1960s that any nation that wanted to have relations with it could not have diplomatic ties with East Germany), opening the way for dual recognition. Not a single country recognized both Seoul and Pyongyang in 1962; by mid-1976 some 49 countries had done so. In contrast, at the end of 1990 some 136 countries maintained diplomatic relations with Beijing and only 28 countries—mostly in Africa and Central America—had recognized Taiwan, and none had recognized both.[17] As South Korea's former foreign minister Han Sung-Joo aptly put it: "Beijing succeeded in creating a kind of 'new math' whereby for Korea, one plus one equaled two, while for China, one plus one was still one."[18]

Thus another major obstacle on China's long march toward normalization with Seoul was removed. After entry of the two Koreas into the United Nations in September 1991, Sino-ROK contacts were accelerated and elevated to the foreign ministerial level, with UN or other multilateral forums providing a venue for talks on issues of common concern. Yet Beijing still resisted the initiation of normalization talks. Immediately after South Korea's UN admission the Chinese and South Korean foreign ministers, Qian Qichen and Lee Sang Ock, met for the first time to discuss bilateral relations. However, Lee's probing elicited only a noncommittal response—the two countries should continue their functional (that is, nonpolitical) cooperation in a low-profile manner. A month later Qian went to Seoul to attend the APEC meeting and again responded to Lee's solicitation with the familiar "not yet" refrain. It was not until April 1992 that "conditions" finally were ripe for normalization talks.

What were the proximate causes that made conditions ripe at that time? Clearly UN membership for both Koreas was the single greatest factor enabling Beijing to overcome Pyongyang's one-Korea angst. The improved state of inter-Korean relations—one of the unspecified preconditions that required ripening—also facilitated the initiation of normalization talks at that juncture. The seven-month period from September 1991 to April 1992 witnessed a remarkable finale to the inter-Korean talks at the prime ministerial level: An Agreement on Reconciliation, Nonaggression, and Exchanges and Cooperation Between the South and the North (signed on December 13, 1991, and entered into force as of February 19, 1992) and the Joint Declaration of the Denuclearization of the Korean Peninsula (signed on December 31, 1991, and entered into force as February 19, 1992).

Another unspoken causal force behind Beijing's decision to have normalization talks was its desire to lead the shaping of a new East Asian order after the demise of the Soviet Union, a point stressed by South Korean interlocutors that was like sweet music to Chinese ears. During much of the cold war China's regional policy remained a stepchild of its global superpower policy—a policy driven by China's centrality to the U.S.-China-Soviet geostrategic triangle. Chinese foreign policy in Asia, and especially on the Korean peninsula, was directed primarily to the United States and the Soviet Union. China was a regional power without a regional policy or identity, as every regional decision (including that regarding its invasion of Vietnam in 1979) was justified primarily in terms of global security imperatives, not as a matter of bilateral or even regional politics or economics. In the post-Tiananmen period, especially since the collapse of the Soviet Union in December 1991, however, Chinese foreign policy has become more Asia-centric.

The escalation of Sino-American trade disputes in 1992, with the mounting "Super 301" pressure from Washington, was another factor contributing to the Asianization of Chinese foreign policy and an acceleration of Beijing's decision-making on normalization. China expressed its receptivity to the idea of gradually establishing "a bilateral, subregional, and regional multichannel and multilayered security dialogue mechanism so as to hold consultations on the issues concerned and to strengthen interchange and confidence."[19] Beijing established, or "renormalized," diplomatic relations with Asian neighbors, including India, Indonesia, Kazakhstan, Kyrgyzstan, Singapore, Turkmenistan, Uzbekistan, and Vietnam, leaving only South Korea out of Beijing's diplomatic circle. Therefore, to recognize Seoul became part of China's newly Asia-centric foreign policy orientation.

Domestic and External Linkages

This is not to suggest that domestic factors played no part in catalyzing Beijing's normalization talks with Seoul. In fact, China's domestic political forces were equally divided between conservative leaders opposed to formal diplomatic ties with the South and senior policy advisors in favor of normalization. The opposition relied on the following assumptions and arguments: China's switch to a formal two-Koreas policy would provide powerful ammunition for advocates of a two-Chinas policy; PRC-ROK normalization would be perceived as a betrayal of China's socialist ally and might consequently accentuate Pyongyang's siege mentality and contribute to, if not precipitate, the collapse of the North Korean system; and Beijing could have its cake and eat it too by continuing its existing one-Korea de jure and two-Koreas de facto policy.

The pro-normalization arguments advanced by senior foreign policy advisors including Foreign Minister Qian Qichen were as follows: given Moscow's growing influence in South Korea, Beijing could not afford to procrastinate if it did not wish to forfeit Chinese influence on the Korean peninsula; there were limits to South Korean patience, and normalization talks had to be completed before the end of President Roh's tenure in December 1992; Beijing could not afford to wait for Japan-DPRK and U.S.-DPRK normalization, because the prospects for such recognition were limited; and Pyongyang could not accuse Beijing of socialist betrayal, because China remained supportive of North Korea in many other ways.[20] In a secret report to the Chinese Communist Party Central Committee Foreign Affairs Leading Small Group, Qian reportedly argued that full normalization of relations with Seoul would have the effect of "downing four birds with one stone": increasing Taiwan's diplomatic isolation, expanding Beijing's economic cooperation with Seoul, diminishing Pyongyang's seemingly endless requests for aid, and enhancing Beijing's bargaining power to defuse mounting "Super 301" pressure from the United States concerning unfair trade practices.[21]

Not surprisingly, Deng Xiaoping had to intervene to settle the matter. Disregarding the assurances he had given Kim Il Sung over the years, Deng cast his decisive vote to proceed with normalization negotiations; therefore, Deng was the decisive player in obtaining domestic ratification of Beijing's two-Koreas decision. In early 1992 Deng launched a major personal campaign to rejuvenate his reform programs through his epochal "southern trip." Deng saw the value of a new "Korean connection" to his campaign to rekindle China's reform and "open" policy, according to Parris Chang, and believed "that the ROK government and Korean business community would be willing and able to provide capital and technology" to further the reform process.[22] No doubt a new Korean connection would also stimulate ROK-Japanese as well as ROK-Taiwan economic competition for the Chinese market, enabling Beijing to obtain more favorable trade and investment terms from all three parties.

It is not clear exactly when Deng made his decision, but it seems that it was made prior to the United Nations Economic and Social Commission for Asia and the Pacific (ESCAP) conference in Beijing in April 1992. According to South Korean sources, it was at the ESCAP meeting that Chinese Foreign Minister Qian Qichen approached ROK Foreign Minister Lee Sang Ock to propose normalization talks. In the April 13, 1992, meeting Qian and Lee agreed upon the basic rules of the game: that normalization negotiations had to be confined to diplomatic channels, that complete secrecy had to be maintained throughout the talks, and that in the event of any press leakage both parties were to immediately deny it. This was designed primarily to respect North Korea's sensibilities and prevent Pyongyang from exercising its negative (nuisance) power.

That Beijing went to some lengths to soothe Pyongyang's one-Korea angst was also evident in Beijing's shuttle diplomacy of 1992. In April 1992 President Yang Shangkun traveled to Pyongyang to personally inform President Kim Il Sung about the future of China's Korea policy, even as his stepbrother General Yang Baibing, secretary general of the Central Military Commission, made an eight-day "goodwill visit" to North Korea. Foreign Minister Qian also made a secret trip to Pyongyang sometime immediately before or after the second round of normalization talks in June 1992. This trip was designed to give a detailed report to Kim Il Sung on the progress of the talks and to assure the "great leader" that PRC-ROK normalization would help accelerate Pyongyang's own normalization talks with Tokyo and Washington, would stabilize the situation on the Korean peninsula, and would contribute to North Korea's system maintenance. In the end Qian managed to obtain Kim's grudging understanding, if not full acceptance, of China's normalization decision.[23] Once Beijing obtained Kim Il Sung's understanding, normalization talks gained momentum for rapid finalization. A Beijing-Taipei diplomatic bidding war over Niger that erupted in June 1992 was not a proximate causal factor, as widely argued, but merely served as an additional factor in accelerating the normalization talks.[24]

One major sticking point in the talks was Seoul's request that China acknowledge its past aggression in Korea. The South Korean negotiators recognized that this was an unrealistic request, but nonetheless made it for the historical record and to ensure domestic considerations. The Chinese negotiators responded that there was no "past issue" to discuss and that any such acknowledgment, let alone an apology, was out of the question.[25] The final PRC-ROK normalization treaty—issued in the form of a six-point joint communiqué[26]—is silent on the past, as if there were no past relationship of any kind. The treaty can also be said to reflect an asymmetrical exchange of mutual legitimization—Seoul's acceptance of the one-China principle in exchange for Beijing's acceptance of the two-Koreas principle. Although there was no Chinese request for aid, Seoul's prompt severance of diplomatic ties with Taipei and handing over of Taiwan's $1.7 billion embassy complex in Seoul to the PRC are widely believed to have been the functional equivalent of Seoul's $3 billion aid package with regard to the Soviet normalization decision in 1990.

THE REMAKING OF THE TWO-KOREAS DECISION

The making of China's two-Koreas decision did not come to a sudden end in August 1992. Rather, this event marked the culmination of the informal bargaining process and the beginning of a process of implementing—and remaking—the two-Koreas decision in a variety of issue areas. The challenge has remained the same—how to maintain China's "special relationship" with Pyongyang while promoting and expanding "normal state relations" with Seoul.[27] As if to test China's ability to live with such contradiction, a series of North Korean crises (such as those related to the nuclear issue, ballistic missiles, suspected underground nuclear site issues, and the future of post-Kim North Korea) arose in rapid succession during the postnormalization period. In order to capture the complex nature of China's two-Koreas policy in the postnormalization period (1992–99), three broad issue areas—economic/functional, military/security, and political/unification—require close examination.

The Economic/Functional Domain

From the perspective of post-Mao reform and opening to China, the South Korean economy represented opportunities to be exploited, whereas North

Korea posed a burden to be lessened without damaging geopolitical ties or causing system collapse. That China has become, in the wake of 1990 Soviet-ROK normalization, North Korea's biggest trading partner and economic patron is a mixed blessing. A highly asymmetric Beijing-Pyongyang-Seoul economic interdependence has emerged, with Sino–North Korean trade representing about 30 percent of Pyongyang's foreign trade, but only about 3 percent of Sino-ROK trade volume and less than one-fourth of 1 percent of China's total trade volume (down from about 4 percent in the 1960s). Seoul had also become a donor of foreign aid to both Beijing and Pyongyang, allowing Beijing to assume the role of broker or balancer between the Koreas.

The 1990 Soviet decision to normalize relations with South Korea played a major role in the restructuring of North Korea's political economy. As if to add economic insult to diplomatic injury, Moscow served notice that Pyongyang would have to start serving its debt to Moscow (estimated at $4.6 billion) and that trade would henceforth be in hard currency. Unsurprisingly, these changes seriously disrupted North Korea's foreign trade regime. The cumulative effect of the sudden withdrawal of Soviet aid and subsidized trade, the collapse of the socialist world market, the structural problems of the command economy, the overallocation of resources to heavy industry and military spending, the inordinate misappropriation of human and natural resources to the deification of the "great leader," and finally, the bad weather of 1995 and 1996 effected a contraction of the North Korean economy by over 50 percent from 1991 to 1996. As late as 1990 the Soviet Union was the DPRK's largest trading partner, accounting for over 50 percent of its total trade, but that relationship quickly soured in the wake of the 1990 Soviet decision.

As a result, China's share of North Korea's foreign trade rose from 10.9 percent in 1990 to 25 percent in 1991 and hovered around 30 percent between 1991 and 1996, although it remained relatively constant in absolute terms. By mid-1994 China accounted for about three-quarters of North Korea's oil and food imports.[28] China's economic policy toward North Korea in the postnormalization period seems to be framed by the conflicting goals of minimizing the financial costs of its support while also minimizing the risk of wider instability.[29] There are several tactics Beijing has employed in its behind-the-scenes diplomatic efforts. Beijing has been applying pressure on Pyongyang to lift its collapsing economy on its own. Growing Sino-ROK economic ties have remained the clearest way of demonstrating the possibilities of inter-Korean economic cooperation. Beijing also followed Moscow's lead in demanding cash payments as of January 1, 1993. Beijing therefore served two-year notice on Pyongyang to adjust its economic bottom line.

Faced with the deepening food crisis, the rise in refugee flows, and the growing danger of system collapse in the post–Kim Il Sung era, especially since early 1996, Beijing has engaged in more active two-level bargaining with Pyongyang. Based on a reliable Beijing source and several internal documents, *Hsin Pao,* a Hong Kong economic journal, provided a rare inside view of the twists and turns of Sino–North Korean relations in the first half of 1996, focusing on Chinese aid.[30] The sequence of actions and reactions can be summarized as follows:

— In early 1996 North Korea asked China for 200,000 tons of grain.
— Because this was seen as too great a demand, China initially promised only 20,000 tons.
— North Korean leader Kim Jong Il flew into a rage when he heard of China's response and threatened to play his "Taipei card"; simultaneously he sent a letter to Jiang Zemin and Li Peng with six new demands: that both Beijing and Pyongyang jointly reaffirm their responsibilities and obligations under the PRC-DPRK Treaty of Friendship, Cooperation, and Mutual Assistance (1961); that China make clear its support for the principles and policies of the Korean Workers' Party and the DPRK government; that senior party and government leaders of both countries exchange state visits in the fourth quarter of 1996 and issue a communiqué of mutual support; that during the 1996 and 1997 fiscal years China provide 5 billion yuan of grain, fuel oil, transportation equipment, heavy-duty machinery, and light industrial products; that China provide the DPRK with $1.5 billion for the purchase of military equipment and replacement parts from Russia; and that China provide the DPRK with three missile speedboats and forty missiles, as well as twelve Jian-7II's (an improved type of MIG-21) and parts for them.
— On July 8, 1996, Zou Jiahua, a member of the Politburo and vice premier of the State Council, announced China's two-point response: (1) the Chinese party, government, and people have always cherished the Sino-DPRK Treaty of Friendship, Cooperation, and Mutual Assistance as a symbol of the traditional friendship between the two countries, but because of a tight work schedule that year for Jiang Zemin and Li Peng the Chinese government could have only Luo Gan, state councilor and secretary general of the State Council, visit the DPRK; and (2) with regard to aid, "we shall try our best, but we are still unable to meet the DPRK's demands."

— Beijing reportedly made it known to Pyongyang that during the 1996 and 1997 fiscal years the Chinese government would provide the DPRK with 480 million yuan (about $59 million) in material aid and $20 million in interest-free loans for a period of ten years.

By providing more aid in a wider variety of forms—direct government-to-government aid, subsidized cross-border trade, and private barter transactions—Beijing thus became more deeply involved, playing a more active role (indeed every year a crucial role) in the politics of regime survival. The exact amount and terms of China's aid to North Korea remain unclear, however. *Chosun Ilbo* (Korea Daily), the largest daily in Seoul, reported in 1996 that Beijing had decided to provide 500,000 tons of grains and 1.3 million tons of petroleum to North Korea each year for the next five years (1996–2000).[31]

In contrast, there is no evidence of high-level Sino-ROK bargaining over economic matters. In the wake of the 1992 normalization decision Sino-ROK economic relations have been making up for lost time. South Korea became China's third largest trading partner, after the United States and Japan. Sino-ROK trade ballooned to $6.4 billion in 1992, $9 billion in 1993, $11.6 billion in 1994, $16.5 billion in 1995, $20 billion in 1996, and $23.7 billion in 1997. By 1997 it was almost three times larger than the Sino-Russian trade volume ($7 billion), seven times the Russo-ROK trade volume ($3 billion), and thirty-four times the Sino–North Korean trade volume ($699 million). In 1993 China became the most preferred country for foreign direct investment (FDI) by South Korean firms, with Seoul authorizing 616 applications for investment in China.[32] By September 1998 South Korean investment in China amounted to $14.26 billion, with $7.11 billion actually used in 10,817 different projects. The two countries have opened up ten air and seven shipping routes to handle the heavy traffic in goods, services, and people.[33]

The expanding Beijing-Pyongyang-Seoul economic triangle reflects the trend of regionalization in China. Many provinces are now trading more with the outside world than domestically, both in real terms and as a percentage of total provincial trade.[34] A center-periphery disparity (thinking nationally but acting locally) in the implementation of the two-Koreas decision is thus especially evident in the northeastern region (Liaoning, Jilin, and Heilongjiang Provinces), particularly in Jilin's Yanbian Korean Autonomous Prefecture (site of Mount Paektu, the mythological birthplace of the Korean nation). It was here more than in any other part of China that regional actors had to cope with the challenges posed by the changing balance of power on the Korean peninsula.

In this regard the Tumen River Area Development Program (TRADP), in which China, North and South Korea, Russia, and Mongolia have all been involved, is tailor-made for exploring the possibilities and limitations of a multi-lateral Northeast Asian economic regime. The TRADP presents a unique case of regime formation involving multiple sets of actors—provincial, national, and international—all engaged in bargaining over the nature, scope, and direction of Northeast Asian economic development. Tellingly, China has been the most active promoter of the TRADP, and without its involvement the program would not have been launched, let alone survived.

The notion of a Northeast Asian cooperative regime was first suggested during a Sino-ROK nongovernmental dialogue at the National Research Center for Science and Technology for Development in 1985.[35] In July 1990 the International Conference for Economic and Technological Development in Northeast Asia (jointly sponsored by the Asia-Pacific Research Institute of Jilin Province and the East-West Center in Hawaii) was held in Changchun, China, with delegates from China, Japan, North and South Korea, Mongolia, the former Soviet Union, the United States, and the United Nations Development Program (UNDP), who adopted a "Changchun Initiative" in which the participants agreed that economic development and political stability should be the common goal of all countries in the region. In July 1991 the UNDP initiated follow-up discussions leading to agreement among the five Northeast Asian countries to cooperate in the economic development of the four subregional areas collectively known as the Tumen River Region.

As originally conceived, the TRADP was an ambitious project to turn the sleepy backwaters of Rajin (North Korea), Hunchun (China), and Posyet (Russia's Far East) into a Northeast Asian Hong Kong by the end of the 1990s: a huge duty-free shipping and processing zone along the Tumen River of North Korea and a large circle of prosperity stretching from Vladivostok south to North Korea's Chongjin and west to Yanji in northeastern Jilin Province. The estimated costs of the project were $30 billion over a fifteen- to twenty-year period. The six participating states—the earlier five plus Japan—were meant to complement one another, with Japan and South Korea providing investment capital, modern technologies, and management and marketing skills; North Korea and China providing cheap labor; and China and Russia providing the coal, timber, minerals, and other raw materials. China needed a port outlet to the Sea of Japan. Russia wanted to integrate the political economy of its Far Eastern region into the dynamics of the Northeast Asian economy. Mongolia, as a landlocked country, obviously wanted access to an international port. North Korea wanted to milk as much from the TRADP as possible in support of its own Rajin-Sonbong free economic and trade zone. South Korea finally saw another open gateway to North Korea.

The economic viability of the TRADP as originally envisioned, however, was tied to the economic and political context of the Soviet Union, Mongolia, and North Korea in the late 1980s and to the willingness of Japan and South Korea to provide the lion's share of the capital needed to launch the project. With the collapse of the Soviet—and consequently the North Korean—economy, this context changed dramatically. Additionally, Japan's interest in the Tumen project was limited from the outset, as was evident in Tokyo's refusal to become a participating member state.

Beijing's somewhat unusual activism suggests that China stands to gain the most from the project. China's enthusiasm has also been inspired by other factors, including the project's potential to expand subregional economic cooperation between the two Koreas. There is also a strategic dimension behind China's push on the TRADP—namely, access to the Sea of Japan. Finally, the project was also seen as a way to stabilize the situation in the Yanbian Korean Autonomous Prefecture (*Yanbian Chaoxian Zizhiqu*) in Jilin Province, which was threatened with economic and political chaos as a result of North Korea's precipitous decline. This would explain Beijing's selection of the latter as its designated area for the TRADP rather than Heilongjiang or Liaoning Province.

The original grandiose, multilateral infrastructure project was consequently downsized into smaller bilateral or trilateral pieces.[36] Because of the limited scope of the TRADP and the size of the Tumen River Basin generally, the TRADP is better viewed as a subset of Northeast Asian regional cooperation than an overall regional cooperation regime. As a Russian participant noted, the TRADP as a mechanism of regional cooperation is "geographically vague, alternating between the border level, the multilateral level, rims, zones, and triangles that are only loosely corresponding."[37] Although the future of the TRADP therefore remains uncertain, China's active participation remains significant and may be seen as an attempt at providing political and economic life support for North Korea.

The TRADP, involving as it does both central and local decision-makers within its five participating states (plus the UNDP), shows that international cooperation becomes exponentially more difficult as the number of actors increases. This is because international cooperation requires both recognition of opportunities for the advancement of mutual interests and policy coordination once such opportunities have been identified and recognized. As the number of actors increases, however, the likelihood of defection increases while the feasibility of sanctioning defectors diminishes. Likewise, the costs of transactions rise with the multiplicity and complexity of each player's "payoff structure" and "mutual interests," thus militating against any easy identification and realization of common interests. A strategy of reciprocity or "seeking common ground while preserving differences" (*qiutong cunyi*) becomes more difficult to carry out.[38]

The Asian financial crisis (AFC) of 1997–98, which first erupted in Thailand in July 1997 and then spread elsewhere, including South Korea, has muddied the waters with uneven effects on Sino-Korean economic relations. Given that China is so deeply enmeshed in the Asian-Pacific economy, why has it emerged relatively unscathed from the AFC? A combination of factors explains China's relative immunity. These include the nonconvertibility of its currency (the yuan), substantial foreign exchange reserves (about $140 billion) to defend against speculative attacks, and a large inflow of FDI, only a small percentage of which is portfolio investment (which is more vulnerable to quick withdrawal in a panic).

Having largely escaped the worst of the AFC and having also won kudos from the international community for its responsible exchange rate policy, Beijing nonetheless faces an unpredictable interplay of domestic and external forces—growing unemployment, rampant corruption, widening regional and social inequality, spreading insolvencies at state banks and state-owned enterprises (SOEs), and another round of searing power struggle between economic reformers and conservatives at home and the slowdown in external demand for and inflows of FDI. China's economy suffered severely from reduced foreign investment from other Asian countries, especially from overseas Chinese in Thailand, Malaysia, and elsewhere in Southeast Asia; more intense export competition; substantial (if unspecified) capital flight through many loopholes; a shrinking export pie; the looming perils of financial liberalization or lack thereof; and a slowdown of the economic growth rate.

The AFC seems to have adversely impacted putatively self-reliant and autarkic North Korea. North Korea's foreign trade declined from $2.2 billion in 1997 to $1.5 billion in 1998, a 30 percent decline. More seriously, the drop in exports (by 40.3 percent, down to $152 million) was greater than that of imports (23.1 percent to $331 million). For the first time in years, Japan surpassed China as North Korea's largest trading partner, even as China's supply of food and energy to North Korean began to drop sharply.[39] Sino-DPRK trade in 1998 stood at a mere $410 million, registering a sizable decline of 37.1 percent from the $699 million in 1997. North Korea's exports to China in 1998 were worth $57 million, a whopping decline of 52.9 percent, due to decreases in timber and steel exports, and North Korea's imports from China fell 34 percent to $350 million due to a decline in exports of grains and mineral fuels.[40] For North Korea and Sino-DPRK relations, then, the AFC proved to be the case of *huo bu danxing*—misfortunes never come singly!

The impact of the AFC on Sino-ROK economic relations has been mixed. In the 1980s Seoul was seen as the emulation model for China's export-oriented development strategy. At the time of the Fifteenth Party Congress in September 1997, two months after the eruption of the AFC, South Korea's *chaebol* (conglomerates) were publicly touted as a model for reforming SOEs. As late as February 1998, more than three months after the IMF responded to Seoul's call for help with the largest ($58 billion) rescue package it granted during the crisis, Korea still seemed to have energized China's attempt to restructure the SOEs into South Korean–style *chaebol* under the banner "grabbing the big, letting go the small," with the state trying to establish an organic link between corporate revival and comprehensive national strength. By mid-1998 Beijing was forced to back away from this approach when the weaknesses of the *chaebol* were brought to light and President Kim Dae Jung was trying hard to dismantle or downsize Korean corporate leviathans.

Sino-ROK trade dropped 22 percent, from $24 billion in 1997 to $18.4 billion in 1998, but rose to $22.6 billion the next year. Thanks in part to China's refusal to devalue its currency, South Korea also managed to generate an all-time trade surplus of $5.5 billion in 1998 and $4.8 billion in 1999, up from a $3.5 billion surplus in 1997, even as Seoul's FDI in China began to fall as much as 59.2 percent.

With the recovery of the South Korean economy from the AFC and the conclusion of U.S.-China negotiations on Beijing's entry into the World Trade Organization (WTO) in late 1999, however, Sino-ROK economic relations entered a new phase with a mixed but cautiously upbeat assessment of near-term challenges and opportunities. China's entry into the WTO is likely to have a positive impact on South Korea's trade with China, with Seoul's trade surplus projected to increase an additional $2.4 billion between 2000 and 2005. Since only 18 percent of South Korea's total exports (such as clothing, textiles, televisions, video cassette recorders, electric irons, earphones, and electric motors) lag behind Chinese products in international competitiveness or compete with them in world markets, the economies of the two countries remain more complementary than competitive.[41]

South Korean firms are increasingly seeking to target the more than sixty million urban middle-class Chinese with per capita incomes of over $5,000. The greatest interest among South Korean businesses currently appears to be in the telecommunications sector. The Chinese market for CDMA (code division multiple access) to its domestic mobile phone makers and operators is expected to increase 63 percent in 2000, to seventy million customers, offering an unprecedented business challenge and competition for Japanese and Korean high-tech business firms. Seoul has also sought to retain a foothold in the Chinese auto assembly market and explore opportunities for Korean companies to develop high-speed railroads in China.

The Military/Security Domain

The single greatest challenge to smooth implementation of the two-Koreas decision has remained Pyongyang's security behavior. The euphoria of 1990–92—engendered by Soviet-ROK normalization, the two Koreas' UN membership, the inter-Korean accords, and Sino-ROK normalization—was greatly overshadowed by the nuclear crisis of 1993–94. North Korea's nuclear brinkmanship created a new set of dangers and opportunities in the management of China's two-Koreas policy at the bilateral, regional, and global levels.

The nuclear standoff can be traced to February 1993, when the International Atomic Energy Agency (IAEA) made an unprecedented request that North Korea submit to a so-called special inspection of two undeclared sites at the Yongbyon nuclear complex. This call for a special inspection was denounced by Pyongyang as an espionage scheme directed at its military facilities. More important, North Korea declared that it was withdrawing from the Nuclear Non-Proliferation Treaty (NPT). The withdrawal announcement caused widespread panic in Seoul, Tokyo, and Washington, as well as in Vienna and New York, because North Korea, once legally out of the NPT, would be legally free to proceed with its nuclear weapons program.

Against this backdrop Foreign Minister Qian made it clear that his government opposed not only economic sanctions, but also any effort to raise the issue at the IAEA or in the UN Security Council. When push came to shove in the Security Council, Beijing issued a thinly veiled threat to veto any proposed resolution. Because China alone among the Perm Five had taken such a hard line, the Security Council had to delay and then dilute its draft resolution so as to make it palatable to China's sovereignty-bound minimalism. On May 11, 1993, the Security Council finally adopted a resolution (S/RES/825) by a vote of 13 to 0, with only China and Pakistan abstaining, simply calling upon the DPRK to reconsider its announced withdrawal from the NPT. Later, on March 28, 1994, China brushed aside demands for a further resolution, successfully insisting on a milder "presidential statement." On May 29, 1994, the Security Council, in diluted diplomatic language acceptable to Beijing, tried again to send a message stating that "further Security Council consideration will take place" to help secure Pyongyang's full compliance with the NPT.

There were several reasons for Beijing's antisanctions strategy. To begin with, for a Chinese government faced with legitimization crises both at home (the Tiananmen carnage) and abroad (the collapse of transnational communism), international sanctions, especially U.S.-sponsored sanctions against a socialist regime, touched too close to home.[42] As one Security Council representative put it, "The Chinese representatives used the North Korean debate as a case to illustrate a deeper point—If you can't force the North Koreans to do what you want, how do you imagine you could ever force the Chinese to do anything? Nothing can be done against the Chinese. . . . We lobbied them as part of the NAM [Nonaligned Movement] countries on the Bosnia and the Haiti missions. Again, they believe in *bilateral dealing;* they come, they smile, they leave."[43]

A second reason for China's resistance to UN action may be greater commitment to maintaining the North Korean regime than to denuclearizing the Korean peninsula. The greatest danger to Beijing would be for its socialist ally to feel so cornered that it would fight back or that economic sanctions would work so well as to produce another collapsing socialist regime on China's northern borders with all its political, economic, and social consequences for China's domestic politics. Third, Beijing may have recognized the limitations of its influence in reshaping Pyongyang's national security behavior. From Pyongyang's vantage point nuclear weapons constitute the most cost-effective deterrent and "strategic equalizer" in its competition with the South. The de facto removal of the Russian nuclear umbrella thus seemed to have strengthened the DPRK's determination to go nuclear as a matter of necessity and regime survival.

In the end China's bargaining strategy played a positive role of sorts by forcing the crisis management to be transferred from the Security Council to direct

U.S.-DPRK negotiations. Thus began a series of high-level talks between the North Koreans and Americans that resulted first in deadlock and then, thanks to former president Jimmy Carter's shuttle diplomacy in the heat of nuclear crisis in June 1994, in a landmark accord, officially known as the U.S.-DPRK Agreed Framework, which was signed on October 21, 1994. As if to take credit for the breakthrough, China praised Carter's "fruitful mediation" as evidence that "dialogue is better than confrontation."[44]

From Beijing's vantage point the Agreed Framework was further seen as opening a window of opportunity to improve economic conditions in North Korea, to bolster the legitimacy of the Kim Jong Il regime, and to enhance the prospects for political stability. Additionally, the Agreed Framework would go some way toward redressing the dangerous imbalance of power between the two Koreas. As such, its full implementation was regarded by China as essential to peace and stability on the Korean peninsula and therefore vital to China's national security interests.[45] Pyongyang seemed determined to refuse any notion that Beijing had anything to do with the breakthrough, stating: "We held the talks independently with the United States on an independent footing, *not relying on someone else's sympathy or advice,*" and "the adoption of the DPRK-U.S. Agreed Framework is a fruition of our independent foreign policy, *not someone's influence,*" with the United States finally accepting "our proposal."[46]

If Beijing wanted to stay out of harm's way with regard to the nuclear crisis of 1993–94, the same cannot be said about the two-plus-two formula, the four-party peace talks formula jointly proposed by Presidents Bill Clinton and Kim Young Sam at their summit meeting in April 1996. In response to this overture Chinese diplomats made clear to Washington that Beijing was quite unhappy, not only because it had not been adequately consulted, but also because Washington was acting prematurely. Although never publicly stated, the Chinese complaint was that both Pyongyang and Beijing were put on the spot without knowing what precisely was being asked of them, much less what response they should give to avoid getting into negotiations that might work to their disadvantage. Worse, according to Chinese diplomats, Pyongyang was once more being asked to do something that would almost inevitably cause North Korea to engage in its long-standing extortion diplomacy. Washington had thus jeopardized the stability of China's delicate geostrategic relationship with North Korea.[47]

The quest for an equidistant posture coupled with the concern about not being viewed as hostile toward Pyongyang defined the outer limits of the possible and the permissible for China's participation in any Northeast Asian regional security dialogues. When Pyongyang continued to press hard for its two-plus-zero or three-plus-zero formula in an obvious attempt to exclude Beijing, China's surprise response was that it suddenly opposed North Korea's two-plus-zero scheme as "unrealistic, unreasonable and impossible." Pyongyang's formula was thus declared to marginalize the China factor in the security complex of the Korean peninsula. "The Korean peninsula issue is no longer a simple dispute between South and North Korea," according to an unnamed PRC expert. "The different attitudes of China and the U.S. on the North Korean nuclear issue is, essentially speaking, a strategic trial of strength between the two countries on the Korean peninsula."[48] As a signatory to the Korean armistice accord, Yu Shaohua, one of China's leading Koreanists, argued, China has every right to be a party in the Four-Party Peace Talks designed to replace the armistice with a peace treaty or mechanism.[49] To prevent a situation in which a major power would dominate the region, argues another scholar, "China takes a neutral stance toward the conflicts between the United States, Japan, and Russia" because it is desirable "for China to maintain an equilibrium among America, Japan, and Russia," ideally to become "a balancer" in the "U.S.-Japan-China or U.S.-Russia-China triangular relations."[50]

Once the Four-Party Talks got under way China's "balancing" strategy of becoming all things to all parties and thereby maximizing its influence became clear. At the first round of preliminary talks in New York in August 1997, Beijing took a relatively neutral position on various differences between North and South Korea, opposing Pyongyang's demand that the issues of U.S. troops' presence in South Korea and a U.S.–North Korean peace treaty be included on the agenda while also refusing to support the joint U.S.-ROK proposal that the talks address tension-reducing and confidence-building measures. Instead Beijing advanced its familiar line— that the four countries should primarily discuss the improvement of bilateral relations.[51] Assistant Foreign Minister Chen Jian, head of the Chinese delegation to the second round of talks in Geneva March 16–21, 1998, explained to the domestic audience that the talks had ended with no agreement because the United States and the DPRK refused to budge. On the other hand, China, the only country with diplomatic ties to all three other parties, was playing a very special role. On all the outstanding issues discussed at the talks China maintained "no specific stance but a flexible attitude"—the reason why the other three parties (supposedly) pinned their hopes on China.

Although no substantive progress was made in the second round of talks, China was said to have played its special role in three ways. First, faced with the DPRK's objection to the seating arrangements, China proposed that at future talks the three parties other than the rotating chair be seated in alphabetical order. Second, as a way of expressing its preference for bilateral negotiations China proposed that half of each conference day be set aside for bilateral contacts. As a result, on the morning of March 17, 1998, China held separate consultations with the United States and both Koreas. Third, thanks to bilateral negotiations the parties agreed to "impasse-breaking proposals that a sub-committee be established on a provisional basis to discuss legal matters, long-term arrangements and confidence-building measures."[52] Similarly, in the third round of talks, in October 1998, China's chief negotiator, Qian Yongnian, is said to have played an important role in persuading North Korean Vice Foreign Minister Kim Gye-gwan to make some concessions in the formation of subcommittees.[53]

Just as Beijing was beginning to play a more proactive role in Geneva, however, the Four-Party Peace Talks were suddenly overshadowed by the political and strategic smoke caused by Pyongyang's submarine incursions into South Korean territorial waters, its suspected underground nuclear construction at Kumchang-ri, and its launching of a three-stage Taepodong-I missile over Japan in the latter half of 1998. This situation dramatically illustrates how difficult it is for Beijing to maintain its Korea policy on a bilateral, two-level game track. Once again Kumchang-ri became a subject of bilateral negotiations, with the United States asking for unconditional access to the site and North Korea demanding $300 million for a one-shot admission ticket. At the end of four rounds of negotiations in mid-March 1999 a quid pro quo agreement was reached—Washington's quid (an additional four hundred thousand tons of food aid) for a single Pyongyang quo (U.S. inspection of the suspected site). In May a large U.S. technical team completed a week of on-site inspection, finding nothing but empty tunnels. However, the August 31, 1998, firing of a Taepodong-I missile seemed aimed at overcoming domestic U.S. opposition to the development of a Theater Missile Defense (TMD) program and to press Tokyo if not Seoul to join the TMD project, all with enormous military and strategic implications for Beijing.

Can China really have its Korean security cake and eat it too? Is a genuine two-Koreas security policy possible despite the PRC-DPRK Treaty of Friendship, Cooperation, and Mutual Assistance? Although the present-day Sino-DPRK relationship is not as close as it once was, neither Beijing nor Pyongyang has shown any interest in modifying the treaty. Unlike the 1961 Soviet-DPRK treaty, the Sino-DPRK treaty cannot be revised or abrogated without prior mutual agreement (Article 7). Still, Beijing let it be known, if only informally at first, that it would not support Pyongyang if North Korea attacked South Korea. During Jiang Zemin's state visit to South Korea in 1995 a Chinese Foreign Ministry spokesperson stated that the alliance does not commit Chinese troops to defending North Korea.[54] On other occasions, however, the formulation has been that Beijing's support would not be provided if the North launched "an unprovoked attack" or that the treaty does not require the dispatch of Chinese military forces or that China was not willing to intervene "automatically." With such seeming impunity Beijing projects a strategic posture of calculated ambiguity, letting it be known to all that the treaty commitment to Pyongyang could be interpreted as Chinese leaders chose or that it does not consider the treaty to be an ipso facto hard and fast commitment and that in a crisis situation Chinese leaders may "change their minds, change their policies, or, of course, even act with reckless abandon."[55]

On the eve of President Kim Dae Jung's first official state visit to China in November 1998, Chinese and South Korean negotiators were engaged in a last-minute tug of war over how to define the "partnership" agreement to be signed by their leaders at the conclusion of the Jiang-Kim summit meeting in Beijing. That is, the behind-the-scenes negotiations were mired in which modifying adjective to use to characterize "partnership"—"strategic," "comprehensive," or "good and friendly." After the two parties hit many rough spots the South Korean side wanted to describe the new relationship as a "partnership without any modifier," whereas the Chinese side insisted on putting "cooperative" ahead of the partnership. "The negotiations went through childbirth pains," according to Park Jie-won, the chief presidential spokesperson for the Blue House in Seoul, and the two parties eventually agreed to call it a "cooperative partnership."[56] The ROK-PRC Joint Statement of November 15, 1998, is long on economic and functional cooperation and short on political and security cooperation, except in the context of global politics.

In early June 1999 a fifty-member North Korean delegation led by Supreme People's Assembly (SPA) President Kim Yong Nam made a high-profile state visit to China. The visit was remarkable for at least three reasons: it was the first high-level state visit since President Kim Il Sung's in late 1991 (compared to myriad summit meetings between South Korean and Chinese leaders in 1992–98); it was a "military-first delegation," headed by SPA President Kim Yong Nam but consisting almost exclusively of military generals and not a single economic official; and the delegation's itinerary included Beijing, Shanghai, and Hangzhou, but not China's showcase special economic zones such as Shenzhen, with Kim Yong Nam telling Chinese Premier Zhu Rongji that Chinese economic reforms "suited China's national conditions." For Pyongyang the visit was a success not only as a symbol of Sino–North Korean strategic partnership, but also for obtaining China's promise of an additional 150,000 tons of grain and 400,000 tons of coal. On the occasion of the fiftieth anniversary of the establishment of diplomatic relations in October, Chinese Foreign Minister Tang Jiaxuan traveled to Pyongyang to discuss ways of expanding bilateral ties.

And yet, as if to demonstrate that there is far more or far less than meets the public's eye in the new Beijing-Moscow-Pyongyang strategic partnership, the Chinese and the South Koreans held their first-ever defense ministers' talks in Beijing August 23–29, 1999, to coincide with the seventh anniversary of Sino-ROK normalization. For Seoul, Defense Minister Cho Sung-tae's visit was part of a diplomatic blitz aimed at winning China's support for President Kim Dae Jung's "sunshine policy," and specifically for helping to stop North Korea from launching Taepodong-II. Moreover, Seoul's requests for broader Sino-ROK security cooperation also included joint PRC-ROK military exercises, a joint maritime search-and-rescue exercise, exchanges of naval port calls, establishing a multilateral arms control and disarmament dialogue to prevent the proliferation of weapons of mass destruction, and a return visit of Chinese Defense Minister Chi Haotian.

Not surprisingly, Beijing responded with the maxi-mini strategy of killing several birds with one stone: accepting Seoul's invitation for Chi's return visit (which was carried out five months later in January 2000); warning Seoul against enhancing military ties with the United States (that is, carrying out the annual Ulchi Focus Lens U.S.-ROK joint military exercises); preaching about the danger of American hegemony (a unipolar world order) in the era of political multipolarization; and dancing away from Seoul's request for Beijing's help or response on the other issues. Beijing remains unwilling to engage Seoul in joint exercises even in basic areas such as search and rescue, humanitarian operations, or the exchange of naval port calls by each other's ships.

Seoul's overeagerness for a more active military and security partnership was on full display on China's home turf. South Korean Defense Minister Cho's remark at the Chinese Military Academy that the United States Forces in Korea (USFK) may eventually be subject to negotiated consensus among Northeast Asian neighboring countries was sweet music to Chinese realpolitik ears because it offers Beijing a kind of unit veto related to the future of the American military presence in Korea. Not surprisingly, the controversial statement generated an instant firestorm of protest in increasingly contentious and fractured domestic politics in Seoul, with sixty-three opposition Grand National Party lawmakers demanding Cho's dismissal. Cho's statement also blew a big hole in President Kim Dae Jung's assurances that the USFK would be a force for regional stability even after Korean reunification.

The first-ever meeting of Chinese and South Korean defense ministers in Beijing (in August 1999) and Seoul (in January 2000), coming on the heels of North Korean "President" Kim Yong Nam's state visit in June 1999, may be seen as a contemporary version of China's traditional stratagem of using barbarians to control barbarians—the "divide-and-rule strategy" of Western realpolitik—except that post-Mao China has considerable economic, political, and military resources to back up such a balancing strategy. Beijing's maximini equidistance strategy is made evident in a two-handed approach whereby it props up North Korea on traditional geostrategic grounds with one hand while simultaneously grabbing South Korea for new military exchange and cooperative partnership with the other hand.

From Seoul's perspective, to engage Beijing in the military and security domain is part and parcel of its sunshine policy of comprehensive but balanced engagement with all neighboring powers. The real challenge is not how to balance Washington against Beijing or to get on the bandwagon regarding the rising China, but to avoid being caught in any crossfire between Beijing and Washington while enhancing its own political, economic, and functional cooperation with China. As Pyongyang seeks to break out of its self-imposed cocoon of isolation and expands and diversifies its diplomacy, one traditionally appealing approach may well be to play the major powers against one another (Washington against Beijing, Taipei against Beijing, Beijing against Tokyo) to see what the geopolitical market will bear.

The Political/Unification Endgame

With the nuclear crisis "resolved" or at least put in abeyance in 1994, North Korea was once again back in the news, this time as East Asia's time bomb seemingly ripe for explosion (or implosion). A deepening systemic crisis in North Korea, reflecting critical shortages of food, energy, and hard currency, has far-reaching ramifications for the DPRK's political stability and even survival. As a result, Korean reunification by Southern absorption or system collapse in the North has entered into Chinese foreign policy thinking and behavior.

It is important to recognize that China's thinking on Korean unification, far from being cast in stone, evolves with the Chinese domestic, Northeast Asian regional, and global situation and with changes in Sino-U.S. relations. In 1993 Chen Qimao, a leading scholar and former president of the Shanghai Institute of International Studies, stated China's position on the Korean unification issue in the following terms: "China supports President Kim Il Sung's plan to reunify North and South Korea in a Confederal Republic of Koryo under the principle of 'one country, one nation; two systems, two governments.' This is not only because of China's traditional friendship with North Korea but also because the Chinese leadership believes this policy meets *the current situation* of Korea and supports Korea's national interest as well as the peace and stability of the region. By contrast, *a dramatic change*—which would be very dangerous and could easily turn into a conflict, even a war—would be a disaster for the Korean nation. Further, it would threaten not only China's security but the security of the entire Asia-Pacific region and even the world as well."[57]

China wanted to have Korean unification both ways, supporting the peaceful coexistence of the two Koreas under Kim Il Sung's "Confederal" formula—"one country, one nation; two systems, two governments"—but also opposing any "dramatic change" (that is, German-style reunification). This was seen as the most feasible way to maintain peace and stability on the Korean peninsula.[58] Despite China's lip service to reunification, the central challenge of post-Mao foreign policy was and remains to create a congenial external environment, especially in Northeast Asia, for its own accelerated march to power and plenty. By mid-1994, when Kim Il Sung suddenly died, Pyongyang's reunification policy had turned into a kind of habit-driven trumpery, devoid of substantive relevance.[59] The real issue for Pyongyang—and for Beijing—was how to avert system collapse, which would threaten not only the survival of the North Korean state, but also China's security environment. With the balance of national strength having already shifted decisively in favor of South Korea, thus enhancing the prospects for reunification by absorption, strengthening ties with the weaker North, albeit in a cost-effective way, has become one of Beijing's central strategic goals.

What heightened Beijing's opposition to the reunification-by-absorption scenario was its perception of U.S. strategy. "To put it bluntly," one pro-China newspaper in Hong Kong wrote, "the United States wants to use this chance to topple the DPRK, and this is a component of U.S. strategy to carry out peaceful evolution [*heping yanbian*] in the socialist countries." As this is so, the United States "will practice a strategy of destruction against North Korea . . . with the aim of enabling South Korea to gobble up North Korea, like West Germany gobbling up East Germany." Such a perceived strategy posed not only an ideological challenge to China, but, more important, a strategic threat, because "China regards the Korean region as an important buffer zone between China and the United States."[60] Apparently this too lay behind Beijing's opposition in the UN Security Council to sanctions against North Korea in 1993–94.

Given its realpolitik perspective and security concerns, there are also other reasons why Beijing takes a skeptical view of Korean reunification. It is hardly surprising that post-Tiananmen China assesses the global and regional situation in terms of how it will affect both internal and external threats. According to Yan Xuetong and Li Zhongcheng, from the Chinese perspective "the major challenge the Chinese state will have to face during the next decade is not global interdependence, but a concerted Western plot to weaken China by giving support to separatists, by exaggerating and taking advantage of differences between the center and the periphery, between factions, and between state and society, and by exerting pressure using such issues as democracy and human rights."[61] Of particular concern to China is that local and ethnonational conflicts, previously overshadowed by the superpower rivalry, are now breaking out throughout the world. According to Yan Xuetong, now that the threat of direct military invasion has subsided, China too is plagued by ethnic separatism and border disputes, with "hypernationalism" (*jiduan minzuzhuyi*) having made extensive inroads among China's separatists.[62]

Moreover, the onset of another round of Sino-American tension (1995–97) introduced a highly charged nationalistic lens for viewing the security situation on the Korean peninsula and particularly America's Korea policy. Situated at the center of Northeast Asia, the Korean peninsula was seen as a battleground of the four great powers' contending strategic plans. Japan views a unified Korea as a great threat to its own military and economic security and therefore is aggressively seeking to arrest the continuing imbalance between the two Koreas. Russia too is trying to get back into the game in order to curb the growing influence of the other major powers, especially Japan. The United States, more than the others, views the three other players as threats to its hegemonic position. The main reason the United States has attached such importance to the Korean peninsula, we are told, is that it wants to contain any growing Chinese, Russian, or Japanese influence. Faced with this situation, China felt obliged to step up its own involvement with the Korean peninsula, hence China's attempts to check American expansionism and hegemonism in the region, thus effectively safeguarding the peace and stability of Northeast Asia.[63]

With the improvement of Sino-American relations since 1997 such anti-American assessments of the Korean situation subsided, especially in the wake of President Jiang Zemin's state visit to the United States. Changes also occurred in the policies of all peripheral players, especially the United States, in 1996–97. Probably reflecting a shift in America's North Korea policy from deterrence to "deterrence plus"—a policy of conditional and reciprocal engagement[64]—the United States was said to have adopted a "coordinating and mediating attitude" instead of taking a concerted united front position with its South Korean ally.[65]

There is far more than meets the public's eye to Beijing's status quo—and antiunification—policy. Apart from maximizing China's leverage as a balancer in Northeast Asia politics, China genuinely fears that North Korea could come to feel cornered and see no choice but to fight back, triggering at least a regional war. Beijing does not doubt that Pyongyang would fight rather than succumb to German-style hegemonic unification. Even if the system in the North simply collapses, moreover, it is likely to be bloody, triggering a civil war rather than immediate absorption by the South. Even the North Korean defector, Hwang Jang-yop warned against the danger of reading too much into his defection: "The republic [North Korea] is in economic difficulty but it remains politically united and there's no danger of its collapse."[66]

Until at least 1996, unification by Southern absorption was regarded by Chinese scholars and policy-makers as wishful thinking on the part of Western analysts. With the economic crisis in North Korea further reflecting and affecting the structural contradictions within the system, an increasing number of Chinese analysts began to acknowledge the possibility of system collapse, even if they doubted such collapse was imminent.[67] In other words, by 1997 not to think about the unthinkable came to be viewed as an exercise in Chinese wishful thinking. In late October 1997 the *Beijing Review,* which touts the party line on every issue, published an unsigned article in which it offered an unprecedented analysis (and rebuke) of the root causes of North Korea's food crisis: "What's more, a heavy military burden is using up much needed resources. . . . The present military expenditure of DPRK is US$6 billion, bringing a huge burden to its economy. For the time being, the United

States, Japan, and the Republic of Korea (ROK) are three main forces in the aid of DPRK. Due to conflicting points of view, however, many political conditions are attached to the aid process. . . . Ultimately, it's up to the [North] Korean people themselves to resolve the grain crisis. It requires spirit and will power to meet the challenge of such reforms as introducing foreign investment and opening up, while maintaining a stable political situation. And Korea needs to be flexible while carrying out diplomatic policies."[68]

Pyongyang's growing dependence on Beijing for its economic and political survival, coupled with Beijing's growing frustration, has bred mutual distrust and resentment. Pyongyang has taken a sleight-of-hand approach by privately asking for more and more aid to avoid getting less and less ("asking for four of something with the hope of getting one"). All the same, North Korean diplomats habitually publicly deny that they have asked for or received any Chinese aid.[69] "The most frightening prospect," according to Hwang Jang-yop, "is not that North Korea will collapse. What I fear most is that Kim Jong Il will bow down to China to get the help he needs, and North Korea will slip into the Chinese orbit."[70]

Even if we accept the heroic assumption that Korean reunification will come about peacefully, without igniting a civil war or generating a massive refugee population, Beijing would still face a wide range of territorial disputes over fisheries and mineral, oil, and gas deposits in the Yellow Sea. China's security dilemma today is largely shaped by the eighty million minority members vying in the strategically sensitive "autonomous" regions that make up roughly 64 percent of China's territory. In this regard, what would a united and nationalistic Korea do about its territorial claims along the Sino-Korean border and in China's northeastern provinces, inhabited by the world's largest concentration of overseas ethnic Koreans? Organizations such as Damui (Reclaim) in South Korea, with more than fifty thousand members, are already advancing the irredentist claim: "Manchuria was ours but was taken away [and] . . . maybe, one day, it'll be ours again." Damui's activities have thus already provoked Beijing's strong protests.[71]

Although Korean reunification looms large in Sino-ROK relations, it is seldom the subject of direct negotiations. In 1998, however, Beijing and Seoul became entangled in intense two-level bargaining over the dual nationality legislative bill the Kim Dae Jung government was set to enact. Seoul's attitude toward Chinese-Koreans in China's northeastern provinces thus came to light in August 1998, when the ROK Ministry of Justice announced a legislative plan to accord all ethnic Koreans abroad legal status virtually equal to that of Korean citizens at home. The main objective of this plan, according to the ministry, was to give overseas Koreans a stronger sense of Korean ethnonational community and to encourage them to contribute to the economic development of their motherland. However, this hypernationalistic stand not only would directly contradict President Kim Dae Jung's professed globalism, but would also create legal and diplomatic disputes with the host countries of overseas Koreans, most of whom (about 60 percent) are by birth or naturalization bona fide citizens of their host states.

China lost no time in making known its strong displeasure and promptly threatened to call off President Kim Dae Jung's scheduled state visit to China. Beijing also implied that it might reject Seoul's persistent request since 1992 to set up a consulate in the sensitive city of Shenyang to take care of Korean business and other matters in Liaoning, Jilin, and Heilongjiang. Against this backdrop and following intense but fruitless bargaining, the ROK Ministry of Foreign Affairs and Trade expressed its opposition to the proposed legislation for fear that it might cause serious diplomatic and legal disputes with China. In the end Seoul was forced to drastically revise the dual-citizenship bill to accommodate Beijing's demands. The revised bill that the National Assembly finally passed on August 12, 1999, would exclude ethnic Koreans in China by extending the benefits of the new law to only those overseas Koreans who emigrated *after* the establishment of the ROK in 1948.

Ultimately, China is not opposed to Korean reunification, we are told, provided that it comes about gradually and peacefully; it is a negotiated unification between the two Koreas, not a hegemonic unification by absorption; and a unified Korea does not harm or threaten China's security or national interests. According to Zhao Gancheng, "China will use her influence to strive for the peaceful unification of Korea, and to keep unified Korea as a friendly, or at best, *neutral* neighbor."[72] A united Korea would be expected, moreover, to be drawn within China's economic and military sphere; China should help shape developments in Korea, not merely follow the lead of the United States and Japan.[73] In short, China has become and will remain a critical factor in North Korea's future—whether it will survive or collapse, or, more accurately, whether it will move from here to there in a system-maintaining, system-reforming, system-decaying, or system-collapsing trajectory.

CONCLUSION

The making of the two-Koreas decision in 1992 was a result of the interaction of domestic and external factors as well as the interaction of long-term (underlying) and medium- and short-term (proximate) causes. What really connected the underlying causes with the most proximate factors was Deng Xiaoping. Political leadership mattered in the sense that the paramount leader in Beijing played the determinative role at the starting and culminating points in the decision-making process (1978–92). In between, China's normalization decision-making process proceeded at a measured pace under a maxi-mini bargaining strategy maximizing China's national interests while minimizing the economic and security costs of winning both international accord and domestic ratification. The prime motive behind Seoul's nordpolitik was initially more political than economic, with Beijing's recognition as the ultimate prize, whereas Beijing sought multiple goals, including economic benefits, enhancing its influence on the Korean peninsula, and expanding and diversifying its foreign policy options.

In implementing the two-Koreas decision in the postnormalization period China had to operate in a more complex strategic setting where contradictory historical, ideological, strategic, and economic factors confronted Chinese policy-makers. Necessarily, China's two-Koreas policy involved a balancing act reflecting and affecting its own interests and requiring its participation in multiple games on various bilateral, regional, and global chessboards. With the demise of the Beijing-Moscow-Washington strategic triangle there emerged what many Chinese strategic analysts term "political multipolarization" and "economic globalization"; in this case study there emerged a complex economic and strategic triangle involving three sets of asymmetrical interests—Beijing-Seoul, Beijing-Pyongyang, and Seoul-Pyongyang.

As I argued in the preceding pages, China has pursued a bargaining strategy of following different but complementary interests—strategic, economic, and antihegemonic—on all sides of the Beijing-Pyongyang-Seoul triangle. On the first and second sides of the triangle Beijing has sought to maintain its strategic ties with North Korea even as it promoted new economic ties to South Korea. On the third side of the triangle, the most turbulent and contentious domain, Beijing has sought to keep out of harm's way with a bargaining strategy of calculated ambiguity and equidistance. As a way of maximizing its influence over Korean affairs China often seeks to be all things to all parties, which always raises questions about its true intentions and ultimate decisions. China has seldom placed itself on the front lines of the Korean conflict as either a mediator or peacemaker for fear it might get burned if something goes wrong.

Applying the logic of the two-level approach, one can see China's two-Koreas policy as a bargaining strategy for winning both Seoul's and Pyongyang's accord and domestic ratification by maintaining a "special relationship" with North Korea while promoting and expanding a "normal state relationship" with South Korea. The same logic of the two-level game is visible in both Pyongyang's and Seoul's efforts to exploit their Beijing connection to gain a bargaining advantage over the other side. Generally, then, China's maxi-mini, two-Korea strategy is more reactive than proactive and is concentrated on the short-term challenge of avoiding constraints; it does not, however, appear to include a long-term strategic vision for the Korean peninsula—except for keeping it as a buffer zone.

From the patterns of China's negotiating behavior described in the preceding pages we can deduce the following axioms ("dos and don'ts"):

— Do not commit to premature specificity on any Korea-specific issue.
— Do not say "yes" or "no" prematurely, especially to Seoul or Washington.
— Do not take any publicly anti-Pyongyang stand so as to make Seoul, Washington, or Tokyo anxious to seek Beijing's assistance.
— Do not become entangled in multilateral negotiations if possible.
— Do seek common ground while preserving differences (*qiutong cunyi*) by taking a "wait-and-see" stance, allowing others to reveal their bottom lines first.
— Do watch out for—and nip in the bud—any anti-China (or pro-Taiwan) unilateral, bilateral, or trilateral move linked to Korean affairs.
— Do bargain with Pyongyang privately, using a carrot-and-stick approach, to moderate its risky behavior.
— Do separate economics from security issues as a way of maintaining a "special security relationship" with North Korea and a "special economic and functional relationship" with South Korea.
— Do participate in multilateral negotiations if there is no alternative, but bifurcate the process into a series of bilateral negotiations, thereby maximizing China's bargaining power.
— Do stay firm in principle, but flexible in tactic (*yuanze de jianding xing he celue de linghuo xing*) by bending even "principled stands" somewhat and making certain eleventh-hour concessions if necessary.

That China has come to interact with the two Koreas in more ways, with more depth and complexity, and on more chessboards than ever before has several consequences for the making and remaking of Chinese foreign policy. More interests are now involved in China's multifaceted two-Koreas policy, which slows the decision-making. This is not unique to China's Korea policy. As China's integration with the outside world deepens, different domestic groups and actors with varied interests will seek to "participate" in the making and implementation (or nonimplementation) of foreign policy goals (see David Lampton's introductory chapter to this volume). Like it or not, China's two-Koreas policy cannot be contained within a state-to-state bilateral straitjacket. Domestic and external third parties with their own agendas and rules constantly move in and out of the making and implementing of China's two-Koreas policy, especially given Pyongyang's ability to generate crisis upon crisis, threatening not only peace and stability on the Korean peninsula, but also global nonproliferation (Nuclear Non-Proliferation Treaty), missile (Missile Technology Control Regime), and food (UN Food and Agricultural Organization / World Food Program) regimes. Increasingly China's two-Koreas policy constitutes more than the sum total of interstate bilateral relations. The remaking of China's two-Koreas policy may thus be seen as the outcome of China's learning through two-level bargaining both domestically (between Beijing and the Northeast region) and internationally (between Beijing and other East Asian regional and global actors). As a result, China's capacity to initiate and implement consistent policies toward the two Koreas is constrained by the positions of important domestic groups and other Northeast Asian states, as well as the United States, Japan, and Russia. Meanwhile, the growing complexity, density, and multilateralization exemplified by the Korean issue have placed pressure on the Chinese foreign policy-making system to develop more effective coordinating mechanisms and means to monitor what is really going on.[74]

Although Beijing today commands a rather unique position as the only major power that maintains good relations with both Koreas, the making and remaking of China's two-Koreas policy underscores three major challenges. First, Beijing has the daunting task of managing the reality that China and Korea remain the last two legacies of cold war divided polity. Given the growing chasm between the two halves of Korea, almost any scenario for Korean reunification has portentous implications for China's own unification drive. Although Beijing stresses the differences between the Chinese and Korean cases, the two-Koreas policy only underscores the fact that the two Chinas are also going their separate ways.

Second, despite (or perhaps because of) the fragmented authoritarian trend in China, coping with the pressures of globalization and localization is likely to remain a central challenge for the third-generation leadership, as well as a major source of their authority and legitimacy. The primal force behind nationalistic behavior in the post-Tiananmen years is not any military threat from without, but the leadership's resolve to project China's national identity as an up-and-coming superpower in the Asia-Pacific region so as to make up for the domestic legitimization and security deficits. Yet China's third-generation leaders will not be able to dominate foreign policy-making the way Mao—and to a lesser extent Deng—did, nor will they be able to make the necessary compromises on a host of sovereignty-bound issues with respect to Hong Kong, Taiwan, Tibet, and other irredentist claims in East Asia. Although the Chinese Koreans in Jilin Province have often been touted as a model minority in a multinational empire, Korean reunification by absorption—or the intrusion of the two Koreas' politics of competitive legitimization and delegitimization into the world's largest Korean Diaspora—hangs over the future of China's two-Koreas policy. Hence, the antinomies between globalization from above and without and localization from below and within enter full force into China's multiple identities and competing role conceptions, with significant implications for the resolution of outstanding territorial disputes with neighboring states and of ethnonational conflicts within China.

Third and finally, in the turbulent post–cold war world, in which contradictory forces are vying for primacy, most states, especially multinational states such as China, are subject to the contradictory pressures of globalization from above and fragmentation from below. The Chinese "totalitarian" party-state is no longer the almighty Leviathan of yore. Rather than making states functionally obsolete or irrelevant, however, globalization has redefined what it takes to be a competent state in an increasingly interdependent and interactive world. Globalization is a double-edged sword in this respect: it threatens both minimalist and maximalist states and thus provides an opportunity for competent and adaptable ones. Increasingly, a state capacity to rapidly absorb, generate, disseminate, and apply knowledge is critical to economic and social well-being—indeed, to China's "comprehensive national strength."[75] The greatest irony of all is that globalization requires fast responses at a time when the system is becoming diffused and protracted because of its maxi-mini, multilevel bargaining approach across multiple issues both at home and abroad.

Notes

1. John Pomfret, "China's Zigzagging Path on Taiwan," *Washington Post,* March 8, 2000, pp. A24, A26.

2. Michael Swaine calls this the "National Strategic Objectives Subarena." See his *The Role of the Chinese Military in National Security Policymaking,* rev. ed. (Santa Monica, Calif.: RAND Center for Asia-Pacific Policy, 1998).

3. Andrew J. Nathan and Robert S. Ross, *The Great Wall and the Empty Fortress* (New York: Norton, 1997), p. 14.

4. Yan Xuetong, *Zhongguo Guojia Liyi Fenxi* (The Analysis of China's National Interest) (Tianjin: Tianjin Renmin Chubanshe, 1996); see also Thomas Christensen, "Chinese Realpolitik," *Foreign Affairs,* Vol. 75, No. 5 (Sept. Oct. 1996), pp. 37–52; see also Alastair Iain Johnston, "Learning versus Adaptation: Explaining Change in Chinese Arms Control Policy in the 1980s and 1990s," *China Journal,* No. 35 (Jan. 1996), pp. 27–62.

5. John W. Lewis, Hua Di, and Xue Litai, "Beijing's Defense Establishment: Solving the Arms-Export Enigma," *International Security,* Vol. 15, No. 4 (Spring 1991), pp. 87–109.

6. Marlowe Hood, "Sourcing the Problem: Why Fuzhou?" in Paul Smith, ed., *Human Smuggling: Chinese Migrant Trafficking and the Challenge to America's*

Immigration Tradition (Washington, D.C.: Center for Strategic and International Studies, 1997), pp. 76–92, especially p. 80.

7. Shi Chen, "Leadership Change in Shanghai: Toward the Dominance of Party Technocrats," *Asian Survey,* Vol. 38, No. 7 (July 1998), pp. 671–87; see also Li Cheng and Lynn White, "The Fifteenth Central Committee of the Chinese Communist Party: Full-Fledged Technocratic Leadership with Partial Control by Jiang Zemin," *Asian Survey,* Vol. 38, No. 3 (March 1998), pp. 231–64.

8. Gao Xin, *Jiang Zemin de Muliao* (Jiang Zemin's Counselors) (New York: Mirror, 1996), pp. 13–67.

9. David M. Lampton, interview with Foreign Ministry official, Feb. 1999.

10. Lu Ning, *The Dynamics of Foreign-Policy Decisionmaking in China* (Boulder, Colo.: Westview, 1997), pp. 40–44.

11. Ibid., pp. 41–42.

12. David M. Lampton, interview with Foreign Ministry official, Feb. 1999.

13. David M. Lampton, conversation with Assistant Minister Long Yongtu, June 11, 1997, Washington, D.C.

14. Harold K. Jacobson and Michel Oksenberg, *China's Participation in the IMF, the World Bank, and GATT* (Ann Arbor, Mich.: University of Michigan Press, 1990), p. 147.

15. David M. Lampton, interview with Chinese official, Feb. 1999.

16. David M. Lampton, "Chinese Politics: The Bargaining Treadmill," *Issues and Studies,* Vol. 23, No. 3 (1987), pp. 11–41.

17. Carol Lee Hamrin and Suisheng Zhao, eds., *Decision-Making in Deng's China: Perspectives from Insiders* (Armonk, N.Y.: Sharpe, 1995), pp. xxxiii–xxxiv.

18. Transcript of meeting with a member of the Standing Committee of the Politburo, April 1993, p. 3.

19. David M. Lampton, conference notes, March 3, 1999.

20. James Mulvenon, *Chinese Military Commerce and U.S. National Security* (Santa Monica, Calif.: RAND Center for Asia-Pacific Policy, June 1997), Fig. 2.

21. Samuel S. Kim, "Taiwan and the International System: The Challenge of Legitimation," in Robert G. Sutter and William R. Johnson, eds., *Taiwan in World Affairs* (Boulder, Colo.: Westview, 1994), p. 151; also Kyodo News Service, "China Severs Diplomatic Ties With Macedonia," February 10, 1999.

22. Samuel S. Kim, "China and the United Nations," in Elizabeth Economy and Michel Oksenberg, eds., *China Joins the World: Progress and Prospects* (New York: Council on Foreign Relations Press, 1999), p. 47; see also Union of International Associations, *Yearbook of International Organizations,* Vol. 2 (Munich: Saur, 1997/1998), Table 3, Appendix 3.

23. World Bank, *1998 World Development Indicators,* CD ROM, "China's Trade (Exports and Imports)," 1978–96, pp. 1–2.

24. World Bank, *China 2020: Development Challenges in the New Century* (Washington, D.C.: World Bank, 1997), pp. 24–25.

25. State Statistical Bureau, *China Statistical Yearbook 1997* (Beijing: China Statistical Publishing, 1998), pp. 247–48.

26. David M. Lampton, interview with Shanghai scholar, August 18, 1998.

27. Director of Central Intelligence, Nonproliferation Center, "Unclassified Report to Congress on the Acquisition of Technology Relating to Weapons of Mass Destruction and Advanced Conventional Munitions," Jan. 1–June 30, 1998, http://www.cia.gov/cia/publications/bian/bian.html.

28. Paul J. Smith, ed., *Human Smuggling* (Washington, D.C.: Center for Strategic and International Studies, 1997).

29. Thomas Moore, Westfields Conference, 1998.

30. Swaine, *Role of the Chinese Military in National Security Policymaking*, pp. 7–18.

31. See Suisheng Zhao, "The Structure of Authority and Decision-Making: A Theoretical Framework," in Hamrin and Zhao, *Decision-Making in Deng's China*, pp. 242–43.

32. Zhao, "Structure of Authority and Decision-Making," p. 242.

33. A. Doak Barnett, *The Making of Foreign Policy in China: Structure and Process* (Boulder, Colo.: Westview, 1985).

34. Lu, *Dynamics of Foreign-Policy Decisionmaking in China*.

35. Swaine, *Role of the Chinese Military in National Security Policymaking*.

36. Hamrin and Zhao, *Decision-Making in Deng's China*.

37. Kenneth Lieberthal, *Governing China: From Revolution through Reform* (New York: Norton, 1995).

38. Thomas J. Christensen, "Chinese Realpolitik"; see also his *Useful Adversaries: Grand Strategy, Domestic Mobilization, and Sino-American Conflict, 1947–1958* (Princeton, N.J.: Princeton University Press, 1996).

39. Nathan and Ross, *The Great Wall and the Empty Fortress*.

40. Johnston, "Learning versus Adaptation."

41. Allen S. Whiting, "Chinese Nationalism and Foreign Policy after Deng," *China Quarterly*, No. 142 (June 1995), pp. 295–316.

42. See, for example, William C. Kirby, "Traditions of Centrality, Authority, and Management in Modern China's Foreign Relations," in Thomas Robinson and David Shambaugh, eds., *Chinese Foreign Policy: Theory and Practice* (London: Oxford University Press, 1997), pp. 13–29; see also David Shambaugh, *Beautiful Imperialist: China Perceives America, 1972–1990* (Princeton, N.J.: Princeton University Press, 1991).

43. Samuel S. Kim, ed., *China and the World: Chinese Foreign Policy in the Post-Mao Era* (Boulder, Colo.: Westview, 1984).

44. Robinson and Shambaugh, *Chinese Foreign Policy.*

45. Nathan and Ross, *The Great Wall and the Empty Fortress.*

46. Lewis et al., "Beijing's Defense Establishment"; John W. Lewis and Xue Litai, *China's Strategic Seapower: The Politics of Force Modernization in the Nuclear Age* (Stanford, Calif.: Stanford University Press, 1994).

47. Evan Feigenbaum, "Soldiers, Weapons and Chinese Development Strategy: The Mao Era Military in China's Economic and Institutional Debate," *China Quarterly*, No. 158 (June 1999), pp. 285–313.

48. Harold K. Jacobson and Michel Oksenberg, *China's Participation in the IMF, the World Bank, and GATT.*

49. Johnston, "Learning versus Adaptation."

50. Robert D. Putnam, "Diplomacy and Domestic Politics: The Logic of Two-Level Games," in Peter B. Evans, Harold K. Jacobson, and Robert D. Putnam, eds., *Double-Edged Diplomacy* (Berkeley, Calif.: University of California Press, 1993), pp. 431-33.

51. Christensen, "Chinese Realpolitik."

52. Peter Bottelier, "Dynamics of Economic Reform and Institutional Development," draft paper, June 1999, p. 5.

CHAPTER 2

1. Yan Huai, "Zhongguo Dalu Zhengzhi Tizhi Qianlun" (Understanding the Political System of Contemporary China), *Papers of the Center for Modern China*, No. 10 (August 1991), p. 2.

2. Ibid.

3. Ibid., p. 6.

4. In the Chinese political system there is a very strict definition of the term *zhongyang lingdao,* the central leadership, more often known in the Chinese media as *dang he guojia lingdaoren,* the party and state leaders. Officially the term refers to members of the CCP Politburo and Secretariat, the secretary of the CCP Central Discipline Inspection Committee, the president and vice president of the state, the premier and vice premiers of the State Council, the state councilors, the chairman and vice chairmen of the National People's Congress (NPC) Standing Committee, the chairman and vice chairmen of the National People's Political Consultative Conference, the president of the Supreme People's Court, the procurator general of the Supreme People's Procurate, and chairman and vice chairmen of the Party Central Military Commission. Yan Huai, "Zhongguo Dalu Zhengzhi Tizhi Qianlun," pp. 15-16.

5. The individuals referred to here are professionals below the ministerial rank.

6. On May 31, 1989, on the eve of the June 4 crackdown, Deng Xiaoping, in talks with CCP Politburo Standing Committee members Li Peng and Yao Yilin, said that the leadership nucleus (*lingdao hexin*) of the CCP's first generation was Mao Zedong, that of the second generation was Deng Xiaoping, and that of the third would be Jiang Zemin. Although the speech was meant to admonish Li and Yao to submit to the leadership of the newly nominated Jiang Zemin, it reveals that in the Chinese political system the ultimate power rests in the hands of a single paramount political leader. *Zhonggong Nianbao 1990* (CCP Yearbook 1990) (Taipei: Institute for the Study of Chinese Communist Problems, 1990).

7. Yan Huai, "Zhongguo Dalu Zhengzhi Tizhi Qianlun," pp. 20-21.

8. Ibid.

9. Personal communications with a senior Chinese MFA official, August 14, 1998, Washington, D.C.

10. At the Seventh Party Congress the following five people were elected secretaries of the Party Secretariat: Mao Zedong, Zhu De, Liu Shaoqi, Zhou Enlai, and

Ren Bishi, who was later replaced by Chen Yun when the former fell seriously ill. The five were later known as the Five Big Secretaries (*wu da shuji*) of the party.

11. Zheng Qian, Pang Song, Han Gang, and Zhang Zhanbin, *Dangdai Zhongguo Zhengzhi Tizhi Fazhan Gaiyao* (An Outline of the Evolution of the Contemporary Chinese Political System) (Beijing: Zhonggong Dangshi Ziliao Chubanshe, 1988), p. 89.

12. Jiang Weiwen, "Zhonggong Gaoceng Jigou Gaige Fangan Da Pilu: Zhonggong Gaoceng Renshi Da Tiaozheng" (A Big Exposé of the Reform Plan for the High-Level CCP Institutions: A Big Reshuffle of the High-ranking CCP Officials), *Guang Jiaojing* (Wide Angle), No. 184 (Jan. 16, 1988), p. 8.

13. See note 9.

14. See the chapter by H. Lyman Miller and Liu Xiaohong in this volume.

15. Zheng et al., *Dangdai Zhongguo Zhengzhi Tizhi Fazhan Gaiyao*, p. 91.

16. Jiang, "Zhonggong Gaoceng Jigou Gaige Fangan Da Pilu," pp. 6–7. The second category includes such Central Committee institutions as the Central General Affairs Office, the Central Organization Department, the Central United Front Work Department, and the Central International Liaison Department. They are responsible for handling the day-to-day work of the CCP under the leadership of the Politburo and its Standing Committee. The third category includes the party newspaper *Renmin Ribao* (People's Daily), the Central Party School, and the Party History Research Office.

17. Si Maqian, "Zhonggong Waishi Xiaozu Quanmian Gaizu: Li Peng Kaishi Zhangguan Zhongguo Waijiao" (A Comprehensive Reorganization of the CCP Foreign Affairs LSG: Li Peng Begins to Control Chinese Diplomacy), *Guang Jiaojing* (Wide Angle), No. 184 (Jan. 16, 1988), p. 11.

18. As in other cases in the Chinese power structure, the Central Foreign Affairs LSG and the SCFAO were one institution, with one team of staffers but with two nameplates (*yiban renma, liangkuai paizi*).

19. Personal communications with an MFA official, Nov. 11, 1997.

20. See the chapter by Miller and Liu.

21. Si, "Zhonggong Waishi Xiaozu Quanmian Gaizu," p. 7.

22. Personal communication with a former leading member of the CCP Central External Propaganda Small Group, March 16, 1998. The group's Chinese name remains the Central External Propaganda Small Group, according to the Xinhua Database.

23. *Guanyu Guowuyuan Jigou Shezhi de Tongzhi* (Circular on the Structuring of State Council Organs), Guofa (1993) No. 25 (April 19, 1993), in Secretariat of the State Council General Office and Comprehensive Department of the Central Committee Staffing Committee Office, *Zhongyang Zhengfu Zuzhi Jigou* (Central Government Organs) (Beijing: Zhongguo Fazhan Chubanshe [China Development Publishing House] 1995), pp. 15–18.

24. Xinhua database (http://info.xinhua.org).

25. For Zhao's State Council appointment, see Xinhua report, April 13, 1998. Official reports on the National External Propaganda Conference confirmed that Zhao

was concurrently the director of the Party International Communication Office. *Renmin Ribao,* Feb. 27, 1999.

26. Huang Wenfang, "Zhudao Duitai Gongzuo, Yisheng Zhongshi Liangan Tongyi" (Leading the Taiwanese Work, Attaching Great Importance to Cross-Strait Unification throughout His Life), *Ming Pao,* Sept. 15, 1998.

27. *Guanyu Guowuyuan Jigou Shezhi de Tongzhi.*

28. *Lianhe Bao* (Taiwan), April 22, 1998.

29. Deng Xiaoping at the time reportedly said that the post of CMC secretary general was optional (*ke she ke bu she*).

30. Yan Kong, "China's Arms Trade Bureaucracy," *Jane's Intelligence Review,* February 1994, p. 80.

31. Government restructuring Web site www.peoplesdaily.com.cn/gwy/a1070.htm.

32. COSTIND was created on May 10, 1982, by merging the Defense Science and Technology Commission, the National Defense Industry Office, and the CMC's Science, Technology, and Equipment Commission. Representing the interests of the defense industry, until 1998 COSTIND was under the dual leadership of the CMC and the State Council. Yan, "China's Arms Trade Bureaucracy."

33. Contrary to some Western literature on the subject, such as Nicholas Eftimiades's *Chinese Intelligence Operations* (Annapolis: Naval Institute Press, 1994), the Chinese intelligence operations are quite small when compared to those of the U.S. Central Intelligence Agency and the Russian KGB, both in scale and resources. This is partly because the top leadership has always put a greater premium on the strategic intent of its adversaries than on their technical capabilities. For instance, with few exceptions (one of them being Hong Kong) Chinese diplomatic missions abroad are forbidden to engage in espionage operations according to the CCP Central Committee regulations. Xu Jiatun, *Xu Jiatun Xianggang Huiyilu* (Xu Jiatun Hongkong Memoirs), Vol. 1 (Hong Kong: Lianhe Bao, 1993), p. 52. The original decision was to impose a blanket ban on all intelligence operations. However, after a personal appeal from Shen Jian, then ambassador to India, who wrote directly to the then-party General Secretary Hu Yaobang asking to make a distinction between espionage and general research, the scale of the ban was narrowed to espionage-related activities. Xiong Zhen (Madam Shen Jian), *Yidui Waijiaoguan Fufu de Zuji* (The Footprints of a Diplomat Couple) (Nanjing: Jiangsu Renmin Chubanshe, 1995), pp. 195–96. From 1978 to 1998 the intelligence community played a very limited role in the making of foreign policy decisions besides being an information provider. However, this description excludes areas that are traditionally not regarded as foreign affairs issues, such as Taiwan. Further, the entry of Xu Yongyue, minister of state security, into the Foreign Affairs LSG in 1998 indicated that the central leadership saw a greater role for the intelligence community in the future.

34. Although Beijing and the Vatican have been conducting secret talks on the normalization of relations, there has been no real incentive for Beijing to compromise. Thus far Beijing has been insisting on a normalization based on its own terms: the Vatican must sever official ties with Taiwan (that is easy) and recognize the official independent church in China (that is difficult).

35. For details of central document types and their respective functions, see Yan Huai, "Zhongguo Mimi Wenjian Gaiyao" (A Survey of China's Secret Documents), *Papers of the Center for Modern China,* Vol. 4, No. 22 (Dec. 1993), pp. 3–9.

36. For examples of and details on the Chinese arms sales and control process, see Lu Ning, *Dynamics.*

37. Yan, "China's Arms Trade Bureaucracy," p. 80.

38. *China Government Organization* (Beijing: Zhongguo Renshi Chubanshe, 1991), p. 328.

39. Yan Huai, "Zhongguo Mimi Wenjian Gaiyao" (Notes on China's Confidential Documents), *Papers of the Center for Modern China,* Vol. 4, No. 12, 1993, pp. 12–13.

40. This principle, first established by Mao during the civil war years and known as "the party commands the gun," has been widely misunderstood. As during the war period, the communist forces consisted of only two basic institutions, the Communist Party and the army. What this really meant was civilian control of the military. However, once the communists came to power a government was set up. It is critically important to understand that because at the top level senior leaders concurrently hold both government and party posts, the essence of the principle—civilian control of the military—remains unchanged.

41. *Ming Pao,* Dec. 2, 1998.

42. See www.peopledaily.com.cn/gwy/a1070.htm.

43. As in the case of the SCFAO, the Foreign Affairs Bureau of the PLA General Staff Department, also known as the Foreign Affairs Bureau of the Ministry of Defense (which in reality does not exist), serves as the executive body of the CMC Foreign Affairs Office in an arrangement that involves one office, one team of staff, and in this case three name plates.

44. Zheng et al., *Dangdai Zhongguo Zhengzhi Tizhi Fazhan Gaiyao,* p. 91.

45. Pang Song and Han Gang, "Dang he Guojia Lingdao Tizhi de Lishi Kaocha yu Gaige Zhanwang" (A Historical Review and Reform Outlook of the Party and State Leadership Systems), *Zhongguo Shehui Kexue,* No. 6 (Nov. 10, 1987), p. 5.

46. Ibid., p. 16.

47. Ibid., p. 20.

48. However, senior appointments (above the bureau level), though usually nominated by the chief executive, are subject to the approval of the CCP Central Organization Department.

49. The exact number of vice ministers, assistant ministers, deputy directors of departments, and deputy division chiefs varies by bureaucracy.

CHAPTER 3

1. Mao Tse-Tung, *Selected Works of Mao Tse-Tung,* Vol. 2 (Beijing: Foreign Languages Press, 1967), p. 224.

2. Michael D. Swaine, *The Role of the Chinese Military in National Security Policy-making* (Santa Monica, Calif.: RAND, 1996), and Jonathan D. Pollack, "Structure and Process in the Chinese Military System," in Kenneth G. Lieberthal and David

M. Lampton, eds., *Bureaucracy, Politics and Decision Making in Post-Mao China* (Berkeley, Calif.: University of California Press, 1992), pp. 151–80.

3. These were the topics discussed during the first, second, and third enlarged sessions of the CMC held in 1954, 1956, and 1957, respectively. See Li Houting and Tang Jinhe, *Zhongguo Wuzhuang Liliang Tongzhan, 1949–1989* (Chronology of China's Armed Power, 1949–1989) (Beijing: Renmin Chubanshe [People's Publishing House], 1990), pp. 404–7.

4. For a fascinating glimpse into the involvement of Ye and the CMC in China's internal upheavals during the mid-1970s, see Fan Shuo, *Ye Jianying Zai 1976* (Ye Jianying in 1976) (Beijing: Zhonggong Zhongyang Dangxiao Chubanshe [Chinese Communist Party Central Party School Publishing House], 1990).

5. Junshi Kexueyuan Junshi Lishi Yanjiubu (Academy of Military Sciences Military History Research Department), *Zhongguo Renmin Jiefangjun Liushinian Dashiji, 1927–1987* (Major Events in the 60 Years of the Chinese People's Liberation Army, 1927–1987) (Beijing: Junshi Kexue Chubanshe [Military Science Publishing House], 1988), pp. 672–85.

6. Deng Xiaoping, *Selected Works of Deng Xiaoping, 1975–1982* (Beijing: Foreign Languages Press, 1984), p. 386.

7. Interview with a Western military attaché, Beijing, May 1998.

8. Interviews, Beijing, Sept. 1987. Policy planners at the Academy of Military Sciences drew up this report. For details see British Broadcasting Corporation, *Summary of World Broadcasts, Far East* (SWB/FE/8318/BII/1), July 23, 1986.

9. *Wen Wei Po* (Hong Kong), March 28, 1988, p. 2.

10. The party CMC's dominant control over the PLA was codified in the Law on National Defense that was passed by the NPC in March 1997. Article 19 of the law states that the armed forces are "subject to the leadership of the Chinese Communist Party." *Law of the People's Republic of China on National Defense,* adopted at the Fifth Session of the Eighth National People's Congress, March 14, 1997.

11. On Jiang Zemin's ties with the PLA see David Shambaugh, "China's Commander-in-Chief: Jiang Zemin and the PLA," in C. Dennison Lane, Mark Weisenbloom, and Dimon Liu, eds., *Chinese Military Modernization* (London: Kegan Paul, 1996), pp. 209–45, and Tai Ming Cheung, "Jiang Zemin at the Helm: His Quest for Power and Paramount Status," unpublished conference paper, September 1997.

12. Interview, Beijing, April 1997.

13. Jiang, for example, no longer attends the weekly CMC work conferences. Interview, Beijing, July 1997.

14. See Kuan Chachia, "Beijing Holds Enlarged Meeting of Central Military Commission: Zhang Wannian Pursues New Ideas on Developing Weapons," *Kuang Chiao Ching* (Wide Angle), Dec. 16, 1997, in *Foreign Broadcast Information Service* (FBIS), Internet version.

15. For analysis of the recent generations of Chinese military leaders see David Shambaugh, "China's Post-Deng Military Leadership," in James R. Lilley and David Shambaugh, eds., *China's Military Faces the Future* (Washington, D.C.: AEI and Sharpe,

1999), pp. 3–35, and Michael Swaine, *The Military and Political Succession in China* (Santa Monica, Calif.: RAND, 1993).

16. Zhang had been considered a strong candidate to replace Liu, but he appears to have been edged out in intensive last-minute political maneuverings by Wei Jianxing. Interviews, Sept. 1997.

17. Interviews, Beijing, Aug. 1991. See Tai Ming Cheung, "Waiting at the Top," *Far Eastern Economic Review,* Sept. 12, 1991, p. 18.

18. Wang was reported to have retired from his military positions at the beginning of 1999.

19. Jia had previously served in the artillery. Interview, Beijing, Jan. 1999.

20. Interview, Beijing, April 1997. See also "Central Military Commission Reportedly Reshuffled," *Ming Pao,* Nov. 9, 1996, p. A11.

21. Swaine, *Military and Political Succession in China,* p. 52.

22. Tang Yan, "Trends and Theories in the System of Army Organization," in Zongcanmoubu Junshi Xunbubian (General Staff Department Training Department), *Guofang Xiandaihua Fazhan Zhanlue Yanjiu* (Research in the Development Strategy of National Defense Modernization) (Beijing: Junshi Fanwen Chubanshe [Military Literature Publishing House], 1987), p. 261.

23. Zhao Qi, "A Major Indication of a Perfect State System: A Visit to Yang Dezhi and Other NPC Deputies on the Occasion of the Birth of the State Central Military Commission," *Liaowang* (Outlook), July 20, 1983, p. 11.

24. Interviews, Beijing, Jan. 1999.

25. Interviews, Beijing, Dec. 1996. See also Serold Hawaii, Inc., *Directory of People's Republic of China Military Personalities, 1998* (Honolulu: Serold Hawaii, Aug. 1998), p. 4.

26. The administrative functions of the CMC general office are similar to those of the general offices of the State Council and the Party Central Committee. The State Council General Office is responsible for the following functions: organizing the meetings of the State Council; handling the implementation of resolutions made at these meetings; drafting notices or announcements for the State Council; reporting to the head of the State Council for decisions on research projects and requests from provincial governments and ministries within the State Council; coordinating the work of related ministries and reporting to the head of the State Council on any disputes, along with opinions on possible solutions; assisting in the handling of events and important matters that require the direct involvement of the State Council; handling all incoming correspondence, receiving groups for visits, and making timely reports to the head of the State Council on suggestions arising from these sources; and investigating, researching, inspecting, and supervising the enforcement of the State Council's decisions and directives. Hong Kong Commercial Daily, *Directory of China's Government Structure* (Hong Kong: Hong Kong Commercial Daily Press, 1997), pp. 10–11.

27. "Xiao Xiangrong," in *Qinghuo Liaoyuan Bianjibu* (Single Spark Editorial Committee), *Jiefangjun Jianglingzhuang Deqiji* (Biographies of Liberation Army Generals), Vol. 7 (Beijing: Jiefangjun Chubanshe [Liberation Army Publishing

House], 1988), p. 254. Xiao was the first CMC General Office director in the early 1950s.

28. These include the *chengyuejian* (reading materials for superiors), *zhuangyuejian* (commentaries on reading materials), and *junban jianbao* (CMC bulletin). Ibid.

29. Serold Hawaii, Inc., *Directory of People's Republic of China Military Personalities, 1999* (Honolulu: Serold Hawaii, 1999), p. ii.

30. Interviews, Beijing, 1987. See also Swaine, *Military and Political Succession in China*, p. 68.

31. For a broad analysis of the secretarial system, see "A Brief History of the Work of Secretaries in the Chinese Communist Party (1921–1949)," *Chinese Law and Government*, Vol. 30, No. 3 (May–June 1997), and Wei Li, *The Chinese Staff System: A Mechanism for Bureaucratic Control and Integration* (Berkeley, Calif.: Institute for East Asian Studies, 1994). See also "'Deng Office' Disbanded, Office Site Handed Over," *Ming Pao*, July 25, 1997, p. A13, in FBIS, Internet version. This report said that Deng's office had more than thirty on staff, including medical workers.

32. Interview, Beijing, Jan. 1997.

33. See Junshi Kexueyuan Junshi Lishi Yanjiubu, *Zhongguo Renmin Jiefangjun Liushinian Dashiji*, pp. 658, 696, and 722.

34. Jiang Siyi, chief ed., *Zhongguo Renmin Jiefangjun Dashidian* (Chinese People's Liberation Army Encyclopedia) (Tianjin: Tianjin Renmin Chubanshe [Tianjin People's Publishing House], 1992), p. 1871.

35. The last reported CMC plenary session was held in December 1977. Junshi Kexueyuan Junshi Lishi Yanjiubu, *Zhongguo Renmin Jiefangjun Liushinian Dashiji*, p. 676.

36. See "'Inside Story' on Drafting Ninth Five Year Plan Outline," *Xinhua News Agency*, March 9, 1996, in FBIS, Internet version.

37. "Ye Jianying: A Great and Brilliant Life," *Xinhua*, Oct. 29, 1986, in British Broadcasting Corporation, *Summary of World Broadcasts* (FE/8405/B11/10), Nov. 1, 1986.

38. Wang Gangyi, "Yang Shangkun Discusses PLA Modernization Program," *China Daily*, March 30, 1988, p. 1.

39. "Yang Shangkun at PLA Financial Discipline Meeting," *Xinhua Domestic Service*, March 11, 1986, in FBIS, March 13, 1986, K23.

40. See Bates Gill's contribution to this volume.

41. Interviews, Beijing, March and Sept. 1994.

42. Interview, Beijing, May 1998.

43. Jiang Zemin, "Continue to Promote the Reunification of the Motherland," *Xinhua News Service*, January 30, 1995.

44. *Jiefangjun Bao* (Liberation Army Daily), Dec. 2, 1994, p. 3.

45. See John W. Lewis, Hua Di, and Xue Litai, "Beijing's Defense Establishment: Solving the Arms Export Enigma," *International Security*, Vol. 15, No. 4 (Spring 1991), pp. 87–109.

46. Arms export regulations published in October 1997 point out that a State Military Articles Trade Bureau is the executive organ of the State Military Articles Trade

Management Committee set up by the State Council and the CMC. "Regulations of the People's Republic of China on Managing Exports of Military Articles," *Xinhua Domestic Service,* October 30, 1997, in FBIS Internet version.

47. Interview with a CMC arms trade bureau official, Moscow, June 1993.

48. Information Office of the State Council, *White Paper on China's National Defense,* July 27, 1998.

49. Interview with a financial official, Beijing, October 1998. For some Chinese military views on the importance of financial security, see Tan Jian, "Who Will Be Responsible for Defending State Economic Security?" *Jiefangjun Bao,* April 30, 1998, p. 5, in FBIS Internet Edition.

50. Interview, Beijing, Oct. 1998.

51. See Serold Hawaii, *Directory of People's Republic of China Military Personalities, 1998,* for a breakdown of the various departments and bureaus.

52. The Liaison Department is said to have been instrumental in persuading Tonga to switch diplomatic ties from Taipei to Beijing in November 1998. Interview, Beijing, Jan. 1999.

53. Interview with Carrie executive, Beijing, September 1995. See also Min Chen, "Market Competition and the Management Systems of PLA Companies," in Jorn Brommelhorster and John Frankenstein, eds., *Mixed Motives, Uncertain Outcomes: Defense Conversion in China* (Boulder, Colo.: Lynne Rienner, 1997), p. 220.

54. For an assessment of COSTIND's general role see Shirley Kan, *Commission of Science, Technology and Industry for National Defense* (Washington, D.C.: Congressional Research Service, Nov. 1996).

55. "Industry Embraces Market Forces," *Jane's Defense Weekly,* Dec. 16, 1998, p. 28.

56. On some of the writings of these researchers see Michael Pillsbury, ed., *Chinese Views of Future War* (Washington D.C.: National Defense University, 1997).

57. See Tai Ming Cheung, "Reforming the Dragon's Tail: Chinese Military Logistics in the Era of High-Technology Warfare and Market Economics," in Lilley and Shambaugh, eds., *China's Military Faces the Future,* pp. 228–46.

58. See Ellis Joffe, "Party-Army Relations in China: Retrospect and Prospect," *China Quarterly,* June 1996, pp. 299–314.

59. On the role of the party Secretariat, see Lu Ning, *The Dynamics of Foreign-Policy Decisionmaking in China* (Boulder, Colo.: Westview, 1997), pp. 10–11.

60. See Carol Lee Hamrin, "The Party Leadership System," in Kenneth G. Lieberthal and David M. Lampton, eds., *Bureaucracy, Politics, and Decision Making in Post-Mao China* (Berkeley, Calif.: University of California Press, 1992), pp. 95–124.

61. This foreign affairs bureau is, in reality, part of the GSD.

62. Interview with a Western diplomat, Hong Kong, Feb. 1998.

63. *Wen Wei Pao* (Hong Kong), May 2, 1994.

64. Zhu Rongji, "Unify Thinking, Strengthen Leadership and Swiftly and Sternly Crack Down on the Criminal Activities of Smuggling," *Qiushi* (Seek Truth from Facts), Sept. 1, 1998.

65. Interviews, Beijing, Jan. 1999.

66. Interview with military business executive, Beijing, Oct. 1998.

67. Interviews with PLA business executives, Beijing, Dec. 1999. See also Tai Ming Cheung's forthcoming book, *The Rise and Fall of China's Entrepreneurial Army.*

68. *Law of the People's Republic of China on National Defense.*

69. *Jiefangjun Bao,* March 17, 1994.

CHAPTER 4

Research for this chapter was supported by a grant from the Committee on Research and Conference Grants and a Faculty Reserve Fund grant from the University of Hong Kong. Special thanks for useful comments on earlier drafts of this chapter are due to Professor David M. Lampton, two anonymous reviewers, and participants in the two conferences organized for this project.

1. Exclusive of Taiwan, China has twenty-two provinces, four centrally administered cities, and five autonomous regions, all enjoying provincial-level status. For the sake of simplicity, the thirty-one units are referred to as provinces in this chapter. *Localities* refers to administrative units at the subprovincial level, such as municipalities or counties. *Regions* refers to groupings of several provinces sharing similar geographical attributes. *The Center (zhongyang)* refers to the "State Council and its commissions, ministries, and leadership small groups in Beijing, as well as the Party Politburo, Secretariat, and the organs of the Central Committee." This is used interchangeably with *the central government* for the sake of simplicity. See Kenneth Lieberthal and Michel Oksenberg, *Policy Making in China: Leaders, Structures, and Processes* (Princeton, N.J.: Princeton University Press, 1988), p. 138. Similarly, the term *province* or *provincial government* is used to refer to provincial party and state authorities. Hong Kong and Macao are special administrative regions directly under the central government and both enjoy a high degree of autonomy under the arrangement of "one country, two systems."

2. See, for example, David S. G. Goodman and Gerald Segal, eds., *China Deconstructs: Politics, Trade and Regionalism* (London: Routledge, 1994); Gerald Segal, *China Changes Shape,* Adelphi Paper No. 287 (London: International Institute for Strategic Studies, 1994); Dali Yang, *Beyond Beijing: Liberalization and the Regions in China* (London: Routledge, 1997); Zheng Yong-nian, "Perforated Sovereignty: Provincial Dynamism and China's Foreign Trade," *Pacific Review,* Vol. 7, No. 3 (1994), pp. 309-21.

3. Data for this study come from both documentary sources and interviews. Documentary data include provincial and national publications, including yearbooks, statistical yearbooks, document compilations, government reports (*zhengbao*), and newspapers and journals; documents and publications on the Chinese economy and foreign policy; and foreign press or magazine coverage of the external activities of the provinces. We have interviewed officials in the foreign affairs systems of four provinces (Guangdong and Shanghai in September and October 1997 and Yunnan and Guangxi in October 1998), as well as Western diplomats in Hong Kong and Mainland China in 1997 and 1998. We have also spoken with Chinese scholars and officials who are knowledgeable about this topic on many other occasions.

4. A useful discussion of central-local tensions arising from foreign trade can be found in Li Jinming and Liu Dake, eds., *Zhongguo Gudai Haiwai Maoyishi* (A History of Ancient China's Overseas Trade) (Nanning: Guangxi Renmin Chubanshe [Guangxi People's Press], 1995). See also Wang Gungwu, "Early Ming Relations with Southeast Asia: A Background Essay" and Mark Mancall, "The Ch'ing Tribute System: An Interpretive Essay," in John K. Fairbank, ed., *The Chinese World Order: Traditional China's Foreign Relations* (Cambridge, Mass.: Harvard University Press, 1968).

5. See "New China's Foreign Policy," in *Zhou Enlai Waijiao Wenxuan* (Selected Works on Foreign Affairs by Zhou Enlai) (Beijing: Zhongyang Wenxian Chubanshe [Central Documents Press], 1990), pp. 1–7.

6. These offices were headed by senior cadres who reported directly to the leadership of the central government. A useful collection of documents on the communist leaders' management of foreign relations in this period is Shuguang Zhang and Jian Chen, eds., *Chinese Communist Foreign Policy and the Cold War in Asia: New Documentary Evidence, 1944–1950* (Chicago: Imprint, 1996).

7. For a study of the role of provincial leaders in China's reform and open-door policy see Peter T. Y. Cheung, Jae Ho Chung, and Zhimin Lin, eds., *Provincial Strategies of Economic Reform in Post-Mao China: Leadership, Politics and Implementation* (Armonk, N.Y.: Sharpe, 1998).

8. The number of provinces has ranged from fifty-two in 1950–51 to twenty-eight in 1955–56 and 1958–66 (this figure and the following ones exclude Taiwan). For details see Zhang Wenfan, ed., *Zhongguo Shengzhi* (China's Provincial System) (Beijing: Zhongguo Dabaike Quanshu Chubanshe [China Encyclopedia Press], 1995), pp. 53–54 and 71–73.

9. The data in this paragraph are from *Zhongguo Tongji Nianjian 1998* (China Statistical Yearbook 1998) (Beijing: Zhongguo Tongji Chubanshe [China Statistics Press], 1998), and Zhou Shunwu, *China Provincial Geography* (Beijing: Foreign Languages Press, 1992).

10. Each of the five most populous provinces, namely Henan, Shandong, Sichuan, Jiangsu, and Guangdong, has a population much larger than that of most countries (between seventy and ninety-two million).

11. Hu Zhao-liang, Wang En-chong, and Han Mao-li, *Zhongguo Jingji Quyu Chayi ji qi Duice* (China's Regional Economic Disparities and Remedial Strategies) (Beijing: Qinghua Daxue Chubanshe [Qinghua University Press], 1997), pp. 46–47; *China Statistical Yearbook 1998,* passim.

12. The coastal provinces include Beijing, Fujian, Hebei, Jiangsu, Shandong, Shanghai, Tianjin, and Zhejiang. The coastal/border provinces include Guangdong, Guangxi, Hainan, and Liaoning. The inland border provinces include Gansu, Heilongjiang, Inner Mongolia, Jilin, Tibet, Xinjiang, and Yunnan. The inland provinces include Anhui, Chongqing, Guizhou, Henan, Hubei, Hunan, Jiangxi, Ningxia, Qinghai, Shaanxi, Shanxi, and Sichuan.

13. See, for example, the chapters by Kevin P. Lanne and Lijian Hong in Cheung, Chung and Lin, eds., *Provincial Strategies of Economic Reform,* pp. 212–50 and 372–411, respectively.

14. The following discussion draws from Yang, *Beyond Beijing,* pp. 43–61.

15. Li Dong-hui, "Ideas on the Problem of Closing the Gap between the East and the West," *Strategy and Management,* No. 4 (1995), pp. 42–44; see also Yang, *Beyond Beijing,* pp. 92–93.

16. The following information draws from *Zhongguo Gaige yu Fazhan Baogao Zhuanjiazu* (China's Reform and Development Report Expert Group), eds., *Zhongguo Gaige yu Fazhan Baogao, 1992–1993* (China's Reform and Development Report, 1992–1993) (Beijing: Zhongguo Caizheng Jingji Chubanshe (China's Finance and Economics Press, 1994), pp. 168–88.

17. Policy measures favoring the inland provinces included putting more emphasis on investment in basic construction and energy exploration, encouraging the relocation of manufacturing industries, adjusting the prices of raw materials, gradually increasing fiscal assistance, organizing more antipoverty projects, and promoting better economic cooperation between the southeastern coastal regions and the central and western regions.

18. This speech, "Jiachang Difang Waishi Gongzuo" (Strengthen Local Foreign Affairs Work), appears in Li Xiannian, *Li Xiannian Wenxuan, 1935–1988* (Selected Essays of Li Xiannian, 1935–1988) (Beijing: Renmin Chubanshe [People's Press], 1989), pp. 425–30.

19. "Regulation on the Scope of Duties of the Foreign Affairs Office of the People's Government in the Provinces, Municipalities, and Autonomous Regions," State Council Document No. 157 (1981), in Labor and Personnel Division of the Ministry of Geology and Mineral Resources, ed., *Waishi Wenjian Huibian, 1978–1987* (A Collection of Foreign Affairs Documents, 1978–1987), internal publication, May 1987, pp. 53–55.

20. This section is based on State Council Document No. 157 (1981) and another recent document on the Guangdong provincial FAO, *Guangdong Zhengbao* (Guangdong Government Report), No. 25 (1995), pp. 1247–49. We have used the sections on external affairs in the *Dangdai Zhongguo* (Contemporary China) series, provincial yearbooks, and interviews with officials from the FAOs.

21. Interview with an official in Shanghai, Oct. 30, 1997.

22. For annual reviews of the external affairs of the Chinese Communist Party, see *Zhongguo Gongchandang Duiwai Gongzuo Gaikuang* (A General Survey of the External Work of the Chinese Communist Party) (Beijing: Dangdai Shijie Chubanshe [Contemporary World Press], 1992–97).

23. *Heilongjiang Duiwaijingjimaoyi Nianjian 1996/97* (Yearbook of Heilongjiang's Foreign Economic Relations and Trade) (Harbin: Heilongjiang Renmin Chubanshe [Heilongjiang People's Press], 1997), p. 1.

24. See, for example, *Hebei Nianjian 1997* (Hebei Yearbook 1997) (Shijiazhuang: Hebei Nianjianshe [Hebei Yearbook Press], 1997), p. 111.

25. *Sichuan Nianjian 1997* (Sichuan Yearbook 1997) (Chengdu: Sichuan Nianjianshe [Sichuan Yearbook Press], 1997), p. 53.

26. *Henan Zhengbao* (Henan Government Report), No. 6 (1995), pp. 12–15.

27. *Zhejiang Nianjian 1997* (Zhejiang Yearbook 1997) (Hangzhou: Zhejiang Renmin Chubanshe [Zhejiang People's Press], 1997), p. 237.

28. *Hubei Nianjian 1997* (Hubei Yearbook 1997) (Wuhan: Hubei Renmin Chubanshe [Hubei People's Press], 1997), p. 102; *Guizhou Nianjian 1997* (Guizhou Yearbook 1997) (Guiyang: Guizhou Renmin Chubanshe [Guizhou People's Press], 1997), p. 157.

29. These are 1992 figures. See *Zhejiang Waishizhi* (History of Zhejiang's External Affairs) (Beijing: Zhonghua Shuju [China Bookstore], 1996), p. 266.

30. Ibid., p. 267.

31. Interview with officials in Nanning, Oct. 7, 1998.

32. The data on Guangdong's provincial organs in this chapter are drawn from *Guangdong Zhengbao* (Guangdong Government Report), 1995, various issues.

33. *Guizhou Nianjian 1996* (Guizhou Yearbook 1996) (Guiyang: Guizhou Renmin Chubanshe, 1996), p. 164.

34. *Hebei Nianjian 1997* (Shijiazhuang: Hebei Nianjianshe, 1997), pp. 108–9.

35. *Henan Zhengbao*, No. 8 (1995), pp. 24–25.

36. *Shandong Nianjian 1998* (Shandong Yearbook 1998) (Jinan: Shandong Nianjianshe [Shandong Yearbook Press], 1998), p. 59.

37. *Guizhou Nianjian 1998* (Guizhou Yearbook 1998) (Guiyang: Guizhou Renmin Chubanshe, 1998), pp. 85–86.

38. See, for example, *Heilongjiang Zhengbao* (Heilongjiang Government Report), No. 19 (1998), pp. 31–34; *Henan Zhengbao*, No. 8 (1995), pp. 24–25.

39. The 1978 and 1985 figures on Jiangsu are from *Jiangsu Shengzhi (Caizhengjuan,* Vol. I) (History of Jiangsu Province, Volume I: Public Finance) (Nanjing: Jiangsu Renmin Chubanshe [Jiangsu People's Press], 1996), pp. 497–98. The 1996 figures in the paragraph are from Caizhengbu Difangshi (Local Finance Division, Ministry of Finance), ed., *Difang Caizheng Tongji Ziliao 1996* (Local Fiscal Statistical Data 1996) (Beijing: Zhongguo Caizheng Jingji Chubanshe [China Finance and Economics Press], 1998), pp. 4 and 341.

40. *Guangxi Nianjian 1997* (Guangxi Yearbook 1997) (Nanning: Guangxi Nianjianshe [Guangxi Yearbook Press], 1997), p. 137.

41. *Liaoning Nianjian 1996* (Liaoning Yearbook 1996) (Beijing: Zhongguo Tongji Chubanshe, 1996), p. 68.

42. They include Australia, Austria, Belgium, Brazil, Canada, Chile, Cuba, the Czech Republic, Denmark, Finland, France, Germany, India, Iran, Israel, Italy, Japan, South Korea, Mexico, the Netherlands, New Zealand, Norway, Poland, Russia, Singapore, Switzerland, Thailand, Turkey, the United Kingdom, and the United States.

43. They include Australia, Canada, France, Germany, Japan, Malaysia, the Philippines, Poland, Thailand, the United Kingdom, the United States, and Vietnam.

44. Consular Department of the Ministry of Foreign Affairs, *Consular Officers List* (Beijing: Consular Department of the Ministry of Foreign Affairs of the People's Republic of China, July 1997) and *Zhongguo Waijiao 1996* (China's Diplomatic Relations 1996) (Beijing: Shijie Zhishi Chubanshe [World Knowledge Press], 1996).

45. *Xinjiang Nianjian 1996* (Xinjiang Yearbook 1996) (Urumqi: Xinjiang Renmin Chubanshe [Xinjiang People's Press], 1996), p. 109, and *Gansu Nianjian 1997* (Gansu Yearbook 1997) (Beijing: Zhongguo Tongji Chubanshe, 1997), p. 59.

46. *Zhongguo Waijiao Gailan 1992* (A Survey of China's Diplomatic Relations 1992), pp. 258–59.

47. Ibid., pp. 315–18.

48. See *Zhongguo Waijiao 1996* (China's Diplomatic Relations 1996) (Beijing: Shijie Zhishi Chubanshe [World Knowledge Press], 1996), pp. 255–59, and *Zhongguo Waijiao 1997* (China's Diplomatic Relations 1997) (Beijing: Shijie Zhishi Chubanshe, 1997), pp. 314–18.

49. See the following reports in the *South China Morning Post:* "France's Project Loss May Be Britain's Gain" (Jan. 5, 1993), "Britain Keen on Subway Finance Job" (Jan. 7, 1993), and "Consulate Doors Shut" (Jan. 22, 1993).

50. *Xinjiang Nianjian 1987* (Urumqi: Xinjiang Renmin Chubanshe, 1987), p. 201; *Yunnan Nianjian 1996* (Yunnan Yearbook 1996) (Kunming: Yunnan Nianjian Zazhishe [Yunnan Yearbook Press], 1996), p. 77; *Liaoning Nianjian 1996* (Beijing: Zhongguo Tongji Chubanshe, 1996), p. 69; *Guangxi Nianjian 1997* (Nanning: Guangxi Nianjianshe, 1996), p. 137. Interviews with Yunnan and Guangxi officials, October–November 1998.

51. For information on cross-boundary issues between Hong Kong and Guangdong please refer to a training booklet prepared by Peter T. Y. Cheung for the Civil Service Training and Development Institute, Hong Kong SAR Government, *Yueguang Chuanjichu* (The Guangdong–Hong Kong Interface), March 1998.

52. *Hainan Nianjian 1997* (Hainan Yearbook 1997), Vol. 2 (Haikou: Hainan Nianjianshe [Hainan Yearbook Press], 1997), pp. 24–25.

53. Sister relations refer to sister arrangements with overseas counties, cities, and provinces. The data for sister city relations are 1996 data, with the exceptions of those for Shanghai, Guangxi, and Jiangxi, where 1995 data are used. The data on sister relations come from provincial yearbooks, except for those for Guangdong and Yunnan. The data for Yunnan come from *A New Survey of Yunnan Province* (Kunming: Yunnan Renmin Chubanshe, 1996), p. 168. The figure for Guangdong as of April 1997 was provided by its Foreign Affairs Office.

54. Approval of sister city arrangements requires authorization of the State Council and the People's Friendship Association in Beijing.

55. Liang Linguang, *Liang Linguang Huiyilu* (Liang Linguang's Memoir) (Beijing: Zhonggong Dangshi Chubanshe [Chinese Communist Party History Press], 1996), pp. 704–44. Liang was the governor of Guangdong from 1981 to 1985.

56. *Qingdao Waishizhi* (History of Qingdao's External Affairs) (Beijing: Xinhua Chubanshe [New China Press], 1995), p. 91.

57. *Tianjin Jingji Nianjian 1997* (Tianjin Economic Yearbook 1997) (Tianjin: Tianjin Renmin Chubanshe [Tianjin People's Press], 1997), p. 345.

58. *Hainan Nianjian 1996* (Hainan Yearbook 1996) (Beijing: Xinhua Chubanshe, 1996), p. 139.

59. *Shandong Nianjian 1997* (Shandong Yearbook 1997) (Jinan: Shandong Nianjianshe, 1997), p. 96.

60. Interview with a Western diplomat stationed in Guangzhou, November 1997.

61. In 1995, for example, the Shanghai municipal government welcomed twenty-four heads of state, forty-five party leaders, thirty-five deputy prime ministers, and eighty-one ministers or vice ministers. *Shanghai Nianjian 1996* (Shanghai Yearbook 1996) (Shanghai: Shanghai Remin Chubanshe [Shanghai People's Press], 1996), p. 375.

62. *Jiangsu Nianjian 1996* (Jiangsu Yearbook 1996) (Nanjing: Nanjing Daxue Chubanshe [Nanjing University Press], 1996), pp. 174–75.

63. Interview with officials in Shanghai, October 30,1997.

64. Chen Pixian, *Lishi de Zhuanzhe zai Hubei (The Historical Turning Point Was in Hubei)* (Beijing: Zhongyang Wenxian Chubanshe, 1996), pp. 142–45. Chen was the party secretary of Hubei from 1978 to 1983. Hubei was the first province for which a sister relationship with an overseas counterpart—in this case the state of Ohio in the United States—was approved by the central government.

65. Interview in Guangzhou, Sept. 12, 1997.

66. *Yunnan Nianjian 1996* (Kunming: Yunnan Nianjian Zazhishe, 1996), p. 75.

67. *Guangxi Nianjian 1996* (Guangxi Yearbook 1996) (Nanning: Guangxi Nianjianshe, 1996), p. 168.

68. *Liaoning Nianjian 1996* (Liaoning Yearbook 1996) (Beijing: Zhongguo Tongji Chubanshe, 1996), p. 68.

69. See Feng Chongyi and David S. G. Goodman, "Hainan: Communal Politics and the Struggle for Identity," in David S. G. Goodman, ed., *China's Provinces in Reform* (London: Routledge, 1997), pp. 75–77.

70. See *Henan Nianjian 1987* (Henan Yearbook 1987) (Zhengzhou: Henan Nianjian Bianjibu [Henan Yearbook Editorial Committee], 1987), p. 209; *Guizhou Nianjian 1996* (Guizhou Yearbook 1996) (Guiyang: Guizhou Renmin Chubanshe, 1996), pp. 164–65; *Hubei Nianjian 1996* (Hubei Yearbook 1996) (Wuhan: Hubei Renmin Chubanshe, 1996), pp. 112 and 238–40.

71. Interview with a Yunnan official who formerly worked in the border region, Kunming, Oct. 7, 1998.

72. Even if the visitors from Hong Kong, Macao, and Taiwan are excluded, the pattern is the same. The unit in which the following data are given is the number of "person times." See *China Statistical Yearbook 1998,* p. 660.

73. *Jiangsu Nianjian 1996* (Nanjing: Nanjing Daxue Chubanshe, 1996), pp. 174–75.

74. This section draws from David S. G. Goodman, "How Open Is Chinese Society?" in David S. G. Goodman and Gerald Segal, eds., *China Rising: Nationalism and Interdependence* (London: Routledge, 1997), pp. 27–52 and especially pp. 43–44.

75. Ibid., p. 44.

76. *Yunnan Nianjian 1996* (Kunming: Yunnan Nianjian Zazhishe, 1996), p. 76. Beijing was originally the host, but it later dropped out of the event.

77. See, for example, Cheung, Chung, and Lin, eds., *Provincial Strategies of Economic Reform in Post-Mao China,* pp. 253–411.

78. Brantly Womack and Guangzhi Zhao, "The Many Worlds of China's Provinces: Foreign Trade and Diversification," in Goodman and Segal, *China Deconstructs,* pp. 131–76.

79. The data given are drawn from the *Almanac of China's Foreign Economic Relations and Trade 1997/1998* (Beijing: Zhongguo Jingji Chubanshe, 1997).

80. This comparison is drawn from a useful table identifying the major provincial export partners in 1990. See Womack and Zhao, "Many Worlds of China's Provinces," p. 165, Table 5.5. The 1996 data in this paragraph are from the source cited in note 79.

81. See Sung Yun-wing, *Hong Kong and South China: The Economic Synergy* (Hong Kong: City University of Hong Kong Press, 1999), especially pp. 1–30.

82. *Zhongguo Tongji Nianjian 1998,* pp. 642 and 644.

83. "Top Minds Have Helped Shanghai Back on Its Feet, Now It Is the SAR's Turn," *South China Morning Post,* Jan. 10, 1999, p. 9; *Shanghai Jingji Nianjian 1998* (Shanghai Economy Yearbook 1998) (Shanghai: Shanghai Jingji Nianjian Chubanshe [Shanghai Economy Yearbook Press], 1998), pp. 103–4.

84. Report by the China–Southeast Asia Commercial Committee, Dec. 1997. See also the official publication of the committee, *Dongnanya Jianbao* (Concise Report on Southeast Asia), No. 35 (Nov. 1997).

85. The following data are drawn from Jae Ho Chung, "Shandong: The Political Economy of Development and Inequality," in Goodman, *China's Provinces in Reform,* p. 138.

86. The number of trading firms includes those owned by both provincial and subprovincial units.

87. *Sichuan Nianjian 1996* (Sichuan Yearbook 1996) (Chengdu: Sichuan Nianjianshe, 1996), p. 212.

88. *Shanxi Zhengbao* (Shanxi Government Report), No. 5 (1997), p. 29.

89. See in particular Yang Jichang and Liu Hanyu, eds., *The Rising of Southwest China* (Nanning: Guangxi Jiaoyu Chubanshe [Guangxi Education Press], 1994). The following discussion draws from the report of the State Council study group of the region in that volume; see pp. 1–60.

90. For a detailed account of this issue see Yong-nian Zheng, "Institutional Change, Local Developmentalism, and Economic Growth: The Making of Semi-Federalism in Reform China," unpublished Ph.D. dissertation, Princeton University, 1995, pp. 215–72.

91. Ibid.

92. For a discussion of economic reform and development in the northeast in the 1980s, see Gaye Christofferson, "Economic Reforms in Northeast Asia: Domestic Determinants," *Asian Survey,* Vol. 28, No. 12 (Dec. 1988), pp. 1245–63, and "The Political Implications of Heilongjiang's Industrial Structure," paper presented at the third workshop China's Provinces in Reform, Kunming, Oct. 6–8, 1998.

93. *Heilongjiang Nianjian 1996* (Heilongjiang Yearbook 1996) (Harbin: Heilongjiang Renmin Chubanshe, 1996), pp. 113–15.

94. Chung, "Shandong," in Goodman, *China's Provinces in Reform,* pp. 135–36.

95. One discussion of the establishment of PRC–South Korean diplomatic relations from a Chinese perspective is Shi Yuanhua, "Jianlu Zhonghan Jianjiao de Lishibeijing" (A Brief Discussion of the Historical Background Leading to the Estab-

lishment of Sino–South Korean Diplomatic Relations), in *Waijiao Xuebao* (Journal of Foreign Affairs College), No. 1 (1995), pp. 30–33. For an account of the Shandong-Liaoning rivalry, see Zhang Yawen, "Zhonghan Jianjiao Miwenlu" (The Secrets in the Establishment of Sino–South Korea Diplomatic Relations), *Nanfang Zhoumo* (Southern Weekend), Oct. 27, 1995, p. 1.

96. Jae Ho Chung, "Shandong's Strategies of Reform in Foreign Economic Relations," in Cheung, Chung, and Lin, eds., *Provincial Strategies of Economic Reform in Post-Mao China,* pp. 281 and 284, Tables 5.10 and 5.13.

97. A good discussion is James Cotton, "China and Tumen River Cooperation: Jilin's Coastal Development Strategy," *Asian Survey,* Vol. 36, No. 11 (Nov. 1996), p. 1094.

98. This account of Jilin's involvement in the Tumen project is based on a collection of documents in *Tumenjiang Tonghaihangxing yu Duiwaikaifang Yanjiuwenji Shujiyi* (Studies on Tumen River's Entry into the Sea of Japan and Opening: Supplementary Vol. 1) (Changchun: Jilin Reminzhengfu Jingji Zishu Shehui Fazhan Yanjiu Zhongxin [Jilin People's Government Economic, Technological and Social Development Research Center], 1990).

99. Gerald Segal, "Deconstructing Foreign Relations," in Goodman and Segal, *China Deconstructs,* pp. 345–50.

CHAPTER 5

1. The biographic data on the Jiang leadership presented in this section have been derived from the two applicable editions of *Who's Who in China: Current Leaders* (Beijing: Foreign Languages Press, 1989 and 1994), supplemented by the biographic sketches disseminated by the *Xinhua* News Agency after the 1992 Fourteenth and 1997 Fifteenth CCP Congresses (*Xinhua,* Oct. 19, 1992, in Foreign Broadcast Information Service [FBIS], *China Report,* Oct. 19, 1992, pp. 13–27, and *Xinhua,* Sept. 19, 1997, via World News Connection) and the 1993 Eighth National People's Congress (*Xinhua,* March 27, 1993, in FBIS, *China Report,* March 29, 1993, pp. 15–16 and 30–40). A prescient analysis of the impact of generational change on Soviet domestic politics and foreign policy is Seweryn Bialer, *Stalin's Successors: Leadership, Stability, and Change in the Soviet Union* (New York: Cambridge University Press, 1980).

2. The locus classicus of this distinction in agenda and the implications it carries for policy and personnel in communist regimes is the work of Richard Lowenthal, including "Development vs. Utopia in Communist Policy," in Chalmers Johnson, ed., *Change in Communist Systems* (Stanford, Calif.: Stanford University Press, 1970), pp. 33–116; "The Ruling Party in a Mature Society," in Mark G. Field, ed., *The Social Consequences of Modernization in Communist Societies* (Baltimore: Johns Hopkins University Press, 1976), pp. 81–118; and "The Post-Revolutionary Phase in China and Russia," *Studies in Comparative Communism,* Vol. 13, No. 3 (Autumn 1981), pp. 191–201.

3. "The Primary Task of Veteran Cadres Is to Select Young and Middle-Aged Cadres for Promotion," in Deng Xiaoping, *Selected Works of Deng Xiaoping, 1975–1982* (Beijing: Foreign Languages Press, 1984), pp. 361–66.

4. A useful survey of these reforms and an evaluation of their impact is James C. Mulvenon, *Professionalization of the Senior Chinese Officer Corps: Trends and Implications* (Santa Monica, Calif.: RAND, 1997).

5. Ibid., pp. 69–75.

6. On this point, in addition to the chapters by Lu Ning, Michael Swaine, and Elizabeth Economy in this volume, see Nina Halpern, *Economic Specialists and the Making of Chinese Economic Policy* (Ann Arbor: University of Michigan Press, 1985).

7. Frederick C. Teiwes, "The Paradoxical Post-Mao Transition: From Obeying the Leader to 'Normal Politics,'" *China Journal*, No. 34 (July 1995), pp. 55–94. These are the integrative themes highlighted in David Lampton's introduction to this volume.

8. This rule following at the top, of course, does not mean that the Jiang leadership, like the Deng leadership before it, has not been ready to ignore constitutional stipulations of political liberties for the populace it governs, such as freedom of speech, freedom of the press, freedom of assembly, and so forth.

9. C. P. Snow's delineation of the sciences and humanities as "two cultures" obscures a deeper demarcation in worldview between scientists and humanists on the one hand and engineers on the other.

10. See Michael Pillsbury, ed., *Chinese Views of Future Warfare*, rev. ed. (Washington, D.C.: National Defense University Press, 1998).

11. The chapters by Lu Ning, Michael Swaine, and Elizabeth Economy are illustrative in this respect.

12. The Taiwan question may be an exception, as the chapters by Tai Ming Cheung and Michael Swaine suggest.

13. Much of the following discussion is distilled from a somewhat longer analysis of trends in China's post–cold war foreign policy in my "The United States, Japan, and Post-Deng China: A Contextual Approach," in Hosoya Chihiro and Shinoda Tomohito, eds., *Redefining the Partnership: The United States and Japan in East Asia* (Lanham, Md.: University Press of America, 1998), pp. 127–58.

14. In the 1950s Beijing allied itself with Moscow against preponderant American strategic power. In the 1960s, a period of growing Soviet-American détente and strategic parity, Beijing pursued a dual-adversary tactic. In the 1970s, amid perceptions of growing Soviet and declining U.S. power, Beijing leaned to the side of Washington and the West. In the 1980s, as the United States reasserted itself strategically and as Soviet power ebbed, Beijing pursued an "independent foreign policy line" that put some distance between itself and Washington (while preserving and expanding bilateral ties) and moved to restore relations with Moscow.

15. "Joint Statement by the People's Republic of China and the Russian Federation on the Multipolarization of the World and the Establishment of a New International Order," April 23, 1997, in *Beijing Review*, May 12–18, 1997, pp. 7–8, and "Sino-French Joint Declaration," May 16, 1997, in *Beijing Review*, June 2–8, 1997, pp. 7–9.

16. The U.S.-PRC joint statement concluded at the October 1997 Jiang-Clinton summit committed both sides to "building toward a constructive strategic partner-

ship," but made no reference to joint opposition to "hegemonism." Judging by comments by administration officials, Beijing did not propose such a reference, nor did the U.S. side propose its inclusion, even though both the 1972 Shanghai Communiqué and the 1978 normalization communiqué did so.

17. For example, see Jiang Zemin's speech at the eighth meeting of diplomatic envoys, Aug. 28, 1998, *Xinhua* Chinese Service (Aug. 28, 1998), as translated in World News Connection (WNC), Sept. 1, 1998, document FBIS-CHI-98-242. See also State Council Foreign Affairs Office Director Liu Huaqiu, "Zhongguo Shizhong Buyu de Fengxing Dulizizhu de Heping Waijiao Zhengce" (China Will Unswervingly Pursue a Peaceful Foreign Policy of Independence and Self-Determination), *Qiushi* (Seeking Truth), No. 23 (1997), pp. 2–9; a translation appears in WNC, March 23, 1998, document FBIS-CHI-98-078.

18. Interviews, Beijing, Sept. 1998.

19. Among numerous statements and commentaries see, for example, the *Renmin Ribao* (People's Daily) commentator article "Establish a New Type of State Relationship for the New Century," Dec. 8, 1997, as translated by FBIS in WNC, Dec. 13, 1997, document FBIS-CHI-97-347; interview with Foreign Minister Qian Qichen, *Renmin Ribao,* Dec. 18, 1997, as translated in WNC, Dec. 23, 1997, document FBIS-CHI-97-357; Dai Xiaohua, "Establishing a New Type of Foreign Relations," *Beijing Review,* Jan. 19–25, 1998, pp. 6–9; speech by Foreign Minister Tang Jiaxuan to central party organs, July 16, 1998, *Xinhua* Chinese Service, July 16, 1998, as translated in WNC, July 17, 1998, document FBIS-CHI-98-197; and Yan Rong, "The Success of Big Power Relations," *Beijing Review,* Nov. 23–29, 1998, pp. 7–9.

20. Speech by Qian Qichen at ASEAN Regional Forum meeting in Jaya, Malaysia, July 27, 1997, *Xinhua* Chinese Service, July 27, 1997, as translated in WNC, Aug. 8, 1997, document FBIS-CHI-97-219; A Ying, "New Security Mechanism Needed for Asian-Pacific Region," *Beijing Review,* August 18–24, 1997, pp. 6–7; speech by Chi Haotian in Tokyo, Feb. 4, 1998, *Xinhua* Chinese Service, Feb. 4, 1998, as translated in WNC, February 6, 1998, document FBIS-CHI-98-035.

21. Speech by Jiang Zemin to the eighth conference of diplomatic envoys; speech by Foreign Minister Tang Jiaxuan to the United Nations General Assembly, Sept. 23, 1998, *Xinhua* Chinese Service, Sept. 23, 1998, as translated in WNC, Sept. 25, 1998, document FBIS-CHI-98-267; "Observer" article, "Economic Globalization Calls for Financial Security," *Renmin Ribao,* Oct. 21, 1998, as translated in WNC, Oct. 22, 1998, document FBIS-CHI-98-294; and speech by Jiang Zemin to an Asia-Pacific Economic Cooperation meeting, Nov. 18, 1998, *Xinhua* English Service, Nov. 18, 1998, in WNC, document FBIS-CHI-98-322.

22. Speech by Chi Haotian to central party organs, July 29, 1997, *Xinhua* Chinese Service, July 29, 1997, as translated in WNC, Aug. 5, 1997, document FBIS-CHI-97-214; and Li Dianren, "A Guide for the Cross-Century Development of Our Army's Modernization Program: Studying Comrade Jiang Zemin's Important Exposition on Army Building," *Jiefangjun Bao* (Liberation Army Daily), Oct. 26, 1998, as translated in WNC, Nov. 13, 1998, document FBIS-CHI-98-315.

23. For more details on these changes see the chapter by Tai Ming Cheung.

24. Interviews, Beijing, Sept. 1998. Former State Council Foreign Affairs Office Director Liu Huaqiu has been identified in PRC media reports as Central Committee Foreign Affairs Office director since October 1998.

25. Song Qiang, Zhang Zangzang, Qiao Bian, et al., *Zhongguo Keyi Shuobu: Lengzhanhou Shidai de Zhengzhi yu Qinggan Jueze* (China Can Say No: Political and Emotional Choices in the Post–Cold War Era) (Beijing: Zhonghua Gongshang Lianhe Chubanshe, 1996).

26. Yan Xuetong, Wang Zaibang, Li Zhongcheng, and Hou Ruoshi, *Zhongguo Jueqi: Guoji Huanjing Pinggu* (China's Rise: An Assessment of the International Environment) (Tianjin: Tianjin Renmin Chubanshe, 1998), and Yan Xuetong, *Zhongguo Guojia Liyi Fenxi* (An Analysis of China's National Interest) (Tianjin: Tianjin Renmin Chubanshe, 1996).

27. Xi Laiwang, *Ershiyi Shiji Zhongguo Zhanlue Dacehua* (The Grand Plan of China's Twenty-first-Century Strategy) (Beijing: Hongqi Chubanshe, 1996).

28. Shen Jiru, *Zhongguo Budang "Buxiansheng": Dangdai Zhongguo de Guoji Zhanlue Wenti* (China Should Not Be "Mr. No": Issues in Contemporary China's International Strategy) (Beijing: Jinri Zhongguo Chubanshe, 1998). Shen summarized the main themes of this book in his essay "Guoji Zhanlue Wenti" (The Issue of International Strategy), in Xu Ming, ed., *Guanjian Shike: Dangdai Zhongguo Jidai Jiejue de Ershiqige Wenti* (A Crucial Moment: Twenty-Seven Issues That Contemporary China Must Resolve) (Beijing: Jinri Zhongguo Chubanshe, 1998), pp. 1–20.

29. The sensitivity this transition occasioned was clear from Beijing's touchy response to Soviet and Albanian criticism in 1977, when it asserted that "in the final analysis, national struggle is a matter of class struggle." See the *Renmin Ribao* Editorial Department article "Chairman Mao's Theory of the Differentiation of the Three Worlds Is a Major Contribution to Marxism-Leninism," *Renmin Ribao,* Nov. 1, 1977, as published in *Beijing Review,* No. 45 (Nov. 4, 1977), pp. 11–12.

30. See, for example, Qian Qichen's September 1993 address to the United Nations General Assembly, in *Beijing Review,* Oct. 11–17, 1993, pp. 8–11, and Jiang Zemin's Oct. 24, 1995, speech in New York on the fiftieth anniversary of the creation of the United Nations, in *Beijing Review,* Nov. 6–12, 1995, pp. 19–22.

31. Speech by Jiang Zemin in Kuala Lumpur, Dec. 15, 1997, *Xinhua* English Service, Dec. 15, 1997, in WNC, Dec. 15, 1997, document FBIS-CHI-97-349; speech by Jiang Zemin at Harvard University, Nov. 1, 1998, in *Beijing Review,* Nov. 24–30, 1998, pp. 7–11.

CHAPTER 6

1. Thomas J. Christensen, *Useful Adversaries: Grand Strategy, Domestic Mobilization, and Sino-American Conflict, 1947–1958* (Princeton, N.J.: Princeton University Press, 1996).

2. John W. Garver, *China's Decision for Rapprochement with the United States, 1968–1971* (Boulder, Colo.: Westview, 1982); and Kenneth Lieberthal, *Sino-Soviet Conflict in the 1970s: Its Evolution and Implication for the Strategic Triangle,* RAND report R-2342-NA (Santa Monica, Calif.: RAND Corporation, 1978).

3. Li Rui, "Jieshou Lishi Jiaoxun, Jiaqiang Dangnei Minzhu" (Accept the Lessons of History, Strengthen Inner-Party Democracy), *Gaige* (Reform), No. 1 (1998): 75–81.

4. A. Doak Barnett, *The Making of Chinese Foreign Policy: Structure and Process* (Boulder, Colo.: Westview, 1985).

5. An important case study of this is China's involvement in international financial institutions and the demands that involvement made on China to cultivate the requisite expertise. See Harold. K. Jacobson and Michel Oksenberg, *China's Participation in the IMF, World Bank, and GATT: Toward a Global Economic Order* (Ann Arbor, Mich.: University of Michigan Press, 1990).

6. Author interview.

7. See, for instance, Sun Li and Zheng Weidong, "1991–1995 Nian Zhongguo 40 ge Chengshi Jumin Manyidu de Genzong Guance" (Tracking the Level of Satisfaction of Residents of 40 Cities between 1991 and 1995), in Lu Xueyi and Li Peilin, eds., *Zhongguo Xinshiqi Shehui Fazhan Baogao (1991–1995)* (Report on China's Social Development in the New Period, 1991–1995) (Shenyang: Liaoning Chubanshe, 1997).

8. Author interviews. There are also occasional reports of leaders commenting on controversial works, such as Jiang Zemin's comments on the recent best-seller *Jiaofeng* (Crossed Swords). See *South China Morning Post,* March 28, 1998, p. 9.

9. Joseph Fewsmith, "China in 1998: Tacking to Stay the Course," *Asian Survey,* Jan. 1999, pp. 99–113.

10. Stanley Rosen, "Public Opinion and Reform in the People's Republic of China," *Studies in Comparative Communism,* Vol. 23, No. 2/3 (Summer–Autumn 1989), pp. 153–70.

11. At least five areas are currently considered off limits for public opinion pollsters in China. Polls are not to be conducted on the rating of state leaders; the assessment of Deng Xiaoping's historical status; the assessment, reevaluation or outcome of the 1989 student movement; attitudes toward the independence of Taiwan; or the government's policy toward national minorities. One prominent pollster asked an official of the Propaganda Department of the CCP Central Committee whether he could conduct a poll on the Taiwan issue. He was told that such a poll could be conducted if it could be guaranteed that 100 percent of those polled opposed independence for Taiwan. Anything less would be unacceptable. Author interviews.

12. Author interview.

13. Horizon Survey Company, State Statistical Bureau, and Chinese Entrepreneurs Investigation System, eds., *Guancha Zhongguo* (Observing China) (Beijing: Gongshang Chubanshe, 1997), pp. 31–52.

14. Stanley Rosen, "Students and the State in China: The Crisis in Ideology and Organization," in Arthur Lewis Rosenbaum, ed., *State and Society in China: The Consequences of Reform* (Boulder, Colo.: Westview, 1992), pp. 167–91.

15. J. H. Zhu, "Origins of the Chinese Student Unrest," *Indianapolis Star,* May 9, 1989.

16. Horizon Survey Company et al., *Guancha Zhongguo,* pp. 31–52.

17. *Daxuesheng* (College Students), No. 1 (Jan. 1998), pp. 55–57.

18. On Chinese nationalism see Jonathan Unger, ed., *Chinese Nationalism* (Armonk, N.Y.: Sharpe, 1996); Michel Oksenberg, "China's Confident Nationalism," *Foreign Affairs*, Vol. 65, No. 3 (1987), pp. 501–23; Allen Whiting, "Chinese Nationalism and Foreign Policy after Deng," *China Quarterly*, No. 142 (June 1995), pp. 295–316; and Suisheng Zhao, "Chinese Intellectuals' Quest for National Greatness and Natonalistic Writing in the 1990s," *China Quarterly*, No. 152 (Dec. 1997), pp. 725–45. On the closely related issue of national identity see Lowell Dittmer and Samuel S. Kim, eds., *China's Quest for National Identity* (Ithaca, N.Y.: Cornell University Press, 1993).

19. Indeed, it is the expression of nationalism that Richard Bernstein and Ross H. Munro responded to in their controversial *The Coming Conflict with China* (New York: Random House, 1997).

20. On China's different orientations to the outside world in the modern era see Michel Oksenberg and Steven Goldstein, "The Chinese Political Spectrum," *Problems of Communism*, Vol. 23, No. 2 (March–April 1974), pp. 1–13; Kenneth Lieberthal, "Domestic Politics and Foreign Policy," in Harry Harding, ed., *China's Foreign Relations in the 1980s* (New Haven, Conn.: Yale University Press, 1984), pp. 43–70; and Joseph Fewsmith, "The Dengist Reforms in Historical Perspective," in Brantly Womack, ed., *Contemporary Chinese Politics in Historical Perspective* (Cambridge: Cambridge University Press, 1991), pp. 23–52.

21. Introduction to inaugural issue of *Wenhua: Zhongguo yu Shijie* (Culture: China and the World), Vol. 1, No. 6 (1987), p. 1. See also Gan Yang, "80 Niandai Wenhua Taolunzhong de Jige Wenti" (Several Problems in the 1980s Discussion of Culture) in the inaugural issue of *Culture: China and the World*. Gan Yang, one of the leading intellectuals in China in the 1980s, was chief editor of the *Culture: China and the World* book series, which included translations of many influential Western writings. See Chen Fong-ching and Jin Guantao, *From Youthful Manuscripts to River Elegy: The Chinese Popular Cultural Movement and Political Transformation, 1979–1989* (Hong Kong: The Chinese University Press, 1997), pp. 159–86. Ironically, in recent years Gan Yang has been leading explorations of nativist traditions. See Gan Yang, "'Jiangcun Jingji' Zairenshi" (Reunderstanding Jiang Village's Economy), *Dushu* (Reading), 1994, No. 10 (Oct.), pp. 50–57.

22. Cited in Jing Wang, *High Culture Fever: Politics, Aesthetics, and Ideology in Deng's China* (Berkeley: University of California Press, 1996), p. 123. Emphasis added by Jing Wang. See also Frederic Wakeman, "All the Rage in China," *New York Review of Books*, March 2, 1989, pp. 19–21.

23. Wang, *High Culture Fever*, p. 123.

24. Chen Fong-ching and Jin Guantao, *From Youthful Manuscripts to River Elegy*. Perhaps the word *cosmopolitanism* does not convey the complexity of China's emotional response to the outside world. As Jing Wang comments: "Chinese [enlightenment] intellectuals [are] at once proud of and hostile toward their own cultural and national heritage, while defiant toward and subservient to the imported Western culture at the same time." See Wang, *High Culture Fever*, p. 124.

25. Ma Licheng and Ling Zhijun, *Jiaofeng* (Crossed Swords) (Beijing: Jinri Zhongguo Chubanshe, 1998). For a review see Joseph Fewsmith, "Review of *Jiaofeng*," *Foreign Policy*, No. 113 (Winter 1998–99), pp. 107–10. See also Ling Zhijun, *Chenfu: Zhongguo Jingji Gaige Beiwanglu, 1989–1997* (Turbulence: A Memoir of China's Economic Reforms, 1989–1997) (Beijing: Dongfang Chuban Zhongxin, 1998).

26. Suisheng Zhao, *In Search of a Right Place? Chinese Nationalism in the Post–Cold War World* (Hong Kong: Hong Kong Institute for Asia-Pacific Studies, Chinese University of Hong Kong, 1997), p. 13.

27. See *Zhongguo Qingnian Bao* (China Youth Daily), Feb. 1, 1997, for a five-part series on survey research and its uses.

28. *Zhongguo Qingnian Bao*, July 14, 1995, p. 8.

29. "Miandui 'Shengtu de Yingdi': Yu Women de Qingnian Jiaoliu" (Facing 'The Camp of the Saints': An Exchange with Our Youth), in *Zhongguo Qingnian Bao*, Aug. 11, 1995, p. 8.

30. Most important, because the survey was conducted by *Zhongguo Qingnian Bao* (China Youth Daily) the respondents were disproportionately from the Communist Youth League (the owner of *China Youth Daily*), and many of the questionnaires were apparently filled out after being discussed in groups. Therefore, it was an "organized" survey and did not represent a free response of individual informants. Indeed, as many as 25 percent of the respondents were in the military. Moreover, the survey was conducted soon after Lee Teng-hui, the president of Taiwan, visited the United States in mid-1995, an event that seriously set back Sino-American relations. Surveys conducted at other times—for example, around the time of President Clinton's 1997 visit to China, to take the other extreme—have produced very different and far more positive results. As one leading public opinion specialist explained in an interview, the attitude toward the American government may change dramatically depending on the overall state of Sino-American relations, but the underlying (positive) attitude toward the United States and toward Americans is far more stable.

Other methodological problems included the fact that the target group of the survey was the readers of the newspaper, not all Chinese youth. The questionnaire was in the newspaper, so the respondents were far from being a scientifically derived random sample; indeed, anyone could fill out the questionnaire. Moreover, the newspaper is directed toward youth in units under the control of the state (*tizhinei qingnian*), because such units are the primary subscribers to the paper. Such units would therefore not include youth in private or joint venture enterprises, individual laborers (*getihu*), or others outside the state system. Therefore, the results were skewed in a conservative direction.

The newspaper did make some attempt to sample youth in direct proportion to their numbers in society, but only after the questionnaires were returned. They received more than a hundred thousand responses from their very unscientific sample and then took gender, profession, and so forth into account. This had several significant consequences. For example, since there were so few responses from *getihu* they simply included all such responses in their sample. But because soldiers were heavily overrepresented, they included the same proportion of soldiers as could be found in society (thus rather arbitrarily eliminating many of the questionnaires submitted from military units). The comments in this note are based on interviews in Beijing, including a visit to the survey office of *China Youth Daily.*

31. "Xun COOL Yidai: Zhongguo Yanhai Diqu Zhongxuesheng Shehui Wenhua Tezheng Yanjiu" (Looking for the Cool Generation: Research on the Social and Cultural Characteristics of Chinese Secondary School Students in the Coastal Regions), Horizon Research Report, Dec. 15, 1999.

32. *Zhongguo Qingnian Bao,* March 18, 1997, p. 1, translated in Foreign Broadcast Information Service (FBIS), *Daily Report, China,* 97-194, May 16, 1997.

33. "Xun COOL Yidai."

34. *China News Digest,* Sept. 23, 1996, citing the *Washington Post.*

35. *China News Digest,* Sept. 18, 1996, citing the *Hong Kong Standard.* For criticisms of Jiang within the government and the military over the Diaoyu Islands dispute, see *Zhengming* (Contending), Oct. 1, 1996, translated in FBIS, *Daily Report, China,* 96-213, Nov. 4, 1996; see also *The Economist,* Sept. 21, 1996, pp. 34 and 39.

36. *Zhengming,* November 1, 1998, translated in FBIS, *Daily Report, China,* 98-307, Nov. 5, 1998.

37. There was a widespread feeling among Chinese in and outside the mainland that the summit was a failure. For example, see Chen Wenhong, "Fang Ri Shi Zhongguo Waijiao de Shibai" (The Visit to Japan Is a Failure of Chinese Foreign Policy), *Ming Pao* (Hong Kong), Nov. 30, 1998, p. A14. One interviewee, a leading public opinion specialist, argued that the Chinese government's lack of any clear policy toward Japan has contributed to the public's assessment of the policy as "weak." Indeed, even though Japanese products are considered of high quality, surveys suggest that many Chinese feel that the Japanese export "second-rate" goods to China, provide poor service, and generally look down on the Chinese.

38. Song Qiang, Zhang Zangzang, and Qiao Bian, *Zhongguo Keyi Shuobu* (China Can Say No) (Beijing: Zhonghua Gongshang Lianhe Chubanshe, 1996), pp. 36, 62, 71, 77, 143, 147, 186, and 243.

39. Ibid., pp. 34, 140, 312, 316, 322, and 326.

40. In a survey of reading habits from 1978 to 1998 commissioned by Central Chinese TV, 0.9 percent of 932 respondents listed *Zhongguo Keyi Shuobu* (China Can Say No) as the book with the greatest influence on them (pp. 58–59). The leaders in the survey were *Hong Lou Meng* (Dream of the Red Chamber), chosen by 17.7 percent of respondents; *Sanguo Yanyi* (Romance of the Three Kingdoms), 13.9 percent; *Gangtie Shi Zenyang Lianchengde* (How the Steel Was Tempered), 13 percent; and *Mao Zedong Xuanji* (Selections from the Works of Mao Zedong), 9.6 percent. The classics did well because of the general wording of the question: "Up till now, which book has had the greatest influence on you?" Although *China Can Say No* finished tied for twenty-fifth place in the overall poll, among books published after 1993 (706 respondents) it came in a close second (2.4 percent), behind only a general category of "books on economics" (2.5 percent) and just ahead of the journal *Dushu* (Reading) (2.3 percent) (pp. 52–54). The authors of the survey stated, "It is worth paying attention to the great influence on readers of the thinly veiled (*lugu*) discussion of nationalist sen-

timent (*minzu zhuyi qingxu*) with regard to international relations in this popular literature," and they noted that *China Can Say No* "unexpectedly" (*juran*) was the most influential book in the period after 1993. See Kang Xiaoguang, Wu Yulun, Liu Dehuan, and Sun Hui, *Zhongguoren Dushu Toushi: 1978–1998 Dazhong Dushu Shenghuo Bianqian Diaocha* (A Perspective on the Reading Habits of the Chinese: An Investigation of the Changes in the Reading Habits of the Masses from 1978 to 1998) (Nanning: Guangxi Jiaoyu Chubanshe, 1998), pp. 52–59.

41. *Zhongguo Haishi Neng Shuobu* (China Still Can Say No) (Hong Kong: Ming Bao, 1996).

42. See Li Xiguang and Liu Kang, *Yaomo Zhongguo de Beihou* (Behind the Demonizing of China) (Beijing: Zhongguo Shehui Kexue Chubanshe, 1996); Peng Qian, Yang Mingjie, and Xu Deren, *Zhongguo Weishenma Shuo Bu?* (Why Does China Say No?) (Beijing: Xinshijie Chubanshe, 1996); Zhang Xueli, *Zhongguo Heyi Shuo Bu* (Why China Says No) (Beijing: Hualing Chubanshe, 1996); Li Shuyi and Yong Jianxiong, eds., *Ershiyi Shiji Zhongguo Jueqi* (The Rise of China in the Twenty-First Century) (Beijing: Zhonggong Zhongyang Chubanshe, 1997); He Jie, Wang Baoling, and Wang Jianji, eds., *Wo Xiangxin Zhongguo* (I Believe in China) (Beijing: Chengshi Chubanshe, 1997); and He Degong, Pu Weizhong, and Jin Yong, *Qingxiang Zhongguo* (Biased toward China) (Guangzhou: Guangdong Renmin Chubanshe, 1997).

43. Song Qiang et al., *Zhongguo Keyi Shuobu*, pp. 64, 90, and 165.

44. Wang Xiaodong, Fang Ning, and Song Qiang, eds., *Quanqiuhua Yingyingxia de Zhongguo Zhilu* (China's Road under the Shadow of Globalization) (Beijing: Zhongguo Shehui Kexue Chubanshe, 1999). Wang Xiaodong and Fang Ning collaborated on the *China Youth Daily* survey discussed earlier, and Song Qiang was one of the writers of *China Can Say No*.

45. Shi Zhong, "Chinese Nationalism and the Future of China," translated in Stanley Rosen, ed., "Nationalism and Neoconservatism in China in the 1990s," *Chinese Law and Government*, Vol. 30, No. 6 (Nov.–Dec. 1997), pp. 8–27. The article had appeared in Chinese in less complete form in *Mingbao Yuekan* (Mingbao Monthly), No. 9 (Sept. 1996) and has since been included in Wang et al., *Quanqiuhua Yinyingxia de Zhongguo Zhilu*, pp. 81–106.

46. Li Ping, *Zhongguo Xiayibu Zenyang Zuo: Dangdai Jingying Dalunzheng* (Where Will China's Next Step Be? Great Debates among Contemporary Elites) (Hong Kong: Mirror, 1998), pp. 115–18 and 190–91.

47. See the following articles by Sheng Hong: "Shenma Shi Wenming?" (What Is Civilization?), *Zhanlue yu Guanli* (Strategy and Management), No. 5 (1995); "Zhongguo Xianqin Zhexue He Xiandai Zhidu Zhuyi" (China's pre-Qin Philosophy and the New Institutionalism), *Guanli Shijie* (Management World), No. 3 (1993); and "Cong Minzu Zhuyi Dao Tianxia Zhuyi" (From Nationalism to Cosmopolitanism), *Zhanlue yu Guanli*, No. 1 (1996).

48. Li, *Zhongguo Xiayibu Zenyang Zuo*, p. 190.

49. See in particular Cui Zhiyuan, *Zhidu Chuangxin yu Di'erci Sixiang Jiefang* (Institutional Renovation and the Second Emancipation of Thought) (Hong Kong: Oxford University Press, 1997).

50. The literature on the New Left in Chinese is extensive, and attitudes toward it differ widely. Yongnian Zheng adopts a generally sympathetic attitude in his *Discovering Chinese Nationalism in China: Modernization, Identity, and International Relations* (Cambridge, U.K.: Cambridge University Press, 1999). In contrast, Ben Xu expresses deep dislike in his *Disenchanted Democracy: Chinese Cultural Criticism after 1989* (Ann Arbor, Mich.: University of Michigan Press, 1999). See also Min Lin, *The Search for Modernity: Chinese Intellectuals and Cultural Discourse in the Post-Mao Era* (New York: St. Martin's, 1999).

51. See, for instance, Anne Thurston, *Muddling Toward Democracy: Political Change in Grassroots China* (Washington, D.C.: United States Institute of Peace, 1998).

52. Feng Chen, "Order and Stability in Social Transition: Neoconservative Political Thought in Post-1989 China," *China Quarterly,* No. 151 (Sept. 1997), pp. 593–613.

53. Jianying Zha, *China Pop: How Soap Operas, Tabloids, and Bestsellers are Transforming a Culture* (New York: New Press, 1995), pp. 38–39.

54. Ibid., p. 38.

55. Ibid., p. 46.

56. Commentator, "Dajia Lai Taolun Zhege Zhongda Keti: Cong Pijiu Hezi Yinqi de Sikao" (Everybody Come Discuss This Important Topic: Thoughts Derived from Joint Ventures in the Beer Industry), *Jingji Ribao* (Economic Daily), June 20, 1996, p. 1.

57. Jiang Po, "'Yanjing' Wei Shenma Bu Hezi?" (Why Doesn't "Yanjing" Form a Joint Venture?), *Jingji Ribao,* July 2, 1996, p. 1.

58. Jiang Po, "Woguo Mingpai Mianlin Yanjun Tiaozhan" (Chinese Famous Brands Are Facing a Serious Challenge), *Jingji Ribao,* July 10, 1996, pp. 1 and 3; Wang Yungui, "Kan RiMeiFa Zhengfu Ruhe Baohu Benguo Gongye" (Looking at How Japan, the United States, and France Protected Their Domestic Industries), *Jingji Ribao,* July 17, 1996, pp. 1 and 3; and "Shanghai 'Zhang Xiaochuan' Jianchi Bumai Pinpai" (Shanghai's "Zhang Xiaochuan" Adamantly Refuses to Sell Its Brand Name), *Jingji Ribao,* July 26, 1996, p. 1.

59. "Zao Gai Zheyang Taolunle" (There Should Have Been This Discussion Long Ago), *Jingji Ribao,* July 18, 1996, p. 1. It should be noted that one of the five letters published that day questioned the premise of the series, saying that before China opened up all of its industries were "national industries"—but they could not compete on the world market. These arguments have animated the domestic debate over China's WTO entrance, pitting "liberals" against "economic nationalists" over what type of economic development strategy is best suited to China and the proper role of foreign direct investment. See Yong Wang, "China's Domesic WTO Debate," *China Business Review,* Vol. 27, No. 1 (Jan.–Feb. 2000), pp. 54–62.

60. See the selections from *Xinmin Wanbao* (New People's Evening News), Sept. 6–12, 1996, translated in Stanley Rosen, ed., "The Contention Over 'Cultural Colonialism,'" *Chinese Sociology and Anthropology,* Vol. 31, No. 4 (Summer 1999), pp. 87–96.

61. Wang Jisi, "The Role of the United States as a Global and Pacific Power: A View from China," *Pacific Review,* Vol. 10, No. 1 (1997), pp. 1–18.

62. Zhang Yunling, *Zhuanbianzhong de Zhong, Mei, Ri Guanxi* (The Changing Relations among China, the United States, and Japan) (Beijing: Zhongguo Shehui Kexue Chubanshe, 1997), pp. 23–25.

63. Yan Xuetong at the China Institute of Contemporary International Relations has been a prominent proponent of analyzing foreign policy in terms of national interest. See his *Zhongguo Guojia Liyi Fenxi* (Analyzing the National Interests of China) (Tianjin: Renmin Chubanshe, 1996). For a survey of Chinese thinking on foreign policy, see Zhang Honglin, "Ershiyi Shiji de ZhongMei Guanxi: Duikang Haishi Hezuo?" (Sino-U.S. Relations in the Twenty-First Century: Conflict or Cooperation?), in *Zhanlue yu Guanli*, No. 3 (1997), pp. 24–25. We are indebted to Alastair Iain Johnston for helping us clarify the differences among these different approaches to international relations.

64. Yong Deng, "The Chinese Conception of International Relations," *China Quarterly*, No. 154 (June 1998), p. 311.

65. "Realistic Responses and Strategic Choices for China after the Soviet Upheaval," reprinted in *Zhongguo Zhi Chun* (China's Spring), No. 104 (Dec. 15, 1991), pp. 35–39.

66. Deng, "Chinese Conception of International Relations," pp. 316–20. It appears that this more liberal interpretation that draws on thinking about complex interdependence suffered greatly within intellectual circles following the bombing of the Chinese embassy.

67. For a good expression of an elite cosmopolitan orientation, see the speech by Long Yongtu, vice minister of the Ministry of Foreign Trade and Economic Cooperation, "Guanyu Jingji Quanqiuhua Wenti" (On Economic Globalization), *Zhonggong Zhongyang Dangxiao Baogaoxuan* (Selections from Reports of the Central Party School of the Communist Party of China), No. 16 (Oct. 30, 1998), pp. 12–20.

68. Alastair Iain Johnston and Paul Evans, "China's Engagement with Multilateral Security Institutions," in Alastair Iain Johnston and Robert Ross, eds., *Engaging China* (London: Routledge, 1999), pp. 235–72, and Michael D. Swaine and Alastair Iain Johnston, "China and Arms Control Institutions," in Elizabeth Economy and Michel Oksenberg, eds., *China Joins the World: Progress and Prospects* (New York: Council on Foreign Relations Press, 1999), pp. 90–135.

69. He Xin, *Wei Zhongguo Shengbian* (Arguing for China) (Jinan: Shandong Youyi Chubanshe, 1996), and He Xin, *Zhonghua Fuxing yu Shijie Weilai* (The Chinese Renaissance and the Future of the World), 2 vols. (Chengdu: Sichuan Renmin Chubanshe, 1996).

70. Shen Jiru, *Zhongguo Bu Dang "Bu Xiansheng"* (China Should Not Be "Mr. No") (Beijing: Jinri Chubanshe, 1998).

71. Liu Junning, ed., *Beida Chuantong yu Jindai Zhongguo* (Beijing University's Tradition and Modern China) (Beijing: Zhongguo Renshi Chubanshe, 1998); Yu Jie, *Huo yu Bing* (Fire and Ice) (Beijing: Jingji Ribao Chubanshe, 1998); Dong Youyu and Shi Binghai, eds., *Zhengzhi Zhongguo* (Political China) (Beijing: Jinri Zhongguo Chubanshe, 1998); and Ling Zhijun, *Chenfu: Zhongguo Jingji Gaige Beiwanglu (1989–1997)* (Turbulence: A Memoir of China's Economic Reforms [1989–1997]) (Beijing: Dongfang Chubanshe, 1998).

72. James N. Rosenau, *Public Opinion and Foreign Policy* (New York: Random House, 1961), p. 4.

73. Ole Holsti, *Public Opinion and American Foreign Policy* (Ann Arbor, Mich.: University of Michigan Press, 1996).

74. Henry Chu and Jim Mann, "Chen Says Preserving Peace Is Top Priority," *Los Angeles Times,* March 20, 2000, p. A12, and *China News Digest,* March 22, 2000.

75. Willy Wo-Lap Lam, "Beijing 'Has Timetable for Unity,'" *South China Morning Post,* March 22, 2000, p. 1.

76. This dimension is limited to the state of Sino-U.S. relations rather than the international environment in general because other international relationships may reverberate through the political system differently. A tense relationship with Japan, for instance, might yield elite consensus rather than division.

77. *Public* is in quotation marks because this article was widely circulated, but not published.

78. "Yingxiang Woguo Guojia Anquan de Ruogan Yinsu" (Several Factors Influencing China's National Security), in Shi Liaozi, ed., *Beijing Dixia "'Wanyanshu"* (Beijing's Underground "10,000-Character Manifestos") (Hong Kong: Mingjing Chubanshe, 1997), pp. 25–48.

79. Author interviews.

80. "Weilai Yi, Ershi Nian Woguo Anquan de Neiwai Xingshi Ji Zhuyao Weixie de Chubu Tantao" (A Preliminary Examination of the Domestic and Foreign Conditions and Primary Threats to Our National Security in the Next Ten to Twenty Years), in *Beijing Dixia "Wanyanshu,"* pp. 134–35.

81. Ibid., pp. 137 and 139.

82. Ibid., p. 141.

83. Ibid., p. 143.

84. Author interviews.

85. The final commentary in the series of articles published by *Jiefangjun Bao* said only that "individual conclusions of Marxism are perhaps out of date [*guoshi*]" and specifically stated that Marxism's fundamental principles (*jiben yuanli*) regarding socialism have been proven to be "completely correct." See "Makesi Zhuyi Yongyuan Shi Women Shengli de Qizhi" (Marxism Is Forever Our Victorious Banner), *Jiefangjun Bao,* May 6, 1996, p. 1.

86. Note that Xing's formulation goes well beyond what the *Jiefangjun Bao* commentator article stated (see note 85). See Xing Bensi, "Jianchi Makesi Zhuyi Bu Dongyao" (Uphold Marxism without Wavering), *Renmin Ribao* (People's Daily), June 6, 1996, p. 9.

87. Li Zehou and Liu Zaifu, *Gaobie Geming: Huiwang Ershi Shiji Zhongguo* (Farewell to Revolution: Looking Back on Twentieth-Century China) (Hong Kong: Cosmos, 1995).

88. Tang Tsou, "Political Change and Reform: The Middle Course," in Tang Tsou, *The Cultural Revolution and Post-Mao Reforms* (Chicago: University of Chicago Press, 1986), p. 222.

89. Weng Jieming, Zhang Ximing, Zhang Tao, and Qu Kemin, eds., *Yu Zong-shuji Tanxin* (Heart-to-Heart Talks with the General Secretary) (Beijing: Zhongguo Shehui Kexue Chubanshe, 1996), pp. 18–19.

90. Author interview.

91. Author interview.

92. *Xinhua,* Feb. 25, 1997.

93. Author interview.

94. "Jiang Zemin's Speech at Party School Sets Keynote for 15th CPC National Congress," *Ming Pao,* June 8, 1997, p. A8, translated in FBIS, *Daily Report, China,* 97-160.

95. Ibid.

96. Jianwei Wang, "Managing Conflict: Chinese Perspectives on Multilateral Diplomacy and Collective Security," in Yong Deng and Fei-Ling Wang, eds., *In the Eyes of the Dragon: China Views the World* (Lanham, Md.: Rowman and Littlefield, 1999), pp. 73–96.

97. Agence France Presse, May 3, 1999.

98. "World Facing Seven Ill Omens at Turn of Century: Interviewing Shen Jiru," *Ta Kung Pao* (Impartial Daily), May 20, 1999, translated in FBIS, *Daily Report, China,* 1999-0608 (June 10, 1999).

99. Fang Ning, Wang Xiaodong, and Song Qiang, *Quanqiuhua Yinyingxia de Zhongguo Zhilu* (China's Road Under the Shadow of Globalization) (Beijing: Zhongguo Shehui Kexue Chubanshe, 1999), p. 21. Other important expressions of nationalism included the unusual publication of a book by two researchers at National Defense University calling for China to develop, and employ if necessary, any and all means to defeat the United States. See Qiao Liang and Wang Xianghui, *Chaoxianzhan* (Unlimited Warfare) (Beijing: Jiefangjun Wenyi Chubanshe, 1999).

100. Fang, Wang, and Song, *Quanqiuhua Yinyingxia de Zhongguo Zhilu,* p. 22.

101. Ibid., pp. 7 and 11.

102. Wang says that, contrary to intellectual opinion in China, American opposition to the war in Vietnam derived not from moral concerns, but simply from the fact that the United States was losing the war. See Fang, Wang, and Song, *Quanqiuhua Yinyingxia de Zhongguo Zhilu,* p. 26.

103. Fang Ning, "Ershiyi Shiji de Liangzhong Qushi" (Two Trends in the Twenty-first Century), in Fang, Wang, and Song, *Quanqiuhua Yinyingxia de Zhongguo Zhilu,* pp. 230–41.

104. Wang Huning, "Wenhua Kuozhang yu Wenhua Zhuquan: Dui Zhuquan Guannian de Tiaozhan" (Cultural Expansionism and Cultural Sovereignty: A Challenge to the Concept of Sovereignty), *Fudan Xuebao* (Fudan University Journal), No. 3 (1994), reprinted in Wang Jisi, ed., *Wenming yu Guoji Zhengzhi: Zhongguo Xuezhe Ping Hengtingdun de Wenming Chongtu Lun* (Culture and International Relations: Chinese Scholars Critique Huntington's Cultural Clash Thesis) (Shanghai: Renmin Chubanshe, 1995), pp. 340–56. The long citation is from p. 356.

105. Fang Li, "Meiguo Quanqiu Zhanlue Zhong de Wenhua Kuozhang yu Cantuo" (Cultural Expansion and Penetration in America's Global Strategy), *Lilun Dongtai* (Theoretical Trends), No. 1446 (June 15, 1999).

106. It should be noted that such arguments were important in the realm of elite politics; the intellectual trends discussed earlier were more important at lower levels.

107. Robert D. Putnam, "Diplomacy and Domestic Politics: The Logic of Two-Level Games," reprinted in Peter D. Evans, Harold K. Jacobson, and Robert D. Putnam, eds., *Double-Edged Diplomacy: International Bargaining and Domestic Politics* (Berkeley: University of California Press, 1993).

108. Author interview.

109. Joseph Fewsmith, "Jiang Zemin Takes Command," *Current History,* Vol. 97, No. 620 (Sept. 1998), pp. 250–56.

110. Suisheng Zhao, "A State-Led Nationalism: The Patriotic Education Campaign in Post-Tiananmen China," *Communist and Post-Communist Studies,* Vol. 31, No. 3 (1998), pp. 287–302.

111. Alastair Iain Johnston has recently argued that much of China's conflict behavior from 1949 to 1992 can be explained by status inconsistency—that is, the gap between the status China thinks it should have and that granted by the major powers. This status inconsistency theory may explain much about China's "reactive nationalism" and foreign policy behavior in the post-Tiananmen period. See his "China's Militarized Dispute Behavior 1949–1992: A First Cut at the Data," *The China Quarterly,* Vol. 153 (March 1998), pp. 1–30.

CHAPTER 7

1. The specific period we examine is from July 1997 to December 1998, recognizing that by most accounts the economic downturn for the region did not end for nearly another year.

2. Wu Yi, "The Asian Financial Crisis and China's Economic Development," *Guoji Shangbao* (International Business), Sept. 9, 1998, pp. 1–2, in Foreign Broadcast Information Service, *China Daily Report,* Internet version (FBIS-CHI-98-274).

3. For a good overview of the literature on foreign policy learning see Jack Levy, "Learning and Foreign Policy: Sweeping a Conceptual Minefield," *International Organization,* Vol. 48, No. 2 (Spring 1994), pp. 279–312. A classic in the field is George Breslauer and Philip Tetlock, eds., *Learning in U.S. and Soviet Foreign Policy* (Boulder, Colo.: Westview, 1991).

4. To a lesser extent, we have also drawn upon non-Mainland sources such as Western newspapers and the Hong Kong media. In order to minimize the number of notes, we cite Chinese and foreign materials only as necessary to document quotations or specific facts asserted in the text. We do not provide citations when our purpose is merely to characterize the general tenor of news reports and similar sources.

5. Harold Jacobson and Michel Oksenberg, *China's Participation in the IMF, World Bank, and GATT* (Ann Arbor, Mich.: University of Michigan Press, 1990). For a more recent survey, see William R. Feeney, "China and the Multilateral Economic Institutions," in Samuel S. Kim, ed., *China and the World,* 4th ed. (Boulder, Colo.: Westview, 1998), pp. 239–63.

6. For a general introduction to the topic, see Peter M. Haas, ed., "Knowledge, Power, and International Policy Coordination," special issue of *International Organization*, Vol. 46, No. 1 (Winter 1992).

7. Yong Wang, "China's Domestic WTO Debate," *China Business Review*, Jan.–Feb. 2000, p. 54.

8. Nicholas R. Lardy, *China's Unfinished Economic Revolution* (Washington, D.C.: Brookings Institution, 1998), p. 191.

9. Mitchell Bernard and John Ravenhill, "Beyond Product Cycles and Flying Geese," *World Politics*, Vol. 47, No. 2 (Jan. 1995), p. 172.

10. For the classic account of Guangdong, see Ezra Vogel, *One Step Ahead in China: Guangdong under Reform* (Cambridge, Mass.: Harvard University Press, 1989). For a more recent examination of South China, with emphasis on Fujian, see You-tien Hsing, *Making Capitalism in China* (New York: Oxford University Press, 1998).

11. Doug Guthrie, *Dragon in a Three-Piece Suit* (Princeton, N.J.: Princeton University Press, 1999).

12. See, for example, Linda Y. C. Lim, "Southeast Asia: Success through International Openness," in Barbara Stallings, ed., *Global Change, Regional Response* (Cambridge: Cambridge University Press, 1995), pp. 238–71, and Stephan Haggard, *Developing Nations and the Politics of Global Integration* (Washington, D.C.: Brookings Institution, 1995), pp. 46–74.

13. That said, China at times has been able to play its huge domestic market off against the demands of foreign capitalists. Prominent examples include Beijing's use of cutthroat competition between Boeing and Airbus, as well as intense rivalry among the world's leading automobile corporations, to extract major technology concessions not available to other countries.

14. Our use of the term *private conditionality* draws on Barbara Stallings, "The New International Context of Development," in Stallings, *Global Change*, p. 362.

15. The most prominent example of the "political" logic is Susan L. Shirk, *How China Opened Its Doors: The Political Success of the PRC's Foreign Trade and Investment Reforms* (Washington, D.C.: Brookings Institution, 1994). Examples of the "economic" logic include Dwight Perkins, "China's Industrial and Foreign Trade Reforms," in Andras Koves and Paul Marer, eds., *Foreign Economic Liberalization: Transformations in Socialist and Market Economies* (Boulder, Colo.: Westview, 1991), pp. 269–81; Cyril Zhiren Lin, "Open-Ended Economic Reform in China," in Victor Nee and David Stark, eds., *Remaking the Economic Institutions of Socialism* (Stanford, Calif.: Stanford University Press, 1989), pp. 95–136; and Barry Naughton, *Growing Out of the Plan* (Cambridge: Cambridge University Press, 1995).

16. This section draws in part on arguments first set forth in Thomas G. Moore, "China as a Latecomer: Toward a Global Logic of the Open Policy," *Journal of Contemporary China*, Vol. 5, No. 12 (Summer 1996), pp. 187–208.

17. The notion of China's economy as "growing out of the plan" belongs to Naughton, *Growing Out of the Plan*. For more on China's "trading out of ISI" see Moore, "China as a Latecomer."

18. Jeffry Frieden and Ronald Rogowski, "The Impact of the International Economy on National Policies: An Analytic Overview," in Robert Keohane and Helen Milner, eds., *Internationalization and Domestic Politics* (New York: Cambridge University Press, 1996), p. 33.

19. Peter Evans, "The Eclipse of the State," *World Politics,* Oct. 1997, pp. 62–87; quote on p. 65.

20. The locus classicus on this subject is Alexander Gerschenkron, *Economic Backwardness in Historical Perspective* (Cambridge: Harvard University Press, 1962).

21. "Crisis to Hit GDP, Exporters," *South China Morning Post,* Feb. 4, 1998, "Business Post," p. 4.

22. "Sino-Japan Ties Set to Leap Backwards," *South China Morning Post,* Aug. 12, 1998, p. 15.

23. "Dynamic Diplomacy Harks Back to Style of Zhou Enlai," *South China Morning Post,* April 5, 1998, p. 6.

24. *Newsweek,* June 29, 1998, p. 26.

25. There were industrial and trading interests that favored a stable currency, of course, but given the proactive stance taken against devaluation in Beijing, their role was limited to background support.

26. MOFTEC had agreed, one interviewee revealed, only to allow Shenzhen to serve as a trial base for direct exports by private enterprises.

27. "Fujian Province Seeks to Attract Overseas Investment," *Xinhua* (New China News Agency), May 14, 1998, in FBIS-CHI-98-133.

28. "New PRC Strategy Benefits Foreign Trade," *Xinhua* (New China News Agency), May 12, 1998, in FBIS-CHI-98-131.

29. Our conclusions here are consistent with other recent analyses of the Chinese foreign policy system. See, for instance, David Bachman, "Structure and Process in the Making of Chinese Foreign Policy," in Kim, *China and the World,* pp. 34–54.

30. Lardy, *China's Unfinished Economic Revolution.*

31. "Zhu Rongji Talks to Academicians about China's Economic Situation," *Ching Pao* (Hong Kong), Aug. 1, 1998, pp. 32–35, in FBIS-CHI-98-222.

32. See, for example, the comments of Foreign Ministry spokesman Zhu Bangzao in "Villainous Taiwan Sabotaging Markets," *South China Morning Post,* March 11, 1998, p. 9. It should be noted that Taiwan's role in the AFC remains controversial, with some foreign observers arguing that Taiwan's behavior has been unfairly maligned. According to this view the Taiwan central bank spent several billion U.S. dollars trying to defend its currency, giving up only in the face of undiminished pressure from speculators.

33. See, for instance, an article by analysts from CASS's Institute of World Economics and Politics entitled "The East Asian Financial Crisis and its Lessons," *Qiushi* (Seeking Truth), March 1, 1998, pp. 41–45, in FBIS-CHI-98-138.

34. For an excellent introduction to these issues see Alastair Iain Johnston, "Learning versus Adaptation: Explaining Change in Chinese Arms Control Policy in the 1980s and 1990s," *China Journal,* No. 35 (January 1996), pp. 27–61.

35. For a similar argument along these lines see Samuel S. Kim, "Chinese Foreign Policy in Theory and Practice," in Kim, *China and the World,* p. 26.

36. For more on this subject see Thomas G. Moore, "China and Globalization," in Samuel S. Kim, ed., *East Asia and Globalization* (Lanham, Md.: Rowman and Littlefield, 2000), pp. 105–31.

37. Areas of relatively strong resistance include security matters and political engagement. By contrast, trade relations, technology transfer, and scientific/academic exchange are areas of weaker resistance. Areas such as financial integration represent a middle ground of resistance.

CHAPTER 8

1. Union of International Associations, *Yearbook of International Organizations 1997/1998,* Vol. 2 (Munich: K. G. Saur, 1997), p. 1747.

2. David M. Lampton, draft proposal for this volume, March 12, 1997, p. 9.

3. For one of the best studies of the impact of international regimes on Chinese foreign policy, see Harold Jacobson and Michel Oksenberg, *China's Participation in the IMF, the World Bank, and GATT* (Ann Arbor, Mich.: University of Michigan Press, 1990).

4. Joint implementation was a scheme proposed by the advanced industrialized countries whereby they would receive credit toward achieving their targets for greenhouse gas reduction by undertaking projects in developing countries (e.g., a U.S. power company could pursue a reforestation effort in Brazil), where the cost of taking action overseas would be substantially lower than the domestic cost.

5. Thomas J. Christensen, "Chinese Realpolitik," *Foreign Affairs,* Vol. 75, No. 5 (Sept.–Oct. 1996), p. 37.

6. Harry Harding and David Shambaugh, "Conclusion," final draft chapter for inclusion in Harry Harding, ed., *China's Cooperative Relationships: Partnerships and Alignments in Modern Chinese Foreign Policy,* p. 2.

7. Samuel S. Kim, "International Organizations in Chinese Foreign Policy," *Annals,* No. 519 (Jan. 1992), p. 151.

8. Harding and Shambaugh, "Conclusion," pp. 6–7.

9. Alastair Iain Johnston, "China's New 'Old Thinking': The Concept of Limited Deterrence," *International Security,* Vol. 20, No. 3 (Winter 1995–96), p. 7.

10. Michel Oksenberg and Elizabeth Economy, *Shaping U.S.-China Relations: A Long-Term Strategy* (New York: Council on Foreign Relations Press, 1997).

11. Fred Tipson, "China and the Telecommunications Regime," in Michel Oksenberg and Elizabeth Economy, eds., *China Joins the World: Progress and Prospects* (New York: Council on Foreign Relations Press, 1999), pp. 231–65.

12. Oksenberg and Economy, *Shaping U.S.-China Relations,* p. 16.

13. Elizabeth Economy, "Negotiating the Terrain of Global Climate Policy in the Soviet Union and China: Linking International and Domestic Decision Making Pathways," Ph.D. dissertation, University of Michigan, 1994.

14. M. Taylor Fravel, "China's Attitude toward U.N. Peacekeeping Operations since 1989," *Asian Survey,* Vol. 36 (Nov. 1996), pp. 1105–6.

15. Oksenberg and Economy, *Shaping U.S.-China Relations,* p. 19.

16. Ibid., p. 18.

17. Johnston, "China's New 'Old Thinking,'" p. 7.

18. Margaret Pearson, "China's Integration into the International Trade and Investment Regime," in Oksenberg and Economy, *China Joins the World*, p. 161.

19. See also ibid., pp. 186–90.

20. Nicholas Lardy, "China and the International Financial System," in Oksenberg and Economy, *China Joins the World*, p. 221.

21. Oksenberg and Economy, *Shaping U.S.-China Relations*, pp. 19–20.

22. Economy, "Negotiating the Terrain of Global Climate Policy," pp. 137–211.

23. Peter Haas, "Knowledge, Power and International Coordination," *International Organization*, Vol. 46, No. 1 (Winter 1992).

24. Elizabeth Economy and Miranda Schreurs, "Domestic and International Linkages in Environmental Politics," in Miranda Schreurs and Elizabeth Economy, eds., *The Internationalization of Environmental Protection* (Cambridge: Cambridge University Press, 1997), pp. 6–7.

25. As will become clear in the case of China, expertise does not exist in many areas and must be developed.

26. Jacobson and Oksenberg, *China's Participation in the IMF*, p. 151.

27. Banning Garrett and Bonnie Glaser, "Chinese Perspectives on Nuclear Arms Control," *International Security*, Vol. 20, No. 3 (Winter 1995–96), p. 46.

28. Samuel S. Kim, "Thinking Globally in Post-Mao China," *Journal of Peace Research*, Vol. 27, No. 2 (1990), p. 198.

29. Jacobson and Oksenberg, *China's Participation in the IMF*, p. 142.

30. For example, this appears to have happened in the case of Chinese accession to the Framework Convention on Global Climate Change, in which officials in the State Planning Commission (SPC) who were assigned to represent SPC interests have, over the years, become far more sympathetic to environmentally proactive measures than their colleagues within the SPC.

31. Oksenberg and Economy, *Shaping U.S.-China Relations*, p. 12.

32. Ibid., p. 13.

33. Author discussion with *Huanjing Bao* (Environmental News) reporter, Beijing, Dec. 6, 1997.

34. Oksenberg and Economy, *Shaping U.S.-China Relations*, p. 29.

35. Samuel Kim, "China's International Organizational Behavior," in Thomas W. Robinson and David Shambaugh, eds., *Chinese Foreign Policy* (Oxford: Oxford University Press, 1994), p. 434.

36. Ibid., p. 432.

37. Kim, "Thinking Globally," p. 203.

38. Jacobson and Oksenberg, *China's Participation in the IMF*, p. 41.

39. Ibid., p. 143.

40. Margaret M. Pearson, *Joint Ventures in the People's Republic of China: The Control of Foreign and Direct Investment under Socialism* (Princeton, N.J.: Princeton University Press, 1991).

41. Yangmin Wang, "The Politics of U.S.-China Economic Relations," *Asian Survey,* Vol. 23, No. 5 (May 1993), p. 459.

42. Ibid., p. 479.

43. Oksenberg and Economy, *Shaping U.S.-China Relations,* p. 29.

44. Garrett and Glaser, "Chinese Perspectives on Nuclear Arms Control," pp. 50–51.

45. Sara E. Mendelson, "Internal Battles and External Wars: Politics, Learning, and the Soviet Withdrawal from Afghanistan," *World Politics,* Vol. 45 (April 1993), pp. 332–33.

46. Alastair Iain Johnston, "Is There Learning in Chinese Arms Control Policy?" paper prepared for the American Political Science Association, New York, Sept. 1–4, 1994.

47. Ibid., p. 43.

48. Jan, "The PRC's Bid to Enter the GATT/WTO," *Issues and Studies,* Vol. 33, No. 6 (June 1997), p. 42.

49. Garrett and Glaser, "Chinese Perspectives on Nuclear Arms Control," p. 53.

50. George Schaller, *The Last Panda* (Chicago: University of Chicago Press, 1993).

51. The case study of China's participation in the Montreal Protocol is excerpted from Michel Oksenberg and Elizabeth Economy, "The China Case: Implementation Under Market Reform," in Harold Jacobson and Edith Brown Weiss, eds., *Engaging Countries: Strengthening Compliance with International Environmental Accords* (Cambridge, Mass.: MIT Press, 1998).

52. An expanded version of the discussion of China's participation in the FCCC can be found in Elizabeth Economy, "Negotiating the Terrain of Global Climate Change Policy," pp. 137–211.

53. The Vienna Convention included no agreement on how the international community should respond to the threat of ozone depletion other than to continue studying the issue and to meet in two years.

54. The source of this prompting will require further exploration.

55. In 1998 the National Environmental Protection Agency was elevated in bureaucratic status to ministerial level and renamed the State Environmental Protection Administration.

56. The Montreal Protocol includes a provision that the parties meet every four years to review the status of implementation and the current science on ozone depletion. China joined the deliberations leading to the 1991 London Amendments to the Protocol.

57. Author interview with MFA official, Beijing, Dec. 1996.

58. Author interview with MFA official, Beijing, Nov. 1998.

59. Jimin Zhao and Leonardo Ortolano, "Implementing the Montreal Protocol in China: Use of Cleaner Technology in Two Industrial Sectors," *Environmental Impact Assessment Review,* Vol. 83, No. 5–6 (Sept.–Nov. 1999), pp. 510–13.

60. These scientific negotiations preceded the political negotiations (1991–92) and were designed to forge an international consensus concerning the likelihood, nature, and impact of global climate change.

61. Since this case study was completed in 1994, a volume of Chinese position papers detailing the internal debates over climate change has emerged. This set of papers would likely be extremely useful in developing a further understanding of the ways in which the international community influenced Chinese thinking.

62. By the time of the negotiations China was the third largest emitter of greenhouse gases in the world after the United States and Japan.

63. China had taken extraordinary steps to ensure that the developing countries would not place pressure on it to take action. For more on this see Elizabeth Economy, "China's Environmental Diplomacy," in Samuel Kim, ed., *China and the World,* 4th ed. (Boulder, Colo.: Westview, 1998). In addition, neither the United States nor Japan was prepared to undertake this task at the time of the negotiations.

64. In the wake of the 1998 administrative reforms, the Administrative Center for China's Agenda 21 is now managed by the Ministry of Science and Technology.

65. Interview with State Science and Technology Commission officials, March 1997.

66. According to two sources, Zhu made these remarks at the November 1998 meeting of the China Council on International Cooperation on Environment and Development.

67. Interview with Chinese NGO official, Beijing, Nov. 18, 1998.

68. Interview with Chinese Academy of Sciences official, Beijing, Nov. 17, 1998.

69. Adaptation means that China will take steps to adapt to the impacts of climate change as they occur. Mitigation means that China would take measures to prevent or slow climate change.

70. http://www.usembassy-china.gov/english/sandt/clchng.htm#TOP.

71. http://www.iisd.ca/linkages/download/asc/enb 1288e.txt.

72. Ibid.

73. Global climate change actually is only one issue among seven to be considered by the U.S.-China Forum on Sustainable Development, Energy, and the Environment, which was inaugurated in April 1996.

74. Briefing by forum participants for U.S. NGOs, Council on Environmental Quality, Washington, D.C., March 3, 2000.

75. Author discussion with Chinese forum participant, Washington, D.C., April 1999.

76. Telephone discussion with World Resources Institute scientist, Washington, D.C., Dec. 10, 1998.

77. Ibid.

78. E-mail exchange with Chinese SEPA official, Dec. 6, 1998.

79. Oksenberg and Economy, *Shaping U.S.-China Relations,* p. 25.

CHAPTER 9

1. Works by Western specialists that specifically address Chinese policy development on nonproliferation and arms control issues include Evan Medeiros and Bates Gill, *Chinese Arms Exports: Policy, Players, and Process* (Carlisle Barracks, Pa.: U.S. Army War College, 2000); Alastair Iain Johnston and Paul Evans, "China's Engagement with Multilateral Security Institutions," in Alastair Iain Johnston and Robert S. Ross, eds.,

Engaging China: The Management of an Emerging Power (New York: Routledge, 1999), pp. 235–72; Alastair Iain Johntson, "Learning versus Adaptation: Explaining Change in Chinese Arms Control Policy in the 1980s and 1990s," *China Journal*, No. 35 (Jan. 1996), pp. 27–61; Karl W. Eikenberry, *Explaining and Influencing Chinese Arms Transfers*, McNair Papers 36 (Washington, D.C.: National Defense University, Feb. 1995); Bates Gill, *Chinese Arms Transfers* (Westport, Conn.: Praeger, 1992); John W. Lewis, Hua Di, and Xue Litai, "Beijing's Defense Establishment: Solving the Arms-Export Enigma," *International Security*, Vol. 14, No. 4 (Spring 1991), pp. 87–109.

2. Major Chinese sources include Jing-dong Yuan, "Culture Matters: Chinese Approaches to Arms Control and Disarmament," *Contemporary Security Policy*, Vol. 19, No. 1 (April 1998), pp. 85–128; Lu Ning, *The Dynamics of Foreign-Policy Decision-making in China* (Boulder, Colo.: Westview, 1997), especially pp. 113–19; Pan Zhenqiang, ed., *Guoji Caijun yu Junbei Kongzhi* (International Disarmament and Arms Control) (Beijing: National Defense University Press, 1996); Du Xiangwan, ed., *He Junbei Kongzhi de Kexue Jishu* (Foundations of Nuclear Arms Control Science and Technology) (Beijing: National Defense Industry Press, 1996); Zhu Mingquan, "The Evolution of China's Nuclear Nonproliferation Policy," *Nonproliferation Review* (Winter 1997); Wu Yun, "China's Policies Towards Arms Control and Disarmament: From Passive Responding to Active Leading," *Pacific Review*, Vol. 9. No. 4 (1996); Zhu Mingquan, *He Kuosan: Weixian yu Fangzhi* (Nuclear Proliferation: Danger and Prevention) (Shanghai: Shanghai Science and Technology Documents Press, 1995). This brief bibliographic survey does not include a burgeoning literature in the open Chinese press, in such journals as *Guoji Wenti* (International Studies), *Xiandai Guoji Wenti* (Contemporary International Studies), and *Guoji Zhanlue* (International Strategy). See also, for example, the bibliographies of *Renmin Ribao* (People's Daily) articles concerned with nonproliferation and arms control, *He Caijun yu Junbei Kongzhi Ziliao: Renmin Ribao Youguan Ziliao Xuanbian, 1990–94* (Nuclear Disarmament and Arms Control Materials: Selected Related References from the People's Daily, 1990–94) (Beijing: People's Daily, 1995), and a subsequent volume in this series. Academic papers delivered by Chinese specialists at international conferences—such as those sponsored by the International School of Disarmament and Arms Control, the National Resources Defense Council, the National Academy of Sciences, the International Network of Engineers and Scientists Against Proliferation, the Union of Concerned Scientists, and the Center for Nonproliferation Studies—are increasingly available.

3. Walter C. Clemens, Jr., "China," in Richard Dean Burns, ed., *Encyclopedia of Arms Control and Disarmament*, Vol. 1 (New York: Scribner's, 1993), p. 66.

4. *China's Proposal on Essential Measures for an Immediate Halt to the Arms Race and for Disarmament*, submitted at the United Nations Second Special Session on Disarmament in New York on June 21, 1982.

5. *Chinese Plenary Statement to the Conference on Disarmament*, statement presented in Geneva on July 17, 1990.

6. Pan et al., *Guoji Caijun*, pp. 123–24. For example, in 1988, fearful that its call for a "50 percent reduction" might become reality, China changed its position on

superpower disarmament, calling on them to make undefined "drastic" and "substantial" reductions in their nuclear arsenals.

7. A widely respected source subsequently estimated the test's yield at 660 kilotons, still China's largest underground test. "Nuclear Notebook," *The Bulletin of the Atomic Scientists,* May 1993, p. 49.

8. *Statement of the Government of the People's Republic of China on the Question of Nuclear Testing,* Oct. 5, 1993, reprinted in part in "China Airs Stand on Nuclear Testing," *Beijing Review,* Oct. 18–24, 1993, p. 4.

9. Pan et al., *Guoji Caijun,* pp. 127–29.

10. "China Says Still Wants Peaceful Nuclear Tests," Reuters, April 23, 1996.

11. See "China Criticizes Draft Nuclear Treaty but Agrees to Submission," *Xinhua,* Aug. 15, 1996, translated in British Broadcasting Corporation, *Summary of World Broadcasts* (FE/D2693/G), Aug. 17, 1996.

12. *Joint U.S.-China Statement,* Oct. 29, 1997. See http://www.china-embassy.org.

13. United Nations Security Council Resolution 1172, S/RES/1172 (1998), June 6, 1998.

14. The Soviet Union's last test was in October 1990; the newly independent state of Russia has not tested since; the last U.S. test was in September 1992; the last U.K test was in November 1991. France participated in the moratorium for nearly four years, from late 1991 to late 1995, when it conducted a final series of tests from September 1995 to January 1996. Also during this period the international community decided to indefinitely extend the Non-Proliferation Treaty (in May 1995), a result achieved in large measure by a commitment of the nuclear powers to engage in meaningful disarmament efforts, such as the CTBT.

15. Michael Littlejohns, "U.N. Votes against N-Testing," *Financial Times,* Dec. 14, 1995, p. 6.

16. "Sources Indicate Plans for Nuclear Test Halted," *Itar-Tass,* in Foreign Broadcast Information Service (FBIS), *Daily Report: China,* FBIS-CHI-95-211, Oct. 31, 1995; "Intention to Grant Yen Loans to PRC Firms Up," *Yomiuri Shimbun,* in FBIS, *Daily Report: East Asia,* FBIS-EAS-95-208, Oct. 26, 1995.

17. Douglas Busvine, "China's Jiang Calls for Nuclear Test Ban Treaty," Reuters, July 5, 1996.

18. *Statement of the Government of the People's Republic of China,* July 29, 1996, Conference on Disarmament Document CD/1410, July 29, 1996.

19. Xiangli Sun, *Implications of a Comprehensive Test Ban for China's Security Policy* (Center for International Security and Arms Control, Stanford University, June 1997), p. 8. Dr. Sun is a physicist working for the Arms Control Research Division of the Institute of Applied Physics and Computational Mathematics within the Chinese strategic weapons research and development complex.

20. *Statement of the Government of the People's Republic of China,* July 29, 1996, Conference on Disarmament Document CD/1410, July 29, 1996.

21. With 45 tests over a period of 381 months (October 1964 through July 1996), China averaged about 0.118 tests every month, or 2.95 tests on average for a period of 25 months. Comparably intensive testing for China occurred over the period Octo-

ber 1975 to December 1978, when China tested nine times over a period of 38 months and four times in 1976 alone.

22. Zou Yunhua, "International Arms Control Situation," in *Guoji Wenti Yanjiu* (International Studies), No. 1 (Jan. 1994). Senior Colonel Zou was posted to COSTIND at the time of her article and served in Geneva with the Chinese delegation to the CD during the CTBT negotiations.

23. These points are made by Sun, "Implications of a Comprehensive Test Ban," p. 11.

24. In a related development it appears that the CTBT negotiations produced a more focused commitment by the Chinese leadership to develop its expertise in arms control research and policy development. Outmaneuvered into accepting a treaty placing considerable constraints on China's future military capability, the Chinese arms control community has grown across a number of institutions since mid- to late 1996. It is likely that this interest stems from a realization that in this era of progress in nonproliferation and arms control, China needs to be better prepared to engage the international community constructively while at the same time preserving Chinese national interests.

25. This process is explained and analyzed in Medeiros and Gill, *Chinese Arms Exports,* and John Frankenstein and Bates Gill, "Challenges to the Chinese Defense Industries," *China Quarterly* (June 1996).

26. *SIPRI Yearbook 1997: Armaments, Disarmament and International Security* (Oxford: Oxford University Press, 1997), Table 9.1, p. 268; the more recent data are drawn from the SIPRI Web site: www.sipri.se.

27. See, for example, State Council and Central Military Commission, *Zhonghua Renmin Gongheguo Junpin Chukou Guanli Tiaoli* (People's Republic of China Military Products Export Management Regulations), Order No. 234, Oct. 22, 1997 (Jan. 1, 1998); State Council, *Zhonghua Renmin Gongheguo He Chukou Guanzhi Tiaoli* (People's Republic of China Nuclear Export Control Regulations), Sept. 11, 1997; Ministry of the Chemical Industry, *Zhonghua Renmin Gongheguo Jiankong Huaxuepin Guanli Shishi Xize* (People's Republic of China Detailed Implementation Regulations for Control and Management of Chemical Products), Order No. 12, March 10, 1997; State Council, *Zhonghua Renmin Gongheguo Jiankong Huaxuepin Guanli Tiaoli* (People's Republic of China Regulations for Control and Management of Chemical Products), Order No. 190, Dec. 27, 1995. China announced in November 2000 that it would soon issue export control regulations for missile-related transfers.

28. UN General Assembly, *Statement by H.E. Sha Zukang, Ambassador of the People's Republic of China for Disarmament Affairs, at the First Committee of the 52nd Session of the United Nations General Assembly,* Oct. 14, 1997. See also UN General Assembly, *Chinese Statement to the 52nd United Nations First Committee on the Draft Resolution of the Role of Science and Technology in the Context of International Security and Disarmament,* Nov. 12, 1997.

29. Nayan Chanda, "Technology Cocooned: U.S. Retaliates Against China's Sale of Silkworm Missiles," *Far Eastern Economic Review,* Nov. 1987, p. 27.

30. This act, also known as the Gore-McCain Act, is targeted at countries that transfer destabilizing weapons to either Iran or Iraq.

31. Benjamin Lim, "Beijing Defends Selling Iran Arms," *Washington Times,* June 4, 1997, p. A4.

32. Bill Gertz, "Senate Asks for Sanctions on China," *Washington Times,* June 18, 1997, p. 13.

33. Steve Erlanger, "U.S. Says Chinese Will Stop Sending Missiles to Iran," *New York Times,* Oct. 18, 1997, p. 1; Laura Myers, "U.S.-China," Associated Press, Oct. 18, 1997, quoting State Department spokesman James P. Rubin.

34. The White House, Office of the Press Secretary, "Fact Sheet: Accomplishments of the U.S.-China Summit," Oct. 30, 1997.

35. Timothy V. McCarthy, *A Chronology of PRC Missile Trade and Developments* (Monterey, Calif.: Monterey Institute of International Studies, 1992).

36. Mark Hibbs, "Sensitive Iran Reactor Deal May Hinge on MFN for China," *Nucleonics Week,* Oct. 1, 1992, pp. 5–6; Steve Coll, "U.S. Halted Nuclear Bid by Iran," *Washington Post,* Nov. 17, 1992, p. A1.

37. Elaine Sciolino, "China Cancels Deal for Selling Iran 2 Reactors," *New York Times,* Sept. 28, 1995, p. A1.

38. "China Said Holding Advance Funds for Conversion Plant Sale to Iran," *Nuclear-Fuel,* Dec. 39, 1996, p. 3.

39. The White House, Office of the Press Secretary, "Press Briefing by Secretary of State Madeleine Albright and National Security Advisor Sandy Berger," Oct. 29, 1997; R. Jeffrey Smith, "China's Pledge to End Iran Nuclear Aid Yields U.S. Help," *Washington Post,* Oct. 30, 1997, p. 1.

40. "China Agrees to End Nuclear Trade with Iran When Two Projects Completed," *NuclearFuel,* Nov. 3, 1997, pp. 3–4.

41. Xie Guang, ed., *Dangdai Zhongguo de Guofang Keji Shiye* (Contemporary China's Defense Science and Technology Undertakings) (Beijing: Contemporary China Press, 1992), pp. 73–81. On Chinese cruise missile–related assistance to Iran see Gordon Jacobs and Tim McCarthy, "China's Missile Sales: Few Changes for the Future," *Jane's Intelligence Review,* Dec. 1992, p. 561.

42. "Beijing Says No Nuclear Cooperation with Iran," *Inside China Today,* Nov. 3, 1997; "China Says It Has No Nuclear Cooperation with Iran," Reuters, Nov. 2, 1997.

43. Interview with MFA official, Dec, 1997.

44. Lu, *Dynamics of Foreign-Policy Decisionmaking,* pp. 113–17.

45. Lewis et al., "Beijing's Defense Establishment," p. 95.

46. State Council, *China: Arms Control and Disarmament* (Beijing: Information Office of the State Council of the People's Republic of China, Nov. 1995).

47. State Council, *Zhonghua Renmin Gongheguo He Chukou Guanli Tiaoli.* See also "Regulations on Nuclear Export Control," *Xinhua,* in FBIS, *Daily Report: China,* FBIS-CHI-97-256, Sept. 11, 1997; Jiang Wandi, "Tighter Export Controls on Nuclear Exports," *Beijing Review,* Dec. 1–7, 1997, pp. 21–23; "Nuclear Product Controls Issued," *Xinhua,* in FBIS, *Daily Report: China,* FBIS-CHI-98-170, June 19, 1998.

48. See Lewis et al., "Beijing's Defense Establishment," p. 95, and Lu, *Dynamics of Foreign-Policy Decisionmaking,* pp. 113–17.

49. Nicholas R. Lardy, *Foreign Trade and Economic Reform in China 1978–1990* (Cambridge: Cambridge University Press, 1992), pp. 16–36; Nicholas R. Lardy, "Chinese Foreign Trade," in Robert Ash and Y. Y. Kueh, eds., *The Chinese Economy under Deng Xiaoping* (Oxford: Clarendon Press, 1996), pp. 217–46.

50. Sha Zukang, quoted in the *Jiefangjun Bao* (Liberation Army Daily), Nov. 16, 1996, p. 4, and reprinted in the *NAPSNet Daily Report,* Nautilus Institute, Nov. 21, 1996.

51. The UNROCA was established by United Nations General Assembly Resolution 46/36L in December 1991. The register first began recording submissions from United Nations members in 1993 for their imports and exports of major conventional weapons in calendar year 1992. China's submissions to the UNROCA for the years 1992–96 are included in its defense white paper of July 1998.

52. China was not alone in this. According to a study of the UNROCA participation of thirty-nine Asia-Pacific states, only six countries (Australia, Canada, Japan, New Zealand, the Republic of Korea, and the United States) included background information with their submissions during the three-year period 1992–94. Bates Gill, "Asia-Pacific Participation in the United Nations Register of Conventional Arms: Prospects for Regionalization," in United Nations Center for Disarmament Affairs, *Workshop on the United Nations Register of Conventional Arms: The Experience of the Asia-Pacific Region* (New York: United Nations, 1996), pp. 21–31.

53. See, for example, Edward J. Laurance, Siemon T. Wezeman, and Herbert Wulf, *Arms Watch: SIPRI Report on the First Year of the UN Register of Conventional Arms* (Oxford: Oxford University Press, 1993), Annexes 1 and 2; Malcolm Chalmers and Owen Greene, *The UN Register in Its Fourth Year,* Bradford Arms Register Series Working Paper No. 2 (Bradford, U.K.: Department of Peace Studies, University of Bradford, Nov. 1996).

54. *Statement by H.E. Ambassador Sha Zukang to the Conference on Disarmament,* June 26, 1997.

55. *SIPRI Yearbook 1997: Armaments, Disarmament and International Security* (Oxford: Oxford University Press, 1997), p. 214.

56. UNROCA submissions are available on the Web at http://domino.un.org/REGISTER.nsf.

57. Interviews, Jan. 1999.

58. State Council, *China: Arms Control and Disarmament.*

59. See Kang Choi and Panitan Wattanayagorn, "Development of Defence White Papers in the Asia-Pacific Region," in Bates Gill and J. N. Mak, eds., *Arms, Transparency and Security in South-East Asia* (Oxford: Oxford University Press, 1997), pp. 79–92.

60. *Chairman's Statement of the Second ASEAN Regional Forum,* Bandar Seri Begawan, Brunei Darussalam, Aug. 1, 1995; reprinted in *NAPSNet,* Nautilus Institute, Sept. 1995.

61. Noriyoshi Itokawa, "Sino-Japanese Security Talks Discussed," *Asahi Shimbun,* Jan. 16, 1996, in FBIS, *Daily Report: China,* FBIS-CHI-96-013, Jan. 16, 1996.

62. Interviews with Chinese military and security think-tank researchers, Nov. 1996.

63. Interviews with senior Chinese arms control official, Jan. 1999.

64. Interviews with current and former PLA officials, Sept. 1998.

65. Johnston, "Learning versus Adaptation."

66. Pan et al., *Guoji Caijun*, pp. 423–24.

67. Interview with high-ranking United Nations disarmament official, Jan. 1998.

68. Pan et al., *Guoji Caijun*, pp. 423–24.

69. In June 1998, during his state visit to China, President Bill Clinton publicly declared what had been official, but usually more muted, U.S. policy: that the United States would not support Taiwan's independence, would not support a "one China, one Taiwan" policy, and would not support Taiwan's membership in international organizations in which statehood is a criterion for membership (such as the United Nations).

70. See Medeiros and Gill, *Chinese Arms Exports.*

CHAPTER 10

1. The research for this chapter, consisting primarily of detailed interviews held in China, Taiwan, and the United States, was largely completed in mid-1998.

2. Mao Zedong reportedly exercised an even greater degree of control over Taiwan policy than Deng Xiaoping. Although Zhou Enlai was closely involved with many aspects of policy regarding Taiwan in the 1950s, 1960s, and early 1970s, Mao alone made the decisions.

3. Despite their putative authority as designated successors to Deng Xiaoping, Hu Yaobang, Zhao Ziyang, and Jiang Zemin did not exercise decisive influence over Taiwan policy while Deng was alive and healthy. According to informants, party and military elders played a more important role than any of his erstwhile successors. This is not to say that Hu, Zhao, and Jiang exerted no influence whatsoever over Taiwan policy while Deng was active. Such influence was simply limited to administration and implementation, as I discuss later.

4. Jiang also exerts indirect influence over Taiwan policy as head of the Foreign Affairs Leading Small Group (FALSG), which he became following Li Peng's retirement from the State Council premiership in early 1998.

5. Chu Yun-han, "Making Sense of Beijing's Policy toward Taiwan: The Prospect of Cross-Strait Relations during Jiang Zemin's Next Five-Year Tenure," paper presented at a conference entitled "The PRC after the Fifteenth Party Congress," sponsored by the Institute for National Policy Research, Taipei, Taiwan, Feb. 1998, p. 4.

6. Because Taiwan was forcibly annexed by Japan as a result of the Sino-Japanese War of 1895 and occupied by the fleeing Nationalists after World War II, its continued political separation from the Mainland is widely viewed in China as the last major legacy of the imperialist era of oppression and humiliation.

7. For these reasons achieving success in the handling of Taiwan policy is viewed as a means of consolidating a supreme leader's personal power and ensuring his historical legacy. This is especially true in the post-Deng era given that leaders of the "third generation" must rely on genuine policy successes to maintain their power and authority, in contrast to leaders of the revolutionary generation, who could rely on status, prestige, and strong personal relations to maintain power.

8. As I discuss in greater detail later, Jiang is reportedly able to exert considerable authority over many Taiwan policy issues through his control of the TALSG. However, for major policy decisions at the level of grand strategy and for important new initiatives Jiang must obtain the approval of the Politburo Standing Committee, especially key members such as Li Peng.

9. Two less important personal advisors on Taiwan policy are Liu Ji, a deputy director of the Chinese Academy of Social Sciences (CASS) and a former Shanghai-based Jiang associate, and Li Chuwen, former head of the Hong Kong Office of the New China News Agency (Xinhuashe) and currently Senior Advisor to Xinhuashe's Hong Kong Office and a foreign affairs advisor to the Shanghai government.

10. In addition, Zhang Wannian was in charge of the military exercises and missile tests carried out near Taiwan in late 1995 and early 1996.

11. Michael D. Swaine, *The Role of the Chinese Military in National Security Policy-Making*, rev. ed. (Santa Monica, Calif.: RAND Corporation, 1998). For additional information on the CMC, see also the chapter by Tai Ming Cheung in this volume.

12. Xiong is also a member of the FALSG.

13. In the military arena this almost certainly includes Xiong Guangkai.

14. Chu, "Making Sense of Beijing's Policy toward Taiwan," p. 6.

15. On most Taiwan policy issues Li Peng reportedly relies heavily on information provided by Qian Qichen. Moreover, Qian probably presides over the TALSG in Jiang Zemin's absence.

16. For more information on the MFA, see the chapter by Lu Ning in this volume.

17. In addition to these central organizations, an increasing array of provincial and municipal units have also become involved in administering aspects of Taiwan policy. However, they have no influence over core elements of China's grand strategy toward Taiwan.

18. Interviews, Beijing, Sept. 1998.

19. George W. Tsai, "The Making of Taiwan Policy in Mainland China: Structure and Process," *Issues & Studies*, Vol. 33, No. 9 (Sept. 1997), p. 13. ARATS has six departments, including a secretariat and research and economic offices.

20. Such functions are generally performed by the CCP Central Committee Taiwan Affairs Office.

21. Leading small groups such as the TALSG are sometimes referred to by the leadership as "advisory bodies" for the Politburo or party Secretariat, and their decisions are often issued in the names of those bodies. However, they can also present policy packages directly to the party's leading organs and can issue orders and instructions directly to line departments.

22. Interviews, Beijing, Sept. 1998.

23. Deng stated in December 1978 that reunification was one of three major tasks to be accomplished during the 1980s.

24. Interviews, Beijing, Sept. 1998.

25. During the 1980s and early 1990s the TALSG membership grew to include at least twelve individuals: a head and deputy head, a vice premier, the director of

the CCP Investigation Department, the director of the Foreign Propaganda Small Group, the chairman of the All-China Federation of Taiwan Compatriots, the director of the Party Central Committee International Liaison Department, the minister of state security, the minister of culture, the minister of public security, the minister of foreign economic relations and trade, and the director of the Party Central Committee United Front Work Department and concurrent head of the Central Committee Taiwan Affairs Office.

26. Yang had served for many years in the PLA and was the senior vice chairman of the Central Military Commission throughout much of the 1980s. In that capacity he served as the primary supervisor of the military reform process.

27. Interviews, Beijing, Sept. 1998.

28. Jiang was named head of the TALSG in June 1993.

29. According to informants, this decrease was carried out as part of an overall reduction in the size of party organs mandated by the Fourteenth Party Congress in fall 1992. The decrease in membership was also reportedly supported by Jiang Zemin in order to increase the overall importance of the TALSG.

30. Hence officials representing party investigation, liaison, and propaganda departments; mass organizations associated with Taiwan compatriots; and ministries in charge of cultural affairs, public security, and foreign economic relations were all dropped from the TALSG. For more details see *Sing Tao Jih Pao* (Sing Tao Daily), Hong Kong, Feb. 7, 1996, p. A 4, in FBIS-CHI-96-026, 2/7/96, p. 23, and Chu, "Making Sense of Beijing's Policy toward Taiwan," p. 4.

31. Chu, "Making Sense of Beijing's Policy toward Taiwan," p. 5.

32. Ibid., pp. 5–6. The largely technical task of coordinating policies among economic and trade ministries and between central and local economic authorities was transferred to the State Council Economic and Trade Policy Toward Taiwan Coordination Small Group, headed by Vice Premier Li Lanqing.

33. Tsai, "Making of Taiwan Policy in Mainland China," p. 6.

34. Hence the relationship of the CCTAO to the TALSG is similar to that of the State Council Foreign Affairs Office to the FALSG. See Swaine, *Role of the Chinese Military,* p. 25.

35. These large meetings are attended by representatives of all Taiwan-related policy organs in the party, state, and military structures. They are supposed to be held every five years and are convened primarily to ratify decisions made by the senior policy echelon and to work out procedures essential to the implementation of those decisions.

36. Tsai, "Making of Taiwan Policy in Mainland China," p. 6; interviews, Beijing, Sept. 1998. The director of the CCTAO is able to exert considerable influence over the Taiwan policy-making process through his control over such activities, which allow him to solicit and absorb expert analysis, structure policy deliberations, and shape senior leadership views.

37. Ibid. Tsai asserts that the CCTAO became "the main channel through which military cadres express their views on Taiwan affairs." Although this might have been the case in the 1980s, such views apparently did not have a major effect on Tai-

wan policy decisions made during that decade, and that is apparently not the case under Jiang Zemin today, as I discuss later.

38. Wang was previously governor of Fujian Province and was extensively involved in Taiwan-related activities.

39. Tsai states that at this time the CCTAO began to handle information from the PLA General Political Department, the State Council, and the Ministry of State Security. However, the CCTAO does not have control of all policy documents and proposals relating to Taiwan. Some materials are routed to the senior leadership via the Central Committee General Office, discussed later. Tsai, "Making of Taiwan Policy in Mainland China," p. 7.

40. In a formal sense the CCTAO, the SCTAO, and other organs responsible for Taiwan policy are to convey all relevant documents and opinions on Taiwan policy to the CCGO, which then evaluates and routes such materials to the senior members of the party Secretariat and the Politburo. However, the aforementioned offices all possess ministry-level status in the bureaucracy, suggesting that the two TAOs are not invariably obligated to submit policy materials to the CCGO. Indeed, as I indicate later, not all policy materials are sent through the CCGO.

41. The CCGO obviously has much broader responsibilities and powers than the CCTAO. Hence, it is unable to concentrate on any one policy arena. Yet its important "gatekeeper" role in mediating contacts and document flows among senior leaders and top organizations, along with its high bureaucratic status as a party organ, give it enormous potential access to and influence over particular policy arenas, including Taiwan policy.

42. Interviews, Taipei, Aug. 1998.

43. Tsai, "Making of Taiwan Policy in Mainland China," p. 15.

44. For more on the CMC, see the chapter by Tai Ming Cheung in this volume.

45. Tsai, "Making of Taiwan Policy in Mainland China," p. 11.

46. Taiwan Affairs Offices have recently been established in virtually all ministries, commissions, and provincial-level governments to oversee Taiwan issues across the central government and among the provincial governments. Although central and provincial-level TAOs have close interactions, the latter are not formally subordinate to the former and have far less power than the SCTAO and its central-level branches. Tsai, "Making of Taiwan Policy in Mainland China," p. 12.

47. Generally known in China as simply strategic assessment and analysis (*zhanlue pingjia yu fenxi*).

48. Taiwan-related research is also conducted by other central and provincial-level agencies, but these entities are far less important to the formulation and evolution of basic Taiwan policy.

49. Its Number One Bureau (*Diyiju*) collects a wide variety of intelligence related to Taiwan issues. Since the 1980s its activities have expanded as the number of the PLA's foreign contacts has grown. It now has branches in Beijing, Shenyang, Shanghai, Nanjing, and Guangzhou. The Guangzhou office is primarily responsible for collecting defense-related intelligence concerning Taiwan. Interviews, Taipei, Aug. 1998.

50. Although formally presented as the MND's major research unit on international security affairs, the CIISS is in reality staffed and directed entirely by the Second Department.

51. Swaine, *Role of the Chinese Military.*

52. The NDU's ISS includes approximately fifty researchers and support personnel versus about nine hundred within the AMS's DSS.

53. Swaine, *Role of the Chinese Military.*

54. Interviews, Taipei, Aug. 1998.

55. In the 1980s TARO reportedly applied a rigid class viewpoint in its analysis. However, its analysis of Taiwan-related issues, especially Taiwan's internal political situation, has improved considerably in recent years as it has acquired many university graduates and utilized an increasing number of Taiwanese publications. It currently receives the most funding of any Taiwan-related research institute in China. Interviews, Taipei, Aug. 1998.

56. The CICIR publishes two internal documents: *Guoji Guanxi Yanjiu* (International Relations Research) and *Shubao Jianxun* (News in Brief from Books and Newspapers), as well as the publicly distributed quarterly *Xiandai Guoji Guanxi* (Contemporary International Relations).

57. Interviews, Taipei, Aug. 1998.

58. Some Chinese observers even assert that many Taiwan policy decisions below the level of grand strategy are made by these senior bodies in a pro forma manner based on the recommendations of the CCTAO and the SCTAO.

59. Interviews, Taipei, Aug. 1998.

60. Interviews, Taipei, Aug. 1998.

61. Alternatively, ministry- and commission-level units occasionally submit their views on important policy issues directly to the TALSG, the State Council, and (in the case of purely military issues) the CMC leadership, bypassing the CCTAO, SCTAO, and CMCGO.

62. In addition to this formal process of bureaucratic consultation and reporting, party, government, and military units also convey views to individual members of the senior party leadership via a variety of informal channels, including personal discussions.

63. Ralph N. Clough, *Reaching across the Taiwan Strait: People-to-People Diplomacy* (Boulder, Colo.: Westview, 1993), p. 126.

64. Some elements of this policy (e.g., the notion of "one China") have existed since at least 1949, but were never explicitly included prior to the 1990s as part of a larger reunification talks initiative.

65. Interviews, Beijing, Sept. 1998.

66. The latter event was soon followed by the August 1982 Sino-U.S. communiqué in which Washington pledged to reduce the level of U.S. arms sales to Taiwan.

67. Interviews, Beijing, Sept. 1998.

68. This task was dropped once it became clear that Taipei was unwilling to enter into reunification talks with the Mainland and that the United States would continue to provide substantial military assistance to the island.

69. Interviews, Beijing, Sept. 1998.

70. Interviews, Beijing, Sept. 1998. Ye Jianying reportedly played a particularly important role in this process. This arose not only from his military connections and personal prestige, but also from his position as chairman of the National People's Congress. In the latter capacity Ye was responsible for the implementation of a wide range of government policies.

71. Interviews, Beijing, Sept. 1998.

72. Interviews, Beijing, Sept. 1998.

73. For the full text of the Jiang Eight Points, see the Web site of the Ministry of Foreign Affairs of the People's Republic of China at http://www.fmprc.gov.cn/english/dhtml/readsubject.asp?pkey=20000121101900.

74. Chu, "Making Sense of Beijing's Policy toward Taiwan," p. 15.

75. Taiwan was admitted to the Asia Pacific Economic Cooperation forum in 1991. In late 1993 and early 1994 Lee Teng-hui paid a series of "unofficial" but highly public visits to the Philippines, Indonesia, and Thailand as part of his so-called vacation diplomacy.

76. By 1993 Taiwan claimed to have unofficial relations with 150 countries, to have established 90 offices in 60 countries that did not maintain diplomatic relations with Taiwan, and to host 37 offices of foreign governments that did not maintain diplomatic relations with Taiwan.

77. One well-informed Chinese informant told me that it was after this event that Lee began to refer publicly to the "one China" policy as a central component of U.S. policy, implying that it was no longer the policy of Taiwan.

78. Chu, "Making Sense of Beijing's Policy toward Taiwan," pp. 13–14.

79. Interviews, Beijing, Sept. 1998.

80. Jiang was reportedly given oversight responsibility for the CCTAO soon after the Tiananmen incident. If this is true, it gave him access to Taiwan policy before he assumed the leadership of the TALSG in mid-1993 or the FALSG in early 1998.

81. Interviews, Shanghai, Sept. 1998.

82. As Chu Yun-han states, "Formulating a new policy guideline on the Taiwan issue was a strong political statement about the coming of Jiang's era." Chu, "Making Sense of Beijing's Policy toward Taiwan," p. 12.

83. Ibid., p. 15; interviews, Taipei, Aug. 1998.

84. Chu, "Making Sense of Beijing's Policy toward Taiwan," p. 15.

85. The timing of the preparation of the Jiang Eight Points suggests that it was not devised in response to the Taiwan Policy Review of the U.S. government, announced in the fall of 1994. Indeed, several Chinese informants indicated that the Taiwan Policy Review had little impact on Beijing's deliberations on Taiwan policy.

86. Interviews, Beijing and Shanghai, fall 1998. During this period Jiang's initiative was apparently criticized as too conciliatory by PBSC rivals such as Qiao Shi and Li Ruihuan. Some observers believe that both individuals sought to use the Taiwan issue to boost their power and weaken Jiang. However, this assessment remains speculative, and there is no indication that these individuals improved their position within the CCP as a result of such a stance.

87. Interviews, Shanghai, Sept. 1998.

88. Tai Ming Cheung, "Chinese Military Preparations against Taiwan over the Next Ten Years," in James R. Lilley and Chuck Downs, eds., *Crisis in the Taiwan Strait* (Washington, D.C.: National Defense University Press, 1997), p. 48.

89. Generals Liu Huaqing and Zhang Zhen had risen to top leadership posts in the military following the ouster of Yang Shangkun from office at the Fourteenth Party Congress in the fall 1992, for factional intrigue against Jiang. Both men, and especially Zhang Zhen, have long held tough positions toward Taiwan. In addition, Zhang was placed in charge of military strategy and threat evaluations, which of course include military calculations regarding Taiwan.

90. Lee Teng-hui's strong push to visit Cornell was at least in part intended to counter-balance the decision to continue the cross-strait dialogue. Taipei was apparently following a two-pronged strategy in which any significant improvement in cross-strait relations was to be accompanied by a parallel measure designed to improve Taiwan's standing in the international community. See Chu, "Making Sense of Beijing's Policy Toward Taiwan," pp. 16–17.

91. This was especially true, in the Chinese view, given Washington's past assurances that the issuance of a visa to Lee Teng-hui would constitute a violation of that policy.

92. For example, reports appeared in late 1995 and early 1996 that the military had seized control of the TALSG, established a special office within the CMC to handle the Taiwan crisis, forced through plans to attack Taiwan after the Taiwanese presidential election in March 1996, and generally cowed the PBSC to support its "militant stance" toward Taiwan.

93. Interviews, Beijing, Sept. 1998.

94. Interviews, Beijing, Sept. 1998.

95. Various retired party and military elders also probably voiced their views informally to the party leadership during the crisis, although their ability to influence events had declined greatly since the early 1990s. Interviews, Beijing, Sept. 1998.

96. You Ji stresses that Beijing's tough response was the product of a strong consensus between Jiang Zemin and Li Peng. See You Ji, "Missile Diplomacy and PRC Domestic Politics," in Greg Austin, ed., *Missile Diplomacy and Taiwan's Future: Innovations in Politics and Military Power* (Canberra: Australian National University, 1997), pp. 38–43.

97. Interviews, Beijing, Sept. 1998.

98. Qian reportedly was angered and embarrassed by the abrupt U.S. about-face and needed to show those who believed his previous stance toward the United States was overly conciliatory that he was not Washington's dupe. Interviews, Beijing, Sept. 1998.

99. According to several informants these individuals pointed to China's greatly increased dependence on the U.S. market as a primary reason for restraint.

100. Interviews, Beijing, Sept. 1998. Informants insisted that the Chinese leadership never considered directly attacking Taiwanese territory, including the offshore islands, because such an act would suggest that Beijing no longer supported a peace-

ful resolution of the Taiwan problem and thus would almost certainly precipitate a strongly adverse U.S. reaction.

101. Interviews, Beijing, Sept. 1998.

102. Interviews, Beijing and Shanghai, Sept. 1998.

103. The military also doubtless supported exercises as a way of improving China's overall military capabilities in the event of confrontation with Taiwan involving a naval blockade, coordinated missile and air attacks, or an invasion.

104. I have been unable to confirm this report through interviews with knowledgeable Chinese observers.

105. Robert G. Sutter, "The Taiwan Crisis of 1995–96 and U.S. Domestic Politics," in Greg Austin, ed., *Missile Diplomacy and Taiwan's Future: Innovations in Politics and Military Power* (Canberra: Australian National University, 1997), p. 68; You, "Missile Diplomacy and PRC Domestic Politics," p. 46.

106. Sutter, "The Taiwan Crisis of 1995–96," p. 69.

107. Clinton administration officials would not agree to preclude any further visits by senior Taiwan officials given the fact that Congress could invite such officials and that U.S. law could not prevent them from visiting the United States as private citizens.

108. In October 1995 the CMC reportedly formed a special headquarters in the newly named "Nanjing Theater" to deal with the November 1995 and February and March 1996 exercises.

109. Chinese leaders did not view the subsequent passage of the U.S. aircraft carrier Nimitz and four escort vessels through the Taiwan Strait (ostensibly to avoid "bad weather") as a signal that Washington would directly intervene in the Taiwan crisis. Although the Chinese leadership expressed concern over the passage, given the rising tensions across the strait, and undoubtedly understood that Washington intended to caution Beijing through the action, the U.S. action did not alter Chinese behavior in any significant manner. Interviews, Beijing and Shanghai, Sept. 1998.

110. Interviews, Beijing, Sept. 1998.

111. Interviews, Beijing, Sept. 1998.

112. Interviews, Beijing and Shanghai, Sept. 1998.

113. By 1999 at the latest (and for reasons discussed later), the Chinese leadership had given up any expectation that Lee Teng-hui would undertake any serious cross-strait talks involving political issues.

114. On April 27–29, 1996, the CCP held a Taiwan Work Conference at which Qian Qichen delivered an important "eight-point" speech reiterating the themes of Jiang's earlier initiative and declaring that further reduction of cross-strait hostility can come only after Taiwan genuinely returns to the "one China" principle. On April 30, 1996, Foreign Ministry spokesman Shen Guofang declared China's willingness to resume a dialogue between the Straits Exchange Foundation (SEF) and the Association for Relations Across the Taiwan Strait (ARATS). On August 24–31, 1996, a delegation of eighty Taiwan businesspeople visited Beijing and met with top leaders.

115. Beijing did, however, eventually drop its demand that Taipei explicitly agree to discuss political relations between the two sides as a precondition to the resumption of cross-strait talks.

116. These statements became known as the "three noes" when President Clinton uttered them in Shanghai during his state visit to China in mid-1998.

117. As Chu Yun-han points out, Beijing argued that it was "in the U.S.'s best interest to urge Taipei to come to the negotiation table under the One China principle; otherwise, as the volatile situation continued to drift, both sides have to face a growing risk of military conflict in the Strait." Chu, "Making Sense of Beijing's Policy Toward Taiwan," p. 10.

118. Since 1996 China has increased its production of short-range ballistic missiles; reached agreements to obtain additional sophisticated naval, air, and air defense assets from Russia; and increased its efforts to acquire the capability to detect, track, target, and attack U.S. carrier battle groups.

119. Chu, "Making Sense of Beijing's Policy Toward Taiwan," p. 2; in elaborating the one-China principle, Chinese officials had routinely stated in the past that "there is only one China, Taiwan is a part of China, and the PRC is the sole legitimate government of China."

120. Interviews, Taipei, Aug. 1998.

121. For a full transcript of Lee's remarks, see http://www.gio.gov.tw/info/99html/99lee/0709.htm.

122. Lee's successor would be selected through a presidential election on March 18, 2000. Chen Shui-bian, the Democratic Progressive Party candidate, was elected by a plurality when Kuomintang votes were split among the official KMT candidate, Lien Chan, and insurgent independent James Soong.

123. Relations between Washington and Beijing had been badly damaged by China's strong opposition to the U.S.-led military action against Serbia, the accidental U.S. bombing of the Chinese embassy in Belgrade during that conflict, and the highly critical assessment of Chinese military modernization and espionage against the United States contained in the controversial Report of the House Select Committee on U.S. National Security and Military/Commercial Concerns with the People's Republic of China (known as the Cox Committee Report).

124. For the full text of the white paper, entitled *The One-China Principle and the Taiwan Issue,* see http://taiwansecurity.org/IS/White-Paper-022100.htm.

125. Interviews, Beijing, Sept. 1998.

126. Some outside observers believe that the military leadership (and perhaps many party figures as well) concluded during the 1995–96 crisis that China will eventually be required to use force to resolve the Taiwan situation. I have been unable to confirm this assertion. If true, it would tend to suggest that a significant gap exists between the military and civilian organs such as the MFA and the TAO over the possibility that a peaceful solution will emerge.

127. This is not to say that there are no disagreements within the leadership over the precise balance to strike between persuasive and coercive elements, especially as presented in the 2000 white paper. For example, it is likely that some policy-makers question the wisdom of formally citing a willingness to use force if Taiwan did not enter into talks.

CHAPTER 11

1. The bilateral agreement between the United States and China was acknowledged by all to be the main step for China's admission. The United States was seen by WTO members as most likely to be able to negotiate a favorable deal with China. Negotiations with other countries and with GATT/WTO itself proceeded simultaneously with Sino-U.S. negotiations, but took a back seat. On the process for entering WTO and the rules established by WTO, respectively, see "WTO Accession: China's Next Steps" and "WTO Basics," both in *China Business Review*, Vol. 27, No. 1 (Jan.–Feb. 2000), pp. 34–38.

2. The idea that the GATT/WTO decision process is a two-level game is central to this chapter. On the two-level game between China and the United States more generally, see Robert S. Ross, *Negotiating Cooperation: The United States and China, 1969–1989* (New York: Columbia University Press, 1995). On the domestic politics of U.S. trade policy, see, for example, I. M. Destler, *American Trade Politics: System Under Stress*, 3rd ed. (Washington, D.C.: Institute for International Economics, 1995).

3. On the cyclic nature of Sino-U.S. relations, see Harry Harding, *A Fragile Relationship: The United States and China since 1972* (Washington, D.C.: Brookings Institution, 1992).

4. The major study of China's early stance toward GATT is Harold K. Jacobson and Michel Oksenberg, *China's Participation in the IMF, World Bank, and GATT: Toward a Global Economic Order* (Ann Arbor, Mich.: University of Michigan Press, 1991).

5. The Multifiber Arrangement is a textile accord that sets quotas on textile exports of member countries. China had strong interests in the accord, as its exports were limited by the quota system.

6. China had been a founding member of the GATT, but the Taiwan government withdrew in 1950. The PRC government claimed that Taipei's withdrawal was not applicable to Beijing, although it recognized it would have to sign a formal protocol of accession.

7. Jacobson and Oksenberg, *China's Participation in the IMF*, p. 105.

8. Ibid., pp. 88–89.

9. Joseph Fewsmith, "China and the WTO: The Politics behind the Agreement," National Bureau of Asian Research Report (online), Nov. 1999.

10. The U.S. trade negotiators argued that the draft accession protocol was only about 30 percent complete. Bhushan Bahree, "China Fails in Bid to Rejoin GATT by Own Deadline," *Wall Street Journal*, Jan. 20, 1994, p. A10.

11. Information on the 1994 mood comes from interviews with Chinese trade and planning officials in October 1996 and with trade officials in March 1998.

12. See Marcus Brauchli and Craig S. Smith, "China Sets Its Sights on Joining WTO after Averting Trade War with the U.S.," *Wall Street Journal*, Feb. 28, 1995, p. A17, and Joseph Kahn, "China Plans to Cut Tariffs, End Quotas in Bid to Join Trade Group," *Wall Street Journal*, Nov. 20, 1995, p. A10.

13. The U.S. trade negotiators claimed that a deal could be reached by the upcoming summit in mid-July of 1997 and that the biggest problem was the U.S.

Congress. Information on the 1997 talks is drawn from discussions with USTR negotiators; Pierre-Louis Girard, chairman of the WTO Working Party on the Accession of China, memo to members of the Working Party and China, March 6, 1997; *Inside U.S. Trade,* March 14, 1997, pp. 6 and 25; and Paul Magnusson, "Slow Dance with the Dragon," *Business Week,* April 7, 1997, pp. 52–53. After the main U.S. negotiators responsible for the 1997 talks, Lee Sands and Deborah Lehr, left their posts in late 1997, many analysts claimed the talks had never progressed as far as these negotiators had suggested.

14. Reported in *China News Digest* (CND)–Global (online), April 23, 1997, Global News GL97-060.

15. See Paul J. Deveney, "World Watch: China Unveils Plan to Cut Tariffs to Placate WTO," *Wall Street Journal,* Sept. 15, 1997, p. A14; and Robert S. Greenberger, "China Tells U.S. It Will Cut Tariff to 10%," *Wall Street Journal,* Oct. 31, 1997, p. A3.

16. On the pessimism of the United States in late 1998 see "Remarks by Secretary of Commerce William M. Daley, 12th U.S.-China Joint Commission on Commerce and Trade, Closing Plenary Session," Washington, D.C., December 18, 1998.

17. Much of the information in this discussion of the events of late 1998 and 1999 is drawn from the excellent analysis by Fewsmith, "China and the WTO."

18. On the question of whether Zhu offered more concessions than he was authorized to offer and a conclusion that he likely did not, see ibid.

19. For a summary of the agreement, see "The U.S.-China Bilateral Agreement and the United States," *China Business Review,* Vol. 27, No. 1 (Jan.–Feb. 2000), pp. 20–27.

20. On fragmented authoritarianism see Kenneth Lieberthal and David M. Lampton, eds., *Bureaucracy, Politics, and Decision Making in Post-Mao China* (Berkeley, Calif.: University of California Press, 1992).

21. In this sense MOFTEC's role is similar to that which Lu Ning describes for the Ministry of Foreign Affairs earlier in this volume. The WTO Division is formally under the International Relations Department of MOFTEC, but reports directly to the vice minister due to the importance of its work.

22. MOFTEC was not a monolithic supporter of WTO accession, however. Support for WTO membership among its Foreign Trade Corporations (FTCs) was less robust than in other parts of the ministry, because FTCs stood to see their monopoly over trade, already weakened by domestic reforms, erode further. In the past FTCs received large revenues from exports, and they stood to lose from the reduction of tariffs.

23. The idea was that there would be a division of labor, with Zhu predominant on economic matters and Jiang predominant on party, personnel, and political matters. This was said to be true despite the fact that Jiang was ultimately the "paramount leader."

24. Wang Lixin and Joseph Fewsmith, "Bulwark of the Planned Economy: The Structure and Role of the State Planning Commission," in Carol Lee Hamrin and Suisheng Zhao, eds., *Decision-Making in Deng's China: Perspectives from Insiders* (Armonk, N.Y.: Sharpe, 1995), p. 51.

25. Susan L. Shirk, *How China Opened Its Door: The Political Success of the PRC's Foreign Trade and Investment Reforms* (Washington, D.C.: Brookings Institution, 1994).

26. Feng Yushu, *Guoji Maoyi Tizhi Xia de Guan Mao Zong Xieding yu Zhongguo* (GATT and China under the International Trade System) (Beijing: Zhongguo Dui Wai Jingji Maoyi Chubanshe [Chinese Foreign Economic Trade Publishers], December 1992), pp. 219–21. On earlier rounds of talks, see Jacobson and Oksenberg, *China's Participation in the IMF,* pp. 147 and 150.

27. Wang Yong, "Mission Seeks Re-Entry to WTO," *China Daily,* March 28, 1998, p. B1.

28. Labor interests were represented through the management (i.e., government bureaucracy) of the particular industry involved.

29. Jacobson and Oksenberg, *China's Participation in the IMF,* pp. 95–97.

30. The literature on learning focuses primarily on issues of arms control—particularly the causes of Gorbachev's "new thinking" about Soviet arms control—but it is also useful with regard to international economic institutions. See Jack S. Levy, "Learning and Foreign Policy: Sweeping a Conceptual Minefield," *International Organization,* Vol. 48 (Spring 1994), pp. 279–312; George W. Breslauer and Philip E. Tetlock, eds., *Learning in U.S. and Soviet Foreign Policy* (Boulder, Colo.: Westview, 1991); and, for an application to China in the area of arms control, Alastair Iain Johnston, "Learning versus Adaptation: Explaining Change in Chinese Arms Control Policy in the 1980s and 1990s," *China Journal,* No. 35 (Jan. 1996), pp. 27–62.

31. Levy, "Learning and Foreign Policy," p. 312, is careful to point out that learning models alone do not provide complete explanations for foreign policy change because they cannot explain how and under what conditions learning by individual leaders is translated into policy.

32. See Margaret M. Pearson, *Joint Ventures in the People's Republic of China* (Princeton, N.J.: Princeton University Press, 1991), pp. 54–58.

33. For example, the IMF and Chinese officials hold annual consultations on exchange rate issues. Lardy notes that many of the most important Chinese decisions on exchange rate policy have been announced within a few weeks of this annual meeting. Nicholas R. Lardy, "China and the International Financial System," in Elizabeth Economy and Michel Oksenberg, eds., *China Joins the World: Progress and Prospects* (New York: Council on Foreign Relations, 1999), p. 210.

34. On these and other policy changes, see Nicholas R. Lardy, *Foreign Trade and Economic Reform in China, 1978–1990* (Cambridge: Cambridge University Press, 1992), pp. 37–82; World Bank, *The Chinese Economy: Fighting Inflation, Deepening Reforms* (Washington, D.C.: World Bank, 1996), p. 8; World Bank, *China: Foreign Trade Reform* (Washington, D.C.: World Bank, 1994), pp. xvi and 15–23; He Chang, "Article Views Prospects of Admission to GATT 'This Year,'" *Zhongguo Tongxun She* (Hong Kong), in Foreign Broadcast Information Service (FBIS), March 17, 1994, p. 2; and Girard, memo to members of the Working Party and China.

35. Japan occasionally was seen as a defector from the quasi-alliance of WTO members, particularly after Prime Minister Hashimoto concluded a number of agreements in bilateral negotiations with China in 1997. U.S. and European negotiators argue

that Japan negotiated weaker terms on these issues on the assumption that the United States would strike a more stringent deal, from which Japan would also benefit.

36. See, for example, Feng, *Guoji Maoyi Tizhi Xia de Guan Mao Zong Xieding yu Zhongguo*, p. 214.

37. Shirk, *How China Opened Its Door*, p. 73.

38. Feng, *Guoji Maoyi Tizhi Xia de Guan Mao Zong Xieding yu Zhongguo*, pp. 215–18.

39. Jacobson and Oksenberg, *China's Participation in the IMF*, pp. 90 and 100–101.

40. Ibid., p. 97.

41. For an excellent summary of the debate and how it has evolved over time, see Yong Wang, "China's Domestic WTO Debate," in *China Business Review*, Vol. 27, No. 1 (Jan.–Feb. 2000), pp. 54–62.

42. On these reasons, see Feng, *Guoji Maoyi Tizhi Xia de Guan Mao Zong Xieding yu Zhongguo*, pp. 214–18; Jacobson and Oksenberg, *China's Participation in the IMF*, pp. 92–93; and Shirk, *How China Opened Its Door*, p. 71.

43. See, for example, Zhang Shuguang, Zhang Yansheng, and Wan Zhongxin, *Measuring the Costs of Protection in China* (Washington, D.C.: Institute for International Economics, 1998). The authors are economists at the independent Unirule Institute of Economics in Beijing. See also "Shijie Maoyi Zuzhi Zhuanji" (Special Edition on the WTO), *Guoji Maoyi Wenti* (Problems of International Trade), Vol. 10 (Oct. 1998), pp. 1–65; and Yi Xiaozhun, "Shi Nian Jian," *Guoji Maoyi* (International Trade), Jan. 1998, pp. 4–6. Yi is deputy director general of the Department of International Trade and International Affairs of MOFTEC.

44. On the historic sensitivity of foreign participation in the economy in the reform era see Pearson, *Joint Ventures in the People's Republic of China*, pp. 38–46.

45. This opinion was reiterated by Feng, *Guoji Maoyi Tizhi Xia de Guan Mao Zong Xieding yu Zhongguo*, and by commercial officers interviewed at the Chinese Embassy in Washington in April 1998.

46. World Bank, *China Engaged: Integration with the Global Economy* (Washington, D.C.: World Bank, 1997), p. 16.

47. Interview, Washington, D.C., Oct. 1998.

48. For example, on the perceived threat to electronics, automobiles, petroleum refining, machine tools, and instruments, see State Planning Commission Economics Research Institute Task Force, "Dui Huifu Guanmao Zongxieding Diwei Hou de Xiaoyi Fenxi He Duice" (Effective Analysis and Countermeasures after China Resumes Its Place in GATT), *Guoji Maoyi*, No. 2 (1993), p. 10. A Chinese Embassy commercial officer (interviewed in Washington, D.C., in May 1996) suggested that the chemical, textiles, agriculture, machinery and electronics, and health industries and the People's Bank of China are "united against WTO." A 1997 World Bank study confirms that WTO accession would show a relative decline in the "output of (capital- and technology-intensive) transport, machinery and equipment, and other heavy manufacturing industries (consistent with China's comparative advantage)." World Bank, *China Engaged: Integration with the Global Economy*, p. 2.

49. China's intention to write industrial policies for its "pillar" industries was announced in June 1994. To be considered a pillar industry a sector must have the

potential for very large output, use of advanced technology, and a large domestic (and potentially foreign) market; World Bank, *Chinese Economy,* p. 18. On the WTO implications of China's industrial policy, especially in automobiles, see U.S.-China Business Council, "China's Accession to the WTO/GATT: Investment/Industrial Policies" (Washington D.C.: U.S.-China Business Council, Sept. 15, 1995).

50. For example, a researcher at an SDPC research institute (interviewed in Beijing in October 1996) dated heightened protectionist concerns to 1992; from then on his institute prepared multiple studies on the provincial impact of WTO membership.

51. Previously the industry was operated directly by the Ministry of Post and Telecommunications (MPT); under the MII, which succeeded the MPT in the reorganization, the industry is theoretically to be held at arm's length from the regulators. This information on the lobbying efforts of the telecommunications industry and the MII comes from interviews with former MOFTEC negotiators in Washington, D.C., in March and October 1998 and with an official of the SDPC in Beijing in October 1996. On the telecommunications industry, see also Fred Tipson, "China and the Information Revolution," in Economy and Oksenberg, *China Joins the World,* pp. 231–65.

52. Bahree, "China Fails in Bid to Rejoin GATT by Own Deadline."

53. Interview, Washington, D.C., Oct. 1998.

54. A think-tank researcher who follows the WTO said that in 1995 there were only six books on GATT/WTO in the national library in Beijing, whereas in 1998 there were two long shelves. Interview, Oct. 1998.

55. See the book by Finance Ministry official and international trade economist Feng, *Guoji Maoyi Tizhi Xia de Guan Mao Zong Xieding yu Zhongguo.* See also Wang Yaotian and Zhou Hanmin, eds., *Shijie Maoyi Zuzhi Zonglun* (Survey of the WTO) (Shanghai: Shanghai Yuandong Chubanshe, December 1995); and Yan Xuejun and Wei Ping, eds., *Chongjin Guanmao Zong Xieding de Jingying Duice* (Management Countermeasures after China Re-Enters GATT) (Hubei: Huazhong Ligong Daxue Chubanshe [Huazhong Science and Engineering University Publishers], 1994).

56. In general, China's "new business elite" was not politically active in the 1990s. See Margaret M. Pearson, *China's New Business Elite: The Political Consequences of Economic Reform* (Berkeley: University of California Press, 1997).

57. Even though government-to-government negotiations had their ups and downs during the period from 1996 to 1999, as indicated previously, public debate on the subject of WTO, although not silent, was muted.

58. Fewsmith, "China and the WTO."

59. Ibid.

60. Andrew P. Cortell and James W. Davis, Jr., "How Do International Institutions Matter? The Domestic Impact of International Rules and Norms," *International Studies Quarterly,* Vol. 40, (1996), p. 455.

61. This argument about domestic structure is based on Thomas Risse-Kappen, "Bringing Transnational Relations Back In: Introduction," in Thomas Risse-Kappen, ed., *Bringing Transnational Relations Back In* (Cambridge: Cambridge University Press,

1995), pp. 3–33, and Matthew Evangelista, "The Paradox of State Strength: Transnational Relations, Domestic Structures and Security Policy in Russia and the Soviet Union," *International Organization*, Vol. 49 (1995), pp. 1–38.

62. Such "negative learning" did not appear to be mere "adaptation," moreover, because China changed as the external environment remained constant. Another version of this argument, in the area of Chinese security studies, appears in Charles Sanderson, "Explaining China's CTBT Decision: Learning Theory and Chinese Security Policy," University of Maryland Department of Government and Politics, December 1998.

CHAPTER 12

I am grateful to Thomas Christensen, David M. Lampton, and Thomas Moore for their helpful comments and suggestions on an earlier version of this chapter.

1. For the official Chinese text of the joint communiqué, see Liu Jinzhi and Yang Huaisheng, eds., *Zhongguo dui Chaoxian he Hanguo Zhengci Wenjian Huibian* (A Collection of Documents on China's Policy toward the Democratic People's Republic of Korea and the Republic of Korea), Vol. 5 (1974–94) (Beijing: Zhongguo Shehui Kexue Chubanshe [Chinese Social Science Press], 1994), pp. 2611–12. It is emblematic of the politics of divided Korea that Seoul and Pyongyang use different words for Korea in Korean—*Chosun* (*Chaoxian* in Chinese) in the North and *Hanguk* (or *Hanguo* in Chinese) in the South. South Korea and North Korea in English seem normatively neutral, but not *Chosun* and *Hanguk* in the politics of everyday life in divided Korea. It is also a reminder of the Chinese ability to live with contradictions, as the Chinese text of the joint communiqué still uses *Chaoxian* to refer to the Korean peninsula (*Chaoxian Bandao*, not *Hanguo Bandao*) and *Chaoxian Minzu* for the Korean people. See ibid., p. 2612.

2. When asked by South Korean President Kim Dae Jung, during his official state visit to China in November 1998, to identify the most difficult challenge he faced during his decade-long service as China's foreign minister, Qian Qichen said it was the establishment of Sino-ROK diplomatic relations. See *Korea Times*, Nov. 13, 1998 (Internet version), at http://www.koreatimes.co.kr.

3. Song Dexing, "Lengzhan hou Dongbei Ya Anquan Xingshe de Bianhua" (Changes in the Post–Cold War Northeast Asian Security Situation), *Xiandai Guoji Guanxi* (Contemporary International Relations), No. 9 (1998), pp. 34–38, especially p. 35.

4. Some of the best works on the structure and process of Chinese foreign policymaking include David Bachman, "Structure and Process in the Making of Chinese Foreign Policy," in Samuel S. Kim, ed., *China and the World: Chinese Foreign Policy Faces the New Millennium* (Boulder, Colo.: Westview, 1998), pp. 34–87; A. Doak Barnett, *The Making of Foreign Policy in China* (Boulder, Colo.: Westview, 1985); Carol Hamrin, "Elite Politics and the Development of China's Foreign Relations," in Thomas Robinson and David Shambaugh, eds., *Chinese Foreign Policy* (Oxford: Oxford University Press, 1994), pp. 70–109; Andrew J. Nathan and Robert S. Ross, *The Great Wall and the Empty Fortress* (New York: Norton, 1997), pp. 123–36; Lu Ning,

The Dynamics of Foreign-Policy Decisionmaking in China, 2nd ed. (Boulder, Colo.: West-view, 2000); Michael Swaine, *The Role of the Chinese Military in National Security Policy-making,* rev. ed. (Santa Monica, Calif.: RAND Corporation, 1998); and Quansheng Zhao, *Interpreting Chinese Foreign Policy: The Micro-Macro Linkage Approach* (Oxford: Oxford University Press, 1996), pp. 18–35.

5. Robert Putnam, "Diplomacy and Domestic Politics: The Logic of Two-Level Games," *International Organization,* Vol. 42 (Summer 1988), pp. 427–60, reprinted as an appendix in Peter B. Evans, Harold K. Jacobson, and Robert Putnam, eds., *Double-Edged Diplomacy: International Bargaining and Domestic Politics* (Berkeley: University of California Press, 1993), pp. 431–68.

6. See Zbigniew Brzezinski, *The Grand Chessboard: American Primacy and Its Geostrategic Imperatives* (New York: Basic Books, 1997), p. 190, and Robert E. Bedeski, "Sino-Korean Relations: Triangle of Tension, or Balancing a Divided Peninsula?" *International Journal,* Vol. 50, No. 3 (Summer 1995), pp. 516–38.

7. See Charles F. Hermann, "International Crisis as a Situational Variable," in James N. Rosenau, ed., *International Politics and Foreign Policy: A Reader in Research and Theory,* rev. ed. (New York: Free Press, 1969), p. 414.

8. In the late 1980s a research group was set up at the Chinese Academy of Social Sciences to explore the South Korean development model. See Dong Sun Kim, "China's Policy toward North Korea and Cooperation between South Korea and China," *Korean Journal of International Studies,* Vol. 25, No. 1 (Spring 1994), p. 36.

9. Not surprisingly, there is an asymmetrical exchange of legitimization in the PRC-ROK joint communiqué, in which China gives only half-hearted legitimacy by calling South Korea *Hanguo* in exchange for the ROK's unqualified acceptance of the PRC as "the sole legal government of China" and its acknowledgment "that there is but one China and Taiwan is part of China" (Article 3). See *Zhongguo dui Chaoxian he Hanguo Zhengci Wenjian Huibian,* Vol. 5 (1974–94), p. 2612.

10. Robert Legvold, "Sino-Soviet Relations: The American Factor," in Robert S. Ross, ed., *China, the United States, and the Soviet Union: Tripolarity and Policy Making in the Cold War* (Armonk, N.Y.: Sharpe, 1993), p. 87.

11. *Beijing Review,* Sept. 17–23, 1990, pp. 12–13.

12. Jia Hao and Zhuang Qubing, "China's Policy toward the Korean Peninsula," *Asian Survey,* Vol. 32, No. 12 (Dec. 1992), p. 1140.

13. See Victor D. Cha, "Engaging China: Seoul-Beijing Détente and Korean Security," *Survival,* Vol. 41, No. 1 (Spring 1999), pp. 73–98. The China-ROK communiqué mentions (Article 2) the UN Charter and the Five Principles of Peaceful Coexistence as outlining the foundational principles for normalization. See *Zhongguo dui Chaoxian he Hanguo Zhengci Wenjian Huibian,* Vol. 5 (1974–94), pp. 2611–12.

14. Chae-Jin Lee, *China and Korea: Dynamic Relations* (Stanford, Calif.: Hoover Institution, 1996), pp. 145–46.

15. In the official Chinese documents South Korea was still referred to as *Nan Chao-xian dangju* (South Korean authorities), not *Da Han Minguo* or *Hanguo* (the Republic of Korea). See *Zhongguo dui Chaoxian he Hanguo Zhengci Wenjian Huibian,* Vol. 5 (1974–94), pp. 2373–74.

16. Pyongyang's "principled stand" was self-defeating as far as UN membership was concerned. Faced with a challenge from the South, the best Pyongyang could do was to recycle Kim Il Sung's 1980 formula for "a Democratic Confederal Republic of Korea" as a transitional step to reunification: to wit, the two Koreas should apply for joint UN membership and each take turns sharing a single seat on an annual basis. See UN Doc. S/21836 (Oct. 2, 1990). For a detailed analysis, see Samuel S. Kim, "North Korea and the United Nations," *International Journal of Korean Studies,* Vol. 1, No. 1 (Spring 1997), pp. 77–109.

17. For further analysis and documentation, see Samuel S. Kim, "Taiwan and the International System: The Challenge of Legitimation," in Robert G. Sutter and William R. Johnson, eds., *Taiwan in World Affairs* (Boulder, Colo.: Westview, 1994), pp. 151–57, and idem, "North Korea and the United Nations," pp. 81–82.

18. Han Sung-Joo, "The Emerging Triangle: Korea between China and the United States," Lecture 1 of a three-part series at Harvard University, Cambridge, Mass., April 1, 1998, and also author's interview in Seoul, May 28, 1998.

19. *Renmin Ribao* (People's Daily), March 24, 1992, p. 4.

20. Parris H. Chang, "Beijing's Policy toward Korea and PRC-ROK Normalization of Relations," in Manwoo Lee and Richard W. Mansbach, eds., *The Changing Order in Northeast Asia and the Korean Peninsula* (Seoul: Institute for Far Eastern Studies, Kyungnam University, 1993), pp. 167–69, and Lee, *China and Korea,* pp. 124–25.

21. See the report by Tokyo's KYODO in English in Foreign Broadcast Information Service (FBIS)–China, Sept. 15, 1992, p. 12.

22. Chang, "Beijing's Policy toward Korea," p. 170.

23. According to Chae-Jin Lee's account, based on field interviews with Chinese scholars, Aug. 1992 and Dec. 1993. See Lee, *China and Korea,* p. 125. My own field interviews in Seoul and Beijing in May–June 1998 confirmed this account.

24. The Beijing-Taipei bidding war over diplomatic relations with Niger in June 1992 was not an important causal factor in promoting the talks, as widely argued, but merely a facilitating one in accelerating the talks. Parris Chang, among others, cites this event as one of the two "decisive" factors for normalization, not realizing that the decision to start normalization talks was made at least two months earlier, in April 1992. See Chang, "Beijing's Policy toward Korea," p. 169. Hong Liu also gives greater importance to this event than is warranted. For a similar argument see Hong Liu, "The Sino-South Korean Normalization: A Triangular Explanation," *Asian Survey,* Vol. 33, No. 11 (Nov. 1993), pp. 1083–94, especially p. 1089.

25. Author's interview with Lee Sang Ock, then ROK foreign minister, Seoul, June 4, 1998.

26. In international law a treaty is defined as any international agreement in written form concluded between two or more states. The legal force of a treaty does not depend on any particular designation or appellation (e.g., treaty, convention, protocol, declaration, communiqué, or memorandum of agreement). Hence the joint communiqué of August 24, 1992, is clearly the PRC-ROK normalization treaty and is treated as such in this chapter.

27. For a characterization of China's Korea policy along these lines, see Song, "Lengzhan hou DongbeiYa Anquan Xingshe de Bianhua," p. 37.

28. *North Korea News,* No. 724 (Feb. 28, 1994), pp. 5–6; *The Economist,* March 26, 1994, p. 39.

29. See Nicholas Eberstadt, "China's Trade with the DPRK, 1990–1994: Pyongyang's Thrifty New Patron," *Korea and World Affairs,* Vol. 19, No. 4 (Winter 1995), pp. 665–85.

30. Jen Hui-wen, "Inside Story of Vicissitudes of Sino-DPRK Relations," *Hsin Pao,* July 19, 1996, p. 15, in FBIS-CHI-96-140 (July 19, 1996) (World News Connection [WNC] Internet version), at http://wnc.fedworld.gov/.

31. *Chosun Ilbo* (Seoul), July 20, 1996 (available on the Internet at http://www.chosun.com/).

32. Sino-ROK trade and investment figures for 1992–97 are available in *Oekyo Paeks 1998* (Diplomatic White Paper 1998) (Seoul: Ministry of Foreign Affairs and Trade, 1998), at http://www.mofat.go.kr/korean/data/98white/4-2-2.htm.

33. Xu Baokang and Wang Linchang, "Sino-ROK Partnership toward New Century Introduced," *Beijing Review,* Vol. 41, No. 48 (Nov. 30–Dec. 6, 1998), p. 6. For details on Sino-ROK economic relations see also Lee, *China and Korea,* pp. 142–51, and Hieyeon Keum, "Normalization and After: Prospects for the Sino-South Korean Relations," *Korea and World Affairs,* Vol. 20, No. 4 (Winter 1996), pp. 572–80.

34. See Gerald Segal, "China's Changing Shape," *Foreign Affairs,* Vol. 73, No. 3 (May–June 1994).

35. Gaye Christoffersen, "Nesting the Sino-Russian Border and the Tumen Project in the Asia-Pacific: Heilongjiang's Regional Relations," *Asian Perspective,* Vol. 20, No. 2 (Fall–Winter 1996), p. 270.

36. Cumulative foreign investment for 1992–97 was only $923 million, less than one-tenth of the $30 billion originally envisioned—$450 million for Russia's Primorsky Territory; $410 million for China's Yanbian Korean Autonomous Prefecture; and $63 million for North Korea's Rajin-Sonbong Economic and Trade Zone. See "Tumen Region Overview," at http://www.tradp.org/overview.htm.

37. Quoted in Christoffersen, "Nesting the Sino-Russian Border and the Tumen Project in the Asia-Pacific," p. 292.

38. For an elaboration of the theoretical and policy implications, see the October 1985 special issue of *World Politics,* Vol. 38, No. 1, especially Kenneth A. Oye, "Explaining Cooperation under Anarchy: Hypotheses and Strategies," pp. 1–24.

39. The Economist Intelligence Unit (EIU), *Country Report: South Korea and North Korea,* 4th quarter 1999 (London: EIU, 1999), p. 43.

40. *The Korea Herald,* March 3, 1999 (Internet version), at http://www.korea-herald.co.kr.

41. Estimates and projections by the Bank of Korea in Seoul. See *The Korea Herald,* March 14, 2000 (Internet version), at http://www.koreaherald.co.kr.

42. For a trenchant attack on U.S. "sanctions diplomacy," see *Renmin Ribao,* July 15, 1994, p. 6.

43. For a more detailed analysis of China's behavior in the Security Council, see Samuel S. Kim, "China and the United Nations," in Elizabeth Economy and Michel

Oksenberg, eds., *China Joins the World: Progress and Prospects* (New York: Council on Foreign Relations Press, 1999), pp. 42–89, especially p. 56.

44. *Renmin Ribao,* June 22, 1994, p. 6.

45. For further analysis along this line, see Banning Garrett and Bonnie Glaser, "Looking across the Yalu: Chinese Assessments of North Korea," *Asian Survey,* Vol. 35, No. 6 (June 1995), pp. 528–45.

46. See *Rodong Sinmun* (Worker's Daily) (Pyongyang), Dec. 1, 1994, p. 1 (emphasis added). For further analysis, see Samuel S. Kim, "North Korea in 1994: Brinkmanship, Breakdown and Breakthrough," *Asian Survey,* Vol. 35, No. 1 (Jan. 1995), pp. 13–27.

47. See Eric A. McVadon, "Chinese Military Strategy for the Korean Peninsula," in James R. Lilley and David Shambaugh, eds., *China's Military Faces the Future* (Armonk, N.Y.: Sharpe, 1999), pp. 289–90.

48. PRC expert, quoted in Jen Hui-wen, "The Chinese-U.S. Strategic Trial of Strength on the Korean Peninsula," *Hsin Pao* (Hong Kong), April 8, 1994, p. 24.

49. See Yu Shaohua, "Chaoxian Bandao Xingshi de Fazhan yu Qianjing" (The Evolving Situation and Future Prospects of the Korean Peninsula), *Guoji Wenti Yanjiu* (International Studies), No. 4 (1997), pp. 12–16, especially p. 15.

50. Yang Chengxu, "Dui Dong Ya Anquan Wenti de Fenxi" (An Analysis of the East Asian Security Problem), *Guoji Wenti Yanjiu,* No. 3 (1994), p. 20.

51. *Korea Herald,* Aug. 23, 1997 (Internet version), at http://www.koreaherald.co.kr.

52. Li Jingchen and Yan Ming, "Korean Peace Talks: One Hitch After Another," Xinhua in English, in FBIS-CHI-98-081, March 22, 1998 (WNC Internet version).

53. *Yonhap* (Seoul), November 13, 1998.

54. *Korea Times,* Nov. 16, 1995 (Internet version).

55. McVadon, "Chinese Military Strategy for the Korean Peninsula," p. 280.

56. *Korea Herald,* Nov. 13, 1998 (Internet version). For a more upbeat assessment, see "Sino-ROK Partnership toward New Century Introduced," p. 6.

57. Chen Qimao, "The Role of the Great Powers in the Process of Korean Reunification," in Amos Jordan, ed., *Korean Unification: Implications for Northeast Asia* (Washington, D.C.: Center for Strategic and International Studies, 1993), p. 70 (emphasis added).

58. According to a major 1995 survey of fifty Koreanists—five each from the United States, Japan, China, Russia, and Germany and twenty-five from South Korea—there was general agreement that Korean reunification would eventually occur, with 2.1 percent of the respondents predicting it would occur within one year (1996); 8.3 percent before 2000, 29.2 percent in 2001–5, 20.8 percent in 2006–10, 16.7 percent in 2010–15, and 16.3 percent after 2015. That is, half predicted that Korean reunification would occur during the first decade of the twenty-first century. Tellingly, the United States and China occupy opposite extremes on Korean unification. A more recent survey shows that "the Chinese tended to be most conservative about [Korean] unification, in the hope that the status quo could be maintained for a considerable period of time." See Lee Young-sun, "Is Korean Reunification Possible?" *Korea Focus,* Vol. 3, No. 3 (May–June 1995), p. 13, and Park Young-ho, "International Perceptions of Korean Unification Issues," *Korea Focus,* Vol. 5, No. 1 (Jan.–Feb. 1998), pp. 72–80 (quote on p. 78).

59. For a trenchant analysis of North Korea's unification policy, see Nicholas Eberstadt, "North Korea's Unification Policy: 1948–1996," in Samuel S. Kim, ed., *North Korean Foreign Relations in the Post–Cold War Era* (New York: Oxford University Press, 1998), pp. 235–57.

60. See *Hsin Pao*, April 8, 1994, p. 24, in FBIS-China, April 12, 1994, pp. 13–15, and *Hsin Pao*, June 24, 1994, p. 25, in FBIS-China, June 24, 1994, pp. 7–8, quotations on pp. 14 and 7, respectively.

61. Yan Xuetong and Li Zhongcheng, "Zhanwang Xia Shiji Chu Guoji Zhengzhi" (Prospects for International Politics in the Beginning of the Next Century), *Xiandai Guoji Guanxi* (Contemporary International Relations), No. 6 (1995), p. 7.

62. Yan Xuetong, "Lengzhan hou Zhongguo de Duiwai Anquan Zhanlue" (China's Post–Cold War External Security Strategy), *Xiandai Guoji Guanxi*, No. 8 (1995), p. 24.

63. See Wang Chunyin, "Chaoxian Bandao Anquan Xingshi Zhanwang" (Prospects for the Security Situation on the Korean Peninsula), *Xiandai Guoji Guanxi*, No. 6 (1996), pp. 10–12.

64. The objective of the deterrence-plus policy is neither to prop up the North Korean system nor to seek its collapse, but to promote a process of dialogue and confidence building that goes beyond deterrence. See (Ambassador) James T. Laney, "North and South Korea: Beyond Deterrence," speech delivered to the Asia Society Corporate Conference, Seoul, Korea, May 11, 1996. The deterrence-plus policy was reformulated as a "comprehensive and integrated two-path strategy" in the Perry Report and became the Clinton administration's official North Korea policy. See William J. Perry, *Review of U.S. Policy toward North Korea: Findings and Recommendations*, Oct. 12, 1999, on the Department of State Web site at http://www.state.gov/www/regions/eap/991012_northkorea_rpt.html.

65. See Yu Shaohua, "Chaoxian Bandao Xingshi de Fazhan yu Qianjing" (The Evolving Situation and Future Prospects of the Korean Peninsula), *Guoji Wenti Yanjiu*, No. 4 (1997), pp. 12–16, especially p. 12.

66. Hwang Jang-yop, quoted in *Far Eastern Economic Review*, Feb. 27, 1997, p. 15.

67. Scott Snyder, "North Korea's Decline and China's Strategic Dilemmas," Special Report, United States Institute of Peace (Washington, D.C.: United States Institute of Peace, October 1997). Because of more than five years of severe food shortages and a total breakdown of the public health system an entire generation of children under seven years old suffers from stunted growth physically and is mentally impaired, according to a new study by international aid groups. See Elisabeth Rosenthal, "In North Korean Hunger, Legacy Is Stunted Children," *New York Times*, Dec. 10, 1998, pp. A1 and A14.

68. "Grain Crisis Causes Hardship for DPRK People," *Beijing Review*, Vol. 40, No. 43 (Oct. 27–Nov. 2, 1997), p. 7. See also Song, "Lengzhan hou DongbeiYa Anquan Xingshe de Bianhua," p. 36.

69. In a closed executive session involving two high-ranking North Korean ambassadors and a dozen U.S. scholars, including me, in New York in late May 1998, the ambassadors categorically denied any Chinese aid, saying: "If we wanted Chinese

aid, we could get one million tons of grain from China tomorrow but it would come with an unacceptably heavy price of 'dependence.'"

70. Hwang's statement in an interview granted to U.S. journalist Selig Harrison. See Selig Harrison, "North Korea from the Inside Out," *Washington Post,* June 21, 1998, p. C01.

71. Paul H. Kreisberg, "Threat Environment for a United Korea: 2010," *Korean Journal of Defense Analysis,* Vol. 8, No. 1 (Summer 1996), pp. 84–85.

72. Zhao Gancheng, "China's Korea Unification Policy," in Tae Hwan Kwak, ed., *The Four Powers and Korean Unification Strategies* (Seoul: Institute for Far Eastern Studies, Kyungnam University, 1997), p. 82 (emphasis added).

73. Cai Jianwei, ed., *Zhongguo da Zhanlue: Lingdao Shijie da Lantu* (China's Grand Strategy: A Blueprint for World Leadership) (Haikou: Hainan Chubanshe, 1996), p. 200.

74. On the problem of instituting more effective coordinating mechanisms, see Bachman, "Structure and Process in the Making of Chinese Foreign Policy," p. 49.

75. World Bank, *World Development Report 1998/99: Knowledge for Development* (New York: Oxford University Press, 1998).

Contributors

Peter T. Y. Cheung is an associate professor in the Department of Politics and Public Administration at the University of Hong Kong. He holds a Ph.D. in political science from the University of Washington, Seattle. He has published on the relations between the central government and Guangdong province, the economic and political development of southern China, and the development strategies of China's coastal cities (Guangzhou, Shanghai, and Tianjin). His recent publications include a volume he co-edited with Jae Ho Chung and Zhimin Lin entitled *Provincial Strategies of Economic Reform in Post-Mao China: Leadership, Politics, and Implementation* (Armonk, N.Y.: Sharpe, 1998). He is a member of the editorial committee of the journal *Provincial China: Research, News, Analysis* and a fellow of the University of New South Wales–University of Technology (Sydney) Center for Research on Provincial China.

Tai Ming Cheung is currently an associate managing director at Kroll Associates in Hong Kong. He has written extensively on the Chinese military, especially its involvement in commercial activities and its defense modernization.

He was previously a research associate at the International Institute for Strategic Studies and has also worked as a correspondent at the *Far Eastern Economic Review.*

Elizabeth Economy is senior fellow for China and deputy director of Asia Studies at the Council on Foreign Relations. She currently directs council projects on China and the environment and on U.S.-China relations. Her most recent publications include a volume she co-edited with Michel Oksenberg, *China Joins the World: Progress and Prospects* (New York: Council on Foreign Relations Press, 1999); "Reforming China," *Survival* (Autumn 1999); and "Painting China Green," *Foreign Affairs* (March–April 1999). She is currently writing a book on environmental politics in China. Dr. Economy received a B.A. from Swarthmore College, an A.M. from Stanford University, and a Ph.D. from the University of Michigan.

Joseph Fewsmith is the director of the East Asian Interdisciplinary Studies Program and professor of International Relations at Boston University. He is the author of *China since Tiananmen: The Politics of Transition* (Cambridge: Cambridge University Press, 2001); *Elite Politics in Contemporary China* (Armonk, N.Y.: Sharpe, 2001); *Dilemmas of Reform in China: Political Conflict and Economic Debate* (Armonk, N.Y.: Sharpe, 1994); and *Party, State and Local Elites in Republican China* (Honolulu: University of Hawaii Press, 1985). He has written numerous articles on the politics and economics of contemporary China and is editor of *The Chinese Economy,* a journal of translations published by M.E. Sharpe.

Bates Gill is senior fellow in Foreign Policy Studies and inaugural director of the Center for Northeast Asian Policy Studies at the Brookings Institution in Washington, D.C. His publications include *Contrasting Visions: United States, China, and World Order* (Washington, D.C.: Brookings Institution, in 2001); *Weathering the Storm: Taiwan, Its Neighbors, and the Asian Financial Crisis* (Washington, D.C.: Brookings Institution, 2000); *Arms, Transparency, and Security in Southeast Asia* (Oxford: Oxford University Press, 1997); *China's Arms Acquisitions from Abroad: A Quest for "Superb and Secret Weapons"* (Oxford: Oxford University Press, 1995); *Chinese Arms Transfers* (Westport, Conn.: Praeger, 1992); and articles in *Foreign Affairs, National Interest, China Quarterly, Survival, SIPRI Yearbook,* and *Far Eastern Economic Review.*

Samuel S. Kim is an adjunct professor of political science and senior research associate at the East Asian Institute of Columbia University. He is the author or editor of over a dozen books on East Asia and world order studies, including most recently *Korea's Globalization* (Cambridge: Cambridge University Press, 2000). His articles have appeared in leading professional journals on China and international relations, including the *American Journal of International Law, China Quarterly, International Journal, International Organization, Journal of Chinese Law, Journal of Peace Research,* and *World Politics.*

David M. Lampton, former president of the National Committee on United States–China Relations (1988–97), is the George and Sadie Hyman professor and director of China Studies at the Paul H. Nitze School of Advanced International Studies of Johns Hopkins University. He is also the director of Chinese Studies at The Nixon Center in Washington, D.C. He is the author of numerous scholarly and popular articles and books on Chinese domestic politics, Chinese foreign policy, and U.S.-China relations. His most recent work is *Same Bed, Different Dreams: Managing U.S.-China Relations, 1989–2000* (Berkeley: University of California Press, 2001). He is also the editor of *Policy Implementation in Post-Mao China* (Berkeley: University of California Press, 1987) and (with Kenneth Lieberthal) *Bureaucracy, Politics, and Decision-Making in Post-Mao China* (Berkeley: University of California Press, 1992).

Liu Xiaohong, a former Chinese Foreign Service officer, received her Ph.D. in China studies from the School of Advanced International Studies (SAIS) at Johns Hopkins University and worked as an associate research fellow at SAIS. Currently she is working on her new book, *Chinese Ambassadors: The Rise of Diplomatic Professionalism since 1949,* which will be published by the University of Washington Press.

Lu Ning is senior correspondent with the *Business Times* of Singapore. Previously he was senior fellow at the Atlantic Council in Washington, D.C., a fellow at the International Center for Developing Policy in Washington, D.C., and a research fellow at the Institute of Southeast Asian Studies in Singapore. He also has served as assistant to the vice foreign minister of the People's Republic of China and an analyst with the Chinese Ministry of Foreign Affairs. He is the author of *The Dynamics of Foreign-Policy Decisionmaking in China* (Boulder, Colo.: Westview, 1997, 2000) and *Flashpoint Spratlys* (Singapore: Dolphin Books, 1995).

H. Lyman Miller is a historian and an associate professor of Chinese affairs at the Naval Postgraduate School in Monterey, California, and visiting scholar at the Hoover Institution, Stanford University. He is the author of *Science and Dissent in Post-Mao China: The Politics of Knowledge* (Seattle: University of Washington Press, 1996).

Thomas G. Moore is an assistant professor of political science at the University of Cincinnati, where he teaches courses on Asian politics, U.S. foreign policy, and international political economy. He holds Ph.D. and master's degrees from Princeton University and a bachelor's degree from Hamilton College. He is the author of several articles on China's participation in the world economy in journals such as *Asian Perspective, Journal of Contemporary China,* and *Journal of East Asian Affairs.* His most recent publication, "China and Globalization," appears in Samuel S. Kim, ed., *East Asia and Globalization* (Lanham, Md.: Rowman and Littlefield, 2000). A book based on his dissertation, *China in the World Market,* is forthcoming from Cambridge University Press.

Margaret M. Pearson is an associate professor of government and politics at the University of Maryland, College Park. She authored, most recently, *China's New Business Elite: The Political Consequences of Economic Reform* (Berkeley: University of California Press, 1997) and several articles on China's growing participation in the global economy.

Stanley Rosen is a professor of political science at the University of Southern California and has done research on various aspects of political, social, and cultural change in China. He is the editor of *Chinese Education and Society.* He is currently engaged in a project entitled "Hollywood and China" that focuses on the reception and impact of American films in the People's Republic of China and on the strategies under consideration within China to ensure survival of the film industry following entrance to the World Trade Organization.

Michael D. Swaine is a senior political scientist in international studies at RAND in Santa Monica, California, and research director of the RAND Center for Asia-Pacific Policy (CAPP). Prior to joining RAND in 1989, Dr. Swaine was a consultant in the business sector; a postdoctoral fellow at the Center for Chinese Studies at the University of California, Berkeley; and a research associate at Harvard University. He holds Ph.D. and master's degrees in political science from Harvard University and a bachelor's degree from

George Washington University. He specializes in Chinese security and foreign policy, U.S.-China relations, and East Asian international relations. Dr. Swaine's recent writings include *Interpreting China's Grand Strategy, Past, Present and Future* (with Ashley J. Tellis) (Santa Monica, Calif.: RAND, 2000), *Taiwan's National Security, Defense Policy, and Weapons Procurement Process* (Santa Monica, Calif.: RAND, 1999), *The Role of the Chinese Military in National Security Policymaking*, revised edition (Santa Monica, Calif.: RAND, 1998), *China: Domestic Change and Foreign Policy* (Santa Monica, Calif.: RAND, 1995), *The Modernization of the Chinese People's Liberation Army: Prospects and Implications for Northeast Asia* (Santa Monica, Calif.: RAND, 1994), and *The Military and Political Succession in China: Leadership, Institutions and Beliefs* (Santa Monica, Calif.: RAND, 1992).

James T. H. Tang is head of and an associate professor in the Department of Politics and Public Administration at the University of Hong Kong. He obtained his Ph.D. from the London School of Economics, an M.Phil. from Cambridge University, and a B.A. from the University of Hong Kong. Before returning to Hong Kong he taught at the National University of Singapore. A specialist in international relations, his recent publications include *Britain's Encounter with Revolutionary China* (London: Macmillan, 1992), *Human Rights and International Relations in the Asia-Pacific Region* (London: Pinter, 1995), and a volume he co-edited with Gerald Postiglione, *Hong Kong's Reunion with China: The Global Dimensions* (Armonk, N.Y.: Sharpe, 1997).

Dixia Yang, a Ph.D. candidate in political science at the University of Cincinnati, received her B.A. from the Foreign Affairs College in Beijing. From 1991 to 1995 she was a lecturer and an international programs coordinator at the Foreign Affairs College. With Thomas G. Moore, she has co-authored "China, APEC and Economic Regionalism in the Asia-Pacific," *Journal of East Asian Affairs,* Vol. 13, No. 2 (Fall–Winter 1999).

Index

Page numbers followed by letters *f, n,* and *t* refer to figures, notes, and tables, respectively.

Multilateral economic institutions (MEIs): as channel of external influence, 194; decentralization and weakening of, 201–2. *See also* World Trade Organization

Multilateral security cooperation, 29

Multilateralism, China and, 181, 222, 226

Multinational corporations (MNCs), as channel of external influence, 195–96

Mutual learning, 239

Myanmar: arms sales to, 265; exports to, 113

Nanjing Military Region, and Taiwan policy, 83–84, 319

Nathan, Andrew, 32

National Defense Law (1997), 88, 416n10

National Defense University (NDU), and Taiwan research, 304

National Environmental Protection Agency (NEPA), China: and climate change research, 244, 245; and Framework Convention on Climate Change, 246; and Montreal Protocol, signing of, 10, 11, 242, 252; renaming of, 445n55

National Machinery and Electronics Import and Export Office, and WTO negotiations, 350

National People's Congress (NPC), and military, 89

National policy. *See* Domestic policy

National security. *See* Security

National technical means (NTM) of verification, 260

Nationalism, 158–72; in 1980s, 158–59; in 1990s, 158, 159, 163–64, 182, 185; pluralization and, 13; dimensions of, 169–71, 170t; as double-edged sword, 182; economic, 166–67; elite discord and, 176–77; and elite politics, 184; high expectations and, 186; populist expressions of, 163–64, 171; as public opinion, 14; Taiwan issue and, 293; wealth and power, 148; WTO negotiations and, 360

Nativism, and nationalism, 165, 170t, 185

Navy, and decision-making, 83

NCA. *See* Nuclear Cooperation Agreement

NDU. *See* National Defense University

Negotiations: pluralization and increased complexity of, 30. *See also specific negotiations*

Neocolonialism, 183

NEPA. *See* National Environmental Protection Agency

New Left, 160, 165; and nationalism, 170, 170t

New Party, Taiwan, 325, 326

New security concept, 144

New Taiwan dollar, devaluation of, 219

NGOs. *See* Nongovernmental organizations

Nie Rongzhen, 126, 127

Niger, Sino-Taiwanese diplomatic bidding war over, 383, 468n24

Ningxia Province: characteristics of, 95t; as tourist destination, 111

Ninth Congress of the Chinese Communist Party (1969), and foreign policy, 148

Noncrisis decisions, process for making, 2

Nongovernmental organizations (NGOs), 238; pluralization and, 13

Nonproliferation, China's policy on, 257–58, 265–66; adaptive approach, 280; benefits of, 282; cautious approach, 282; challenges to, 288; external influences on, 267–68, 281–83; internal dynamics and, 271–74, 284–87; military transparency and, 280; shifts in, 280, 287; U.S. pressures and, 268–72, 283–84; white paper on, 277. *See also* Arms control

Nordpolitik, South Korea and, 376–78, 405

Norinco, 55

Normal trade relations (NTR), annual debate on, 339

Norms, international. *See* Global norms and values

North Korea: 1999 delegation to China, 397–98; Asian Financial Crisis and, 390–91; China's relations with, 22, 23, 396–98, 403; collapse of, scenarios for, 402; dependence on China, 403;